Avizandum Statutes on

# The Scots Law of Obligations
## 2003–2004

# Avizandum Statutes on

# The Scots Law of Obligations
## 2003–2004

Editor

**Laura J Macgregor** LLM, Solicitor
Senior lecturer in commercial law,
University of Edinburgh

Avizandum Publishing Ltd
Edinburgh
2003

Published by
Avizandum Publishing Ltd
58 Candlemaker Row
Edinburgh EH1 2QE


First published 2003

© Avizandum Publishing Ltd

ISBN 0-9543423-1-3

British Library Cataloguing in Publication Data
A catalogue record for this book is available from the British Library.

Typeset by AFS Image Setters Ltd, Glasgow
Printed and bound by Bell & Bain Ltd, Glasgow

# AVIZANDUM STATUTES ON
# THE SCOTS LAW OF OBLIGATIONS
# 2003–2004

## ERRATA

### Sale of Goods Act 1979, sections 14 and 15

**page 59:** Section 14(2) of the Sale of Goods Act 1979 should appear as follows:

[(2) Where the seller sells goods in the course of a business, there is an implied term that the goods supplied under the contract are of satisfactory quality.

(2A) For the purposes of this Act, goods are of satisfactory quality if they meet the standard that a reasonable person would regard as satisfactory, taking account of any description of the goods, the price (if relevant) and all the other relevant circumstances.

(2B) For the purposes of this Act, the quality of goods includes their state and condition and the following (among others) are in appropriate cases aspects of the quality of goods—

(a) fitness for all the purposes for which goods of the kind in question are commonly supplied,

(b) appearance and finish,

(c) freedom from minor defects,

(d) safety, and

(e) durability.

(2C) The term implied by subsection (2) above does not extend to any matter making the quality of goods unsatisfactory—

(a) which is specifically drawn to the buyer's attention before the contract is made,

(b) where the buyer examines the goods before the contract is made, which that examination ought to reveal, or

(c) in the case of a contract for sale by sample, which would have been apparent on a reasonable examination of the sample.]

**page 60:** Section 15(2) of the Sale of Goods Act 1979 should appear as follows:

(2) In the case of a contract for sale by sample there is an implied [term]—

(a) that the bulk will correspond with the sample in quality;

. . .

(c) that the goods will be free from any defect, [making their quality unsatisfactory], which would not be apparent on reasonable examination of the sample.

**AVIZANDUM PUBLISHING LTD**
**February 2003**

# EDITOR'S PREFACE

This collection of statutes has been produced specifically for the use of students studying obligations at undergraduate level as part of a law degree in Scotland. The aim was to produce a low-cost collection of statutes which would provide the relevant material in an easily accessible form.

Selecting the necessary material was by no means an easy task. The statutes have been published at a time of great change in the curricula of Scots law degrees. The form of the individual courses in which students study obligations now varies significantly from university to university. I must acknowledge with thanks my debt to the individual lecturers who provided me with an indication of the statutes they considered would be useful to support the study of obligations in their individual universities. Particular thanks in this respect must go to Professor Kenneth Norrie and Professor Bill McBryde.

The editor must also tackle the difficulty of how much or how little of individual statutes to include. Clearly, most users would prefer to have access to the entire statute. However, to take this approach would have made the statutes prohibitively expensive, and would ultimately have defeated the overall aim of producing affordable and usable statutes. Some readers may be disappointed that only selections of certain statutes are included. However, the most important statutes are reproduced in full. This is the case where, on the basis of feedback received, it was clear to me that the statute was of central importance to the individual obligations courses.

The statutes were also produced in the knowledge that a companion volume of *Avizandum Statutes on Scots Commercial Law* was being prepared and is shortly to be published. Certain statutes which might otherwise have been included in this volume have been omitted because they will appear in this companion volume edited by Jenny Hamilton.

It should be noted that this volume also includes many important bills relating to the law of contract. Such bills, produced by the Scottish Law Commission, but not yet considered by the Scottish Parliament, are central to the understanding of the law in this area. Certain major international codes or models laws are also included.

Thanks must go first to Margaret Cherry who originally had the idea of producing a Scottish volume of statutes on obligations. Without her enthusiasm and hard work, this volume would not have been published. Geraldine Gobbi must also receive my thanks for collating the statutes which was a long and arduous task.

Given the fact that this is a new enterprise, all of those involved in its production would be grateful to receive feedback on the material which users consider should or should not have been included in the volume. We have endeavoured to update the materials to the end of 2002. Material which was not in the statute as originally enacted is enclosed in square brackets.

Laura Macgregor
University of Edinburgh
*January 2003*

# CONTENTS

# PART I
# STATUTES

## LAWBURROWS ACT 1429

**5** ITEM it is ftatute ande ordanit þat quhare a borgħ is fundyn in a courte apoñ a weir of law þat þe pty defendour as to þat borgħ fal haf fredome to be avifit and afk leve þarto ande fal haf leve ande quheþ' he wil be avifit w'in courte or oute of courte findande borowis of his entre 't his anfuer withïn the hour of caufe at the confid'acioun of the Juge 't the courte.

## LAWBURROWS ACT 1581

Additioun to the act of Lawborrowis.

FORSAMEKILL / as findrie guid actis hes bene maid anent finding of Lawborrowis for preferuatioun of the trew and obedient fubiectis from iniuft force / and violence / and laitlie for þair greitter confort It wes weill ordanit / þat þe panes of lawborrowis fuld be deuidit betuix þe king and þe pairte offendit vnto. Neuerþeles / feing þe panes of lawborrowis hes extendit onlie in tyme bigane in faulftie of bodilie harme from þe perfone of þe complenar / The malice of [the] wickit fa increffis as þei ceif' not be indirect meanis / and hunding out of lȳmaris / vagaboundis / and vþeris not refponfall / to Inuaid þe Innocent perfonis / not onlie in þair bodeis bot to reif / fteill hoch / or flay þair oxin / and vþeris cattell / cut or diftroy þair coirnis / or to cauf' eit þe famȳ wᵗʰ beftiall / to hund and flay þair fcheip wᵗʰ doggis / boift þame felf in fic fort as þai dar not ly in þair awin houff' / or to manas þair feruād𝓵 to leve pair fernice / quhairthrow þair ground may be lyed waift / to þe vttir wrak and depaupering of þe Innocent𝓵 Quhairfoir oure fouerane lord wᵗʰ aduife of his thre eftatis in þis prefent parliament / Ordanis þat all letteris of lawborrowis falbe direct in tyme cūing at þe inftance of þe pairteis complenand / chargeing þe perfonis cōplenit vpoun to find ficker fouertie and lawborrowis / that þe complenaris / thair wyffis bairnis / tenentis and feruandis / falbe harmeles and fkaithles / in þair bodeis landis / takkis / poffeffionis / guidis / and geir / and on na wayis to be moleftit or trublit thairin be þe perfonis complenit vpoun / nor na vþeris of þair caufing / fending hunding out refetting cōmand / affiftance / and ratihabitioun / quhome þai may ftop or let direclie or Indireclie / vþirwayis nor be þe ordoure of law and iuftice vnder greit panes to be modifeit be þe lordis of feffioun / Or vþeris ordinar Judges / Be quhome in caif' þe faid lawborrowis / falbe dewlie tryit / to be brokin / the ane half of þe pane fall pertene to oure fouerane lord / and þe vþir half to þe pairte grevit / according to þe effect' 't meaning of þe faid act' / maid to þat effect' of befoir.

## COMPENSATION ACT 1592

THAT Compenſatioun de liquido ad liquidum be admittit in all Jugementis.

OURE SOUERANE LORD and eſtaitis of parliament ſtatutis and Ordanis that ony debt de liquido ad liquidum inſtantlie verifiet be wreit or aith of the partie befoir the geving of decreit be admittit be all Jugis w<sup>th</sup>in this realme be way of exceptioun Bot no‘ eftir the geving thairof / In the ſuſpenſioun or in reductioun of þe fame decreit.

## PARLIAMENTARY PAPERS ACT 1840
### (3 & 4 Vict, c 9)

Whereas it is essential to the due and effectual exercise and discharge of the functions and duties of Parliament, and to the promotion of wise legislation, that no obstructions or impediments should exist to the publication of such of the reports, papers, votes, or proceedings of either House of Parliament as such House of Parliament may deem fit or necessary to be published: And whereas obstructions or impediments to such publication have arisen, and hereafter may arise, by means of civil or criminal proceedings being taken against persons employed by or acting under the authority of the Houses of Parliament, or one of them, in the publication of such reports, papers, votes, or proceedings; by reason and for remedy whereof it is expedient that more speedy protection should be afforded to all persons acting under the authority aforesaid, and that all such civil or criminal proceedings should be summarily put an end to and determined in manner herein-after mentioned: Be it therefore enacted by the Queen's most excellent Majesty, by and with the advice and consent of the lords spiritual and temporal, and commons, in this present Parliament assembled, and by the authority of the same, that

### 1.   Proceedings, criminal or civil, against persons for publication of papers printed by order of Parliament, to be stayed upon delivery of a certificate and affidavit to the effect that such publication is by order of either House of Parliament

It shall and may be lawful for any person or persons who now is or are, or hereafter shall be, a defendant or defendants in any civil or criminal proceeding commenced or prosecuted in any manner soever, for or on account or in respect of the publication of any such report, paper, votes, or proceedings by such person or persons, or by his, her, or their servant or servants, by or under the authority of either House of Parliament, to bring before the court in which such proceeding shall have been or shall be so commenced or prosecuted, or before any judge of the same (if one of the superior courts at Westminster), first giving twenty-four hours notice of his intention so to do to the prosecutor or plaintiff in such proceeding, a certificate under the hand of the lord high chancellor of Great Britain, or the lord keeper of the great seal, or of the speaker of the House of Lords, for the time being, or of the clerk of the Parliaments, or of the speaker of the House of Commons, or of the clerk of the same house, stating that the report, paper, votes, or proceedings, as the case may be, in respect whereof such civil or criminal proceeding shall have been commenced or prosecuted, was published by such person or persons, or by his, her, or their servant or servants, by order or under the authority of the House of Lords or of the House of Commons, as the case may be, together with an affidavit verifying such certificate; and such court or judge shall thereupon immediately stay such civil or criminal proceeding; and the same, and every writ or process issued therein, shall be and shall be deemed and taken to be finally put an end to, determined, and superseded by virtue of this Act.

### 2. Proceedings to be stayed when commenced in respect of a copy of an authenticated report, &c.

And be it enacted, that in case of any civil or criminal proceeding hereafter to be commenced or prosecuted for or on account or in respect of the publication of any copy of such report, paper, votes, or proceedings, it shall be lawful for the defendant or defendants at any stage of the proceedings to lay before the court or judge such report, paper, votes, or proceedings, and such copy, with an affidavit verifying such report, paper, votes, or proceedings, and the correctness of such copy, and the court or judge shall immediately stay such civil or criminal proceeding; and the same, and every writ or process issued therein, shall be and shall be deemed and taken to be finally put an end to, determined, and superseded by virtue of this Act.

### 3. In proceedings for printing any extract or abstract of a paper, it may be shewn that such extract was bonâ fide made

And be it enacted, that it shall be lawful in any civil or criminal proceeding to be commenced or prosecuted for printing any extract from or abstract of such report, paper, votes, or proceedings, to give in evidence . . . such report, paper, votes, or proceedings, and to show that such extract or abstract was published bonâ fide and without malice; and if such shall be the opinion of the jury, a verdict of not guilty shall be entered for the defendant or defendants.

### 4. Act not to affect the privileges of Parliament

Provided always, and it is hereby expressly declared and enacted, that nothing herein contained shall be deemed or taken, or held or construed, directly or indirectly, by implication or otherwise, to affect the privileges of Parliament in any manner whatsoever.

## TRESPASS (SCOTLAND) ACT 1865
### (1865, c lvi)

### I.  Short Title
This Act may be cited for all Purposes as 'The Trespass (*Scotland*) Act, 1865.'

### II.  Interpretation of Terms
In this Act the following Words shall have the Meanings hereby assigned to them:

'Premises' shall mean and include any House, Barn, Stable, Shed, Loft, Granary, Outhouse, Garden, Stackyard, Court, Close, or inclosed Place:

'Magistrate' shall mean and include the Sheriff and Sheriff Substitute, or any One or more Justice or Justices of the Peace, or any One or more Magistrate or Magistrates, having Jurisdiction respectively in the County or Burgh where any Offence against the Provisions of this Act is committed, or where any Person charged with such Offence is found or brought to Trial:

'Procurator Fiscal' shall mean and include the Procurator Fiscal of the Court having such Jurisdiction.

['Road' shall mean and include any way, other than—
    (a)   a waterway; or
    (b)   without prejudice to section 100(c) (damage to roads by fire) or 129(4) (camping in a road) of the Roads (Scotland) Act 1984, a road within the meaning of that Act.]

### III.  Parties lodging in Premises or encamping on Land, without Permission, guilty of an Offence
Every Person who lodges in any Premises, or occupies or encamps on any

Land, being private Property, without the Consent and Permission of the Owner or legal Occupier of such Premises or Land, and every Person who encamps or lights a Fire on or near any . . . Road or inclosed or cultivated Land, or in or near any Plantation, without the Consent and Permission of the Owner or Legal Occupier of such Road, Land, or Plantation, . . . shall be guilty of an Offence punishable as herein-after provided.

### IV.  Apprehension and Punishment of Offenders
Every Person who commits any Offence against the Provisions of this Act may, if found in the Act of committing the same by any Officer of Police or Constable, be apprehended by such Officer or Constable, and detained in any Prison, Police Station, Lock-up, or other Place of safe Custody, and not later than in the course of the next lawful Day after he shall have been so taken into Custody shall be brought before a Magistrate; and every Person charged with the Commission of any such Offence may, if not so taken into Custody, or if he shall have been liberated on Bail or Pledge, be summoned to appear before a Magistrate, [and every person committing an offence against the provisions of this Act shall be liable, on summary conviction, to a fine not exceeding level 1 on the standard scale.]

### V.  As to Prosecutions under Act
Every Prosecution for an Offence against the Provisions of this Act shall be raised and proceeded in at the Instance of the Procurator Fiscal, and shall be heard and determined by One or more Magistrate or Magistrates in a summary Form; and every such Prosecution shall be commenced within One Month after the Offence has been committed.

### BILLS OF EXCHANGE ACT 1882
#### (1882, c 61)

### 3.  Bill of exchange defined
(1)  A bill of exchange is an unconditional order in writing, addressed by one person to another, signed by the person giving it, requiring the person to whom it is addressed to pay on demand or at a fixed or determinable future time a sum certain in money to or to the order of a specified person, or to bearer.

(2)  An instrument which does not comply with these conditions, or which orders any act to be done in addition to the payment of money, is not a bill of exchange.

(3)  An order to pay out of a particular fund is not unconditional within the meaning of this section; but an unqualified order to pay, coupled with (a) an indication of a particular fund out of which the drawee is to re-imburse himself or a particular account to be debited with the amount, or (b) a statement of the transaction which gives rise to the bill, is unconditional.

(4)  A bill is not invalid by reason—
  (a)  That it is not dated;
  (b)  That it does not specify the value given, or that any value has been given therefor;
  (c)  That it does not specify the place where it is drawn or the place where it is payable.

### 73.  Cheque defined
A cheque is a bill of exchange drawn on a banker payable on demand.

Except as otherwise provided in this Part, the provisions of this Act applicable to a bill of exchange payable on demand apply to a cheque.

### 83.  Promissory note defined
(1)  A promissory note is an unconditional promise in writing made by one person to another signed by the maker, engaging to pay, on demand, or at a

fixed or determinable future time, a sum certain in money, to, or to the order of, a specified person or to bearer.

(2)   An instrument in the form of a note payable to maker's order is not a note within the meaning of this section unless and until it is indorsed by the maker.

(3)   A note is not invalid by reason only that it contains also a pledge of collateral security with authority to sell or dispose thereof.

(4)   A note which is, or on the face of it purports to be, both made and payable within the British Islands is an inland note. Any other note is a foreign note.


## FACTORS ACT 1889
### (52 & 53 Vict, c 45)

*Preliminary*

### 1.   Definitions

For the purposes of this Act—

(1)   The expression 'mercantile agent' shall mean a mercantile agent having in the customary course of his business as such agent authority either to sell goods or to consign goods for the purpose of sale, or to buy goods, or to raise money on the security of goods:

(2)   A person shall be deemed to be in possession of goods or of the documents of title to goods, where the goods or documents are in the actual custody or are held by any other person subject to his control or for him or on his behalf:

(3)   The expression 'goods' shall include wares and merchandise:

(4)   The expression 'document of title' shall include any bill of lading, dock warrant, warehouse-keeper's certificate, and warrant or order for the delivery of goods, and any other document used in the ordinary course of business as proof of the possession or control of goods, or authorising or purporting to authorise, either by endorsement or by delivery, the possessor of the document to transfer or receive goods thereby represented:

(5)   The expression 'pledge' shall include any contract pledging, or giving a lien or security on, goods, whether in consideration of an original advance or of any further or continuing advance or of any pecuniary liability:

(6)   The expression 'person' shall include any body of persons corporate or unincorporate.

*Dispositions by mercantile agents*

### 2.   Powers of mercantile agent with respect to disposition of goods

(1)   Where a mercantile agent is, with the consent of the owner, in possession of goods or of the documents of title to goods, any sale, pledge, or other disposition of the goods, made by him when acting in the ordinary course of business of a mercantile agent, shall, subject to the provisions of this Act, be as valid as if he were expressly authorised by the owner of the goods to make the same; provided that the person taking under the disposition acts in good faith, and has not at the time of the disposition notice that the person making the disposition has not authority to make the same.

(2)   Where a mercantile agent has, with the consent of the owner, been in possession of goods or of the documents of title to goods, any sale, pledge, or other disposition, which would have been valid if the consent had continued, shall be valid notwithstanding the determination of the consent; provided that the person taking under the disposition has not at the time thereof notice that the consent has been determined.

(3)   Where a mercantile agent has obtained possession of any documents of title to goods by reason of his being or having been, with the consent of the owner, in possession of the goods represented thereby, or of any other documents of title to the goods, his possession of the first-mentioned documents shall, for the purposes of this Act, be deemed to be with the consent of the owner.

(4)   For the purposes of this Act the consent of the owner shall be presumed in the absence of evidence to the contrary.

### 3.   Effect of pledges of documents of title
A pledge of the documents of title to goods shall be deemed to be a pledge of the goods.

### 4.   Pledge for antecedent debt
Where a mercantile agent pledges goods as security for a debt or liability due from the pledgor to the pledgee before the time of the pledge, the pledgee shall acquire no further right to the goods than could have been enforced by the pledgor at the time of the pledge.

### 5.   Rights acquired by exchange of goods or documents
The consideration necessary for the validity of a sale, pledge, or other disposition of goods, in pursuance of this Act, may be either a payment in cash, or the delivery or transfer of other goods, or of a document of title to goods, or of a negotiable security, or any other valuable consideration; but where goods are pledged by a mercantile agent in consideration of the delivery or transfer of other goods, or of a document of title to goods, or of a negotiable security, the pledgee shall acquire no right or interest in the goods so pledged in excess of the value of the goods, documents, or security when so delivered or transferred in exchange.

### 6.   Agreements through clerks, &c.
For the purposes of this Act an agreement made with a mercantile agent through a clerk or other person authorised in the ordinary course of business to make contracts of sale or pledge on his behalf shall be deemed to be an agreement with the agent.

### 7.   Provisions as to consignors and consignees
(1)   Where the owner of goods has given possession of the goods to another person for the purpose of consignment or sale, or has shipped the goods in the name of another person, and the consignee of the goods has not had notice that such person is not the owner of the goods, the consignee shall, in respect of advances made to or for the use of such person, have the same lien on the goods as if such person were the owner of the goods, and may transfer any such lien to another person.

(2)   Nothing in this section shall limit or affect the validity of any sale, pledge, or disposition, by a mercantile agent.

*Dispositions by sellers and buyers of goods*

### 8.   Disposition by seller remaining in possession
Where a person, having sold goods, continues, or is, in possession of the goods or of the documents of title to the goods, the delivery or transfer by that person, or by a mercantile agent acting for him, of the goods or documents of title under any sale, pledge, or other disposition thereof, or under any agreement for sale, pledge, or other disposition thereof, to any person receiving the same in good faith and without notice of the previous sale, shall have the same effect as if the person making the delivery or transfer were expressly authorised by the owner of the goods to make the same.

### 9.  Disposition by buyer obtaining possession

Where a person, having bought or agreed to buy goods, obtains with the consent of the seller possession of the goods or the documents of title to the goods, the delivery or transfer, by that person or by a mercantile agent acting for him, of the goods or documents of title under any sale, pledge, or other disposition thereof, or under any agreement for sale, pledge, or other disposition thereof, to any person receiving the same in good faith and without notice of any lien or other right of the original seller in respect of the goods, shall have the same effect as if the person making the delivery or transfer were a mercantile agent in possession of the goods or documents of title with the consent of the owner.

[For the purposes of this section—

(i)   the buyer under a conditional sale agreement shall be deemed not to be a person who has bought or agreed to buy goods, and

(ii)   'conditional sale agreement' means an agreement for the sale of goods which is a consumer credit agreement within the meaning of the Consumer Credit Act 1974 under which the purchase price or part of it is payable in instalments, and the property in the goods is to remain in the seller (notwithstanding that the buyer is to be in possession of the goods) until such conditions as to the payment of instalments or otherwise as may be specified in the agreement are fulfilled.]

### 10.  Effect of transfer of documents on vendor's lien or right of stoppage in transitu

Where a document of title to goods has been lawfully transferred to a person as a buyer or owner of the goods, and that person transfers the document to a person who takes the document in good faith and for valuable consideration, the last-mentioned transfer shall have the same effect for defeating any vendor's lien or right of stoppage in transitu as the transfer of a bill of lading has for defeating the right of stoppage in transitu.

*Supplemental*

### 11.  Mode of transferring documents

For the purposes of this Act, the transfer of a document may be by endorsement, or, where the document is by custom or by its express terms transferable by delivery or makes the goods deliverable to the bearer, then by delivery.

### 12.  Saving for rights of true owner

(1)   Nothing in this Act shall authorise an agent to exceed or depart from his authority as between himself and his principal, or exempt him from any liability, civil or criminal, for so doing.

(2)   Nothing in this Act shall prevent the owner of goods from recovering the goods from any agent or his trustee in bankruptcy at any time before the sale or pledge thereof, or shall prevent the owner of goods pledged by an agent from having the right to redeem the goods at any time before the sale thereof, on satisfying the claim for which the goods were pledged, and paying to the agent, if by him required, any money in respect of which the agent would by law be entitled to retain the goods or the documents of title thereto, or any of them, by way of lien as against the owner, or from recovering from any person with whom the goods have been pledged any balance of money remaining in his hands as the produce of the sale of the goods after deducting the amount of his lien.

(3)   Nothing in this Act shall prevent the owner of goods sold by an agent from recovering from the buyer the price agreed to be paid for the same, or any

part of that price, subject to any right of set off on the part of the buyer against the agent.

### 13. Saving for common law powers of agent

The provisions of this Act shall be construed in amplification and not in derogation of the powers exercisable by an agent independently of this Act.

[. . .]

### 16. Extent of Act

This Act shall not extend to Scotland.

### 17. Short title

This Act may be cited as the Factors Act, 1889.

## FACTORS (SCOTLAND) ACT 1890
### (1890, c 40)

### 1. Application of 52 & 53 Vict. c 45 to Scotland

Subject to the following provisions, the Factors Act, 1889, shall apply to Scotland:—

(1) The expression 'lien' shall mean and include right of retention; the expression 'vendor's lien' shall mean and include any right of retention competent to the original owner or vendor; and the expression 'set off' shall mean and include compensation.

(2) In the application of section five of the recited Act, a sale, pledge, or other disposition of goods shall not be valid unless made for valuable consideration.

### 2. Short title

This Act may be cited as the Factors (Scotland) Act, 1890.

## PARTNERSHIP ACT 1890
### (1890, c 39)

### 2. Rules for determining existence of partnership

In determining whether a partnership does or does not exist, regard shall be had to the following rules:

(1) Joint tenancy, tenancy in common, joint property, common property, or part ownership does not of itself create a partnership as to anything so held or owned, whether the tenants or owners do or do not share any profits made by the use thereof.

(2) The sharing of gross returns does not of itself create a partnership, whether the persons sharing such returns have or have not a joint or common right or interest in any property from which or from the use of which the returns are derived.

(3) The receipt by a person of a share of the profits of a business is *primâ facie* evidence that he is a partner in the business, but the receipt of such a share, or of a payment contingent on or varying with the profits of a business, does not of itself make him a partner in the business; and in particular—

(a) The receipt by a person of a debt or other liquidated amount by instalments or otherwise out of the accruing profits of a business does not of itself make him a partner in the business or liable as such:

(b) A contract for the remuneration of a servant or agent of a person engaged in a business by a share of the profits of the business does not of itself make the servant or agent a partner in the business or liable as such:

(c) A person being the widow or child of a deceased partner, and receiving by way of annuity a portion of the profits made in the business in which the deceased person was a partner, is not by reason only of such receipt a partner in the business or liable as such:

(d)   The advance of money by way of loan to a person engaged or about to engage in any business on a contract with that person that the lender shall receive a rate of interest varying with the profits, or shall receive a share of the profits arising from carrying on the business, does not of itself make the lender a partner with the person or persons carrying on the business or liable as such. Provided that the contract is in writing, and signed by or on behalf of all the parties thereto:

(e)   A person receiving by way of annuity or otherwise a portion of the profits of a business in consideration of the sale by him of the goodwill of the business is not by reason only of such receipt a partner in the business or liable as such.

## MARINE INSURANCE ACT 1906
### (1906, c 41)

#### 22.   Contract must be embodied in policy

Subject to the provisions of any statute, a contract of marine insurance is inadmissible in evidence unless it is embodied in a marine policy in accordance with this Act. The policy may be executed and issued either at the time when the contract is concluded, or afterwards.

## LAW REFORM (MISCELLANEOUS PROVISIONS) (SCOTLAND) ACT 1940
### (1940, c 42)

#### 1.   Amendment of the law as to enforcement of decrees ad factum praestandum

(1)   No person shall be apprehended or imprisoned on account of his failure to comply with a decree ad factum praestandum except in accordance with the following provisions—

(i)   On an application by the person in right of such a decree (hereinafter referred to as the applicant) to the court by which the decree was granted, the court may, if it is satisfied that the person against whom such decree was granted (hereinafter referred to as the respondent) is wilfully refusing to comply with the decree, grant warrant for his imprisonment for any period not exceeding six months;

(ii)   Where the court is satisfied that a person undergoing imprisonment in pursuance of a warrant granted under this section has complied, or is no longer wilfully refusing to comply, with the decree, the court shall, notwithstanding any period specified in the warrant, order the immediate liberation of such person, and it shall be the duty of the applicant, as soon as he is satisfied that the decree has been complied with, forthwith to inform the clerk of the court of such compliance;

(iii)   Imprisonment under a warrant granted under this subsection shall not operate to extinguish the obligation imposed by the decree on which the application proceeds;

(iv)   The person on whose application a warrant for imprisonment has been granted under this subsection shall not be liable to aliment, or to contribute to the aliment of, the respondent while in prison.

(2)   On any application in pursuance of the foregoing subsection, the court may, in lieu of granting warrant for imprisonment, recall the decree on which the application proceeds and make an order for the payment by the respondent to the applicant of a specified sum or make such other order as appears to the court to be just and equitable in the circumstances, including, in the case where the decree on which the application proceeds is a decree for delivery of

corporeal moveables, a warrant to officers of court to search any premises in the occupation of the respondent or of such other person as may be named in the warrant, and to take possession of, and deliver to the applicant, any such moveables which may be found in such premises.

(3)   Any warrant granted under the last foregoing subsection shall be deemed to include authority to open shut and lockfast places for the purpose of carrying the warrant into lawful execution.

### 3.   Contribution among joint wrongdoers

(1)   Where in any action of damages in respect of loss or damage arising from any wrongful acts or negligent acts or omissions two or more persons are, in pursuance of the verdict of a jury or the judgment of a court found jointly and severally liable in damages or expenses, they shall be liable *inter se* to contribute to such damages or expenses in such proportions as the jury or the court, as the case may be, may deem just: Provided that nothing in this subsection shall affect the right of the person to whom such damages or expenses have been awarded to obtain a joint and several decree therefor against the persons so found liable.

(2)   Where any person has paid any damages or expenses in which he has been found liable in any such action as aforesaid, he shall be entitled to recover from any other person who, if sued, might also have been held liable in respect of the loss or damage on which the action was founded, such contribution, if any, as the court may deem just.

(3)   Nothing in this section shall—

(a)   apply to any action in respect of loss or damage suffered before the commencement of this Act; or

(b)   affect any contractual or other right of relief or indemnity or render enforceable any agreement for indemnity which could not have been enforced if this section had not been enacted.

**LAW REFORM (CONTRIBUTORY NEGLIGENCE) ACT 1945**
**(1945, c 28)**

### 1.   Apportionment of liability in case of contributory negligence

(1)   Where any person suffers damage as the result partly of his own fault and partly of the fault of any other person or persons, a claim in respect of that damage shall not be defeated by reason of the fault of the person suffering the damage, but the damages recoverable in respect thereof shall be reduced to such extent as the court thinks just and equitable having regard to the claimant's share in the responsibility for the damage:

Provided that—

(a)   this subsection shall not operate to defeat any defence arising under a contract;

(b)   where any contract or enactment providing for the limitation of liability is applicable to the claim, the amount of damages recoverable by the claimant by virtue of this subsection shall not exceed the maximum limit so applicable.

(2)   Where damages are recoverable by any person by virtue of the foregoing subsection subject to such reduction as is therein mentioned, the court shall find and record the total damages which would have been recoverable if the claimant had not been at fault.

. . .

(5)   Where, in any case to which subsection (1) of this section applies, one of the persons at fault avoids liability to any other such person or his personal representative by pleading the Limitation Act, 1939, or any other enactment limiting the time within which proceedings may be taken, he shall not be

entitled to recover any damages . . . from that other person or representative by virtue of the said subsection.

(6)   Where any case to which subsection (1) of this section applies is tried with a jury, the jury shall determine the total damages which would have been recoverable if the claimant had not been at fault and the extent to which those damages are to be reduced.

## 2.   Provisions as to workmen and employers

(1)   Where, within the time limited for the taking of proceedings under the Workmen's Compensation Acts, 1925 to 1943, an action is brought to recover damages independently of the said Acts in respect of an injury or disease giving rise to a claim for compensation under the said Acts, and it is determined in that action that—

(a)   damages are recoverable independently of the said Acts subject to such reduction as is mentioned in subsection (1) of the foregoing section of this Act; and

(b)   the employer would have been liable to pay compensation under the Workmen's Compensation Acts, 1925 to 1943;

subsection (2) of section twenty-nine of the Workmen's Compensation Act, 1925, (which enables the court, on the dismissal of an action to recover damages independently of the said Acts, to assess and award compensation under the said Acts) shall apply in all respects as if the action had been dismissed, and, if the claimant chooses to have compensation assessed and awarded in accordance with the said subsection (2), no damages shall be recoverable in the said action.

This subsection shall apply, with the necessary adaptations, in any case where compensation is recoverable under a scheme certified or made under the Workmen's Compensation Acts, 1925 to 1943, or under the Workmen's Compensation and Benefit (Byssinosis) Act, 1940, if the scheme applies section twenty-nine of the Workmen's Compensation Act, 1925, or contains any provision similar to that section.

(2)   Where a workman or his personal representative or dependant has recovered compensation under the Workmen's Compensation Acts, 1925 to 1943, or under any scheme certified under the Workmen's Compensation Act, 1925, in respect of an injury caused under circumstances which would give a right to recover reduced damages in respect thereof by virtue of section one of this Act from some person other than the employer (hereinafter referred to as 'the third party'), any right conferred by section thirty of the Workmen's Compensation Act, 1925, on the person by whom the compensation was paid, or on any person called on to pay an indemnity under section six of that Act, to be indemnified by the third party shall be limited to a right to be indemnified in respect of such part only of the sum paid or payable by the said person as bears to the total sum so paid or payable the same proportion as the said reduced damages bear to the total damages which would have been recoverable if the workman had not been at fault.

## 3.   Saving for Maritime Conventions Act, 1911, and past cases

(1)   This Act shall not apply to any claim to which section one of the Maritime Conventions Act, 1911, applies and that Act shall have effect as if this Act had not passed.

(2)   This Act shall not apply to any case where the acts or omissions giving rise to the claim occurred before the passing of this Act.

## 4.   Interpretation

The following expressions have the meanings hereby respectively assigned to them, that is to say—

'court' means, in relation to any claim, the court or arbitrator by or before whom the claim falls to be determined;

'damage' includes loss of life and personal injury;

. . .

'employer' and 'workman' have the same meaning as in the Workmen's Compensation Act, 1925, as amended by any subsequent enactment;

'fault' means negligence, breach of statutory duty or other act or omission which gives rise to a liability in tort or would, apart from this Act, give rise to the defence of contributory negligence.

### 5.  Application to Scotland
In the application of this Act to Scotland—

(a)  the expression 'dependant' means, in relation to any person, any person who would in the event of such first mentioned person's death through the fault of a third party be entitled to sue that third party for damages or solatium; and the expression 'fault' means wrongful act, breach of statutory duty or negligent act or omission which gives rise to liability in damages, or would apart from this Act, give rise to the defence of contributory negligence;

[(b)  section 3 of the Law Reform (Miscellaneous Provisions) (Scotland) Act 1940 (contribution among joint wrongdoers) shall apply in any case where two or more persons are liable, or would if they had all been sued be liable, by virtue of section 1(1) of this Act in respect of the damage suffered by any person.]

(c)  for subsection (4) of section one the following subsection shall be substituted—

(4)   Where any person dies as the result partly of his own fault and partly of the fault of any other person or persons, a claim by any dependant of the first mentioned person for damages or solatium in respect of that person's death shall not be defeated by reason of his fault, but the damages or solatium recoverable shall be reduced to such extent as the court thinks just and equitable having regard to the share of the said person in the responsibility for his death.

### 6.  Provisions as to Northern Ireland
(2)   This Act shall not extend to Northern Ireland.

### 7.  Short title and extent
This Act may be cited as the Law Reform (Contributory Negligence) Act, 1945.

## DEFAMATION ACT 1952
### (1952, c 66)

### 3.  Actions for verbal injury
In any action for verbal injury it shall not be necessary for the pursuer to aver or prove special damage if the words on which the action is founded are calculated to cause pecuniary damage to the pursuer.

### 4.  [*repealed*]

### 5.  Justification
In an action for libel or slander in respect of words containing two or more distinct charges against the plaintiff, a defence of justification shall not fail by reason only that the truth of every charge is not proved if the words not proved to be true do not materially injure the plaintiff's reputation having regard to the truth of the remaining charges.

### 6.  Fair comment
In an action for libel or slander in respect of words consisting partly of allegations of fact and partly of expression of opinion, a defence of fair comment shall not fail by reason only that the truth of every allegation or fact

is not proved if the expression of opinion is fair comment having regard to such of the facts alleged or referred to in the words complained of as are proved.

**7, 8.**   [*repealed*]

### 9.   Extension of certain defences to broadcasting

(1)   Section three of the Parliamentary Papers Act, 1840 (which confers protection in respect of proceedings for printing extracts from or abstracts of parliamentary papers) shall have effect as if the reference to printing included a reference to broadcasting by means of wireless telegraphy.

(2), (3)   [*repealed*]

### 10.   Limitation on privilege at elections

A defamatory statement published by or on behalf of a candidate in any election to local government authority [, to the Scottish Parliament] or to Parliament shall not be deemed to be published on a privileged occasion on the ground that it is material to a question in issue in the election, whether or not the person by whom it is published is qualified to vote at the election.

### 11.   Agreements for indemnity

An agreement for indemnifying any person against civil liability for libel in respect of the publication of any matter shall not be unlawful unless at the time of the publication that person knows that the matter is defamatory, and does not reasonably believe that there is a good defence to any action brought upon it.

### 12.   Evidence of other damages recovered by plaintiff

In any action for libel or slander the defendant may give evidence in mitigation of damages that the plaintiff has recovered damages, or has brought actions for damages, for libel or slander in respect of the publication of words to the same effect as the words on which the action is founded, or has received or agreed to receive compensation in respect of any such publication.

### 14.   Application of Act to Scotland

This Act shall apply to Scotland subject to the following modifications, that is to say—

(a)   sections one, two, eight and thirteen shall be omitted;

(b)   for section three there shall be substituted the following section [*see s 3 above*];

.   .   .

(d)   for any reference to libel, or to libel or slander, there shall be substituted a reference to defamation; the expression 'plaintiff' means pursuer; the expression 'defendant' means defender; for any reference to an affidavit made by any person there shall be substituted a reference to a written declaration signed by that person; for any reference to the High Court there shall be substituted a reference to the Court of Session or, if an action of defamation is depending in the sheriff court in respect of the publication in question, the sheriff; the expression 'costs' means expenses; and for any reference to a defence of justification there shall be substituted a reference to a defence of veritas.

### 16.   Interpretation

(1)   Any reference in this Act to words shall be construed as including a reference to pictures, visual images, gestures and other methods of signifying meaning.

### 17.   Proceedings affected and savings

(2)   Nothing in this Act affects the law relating to criminal libel.

## FINANCE ACT 1956
### (1956, c 54)

*Retirement annuities and related matters*

**22.  Retirement annuities (relief for premiums, and earned income relief)**

(1)  Where, in the year 1956–57 or any subsequent year of assessment, an individual—

(a)  is (or would but for an insufficiency of profits or gains be) chargeable to tax in respect of relevant earnings from any trade, profession, vocation, office or employment carried on or held by him; and

(b)  pays a premium or other consideration under an annuity contract for the time being approved by the Commissioners of Inland Revenue as having for its main object the provision for the individual of a life annuity in old age (hereafter in this Part of this Act referred to as 'a qualifying premium');

then relief from tax may be given in respect of the qualifying premium under the next following section, and any annuity payable to the same or another individual shall be treated as earned income of the annuitant to the extent to which it is payable in return for any amount on which relief is so given.

(2)  Subject to the next following subsection, the Commissioners shall not approve a contract unless it appears to them to satisfy the conditions that it is made by the individual with a person lawfully carrying on in the United Kingdom the business of granting annuities on human life, and that it does not—

(a)  provide for the payment by that person during the life of the individual of any sum except sums payable by way of annuity to the individual; or

(b)  provide for the annuity payable to the individual to commence before he attains the age of sixty or after he attains the age of seventy; or

(c)  provide for the payment by that person of any other sums except sums payable by way of annuity to the individual's widow or widower and any sums which, in the event of no annuity becoming payable either to the individual or to a widow or widower, are payable to the individual's personal representatives by way of return of premiums, by way of reasonable interest on premiums or by way of bonuses out of profits; or

(d)  provide for the annuity, if any, payable to a widow or widower of the individual to be of a greater annual amount than that paid or payable to the individual; or

(e)  provide for the payment of any annuity otherwise than for the life of the annuitant;

and that it does include provision securing that no annuity payable under it shall be capable in whole or in part of surrender, commutation or assignment.

(3)  The Commissioners may, if they think fit, and subject to any conditions they think proper to impose, approve a contract otherwise satisfying the foregoing conditions, notwithstanding that the contract provides for one or more of the following matters, that is to say,—

(a)  for the payment after the individual's death of an annuity to a dependant not the widow or widower of the individual;

(b)  for the payment to the individual of an annuity commencing before he attains the age of sixty, if the annuity is payable on his becoming incapable through infirmity of mind or body of carrying on his own occupation or any occupation of a similar nature for which he is trained or fitted;

(c)  if the individual's occupation is one in which persons customarily retire before attaining the age of sixty, for the annuity to commence before he attains that age (but not before he attains the age of fifty);

(d)  for the annuity payable to any person to continue for a term certain (not exceeding ten years), notwithstanding his death within that term, or for the annuity payable to any person to terminate, or be suspended, on marriage (or remarriage) or in other circumstances;

(e)   in the case of an annuity which is to continue for a term certain, for the annuity to be assignable by will, and in the event of any person dying entitled to it, for it to be assignable by his personal representatives in the distribution of the estate so as to give effect to a testamentary disposition, or to the rights of those entitled on intestacy, or to an appropriation of it to a legacy or to a share or interest in the estate.

(4)   So much of subsection (1) of this section as provides that an annuity shall be treated, in whole or in part, as earned income of the annuitant shall apply only in relation to the annuitant to whom the annuity is made payable by the terms of the contract.

(5)   The foregoing provisions of this section shall apply in relation to a contribution under a trust scheme approved by the Commissioners of Inland Revenue as they apply in relation to a premium under an annuity contract so approved, with the modification that, for the condition as to the person with whom the contract is made, there shall be substituted a condition that the scheme—

(a)   is established under the law of any part of, and administered in, the United Kingdom; and

(b)   is established for the benefit of individuals engaged in or connected with a particular occupation (or one or other of a group of occupations), and for the purpose of providing retirement annuities for them, with or without subsidiary benefits for their families or dependants; and

(c)   is so established under irrevocable trusts by a body of persons comprising or representing a substantial proportion of the individuals so engaged in the United Kingdom, or of those so engaged in England, Wales, Scotland or Northern Ireland;

and with the necessary adaptations of other references to the contract or the person with whom it is made; and exemption from income tax shall be allowed in respect of income derived from investments or deposits of any fund maintained for the purpose aforesaid under a scheme for the time being approved under this subsection.

(6)   The Commissioners may at any time, by notice in writing given to the persons by and to whom premiums are payable under any contract for the time being approved under this section, or to the trustees or other persons having the management of any scheme so approved, withdraw that approval on such grounds and from such date as may be specified in the notice.

(7)   For the purposes of this Part of this Act, a married woman's relevant earnings shall not be treated as her husband's relevant earnings, notwithstanding that her income chargeable to tax is treated as his income.

(8)   Subject to the last foregoing subsection, 'relevant earnings' in relation to any individual means for the purposes of this Part of this Act any income of his chargeable to tax for the year of assessment in question, being either—

(a)   income arising in respect of remuneration from an office or employment of profit held by him other than a pensionable office or employment; or

(b)   income from any property which is attached to or forms part of the emoluments of any such office or employment of profit held by him; or

(c)   income which is chargeable under Schedule B or Schedule D and is immediately derived by him from the carrying on or exercise by him of his trade, profession or vocation either as an individual or, in the case of a partnership, as a partner personally acting therein; or

(d)   income treated as earned income by virtue of paragraph (d) (which relates to patent rights) of subsection (2) of section five hundred and twenty-five of the Income Tax Act, 1952;

but does not include any remuneration as director of an investment company (as defined in section two hundred and fifty-seven of the Income Tax Act, 1952) of which he is a controlling director (as defined in subsection (1) of section three hundred and ninety of that Act).

(9)  For the purposes of this Part of this Act, an office or employment is a pensionable office or employment if, and only if, service in it is service to which a sponsored superannuation scheme relates (not being a scheme under which the benefits provided in respect of that service are limited to a lump sum payable on the termination of the service through death or disability before the age of seventy or some lower age); but references to a pensionable office or employment apply whether or not the duties are performed wholly or partly in the United Kingdom or the holder is chargeable to tax in respect of it.

Service in an office or employment shall not for the purposes of this definition be treated as service to which a sponsored superannuation scheme relates by reason only of the fact that the holder of the office or employment might (though he does not) participate in the scheme by exercising or refraining from exercising an option open to him by virtue of that service.

(10)  In the last foregoing subsection 'a sponsored superannuation scheme' means a scheme or arrangement relating to service in particular offices or employments and having for its object or one of its objects to make provision in respect of persons serving therein against future retirement or partial retirement, against future termination of service through death or disability, or against similar matters, being a scheme or arrangement under which any part of the cost of the provision so made is or has been borne otherwise than by those persons by reason of their service (whether it is the cost or part of the cost of the benefits provided, or of paying premiums or other sums in order to provide those benefits, or of administering or instituting the scheme or arrangement); but for this purpose a person shall be treated as bearing by reason of his service the cost of any payment made or agreed to be made in respect of his service, if that payment or the agreement to make it is treated under the Income Tax Acts as increasing his income, or would be so treated if he were chargeable to tax under Case I of Schedule E in respect of his emoluments from that service.

(11)  Nothing in sections four and six of the Policies of Assurance Act, 1867 (which put on assurance companies certain obligations in relation to notices of assignment of policies of life assurance), shall be taken to apply to any contract approved under this section.

## INTEREST ON DAMAGES (SCOTLAND) ACT 1958
### (1958, c 61)

### 1.  Power of courts to grant interest on damages

[(1)  Where a court pronounces an interlocutor decerning for payment by any person of a sum of money as damages, the interlocutor may include decree for payment by that person of interest, at such rate or rates as may be specified in the interlocutor, on the whole or any part of that sum for the whole or any part of the period between the date when the right of action arose and the date of the interlocutor.

(1A)  Where a court pronounces an interlocutor decerning for payment of a sum which consists of or includes damages or solatium in respect of personal injuries sustained by the pursuer or any other person, then (without prejudice to the exercise of the power conferred by subsection (1) of this section in relation to any part of that sum which does not represent such damages or solatium) the court shall exercise that power so as to include in that sum interest on those damages and on that solatium or on such part of each as the court considers appropriate, unless the court is satisfied that there are reasons special to the case why no interest should be given in respect thereof.

(1B) For the avoidance of doubt, it is hereby declared that where, in any action in which it is competent for the court to award interest under this Act, a tender is made in the course of the action, the tender shall, unless otherwise stated therein, be in full satisfaction of any claim to interest thereunder by any person in whose favour the tender is made; and in considering in any such action whether an award is equal to or greater than an amount tendered in the action, the court shall take account of the amount of any interest awarded under this Act, or such part of that interest as the court considers appropriate.]

(2) Nothing in this section shall—

(a) authorise the granting of interest upon interest, or

(b) prejudice any other power of the court as to the granting of interest, or

(c) affect the running of any interest which apart from this section would run by virtue of any enactment or rule of law.

## 2. Amendment of s 31 of Sheriff Courts (Scotland) Act, 1907

Section thirty-one of the Sheriff Courts (Scotland) Act, 1907 (which among other things specifies the grounds on which an interlocutor of a sheriff entering judgment under that section may be appealed to the Court of Session) shall have effect as if after head (4) thereof there were inserted the following head—

'(5) That no grant of interest on the damages (if any) has been included in the interlocutor or that any such grant so included is inadequate or is excessive.'

and as if there were added at the end of the section the words 'and upon any such appeal so far as based on the ground specified in head (5) of this section the court may make such order as to it seems just.'

## 3. Citation, interpretation, extent and commencement

(1) This Act may be cited as the Interest on Damages (Scotland) Act, 1958.

[(2) In this Act, 'personal injuries' includes any disease and any impairment of a person's physical or mental condition.]

(3) This Act shall extend to Scotland only, and shall not apply to any action commenced against any person before the passing of this Act.

### FINANCE ACT 1959
### (1959, c 30)

### PART IV. STAMP DUTIES

## 30. Stamp duty on policies of insurance

(1) In the first Schedule to the Stamp Act, 1891, before the head of charge 'Policy of Life Insurance' there shall be inserted the following—

|  | £ | s. | d. |
|---|---|---|---|
| 'Policy of Insurance other than Life Insurance | 0 | 0 | 6', |

and the head of charge 'Policy of Sea Insurance' and the head of charge beginning 'Policy of Insurance against Accident' shall be omitted.

(2) The following shall be exempt from all stamp duties:—

(a) cover notes, slips and other instruments usually made in anticipation of the issue of a formal policy, not being instruments relating to life insurance;

(b) instruments embodying alterations of the terms or conditions of any policy of insurance other than life insurance;

(c) policies of insurance on baggage or personal and household effects only, if made or executed out of Great Britain;

and an instrument exempted by virtue of paragraph (a) of this subsection shall not be taken for the purposes of the Stamp Act, 1891, to be a policy of insurance.

(3) An instrument shall not be charged with duty exceeding sixpence by reason only that it contains or relates to two or more distinct matters each falling within the head of charge inserted by subsection (1) of this section.

(4) . . .

(c) section one hundred and sixteen (which enables composition to be made for stamp duty on accident policies) shall apply in relation to all policies of insurance other than life insurance, and the second part of the Second Schedule shall have effect accordingly;
. . .

(6) Notwithstanding the repeal of section ninety-three of the Stamp Act, 1891, a contract for such insurance as is mentioned in section five hundred and six of the Merchant Shipping Act, 1894, shall continue to be admissible in evidence although not embodied in a marine policy as required by section twenty-two of the Marine Insurance Act, 1906.

(7) This section shall apply in relation to instruments made or executed after the beginning of August, nineteen hundred and fifty-nine.

## OCCUPIERS' LIABILITY (SCOTLAND) ACT 1960
### (1960, c 30)

**1. Variation of rules of common law as to duty of care owed by occupiers**

(1) The provisions of the next following section of this Act shall have effect, in place of the rules of the common law, for the purpose of determining the care which a person occupying or having control of land or other premises (in this Act referred to as an 'occupier of premises') is required, by reason of such occupation or control, to show towards persons entering on the premises in respect of dangers which are due to the state of the premises or to anything done or omitted to be done on them and for which he is in law responsible.

(2) Nothing in those provisions shall be taken to alter the rules of the common law which determine the person on whom in relation to any premises a duty to show care as aforesaid towards persons entering thereon is incumbent.

(3) Those provisions shall apply, in like manner and to the same extent as they do in relation to an occupier of premises and to persons entering thereon,—

(a) in relation to a person occupying or having control of any fixed or moveable structure, including any vessel, vehicle or aircraft, and to persons entering thereon; and

(b) in relation to an occupier of premises or a person occupying or having control of any such structure and to property thereon, including the property of persons who have not themselves entered on the premises or structure.

**2. Extent of occupier's duty to show care**

(1) The care which an occupier of premises is required, by reason of his occupation or control of the premises, to show towards a person entering thereon in respect of dangers which are due to the state of the premises or to anything done or omitted to be done on them and for which the occupier is in law responsible shall, except in so far as he is entitled to and does extend, restrict, modify or exclude by agreement his obligations towards that person, be such care as in all the circumstances of the case is reasonable to see that that person will not suffer injury or damage by reason of any such danger.

(2) Nothing in the foregoing subsection shall relieve an occupier of premises of any duty to show in any particular case any higher standard of care which

in that case is incumbent on him by virtue of any enactment or rule of law imposing special standards of care on particular classes of persons.

(3) Nothing in the foregoing provisions of this Act shall be held to impose on an occupier any obligation to a person entering on his premises in respect of risks which that person has willingly accepted as his; and any question whether a risk was so accepted shall be decided on the same principles as in other cases in which one person owes to another a duty to show care.

### 3. Landlord's liability by virtue of responsibility for repairs

(1) Where premises are occupied or used by virtue of a tenancy under which the landlord is responsible for the maintenance or repair of the premises, it shall be the duty of the landlord to show towards any persons who or whose property may from time to time be on the premises the same care in respect of dangers arising from any failure on his part in carrying out his responsibility aforesaid as is required by virtue of the foregoing provisions of this Act to be shown by an occupier of premises towards persons entering on them.

(2) Where premises are occupied or used by virtue of a subtenancy, the foregoing subsection shall apply to any landlord who is responsible for the maintenance or repair of the premises comprised in the sub-tenancy.

(3) Nothing in this section shall relieve a landlord of any duty which he is under apart from this section.

(4) For the purposes of this section, any obligation imposed on a landlord by any enactment by reason of the premises being subject to a tenancy shall be treated as if it were an obligation imposed on him by the tenancy, 'tenancy' includes a statutory tenancy which does not in law amount to a tenancy and includes also any contract conferring a right of occupation, and 'landlord' shall be construed accordingly.

(5) This section shall apply to tenancies created before the commencement of this Act as well as to tenancies created after its commencement.

### 4. Application to Crown

This Act shall bind the Crown, but as regards the liability of the Crown for any wrongful or negligent act or omission giving rise to liability in reparation shall not bind the Crown any further than the Crown is made liable in respect of such acts or omissions by the Crown Proceedings Act, 1947, and that Act and in particular section two thereof shall apply in relation to duties under section two or section three of this Act as statutory duties.

### 5. Short title, extent and commencement

(1) This Act may be cited as the Occupiers' Liability (Scotland) Act 1960, and shall extend to Scotland only.

(2) This Act shall come into operation at the end of the period of three months beginning with the day on which it is passed.

## LAW REFORM (HUSBAND AND WIFE) ACT 1962
### (1962, c 48)

### 2. Proceedings between husband and wife in respect of delict

(1) Subject to the provisions of this section, each of the parties to a marriage shall have the like right to bring proceedings against the other in respect of a wrongful or negligent act or omission, or for the prevention of a wrongful act, as if they were not married.

(2) Where any such proceedings are brought by one of the parties to a marriage against the other during the subsistence of the marriage, the court may dismiss the proceedings if it appears that no substantial benefit would accrue to either party from the continuation thereof; and it shall be the duty of the court

to consider at an early stage of the proceedings whether the power to dismiss the proceedings under this subsection should or should not be exercised.

(3)   This section extends to Scotland only.

## HIRE-PURCHASE ACT 1964
### (1964, c 53)

[PART III. TITLE TO MOTOR VEHICLES ON HIRE-PURCHASE OR CONDITIONAL SALE

### 27. Protection of purchasers of motor vehicles

(1)   This section applies where a motor vehicle has been bailed or (in Scotland) hired under a hire-purchase agreement, or has been agreed to be sold under a conditional sale agreement, and, before the property in the vehicle has become vested in the debtor, he disposes of the vehicle to another person.

(2)   Where the disposition referred to in subsection (1) above is to a private purchaser, and he is a purchaser of the motor vehicle in good faith without notice of the hire-purchase or conditional sale agreement (the 'relevant agreement') that disposition shall have effect as if the creditor's title to the vehicle has been vested in the debtor immediately before that disposition.

(3)   Where the person to whom the disposition referred to in subsection (1) above is made (the 'original purchaser') is a trade or finance purchaser, then if the person who is the first private purchaser of the motor vehicle after that disposition (the 'first private purchaser') is a purchaser of the vehicle in good faith without notice of the relevant agreement, the disposition of the vehicle to the first private purchaser shall have effect as if the title of the creditor to the vehicle had been vested in the debtor immediately before he disposed of it to the original purchaser.

(4)   Where, in a case within subsection (3) above—

(a)   the disposition by which the first private purchaser becomes a purchaser of the motor vehicle in good faith without notice of the relevant agreement is itself a bailment or hiring under a hire-purchase agreement, and

(b)   the person who is the creditor in relation to that agreement disposes of the vehicle to the first private purchaser, or a person claiming under him, by transferring to him the property in the vehicle in pursuance of a provision in the agreement in that behalf, the disposition referred to in paragraph (b) above (whether or not the person to whom it is made is a purchaser in good faith without notice of the relevant agreement) shall as well as the disposition referred to in paragraph (a) above, have effect as mentioned in subsection (3) above.

(5)   The preceding provisions of this section apply—

(a)   notwithstanding anything in [section 21 of the Sale of Goods Act 1979] (sale of goods by a person not the owner), but

(b)   without prejudice to the provisions of the Factors Acts (as defined by [section 61(1) of the said Act of 1979]) or any other enactment enabling the apparent owner of goods to dispose of them as if he were the true owner.

(6)   Nothing in this section shall exonerate the debtor from any liability (whether criminal or civil) to which he would be subject apart from this section; and, in a case where the debtor disposes of the motor vehicle to a trade or finance purchaser, nothing in this section shall exonerate—

(a)   that trade or finance purchaser, or

(b)   any other trade or finance purchaser who becomes a purchaser of the vehicle and is not a person claiming under the first private purchaser,

from any liability (whether criminal or civil) to which he would be subject apart from this section.

### 28. Presumptions relating to dealings with motor vehicles

(1)   Where in any proceedings (whether criminal or civil) relating to a motor vehicle it is proved—

(a)   that the vehicle was bailed or (in Scotland) hired under a hire-purchase agreement, or was agreed to be sold under a conditional sale agreement and

(b)   that a person (whether a party to the proceedings or not) became a private purchaser of the vehicle in good faith without notice of the hire-purchase or conditional sale agreement (the 'relevant agreement'), this section shall have effect for the purposes of the operation of section 27 of this Act in relation to those proceedings.

(2)   It shall be presumed for those purposes unless the contrary is proved, that the disposition of the vehicle to the person referred to in subsection (1)(b) above (the 'relevant purchaser') was made by the debtor.

(3)   If it is proved that that disposition was not made by the debtor, then it shall be presumed for those purposes, unless the contrary is proved—

(a)   that the debtor disposed of the vehicle to a private purchaser purchasing in good faith without notice of the relevant agreement, and

(b)   that the relevant purchaser is or was a person claiming under the person to whom the debtor so disposed of the vehicle.

(4)   If it is proved that the disposition of the vehicle to the relevant purchaser was not made by the debtor, and that the person to whom the debtor disposed of the vehicle (the 'original purchaser') was a trade or finance purchaser, then it shall be presumed for those purposes, unless the contrary is proved—

(a)   that the person who, after the disposition of the vehicle to the original purchaser, first became a private purchaser of the vehicle was a purchaser in good faith without notice of the relevant agreement, and

(b)   that the relevant purchaser is or was a person claiming under the original purchaser.

(5)   Without prejudice to any other method of proof, where in any proceedings a party thereto admits a fact, that fact shall, for the purposes of this section, be taken as against him to be proved in relation to those proceedings.

### 29. Interpretation of Part III

(1)   In this Part of this Act—

'conditional sale agreement' means an agreement for the sale of goods under which the purchase price or part of it is payable by instalments, and the property in the goods is to remain in the seller (notwithstanding that the buyer is to be in possession of the goods) until such conditions as to the payment of instalments or otherwise as may be specified in the agreement are fulfilled;

'creditor' means the person by whom goods are bailed or (in Scotland) hired under a hire-purchase agreement or as the case may be, the seller under a conditional sale agreement, or the person to whom his rights and duties have passed by assignment or operation of law;

'disposition' means any sale or contract of sale (including a conditional sale agreement), any bailment or (in Scotland) hiring under a hire-purchase agreement and any transfer of the property of goods in pursuance of a provision in that behalf contained in a hire-purchase agreement, and includes any transaction purporting to be a disposition (as so defined), and 'dispose of' shall be construed accordingly;

'hire-purchase agreement' means an agreement, other than a conditional sale agreement, under which—

(a)   goods are bailed or (in Scotland) hired in return for periodical payments by the person to whom they are bailed or hired, and

(b)   the property in the goods will pass to that person if the terms of the agreement are complied with and one or more of the following occurs—

(i)   the exercise of an option to purchase by that person,

(ii)  the doing of any other specified act by any party to the agreement,

(iii)  the happening of any other specified events; and

'motor vehicle' means a mechanically propelled vehicle intended or adapted for use on roads to which the public has access.

(2)  In this Part of this Act 'trade or finance purchaser' means a purchaser who, at the time of the disposition made to him, carries on a business which consists, wholly or partly—

(a)  of purchasing motor vehicles for the purpose of offering or exposing them for sale, or

(b)  of providing finance by purchasing motor vehicles for the purpose of bailing or (in Scotland) hiring them under hire-purchase agreements or agreeing to sell them under conditional sale agreements,

and 'private purchaser' means a purchaser who, at the time of the disposition made to him, does not carry on any such business.

(3)  For the purposes of this Part of this Act a person becomes a purchaser of a motor vehicle if, and at the time when, a disposition of the vehicle is made to him; and a person shall be taken to be a purchaser of a motor vehicle without notice of a hire-purchase agreement or conditional sale agreement if, at the time of the disposition made to him, he has no actual notice that the vehicle is or was the subject of any such agreement.

(4)  In this Part of this Act the 'debtor' in relation to a motor vehicle which has been bailed or hired under a hire-purchase agreement, or, as the case may be, agreed to be sold under a conditional sale agreement, means the person who at the material time (whether the agreement has before that time been terminated or not) either—

(a)  is the person to whom the vehicle is bailed or hired under that agreement, or

(b)  is, in relation to the agreement, the buyer,

including a person who at that time is, by virtue of section 130(4) of the Consumer Credit Act 1974 treated as a bailee or (in Scotland) a custodier of the vehicle.

(5)  In this Part of this Act any reference to the title of the creditor to a motor vehicle which has been bailed or (in Scotland) hired under a hire-purchase agreement or agreed to be sold under a conditional sale agreement, and is disposed of by the debtor, is a reference to such title (if any) to the vehicle as, immediately before that disposition, was vested in the person who then was the creditor in relation to the agreement.]

## EMPLOYERS' LIABILITY (DEFECTIVE EQUIPMENT) ACT 1969
### (1969, c 37)

### 1. Extension of employer's liability for defective equipment

(1)  Where after the commencement of this Act—

(a)  an employee suffers personal injury in the course of his employment in consequence of a defect in equipment provided by his employer for the purposes of the employer's business; and

(b)  the defect is attributable wholly or partly to the fault of a third party (whether identified or not),

the injury shall be deemed to be also attributable to negligence on the part of the employer (whether or not he is liable in respect of the injury apart from this subsection), but without prejudice to the law relating to contributory negligence and to any remedy by way of contribution or in contract or otherwise which is available to the employer in respect of the injury.

(2)  In so far as any agreement purports to exclude or limit any liability of an employer arising under subsection (1) of this section, the agreement shall be void.

(3)   In this section—

'business' includes the activities carried on by any public body;

'employee' means a person who is employed by another person under a contract of service or apprenticeship and is so employed for the purposes of a business carried on by that other person, and 'employer' shall be construed accordingly;

'equipment' includes any plant and machinery, vehicle, aircraft and clothing;

'fault' means negligence, breach of statutory duty or other act or omission which gives rise to liability in tort in England and Wales or which is wrongful and gives rise to liability in damages in Scotland; and

'personal injury' includes loss of life, any impairment of a person's physical or mental condition and any disease.

(4)   This section binds the Crown, and persons in the service of the Crown shall accordingly be treated for the purposes of this section as employees of the Crown if they would not be so treated apart from this subsection.

## EMPLOYERS' LIABILITY (COMPULSORY INSURANCE) ACT 1969
### (1969, c 57)

### 1.   Insurance against liability for employees

(1)   Except as otherwise provided by this Act, every employer ... shall insure, and maintain insurance, under one or more approved policies with an authorised insurer or insurers against liability for bodily injury or disease sustained by [those of his relevant employees who are employed by him for work on or from an offshore installation, or on or from an associated structure in the course of an activity undertaken on or in connection with an offshore installation, and arising out of and in the course of their employment for that work.]

(2)   Regulations may provide that the amount for which an employer is required by this Act to insure and maintain insurance shall, either generally or in such cases or classes of case as may be prescribed by the regulations, be limited in such manner as may be so prescribed.

### 2.   Employees to be covered

(1)   For the purposes of this Act the term 'employee' means an individual who has entered into or works under a contract of service or apprenticeship with an employer whether by way of manual labour, clerical work or otherwise, whether such contract is expressed or implied, oral or in writing.

(2)   This Act shall not require an employer to insure—

(a)   in respect of an employee of whom the employer is the husband, wife, father, mother, grandfather, grandmother, step-father, step-mother, son, daughter, grandson, granddaughter, stepson, stepdaughter, brother, sister, half-brother, half-sister.

## INCOME AND CORPORATION TAXES ACT 1970
### (1970, c 10)

### CHAPTER III. RETIREMENT ANNUITIES

### 226.   Approval of retirement annuity contracts and trust schemes

(1)   Where, in any year of assessment, an individual—

(a)   is (or would but for an insufficiency of profits or gains be) chargeable to income tax in respect of relevant earnings from any trade, profession, vocation, office or employment carried on or held by him, and

(b)   pays a premium or other consideration under an annuity contract for the time being approved by the Board as having for its main object the

provision for the individual of a life annuity in old age [or under a contract
for the time being approved under section 226A of this Act] (hereafter in this
Chapter referred to as 'a qualifying premium'),
then relief from income tax may be given in respect of the qualifying premium
under section 227 below, and any annuity payable to the same or another
individual shall be treated as earned income of the annuitant to the extent to
which it is payable in return for any amount on which relief is so given.

(2)  Subject to subsection (3) below, the Board shall not approve a contract
unless it appears to them to satisfy the conditions that it is made by the
individual with a person lawfully carrying on in the United Kingdom the
business of granting annuities on human life, and that it does not—

(a)  provide for the payment by that person during the life of the
individual of any sum except sums payable by way of annuity to the
individual, or

(b)  provide for the annuity payable to the individual to commence before
he attains the age of sixty or after he attains the age of seventy, or

(c)  provide for the payment by that person of any other sums except
sums payable by way of annuity to the individual's widow or widower and
any sums which, in the event of no annuity becoming payable either to the
individual or to a widow or widower, are payable to the individual's personal
representatives by way of return of premiums, by way of reasonable interest
on premiums or by way of bonuses out of profits, or

(d)  provide for the annuity, if any, payable to a widow or widower of the
individual to be of a greater annual amount than that paid or payable to the
individual, or

(e)  provide for the payment of any annuity otherwise than for the life of
the annuitant,
and that it does include provision securing that no annuity payable under it
shall be capable in whole or in part of surrender, commutation or assignment
[provided that the contract may give the individual the right to receive, by way
of commutation of part of the annuity payable to him, a lump sum not
exceeding three times the annual amount of the remaining part of the annuity
taking, where the annual amount is or may be different in different years, the
initial annual amount, and shall make any such right depend on the exercise by
the individual of an election at or before the time when the annuity first
becomes payable to him].

(3)  The Board may, if they think fit, and subject to any conditions they think
proper to impose, approve a contract otherwise satisfying the preceding
conditions, notwithstanding that the contract provides for one or more of the
following matters—

(a)  for the payment after the individual's death of an annuity to a
dependant not the widow or widower of the individual,

(b)  for the payment to the individual of an annuity commencing before he
attains the age of sixty, if the annuity is payable on his becoming incapable
through infirmity of body or mind of carrying on his own occupation or any
occupation of a similar nature for which he is trained or fitted,

(c)  if the individual's occupation is one in which persons customarily
retire before attaining the age of sixty, for the annuity to commence before he
attains that age (but not before he attains the age of fifty),

(d)  for the annuity payable to any person to continue for a term certain
(not exceeding two years), notwithstanding his death within that term, or for
the annuity payable to any person to terminate, or be suspended, on marriage
(or re-marriage) or in other circumstances,

(e)  in the case of an annuity which is to continue for a term certain, for
the annuity to be assignable by will, and in the event of any person dying
entitled to it, for it to be assignable by his personal representatives in the

distribution of the estate so as to give effect to a testamentary disposition, or to the rights of those entitled on intestacy, or to an appropriation of it to a legacy or to a share or interest in the estate.

(4) So much of subsection (1) above as provides that an annuity shall be treated, in whole or in part, as earned income of the annuitant shall apply only in relation to the annuitant to whom the annuity is made payable by the terms of the contract.

(5) The preceding provisions of this section shall apply in relation to a contribution under a trust scheme approved by the Board as they apply in relation to a premium under an annuity contract so approved, with the modification that, for the condition as to the person with whom the contract is made, there shall be substituted a condition that the scheme—

(a) is established under the law of any part of, and administered in, the United Kingdom, and

(b) is established for the benefit of individuals engaged in or connected with a particular occupation (or one or other of a group of occupations), and for the purpose of providing retirement annuities for them, with or without subsidiary benefits for their families or dependants, and

(c) is so established under irrevocable trusts by a body of persons comprising or representing a substantial proportion of the individuals so engaged in the United Kingdom, or of those so engaged in England, Wales, Scotland or Northern Ireland,

and with the necessary adaptations of other references to the contract or the person with whom it is made.

(6) Exemption from income tax . . . shall not be a chargeable gain for the purposes of capital gains tax.

(7) The Board may at any time, by notice in writing given to the persons by and to whom premiums are payable under any contract for the time being approved under this section, or to the trustees or other persons having the management of any scheme so approved, withdraw that approval on such grounds and from such date as may be specified in the notice.

(8) For the purposes of this Chapter, a married woman's relevant earnings shall not be treated as her husband's relevant earnings, notwithstanding that her income chargeable to tax is treated as his income.

(9) Subject to subsection (8) above, 'relevant earnings', in relation to any individual, means for the purposes of this Chapter any income of his chargeable to tax for the year of assessment in question, being either—

(a) income arising in respect of remuneration from an office or employment held by him other than a pensionable office or employment, or

(b) income from any property which is attached to or forms part of the emoluments of any such office or employment held by him, or

(c) income which is chargeable under Schedule A or Schedule D and is immediately derived by him from the carrying on or exercise by him of his trade, profession or vocation either as an individual or, in the case of a partnership, as a partner personally acting therein, or

(d) income treated as earned income by virtue of section 383 of this Act (patent rights),

but does not include any remuneration as director of a company whose income consists wholly or mainly of investment income (construed in accordance with section 292(1) of this Act), being a company of which he is a controlling director (as defined in section 224(1) above).

(10) For the purposes of this Chapter, an office or employment is a pensionable office or employment if, and only if, service in it is service to which a sponsored superannuation scheme relates (not being a scheme under which the benefits provided in respect of that service are limited to a lump sum payable on the termination of the service through death or disability before the

age of seventy or some lower age); but references to a pensionable office or employment apply whether or not the duties are performed wholly or partly in the United Kingdom or the holder is chargeable to tax in respect of it.

Service in an office or employment shall not for the purposes of this definition be treated as service to which a sponsored superannuation scheme relates by reason only of the fact that the holder of the office or employment might (though he does not) participate in the scheme by exercising or refraining from exercising an option open to him by virtue of that service.

(11) In subsection (10) above 'a sponsored superannuation scheme' means a scheme or arrangement relating to service in particular offices or employments and having for its object or one of its objects to make provision in respect of persons serving therein against future retirement or partial retirement, against future termination of service through death or disability, or against similar matters, being a scheme or arrangement under which any part of the cost of the provision so made is or has been borne otherwise than by those persons by reason of their service (whether it is the cost or part of the cost of the benefits provided, or of paying premiums or other sums in order to provide those benefits, or of administering or instituting the scheme or arrangement); but for this purpose a person shall be treated as bearing by reason of his service the cost of any payment made or agreed to be made in respect of his service, if that payment or the agreement to make it is treated under the Income Tax Acts as increasing his income, or would be so treated if he were chargeable to tax under Case I of Schedule E in respect of his emoluments from that service.

(12) Nothing in sections 4 and 6 of the Policies of Assurance Act 1867 (which put on assurance companies certain obligations in relation to notices of assignment of policies of life assurance) shall be taken to apply to any contract approved under this section.

(13) For the purposes of any provision applying this subsection 'approved annuities' means annuities under contracts approved by the Board under this section, being annuities payable wholly in return for premiums or other consideration paid by a person who (when the premiums or other consideration are or is payable) is, or would but for an insufficiency of profits or gains be, chargeable to tax in respect of relevant earnings from a trade, profession, vocation, office or employment carried on or held by him.

**[226A.   Contracts for dependants or life insurance**

(1) The Board may approve under this section—

(a) a contract the main object of which is the provision of an annuity for the wife or husband of the individual, or for any one or more dependants of the individual,

(b) a contract the sole object of which is the provision of a lump sum on the death of the individual before he attains the age of 70, being a lump sum payable to his personal representatives.

(2) The Board shall not approve the contract unless it appears to them that it is made by the individual with a person lawfully carrying on in the United Kingdom the business of granting annuities on human life.

(3) The Board shall not approve a contract under subsection (1)(a) above unless it appears to them to satisfy all the following conditions, that is—

(a) that any annuity payable to the wife or husband or dependant of the individual commences on the death of the individual,

(b) that any annuity payable to the individual commences at a time after the individual attains the age of 60, and, unless the individual's annuity is one to commence on the death of a person to whom an annuity would be payable under the contract if that person survived the individual, can not commence after the time when the individual attains the age of 70,

(c) that the contract does not provide for the payment by the person contracting with the individual of any sum, other than any annuity payable to the individual's wife or husband or dependant, or to the individual except, in the event of no annuity becoming payable under the contract, any sums payable to the individual's personal representatives by way of return of premiums, by way of reasonable interest on premiums or by way of bonuses out of profits,

(d) that the contract does not provide for the payment of any annuity otherwise than for the life of the annuitant,

(e) that the contract does include provision securing that no annuity payable under it shall be capable in whole or in part of surrender, commutation or assignment.

(4) The Board may, if they think fit, and subject to any conditions that they think proper to impose, approve a contract under subsection (1)(a) above notwithstanding that, in one or more respects, they are not satisfied that the contract complies with the provisions of paragraphs (a) to (e) of subsection (3) above.

(5) Subsections (2) and (3) of section 226 above shall not apply to the approval of a contract under this section.

(6) The main purpose of a trust scheme, or part of a trust scheme, within section 226(5) above may be to provide annuities for the wives, husbands and dependants of the individuals, or lump sums payable to the individuals' personal representatives on death and in that case—

(a) approval of the trust scheme shall be subject to the preceding provisions of this section with any necessary modifications, and not subject to subsections (2) and (3) of section 226 above,

(b) the provisions of this Chapter shall apply to the scheme or part of the scheme when duly approved as it applies to a contract approved under this section,

(c) section 226(6) above (tax relief for investments or deposits of the fund) shall apply to any duly approved trust scheme, or part of a trust scheme.

(7) Except as otherwise provided in this Chapter, any reference in the Tax Acts to a contract or scheme approved under section 226 above shall include a reference to a contract or scheme approved under this section.]

## PRESCRIPTION AND LIMITATION (SCOTLAND) ACT 1973
### (1973, c 52)

*Negative prescription*

### 6. Extinction of obligations by prescriptive periods of five years

(1) If, after the appropriate date, an obligation to which this section applies has subsisted for a continuous period of five years—

(a) without any relevant claim having been made in relation to the obligation, and

(b) without the subsistence of the obligation having been relevantly acknowledged,

then as from the expiration of that period the obligation shall be extinguished:

Provided that in its application to an obligation under a bill of exchange or a promissory note this subsection shall have effect as if paragraph (b) thereof were omitted.

(2) Schedule 1 to this Act shall have effect for defining the obligations to which this section applies.

(3) In subsection (1) above the reference to the appropriate date, in relation to an obligation of any kind specified in Schedule 2 to this Act is a reference to the date specified in that Schedule in relation to obligations of that kind, and in

relation to an obligation of any other kind is a reference to the date when the obligation became enforceable.

(4) In the computation of a prescriptive period in relation to any obligation for the purposes of this section—

(a) any period during which by reason of—

(i) fraud on the part of the debtor or any person acting on his behalf, or

(ii) error induced by words or conduct of the debtor or any person acting on his behalf,

the creditor was induced to refrain from making a relevant claim in relation to the obligation, and

(b) any period during which the original creditor (while he is the creditor) was under legal disability,

shall not be reckoned as, or as part of, the prescriptive period:

Provided that any period such as is mentioned in paragraph (a) of this subsection shall not include any time occurring after the creditor could with reasonable diligence have discovered the fraud or error, as the case may be, referred to in that paragraph.

(5) Any period such as is mentioned in paragraph (a) or (b) of subsection (4) of this section shall not be regarded as separating the time immediately before it from the time immediately after it.

**7. Extinctions of obligations by prescriptive periods of twenty years**

(1) If, after the date when any obligation to which this section applies has become enforceable, the obligation has subsisted for a continuous period of twenty years—

(a) without any relevant claim having been made in relation to the obligation, and

(b) without the subsistence of the obligation having been relevantly acknowledged,

then as from the expiration of that period the obligation shall be extinguished:

Provided that in its application to an obligation under a bill of exchange or a promissory note this subsection shall have effect as if paragraph (b) thereof were omitted.

(2) This section applies to an obligation of any kind (including an obligation [to which section 22A of this Act applies or an obligation] to which section 6 of this Act applies), not being an obligation specified in Schedule 3 to this Act as an imprescriptible obligation [or an obligation to make reparation in respect of personal injuries within the meaning of Part II of this Act or in respect of the death of any person as a result of such injuries.]

**11. Obligations to make reparation**

(1) Subject to subsections (2) and (3) below, any obligation (whether arising from any enactment, or from any rule of law or from, or by reason of any breach of, a contract or promise) to make reparation for loss, injury or damage caused by an act, neglect or default shall be regarded for the purposes of section 6 of this Act as having become enforceable on the date when the loss, injury or damage occurred.

(2) Where as a result of a continuing act, neglect or default loss, injury or damage has occurred before the cessation of the act, neglect or default the loss, injury or damage shall be deemed for the purposes of subsection (1) above to have occurred on the date when the act, neglect or default ceased.

(3) In relation to a case where on the date referred to in subsection (1) above (or, as the case may be, that subsection as modified by subsection (2) above) the creditor was not aware, and could not with reasonable diligence have been aware, that loss, injury or damage caused as aforesaid had occurred, the said subsection (1) shall have effect as if for the reference therein to that date there

were substituted a reference to the date when the creditor first became, or could with reasonable diligence have become, so aware.

(4)   Subsections (1) and (2) above (with the omission of any reference therein to subsection (3) above) shall have effect for the purposes of section 7 of this Act as they have effect for the purposes of section 6 of this Act; . . .

### [17.   Actions in respect of personal injuries not resulting in death

(1)   This section applies to an action of damages where the damages claimed consist of or include damages in respect of personal injuries, being an action (other than an action to which section 18 of this Act applies) brought by the person who sustained the injuries or any other person.

(2)   Subject to subsection (3) below and section 19A of this Act, no action to which this section applies shall be brought unless it is commenced within a period of 3 years after—

(a)   the date on which the injuries were sustained or, where the act or omission to which the injuries were attributable was a continuing one, that date or the date on which the act or omission ceased, whichever is the later; or

(b)   the date (if later than any date mentioned in paragraph (a) above) on which the pursuer in the action became, or on which, in the opinion of the court, it would have been reasonably practicable for him in all the circumstances to become, aware of all the following facts—

(i)   that the injuries in question were sufficiently serious to justify his bringing an action of damages on the assumption that the person against whom the action was brought did not dispute liability and was able to satisfy a decree;

(ii)   that the injuries were attributable in whole or in part to an act or omission; and

(iii)   that the defender was a person to whose act or omission the injuries were attributable in whole or in part or the employer or principal of such a person.

(3)   In the computation of the period specified in subsection (2) above there shall be disregarded any time during which the person who sustained the injuries was under legal disability by reason of nonage or unsoundness of mind.

### 18.   Actions where death has resulted from personal injuries

(1)   This section applies to any action in which, following the death of any person from personal injuries, damages are claimed in respect of the injuries or the death.

(2)   Subject to subsections (3) and (4) below and section 19A of this Act, no action to which this section applies shall be brought unless it is commenced within a period of 3 years after—

(a)   the date of death of the deceased; or

(b)   the date (if later than the date of death) on which the pursuer in the action became, or on which, in the opinion of the court, it would have been reasonably practicable for him in all the circumstances to become, aware of both of the following facts—

(i)   that the injuries of the deceased were attributable in whole or in part to an act or omission; and

(ii)   that the defender was a person to whose act or omission the injuries were attributable in whole or in part or the employer or principal of such a person.

(3)   Where the pursuer is a relative of the deceased, there shall be disregarded in the computation of the period specified in subsection (2) above any time during which the relative was under legal disability by reason of nonage or unsoundness of mind.

(4)   Subject to section 19A of this Act, where an action of damages has not

been brought by or on behalf of a person who has sustained personal injuries within the period specified in section 17(2) of this Act and that person subsequently dies in consequence of those injuries, no action to which this section applies shall be brought in respect of those injuries or the death from those injuries.

(5) In this section 'relative' has the same meaning as in Schedule 1 to the Damages (Scotland) Act 1976.

**18A. Limitation of defamation and other actions**

(1) Subject to subsections (2) and (3) below and section 19A of this Act, no action for defamation shall be brought unless it is commenced within a period of 3 years after the date when the right of action accrued.

(2) In the computation of the period specified in subsection (1) above there shall be disregarded any time during which the person alleged to have been defamed was under legal disability by reason of nonage or unsoundness of mind.

(3) Nothing in this section shall affect any right of action which accrued before the commencement of this section.

(4) In this section—

(a) 'defamation' includes *convicium* and malicious falsehood, and 'defamed' shall be construed accordingly; and

(b) references to the date when a right of action accrued shall be construed as references to the date when the publication or communication in respect of which the action for defamation is to be brought first came to the notice of the pursuer.

**18B. Actions of harassment**

(1) This section applies to actions of harassment (within the meaning of section 8 of the Protection from Harassment Act 1997) which include a claim for damages.

(2) Subject to subsection (3) below and to section 19A of this Act, no action to which this section applies shall be brought unless it is commenced within a period of 3 years after—

(a) the date on which the alleged harassment ceased; or

(b) the date (if later than the date mentioned in paragraph (a) above) on which the pursuer in the action became, or on which, in the opinion of the court, it would have been reasonably practicable for him in all the circumstances to have become, aware, that the defender was a person responsible for the alleged harassment or the employer or principal of such a person.

(3) In the computation of the period specified in subsection (2) above there shall be disregarded any time during which the person who is alleged to have suffered the harassment was under legal disability by reason of nonage or unsoundness of mind.]

**[19A. Power of court to override time-limits etc.**

(1) Where a person would be entitled, but for any of the provisions of sections 17, [18, 18A or 18B] of this Act, to bring an action, the court may, if it seems to it equitable to do so, allow him to bring the action notwithstanding that provision.

(2) The provisions of subsection (1) above shall have effect not only as regards rights of action accruing after the commencement of this section but also as regards those, in respect of which a final judgment has not been pronounced, accruing before such commencement.

(3) In subsection (2) above, the expression 'final judgment' means an interlocutor of a court of first instance which, by itself, or taken along with previous interlocutors, disposes of the subject matter of a cause notwithstanding

that judgment may not have been pronounced on every question raised or that the expenses found due may not have been modified, taxed or decerned for; but the expression does not include an interlocutor dismissing a cause by reason only of a provision mentioned in subsection (1) above.

(4) An action which would not be entertained but for this section shall not be tried by jury.]

**[22. Interpretation of Part II and supplementary provisions**

(1) In this Part of this Act—

'the court' means the Court of Session or the sheriff court; and

'personal injuries' includes any disease and any impairment of a person's physical or mental condition.

(2) Where the pursuer in an action to which section 17, 18 [or 18A] of this Act applies is pursuing the action by virtue of the assignation of a right of action, the reference in subsection (2)(b) of the said section 17 or, [of the said section, or, as the case may be, subsection (4)(b) of the said section 18A] to the pursuer in the action shall be construed as a reference to the assignor of the right of action.

(3) For the purposes of the said subsection (2)(b) knowledge that any act or omission was or was not, as a matter of law, actionable, is irrelevant.

(4) An action which would not be entertained but for the said subsection (2)(b) shall not be tried by jury.]

[PART IIA. PRESCRIPTION OF OBLIGATIONS AND LIMITATION OF ACTIONS UNDER PART I OF THE CONSUMER PROTECTION ACT 1987

*Prescription of obligations*

**[22A. Ten years' prescription of obligations**

(1) An obligation arising from liability under section 2 of the 1987 Act (to make reparation for damage caused wholly or partly by a defect in a product) shall be extinguished if a period of 10 years has expired from the relevant time, unless a relevant claim was made within that period and has not been finally disposed of, and no such obligation shall come into existence after the expiration of the said period.

(2) If, at the expiration of the period of 10 years mentioned in subsection (1) above, a relevant claim has been made but has not been finally disposed of, the obligation to which the claim relates shall be extinguished when the claim is finally disposed of.

(3) In this section a claim is finally disposed of when—

(a) a decision disposing of the claim has been made against which no appeal is competent;

(b) an appeal against such a decision is competent with leave, and the time limit for leave has expired and no application has been made or leave has been refused;

(c) leave to appeal against such a decision is granted or is not required, and no appeal is made within the time limit for appeal; or

(d) the claim is abandoned;

'relevant claim' in relation to an obligation means a claim made by or on behalf of the creditor for implement or part implement of the obligation, being a claim made—

(a) in appropriate proceedings within the meaning of section 4(2) of this Act; or

(b) by the presentation of, or the concurring in, a petition for sequestration or by the submission of a claim under section 22 or 48 of the Bankruptcy (Scotland) Act 1985; or

(c) by the presentation of, or the concurring in, a petition for the winding up of a company or by the submission of a claim in a liquidation in accordance with the rules made under section 411 of the Insolvency Act 1986; 'relevant time' has the meaning given in section 4(2) of the 1987 Act.

(4)   Where a relevant claim is made in an arbitration, and the nature of the claim has been stated in a preliminary notice (within the meaning of section 4(4) of this Act) relating to that arbitration, the date when the notice is served shall be taken for those purposes to be the date of the making of the claim.]

*Limitation of actions*

**[22B.   3 year limitation of actions**

(1)   This section shall apply to an action to enforce an obligation arising from liability under section 2 of the 1987 Act (to make reparation for damage caused wholly or partly by a defect in a product), except where section 22C of this Act applies.

(2)   Subject to subsection (4) below, an action to which this section applies shall not be competent unless it is commenced within the period of 3 years after the earliest date on which the person seeking to bring (or a person who could at an earlier date have brought) the action was aware, or on which, in the opinion of the court, it was reasonably practicable for him in all the circumstances to become aware, of all the facts mentioned in subsection (3) below.

(3)   The facts referred to in subsection (2) above are—

  (a)   that there was a defect in a product;

  (b)   that the damage was caused or partly caused by the defect;

  (c)   that the damage was sufficiently serious to justify the pursuer (or other person referred to in subsection (2) above) in bringing an action to which this section applies on the assumption that the defender did not dispute liability and was able to satisfy a decree;

  (d)   that the defender was a person liable for the damage under the said section 2.

(4)   In the computation of the period of 3 years mentioned in subsection (2) above, there shall be disregarded any period during which the person seeking to bring the action was under legal disability by reason of nonage or unsoundness of mind.

(5)   The facts mentioned in subsection (3) above do not include knowledge of whether particular facts and circumstances would or would not, as a matter of law, result in liability for damage under the said section 2.

(6)   Where a person would be entitled, but for this section, to bring an action for reparation other than one in which the damages claimed are confined to damages for loss of or damage to property, the court may, if it seems to it equitable to do so, allow him to bring the action notwithstanding this section.

**22C.   Actions under the 1987 Act where death has resulted from personal injuries**

(1)   This section shall apply to an action to enforce an obligation arising from liability under section 2 of the 1987 Act (to make reparation for damage caused wholly or partly by a defect in a product) where a person has died from personal injuries and the damages claimed include damages for those personal injuries or that death.

(2)   Subject to subsection (4) below, an action to which this section applies shall not be competent unless it is commenced within the period of 3 years after the later of—

  (a)   the date of death of the injured person;

  (b)   the earliest date on which the person seeking to make (or a person who could at an earlier date have made) the claim was aware, or on which, in the opinion of the court, it was reasonably practicable for him in all the circumstances to become aware—

    (i)   that there was a defect in the product;

    (ii)   that the injuries of the deceased were caused (or partly caused) by the defect; and

    (iii)   that the defender was a person liable for the damage under the said section 2.

(3)   Where the person seeking to make the claim is a relative of the deceased, there shall be disregarded in the computation of the period mentioned in subsection (2) above any period during which that relative was under legal disability by reason of nonage or unsoundness of mind.

(4)   Where an action to which section 22B of this Act applies has not been brought within the period mentioned in subsection (2) of that section and the person subsequently dies in consequence of his injuries, an action to which this section applies shall not be competent in respect of those injuries or that death.

(5)   Where a person would be entitled, but for this section, to bring an action for reparation other than one in which the damages claimed are confined to damages for loss of or damage to property, the court may, if it seems to it equitable to do so, allow him to bring the action notwithstanding this section.

(6)   In this section 'relative' has the same meaning as in the Damages (Scotland) Act 1976.

(7)   For the purposes of subsection (2)(b) above there shall be disregarded knowledge of whether particular facts and circumstances would or would not, as a matter of law, result in liability for damage under the said section 2.]

*Supplementary*

### [22D.   Interpretation of this Part

(1)   Expressions used in this Part and in Part I of the 1987 Act shall have the same meanings in this Part as in the said Part I.

(2)   For the purposes of section 1(1) of the 1987 Act, this Part shall have effect and be construed as if it were contained in Part I of that Act.

(3)   In this Part, 'the 1987 Act' means the Consumer Protection Act 1987.]

### 23A.   Private international law application

(1)   Where the substantive law of a country other than Scotland falls to be applied by a Scottish court as the law governing an obligation, the court shall apply the relevant rules of law of that country relating to the extinction of the obligations or the limitation of time within which proceedings may be brought to enforce the obligation to the exclusion of any corresponding rule of Scots law.

(2)   This section shall not apply where it appears to the court that the application of the relevant foreign rule of law would be incompatible with the principles of public policy applied by the court.

(3)   This section shall not apply in any case where the application of the corresponding rule of Scots law has extinguished the obligation, or barred the bringing of proceedings prior to the coming into force of the Prescription and Limitation (Scotland) Act 1984.

## SCHEDULES

## SCHEDULE 1. OBLIGATIONS AFFECTED BY PRESCRIPTIVE PERIODS OF FIVE YEARS UNDER SECTION 6

1.  Subject to paragraph 2 below, section 6 of this Act applies—
    (a)  to any obligation to pay a sum of money due in respect of a particular period—
        (i)  by way of interest;
        (ii)  by way of an instalment of an annuity;
        (iii)  by way of feuduty or other periodical payment under a feu grant;
        (iv)  by way of ground annual or other periodical payment under a contract of ground annual;
        (v)  by way of rent or other periodical payment under a lease;
        (vi)  by way of a periodical payment in respect of the occupancy or use of land, not being an obligation falling within any other provision of this sub-paragraph;
        (vii)  by way of a periodical payment under a land obligation, not being an obligation falling within any other provision of this sub-paragraph;
    (b)  to any obligation based on redress of unjustified enrichment, including without prejudice to that generality any obligation of restitution, repetition or recompense;
    (c)  to any obligation arising from *negotiorum gestio*;
    (d)  to any obligation arising from liability (whether arising from any enactment or from any rule of law) to make reparation;
    (e)  to any obligation under a bill of exchange or a promissory note;
    (f)  to any obligation of accounting, other than accounting for trust funds;
    (g)  to any obligation arising from, or by reason of any breach of, a contract or promise, not being an obligation falling within any other provision of this paragraph.

2.  Notwithstanding anything in the foregoing paragraph, section 6 of this Act does not apply—
    (a)  to any obligation to recognise or obtemper a decree of court, an arbitration award or an order of a tribunal or authority exercising jurisdiction under any enactment;
    (b)  to any obligation arising from the issue of a bank note;
    . . .
    (d)  to any obligation under a contract of partnership or of agency, not being an obligation remaining, or becoming, prestable on or after the termination of the relationship between the parties under the contract;
    (e)  except as provided in paragraph 1(a) of this Schedule, to any obligation relating to land (including an obligation to recognise a servitude);
    (f)  to any obligation to satisfy any claim to terce, courtesy, legitim, *jus relicti* or *jus relictae*, or to any prior right of a surviving spouse under section 8 or 9 of the Succession (Scotland) Act 1964;
    (g)  to any obligation to make reparation in respect of personal injuries within the meaning of Part II of this Act or in respect of the death of any person as a result of such injuries;
    [(gg)  to any obligation to make reparation or otherwise make good in respect of defamation within the meaning of section 18A of this Act;
    (ggg)  to any obligation arising from liability under section 2 of the Consumer Protection Act 1987 (to make reparation for damage caused wholly or partly by a defect in a product)]
    (h)  to any obligation specified in Schedule 3 to this Act as an imprescriptible obligation.

. . .

4.   In this Schedule—
(a)   'land obligation' has the same meaning as it has for the purposes of the Conveyancing and Feudal Reform (Scotland) Act 1970;
. . .

## SUPPLY OF GOODS (IMPLIED TERMS) ACT 1973
### (1973, c 13)

**8.   Implied terms as title**

[(1)   In every hire-purchase agreement, other than one to which subsection (2) below applies, there is—
(a)   an implied term on the part of the creditor that he will have a right to sell the goods at the time when the property is to pass; and
(b)   an implied term that—
(i)   the goods are free, and will remain free until the time when the property is to pass, from any charge or encumbrance not disclosed or known to the person to whom the goods are bailed or (in Scotland) hired before the agreement is made, and
(ii)   that person will enjoy quiet possession of the goods except so far as it may be disturbed by any person entitled to the benefit of any charge or encumbrance so disclosed or known.
(2)   In a hire-purchase agreement, in the case of which there appears from the agreement or is to be inferred from the circumstances of the agreement an intention that the creditor should transfer only such title as he or a third person may have, there is—
(a)   an implied term that all charges or encumbrances known to the creditor and not known to the person to whom the goods are bailed or hired have been disclosed to that person before the agreement is made; and
(b)   an implied term that neither—
(i)   the creditor; nor
(ii)   in a case where the parties to the agreement intend that any title which may be transferred shall be only such title as a third person may have, that person; nor
(iii)   anyone claiming through or under the creditor or that third person not otherwise than under a charge or encumbrance disclosed or known to the person to whom the goods are bailed or hired, before the agreement is made;
will disturb the quiet possession of the person to whom the goods are bailed or hired.
(3)   As regards England and Wales and Northern Ireland, the term implied by subsection (1)(a) above is a condition and the terms implied by subsections (1)(b), (2)(a) and (2)(b) above are warranties.]

**9.   Bailing or hiring by description**

[(1)   Where under a hire-purchase agreement goods are bailed or (in Scotland) hired by description, there is an implied term that the goods will correspond with the description, and if under the agreement the goods are bailed or hired by reference to a sample as well as a description, it is not sufficient that the bulk of the goods corresponds with the sample if the goods do not also correspond with the description.
(1A)   As regards England and Wales and Northern Ireland, the term implied by subsection (1) above is a condition.
(2)   Goods shall not be prevented from being bailed or hired by description by reason only that, being exposed for sale, bailment or hire, they are selected by the person to whom they are bailed or hired.]

## 10. Implied undertakings as to quality or fitness

[(1)  Except as provided by this section and section 11 below and subject to the provisions of any other enactment, including any enactment of the Parliament of Northern Ireland or the Northern Ireland Assembly, there is no implied term as to the quality or fitness for any particular purpose of goods bailed or (in Scotland) hired under a hire-purchase agreement.

(2)  Where the creditor bails or hires goods under a hire-purchase agreement in the course of a business, there is an implied term that the goods supplied under the agreement are of satisfactory quality.

(2A)  For the purposes of this Act, goods are of satisfactory quality if they meet the standard that a reasonable person would regard as satisfactory, taking account of any description of the goods, the price (if relevant) and all the other relevant circumstances.

(2B)  For the purposes of this Act, the quality of goods includes their state and condition and the following (among others) are in appropriate cases aspects of the quality of goods—

(a)  fitness for all the purposes for which goods of the kind in question are commonly supplied,

(b)  appearance and finish,

(c)  freedom from minor defects,

(d)  safety, and

(e)  durability.

(2C)  The term implied by subsection (2) above does not extend to any matter making the quality of goods unsatisfactory—

(a)  which is specifically drawn to the attention of the person to whom the goods are bailed or hired before the agreement is made,

(b)  where that person examines the goods before the agreement is made, which that examination ought to reveal, or

(c)  where the goods are bailed or hired by reference to a sample, which would have been apparent on a reasonable examination of the sample.

(3)  Where the creditor bails or hires goods under a hire-purchase agreement in the course of a business and the person to whom the goods are bailed or hired, expressly or by implication, makes known—

(a)  to the creditor in the course of negotiations conducted by the creditor in relation to the making of the hire-purchase agreement, or

(b)  to a credit-broker in the course of negotiations conducted by that broker in relation to goods sold by him to the creditor before forming the subject matter of the hire-purchase agreement,

any particular purpose for which the goods are being bailed or hired, there is an implied term that the goods supplied under the agreement are reasonably fit for that purpose, whether or not that is a purpose for which such goods are commonly supplied, except where the circumstances show that the person to whom the goods are bailed or hired does not rely, or that it is unreasonable for him to rely, on the skill or judgment of the creditor or credit-broker.

(4)  An implied term as to quality or fitness for a particular purpose may be annexed to a hire-purchase agreement by usage.

(5)  The preceding provisions of this section apply to a hire-purchase agreement made by a person who in the course of a business is acting as agent for the creditor as they apply to an agreement made by the creditor in the course of a business, except where the creditor is not bailing or hiring in the course of a business and either the person to whom the goods are bailed or hired knows that fact or reasonable steps are taken to bring it to the notice of that person before the agreement is made.

(6)  In subsection (3) above and this subsection—

(a)  'credit-broker' means a person acting in the course of a business of credit brokerage;

(b) 'credit brokerage' means the effecting of introductions of individuals desiring to obtain credit—
    (i)   to persons carrying on any business so far as it relates to the provision of credit, or
    (ii)  to other persons engaged in credit brokerage.
(7)  As regards England and Wales and Northern Ireland, the terms implied by subsections (2) and (3) above are conditions.]

## 11.  Samples
[(1)  Where under a hire-purchase agreement goods are bailed or (in Scotland) hired by reference to a sample, there is an implied term—
    (a)   that the bulk will correspond with the sample in quality; and
    (b)   that the person to whom the goods are bailed or hired will have a reasonable opportunity of comparing the bulk with the sample; and
    (c)   that the goods will be free from any defect, making their quality unsatisfactory, which would not be apparent on reasonable examination of the sample.
(2)  As regards England and Wales and Northern Ireland, the term implied by subsection (1) above is a condition.]

## [12.  Exclusion of implied terms
An express term does not negative a term implied by this Act unless inconsistent with it.]

## [12A.  Remedies for breach of hire-purchase agreement as respects Scotland
(1)  Where in a hire-purchase agreement the creditor is in breach of any term of the agreement (express or implied), the person to whom the goods are hired shall be entitled—
    (a)   to claim damages, and
    (b)   if the breach is material, to reject any goods delivered under the agreement and treat it as repudiated.
(2)  Where a hire-purchase agreement is a consumer contract, then, for the purposes of subsection (1) above, breach by the creditor of any term (express or implied)—
    (a)   as to the quality of the goods or their fitness for a purpose,
    (b)   if the goods are, or are to be, hired by description, that the goods will correspond with the description,
    (c)   if the goods are, or are to be, hired by reference to a sample, that the bulk will correspond with the sample in quality,
shall be deemed to be a material breach.
(3)  In subsection (2) above 'consumer contract' has the same meaning as in section 25(1) of the Unfair Contract Terms Act 1977; and for the purposes of that subsection the onus of proving that a hire-purchase agreement is not to be regarded as a consumer contract shall lie on the creditor.
(4)  This section applies to Scotland only.]

## 14.  Special provisions as to conditional sale agreements
[(1)  Section 11(4) of the Sale of Goods Act 1979 (whereby in certain circumstances a breach of a condition in a contract of sale is treated only as a breach of warranty) shall not apply to [a conditional sale agreement where the buyer deals as consumer within Part I of the Unfair Contract Terms Act 1977 or, in Scotland, the agreement is a consumer contract within Part II of that Act.]

## 15.  Supplementary
[(1)  In sections 8 to 14 above and this section—
'business' includes a profession and the activities of any government department (including a Northern Ireland department), [or local or public authority];

'buyer' and 'seller' includes a person to whom rights and duties under a conditional sale agreement have passed by assignment or operation of law;

'conditional sale agreement' means an agreement for the sale of goods under which the purchase price or part of it is payable by instalments, and the property in the goods is to remain in the seller (notwithstanding that the buyer is to be in possession of the goods) until such conditions as to the payment of instalments or otherwise as may be specified in the agreement are fulfilled;

['consumer sale' has the same meaning as in section 55 of the Sale of Goods Act 1979 (as set out in paragraph 11 of Schedule 1 to that Act)];

'creditor' means the person by whom the goods are bailed or (in Scotland) hired under a hire-purchase agreement or the person to whom his rights and duties under the agreement have passed by assignment or operation of law; and

'hire-purchase agreement' means an agreement, other than conditional sale agreement, under which—

(a)   goods are bailed or (in Scotland) hired in return for periodical payments by the person to whom they are bailed or hired, and

(b)   the property in the goods will pass to that person if the terms of the agreement are complied with and one or more of the following occurs—

(i)   the exercise of an option to purchase by that person,

(ii)   the doing of any other specified act by any party to the agreement,

(iii)   the happening of any other specified event.

(3)   In section 14(2) above 'corresponding hire-purchase agreement' means, in relation to a conditional sale agreement, a hire-purchase agreement relating to the same goods as the conditional sale agreement and made between the same parties and at the same time and in the same circumstances and, as nearly as may be, in the same terms as the conditional sale agreement.

(4)   Nothing in sections 8 to 13 above shall prejudice the operation of any other enactment including any enactment of the Parliament of Northern Ireland or the Northern Ireland Assembly or any rule of law whereby any term, other than one relating to quality or fitness, is to be implied in any hire-purchase agreement.]

## CONSUMER CREDIT ACT 1974
### (1974, c 39)

**61.   Signing of agreement**

(1)   A regulated agreement is not properly executed unless—

(a)   a document in the prescribed form itself containing all the prescribed terms and conforming to regulations under section 60(1) is signed in the prescribed manner both by the debtor or hirer and by or on behalf of the creditor or owner, and

(b)   the document embodies all the terms of the agreement, other than implied terms, and

(c)   the document is, when presented or sent to the debtor or hirer for signature, in such a state that all its terms are readily legible.

(2)   In addition, where the agreement is one to which section 58(1) applies, it is not properly executed unless—

(a)   the requirements of section 58(1) were complied with, and

(b)   the unexecuted agreement was sent, for his signature, to the debtor or hirer by post not less than seven days after a copy of it was given to him under section 58(1), and

(c)   during the consideration period, the creditor or owner refrained from approaching the debtor or hirer (whether in person, by telephone or letter, or in any other way) except in response to a specific request made by the debtor or hirer after the beginning of the consideration period, and

(d)   no notice of withdrawal by the debtor or hirer was received by the creditor or owner before the sending of the unexecuted agreement.

(3)   In subsection (2)(c), 'the consideration period' means the period beginning with the giving of the copy under section 58(1) and ending—

(a)   at the expiry of seven days after the day on which the unexecuted agreement is sent, for his signature, to the debtor or hirer, or

(b)   on its return by the debtor or hirer after signature by him, whichever first occurs.

(4)   Where the debtor or hirer is a partnership or an unincorporated body of persons, subsection (1)(a) shall apply with the substitution for 'by the debtor or hirer' of 'by or on behalf of the debtor or hirer'.

## 67.  Cancellable agreements

A regulated agreement may be cancelled by the debtor or hirer in accordance with this Part if the antecedent negotiations included oral representations made when in the presence of the debtor or hirer by an individual acting as, or on behalf of, the negotiator, unless—

(a)   the agreement is secured on land, or is a restricted-use credit agreement to finance the purchase of land or is an agreement for a bridging loan in connection with the purchase of land, or

(b)   the unexecuted agreement is signed by the debtor or hirer at premises at which any of the following is carrying on any business (whether on a permanent or temporary basis)—

(i)   the creditor or owner;

(ii)   any party to a linked transaction (other than the debtor or hirer or a relative of his);

(iii)   the negotiator in any antecedent negotiations.

## 68.  Cooling-off period

The debtor or hirer may serve notice of cancellation of a cancellable agreement between his signing of the unexecuted agreement and—

(a)   the end of the fifth day following the day on which he received a copy under section 63(2) or a notice under section 64(1)(b), or

(b)   if (by virtue of regulations made under section 64(4)) section 64(1)(b) does not apply, the end of the fourteenth day following the day on which he signed the unexecuted agreement.

## 69.  Notice of cancellation

(1)   If within the period specified in section 68 the debtor or hirer under a cancellable agreement serves on—

(a)   the creditor or owner, or

(b)   the person specified in the notice under section 64(1), or

(c)   a person who (whether by virtue of subsection (6) or otherwise) is the agent of the creditor or owner,

a notice (a 'notice of cancellation') which, however expressed and whether or not conforming to the notice given under section 64(1), indicates the intention of the debtor or hirer to withdraw from the agreement, the notice shall operate—

(i)   to cancel the agreement, and any linked transaction, and

(ii)   to withdraw any offer by the debtor or hirer, or his relative, to enter into a linked transaction.

(2)   In the case of a debtor-creditor-supplier agreement for restricted-use credit financing—

(a)   the doing of work or supply of goods to meet an emergency, or

(b)   the supply of goods which, before service of the notice of cancellation, had by the act of the debtor or his relative become incorporated in any land or thing not comprised in the agreement or any linked transaction, subsection (1) shall apply with the substitution of the following for paragraph (i)—

'(i)    to cancel only such provisions of the agreement and any linked transaction as—

(aa)   relate to the provision of credit, or

(bb)   require the debtor to pay an item in the total charge for credit, or

(cc)   subject the debtor to any obligation other than to pay for the doing of the said work, or the supply of the said goods'.

(3)    Except so far as is otherwise provided, references in this Act to the cancellation of an agreement or transaction do not include a case within subsection (2).

(4)    Except as otherwise provided by or under this Act, an agreement or transaction cancelled under subsection (1) shall be treated as if it had never been entered into.

(5)    Regulations may exclude linked transactions of the prescribed description from subsection (1)(i) or (ii).

(6)    Each of the following shall be deemed to be the agent of the creditor or owner for the purpose of receiving a notice of cancellation—

(a)    a credit-broker or supplier who is the negotiator in antecedent negotiations, and

(b)    any person who, in the course of a business carried on by him, acts on behalf of the debtor or hirer in any negotiations for the agreement.

(7)    Whether or not it is actually received by him, a notice of cancellation sent by post to a person shall be deemed to be served on him at the time of posting.

## 70.  Cancellation: recovery of money paid by debtor or hirer

(1)    On the cancellation of a regulated agreement, and of any linked transaction,—

(a)    any sum paid by the debtor or hirer, or his relative, under or in contemplation of the agreement or transaction, including any item in the total charge for credit, shall become repayable, and

(b)    any sum, including any item in the total charge for credit, which but for the cancellation is, or would or might become, payable by the debtor or hirer, or his relative, under the agreement or transaction shall cease to be, or shall not become, so payable, and

(c)    in the case of a debtor-creditor-supplier agreement falling within section 12(b), any sum paid on the debtor's behalf by the creditor to the supplier shall become repayable to the creditor.

(2)    If, under the terms of a cancelled agreement or transaction, the debtor or hirer, or his relative, is in possession of any goods, he shall have a lien on them for any sum repayable to him under subsection (1) in respect of that agreement or transaction, or any other linked transaction.

(3)    A sum repayable under subsection (1) is repayable by the person to whom it was originally paid, but in the case of a debtor-creditor-supplier agreement falling within section 12(b) the creditor and the supplier shall be under a joint and several liability to repay sums paid by the debtor, or his relative, under the agreement or under a linked transaction falling within section 19(1)(b) and accordingly, in such a case, the creditor shall be entitled, in accordance with rules of court, to have the supplier made a party to any proceedings brought against the creditor to recover any such sums.

(4)    Subject to any agreement between them, the creditor shall be entitled to be indemnified by the supplier for loss suffered by the creditor in satisfying his liability under subsection (3), including costs reasonably incurred by him in defending proceedings instituted by the debtor.

(5)    Subsection (1) does not apply to any sum which, if not paid by a debtor,

would be payable by virtue of section 71, and applies to a sum paid or payable by a debtor for the issue of a credit-token only where the credit-token has been returned to the creditor or surrendered to a supplier.

(6) If the total charge for credit includes an item in respect of a fee or commission charged by a credit-broker, the amount repayable under subsection (1) in respect of that item shall be the excess over [£5] of the fee or commission.

(7) If the total charge for credit includes any sum payable or paid by the debtor to a credit-broker otherwise than in respect of a fee or commission charged by him, that sum shall for the purposes of subsection (6) be treated as if it were such a fee or commission.

(8) So far only as is necessary to give effect to section 69(2), this section applies to an agreement or transaction within that subsection as it applies to a cancelled agreement or transaction.

### 71. Cancellation: repayment of credit

(1) Notwithstanding the cancellation of a regulated consumer credit agreement, other than a debtor-creditor-supplier agreement for restricted-use credit, the agreement shall continue in force so far as it relates to repayment of credit and payment of interest.

(2) If, following the cancellation of a regulated consumer credit agreement, the debtor repays the whole or a portion of the credit—

(a) before the expiry of one month following service of the notice of cancellation, or

(b) in the case of a credit repayable by instalments, before the date on which the first instalment is due,

no interest shall be payable on the amount repaid.

(3) If the whole of a credit repayable by instalments is not repaid on or before the date specified in subsection (2)(b), the debtor shall not be liable to repay any of the credit except on receipt of a request in writing in the prescribed form, signed by or on behalf of the creditor, stating the amounts of the remaining instalments (recalculated by the creditor as nearly as may be in accordance with the agreement and without extending the repayment period), but excluding any sum other than principal and interest.

(4) Repayment of a credit, or payment of interest, under a cancelled agreement shall be treated as duly made if it is made to any person on whom, under section 69, a notice of cancellation could have been served, other than a person referred to in section 69(6)(b).

### 72. Cancellation: return of goods

(1) This section applies where any agreement or transaction relating to goods, being—

(a) a restricted-use debtor-creditor-supplier agreement, a consumer hire agreement, or a linked transaction to which the debtor or hirer under any regulated agreement is a party, or

(b) a linked transaction to which a relative of the debtor or hirer under any regulated agreement is a party,

is cancelled after the debtor or hirer (in a case within paragraph (a)) or the relative (in a case within paragraph (b)) has acquired possession of the goods by virtue of the agreement or transaction.

(2) In this section—

(a) 'the possessor' means the person who has acquired possession of the goods as mentioned in subsection (1),

(b) 'the other party' means the person from whom the possessor acquired possession, and

(c) 'the pre-cancellation period' means the period beginning when the possessor acquired possession and ending with the cancellation.

(3)   The possessor shall be treated as having been under a duty throughout the pre-cancellation period—
>    (a)   to retain possession of the goods, and
>    (b)   to take reasonable care of them.

(4)   On the cancellation, the possessor shall be under a duty, subject to any lien, to restore the goods to the other party in accordance with this section, and meanwhile to retain possession of the goods and take reasonable care of them.

(5)   The possessor shall not be under any duty to deliver the goods except at his own premises and in pursuance of a request in writing signed by or on behalf of the other party and served on the possessor either before, or at the time when, the goods are collected from those premises.

(6)   If the possessor—
>    (a)   delivers the goods (whether at his own premises or elsewhere) to any person on whom, under section 69, a notice of cancellation could have been served (other than a person referred to in section 69(6)(b)), or
>    (b)   sends the goods at his own expense to such a person,

he shall be discharged from any duty to retain the goods or deliver them to any person.

(7)   Where the possessor delivers the goods as mentioned in subsection (6)(a), his obligation to take care of the goods shall cease; and if he sends the goods as mentioned in subsection (6)(b), he shall be under a duty to take reasonable care to see that they are received by the other party and not damaged in transit, but in other respects his duty to take care of the goods shall cease.

(8)   Where, at any time during the period of 21 days following the cancellation, the possessor receives such a request as is mentioned in subsection (5), and unreasonably refuses or unreasonably fails to comply with it, his duty to take reasonable care of the goods shall continue until he delivers or sends the goods as mentioned in subsection (6), but if within that period he does not receive such a request his duty to take reasonable care of the goods shall cease at the end of that period.

(9)   The preceding provisions of this section do not apply to—
>    (a)   perishable goods, or
>    (b)   goods which by their nature are consumed by use and which, before the cancellation, were so consumed, or
>    (c)   goods supplied to meet an emergency, or
>    (d)   goods which, before the cancellation, had become incorporated in any land or thing not comprised in the cancelled agreement or a linked transaction.

(10)   Where the address of the possessor is specified in the executed agreement, references in this section to his own premises are to that address and no other.

(11)   Breach of a duty imposed by this section is actionable as a breach of statutory duty.

### 73.   Cancellation: goods given in part-exchange

(1)   This section applies on the cancellation of a regulated agreement where, in antecedent negotiations, the negotiator agreed to take goods in part-exchange (the 'part-exchange goods') and those goods have been delivered to him.

(2)   Unless, before the end of the period of ten days beginning with the date of cancellation, the part-exchange goods are returned to the debtor or hirer in a condition substantially as good as when they were delivered to the negotiator, the debtor or hirer shall be entitled to recover from the negotiator a sum equal to the part-exchange allowance (as defined in subsection (7)(b)).

(3)   In the case of a debtor-creditor-supplier agreement within section 12(b), the negotiator and the creditor shall be under a joint and several liability to pay to the debtor a sum recoverable under subsection (2).

(4)   Subject to any agreement between them, the creditor shall be entitled to be indemnified by the negotiator for loss suffered by the creditor in satisfying his liability under subsection (3), including costs reasonably incurred by him in defending proceedings instituted by the debtor.

(5)   During the period of ten days beginning with the date of cancellation, the debtor or hirer, if he is in possession of goods to which the cancelled agreement relates, shall have a lien on them for—

(a)   delivery of the part-exchange goods, in a condition substantially as good as when they were delivered to the negotiator, or

(b)   a sum equal to the part-exchange allowance;

and if the lien continues to the end of that period it shall thereafter subsist only as a lien for a sum equal to the part-exchange allowance.

(6)   Where the debtor or hirer recovers from the negotiator or creditor, or both of them jointly, a sum equal to the part-exchange allowance, then, if the title of the debtor or hirer to the part-exchange goods has not vested in the negotiator, it shall so vest on the recovery of that sum.

(7)   For the purposes of this section—

(a)   the negotiator shall be treated as having agreed to take goods in part-exchange if, in pursuance of the antecedent negotiations, he either purchased or agreed to purchase those goods or accepted or agreed to accept them as part of the consideration for the cancelled agreement, and

(b)   the part-exchange allowance shall be the sum agreed as such in the antecedent negotiations or, if no such agreement was arrived at, such sum as it would have been reasonable to allow in respect of the part-exchange goods if no notice of cancellation had been served.

(8)   In an action brought against the creditor for a sum recoverable under subsection (2), he shall be entitled, in accordance with rules of court, to have the negotiator made a party to the proceedings.

## 74.   Exclusion of certain agreements from Part V

(1)   This Part (except section 56) does not apply to—

(a)   a non-commercial agreement, or

(b)   a debtor-creditor agreement enabling the debtor to overdraw on a current account, or

(c)   a debtor-creditor agreement to finance the making of such payments arising on, or connected with, the death of a person as may be prescribed.

(2)   This Part (except sections 55 and 56) does not apply to a small debtor-creditor-supplier agreement for restricted-use credit.

(3)   Subsection (1)(b) or (c) applies only where the Director so determines, and such a determination—

(a)   may be made subject to such conditions as the Director thinks fit, and

(b)   shall be made only if the Director is of opinion that it is not against the interests of debtors.

[(3A)   Notwithstanding anything in subsection (3)(b) above, in relation to a debtor-creditor agreement under which the creditor is the Bank of England or a bank within the meaning of the Bankers' Books Evidence Act 1879, the Director shall make a determination that subsection (1)(b) above applies unless he considers that it would be against the public interest to do so.

(4)   If any term of an 'agreement falling within subsection [(1)(c)] or (2) is expressed in writing, regulations under section 60(1) shall apply to that term (subject to section 60(3)) as if the agreement were a regulated agreement not falling within subsection [(1)(c)] or (2).

## 75.   Liability of creditor for breaches by supplier

(1)   If the debtor under a debtor-creditor-supplier agreement falling within section 12(b) or (c) has, in relation to a transaction financed by the agreement,

any claim against the supplier in respect of a misrepresentation or breach of contract, he shall have a like claim against the creditor, who, with the supplier, shall accordingly be jointly and severally liable to the debtor.

(2)   Subject to any agreement between them, the creditor shall be entitled to be indemnified by the supplier for loss suffered by the creditor in satisfying his liability under subsection (1), including costs reasonably incurred by him in defending proceedings instituted by the debtor.

(3)   Subsection (1) does not apply to a claim—

(a)   under a non-commercial agreement, or

(b)   so far as the claim relates to any single item to which the supplier has attached a cash price not exceeding [£100] or more than [£30,000].

(4)   This section applies notwithstanding that the debtor, in entering into the transaction, exceeded the credit limit or otherwise contravened any term of the agreement.

(5)   In an action brought against the creditor under subsection (1) he shall be entitled, in accordance with rules of court, to have the supplier made a party to the proceedings.

**105.   Form and content of securities**

(1)   Any security provided in relation to a regulated agreement shall be expressed in writing.

(2)   Regulations may prescribe the form and content of documents ('security instruments') to be made in compliance with subsection (1).

(3)   Regulations under subsection (2) may in particular—

(a)   require specified information to be included in the prescribed manner in documents, and other specified material to be excluded;

(b)   contain requirements to ensure that specified information is clearly brought to the attention of the surety, and that one part of a document is not given insufficient or excessive prominence compared with another.

(4)   A security instrument is not properly executed unless—

(a)   a document in the prescribed form, itself containing all the prescribed terms and conforming to regulations under subsection (2), is signed in the prescribed manner by or on behalf of the surety, and

(b)   the document embodies all the terms of the security, other than implied terms, and

(c)   the document, when presented, or sent for the purpose of being signed by or on behalf of the surety, is in such state that its terms are readily legible, and

(d)   when the document is presented or sent for the purpose of being signed by or on behalf of the surety there is also presented or sent a copy of the document.

(5)   A security instrument is not properly executed unless—

(a)   where the security is provided after, or at the time when, the regulated agreement is made, a copy of the executed agreement, together with a copy of any other document referred to in it, is given to the surety at the time the security is provided, or

(b)   where the security is provided before the regulated agreement is made, a copy of the executed agreement, together with a copy of any other document referred to in it, is given to the surety within seven days after the regulated agreement is made.

(6)   Subsection (1) does not apply to a security provided by the debtor or hirer.

(7)   If—

(a)   in contravention of subsection (1) a security is not expressed in writing, or

(b)   a security instrument is improperly executed,

the security, so far as provided in relation to a regulated agreement, is enforceable against the surety on an order of the court only.

(8) If an application for an order under subsection (7) is dismissed (except on technical grounds only) section 106 (ineffective securities) shall apply to the security.

(9) Regulations under section 60(1) shall include provision requiring documents embodying regulated agreements also to embody any security provided in relation to a regulated agreement by the debtor or hirer.

### 137. Extortionate credit bargains

(1) If the court finds a credit bargain extortionate it may reopen the credit agreement so as to do justice between the parties.

(2) In this section and sections 138 to 140,—

(a) 'credit agreement' means any agreement [(other than an agreement which is an exempt agreement as a result of section 16(6C))] between an individual (the 'debtor') and any other person (the 'creditor') by which the creditor provides the debtor with credit of any amount, and

(b) 'credit bargain'—

(i) where no transaction other than the credit agreement is to be taken into account in computing the total charge for credit, means the credit agreement, or

(ii) where one or more other transactions are to be so taken into account, means the credit agreement and those other transactions, taken together.

### 138. When bargains are extortionate

(1) A credit bargain is extortionate if it—

(a) requires the debtor or a relative of his to make payments (whether unconditionally, or on certain contingencies) which are grossly exorbitant, or

(b) otherwise grossly contravenes ordinary principles of fair dealing.

(2) In determining whether a credit bargain is extortionate, regard shall be had to such evidence as is adduced concerning—

(a) interest rates prevailing at the time it was made,

(b) the factors mentioned in subsection (3) to (5), and

(c) any other relevant considerations.

(3) Factors applicable under subsection (2) in relation to the debtor include—

(a) his age, experience, business capacity and state of health; and

(b) the degree to which, at the time of making the credit bargain, he was under financial pressure, and the nature of that pressure.

(4) Factors applicable under subsection (2) in relation to the creditor include—

(a) the degree of risk accepted by him, having regard to the value of any security provided;

(b) his relationship to the debtor; and

(c) whether or not a colourable cash price was quoted for any goods or services included in the credit bargain.

(5) Factors applicable under subsection (2) in relation to a linked transaction include the question how far the transaction was reasonably required for the protection of debtor or creditor, or was in the interest of the debtor.

### 139. Reopening of extortionate agreements

(1) A credit agreement may, if the court thinks just, be reopened on the ground that the credit bargain is extortionate—

(a) on an application for the purpose made by the debtor or any surety to the High Court, county court or sheriff court; or

(b) at the instance of the debtor or a surety in any proceedings to which the debtor and creditor are parties, being proceedings to enforce the credit agreement, any security relating to it, or any linked transaction; or

(c)   at the instance of the debtor or a surety in other proceedings in any court where the amount paid or payable under the credit agreement is relevant.

(2)   In reopening the agreement, the court may, for the purpose of relieving the debtor or a surety from payment of any sum in excess of that fairly due and reasonable, by order—

(a)   direct accounts to be taken, or (in Scotland) an accounting to be made, between any persons,

(b)   set aside the whole or part of any obligation imposed on the debtor or a surety by the credit bargain or any related agreement,

(c)   require the creditor to repay the whole or part of any sum paid under the credit bargain or any related agreement by the debtor or a surety, whether paid to the creditor or any other person,

(d)   direct the return to the surety of any property provided for the purposes of the security, or

(e)   alter the terms of the credit agreement or any security instrument.

(3)   An order may be made under subsection (2) notwithstanding that its effect is to place a burden on the creditor in respect of an advantage unfairly enjoyed by another person who is a party to a linked transaction.

(4)   An order under subsection (2) shall not alter the effect of any judgment.

(5)   In England and Wales an application under subsection (1)(a) shall be brought only in the county court in the case of—

(a)   a regulated agreement, or

(b)   an agreement (not being a regulated agreement) under which the creditor provides the debtor with fixed-sum credit or running-account credit.

(6)   In Scotland an application under subsection (1)(a) may be brought in the sheriff court for the district in which the debtor or surety resides or carries on business.

(7)   In Northern Ireland an application under subsection (1)(a) may be brought in the county court in the case of—

(a)   a regulated agreement, or

(b)   an agreement (not being a regulated agreement) under which the creditor provides the debtor with fixed-sum credit not exceeding [£1,000] or running-account credit on which the credit limit does not exceed [£1,000].

**140.   Interpretation of sections 137 to 139**

Where the credit agreement is not a regulated agreement, expressions used in sections 137 to 139 which, apart from this section, apply only to regulated agreements, shall be construed as nearly as may be as if the credit agreement were a regulated agreement.

**GUARD DOGS ACT 1975**
**(1975, c 50)**

**1.   Control of guard dogs**

(1)   A person shall not use or permit the use of a guard dog at any premises unless a person ('the handler') who is capable of controlling the dog is present on the premises and the dog is under the control of the handler at all times while it is being so used except while it is secured so that it is not at liberty to go freely about the premises.

(2)   The handler of a guard dog shall keep the dog under his control at all times while it is being used as a guard dog at any premises except—

(a)   while another handler has control over the dog; or

(b)   while the dog is secured so that it is not at liberty to go freely about the premises.

(3)   A person shall not use or permit the use of a guard dog at any premises unless a notice containing a warning that a guard dog is present is clearly exhibited at each entrance to the premises.

## DAMAGES (SCOTLAND) ACT 1976
### (1976, c 13)

### 1.   Rights of relatives of a deceased person

(1)   Where a person dies in consequence of personal injuries sustained by him as a result of an act or omission of another person, being an act or omission giving rise to liability to pay damages to the injured person or his executor, then, subject to the following provisions of this Act, the person liable to pay those damages (in this section referred to as 'the responsible person') shall also be liable to pay damages in accordance with this section to any relative of the deceased, being a relative within the meaning of Schedule 1 to this Act.

(2)   No liability shall arise under this section if the liability to the deceased or his executor in respect of the act or omission has been excluded or discharged (whether by antecedent agreement or otherwise) by the deceased before his death, or is excluded by virtue of any enactment.

(3)   The damages which the responsible person shall be liable to pay to a relative of a deceased under this section shall (subject to the provisions of this Act) be such as will compensate the relative for any loss of support suffered by him since the date of the deceased's death or likely to be suffered by him as a result of the act or omission in question, together with any reasonable expense incurred by him in connection with the deceased's funeral.

(4)   If the relative is a member of the deceased's immediate family (within the meaning of section 10(2) of this Act) there shall be awarded, without prejudice to any claim under subsection (3) above, such sum of damages, if any, as the court thinks just by way of compensation for the loss of [all or any of the following—

(a)   distress and anxiety endured by the relative in contemplation of the suffering of the deceased before his death;

(b)   grief and sorrow of the relative caused by the deceased's death;

(c)   the loss of such non-patrimonial benefit as the relative might have been expected to derive from the deceased's society and guidance if the deceased had not died,

and the court in making an award under this subsection shall not be required to ascribe specifically any part of the award to any of paragraphs (a), (b) and (c) above.]

(5)   [Subject to subsection (5A) below] in assessing for the purposes of this section the amount of any loss of support suffered by a relative of a deceased no account shall be taken of—

(a)   any patrimonial gain or advantage which has accrued or will or may accrue to the relative from the deceased or from any other person by way of succession or settlement;

(b)   any insurance money, benefit, pension or gratuity which has been, or will be or may be, paid as a result of the deceased's death;

and in this subsection—

'benefit' means benefit under the Social Security Act 1975 or the Social Security (Northern Ireland) Act 1975, and any payment by a friendly society or trade union for the relief or maintenance of a member's dependants;

'insurance money' includes a return of premiums; and

'pension' includes a return of contributions and any payment of a lump sum in respect of a person's employment.

[(5A) Where a deceased has been awarded a provisional award of damages under section 12(2) of the Administration of Justice Act 1982, the making of that award does not prevent liability from arising under this section but in assessing for the purposes of this section the amount of any loss of support suffered by a relative of the deceased the court shall take into account such part of the provisional award relating to future patrimonial loss as was intended to compensate the deceased for a period beyond the date on which he died.]

(6) In order to establish loss of support for the purposes of this section it shall not be essential for a claimant to show that the deceased was, or might have become, subject to a duty in law to provide or contribute to the support of the claimant; but if any such fact is established it may be taken into account in determining whether, and if so to what extent, the deceased, if he had not died, would have been likely to provide or contribute to such support.

(7) Except as provided in this section [or in Part II of the Administration of Justice Act 1982 or under section 1 of the International Transport Conventions Act 1983] no person shall be entitled by reason of relationship to damages (including damages by way of solatium) in respect of the death of another person.

## [1A. Transmissibility to executor of rights of deceased relative

Any right to damages under any provision of section 1 of this Act which is vested in the relative concerned immediately before his death shall be transmitted to the relative's executor; but, in determining the amount of damages payable to an executor by virtue of this section, the court shall have regard only to the period ending immediately before the relative's death.]

## [2. Rights transmitted to executor in respect of deceased person's injuries

(1) Subject to the following provisions of this section, there shall be transmitted to the executor of a deceased person the like rights to damages in respect of personal injuries (including a right to damages by way of solatium) sustained by the deceased as were vested in him immediately before his death.

(2) There shall not be transmitted to the executor under this section a right to damages by way of compensation for patrimonial loss attributable to any period after the deceased's death.

(3) In determining the amount of damages by way of solatium payable to an executor by virtue of this section, the court shall have regard only to the period ending immediately before the deceased's death.

(4) In so far as a right to damages vested in the deceased comprised a right to damages (other than for patrimonial loss) in respect of injury resulting from defamation or any other verbal injury or other injury to reputation sustained by the deceased, that right shall be transmitted to the deceased's executor only if an action to enforce that right had been brought by the deceased before his death and had not been concluded by then within the meaning of section 2A(2) of this Act.]

## [2A. Enforcement by executor of rights transmitted to him

(1) For the purpose of enforcing any right transmitted to an executor under section 1A or 2 of this Act the executor shall be entitled—

(a) to bring an action; or

(b) if an action for that purpose had been brought by the deceased but had not been concluded before his death, to be sisted as pursuer in that action.

(2) For the purpose of subsection (1) above, an action shall not be taken to be concluded while any appeal is competent or before any appeal taken has been disposed of.]

**[4. Executor's claim not to be excluded by relatives' claim: and vice versa**
A claim by the executor of a deceased person for damages under section 2 of
this Act is not excluded by the making of a claim by a relative of the deceased
for damages under section 1 of this Act [or by a deceased relative's executor
under section 1A of this Act; nor is a claim by a relative of a deceased person
or by a deceased relative's executor for damages under the said section 1 or (as
the case may be) the said section 1A].

**6.  Limitation of total amount of liability**
(1)  Where in any action to which [this] section applies, so far as directed
against any defender, it is shown that by antecedent agreement, compromise or
otherwise, the liability arising in relation to that defender from the personal
injuries in question had, before the deceased's death, been limited to damages
of a specified or ascertainable amount, or where that liability is so limited by
virtue of any enactment, nothing in this Act shall make the defender liable to
pay damages exceeding that amount; and accordingly where in such an action
there are two or more pursuers any damages to which they would respectively
be entitled under this Act apart from the said limitation shall, if necessary, be
reduced *pro rata*.
(2)  Where two or more such actions are conjoined, the conjoined actions
shall be treated for the purposes of this section as if they were a single action.
[(3)  This section applies to any action in which, following the death of any
person from personal injuries, damages are claimed—
    (a)  by the executor of the deceased, in respect of the injuries from which
the deceased died;
    (b)  in respect of the death of the deceased, by any relative of his [or, if
the relative has died, by the relative's executor].]

**7.  Amendment of references in other Acts**
In any Act passed before this Act, unless the context otherwise requires, any
reference to solatium in respect of the death of any person (however expressed)
shall be construed as a reference to a loss of society award within the meaning
of section 1 of this Act; and any reference to a dependant of a deceased person,
in relation to an action claiming damages in respect of the deceased person's
death, shall be construed as including a reference to a relative of the deceased
person within the meaning of this Act.

**8.  Abolition of right of assythment**
After the commencement of this Act no person shall in any circumstances have
a right to assythment, and accordingly any action claiming that remedy shall (to
the extent that it does so) be incompetent.

**9.  Damages due to injured person for patrimonial loss caused by personal
injuries whereby expectation of life is diminished**
(1)  This section applies to any action for damages in respect of personal
injuries sustained by the pursuer where his expected date of death is earlier
than it would have been if he had not sustained the injuries.
(2)  In assessing, in any action to which this section applies, the amount of
any patrimonial loss in respect of the period after the date of decree—
    (a)  it shall be assumed that the pursuer will live until the date when he
would have been expected to die if he had not sustained the injuries
(hereinafter referred to as the 'notional date of death');
    (b)  the court may have regard to any amount, whether or not it is an
amount related to earnings by the pursuer's own labour or other gainful
activity, which in its opinion the pursuer, if he had not sustained the injuries
in question, would have received in the period up to his notional date of
death by way of benefits in money or money's worth, being benefits derived
from sources other than the pursuer's own estate;

(c)   the court shall have regard to any diminution of any such amount as aforesaid by virtue of expenses which in the opinion of the court the pursuer, if he had not sustained the injuries in question, would reasonably have incurred in the said period by way of living expenses.

**[9A.   Solatium for loss of expectation of life**
(1)   In assessing, in an action for damages in respect of personal injuries, the amount of damages by way of solatium, the court shall, if—
(a)   the injured person's expectation of life has been reduced by the injuries; and
(b)   the injured person is, was at any time or is likely to become, aware of that reduction,
have regard to the extent that, in consequence of that awareness, he has suffered or is likely to suffer.
(2)   Subject to subsection (1) above, no damages by way of solatium shall be recoverable in respect of loss of expectation of life.
(3)   The court in making an award of damages by way of solatium shall not be required to ascribe specifically any part of the award to loss of expectation of life.]

**10.   Interpretation**
(1)   In this Act, unless the context otherwise requires—
. . .
'personal injuries' includes any disease or any impairment of a person's physical or mental condition [and injury resulting from defamation or any other verbal injury or other injury to reputation or injury resulting from harassment actionable under section 8 of the Protection from Harassment Act 1997;]
'relative', in relation to a deceased person, has the meaning assigned to it by Schedule 1 to this Act.
(2)   References in this Act to a member of a deceased person's immediate family are references to any relative of his who falls within subparagraph (a), [(aa)], (b) or (c) of paragraph 1 of Schedule 1 to this Act.
(3)   References in this Act to any other Act are references to that Act as amended, extended or applied by any other enactment, including this Act.
. . .

**12.   Citation, application to Crown, commencement and extent**
(1)   This Act may be cited as the Damages (Scotland) Act 1976.
(2)   This Act binds the Crown.
. . .
(5)   This Act extends to Scotland only.

SCHEDULE 1. DEFINITION OF 'RELATIVE'

(1)   In this Act 'relative' in relation to a deceased person includes—
(a)   any person who immediately before the deceased's death was the spouse of the deceased;
[(aa) any person, not being the spouse of the deceased, who was, immediately before the deceased's death, living with the deceased as husband or wife;]
(b)   any person who was a parent or child of the deceased;
(c)   any person not falling within paragraph (b) above who was accepted by the deceased as a child of his family;
(d)   any person who was an ascendant or descendant (other than a parent or child) of the deceased;
(e)   any person who was, or was the issue of, a brother, sister, uncle or aunt of the deceased; and

(f)    any person who, having been a spouse of the deceased, had ceased to be so by virtue of a divorce;
but does not include any other person.

(2) In deducing any relationship for the purposes of the foregoing paragraph—

(a)    any relationship by affinity shall be treated as a relationship by consanguinity; any relationship of the half blood shall be treated as a relationship of the whole blood; and the stepchild of any person shall be treated as his child; and

(b)    section 1(1) of the Law Reform (Parent and Child) (Scotland) Act 1986 shall apply; and any reference (however expressed) in this Act to a relative shall be construed accordingly.

## DANGEROUS WILD ANIMALS ACT 1976
### (1976, c 38)

### 7.  Interpretation

(1)   Subject to subsection (2) of this section, for the purposes of this Act a person is a keeper of an animal if he has it in his possession; and if at any time an animal ceases to be in the possession of a person, any person who immediately before that time was a keeper thereof by virtue of the preceding provisions of this subsection continues to be a keeper of the animal until another person becomes a keeper thereof by virtue of those provisions.

(2)   Where an animal is in the possession of any person for the purpose of—

(a)    preventing it from causing damage,

(b)    restoring it to its owner,

(c)    undergoing veterinary treatment, or

(d)    being transported on behalf of another person,

the person having such possession shall not by virtue only of that possession be treated for the purposes of this Act as a keeper of the animal.

(3)   In this Act expressions cognate with 'keeper' shall be construed in accordance with subsections (1) and (2) of this section.

(4)   In this Act, unless the context otherwise requires, the following expressions have the meanings hereby respectively assigned to them, that is to say—

'circus' includes any place where animals are kept or introduced wholly or mainly for the purpose of performing tricks or manoeuvres;

'damage' includes the death of, or injury to, any person;

'dangerous wild animal' means any animal of a kind for the time being specified in the first column of the Schedule to this Act;

'local authority' means in relation to England . . . a district council, a London borough council or the Common Council of the City of London [, in relation to Wales, a county council or county borough council] and, in relation to Scotland, [a council constituted under section 2 of the Local Government etc. (Scotland) Act 1994];

'premises' includes any place;

'veterinary practitioner' means a person who is for the time being registered in the supplementary veterinary register;

'veterinary surgeon' means a person who is for the time being registered in the register of veterinary surgeons;

. . .

(5)   The second column of the Schedule to this Act is included by way of explanation only; in the event of any dispute or proceedings, only the first column is to be taken into account.

[SCHEDULE. KINDS OF DANGEROUS WILD ANIMALS

NOTE: See section 7(5) of this Act for the effect of the second column of this schedule.

| Scientific name | Common name or names |
| --- | --- |
| Antilocapridae | Pronghorn |
| Bovidae except the species Cephalophus, Sylvicapra grimmia, Oreotragus oreotragus, Ourebia, Raphicerus, Nesotragus moschatus, Neotragus pygmeaus, Madoqua, any domestic form of Capra hircus, Dorcatragus megalotis, Ovis aries and all species of the genera Bos and Bubalus. | These include cattle, antelopes, gazelles, goats and sheep except that duikers, grey duiker, klipspringer, oribi, grysbok, suni, royal antelope, dik-dik, domestic goat, Beira antelope, domestic sheep and domestic cattle are specifically excluded |
| Camelidae except the species Lama glama and Lama pacos. | This kind includes the bactrian camel and Arabian camel except that llama and alpaca are specifically excluded. |
| Canidae except the species Canis familiaris, all species of the genera Vulpes, Alopex, Dusicyon and Otocyon | This kind includes the wild dog, wolf, jackal, coyote except that the domestic dog and all foxes are specifically excluded |
| Casuariidae | Cassowary |
| Cercopithecidae | Old world monkeys, including langur, colobus, macaque, guenon, patas, mangabey, baboon and mandrill |
| Crocodylia | Ths kind includes the alligator, crocodile, gharial, false gharial and caiman |
| Dromaiidae | Emu |
| Elapidae (including Hydrophiidae) | This kind includes the cobra, krait, mamba, coral snake and sea snake, and all Australian poisonous snakes including the death adder |
| Equidae except the species Equus caballus, Equus asinus and Equus caballus x Equus asinus | Horses except that the domestic horse, domestic donkey, mules and hinny are specifically excluded |
| Felidae, except the species Felis catus | This kind includes the lynx, caracal, serval, bobcat, cheetah, lion, tiger, leopard, panther, jaguar, puma, cougar and ocelot, except that the domestic cat is specifically excluded |
| Giraffidae | This kind includes the giraffe and okapi |
| Helodermatidae | Gila monster and Mexican beaded lizard |

| Scientific name | Common name or names |
| --- | --- |
| Hippopotamidae | This kind includes the hippopotamus and pygmy hippopotamus |
| Hyaenidae except the species Proteles cristatus | Hyaenas except that the aardwolf is specifically excluded |
| Hylobatidae | Gibbon |
| Pongidae | Anthropoid apes including orang utan, gorilla and chimpanzee |
| Proboscidae | Elephants including the African and Indian elephant |
| Rhinocerotidae | Rhinoceros |
| Struthionidae | Ostrich |
| Suidae except any domestic form of Sus scrofa | Old world pigs except that the domestic pig is specifically excluded |
| Tapiridae | Tapirs |
| Tayassuidae | New world pigs including the collared peccary and white lipped peccary |
| Ursidae | This kind includes the polar bear, brown bear and grizzly bear |
| Viperidae (including Crotalidae) | This kind includes—<br>(a) most snakes known as vipers and adders, and<br>(b) the rattlesnake, bushmaster, fer-delance, water moccasin and copperhead.] |

## UNFAIR CONTRACT TERMS ACT 1977
### (1977, c 50)

## PART II. AMENDMENT OF LAW FOR SCOTLAND

**15.  Scope of Part II**

(1)  This Part of this Act [ . . . ] is subject to Part III of this Act and does not affect the validity of any discharge or indemnity given by a person in consideration of the receipt by him of compensation in settlement of any claim which he has.

(2)  Subject to subsection (3) below, sections 16 to 18 of this Act apply to any contract only to the extent that the contract—

(a)  relates to the transfer of the ownership or possession of goods from one person to another (with or without work having been done on them);

(b)  constitutes a contract of service or apprenticeship;

(c)  relates to services of whatever kind, including (without prejudice to the foregoing generality) carriage, deposit and pledge, care and custody, mandate, agency, loan and services relating to the use of land;

(d)  relates to the liability of an occupier of land to persons entering upon or using that land;

(e)  relates to a grant of any right or permission to enter upon or use land not amounting to an estate or interest in the land.

(3)  Notwithstanding anything in subsection (2) above, sections 16 to 18—

(a)  do not apply to any contract to the extent that the contract—

(i)    is a contract of insurance (including a contract to pay an annuity on human life);

(ii)    relates to the formation, constitution or dissolution of any body corporate or unincorporated association or partnership;

(b)    apply to—

a contract of marine salvage or towage;

a charter party of a ship or hovercraft;

a contract for the carriage of goods by ship or hovercraft; or

a contract to which subsection (4) below relates,

only to the extent that—

(i)    both parties deal or hold themselves out as dealing in the course of a business (and then only in so far as the contract purports to exclude or restrict liability for breach of duty in respect of death or personal injury); or

(ii)    the contract is a consumer contract (and then only in favour of the consumer).

(4)    This subsection relates to a contract in pursuance of which goods are carried by ship or hovercraft and which either—

(a)    specifies ship or hovercraft as the means of carriage over part of the journey to be covered; or

(b)    makes no provision as to the means of carriage and does not exclude ship or hovercraft as that means,

in so far as the contract operates for and in relation to the carriage of the goods by that means.

### 16.   Liability for breach of duty

(1)    [Subject to subsection (1A) below,] where a term of a contract [, or a provision of a notice given to persons generally or to particular persons,] purports to exclude or restrict liability for breach of duty arising in the course of any business or from the occupation of any premises used for business purposes of the occupier, that term [or provision]—

(a)    shall be void in any case where such exclusion or restriction is in respect of death or personal injury;

(b)    shall, in any other case, have no effect if it was not fair and reasonable to incorporate the term in the contract [or, as the case may be, if it is not fair and reasonable to allow reliance on the provision].

[(1A)    Nothing in paragraph (b) of subsection (1) above shall be taken as implying that a provision of a notice has effect in circumstances where, apart from that paragraph, it would not have effect.]

(2)    Subsection (1)(a) above does not affect the validity of any discharge and indemnity given by a person, on or in connection with an award to him of compensation for pneumoconiosis attributable to employment in the coal industry, in respect of any further claim arising from his contracting that disease.

(3)    Where under subsection (1) above a term of a contract [or a provision of a notice] is void or has no effect, the fact that a person agreed to, or was aware of, the term [or provision] shall not of itself be sufficient evidence that he knowingly and voluntarily assumed any risk.

### 17.   Control of unreasonable exemptions in consumer or standard form contracts

(1)    Any term of a contract which is a consumer contract or a standard form contract shall have no effect for the purpose of enabling a party to the contract—

(a)    who is in breach of a contractual obligation, to exclude or restrict any liability of his to the consumer or customer in respect of the breach;

(b)    in respect of a contractual obligation, to render no performance, or to render a performance substantially different from that which the consumer or customer reasonably expected from the contract;

if it was not fair and reasonable to incorporate the term in the contract.

(2) In this section 'customer' means a party to a standard form contract who deals on the basis of written standard terms of business of the other party to the contract who himself deals in the course of a business.

### 18. Unreasonable indemnity clauses in consumer contracts

(1) Any term of a contract which is a consumer contract shall have no effect for the purpose of making the consumer indemnify another person (whether a party to the contract or not) in respect of liability which that other person may incur as a result of breach of duty or breach of contract, if it was not fair and reasonable to incorporate the term in the contract.

(2) In this section 'liability' means liability arising in the course of any business or from the occupation of any premises used for business purposes of the occupier.

### 19. 'Guarantee' of consumer goods

(1) This section applies to a guarantee—

  (a)  in relation to goods which are of a type ordinarily supplied for private use or consumption; and

  (b)  which is not a guarantee given by one party to the other party to a contract under or in pursuance of which the ownership or possession of the goods to which the guarantee relates is transferred.

(2) A term of a guarantee to which this section applies shall be void in so far as it purports to exclude or restrict liability for loss or damage (including death or personal injury)—

  (a)  arising from the goods proving defective while—

    (i)  in use otherwise than exclusively for the purposes of a business; or

    (ii)  in the possession of a person for such use; and

  (b)  resulting from the breach of duty of a person concerned in the manufacture or distribution of the goods.

(3) For the purposes of this section, any document is a guarantee if it contains or purports to contain some promise or assurance (however worded or presented) that defects will be made good by complete or partial replacement, or by repair, monetary compensation or otherwise.

### 20. Obligations implied by law in sale and hire-purchase contracts

(1) Any term of a contract which purports to exclude or restrict liability for breach of the obligations arising from—

  (a)  section 12 of the Sale of Goods Act [1979] (seller's implied undertakings as to title etc.);

  (b)  section 8 of the Supply of Goods (Implied Terms) Act 1973 (implied terms as to title in hire-purchase agreements),

shall be void.

(2) Any term of a contract which purports to exclude or restrict liability for breach of the obligations arising from—

  (a)  section 13, 14 or 15 of the said Act of [1979] (seller's implied undertakings as to conformity of goods with description or sample, or as to their quality or fitness for a particular purpose);

  (b)  section 9, 10 or 11 of the said Act of 1973 (the corresponding provisions in relation to hire-purchase),

shall—

    (i)  in the case of a consumer contract, be void against the consumer;

    (ii)  in any other case, have no effect if it was not fair and reasonable to incorporate the term in the contract.

### 21. Obligations implied by law in other contracts for the supply of goods

(1)   Any term of a contract to which this section applies purporting to exclude or restrict liability for breach of an obligation—

(a)   such as is referred to in subsection (3)(a) below—

(i)   in the case of a consumer contract, shall be void against the consumer, and

(ii)   in any other case, shall have no effect if it was not fair and reasonable to incorporate the term in the contract;

(b)   such as is referred to in subsection (3)(b) below, shall have no effect if it was not fair and reasonable to incorporate the term in the contract.

(2)   This section applies to any contract to the extent that it relates to any such matter as is referred to in section 15(2)(a) of this Act, but does not apply to—

(a)   a contract of sale of goods or a hire-purchase agreement; or

(b)   a charterparty of a ship or hovercraft unless it is a consumer contract (and then only in favour of the consumer).

(3)   An obligation referred to in this subsection is an obligation incurred under a contract in the course of a business and arising by implication of law from the nature of the contract which relates—

(a)   to the correspondence of goods with description or sample, or to the quality or fitness of goods for any particular purpose; or

(b)   to any right to transfer ownership or possession of goods, or to the enjoyment of quiet possession of goods.

[(3A)   Notwithstanding anything in the foregoing provisions of this section, any term of a contract which purports to exclude or restrict liability for breach of the obligations arising under section 11B of the Supply of Goods and Services Act 1982 (implied terms about title, freedom from encumbrances and quiet possession in certain contracts for the transfer of property in goods) shall be void.]

(4)   Nothing in this section applies to the supply of goods on a redemption of trading stamps within the Trading Stamps Act 1964.

### 22.   Consequence of breach

For the avoidance of doubt, where any provision of this Part of this Act requires that the incorporation of a term in a contract must be fair and reasonable for that term to have effect—

(a)   if that requirement is satisfied, the term may be given effect to notwithstanding that the contract has been terminated in consequence of breach of that contract;

(b)   for the term to be given effect to, that requirement must be satisfied even where a party who is entitled to rescind the contract elects not to rescind it.

### 23.   Evasion by means of secondary contract

Any term of any contract shall be void which purports to exclude or restrict, or has the effect of excluding or restricting—

(a)   the exercise, by a party to any other contract, of any right or remedy which arises in respect of that other contract in consequence of breach of duty, or of obligation, liability for which could not by virtue of the provisions of this Part of this Act be excluded or restricted by a term of that other contract;

(b)   the application of the provisions of this Part of this Act in respect of that or any other contract.

### 24.   The 'reasonableness' test

(1)   In determining for the purposes of this Part of this Act whether it was fair and reasonable to incorporate a term in a contract, regard shall be had only to the circumstances which were, or ought reasonably to have been, known to

or in the contemplation of the parties to the contract at the time the contract was made.

(2)   In determining for the purposes of section 20 or 21 of this Act whether it was fair and reasonable to incorporate a term in a contract, regard shall be had in particular to the matters specified in Schedule 2 to this Act; but this sub-section shall not prevent a court or arbiter from holding in accordance with any rule of law, that a term which purports to exclude or restrict any relevant liability is not a term of the contract.

[(2A)   In determining for the purposes of this Part of this Act whether it is fair and reasonable to allow reliance on a provision of a notice (not being a notice having contractual effect), regard shall be had to all the circumstances obtaining when the liability arose or (but for the provision) would have arisen.]

(3)   Where a term in a contract [or a provision of a notice] purports to restrict liability to a specified sum of money, and the question arises for the purposes of this Part of this Act whether it was fair and reasonable to incorporate the term in the contract [or whether it is fair and reasonable to allow reliance on the provision], then, without prejudice to subsection (2) above [in the case of a term in a contract], regard shall be had in particular to—

(a)   the resources which the party seeking to rely on that term [or provision] could expect to be available to him for the purpose of meeting the liability should it arise;

(b)   how far it was open to that party to cover himself by insurance.

(4)   The onus of proving that it was fair and reasonable to incorporate a term in a contract [or that it is fair and reasonable to allow reliance on a provision of a notice] shall lie on the party so contending.

## 25.   Interpretation of Part II

(1)   In this Part of this Act—

'breach of duty' means the breach—

(a)   of any obligation, arising from the express or implied terms of a contract, to take reasonable care or exercise reasonable skill in the performance of the contract;

(b)   of any common law duty to take reasonable care or exercise reasonable skill;

(c)   of the duty of reasonable care imposed by section 2(1) of the Occupiers' Liability (Scotland) Act 1960;

'business' includes a profession and the activities of any government department or local or public authority;

'consumer' has the meaning assigned to that expression in the definition in this section of 'consumer contract';

'consumer contract' means a contract (not being a contract of sale by auction or competitive tender) in which—

(a)   one party to the contract deals, and the other party to the contract ('the consumer') does not deal or hold himself out as dealing, in the course of a business, and

(b)   in the case of a contract such as is mentioned in section 15(2)(a) of this Act, the goods are of a type ordinarily supplied for private use or consumption;

and for the purposes of this Part of this Act the onus of proving that a contract is not to be regarded as a consumer contract shall lie on the party so contending;

'goods' has the same meaning as in the Sale of Goods Act [1979];

'hire-purchase agreement' has the same meaning as in section 189(1) of the Consumer Credit Act 1974;

['notice' includes an announcement, whether or not in writing, and any other communication or pretended communication;]

'personal injury' includes any disease and any impairment of physical or mental condition.

(2)   In relation to any breach of duty or obligation, it is immaterial for any purpose of this Part of this Act whether the act or omission giving rise to that breach was inadvertent or intentional or whether liability for it arises directly or vicariously.

(3)   In this Part of this Act, any reference to excluding or restricting any liability includes—

(a)   making the liability or its enforcement subject to any restrictive or onerous conditions;

(b)   excluding or restricting any right or remedy in respect of the liability, or subjecting a person to any prejudice in consequence of his pursuing any such right or remedy;

(c)   excluding or restricting any rule of evidence or procedure;

[ . . . ]

(5)   In section 15 and 16 and 19 to 21 of this Act, any reference to excluding or restricting liability for breach of any obligation or duty shall include a reference to excluding or restricting the obligation or duty itself.

## SALE OF GOODS ACT 1979
### (1979, c 54)

### PART II. FORMATION OF THE CONTRACT

**6.   Goods which have perished**

Where there is a contract for the sale of specific goods, and the goods without the knowledge of the seller have perished at the time when the contract is made, the contract is void.

*The price*

**8.   Ascertainment of price**

(1)   The price in a contract of sale may be fixed by the contract, or may be left to be fixed in a manner agreed by the contract, or may be determined by the course of dealing between the parties.

(2)   Where the price is not determined as mentioned in subsection (1) above the buyer must pay a reasonable price.

(3)   What is a reasonable price is a question of fact dependent on the circumstances of each particular case.

**12.   Implied terms about title, etc.**

(1)   In a contract of sale, other than one to which subsection (3) below applies, there is an implied [term] on the part of the seller that in the case of a sale he has a right to sell the goods, and in the case of an agreement to sell he will have such a right at the time when the property is to pass.

(2)   In a contract of sale, other than one to which subsection (3) below applies, there is also an implied [term] that—

(a)   the goods are free, and will remain free until the time when the property is to pass, from any charge or encumbrance not disclosed or known to the buyer before the contract is made, and

(b)   the buyer will enjoy quiet possession of the goods except so far as it may be disturbed by the owner or other person entitled to the benefit of any charge or encumbrance so disclosed or known.

(3)   This subsection applies to a contract of sale in the case of which there appears from the contract or is to be inferred from its circumstances an intention that the seller should transfer only such title as he or a third person may have.

(4)   In a contract to which subsection (3) above applies there is an implied [term] that all charges or encumbrances known to the seller and not known to the buyer have been disclosed to the buyer before the contract is made.

(5)   In a contract to which subsection (3) above applies there is also an implied [term] that none of the following will disturb the buyer's quiet possession of the goods, namely—

(a)   the seller;

(b)   in a case where the parties to the contract intend that the seller should transfer only such title as a third person may have, that person;

(c)   anyone claiming through or under the seller or that third person otherwise than under a charge or encumbrance disclosed or known to the buyer before the contract is made.

[(5A)   As regards England and Wales and Northern Ireland, the term implied by subsection (1) above is a condition and the terms implied by subsections (2), (4) and (5) above are warranties.]

(6)   Paragraph 3 of Schedule 1 below applies in relation to a contract made before 18 May 1973.

### 13.   Sale by description

(1)   Where there is a contract for the sale of goods by description, there is an implied [term] that the goods will correspond with the description.

[(1A)   As regards England and Wales and Northern Ireland, the term implied by subsection (1) above is a condition.]

(2)   If the sale is by sample as well as by description it is not sufficient that the bulk of the goods corresponds with the sample if the goods do not also correspond with the description.

(3)   A sale of goods is not prevented from being a sale by description by reason only that, being exposed for sale or hire, they are selected by the buyer.

(4)   Paragraph 4 of Schedule 1 below applies in relation to a contract made before 18 May 1973.

### 14.   Implied terms about quality or fitness

(1)   Except as provided by this section and section 15 below and subject to any other enactment, there is no implied [term] about the quality or fitness for any particular purpose of goods supplied under a contract of sale.

(2)   Where the seller sells goods in the course of a business, there is an implied condition that the goods supplied under the contract are of merchantable quality, except that there is no such condition—

(a)   as regards defects specifically drawn to the buyer's attention before the contract is made; or

(b)   if the buyer examines the goods before the contract is made, as regards defects which that examination ought to reveal.

(3)   Where the seller sells goods in the course of a business and the buyer, expressly or by implication, makes known—

(a)   to the seller, or

(b)   where the purchase price or part of it is payable by instalments and the goods were previously sold by a credit-broker to the seller, to that credit-broker,

any particular purpose for which the goods are being bought, there is an implied [term] that the goods supplied under the contract are reasonably fit for that purpose, whether or not that is a purpose for which such goods are commonly supplied, except where the circumstances show that the buyer does not rely, or that it is unreasonable for him to rely, on the skill or judgment of the seller or credit-broker.

(4)   An implied [term] about quality or fitness for a particular purpose may be annexed to a contract of sale by usage.

(5)   The preceding provisions of this section apply to a sale by a person who

in the course of a business is acting as agent for another as they apply to a sale by a principal in the course of a business, except where that other is not selling in the course of a business and either the buyer knows that fact or reasonable steps are taken to bring it to the notice of the buyer before the contract is made.

[(6)   As regards England and Wales and Northern Ireland, the terms implied by subsections (2) and (3) above are conditions.]

(7)   Paragraph 5 of Schedule 1 below applies in relation to a contract made on or after 18 May 1973 and before the appointed day, and paragraph 6 in relation to one made before 18 May 1973.

(8)   In subsection (7) above and paragraph 5 of Schedule 1 below references to the appointed day are to the day appointed for the purposes of those provisions by an order of the Secretary of State made by statutory instrument.

*Sale by sample*

## 15.   Sale by sample

(1)   A contract of sale is a contract for sale by sample where there is an express or implied term to that effect in the contract.

(2)   In the case of a contract for sale by sample there is an implied [term]—

    (a)   that the bulk will correspond with the sample in quality;

. . .

    (c)   that the goods will be free from any defect, rendering them unmerchantable, which would not be apparent on reasonable examination of the sample.

[(3)   As regards England and Wales and Northern Ireland, the term implied by subsection (2) above is a condition.]

(4)   Paragraph 7 of Schedule 1 below applies in relation to a contract made before 18 May 1973.

*[Miscellaneous*

## [15B.   Remedies for breach of contract as respects Scotland

(1)   Where in a contract of sale the seller is in breach of any term of the contract (express or implied), the buyer shall be entitled—

    (a)   to claim damages, and

    (b)   if the breach is material, to reject any goods delivered under the contract and treat it as repudiated.

(2)   Where a contract of sale is a consumer contract, then, for the purposes of subsection (1)(b) above, breach by the seller of any term (express or implied)—

    (a)   as to the quality of the goods or their fitness for a purpose,

    (b)   if the goods are, or are to be, sold by description, that the goods will correspond with the description,

    (c)   if the goods are, or are to be, sold by reference to a sample, that the bulk will correspond with the sample in quality,

shall be deemed to be a material breach.

(3)   This section applies to Scotland only.]

## PART III. EFFECTS OF THE CONTRACT

*Transfer of property as between seller and buyer*

## 16.   Goods must be ascertained

[Subject to section 20A below] where there is a contract for the sale of unascertained goods no property in the goods is transferred to the buyer unless and until the goods are ascertained.

## 17.   Property passes when intended to pass

(1)   Where there is a contract for the sale of specific or ascertained goods the

property in them is transferred to the buyer at such time as the parties to the contract intend it to be transferred.

(2) For the purpose of ascertaining the intention of the parties regard shall be had to the terms of the contract, the conduct of the parties and the circumstances of the case.

## 18. Rules for ascertaining intention

Unless a different intention appears, the following are rules for ascertaining the intention of the parties as to the time at which the property in the goods is to pass to the buyer.

*Rule 1.*—Where there is an unconditional contract for the sale of specific goods in a deliverable state the property in the goods passes to the buyer when the contract is made, and it is immaterial whether the time of payment or the time of delivery, or both, be postponed.

*Rule 2.*—Where there is a contract for the sale of specific goods and the seller is bound to do something to the goods for the purpose of putting them into a deliverable state, the property does not pass until the thing is done and the buyer has notice that it has been done.

*Rule 3.*—Where there is a contract for the sale of specific goods in a deliverable state but the seller is bound to weigh, measure, test, or do some other act or thing with reference to the goods for the purpose of ascertaining the price, the property does not pass until the act or thing is done and the buyer has notice that it has been done.

*Rule 4.*—When goods are delivered to the buyer on approval or on sale or return or other similar terms the property in the goods passes to the buyer:—

(a) when he signifies his approval or acceptance to the seller or does any other act adopting the transaction;

(b) if he does not signify his approval or acceptance to the seller but retains the goods without giving notice of rejection, then, if a time has been fixed for the return of the goods, on the expiration of that time, and, if no time has been fixed, on the expiration of a reasonable time.

*Rule 5.*—(1) Where there is a contract for the sale of unascertained or future goods by description, and goods of that description and in a deliverable state are unconditionally appropriated to the contract, either by the seller with the assent of the buyer or by the buyer with the assent of the seller, the property in the goods then passes to the buyer; and the assent may be express or implied, and may be given either before or after the appropriation is made.

(2) Where, in pursuance of the contract, the seller delivers the goods to the buyer or to a carrier or other bailee or custodier (whether named by the buyer or not) for the purpose of transmission to the buyer, and does not reserve the right of disposal, he is to be taken to have unconditionally appropriated the goods to the contract.

[(3) Where there is a contract for the sale of a specified quantity of unascertained goods in a deliverable state forming part of a bulk which is identified either in the contract or by subsequent agreement between the parties and the bulk is reduced to (or to less than) that quantity, then, if the buyer under that contract is the only buyer to whom goods are then due out of the bulk—

(a) the remaining goods are to be taken as appropriated to that contract at the time when the bulk is so reduced; and

(b) the property in those goods then passes to that buyer.

(4) Paragraph (3) above applies also (with the necessary modifications) where a bulk is reduced to (or to less than) the aggregate of the quantities due to a single buyer under separate contracts relating to that bulk and he is the only buyer to whom goods are then due out of that bulk.]

### 19.   Reservation of right of disposal

(1)   Where there is a contract for the sale of specific goods or where goods are subsequently appropriated to the contract, the seller may, by the terms of the contract or appropriation, reserve the right of disposal of the goods until certain conditions are fulfilled; and in such a case, notwithstanding the delivery of the goods to the buyer, or to a carrier or other bailee or custodier for the purpose of transmission to the buyer, the property in the goods does not pass to the buyer until the conditions imposed by the seller are fulfilled.

(2)   Where goods are shipped, and by the bill of lading the goods are deliverable to the order of the seller or his agent, the seller is prima facie to be taken to reserve the right of disposal.

### 23.   Sale under voidable title

When the seller of goods has a voidable title to them, but his title has not been avoided at the time of the sale, the buyer acquires a good title to the goods, provided he buys them in good faith and without notice of the seller's defect of title.

## PART IV. PERFORMANCE OF THE CONTRACT

### 27.   Duties of seller and buyer

It is the duty of the seller to deliver the goods, and of the buyer to accept and pay for them, in accordance with the terms of the contract of sale.

### 35.   Acceptance

(1)   The buyer is deemed to have accepted the goods [subject to subsection (2) below—

(a)   when he intimates to the seller that he has accepted them, or

(b)   when the goods have been delivered to him and he does any act in relation to them which is inconsistent with the ownership of the seller.

(2)   Where goods are delivered to the buyer, and he has not previously examined them, he is not deemed to have accepted them under subsection (1) above until he has had a reasonable opportunity of examining them for the purpose—

(a)   of ascertaining whether they are in conformity with the contract, and

(b)   in the case of a contract for sale by sample, of comparing the bulk with the sample.

(3)   Where the buyer deals as consumer or (in Scotland) the contract of sale is a consumer contract, the buyer cannot lose his right to rely on subsection (2) above by agreement, waiver or otherwise.

(4)   The buyer is also deemed to have accepted the goods when after the lapse of a reasonable time he retains the goods without intimating to the seller that he has rejected them.

(5)   The questions that are material in determining for the purposes of subsection (4) above whether a reasonable time has elapsed include whether the buyer has had a reasonable opportunity of examining the goods for the purpose mentioned in subsection (2) above.

(6)   The buyer is not by virtue of this section deemed to have accepted the goods merely because—

(a)   he asks for, or agrees to, their repair by or under an arrangement with the seller, or

(b)   the goods are delivered to another under a sub-sale or other disposition.

(7)   Where the contract is for the sale of goods making one or more commercial units, a buyer accepting any goods included in a unit is deemed to have accepted all the goods making the unit; and in this subsection 'commercial

unit' means a unit division of which would materially impair the value of the goods or the character of the unit.]

[(8)   Paragraph 10 of Schedule 1 below applies in relation to a contract made before 22 April 1967 or (in the application of this Act to Northern Ireland) 28 July 1967.]

## [35A.   Right of partial rejection

(1)   If the buyer—

(a)   has the right to reject the goods by reason of a breach on the part of the seller that affects some or all of them, but

(b)   accepts some of the goods, including, where there are any goods unaffected by the breach, all such goods,

he does not by accepting them lose his right to reject the rest.

(2)   In the case of a buyer having the right to reject an instalment of goods, subsection (1) above applies as if references to the goods were references to the goods comprised in the instalment.

(3)   For the purposes of subsection (1) above, goods are affected by a breach if by reason of the breach they are not in conformity with the contract.

(4)   This section applies unless a contrary intention appears in, or is to be implied from, the contract.]

## 53.   Remedy for breach of warranty

(1)   Where there is a breach of warranty by the seller, or where the buyer elects (or is compelled) to treat any breach of a condition on the part of the seller as a breach of warranty, the buyer is not by reason only of such breach of warranty entitled to reject the goods; but he may—

(a)   set up against the seller the breach of warranty in diminution or extinction of the price, or

(b)   maintain an action against the seller for damages for the breach of warranty.

(2)   The measure of damages for breach of warranty is the estimated loss directly and naturally resulting, in the ordinary course of events, from the breach of warranty.

(3)   In the case of breach of warranty of quality such loss is prima facie the difference between the value of the goods at the time of delivery to the buyer and the value they would have had if they had fulfilled the warranty.

(4)   The fact that the buyer has set up the breach of warranty in diminution or extinction of the price does not prevent him from maintaining an action for the same breach of warranty if he has suffered further damage.

## [53A.   Measure of damages as respects Scotland

(1)   The measure of damages for the seller's breach of contract is the estimated loss directly and naturally resulting, in the ordinary course of events, from the breach.

(2)   Where the seller's breach consists of the delivery of goods which are not of the quality required by the contract and the buyer retains the goods, such loss as aforesaid is prima facie the difference between the value of the goods at the time of delivery to the buyer and the value they would have had if they had fulfilled the contract.

(3)   This section applies to Scotland only.]

## PART VII. SUPPLEMENTARY

## 55.   Exclusion of implied terms

(1)   Where a right, duty or liability would arise under a contract of sale of goods by implication of law, it may (subject to the Unfair Contract Terms Act 1977) be negatived or varied by express agreement, or by the course of dealing between the parties, or by such usage as binds both parties to the contract.

(2) An express [term] does not negative a condition or warranty implied by this Act unless inconsistent with it.

(3) Paragraph 11 of Schedule 1 below applies in relation to a contract made on or after 18 May 1973 and before 1 February 1978, and paragraph 12 in relation to one made before 18 May 1973.

## ADMINISTRATION OF JUSTICE ACT 1982
### (1982, c 53)

### 8. Services rendered to injured person

(1) Where necessary services have been rendered to the injured person by a relative in consequence of the injuries in question, then, unless the relative has expressly agreed in the knowledge that an action for damages has been raised or is in contemplation that no payment should be made in respect of those services, the responsible person shall be liable to pay to the injured person by way of damages such sum as represents reasonable remuneration for those services and repayment of reasonable expenses incurred in connection therewith.

[(2) The injured person shall be under an obligation to account to the relative for any damages recovered from the responsible person under subsection (1) above.

(3) Where, at the date of an award of damages in favour of the injured person, it is likely that necessary services will, after that date, be rendered to him by a relative in consequence of the injuries in question, then, unless the relative has expressly agreed that no payment shall be made in respect of those services, the responsible person shall be liable to pay to the injured person by way of damages such sum as represents—

    (a) reasonable remuneration for those services; and

    (b) reasonable expenses which are likely to be incurred in connection therewith.

(4) The relative shall have no direct right of action in delict against the responsible person in respect of any services or expenses referred to in this section.]

### 9. Services to injured person's relative

(1) The responsible person shall be liable to pay to the injured person a reasonable sum by way of damages in respect of the inability of the injured person to render the personal services referred to in subsection (3) below.

(2) Where the injured person has died, any relative of his entitled to damages in respect of loss of support under section 1(3) of the Damages (Scotland) Act 1976 shall be entitled to include as a head of damage under that section a reasonable sum in respect of the loss to him of the personal services mentioned in subsection (3) below.

(3) The personal services referred to in subsections (1) and (2) above are personal services—

    (a) which were or might have been expected to have been rendered by the injured person before the occurrence of the act or omission giving rise to liability,

    (b) of a kind which, when rendered by a person other than a relative, would ordinarily be obtainable on payment, and

    (c) which the injured person but for the injuries in question might have been expected to render gratuitously to a relative.

(4) Subject to subsection (2) above, the relative shall have no direct right of action in delict against the responsible person in respect of the personal services mentioned in subsection (3) above.

### 10. Assessment of damages for personal injuries

Subject to any agreement to the contrary, in assessing the amount of damages payable to the injured person in respect of personal injuries there shall not be taken into account so as to reduce that amount—

(a)   any contractual pension or benefit (including any payment by a friendly society or trade union);

(b)   any pension or retirement benefit payable from public funds other than any pension or benefit to which section 2(1) of the Law Reform (Personal Injuries) Act 1948 applies;

(c)   any benefit payable from public funds, in respect of any period after the date of the award of damages, designed to secure to the injured person or any relative of his a minimum level of subsistence;

(d)   any redundancy payment under the [Employment Rights Act 1996], or any payment made in circumstances corresponding to those in which a right to a redundancy payment would have accrued if section 135 of that Act had applied;

(e)   any payment made to the injured person or to any relative of his by the injured person's employer following upon the injuries in question where the recipient is under an obligation to reimburse the employer in the event of damages being recovered in respect of those injuries;

(f)   subject to paragraph (iv) below, any payment of a benevolent character made to the injured person or to any relative of his by any person following upon the injuries in question;

but there shall be taken into account—

(i)   any remuneration or earnings from employment;

(ii)   any [contribution-based jobseeker's allowance (payable under the Jobseekers Act 1995)];

(iii)   any benefit referred to in paragraph (c) above payable in respect of any period prior to the date of the award of damages;

(iv)   any payment of a benevolent character made to the injured person or to any relative of his by the responsible person following on the injuries in question, where such a payment is made directly and not through a trust or other fund from which the injured person or his relatives have benefited or may benefit.

## 11.   Maintenance at public expense to be taken into account in assessment of damages: Scotland

In an action for damages for personal injuries (including any such action arising out of a contract) any saving to the injured person which is attributable to his maintenance wholly or partly at public expense in—

(a)   a hospital . . . or other institution

[(b)   accommodation provided by a care home service (as defined by section 2(3) of the Regulation of Care (Scotland) Act 2001 (asp 8)).]

shall be set off against any income lost by him as a result of the injuries.

## 12.   Award of provisional damages for personal injuries: Scotland

(1)   This section applies to an action for damages for personal injuries in which—

(a)   there is proved or admitted to be a risk that at some definite or indefinite time in the future the injured person will, as a result of the act or omission which gave rise to the cause of the action, develop some serious disease or suffer some serious deterioration in his physical or mental condition; and

(b)   the responsible person was, at the time of the act or omission giving rise to the cause of the action,

(i)   a public authority or public corporation; or

(ii)   insured or otherwise indemnified in respect of the claim.

(2)  In any case to which this section applies, the court may, on the application of the injured person, order—

(a)   that the damages referred to in subsection (4)(a) below be awarded to the injured person; and

(b)   that the injured person may apply for the further award of damages referred to in subsection (4)(b) below,

and the court may, if it considers it appropriate, order that an application under paragraph (b) above may be made only within a specified period.

(3)   Where an injured person in respect of whom an award has been made under subsection (2)(a) above applies to the court for an award under subsection (2)(b) above, the court may award to the injured person the further damages referred to in subsection (4)(b) below.

(4)   The damages referred to in subsections (2) and (3) above are—

(a)   damages assessed on the assumption that the injured person will not develop the disease or suffer the deterioration in his condition; and

(b)   further damages if he develops the disease or suffers the deterioration.

(5)   Nothing in this section shall be construed—

(a)   as affecting the exercise of any power relating to expenses including a power to make rules of court relating to expenses; or

(b)   as prejudicing any duty of the court under any enactment or rule of law to reduce or limit the total damages which would have been recoverable apart from any such duty.

(6)   The Secretary of State may, by order, provide that categories of defenders shall, for the purposes of paragraph (b) of subsection (1) above, become or cease to be responsible persons, and may make such modifications of that paragraph as appear to him to be necessary for the purpose.

And an order under this subsection shall be made by statutory instrument subject to annulment in pursuance of a resolution of either House of Parliament.

## 13.  Supplementary

(1)   In this Part of this Act, unless the context otherwise requires—

'personal injuries' includes any disease or any impairment of a person's physical or mental condition [and injury resulting from defamation or any other verbal injury or other injury to reputation].

'relative', in relation to the injured person, means—

(a)   the spouse or divorced spouse;

(b)   any person, not being the spouse of the injured person, who was, at the time of the act or omission giving rise to liability in the responsible person, living with the injured person as husband or wife;

(c)   any ascendant or descendant;

(d)   any brother, sister, uncle or aunt; or any issue of any such person;

(e)   any person accepted by the injured person as a child of his family.

In deducing any relationship for the purposes of the foregoing definition—

(a)   any relationship by affinity shall be treated as a relationship by consanguinity; any relationship of the half blood shall be treated as a relationship of the whole blood; and the stepchild of any person shall be treated as his child; and

(b)   [section 1(1) of the Law Reform (Parent and Child) (Scotland) Act 1986 shall apply; and any reference (however expressed) in this Part of this Act to a relative shall be construed accordingly.]

(2)   Any reference in this Part of this Act to a payment, benefit or pension shall be construed as a reference to any such payment, benefit or pension whether in cash or in kind.

(3)   This Part of this Act binds the Crown.

# CIVIL AVIATION ACT 1982
## (1982, c 16)

*Trespass by aircraft and aircraft nuisance, noise, etc.*

**76.  Liability of aircraft in respect of trespass, nuisance and surface damage**

(1)  No action shall lie in respect of trespass or in respect of nuisance, by reason only of the flight of an aircraft over any property at a height above the ground which, having regard to wind, weather and all the circumstances of the case is reasonable, or the ordinary incidents of such flight, so long as the provisions of any Air Navigation Order and of any orders under section 62 above have been duly complied with and there has been no breach of section 81 below.

(2)  Subject to subsection (3) below, where material loss or damage is caused to any person or property on land or water by, or by a person in, or an article, animal or person falling from, an aircraft while in flight, taking off or landing, then unless the loss or damage was caused or contributed to by the negligence of the person by whom it was suffered, damages in respect of the loss or damage shall be recoverable without proof of negligence or intention or other cause of action, as if the loss or damage had been caused by the wilful act, neglect, or default of the owner of the aircraft.

(3)  Where material loss or damage is caused as aforesaid in circumstances in which—

(a)  damages are recoverable in respect of the said loss or damage by virtue only of subsection (2) above, and

(b)  a legal liability is created in some person other than the owner to pay damages in respect of the said loss or damage,

the owner shall be entitled to be indemnified by that other person against any claim in respect of the said loss or damage.

*Rights etc. in relation to aircraft*

**86.  Power to provide for the mortgaging of aircraft**

(1)  Her Majesty may by Order in Council make provision for the mortgaging of aircraft registered in the United Kingdom or capable of being so registered.

(2)  Without prejudice to the generality of the powers conferred by subsection (1) above, an Order in Council under this section may, in particular—

(a)  include provisions which correspond (subject to such modifications as appear to Her Majesty in Council to be necessary or expedient) to any of the provisions of the Merchant Shipping Act [1995] relating to the mortgaging of ships;

(b)  make provision as respects the rights and liabilities of mortgagors and mortgagees of such aircraft as are mentioned in subsection (1) above, and as respects the priority inter se of such rights and the relationship of such rights to other rights in or over such aircraft, including possessory liens for work done to such aircraft and rights under section 88 below or under regulations made by virtue of [section 83 of the Transport Act 2000 (detention and sale of aircraft)];

(c)  make provision as respects the operation, in relation to such aircraft as aforesaid, of any of the enactments in force in any part of the United Kingdom relating to bills of sale or the registration of charges on the property or undertaking of companies;

(d)  provide for the rights of mortgagees of such aircraft to be exercisable, in such circumstances as may be specified in the Order, in relation to payments for the use of the aircraft;

(e)  confer on courts in the United Kingdom powers in respect of any register maintained in pursuance of the Order and in respect of transactions affecting aircraft registered therein;

(f)  make provision for enabling the mortgage of an aircraft to extend to any store of spare parts for that aircraft and for applying, for that purpose, to any such spare parts provisions such as are mentioned in the preceding paragraphs of this subsection;

(g)  make provision specifying, subject to the consent of the Treasury, the fees to be paid in respect of the making or deletion of entries in any such register as aforesaid and in respect of any other matters in respect of which it appears to Her Majesty in Council to be expedient for the purposes of the Order to charge fees;

(h)  provide for the imposition of penalties in respect of the making of false statements in connection with matters dealt with in the Order and in respect of the forgery of documents relating to such matters.

## SUPPLY OF GOODS AND SERVICES ACT 1982
### (1982, c 29)

## [PART IA. SUPPLY OF GOODS AS RESPECTS SCOTLAND

*Contracts for the transfer of property in goods*

**11A.  The contracts concerned**

(1)  In this Act in its application to Scotland a 'contract for the transfer of goods' means a contract under which one person transfers or agrees to transfer to another the property in goods, other than an excepted contract.

(2)  For the purposes of this section an excepted contract means any of the following—

(a)  a contract of sale of goods;

(b)  a hire-purchase agreement;

(c)  a contract under which the property in goods is (or is to be) transferred in exchange for trading stamps on their redemption;

(d)  a transfer or agreement to transfer for which there is no consideration;

(e)  a contract intended to operate by way of mortgage, pledge, charge or other security.

(3)  For the purposes of this Act in its application to Scotland a contract is a contract for the transfer of goods whether or not services are also provided or to be provided under the contract, and (subject to subsection (2) above) whatever is the nature of the consideration for the transfer or agreement to transfer.

**11B.  Implied terms about title, etc.**

(1)  In a contract for the transfer of goods, other than one to which subsection (3) below applies, there is an implied term on the part of the transferor that in the case of a transfer of the property in the goods he has a right to transfer the property and in the case of an agreement to transfer the property in the goods he will have such a right at the time when the property is to be transferred.

(2)  In a contract for the transfer of goods, other than one to which subsection (3) below applies, there is also an implied term that—

(a)  the goods are free, and will remain free until the time when the property is to be transferred, from any charge or encumbrance not disclosed or known to the transferee before the contract is made, and

(b)  the transferee will enjoy quiet possession of the goods except so far as it may be disturbed by the owner or other person entitled to the benefit of any charge or encumbrance so disclosed or known.

(3)  This subsection applies to a contract for the transfer of goods in the case

of which there appears from the contract or is to be inferred from its circumstances an intention that the transferor should transfer only such title as he or a third person may have.

(4)   In a contract to which subsection (3) above applies there is an implied term that all charges or encumbrances known to the transferor and not known to the transferee have been disclosed to the transferee before the contract is made.

(5)   In a contract to which subsection (3) above applies there is also an implied term that none of the following will disturb the transferee's quiet possession of the goods, namely—

(a)   the transferor;

(b)   in a case where the parties to the contract intend that the transferor should transfer only such title as a third person may have, that person;

(c)   anyone claiming through or under the transferor or that third person otherwise than under a charge or encumbrance disclosed or known to the transferee before the contract is made.

(6)   [amends Unfair Contract Terms Act 1977]

**11C.   Implied terms where transfer is by description**

(1)   This section applies where, under a contract for the transfer of goods, the transferor transfers or agrees to transfer the property in the goods by description.

(2)   In such a case there is an implied term that the goods will correspond with the description.

(3)   If the transferor transfers or agrees to transfer the property in the goods by reference to a sample as well as by description it is not sufficient that the bulk of the goods corresponds with the sample if the goods do not also correspond with the description.

(4)   A contract is not prevented from falling within subsection (1) above by reason only that, being exposed for supply, the goods are selected by the transferee.

**11D.   Implied terms about quality or fitness**

(1)   Except as provided by this section and section 11E below and subject to the provisions of any other enactment, there is no implied term about the quality or fitness for any particular purpose of goods supplied under a contract for the transfer of goods.

(2)   Where, under such a contract, the transferor transfers the property in goods in the course of a business, there is an implied term that the goods supplied under the contract are of satisfactory quality.

(3)   For the purposes of this section and section 11E below, goods are of satisfactory quality if they meet the standard that a reasonable person would regard as satisfactory, taking account of any description of the goods, the price (if relevant) and all the other relevant circumstances.

(4)   The term implied by subsection (2) above does not extend to any matter making the quality of goods unsatisfactory—

(a)   which is specifically drawn to the transferee's attention before the contract is made,

(b)   where the transferee examines the goods before the contract is made, which that examination ought to reveal, or

(c)   where the property in the goods is, or is to be, transferred by reference to a sample, which would have been apparent on a reasonable examination of the sample.

(5)   Subsection (6) below applies where, under a contract for the transfer of goods, the transferor transfers the property in goods in the course of a business and the transferee, expressly or by implication, makes known—

(a)   to the transferor, or

(b)   where the consideration or part of the consideration for the transfer is a sum payable by instalments and the goods were previously sold by a credit-broker to the transferor, to that credit-broker,
any particular purpose for which the goods are being acquired.

(6)   In that case there is (subject to subsection (7) below) an implied term that the goods supplied under the contract are reasonably fit for the purpose, whether or not that is a purpose for which such goods are commonly supplied.

(7)   Subsection (6) above does not apply where the circumstances show that the transferee does not rely, or that it is unreasonable for him to rely, on the skill or judgment of the transferor or credit-broker.

(8)   An implied term about quality or fitness for a particular purpose may be annexed by usage to a contract for the transfer of goods.

(9)   The preceding provisions of this section apply to a transfer by a person who in the course of a business is acting as agent for another as they apply to a transfer by a principal in the course of a business, except where that other is not transferring in the course of a business and either the transferee knows that fact or reasonable steps are taken to bring it to the transferee's notice before the contract concerned is made.

**11E.   Implied terms where transfer is by sample**

(1)   This section applies where, under a contract for the transfer of goods, the transferor transfers or agrees to transfer the property in the goods by reference to a sample.

(2)   In such a case there is an implied term—
(a)   that the bulk will correspond with the sample in quality;
(b)   that the transferee will have a reasonable opportunity of comparing the bulk with the sample; and
(c)   that the goods will be free from any defect, making their quality unsatisfactory, which would not be apparent on reasonable examination of the sample.

(3)   For the purposes of this section a transferor transfers or agrees to transfer the property in goods by reference to a sample where there is an express or implied term to that effect in the contract concerned.

**11F.   Remedies for breach of contract**

(1)   Where in a contract for the transfer of goods a transferor is in breach of any term of the contract (express or implied), the other party to the contract (in this section referred to as 'the transferee') shall be entitled—
(a)   to claim damages; and
(b)   if the breach is material, to reject any goods delivered under the contract and treat it as repudiated.

(2)   Where a contract for the transfer of goods is a consumer contract and the transferee is the consumer, then, for the purposes of subsection (1)(b) above, breach by the transferor of any term (express or implied)—
(a)   as to the quality of the goods or their fitness for a purpose;
(b)   if the goods are, or are to be, transferred by description, that the goods will correspond with the description;
(c)   if the goods are, or are to be, transferred by reference to a sample, that the bulk will correspond with the sample in quality,
shall be deemed to be a material breach.

(3)   In subsection (2) above, 'consumer contract' has the same meaning as in section 25(1) of the 1977 Act; and for the purposes of that subsection the onus of proving that a contract is not to be regarded as a consumer contract shall lie on the transferor.

*Contracts for the hire of goods*

**11G.  The contracts concerned**

(1)   In this Act in its application to Scotland a 'contract for the hire of goods' means a contract under which one person ('the supplier') hires or agrees to hire goods to another, other than an excepted contract.

(2)   For the purposes of this section, an excepted contract means any of the following—

(a)   a hire-purchase agreement;

(b)   a contract under which goods are (or are to be) hired in exchange for trading stamps on their redemption.

(3)   For the purposes of this Act in its application to Scotland a contract is a contract for the hire of goods whether or not services are also provided or to be provided under the contract, and (subject to subsection (2) above) whatever is the nature of the consideration for the hire or agreement to hire.

**11H.  Implied terms about right to transfer possession etc.**

(1)   In a contract for the hire of goods there is an implied term on the part of the supplier that—

(a)   in the case of a hire, he has a right to transfer possession of the goods by way of hire for the period of the hire; and

(b)   in the case of an agreement to hire, he will have such a right at the time of commencement of the period of the hire.

(2)   In a contract for the hire of goods there is also an implied term that the person to whom the goods are hired will enjoy quiet possession of the goods for the period of the hire except so far as the possession may be disturbed by the owner or other person entitled to the benefit of any charge or encumbrance disclosed or known to the person to whom the goods are hired before the contract is made.

(3)   The preceding provisions of this section do not affect the right of the supplier to repossess the goods under an express or implied term of the contract.

**11I.  Implied terms where hire is by description**

(1)   This section applies where, under a contract for the hire of goods, the supplier hires or agrees to hire the goods by description.

(2)   In such a case there is an implied term that the goods will correspond with the description.

(3)   If under the contract the supplier hires or agrees to hire the goods by reference to a sample as well as by description it is not sufficient that the bulk of the goods corresponds with the sample if the goods do not also correspond with the description.

(4)   A contract is not prevented from falling within subsection (1) above by reason only that, being exposed for supply, the goods are selected by the person to whom the goods are hired.

**11J.  Implied terms about quality or fitness**

(1)   Except as provided by this section and section 11K below and subject to the provisions of any other enactment, there is no implied term about the quality or fitness for any particular purpose of goods hired under a contract for the hire of goods.

(2)   Where, under such a contract, the supplier hires goods in the course of a business, there is an implied term that the goods supplied under the contract are of satisfactory quality.

(3)   For the purposes of this section and section 11K below, goods are of satisfactory quality if they meet the standard that a reasonable person would regard as satisfactory, taking account of any description of the goods, the consideration for the hire (if relevant) and all the other relevant circumstances.

(4)   The term implied by subsection (2) above does not extend to any matter making the quality of goods unsatisfactory—
(a)   which is specifically drawn to the attention of the person to whom the goods are hired before the contract is made, or
(b)   where that person examines the goods before the contract is made, which that examination ought to reveal; or
(c)   where the goods are hired by reference to a sample, which would have been apparent on reasonable examination of the sample.
(5)   Subsection (6) below applies where, under a contract for the hire of goods, the supplier hires goods in the course of a business and the person to whom the goods are hired, expressly or by implication, makes known—
(a)   to the supplier in the course of negotiations conducted by him in relation to the making of the contract; or
(b)   to a credit-broker in the course of negotiations conducted by that broker in relation to goods sold by him to the supplier before forming the subject matter of the contract,
any particular purpose for which the goods are being hired.
(6)   In that case there is (subject to subsection (7) below) an implied term that the goods supplied under the contract are reasonably fit for that purpose, whether or not that is a purpose for which such goods are commonly supplied.
(7)   Subsection (6) above does not apply where the circumstances show that the person to whom the goods are hired does not rely, or that it is unreasonable for him to rely, on the skill or judgment of the hirer or credit-broker.
(8)   An implied term about quality or fitness for a particular purpose may be annexed by usage to a contract for the hire of goods.
(9)   The preceding provisions of this section apply to a hire by a person who in the course of a business is acting as agent for another as they apply to a hire by a principal in the course of a business, except where that other is not hiring in the course of a business and either the person to whom the goods are hired knows that fact or reasonable steps are taken to bring it to that person's notice before the contract concerned is made.

**11K.   Implied terms where hire is by sample**
(1)   This section applies where, under a contract for the hire of goods, the supplier hires or agrees to hire the goods by reference to a sample.
(2)   In such a case there is an implied term—
(a)   that the bulk will correspond with the sample in quality; and
(b)   that the person to whom the goods are hired will have a reasonable opportunity of comparing the bulk with the sample; and
(c)   that the goods will be free from any defect, making their quality unsatisfactory, which would not be apparent on reasonable examination of the sample.
(3)   For the purposes of this section a supplier hires or agrees to hire goods by reference to a sample where there is an express or implied term to that effect in the contract concerned.

*Exclusion of implied terms, etc.*

**11L.   Exclusion of implied terms etc.**
(1)   Where a right, duty or liability would arise under a contract for the transfer of goods or a contract for the hire of goods by implication of law, it may (subject to subsection (2) below and the 1977 Act) be negatived or varied by express agreement, or by the course of dealing between the parties, or by such usage as binds both parties to the contract.
(2)   An express term does not negative a term implied by the preceding provisions of this Part of this Act unless inconsistent with it.
(3)   Nothing in the preceding provisions of this Part of this Act prejudices

the operation of any other enactment or any rule of law whereby any term (other than one relating to quality or fitness) is to be implied in a contract for the transfer of goods or a contract for the hire of goods.]

## PART II. SUPPLY OF SERVICES

### 12. The contracts concerned

(1) In this Act a 'contract for the supply of a service' means, subject to subsection (2) below, a contract under which a person ('the supplier') agrees to carry out a service.

(2) For the purposes of this Act, a contract of service or apprenticeship is not a contract for the supply of a service.

(3) Subject to subsection (2) above, a contract is a contract for the supply of a service for the purposes of this Act whether or not goods are also—

(a) transferred or to be transferred, or

(b) bailed or to be bailed by way of hire,

under the contract, and whatever is the nature of the consideration for which the service is to be carried out.

(4) The Secretary of State may by order provide that one or more of sections 13 to 15 below shall not apply to services of a description specified in the order, and such an order may make different provision for different circumstances.

(5) The power to make an order under subsection (4) above shall be exercisable by statutory instrument subject to annulment in pursuance of a resolution of either House of Parliament.

### 13. Implied term about care and skill

In a contract for the supply of a service where the supplier is acting in the course of a business, there is an implied term that the supplier will carry out the service with reasonable care and skill.

### 14. Implied term about time for performance

(1) Where, under a contract for the supply of a service by a supplier acting in the course of a business, the time for the service to be carried out is not fixed by the contract, left to be fixed in a manner agreed by the contract or determined by the course of dealing between the parties, there is an implied term that the supplier will carry out the service within a reasonable time.

(2) What is a reasonable time is a question of fact.

### 15. Implied term about consideration

(1) Where, under a contract for the supply of a service, the consideration for the service is not determined by the contract, left to be determined in a manner agreed by the contract or determined by the course of dealing between the parties, there is an implied term that the party contracting with the supplier will pay a reasonable charge.

(2) What is a reasonable charge is a question of fact.

### 16. Exclusion of implied terms, etc.

(1) Where a right, duty or liability would arise under a contract for the supply of a service by virtue of this Part of this Act, it may (subject to subsection (2) below and the 1977 Act) be negatived or varied by express agreement, or by the course of dealing between the parties, or by such usage as binds both parties to the contract.

(2) An express term does not negative a term implied by this Part of this Act unless inconsistent with it.

(3) Nothing in this Part of this Act prejudices—

(a) any rule of law which imposes on the supplier a duty stricter than that imposed by section 13 or 14 above; or

(b) subject to paragraph (a) above, any rule of law whereby any term not inconsistent with this Part of this Act is to be implied in a contract for the supply of a service.

(4) This Part of this Act has effect subject to any other enactment which defines or restricts the rights, duties or liabilities arising in connection with a service of any description.

## PART III. SUPPLEMENTARY

### 18. Interpretation: general

(1) In the preceding provisions of this Act and this section—

'bailee', in relation to a contract for the hire of goods means (depending on the context) a person to whom the goods are bailed under the contract, or a person to whom they are to be so bailed, or a person to whom the rights under the contract of either of those persons have passed;

'bailor', in relation to a contract for the hire of goods, means (depending on the context) a person who bails the goods under the contract, or a person who agrees to do so, or a person to whom the duties under the contract of either of those persons have passed;

'business' includes a profession and the activities of any government department or local or public authority;

'credit-broker' means a person acting in the course of a business of credit brokerage carried on by him;

'credit brokerage' means the effecting of introductions—

(a) of individuals desiring to obtain credit to persons carrying on any business so far as it relates to the provision of credit; or

(b) of individuals desiring to obtain goods on hire to persons carrying on a business which comprises or relates to the bailment [or as regards Scotland the hire] of goods under a contract for the hire of goods; or

(c) of individuals desiring to obtain credit, or to obtain goods on hire, to other credit-brokers;

'enactment' means any legislation (including subordinate legislation) of the United Kingdom or Northern Ireland;

'goods' includes all personal chattels, [other than things in action and money, and as regards Scotland all corporeal moveables; and in particular 'goods' includes] emblements, industrial growing crops, and things attached to or forming part of the land which are agreed to be severed before the transfer, [bailment or hire] concerned or under the contract concerned . . .;

'hire-purchase agreement' has the same meaning as in the 1974 Act;

'property', in relation to goods, means the general property in them and not merely a special property;

'redemption', in relation to trading stamps, has the same meaning as in the Trading Stamps Act 1964 or, as respects Northern Ireland, the Trading Stamps Act (Northern Ireland) 1965;

'trading stamps' has the same meaning as in the said Act of 1964 or, as respects Northern Ireland, the said Act of 1965;

'transferee', in relation to a contract for the transfer of goods, means (depending on the context) a person to whom the property in the goods is transferred under the contract, or a person to whom the property is to be so transferred, or a person to whom the rights under the contract of either of those persons have passed;

'transferor', in relation to a contract for the transfer of goods, means (depending on the context) a person who transfers the property in the goods under the contract, or a person who agrees to do so, or a person to whom the duties under the contract of either of those persons have passed.

(2) In subsection (1) above, in the definitions of bailee, bailor, transferee and

transferor, a reference to rights or duties passing is to their passing by assignment, [assignation,] operation of law or otherwise.

[(3)   For the purposes of this Act, the quality of goods includes their state and condition and the following (among others) are in appropriate cases aspects of the quality of goods—

(a)   fitness for all the purposes for which goods of the kind in question are commonly supplied,

(b)   appearance and finish,

(c)   freedom from minor defects,

(d)   safety, and

(e)   durability.

(4)   References in this Act to dealing as consumer are to be construed in accordance with Part I of the Unfair Contract Terms Act 1977; and, for the purposes of this Act, it is for the transferor or bailor claiming that the transferee or bailee does not deal as consumer to show that he does not.]

### 19.   Interpretation: references to Acts

In this Act—

'the 1973 Act' means the Supply of Goods (Implied Terms) Act 1973;

'the 1974 Act' means the Consumer Credit Act 1974;

'the 1977 Act' means the Unfair Contract Terms Act 1977; and

'the 1979 Act' means the Sale of Goods Act 1979.

### 20.   Citation, transitional provisions, commencement and extent

(1)   This Act may be cited as the Supply of Goods and Services Act 1982.

(2)   The transitional provisions in the Schedule to this Act shall have effect.

(3)   Part I of this Act together with section 17 and so much of sections 18 and 19 above as relates to that Part shall not come into operation until 4th January 1983; and Part II of this Act together with so much of sections 18 and 19 above as relates to that Part shall not come into operation until such day as may be appointed by an order made by the Secretary of State.

(4)   The power to make an order under subsection (3) above shall be exercisable by statutory instrument.

(5)   No provision of this Act applies to a contract made before the provision comes into operation.

(6)   This Act [except Part IA, which extends only to Scotland] extends to Northern Ireland [and Parts I and II do not extend] to Scotland.

## MOBILE HOMES ACT 1983
### (1983, c 34)

### 1.   Particulars of agreements

(1)   This Act applies to any agreement under which a person ('the occupier') is entitled—

(a)   to station a mobile home on land forming part of a protected site; and

(b)   to occupy the mobile home as his only or main residence.

(2)   Within three months of the making of an agreement to which this Act applies, the owner of the protected site ('the owner') shall give to the occupier a written statement which—

(a)   specifies the names and addresses of the parties and the date of commencement of the agreement;

(b)   includes particulars of the land on which the occupier is entitled to station the mobile home sufficient to identify it;

(c)   sets out the express terms of the agreement;

(d)   sets out the terms implied by section 2(1) below; and

(e)   complies with such other requirements as may be prescribed by regulations made by the Secretary of State.

(3)   If the agreement was made before the day on which this Act comes into force, the written statement shall be given within six months of that day.

(4)   Any reference in subsection (2) or (3) above to the making of an agreement to which this Act applies includes a reference to any variation of an agreement by virtue of which the agreement becomes one to which this Act applies.

(5)   If the owner fails to comply with this section, the occupier may apply to the court for an order requiring the owner so to comply.

(6)   Regulations under this section—
    (a)   shall be made by statutory instrument; and
    (b)   may make different provision with respect to different cases or descriptions of case, including different provision for different areas.

## 2.   Terms of agreements

(1)   In any agreement to which this Act applies there shall be implied the terms set out in Part I of Schedule 1 to this Act; and this subsection shall have effect notwithstanding any express term of the agreement.

(2)   The court may, on the application of either party made within six months of the giving of the statement under section 1(2) above, order that there shall be implied in the agreement terms concerning the matters mentioned in Part II of Schedule 1 to this Act.

(3)   The court may, on the application of either party made within the said period of six months, by order vary or delete any express term of the agreement.

(4)   On an application under this section, the court shall make such provision as the court considers just and equitable in the circumstances.

## 3.   Successors in title

(1)   An agreement to which this Act applies shall be binding on and enure for the benefit of any successor in title of the owner and any person claiming through or under the owner or any such successor.

(2)   Where an agreement to which this Act applies is lawfully assigned to any person, the agreement shall enure for the benefit of and be binding on that person.

(3)   Where a person entitled to the benefit of and bound by an agreement to which this Act applies dies at a time when he is occupying the mobile home as his only or main residence, the agreement shall enure for the benefit of and be binding on—
    (a)   any person residing with that person ('the deceased') at that time being—
        (i)   the widow or widower of the deceased; or
        (ii)   in default of a widow or widower so residing, any member of the deceased's family; or
    (b)   in default of any such person so residing, the person entitled to the mobile home by virtue of the deceased's will or under the law relating to intestacy but subject to subsection (4) below.

(4)   An agreement to which this Act applies shall not enure for the benefit of or be binding on a person by virtue of subsection (3)(b) above in so far as—
    (a)   it would, but for this subsection, enable or require that person to occupy the mobile home; or
    (b)   it includes terms implied by virtue of paragraph 5 or 9 of Part I of Schedule 1 to this Act.

## 4.   Jurisdiction of the court

The court shall have jurisdiction to determine any question arising under this Act or any agreement to which it applies, and to entertain any proceedings brought under this Act or any such agreement.

### 5. Interpretation

(1) In this Act, unless the context otherwise requires—

'the court' means—

(a) in relation to England and Wales, the county court for the district in which the protected site is situated or, where the parties have agreed in writing to submit any question arising under this Act or, as the case may be, any agreement to which it applies to arbitration, the arbitrator;

(b) in relation to Scotland, the sheriff having jurisdiction where the protected site is situated or, where the parties have so agreed, the arbiter;

'local authority' has the same meaning as in Part I of the Caravan Sites and Control of Development Act 1960;

'mobile home' has the same meaning as 'caravan' has in that Part of that Act;

'owner', in relation to a protected site, means the person who, by virtue of an estate or interest held by him, is entitled to possession of the site or would be so entitled but for the rights of any persons to station mobile homes on land forming part of the site;

'planning permission' means permission under Part III of the Town and Country Planning Act [1990] or Part III of the Town and Country Planning (Scotland) Act [1997];

'protected site' does not include any land occupied by a local authority as a caravan site providing accommodation for gipsies or, in Scotland, for persons to whom section 24(8A) of the Caravan Sites and Control of Development Act 1960 applies but, subject to that, has the same meaning as in Part I of the Caravan Sites Act 1968.

(2) In relation to an agreement to which this Act applies—

(a) any reference in this Act to the owner includes a reference to any person who is bound by and entitled to the benefit of the agreement by virtue of subsection (1) of section 3 above; and

(b) subject to subsection (4) of that section, any reference in this Act to the occupier includes a reference to any person who is entitled to the benefit of and bound by the agreement by virtue of subsection (2) or (3) of that section.

(3) A person is a member of another's family within the meaning of this Act if he is his spouse, parent, grandparent, child, grandchild, brother, sister, uncle, aunt, nephew or niece; treating—

(a) any relationship by marriage as a relationship by blood, any relationship of the half blood as a relationship of the whole blood and the stepchild of any person as his child; and

(b) an illegitimate person as the legitimate child of his mother and reputed father;

or if they live together as husband and wife.

(4) In relation to land in Scotland, any reference in this Act to an 'estate or interest' shall be construed as a reference to a right in, or to, the land.

### 6. Short title, repeals, commencement and extent

(1) This Act may be cited as the Mobile Homes Act 1983.

(2) The enactments mentioned in Schedule 2 to this Act are hereby repealed to the extent specified in the third column of that Schedule.

(3) This Act shall come into force on the expiry of the period of one week beginning with the day on which it is passed.

(4) This Act does not extend to Northern Ireland.

# SCHEDULES

## SCHEDULE 1. AGREEMENTS UNDER ACT

### PART I. TERMS IMPLIED BY ACT

#### Duration of agreement

1. Subject to paragraph 2 below, the right to station the mobile home on land forming part of the protected site shall subsist until the agreement is determined under paragraph 3, 4, 5 or 6 below.

2.—(1) If the owner's estate or interest is insufficient to enable him to grant the right for an indefinite period, the period for which the right subsists shall not extend beyond the date when the owner's estate or interest determines.

(2) If planning permission for the use of the protected site as a site for mobile homes has been granted in terms such that it will expire at the end of a specified period, the period for which the right subsists shall not extend beyond the date when the planning permission expires.

(3) If before the end of a period determined by this paragraph there is a change in circumstances which allows a longer period, account shall be taken of that change.

#### Termination by occupier

3. The occupier shall be entitled to terminate the agreement by notice in writing given to the owner not less than four weeks before the date on which it is to take effect.

#### Termination by owner

4. The owner shall be entitled to terminate the agreement forthwith if, on the application of the owner, the court—

(a) is satisfied that the occupier has breached a term of the agreement and, after service of a notice to remedy the breach, has not complied with the notice within a reasonable time; and

(b) considers it reasonable for the agreement to be terminated.

5. The owner shall be entitled to terminate the agreement forthwith if, on the application of the owner, the court is satisfied that the occupier is not occupying the mobile home as his only or main residence.

6.—(1) The owner shall be entitled to terminate the agreement at the end of a relevant period if, on the application of the owner, the court is satisfied that, having regard to its age and condition, the mobile home—

(a) is having a detrimental effect on the amenity of the site; or

(b) is likely to have such an effect before the end of the next relevant period.

(2) In sub-paragraph (1) above 'relevant period' means the period of five years beginning with the commencement of the agreement and each succeeding period of five years.

#### Recovery of overpayments by occupier

7. Where the agreement is terminated as mentioned in paragraph 3, 4, 5 or 6 above, the occupier shall be entitled to recover from the owner so much of any payment made by him in pursuance of the agreement as is attributable to a period beginning after the termination.

*Sale of mobile home*

8.—(1)  The occupier shall be entitled to sell the mobile home, and to assign the agreement, to a person approved of by the owner, whose approval shall not be unreasonably withheld.

(2)  Where the occupier sells the mobile home, and assigns the agreement, as mentioned in sub-paragraph (1) above, the owner shall be entitled to receive a commission on the sale at a rate not exceeding such rate as may be specified by an order made by the Secretary of State.

(3)  An order under this paragraph—

(a)  shall be made by statutory instrument which shall be subject to annulment in pursuance of a resolution of either House of Parliament; and

(b)  may make different provision for different areas or for sales at different prices.

*Gift of mobile home*

9.  The occupier shall be entitled to give the mobile home, and to assign the agreement, to a member of his family approved by the owner, whose approval shall not be unreasonably withheld.

*Re-siting of mobile home*

10.  If the owner is entitled to require that the occupier's right to station the mobile home shall be exercisable for any period in relation to other land forming part of the protected site—

(a)  that other land shall be broadly comparable to the land on which the occupier was originally entitled to station the mobile home; and

(b)  all costs and expenses incurred in consequence of the requirement shall be paid by the owner.

## PART II. MATTERS CONCERNING WHICH TERMS MAY BE IMPLIED BY COURT

1.  The right of the occupier to quiet enjoyment or, in Scotland, undisturbed possession of the mobile home.

2.  The sums payable by the occupier in pursuance of the agreement and the times at which they are to be paid.

3.  The review at yearly intervals of the sums so payable.

4.  The provision or improvement of services available on the protected site, and the use by the occupier of such services.

5.  The preservation of the amenity of the protected site.

6.  The maintenance and repair of the protected site by the owner, and the maintenance and repair of the mobile home by the occupier.

7.  Access by the owner to the land on which the occupier is entitled to station the mobile home.

## LAW REFORM (HUSBAND AND WIFE) (SCOTLAND) ACT 1984
### (1984, c 15)

*Abolition of actions of breach of promise of marriage, adherence and enticement*

### 1.  Promise of marriage not an enforceable obligation

(1)  No promise of marriage or agreement between two persons to marry one another shall have effect under the law of Scotland to create any rights or obligations; and no action for breach of any such promise or agreement may be

brought in any court in Scotland, whatever the law applicable to the promise or agreement.

(2) This section shall have effect in relation to any promise made or agreement entered into before it comes into force, but shall not affect any action commenced before it comes into force.

## 2. Actions of adherence and enticement abolished

(1) No spouse shall be entitled to apply for a decree from any court in Scotland ordaining the other spouse to adhere.

(2) No person shall be liable in delict to any person by reason only of having induced the spouse of that person to leave or remain apart from that person.

(3) This section shall not affect any action commenced before this Act comes into force.


## BANKRUPTCY (SCOTLAND) ACT 1985
### (1985, c 66)

## 5. Sequestration of the estate of living or deceased debtor

(1) The estate of a debtor may be sequestrated in accordance with the provisions of this Act.

(2) The sequestration of the estate of a living debtor shall be on the petition of—

    (a) the debtor, [if either subsection (2A) or (2B) below applies to him];

    (b) a qualified creditor or qualified creditors, if the debtor is apparently insolvent; or

    (c) the trustee acting under a . . . trust deed [if, and only if, one or more of the conditions in subsection (2C) below is satisfied].

[(2A) This subsection applies to the debtor if a qualified creditor or qualified creditors concur in the petition.

(2B) This subsection applies to the debtor where—

    (a) the total amount of his debts (including interest) at the date of presentation of the petition is not less than £1,500;

    (b) an award of sequestration has not been made against him in the period of 5 years ending on the day before the date of presentation of the petition; and

    (c) the debtor either—

        (i) is apparently insolvent; or

        (ii) has granted a trust deed and the trustee has complied with the requirements of sub-sub-paragraphs (a) to (c) of paragraph 5(1) of Schedule 5 to this Act but has received notification as mentioned in sub-sub-paragraph (d) of that paragraph,

and for the purposes of this paragraph a debtor shall not be apparently insolvent by reason only that he has granted a trust deed or that he has given notice to his creditors as mentioned in paragraph (b) of section 7(1) of this Act.

(2C) The conditions mentioned in subsection (2)(c) above are—

    (a) that the debtor has failed to comply—

        (i) with any obligation imposed on him under the trust deed with which he could reasonably have complied; or

        (ii) with any instruction or requirement reasonably given to or made of him by the trustee for the purposes of the trust deed; or

    (b) that the trustee avers in his petition that it would be in the best interests of the creditors that an award of sequestration be made.]

(3) The sequestration of the estate of a deceased debtor shall be on the petition of—

(a)   an executor or a person entitled to be appointed as executor on the estate;

(b)   a qualified creditor or qualified creditors of the deceased debtor; or

(c)   the trustee acting under a trust deed.

(4)   In this Act 'qualified creditor' means a creditor who, at the date of the presentation of the petition, is a creditor of the debtor in respect of liquid or illiquid debts (other than contingent or future debts) [or amounts payable under a confiscation order], whether secure or unsecured, which amount (or of one such debt which amounts) to not less than [£1,500] or such sum as may be prescribed; and 'qualified creditors' means creditors who at the said date are creditors of the debtor in respect of such debts as aforesaid amounting in aggregate to not less than [£1,500] or such sum as may be prescribed [and in the foregoing provisions of this subsection 'confiscation order' has the meaning assigned by section 2(9) of the Drug Trafficking Act 1994 or by section 49(1) of the Proceeds of Crime (Scotland) Act 1995.

(4A)   In this Act, 'trust deed' means a voluntary trust deed granted by or on behalf of the debtor whereby his estate (other than such of his estate as would not, under section 33(1) of this Act, vest in the permanent trustee if his estate were sequestrated) is conveyed to the trustee for the benefit of his creditors generally.]

(5)   Paragraphs 1(1) and (3), 2(1)(a) and (2) and 6 of Schedule 1 to this Act shall apply in order to ascertain the amount of the debt or debts for the purposes of subsection (4) above as they apply in order to ascertain the amount which a creditor is entitled to claim, but as if for any reference to the date of sequestration there were substituted a reference to the date of presentation of the petition.

(6)   The petitioner shall [on the day of the petition for sequestration under this section] send a copy of [the] petition . . . to the Accountant in Bankruptcy.

[(6A)   Where the petitioner is the debtor—

(a)   he shall lodge with the petition, a statement of assets and liabilities; and

(b)   he shall, on the day the petition is presented, send to the Accountant in Bankruptcy such statement of assets and liabilities as was lodged in court in pursuance of paragraph (a) above.]

(7)   Where, after a petition for sequestration has been presented but before the sequestration has been awarded, the debtor dies then—

(a)   if the petitioner was the debtor, the petition shall fall;

(b)   if the petitioner is a creditor, the proceedings shall continue in accordance with this Act so far as circumstances will permit.

(8)   Where, after a petition for sequestration has been presented under this section but before the sequestration has been awarded, a creditor who—

(a)   is the petitioner or concurs in a petition by the debtor; or

(b)   has lodged answers to the petition,

withdraws or dies, there may be sisted in the place of—

(i)   the creditor mentioned in paragraph (a) above, any creditor who was a qualified creditor at the date when the petition was presented and who remains so qualified at the date of the sist;

(ii)   the creditor mentioned in paragraph (b) above, any other creditor.

[(9)   If the debtor—

(a)   fails to send to the Accountant in Bankruptcy in accordance with subsection (6A)(b) above such statement of assets and liabilities; or

(b)   fails to disclose any material fact in such statement of assets and liabilities; or

(c)   makes a material misstatement in such statement of assets and liabilities,

he shall be guilty of an offence and liable on summary conviction to a fine not exceeding level 5 on the standard scale or to imprisonment for a term not exceeding 3 months or to both such fine and imprisonment.

(10)  In any proceedings for an offence under subsection (9) above, it shall be a defence for the accused to show that he had a reasonable excuse for—

(a)  failing to send to the Accountant in Bankruptcy in accordance with subsection (6A)(b) above such statement of assets and liabilities; or

(b)  failing to disclose a material fact; or

(c)  making a material misstatement.]

### 61.  Extortionate credit transactions

(1)  This section applies where the debtor is or has been a party to a transaction for, or involving, the provision to him of credit and his estate is sequestrated.

(2)  The court may, on the application of the permanent trustee, make an order with respect to the transaction if the transaction is or was extortionate and was not entered into more than three years before the date of sequestration.

(3)  For the purposes of this section a transaction is extortionate if, having regard to the risk accepted by the person providing the credit—

(a)  the terms of it are or were such as to require grossly exorbitant payments to be made (whether unconditionally or in certain contingencies) in respect of the provision of the credit; or

(b)  it otherwise grossly contravened ordinary principles of fair dealing; and it shall be presumed, unless the contrary is proved, that a transaction with respect to which an application is made under this section is, or as the case may be was, extortionate.

(4)  An order under this section with respect to any transaction may contain such one or more of the following as the court thinks fit—

(a)  provision setting aside the whole or part of any obligation created by the transaction;

(b)  provision otherwise varying the terms of the transaction or varying the terms on which any security for the purposes of the transaction is held;

(c)  provision requiring any person who is a party to the transaction to pay to the permanent trustee any sums paid to that person, by virtue of the transaction, by the debtor;

(d)  provision requiring any person to surrender to the permanent trustee any property held by him as security for the purposes of the transaction;

(e)  provision directing accounts to be taken between any persons.

(5)  Any sums or property required to be paid or surrendered to the permanent trustee in accordance with an order under this section shall vest in the permanent trustee.

(6)  Neither—

(a)  the permanent trustee; nor

(b)  a debtor who has not been discharged,

shall be entitled to make an application under section 139(1)(a) of the Consumer Credit Act 1974 (re-opening of extortionate credit agreements) for any agreement by which credit is or has been provided to the debtor to be re-opened; but the powers conferred by this section shall be exercisable in relation to any transaction concurrently with any powers exercisable under this Act in relation to that transaction as a gratuitous alienation or unfair preference.

(7)  In this section 'credit' has the same meaning as in the said Act of 1974.

# SCHEDULES

## SCHEDULE 1. DETERMINATION OF AMOUNT OF CREDITOR'S CLAIM

*Amount which may be claimed generally*

1.—(1)  Subject to the provisions of this Schedule, the amount in respect of which a creditor shall be entitled to claim shall be the accumulated sum of principal and any interest which is due on the debt as at the date of sequestration.

(2)  If a debt does not depend on a contingency but would not be payable but for the sequestration until after the date of sequestration, the amount of the claim shall be calculated as if the debt were payable on the date of sequestration but subject to the deduction of interest at the rate specified in section 51(7) of this Act from the said date until the date for payment of the debt.

(3)  In calculating the amount of his claim, a creditor shall deduct any discount (other than any discount for payment in cash) which is allowable by contract or course of dealing between the creditor and the debtor or by the usage of trade.

*Claims for aliment and periodical allowance on divorce*

2.—(1)  A person entitled to aliment, however arising, from a living debtor as at the date of sequestration, or from a deceased debtor immediately before his death, shall not be entitled to include in the amount of his claim—

(a)  any unpaid aliment for any period before the date of sequestration unless the amount of the aliment has been quantified by court decree or by any legally binding obligation which is supported by evidence in writing, and, in the case of spouses (or, where the aliment is payable to a divorced person in respect of a child, former spouses) they were living apart during that period;

(b)  any aliment for any period after the date of sequestration.

(2)  Sub-paragraph (1) above shall apply to a periodical allowance payable on divorce—

(a)  by virtue of a court order; or

(b)  under any legally binding obligation which is supported by evidence in writing,

as it applies to aliment and as if for the words from 'in the case' to 'they' there were substituted the words 'the payer and payee'.

*Debts depending on contingency*

3.—(1)  Subject to sub-paragraph (2) below, the amount which a creditor shall be entitled to claim shall not include a debt in so far as its existence or amount depends upon a contingency.

(2)  On an application by the creditor—

(a)  to the permanent trustee; or

(b)  if there is no permanent trustee, to the sheriff,

the permanent trustee or sheriff shall put a value on the debt in so far as it is contingent, and the amount in respect of which the creditor shall then be entitled to claim shall be that value but no more; and, where the contingent debt is an annuity, a cautioner may not then be sued for more than that value.

(3)  Any interested person may appeal to the sheriff against a valuation under sub-paragraph (2) above by the permanent trustee, and the sheriff may affirm or vary that valuation.

*Debts due under composition contracts*

4. Where in the course of a sequestration the debtor is discharged following approval by the sheriff of a composition offered by the debtor but the sequestration is subsequently revived, the amount in respect of which a creditor shall be entitled to claim shall be the same amount as if the composition had not been so approved less any payment already made to him under the composition contract.

*Secured debts*

5.—(1) In calculating the amount of his claim, a secured creditor shall deduct the value of any security as estimated by him:

Provided that if he surrenders, or undertakes in writing to surrender, a security for the benefit of the debtor's estate, he shall not be required to make a deduction of the value of that security.

(2) The permanent trustee may, at any time after the expiry of 12 weeks from the date of sequestration, require a secured creditor at the expense of the debtor's estate to discharge the security or convey or assign it to the permanent trustee on payment to the creditor of the value specified by the creditor; and the amount in respect of which the creditor shall then be entitled to claim shall be any balance of his debt remaining after receipt of such payment.

(3) In calculating the amount of his claim, a creditor whose security has been realised shall deduct the amount (less the expenses of realisation) which he has received, or is entitled to receive, from the realisation.

*Valuation of claims against partners for debts of the partnership*

6. Where a creditor claims in respect of a debt of a partnership, against the estate of one of its partners, the creditor shall estimate the value of—

(a) the debt to the creditor from the firm's estate where that estate has not been sequestrated; or

(b) the creditor's claim against that estate where it has been sequestrated, and deduct that value from his claim against the partner's estate; and the amount in respect of which he shall be entitled to claim on the partner's estate shall be the balance remaining after that deduction has been made.

## COMPANIES ACT 1985
### (1985, c 6)

**2. Requirements with respect to memorandum**

(1) The memorandum of every company must state—

(a) the name of the company;

(b) whether the registered office of the company is to be situated in England and Wales, or in Scotland;

(c) the objects of the company.

(2) Alternatively to subsection (1)(b), the memorandum may contain a statement that the company's registered office is to be situated in Wales; and a company whose registered office is situated in Wales may by special resolution alter its memorandum so as to provide that its registered office is to be so situated.

(3) The memorandum of a company limited by shares or by guarantee must also state that the liability of its members is limited.

(4) The memorandum of a company limited by guarantee must also state that each member undertakes to contribute to the assets of the company if it should be wound up while he is a member, or within one year after he ceases

to be a member, for payment of the debts and liabilities of the company contracted before he ceases to be a member, and of the costs, charges and expenses of winding up, and for adjustment of the rights of the contributories among themselves, such amount as may be required, not exceeding a specified amount.

(5) In the case of a company having a share capital—

(a) the memorandum must also (unless it is an unlimited company) state the amount of the share capital with which the company proposes to be registered and the division of the share capital into shares of a fixed amount;

(6) [Subject to subsection (3A) the memorandum] must be signed by each subscriber in the presence of at least one witness, who must attest the signature.

[(6A) Where the memorandum is delivered to the registrar otherwise than in legible form and is authenticated by each subscriber in such manner as is directed by the registrar, the requirements in subsection (6) for signature in the presence of at least one witness and for attestation of the signature do not apply.]

(7) A company may not alter the conditions contained in its memorandum except in the cases, in the mode and to the extent, for which express provision is made by this Act.

## 7. Articles prescribing regulations for companies

(1) There may in the case of a company limited by shares, and there shall in the case of a company limited by guarantee or unlimited, be registered with the memorandum articles of association prescribing regulations for the company.

(2) In the case of an unlimited company having a share capital, the articles must state the amount of share capital with which the company proposes to be registered.

(3) Articles must—

(a) be printed,

(b) be divided into paragraphs numbered consecutively.

. . .

## [35. A company's capacity not limited by its memorandum

(1) The validity of an act done by a company shall not be called into question on the ground of lack of capacity by reason of anything in the company's memorandum.

(2) A member of a company may bring proceedings to restrain the doing of an act which but for subsection (1) would be beyond the company's capacity; but no such proceedings shall lie in respect of an act to be done in fulfilment of a legal obligation arising from a previous act of the company.

(3) It remains the duty of the directors to observe any limitations on their powers flowing from the company's memorandum; and action by the directors which but for subsection (1) would be beyond the company's capacity may only be ratified by the company by special resolution.

A resolution ratifying such action shall not affect any liability incurred by the directors or any other person; relief from any such liability must be agreed to separately by special resolution.

(4) The operation of this section is restricted by [section 65(1) of the Charities Act 1993] and section 112(3) of the Companies Act 1989 in relation to companies which are charities; and section 322A below (invalidity of certain transactions to which directors or their associates are parties) has effect notwithstanding this section.]

## [35A. Power of directors to bind the company

(1) In favour of a person dealing with a company in good faith, the power of the board of directors to bind the company, or authorise others to do so, shall be deemed to be free of any limitation under the company's constitution.

(2)   For this purpose—
(a)   a person 'deals with' a company if he is a party to any transaction or other act to which the company is a party;
(b)   a person shall not be regarded as acting in bad faith by reason only of his knowing that an act is beyond the powers of the directors under the company's constitution; and
(c)   a person shall be presumed to have acted in good faith unless the contrary is proved.
(3)   The references above to limitations on the directors' powers under the company's constitution include limitations deriving—
(a)   from a resolution of the company in general meeting or a meeting of any class of shareholders, or
(b)   from any agreement between the members of the company or of any class of shareholders.
(4)   Subsection (1) does not affect any right of a member of the company to bring proceedings to restrain the doing of an act which is beyond the powers of the directors; but no such proceedings shall lie in respect of an act to be done in fulfilment of a legal obligation arising from a previous act of the company.
(5)   Nor does that subsection affect any liability incurred by the directors, or any other person, by reason of the directors' exceeding their powers.
(6)   The operation of this section is restricted by [section 65(1) of the Charities Act 1993] and section 112(3) of the Companies Act 1989 in relation to companies which are charities; and section 322A below (invalidity of certain transactions to which directors or their associates are parties) has effect notwithstanding this section.

**35B.   No duty to enquire as to capacity of company or authority of directors**
A party to a transaction with a company is not bound to enquire as to whether it is permitted by the company's memorandum or as to any limitation on the powers of the board of directors to bind the company or authorise others to do so.]
. . .

**108.   Valuation and report (s. 103)**
(1)   The valuation and report required by section 103 (or, where applicable, section 44) shall be made by an independent person, that is to say a person qualified at the time of the report to be appointed, or continue to be, an auditor of the company.
(2)   However, where it appears to the independent person (from here on referred to as 'the valuer') to be reasonable for the valuation of the consideration, or part of it, to be made (or for him to accept such a valuation) by another person who—
(a)   appears to him to have the requisite knowledge and experience to value the consideration or that part of it; and
(b)   is not an officer or servant of the company or any other body corporate which is that company's subsidiary or holding company or a subsidiary of that company's holding company or a partner or employee of such an officer or servant,
he may arrange for or accept such a valuation, together with a report which will enable him to make his own report under this section and provide the note required by subsection (6) below.
(3)   The reference in subsection (2)(b) to an officer or servant does not include an auditor.
(4)   The valuer's report shall state—
(a)   the nominal value of the shares to be wholly or partly paid for by the consideration in question;
(b)   the amount of any premium payable on the shares;

(c) the description of the consideration and, as respects so much of the consideration as he himself has valued, a description of that part of the consideration, the method used to value it and the date of the valuation;

(d) the extent to which the nominal value of the shares and any premium are to be treated as paid up—

(i) by the consideration;

(ii) in cash.

(5) Where the consideration or part of it is valued by a person other than the valuer himself, the latter's report shall state that fact and shall also—

(a) state the former's name and what knowledge and experience he has to carry out the valuation, and

(b) describe so much of the consideration as was valued by the other person, and the method used to value it, and specify the date of the valuation.

(6) The valuer's report shall contain or be accompanied by a note by him—

(a) in the case of a valuation made by a person other than himself, that it appeared to himself reasonable to arrange for it to be so made or to accept a valuation so made;

(b) whoever made the valuation, that the method of valuation was reasonable in all the circumstances;

(c) that it appears to the valuer that there has been no material change in the value of the consideration in question since the valuation; and

(d) that on the basis of the valuation the value of the consideration, together with any cash by which the nominal value of the shares or any premium payable on them is to be paid up, is not less than so much of the aggregate of the nominal value and the whole of any such premium as is treated as paid up by the consideration and any such cash.

(7) Where the consideration to be valued is accepted partly in payment up of the nominal value of the shares and any premium and partly for some other consideration given by the company, section 103 (and, where applicable, section 44) and the foregoing provisions of this section apply as if references to the consideration accepted by the company included the proportion of that consideration which is properly attributable to the payment up of that value and any premium; and—

(a) the valuer shall carry out, or arrange for, such other valuations as will enable him to determine that proportion; and

(b) his report shall state what valuations have been made under this subsection and also the reason for, and method and date of, any such valuation and any other matters which may be relevant to that determination.

## PART XVIII. FLOATING CHARGES AND RECEIVERS (SCOTLAND)

### CHAPTER I. FLOATING CHARGES

**462. Power of incorporated company to create floating charge**

(1) It is competent under the law of Scotland for [a limited liability partnership], for the purpose of securing any debt or other obligation (including a cautionary obligation) incurred or to be incurred by, or binding upon, the company or any other person, to create in favour of the creditor in the debt or obligation a charge, in this Part referred to as a floating charge, over all or any part of the property . . . which may from time to time be comprised in its property and undertaking.

. . .

(4) References in this Part to the instrument by which a floating charge was created are, in the case of a floating charge created by words in a bond or other

written acknowledgment, references to the bond or, as the case may be, the other written acknowledgment.

(5) Subject to this Act, a floating charge has effect in accordance with this Part [and Part III of the Insolvency Act 1986] in relation to any heritable property in Scotland to which it relates, notwithstanding that the instrument creating it is not recorded in the Register of Sasines or, as appropriate, registered in accordance with the Land Registration (Scotland) Act 1979.

## LAW REFORM (MISCELLANEOUS PROVISIONS) (SCOTLAND) ACT 1985
### (1985, c 73)

*Provisions relating to leases*

. . .

### 4. Irritancy clauses etc. relating to monetary breaches of lease

(1) A landlord shall not, for the purpose of treating a lease as terminated or terminating it, be entitled to rely—

(a) on a provision in the lease which purports to terminate it, or to enable him to terminate it, in the event of a failure of the tenant to pay rent, or to make any other payment, on or before the due date therefor or such later date or within such period as may be provided for in the lease; or

(b) on the fact that such a failure is, or is deemed by a provision of the lease to be, a material breach of contract,

unless subsection (2) or (5) below applies.

(2) This subsection applies if—

(a) the landlord has, at any time after the payment of rent or other payment mentioned in subsection (1) above has become due, served a notice on the tenant—

(i) requiring the tenant to make payment of the sum which he has failed to pay together with any interest thereon in terms of the lease within the period specified in the notice; and

(ii) stating that, if the tenant does not comply with the requirement mentioned in sub-paragraph (i) above, the lease may be terminated; and

(b) the tenant has not complied with that requirement.

(3) The period to be specified in any such notice shall be not less than—

(a) a period of 14 days immediately following the service of the notice; or

(b) if any period remaining between the service of the notice and the expiry of any time provided for in the lease or otherwise for the late payment of the sum which the tenant has failed to pay is greater than 14 days, that greater period.

(4) Any notice served under subsection (2) above shall be sent by recorded delivery and shall be sufficiently served if it is sent to the tenant's last business or residential address in the United Kingdom known to the landlord or to the last address in the United Kingdom provided to the landlord by the tenant for the purpose of such service.

(5) This subsection applies if the tenant does not have an address in the United Kingdom known to the landlord and has not provided an address in the United Kingdom to the landlord for the purpose of service.

### 5. Irritancy clauses etc. not relating to monetary breaches of leases

(1) Subject to subsection (2) below, a landlord shall not, for the purpose of treating a lease as terminated or terminating it, be entitled to rely—

(a) on a provision in the lease which purports to terminate it, or to enable the landlord to terminate it, in the event of an act or omission by the tenant (other than such a failure as is mentioned in section 4(1)(a) of this Act) or of a change in the tenant's circumstances; or

(b)   on the fact that such act or omission or change is, or is deemed by a provision of the lease to be, a material breach of contract,
if in all the circumstances of the case a fair and reasonable landlord would not seek so to rely.

(2)   No provision of a lease shall of itself, irrespective of the particular circumstances of the case, be held to be unenforceable by virtue of subsection (1) above.

(3)   In the consideration, for the purposes of subsection (1)(a) or (b) above, of the circumstances of a case where—

(a)   an act, omission or change is alleged to constitute a breach of a provision of the lease or a breach of contract; and

(b)   the breach is capable of being remedied in reasonable time,
regard shall be had to whether a reasonable opportunity has been afforded to the tenant to enable the breach to be remedied.

## 6.   Supplementary and transitional provisions relating to sections 4 and 5

(1)   The parties to a lease shall not be entitled to disapply any provision of section 4 or 5 of this Act from it.

(2)   Where circumstances have occurred before the commencement of sections 4 and 5 of this Act which would have entitled a landlord to terminate a lease in reliance on a provision in the lease or on the ground that the circumstances constituted a material breach of contract, but the landlord has not before such commencement given written notice to the tenant of his intention to terminate the lease in respect of those circumstances, he shall, after such commencement, be entitled to terminate the lease in respect of those circumstances only in accordance with the provisions of section 4 or 5 (as the case may be) of this Act.

(3)   Nothing in section 4 or 5 of this Act shall apply in relation to any payment which has to be made, or any other condition which has to be fulfilled, before a tenant is entitled to entry under a lease.

## 7.   Interpretation of sections 4 to 6

(1)   In sections 4 to 6 of this Act 'lease' means a lease of land, whether entered into before or after the commencement of those sections, but does not include a lease of land—

(a)   used wholly or mainly for residential purposes; or

(b)   comprising an agricultural holding, a croft, the subject of a cottar or the holding of a landholder or a statutory small tenant.

(2)   In subsection (1) above—
'agricultural holding' has the same meaning as in section 1 of the Agricultural Holdings (Scotland) Act 1991;
'cottar' has the same meaning as in section 28(4) of the Crofters (Scotland) Act 1955;
'croft' has the same meaning as in section 3 of the Crofters (Scotland) Act 1955; and
'holding' (in relation to a landholder or statutory small tenant), 'landholder' and 'statutory small tenant' have the same meanings as in the Small Landholders (Scotland) Acts 1886 to 1931.

*Provisions relating to other contracts and obligations*

## 8.   Rectification of defectively expressed documents

(1)   Subject to section 9 of this Act, where the court is satisfied, on an application made to it, that—

(a)   a document intended to express or to give effect to an agreement fails to express accurately the common intention of the parties to the agreement at the date when it was made; or

(b) a document intended to create, transfer, vary or renounce a right, not being a document falling within paragraph (a) above, fails to express accurately the intention of the grantor of the document at the date when it was executed,

it may order the document to be rectified in any manner that it may specify in order to give effect to that intention.

(2) For the purposes of subsection (1) above, the court shall be entitled to have regard to all relevant evidence, whether written or oral.

(3) Subject to section 9 of this Act, in ordering the rectification of a document under subsection (1) above (in this subsection referred to as 'the original document'), the court may, at its own instance or on an application made to it, order the rectification of any other document intended for any of the purposes mentioned in paragraph (a) or (b) of subsection (1) above which is defectively expressed by reason of the defect in the original document.

(4) Subject to section 9(4) of this Act, a document ordered to be rectified under this section shall have effect as if it had always been so rectified.

(5) Subject to section 9(5) of this Act, where a document recorded in the Register of Sasines is ordered to be rectified under this section and the order is likewise recorded, the document shall be treated as having been always so recorded as rectified.

(6) Nothing in this section shall apply to a document of a testamentary nature.

(7) It shall be competent to register in the Register of Inhibitions and Adjudications a notice of an application under this section for the rectification of a deed relating to land, being an application in respect of which authority for service or citation has been granted; and the land to which the application relates shall be rendered litigious as from the date of registration of such a notice.

(8) A notice under subsection (7) above shall specify the names and designations of the parties to the application and the date when authority for service or citation was granted and contain a description of the land to which the application relates.

(9) In this section and section 9 of this Act 'the court' means the Court of Session or the sheriff.

## 9. Provisions supplementary to section 8: protection of other interest

(1) The court shall order a document to be rectified under section 8 of this Act only where it is satisfied—

(a) that the interests of a person to whom this section applies would not be adversely affected to a material extent by the rectification; or

(b) that that person has consented to the proposed rectification.

(2) Subject to subsection (3) below, this section applies to a person (other than a party to the agreement or the grantor of the document) who has acted or refrained from acting in reliance on the terms of the document or on the title sheet of an interest in land registered in the Land Register of Scotland being an interest to which the document relates, with the result that his position has been affected to a material extent.

(3) This section does not apply to a person—

(a) who, at the time when he acted or refrained from acting as mentioned in subsection (2) above, knew, or ought in the circumstances known to him at that time to have been aware, that the document or (as the case may be) the title sheet failed accurately to express the common intention of the parties to the agreement or, as the case may be, the intention of the grantor of the document; or

(b) whose reliance on the terms of the document or on the title sheet was otherwise unreasonable.

(4) Notwithstanding subsection (4) of section 8 of this Act and without prejudice to subsection (5) below, the court may, for the purpose of protecting the interests of a person to whom this section applies, order that the rectification of a document shall have effect as at such date as it may specify, being a date later than that as at which it would have effect by virtue of the said subsection (4).

(5) Notwithstanding subsection (5) of section 8 of this Act and without prejudice to subsection (4) above, the court may, for the purpose of protecting the interests of a person to whom this section applies, order that a document as rectified shall be treated as having been recorded as mentioned in the said subsection (5) at such date as it may specify, being a date later than that as at which it would be treated by virtue of that subsection as having been so recorded.

(6) For the purposes of subsection (1) above, the court may require the Keeper of the Registers of Scotland to produce such information as he has in his possession relating to any persons who have asked him to supply details with regard to a title sheet mentioned in subsection (2) above; and any expense incurred by the Keeper under this subsection shall be borne by the applicant for the order.

(7) Where a person to whom this section applies was unaware, before a document was ordered to be rectified under section 8 of this Act, that an application had been made under that section for the rectification of the document, the Court of Session, on an application made by that person within the time specified in subsection (8) below, may—

(a) reduce the rectifying order; or

(b) order the applicant for the rectifying order to pay such compensation to that person as it thinks fit in respect of his reliance on the terms of the document or on the title sheet.

(8) The time referred to in subsection (7) above is whichever is the earlier of the following—

(a) the expiry of 5 years after the making of the rectifying order;

(b) the expiry of 2 years after the making of that order first came to the notice of the person referred to in that subsection.

## 10. Negligent misrepresentation

(1) A party to a contract who has been induced to enter into it by negligent misrepresentation made by or on behalf of another party to the contract shall not be disentitled, by reason only that the misrepresentation is not fraudulent, from recovering damages from the other party in respect of any loss or damage he has suffered as a result of the misrepresentation; and any rule of law that such damages cannot be recovered unless fraud is proved shall cease to have effect.

(2) Subsection (1) applies to any proceedings commenced on or after the date on which it comes into force, whether or not the negligent misrepresentation was made before or after that date, but does not apply to any proceedings commenced before that date.

**INSOLVENCY ACT 1986**
**(1986, c 45)**

## 124. Application for winding up

(1) Subject to the provisions of this section, an application to the court for the winding up of a company shall be by petition presented either by the company, or the directors, or by any creditor or creditors (including any contingent or prospective creditor or creditors), contributory or contributories [, or by a liquidator (within the meaning of Article 2(b) of the EC Regulation) appointed

in proceedings by virtue of Article 3(1) of the EC Regulation or a temporary administrator (within the meaning of Article 38 of the EC Regulation), by a justices' chief executive in the exercise of the power conferred by section 87A of the Magistrates' Courts Act 1980 (enforcement of fines imposed on companies)] or by all or any of those parties, together or separately.

(2), (3)   [*repealed*]

(4)   A winding-up petition may be presented by the Secretary of State—

   (a)   [*repealed*]

   (b)   in a case falling within section [124A below].

(5)   Where a company is being wound up voluntarily in England and Wales, a winding-up petition may be presented by the official receiver attached to the court as well as by any other person authorised in that behalf under the other provisions of this section; but the court shall not make a winding-up order on the petition unless it is satisfied that the voluntary winding up cannot be continued with due regard to the interests of the creditors or contributories.

### [124A.   Petition for winding up on grounds of public interest

(1)   Where it appears to the Secretary of State from—

   (a)   any report made or information obtained under Part XIV of the Companies Act 1985 (company investigations, &c.),

   (b)   any report made by inspectors under—

      (i)   section 167, 168, 169 or 284 of the Financial Services and Markets Act 2000, or

      (ii)   where the company is an open-ended investment company (within the meaning of that Act), regulations made as a result of section 262(2)(k) of that Act;

   (bb)   any information or documents obtained under section 165, 171, 172, 173 or 175 of that Act,

   (c)   any information obtained under section 2 of the Criminal Justice Act 1987 or section 52 of the Criminal Justice (Scotland) Act 1987 (fraud investigations), or

   (d)   any information obtained under section 83 of the Companies Act 1989 (powers exercisable for purpose of assisting overseas regulatory authorities),

that it is expedient in the public interest that a company should be wound up, he may present a petition for it to be wound up if the court thinks it just and equitable for it to be so.

(2)   This section does not apply if the company is already being wound up by the court.]

### 244.   Extortionate credit transactions

(1)   This section applies as does section 238, and where the company is, or has been, a party to a transaction for, or involving, the provision of credit to the company.

(2)   The court may, on the application of the office-holder, make an order with respect to the transaction if the transaction is or was extortionate and was entered into in the period of 3 years ending with the day on which the administration order was made or (as the case may be) the company went into liquidation.

(3)   For the purposes of this section a transaction is extortionate if, having regard to the risk accepted by the person providing the credit—

   (a)   the terms of it are or were such as to require grossly exorbitant payments to be made (whether unconditionally or in certain contingencies) in respect of the provision of the credit, or

   (b)   it otherwise grossly contravened ordinary principles of fair dealing;

and it shall be presumed, unless the contrary is proved, that a transaction with respect to which an application is made under this section is or, as the case may be, was extortionate.

(4) An order under this section with respect to any transaction may contain such one or more of the following as the court thinks fit, that is to say—

(a) provision setting aside the whole or part of any obligation created by the transaction,

(b) provision otherwise varying the terms of the transaction or varying the terms on which any security for the purposes of the transaction is held,

(c) provision requiring any person who is or was a party to the transaction to pay to the office-holder any sums paid to that person, by virtue of the transaction, by the company,

(d) provision requiring any person to surrender to the officeholder any property held by him as security for the purposes of the transaction,

(e) provision directing accounts to be taken between any persons.

(5) The powers conferred by this section are exercisable in relation to any transaction concurrently with any powers exercisable in relation to that transaction as a transaction at an undervalue or under section 242 (gratuitous alienations in Scotland).

## ANIMALS (SCOTLAND) ACT 1987
### (1987, c 9)

**1. New provisions as to strict liability for injury or damage caused by animals**

(1) Subject to subsection (4) and (5) below and section 2 of this Act, a person shall be liable for any injury or damage caused by an animal if—

(a) at the time of the injury or damage complained of, he was a keeper of the animal;

(b) the animal belongs to a species whose members generally are by virtue of their physical attributes or habits likely (unless controlled or restrained) to injure severely or kill persons or animals, or damage property to a material extent; and

(c) the injury or damage complained of is directly referable to such physical attributes or habits.

(2) In this section 'species' includes—

(a) a form or variety of the species or a sub-division of the species, or the form or variety, identifiable by age, sex or such other criteria as are relevant to the behaviour of animals; and

(b) a kind which is the product of hybridisation.

(3) For the purposes of subsection (1)(b) above—

(a) dogs, and dangerous wild animals within the meaning of section 7(4) of the Dangerous Wild Animals Act 1976, shall be deemed to be likely (unless controlled or restrained) to injure severely or kill persons or animals by biting or otherwise savaging, attacking or harrying; and

(b) any of the following animals in the course of foraging, namely—

cattle, horses, asses, mules, hinnies, sheep, pigs, goats and deer,

shall be deemed to be likely (unless controlled or restrained) to damage to a material extent land or the produce of land, whether harvested or not.

(4) Subsection (1) above shall not apply to any injury caused by an animal where the injury consists of disease transmitted by means which are unlikely to cause severe injury other than disease.

(5) Subsection (1) above shall not apply to injury or damage caused by the mere fact that an animal is present on a road or in any other place.

(6) For the purposes of the Law Reform (Contributory Negligence) Act 1945, any injury or damage for which a person is liable under this section shall be treated as due to his fault as defined in that Act.

(7) Subsections (1) and (2) of section 3 of the Law Reform (Miscellaneous Provisions) (Scotland) Act 1940 (contribution among joint wrongdoers) shall, subject to any necessary modifications, apply in relation to an action of damages in respect of injury or damage which is brought in pursuance of this section as they apply in relation to an action of damages in respect of loss or damage arising from any wrongful acts or omissions; but nothing in this subsection shall affect any contractual, or (except as aforesaid) any other, right of relief or indemnity.

(8) The foregoing provisions of this section and section 2 of this Act replace—

  (a)  any rule of law which imposes liability, without proof of a negligent act or omission, on the owner or possessor of an animal for injury or damage caused by that animal on the ground that the animal is *ferae naturae* or is otherwise known to be dangerous or harmful;

  (b)  the Winter Herding Act 1686;

  (c)  section 1(1) and (2) of the Dogs Act 1906 (injury to cattle or poultry).

## 2. Exceptions from liability under section 1

(1)  A person shall not be liable under section 1(1) of this Act if—

  (a)  the injury or damage was due wholly to the fault of—

    (i)  the person sustaining it; or

    (ii)  in the case of injury sustained by an animal, a keeper of the animal;

  (b)  the person sustaining the injury or damage or a keeper of the animal sustaining the injury willingly accepted the risk of it as his; or

  (c)  subject to subsection (2) below, the injury or damage was sustained on, or in consequence of the person or animal sustaining the injury or damage coming on to, land which was occupied by a person who was a keeper, or by another person who authorised the presence on the land, of the animal which caused the injury or damage; and, either—

    (i)  the person sustaining the injury or damage was not authorised or entitled to be on that land; or (as the case may be)

    (ii)  no keeper of the animal sustaining the injury was authorised or entitled to have the animal present on that land.

(2)  A person shall not be exempt from liability by virtue of subsection (1)(c) above if the animal causing the injury or damage was kept on the land wholly or partly for the purpose of protecting persons or property, unless the keeping of the animal there, and the use made of the animal, for that purpose was reasonable, and, if the animal was a guard dog within the meaning of the Guard Dogs Act 1975, unless there was compliance with section 1 of that Act.

(3)  In subsection (1) above—

  (a)  in paragraph (a) 'fault' has the same meaning as in the Law Reform (Contributory Negligence) Act 1945;

  (b)  in paragraph (c) 'authorised' means expressly or impliedly authorised.

## 3. Detention of straying animals

(1)  Without prejudice to section 98 of the Roads (Scotland) Act 1984, where an animal strays on to any land and is not then under the control of any person, the occupier of the land may detain the animal for the purpose of preventing injury or damage by it.

(2)  Part VI of the Civic Government (Scotland) Act 1982 (lost and abandoned property) shall apply in relation to an animal, other than a stray dog, detained under subsection (1) above as it applies in relation to any property taken possession of under section 67 of that Act subject to the omission from section 74 of the words from 'or livestock' to '129 of this Act' and to any other necessary modifications; and section 4 of the Dogs Act 1906 shall, subject to any necessary modifications, apply to a stray dog detained under subsection (1) above as it applies to a stray dog taken possession of under that section.

## 4. Killing of, or injury to, animals attacking or harrying persons or livestock

(1) Subject to subsection (2) below, in any civil proceedings against a person for killing or causing injury to an animal, it shall be a defence for him to prove—

(a) that he acted—

(i) in self-defence;

(ii) for the protection of any other person; or

(iii) for the protection of any livestock and was one of the persons mentioned in subsection (3) below; and

(b) that within 48 hours after the killing or injury notice thereof was given by him or on his behalf at a police station or to a constable.

(2) There shall be no defence available under subsection (1) above to a person killing or causing injury to an animal where the killing or injury—

(a) occurred at or near a place where the person was present for the purpose of engaging in a criminal activity; and

(b) was in furtherance of that activity.

(3) The persons referred to in subsection (1)(a)(iii) above are—

(a) a person who, at the time of the injury or killing complained of, was a keeper of the livestock concerned;

(b) the owner or occupier of the land where the livestock was present; and

(c) a person authorised (either expressly or impliedly) to act for the protection of the livestock by such a keeper of the livestock or by the owner or occupier of the land where the livestock was present.

(4) A person killing or causing injury to an animal ('the defender') shall be regarded, for the purposes of this section, as acting in self defence or for the protection of another person or any livestock if, and only if—

(a) the animal is attacking him or that other person or that livestock and (whether or not the animal is under the control of anyone) the defender has reasonable grounds for believing that there are no other practicable means of ending the attack; or

(b) the defender has reasonable grounds for believing—

(i) that the animal is about to attack him, such person or livestock and that (whether or not the animal is under the control of anyone) there are no other practicable means of preventing the attack; or

(ii) that the animal has been attacking a person or livestock, is not under the control of anyone and has not left the vicinity where the attack took place, and that there are no other practicable means of preventing a further attack by the animal while it is still in that vicinity.

(5) In subsection (4) above 'attack' or 'attacking' includes 'harry' or 'harrying'.

(6) In this section—

'livestock' means any animal of a domestic variety (including in particular sheep, cattle and horses) and, while they are in captivity, any other animals.

## 5. Meaning of a keeper of an animal

(1) Subject to subsection (2) below, for the purposes of this Act a person is a keeper of an animal if—

(a) he owns the animal or has possession of it; or

(b) he has actual care and control of a child under the age of 16 who owns the animal or has possession of it.

(2) For the purposes of this section—

(a) a person shall not be regarded as having possession of an animal by reason only that he is detaining it under section 3 of this Act or is otherwise temporarily detaining it for the purpose of protecting it or any person or other animal or of restoring it as soon as is reasonably practicable to its owner or a possessor of it;

(b)   if an animal has been abandoned or has escaped, a person who at the time of the abandonment or escape was the owner of it or had it in his possession shall remain its owner or shall be regarded as continuing to have possession of it until another person acquires its ownership or (as the case may be) comes into possession of it; and

(c)   the Crown shall not acquire ownership of an animal on its abandonment.

### 6.  Application to Crown
This Act binds the Crown, but this section shall not authorise proceedings to be brought against Her Majesty in her private capacity.

### 7.  Interpretation
In this Act, unless the context otherwise requires—

'animal' does not include viruses, bacteria, algae, fungi or protozoa;

'harry' includes chase in such a way as may be likely to cause injury or suffering; and 'harrying' shall be construed accordingly;

'injury' includes death, any abortion or other impairment of physical or mental condition and any loss of or diminution in the produce of an animal and, subject to section 1(4) of this Act, disease.

### 8.  Transitional provision and repeals
(1)   This Act shall apply only in relation to injury or damage caused after the commencement of the Act.

(2)   The enactments mentioned in the Schedule to this Act are hereby repealed to the extent specified in the third column of that Schedule.

### 9.  Short title, commencement and extent
(1)   This Act may be cited as the Animals (Scotland) Act 1987.

(2)   This Act shall come into force at the end of a period of 2 months beginning with the date on which it is passed.

(3)   This Act extends to Scotland only.


### CONSUMER PROTECTION ACT 1987
### (1987, c 43)


## PART I. PRODUCT LIABILITY

### 1.  Purpose and construction of Part I
(1)   This Part shall have effect for the purpose of making such provision as is necessary in order to comply with the product liability Directive and shall be construed accordingly.

(2)   In this Part, except in so far as the context otherwise requires—

. . .

'dependant' and 'relative' have the same meaning as they have in, respectively, the Fatal Accidents Act 1976 and the Damages (Scotland) Act 1976;

'producer', in relation to a product, means—

(a)   the person who manufactured it;

(b)   in the case of a substance which has not been manufactured but has been won or abstracted, the person who won or abstracted it;

(c)   in the case of a product which has not been manufactured, won or abstracted but essential characteristics of which are attributable to an industrial or other process having been carried out (for example, in relation to agricultural produce), the person who carried out that process;

'product' means any goods or electricity and (subject to subsection (3) below) includes a product which is comprised in another product, whether by virtue of being a component part or raw material or otherwise; and

'the product liability Directive' means the Directive of the Council of the European Communities, dated 25th July 1985, (No 85/374/EEC) on the approximation of the laws, regulations and administrative provisions of the member States concerning liability for defective products.

(3)   For the purposes of this Part a person who supplies any product in which products are comprised, whether by virtue of being component parts or raw materials or otherwise, shall not be treated by reason only of his supply of that product as supplying any of the products so comprised.

## 2.   Liability for defective products

(1)   Subject to the following provisions of this Part, where any damage is caused wholly or partly by a defect in a product, every person to whom subsection (2) below applies shall be liable for the damage.

(2)   This subsection applies to—

(a)   the producer of the product;

(b)   any person who, by putting his name on the product or using a trade mark or other distinguishing mark in relation to the product, has held himself out to be the producer of the product;

(c)   any person who has imported the product into a member State from a place outside the member States in order, in the course of any business of his, to supply it to another.

(3)   Subject as aforesaid, where any damage is caused wholly or partly by a defect in a product, any person who supplied the product (whether to the person who suffered the damage, to the producer of any product in which the product in question is comprised or to any other person) shall be liable for the damage if—

(a)   the person who suffered the damage requests the supplier to identify one or more of the persons (whether still in existence or not) to whom subsection (2) above applies in relation to the product;

(b)   that request is made within a reasonable period after the damage occurs and at a time when it is not reasonably practicable for the person making the request to identify all those persons; and

(c)   the supplier fails, within a reasonable period after receiving the request, either to comply with the request or to identify the person who supplied the product to him.

(4)   (*repealed*)

(5)   Where two or more persons are liable by virtue of this Part for the same damage, their liability shall be joint and several.

(6)   This section shall be without prejudice to any liability arising otherwise than by virtue of this Part.

## 3.   Meaning of 'defect'

(1)   Subject to the following provisions of the section, there is a defect in a product for the purposes of this Part if the safety of the product is not such as persons generally are entitled to expect; and for those purposes 'safety', in relation to a product, shall include safety with respect to products comprised in that product and safety in the context of risks of damage to property, as well as in the context of risks of death or personal injury.

(2)   In determining for the purposes of subsection (1) above what persons generally are entitled to expect in relation to a product all the circumstances shall be taken into account, including—

(a)   the manner in which, and purposes for which, the product has been marketed, its get-up, the use of any mark in relation to the product and any instructions for, or warnings with respect to, doing or refraining from doing anything with or in relation to the product;

(b)   what might reasonably be expected to be done with or in relation to the product; and

(c)   the time when the product was supplied by its producer to another; and nothing in this section shall require a defect to be inferred from the fact alone that the safety of a product which is supplied after that time is greater than the safety of the product in question.

## 4.  Defences

(1)   In any civil proceedings by virtue of this Part against any person ('the person proceeded against') in respect of a defect in a product it shall be a defence for him to show—

(a)   that the defect is attributable to compliance with any requirement imposed by or under any enactment or with any Community obligation; or

(b)   that the person proceeded against did not at any time supply the product to another; or

(c)   that the following conditions are satisfied, that is to say—

(i)   that the only supply of the product to another by the person proceeded against was otherwise than in the course of a business of that person's; and

(ii)   that section 2(2) above does not apply to that person or applies to him by virtue only of things done otherwise than with a view to profit; or

(d)   that the defect did not exist in the product at the relevant time; or

(e)   that the state of scientific and technical knowledge at the relevant time was not such that a producer of products of the same description as the product in question might be expected to have discovered the defect if it had existed in his products while they were under his control; or

(f)   that the defect—

(i)   constituted a defect in a product ('the subsequent product') in which the product in question had been comprised; and

(ii)   was wholly attributable to the design of the subsequent product or to compliance by the producer of the product in question with instructions given by the producer of the subsequent product.

(2)   In this section 'the relevant time', in relation to electricity, means the time at which it was generated, being a time before it was transmitted or distributed, and in relation to any other product, means—

(a)   if the person proceeded against is a person to whom subsection (2) of section 2 above applies in relation to the product, the time when he supplied the product to another;

(b)   if that subsection does not apply to that person in relation to the product, the time when the product was last supplied by a person to whom that subsection does apply in relation to the product.

## 5.  Damage giving rise to liability

(1)   Subject to the following provisions of this section, in this Part 'damages' means death or personal injury or any loss of or damage to any property (including land).

(2)   A person shall not be liable under section 2 above in respect of any defect in a product for the loss of or any damage to the product itself or for the loss of or any damage to the whole or any part of any product which has been supplied with the product in question comprised in it.

(3)   A person shall not be liable under section 2 above for any loss of or damage to any property which, at the time it is lost or damaged, is not—

(a)   of a description of property ordinarily intended for private use, occupation or consumption; and

(b)   intended by the person suffering the loss or damage mainly for his own private use, occupation or consumption.

(4)   No damages shall be awarded to any person by virtue of this Part in

respect of any loss of or damage to any property if the amount which would fall to be so awarded to that person, apart from this subsection and any liability for interest, does not exceed £275.

(5) In determining for the purposes of this Part who has suffered any loss of or damage to property and when any such loss or damage occurred, the loss or damage shall be regarded as having occurred at the earliest time at which a person with an interest in the property had knowledge of the material facts about the loss or damage.

(6) For the purposes of subsection (5) above the material facts about any loss of or damage to any property are such facts about the loss or damage as would lead a reasonable person with an interest in the property to consider the loss or damage sufficiently serious to justify his instituting proceedings for damages against a defendant who did not dispute liability and was able to satisfy a judgment.

(7) For the purposes of subsection (5) above a person's knowledge includes knowledge which he might reasonably have been expected to acquire—

(a) from facts observable or ascertainable by him; or

(b) from facts ascertainable by him with help of appropriate expert advice which it is reasonable for him to seek;

but a person shall not be taken by virtue of this subsection to have knowledge of a fact ascertainable by him only with the help of expert advice unless he has failed to take all reasonable steps to obtain (and, where appropriate, to act on) that advice.

(8) Subsections (5) to (7) above shall not extend to Scotland.

## 6. Application of certain enactments etc.

(1) Any damage for which a person is liable under section 2 above shall be deemed to have been caused—

(a) for the purposes of the Fatal Accidents Act 1976, by that person's wrongful act, neglect or default;

(b) for the purposes of section 3 of the Law Reform (Miscellaneous Provisions) (Scotland) Act 1940 (contribution among joint wrongdoers), by that person's wrongful act or negligent act or omission;

(c) for the purposes of section 1 of the Damages (Scotland) Act 1976 (rights of relatives of a deceased), by that person's act or omission, and

(d) for the purposes of Part II of the Administration of Justice Act 1982 (damages for personal injuries, etc.—Scotland), by an act or omission giving rise to liability in that person to pay damages.

(2) Where—

(a) a person's death is caused wholly or partly by a defect in a product, or a person dies after suffering damage which has been so caused;

(b) a request such as mentioned in paragraph (a) of subsection (3) of section 2 above is made to a supplier of the product by that person's personal representatives or, in the case of a person whose death is caused wholly or partly by the defect, by any dependant or relative of that person; and

(c) the conditions specified in paragraphs (b) and (c) of that subsection are satisfied in relation to that request,

this Part shall have effect for the purposes of the Law Reform (Miscellaneous Provisions) Act 1934, the Fatal Accidents Acts 1976 and the Damages (Scotland) Act 1976 as if liability of the supplier to that person under that subsection did not depend on that person having requested the supplier to identify certain persons or on the said conditions having been satisfied in relation to a request made by that person.

(3) Section 1 of the Congenital Disabilities (Civil Liability) Act 1976 shall have effect for the purposes of this Part as if—

(a) a person were answerable to a child in respect of an occurrence caused wholly or partly by a defect in a product if he is or has been liable under section 2 above in respect of any effect of the occurrence on a parent of the child, or would be so liable if the occurrence caused a parent of the child to suffer damage;

(b) the provisions of this Part relating to liability under section 2 above applied in relation to liability by virtue of paragraph (a) above under the said section 1; and

(c) subsection (6) of the said section 1 (exclusion of liability) were omitted.

(4) Where any damage is caused partly by a defect in a product and partly by the fault of the person suffering the damage, the Law Reform (Contributory Negligence) Act 1945 and section 5 of the Fatal Accidents Act 1976 (contributory negligence) shall have effect as if the defect were the fault of every person liable by virtue of this Part for the damage caused by the defect.

(5) In subsection (4) above 'fault' has the same meaning as in the said Act of 1945.

(6) Schedule 1 to this Act shall have effect for the purpose of amending the Limitation Act 1980 and the Prescription and Limitation (Scotland) Act 1973 in their application in relation to the bringing of actions by virtue of this Part.

(7) It is hereby declared that liability by virtue of this Part is to be treated as liability in tort for the purposes of any enactment conferring jurisdiction on any court with respect to any matter.

(8) Nothing in this Part shall prejudice the operation of section 12 of the Nuclear Installations Act 1965 (rights to compensation for certain breaches of duties confined to rights under that Act).

### 7. Prohibition on exclusions from liability
The liability of a person by virtue of this Part to person who has suffered damage caused wholly or partly by a defect in a product, or to a dependant or relative of such a person, shall not be limited or excluded by any contract term, by any notice or by any other provision.

### 8. Power to modify Part I
(1) Her Majesty may by Order in Council make such modifications of this Part and of any other enactment (including an enactment contained in the following Parts of this Act, or in an Act passed after this Act) as appear to Her Majesty in Council to be necessary or expedient in consequence of any modification of the product liability Directive which is made at any time after the passing of this Act.

(2) An Order in Council under subsection (1) above shall not be submitted to Her Majesty in Council unless a draft of the Order has been laid before, and approved by a resolution of, each House of Parliament.

### 9. Application of Part I to Crown
(1) Subject to subsection (2) below, this Part shall bind the Crown.

(2) The Crown shall not, as regards the Crown's liability by virtue of this Part, be bound by this Part further than the Crown is made liable in tort or in reparation under the Crown Proceedings Act 1947, as that Act has effect from time to time.

### 45. Interpretation
(1) In this Act, except in so far as the context otherwise requires—

'aircraft' includes gliders, balloons and hovercraft;

'business' includes a trade or profession and the activities of a professional or trade association or of a local authority or other public authority;

'conditional sale agreement', 'credit-sale agreement' and 'hire-purchase agreement' have the same meanings as in the Consumer Credit Act 1974 but as if in the definitions in that Act 'goods' had the same meaning as in this Act;

'contravention' includes a failure to comply and cognate expressions shall be construed accordingly;

'enforcement authority' means the Secretary of State, any other Minister of the Crown in charge of a Government department, any such department and any authority, council or other person on whom functions under this Act are conferred by or under section 27 above;

'gas' has the same meaning as in Part I of the Gas Act 1986;

'goods' includes substances, growing crops and things comprised in land by virtue of being attached to it and any ship, aircraft or vehicle;

'information' includes accounts, estimates and returns;

'magistrates' court', in relation to Northern Ireland, means a court of summary jurisdiction;

'modifications' includes additions, alterations and omissions, and cognate expressions shall be construed accordingly;

'motor vehicle' has the same meaning as in the Road Traffic Act 1972;

'notice' means a notice in writing;

'notice to warn' means a notice under section 13(1)(b) above;

'officer', in relation to an enforcement authority, means a person authorised in writing to assist the authority in carrying out its functions under or for the purposes of the enforcement of any of the safety provisions or of any of the provisions made by or under Part III of this Act;

'personal injury' includes any disease and any other impairment of a person's physical or mental condition;

'premises' includes any place and any ship, aircraft or vehicle;

'prohibition notice' means a notice under section 13(1)(a) above;

'records' includes any books or documents and any records in non-documentary form;

'safety provision' means the general safety requirement in section 10 above or any provision of safety regulations, a prohibition notice or a suspension notice;

'safety regulations' means regulations under section 11 above;

'ship' includes any boat and any other description of vessel used in navigation;

'subordinate legislation' has the same meaning as in the Interpretation Act 1978;

'substance' means any natural or artificial substance, whether in solid, liquid or gaseous form or in the form of a vapour, and includes substances that are comprised in or mixed with other goods;

'supply' and cognate expressions shall be construed in accordance with section 46 below;

'suspension notice' means a notice under section 14 above.

(2)   Except in so far as the context otherwise requires, references in this Act to a contravention of a safety provision shall, in relation to any goods, include references to anything which would constitute such a contravention if the goods were supplied to any person.

(3)   References in this Act to any goods in relation to which any safety provision has been or may have been contravened shall include references to any goods which it is not reasonably practicable to separate from any such goods.

(4)   Section 68(2) of the Trade Marks Act 1938 (construction of references to use of a mark) shall apply for the purposes of this Act as it applies for the purposes of that Act.

(5)   In Scotland, any reference in this Act to things comprised in land by virtue of being attached to it is a reference to moveables which have become heritable by accession to heritable property.

## COURT OF SESSION ACT 1988
### (1988, c 36)

**46. Specific relief may be granted in interdict proceedings**

Where a respondent in any application or proceedings in the Court, whether before or after the institution of such proceedings or application, has done any act which the Court might have prohibited by interdict, the Court may ordain the respondent to perform any act which may be necessary for reinstating the petitioner in his possessory right, or for granting specific relief against the illegal act complained of.

**47. Interim interdict and other interim orders**

(1) In any cause containing a conclusion or a crave for interdict or liberation, the Division of the Inner House or the Lord Ordinary (as the case may be) may, on the motion of any party to the cause, grant interim interdict or liberation; and it shall be competent for the Division of the Inner House or the Lord Ordinary before whom any cause in which interim interdict has been granted is pending to deal with any breach of the interim interdict without the presentation of a petition and complaint.

(2) In any cause in dependence before the Court, the Court may, on the motion of any party to the cause, make such order regarding the interim possession of any property to which the cause relates, or regarding the subject matter of the cause, as the Court may think fit.

(3) Every interim act, warrant and decree granted during the dependence of a cause in the Court shall, unless the Court otherwise directs, be extractible *ad interim*.

## ROAD TRAFFIC ACT 1988
### (1988, c 52)

*Driving offences*

**[1. Causing death by dangerous driving**

A person who causes the death of another person by driving a mechanically propelled vehicle dangerously on a road or other public place is guilty of an offence.

**2. Dangerous driving**

A person who drives a mechanically propelled vehicle dangerously on a road or other public place is guilty of an offence.

**2A. Meaning of dangerous driving**

(1) For the purposes of sections 1 and 2 above a person is to be regarded as driving dangerously if (and, subject to subsection (2) below, only if)—

(a) the way he drives falls far below what would be expected of a competent and careful driver, and

(b) it would be obvious to a competent and careful driver that driving in that way would be dangerous.

(2) A person is also to be regarded as driving dangerously for the purposes of sections 1 and 2 above if it would be obvious to a competent and careful driver that driving the vehicle in its current state would be dangerous.

(3) In subsections (1) and (2) above 'dangerous' refers to danger either of injury to any person or of serious damage to property; and in determining for the purposes of those subsections what would be expected of, or obvious to, a competent and careful driver in a particular case, regard shall be had not only to the circumstances of which he could be expected to be aware but also to any circumstances shown to have been within the knowledge of the accused.

(4) In determining for the purposes of subsection (2) above the state of a

vehicle, regard may be had to anything attached to or carried on or in it and to the manner in which it is attached or carried.

### 3. Careless, and inconsiderate, driving

If a person drives a mechanically propelled vehicle on a road or other public place without due care and attention, or without reasonable consideration for other persons using the road or place, he is guilty of an offence.

### 3A. Causing death by careless driving when under influence of drink or drugs

(1)   If a person causes the death of another person by driving a mechanically propelled vehicle on a road or other public place without due care and attention, or without reasonable consideration for other persons using the road or place, and—

(a)   he is, at the time when he is driving, unfit to drive through drink or drugs, or

(b)   he has consumed so much alcohol that the proportion of it in his breath, blood or urine at that time exceeds the prescribed limit, or

(c)   he is, within 18 hours after that time, required to provide a specimen in pursuance of section 7 of this Act, but without reasonable excuse fails to provide it,

he is guilty of an offence.

(2)   For the purposes of this section a person shall be taken to be unfit to drive at any time when his ability to drive properly is impaired.

(3)   Subsection (1)(b) and (c) above shall not apply in relation to a person driving a mechanically propelled vehicle other than a motor vehicle.]

*Promotion of road safety*

### 38. The Highway Code

(1)   The Highway Code shall continue to have effect, subject however to revision in accordance with the following provisions of this section.

(2)   Subject to the following provisions of this section, the Secretary of State may from time to time revise the Highway Code by revoking, varying, amending or adding to the provisions of the Code in such manner as he thinks fit.

(3)   Where the Secretary of State proposes to revise the Highway Code by making any alterations in the provisions of the Code (other than alterations merely consequential on the passing, amendment or repeal of any statutory provision) he must lay the proposed alterations before both Houses of Parliament and must not make the proposed revision until after the end of a period of forty days beginning with the day on which the alterations were so laid.

(4)   If within the period mentioned in subsection (3) above either House resolves that the proposed alterations be not made, the Secretary of State must not make the proposed revision (but without prejudice to the laying before Parliament of further proposals for alteration in accordance with that subsection).

(5)   Before revising the Highway Code by making any alterations in its provisions which are required by subsection (3) above to be laid before Parliament, the Secretary of State must consult with such representative organisations as he thinks fit.

(6)   The Secretary of State must cause the Highway Code to be printed and may cause copies of it to be sold to the public at such price as he may determine.

(7)   A failure on the part of a person to observe a provision of the Highway Code shall not of itself render that person liable to criminal proceedings of any

kind but any such failure may in any proceedings (whether civil or criminal, and including proceedings for an offence under the Traffic Acts, the Public Passenger Vehicles Act 1981 or sections 18 to 23 of the Transport Act 1985) be relied upon by any party to the proceedings as tending to establish or negative any liability which is in question in those proceedings.

(8)   In this section 'the Highway Code' means the code comprising directions for the guidance of persons using roads issued under section 45 of the Road Traffic Act 1930, as from time to time revised under this section or under any previous enactment.

(9)   For the purposes of subsection (3) above—

(a)   'statutory provision' means a provision contained in an Act or in subordinate legislation within the meaning of the Interpretation Act 1978 (and the reference to the passing or repeal of any such provision accordingly includes the making or revocation of any such provision),

(b)   where the proposed alterations are laid before each House of Parliament on different days, the later day shall be taken to be the day on which they were laid before both Houses, and

(c)   in reckoning any period of forty days, no account shall be taken of any time during which Parliament is dissolved or prorogued or during which both Houses are adjourned for more than four days.

## PART VI. THIRD-PARTY LIABILITIES

*Compulsory insurance or security against third party risks*

### 143.   Users of motor vehicles to be insured or secured against third-party risks

(1)   Subject to the provisions of this Part of this Act—

(a)   a person must not use a motor vehicle on a road [or other public place] unless there is in force in relation to the use of the vehicle by that person such a policy of insurance or such a security in respect of third party risks as complies with the requirements of this Part of this Act, and

(b)   a person must not cause or permit any other person to use a motor vehicle on a road [or other public place] unless there is in force in relation to the use of the vehicle by that other person such a policy of insurance or such a security in respect of third party risks as complies with the requirements of this Part of this Act.

(2)   If a person acts in contravention of subsection (1) above he is guilty of an offence.

(3)   A person charged with using a motor vehicle in contravention of this section shall not be convicted if he proves—

(a)   that the vehicle did not belong to him and was not in his possession under a contract of hiring or of loan,

(b)   that he was using the vehicle in the course of his employment, and

(c)   that he neither knew nor had reason to believe that there was not in force in relation to the vehicle such a policy of insurance or security as is mentioned in subsection (1) above.

(4)   This Part of this Act does not apply to invalid carriages.

### 149.   Avoidance of certain agreements as to liability towards passengers

(1)   This section applies where a person uses a motor vehicle in circumstances such that under section 143 of this Act there is required to be in force in relation to his use of it such a policy of insurance or such a security in respect of third-party risks as complies with the requirements of this Part of this Act.

(2)   If any other person is carried in or upon the vehicle while the user is so using it, any antecedent agreement or understanding between them (whether

intended to be legally binding or not) shall be of no effect so far as it purports or might be held—

(a)   to negative or restrict any such liability of the user in respect of persons carried in or upon the vehicle as is required by section 145 of this Act to be covered by a policy of insurance, or

(b)   to impose any conditions with respect to the enforcement of any such liability of the user.

(3)   The fact that a person so carried has willingly accepted as his the risk of negligence on the part of the user shall not be treated as negativing any such liability of the user.

(4)   For the purposes of this section—

(a)   references to a person being carried in or upon a vehicle include references to a person entering or getting on to, or alighting from, the vehicle, and

(b)   the reference to an antecedent agreement is to one made at any time before the liability arose.

## CONTRACTS (APPLICABLE LAW) ACT 1990
### (1990, c 36)

### 1.   Meaning of 'the Conventions'

In this Act—

(a)   'the Rome Convention' means the Convention on the law applicable to contractual obligations opened for signature in Rome on 19th June 1980 and signed by the United Kingdom on 7th December 1981;

(b)   'the Luxembourg Convention' means the Convention on the accession of the Hellenic Republic to the Rome Convention signed by the United Kingdom in Luxembourg on 10th April 1984; and

(c)   'the Brussels Protocol' means the first Protocol on the interpretation of the Rome Convention by the European Court signed by the United Kingdom in Brussels on 19th December 1988;

[(d)   'the Funchal Convention' means the Convention on the accession of the Kingdom of Spain and the Portuguese Republic to the Rome Convention and the Brussels Protocol, with adjustments made to the Rome Convention by the Luxembourg Convention, signed by the United Kingdom in Funchal on 18th May 1992;

(e)   'the 1996 Accession Convention' means the Convention on the accession of the Republic of Austria, the Republic of Finland and the Kingdom of Sweden to the Rome Convention and the Brussels Protocol, with the adjustments made to the Rome Convention by the Luxembourg Convention and the Funchal Convention, signed by the United Kingdom in Brussels on 29th November 1996; and these Conventions and this Protocol are together referred to as 'the Conventions'.

### 2.   Conventions to have force of law

(1)   Subject to subsections (2) and (3) below, the Conventions shall have the force of law in the United Kingdom.

[(1A)   The internal law for the purposes of Article 1(3) of the Rome Convention is the provisions of the regulations for the time being in force under section 424(3) of the Financial Services and Markets Act 2000.]

(2)   Articles 7(1) and 10(1)(e) of the Rome Convention shall not have the force of law in the United Kingdom.

(3)   Notwithstanding Article 19(2) of the Rome Convention the Conventions shall apply in the case of conflicts between the laws of different parts of the United Kingdom.

(4)   For ease of reference there are set out in Schedules [1, 2, 3, 3A and 3B to this Act respectively the English texts of—
  (a)   the Rome Convention;
  (b)   the Luxembourg Convention; . . .
  (c)   the Brussels Protocol;
  (d)   the Funchal Convention; and
  [(e)   the 1996 Accession Convention.]

### 3.   Interpretation of Conventions

(1)   Any question as to the meaning or effect of any provision of the Conventions shall, if not referred to the European Court in accordance with the Brussels Protocol, be determined in accordance with the principles laid down by and any relevant decision of, the European Court.

(2)   Judicial notice shall be taken of any decision of, or expression of opinion by, the European Court on any such question.

(3)   Without prejudice to any practice of the courts as to the matters which may be considered apart from this subsection—
  (a)   the report on the Rome Convention by Professor Mario Giuliano and Professor Paul Lagarde which is reproduced in the Official Journal of the Communities of 31st October 1980 may be considered in ascertaining the meaning or effect of any provision of that Convention; and
  (b)   any report on the Brussels Protocol which is reproduced in the Official Journal of the Communities may be considered in ascertaining the meaning or effect of any provision of that Protocol.

### 4.   Revision of Conventions etc.

(1)   If at any time it appears to Her Majesty in Council that Her Majesty's Government in the United Kingdom—
  (a)   have agreed to a revision of any of the Conventions (including, in particular, any revision connected with the accession to the Rome Convention of any state), or
  (b)   have given notification in accordance with Article 22(3) of the Rome Convention that either or both of the provisions mentioned in section 2(2) above shall have the force of law in the United Kingdom,
Her Majesty may by Order in Council make such consequential modifications of this Act or any other statutory provision, whenever passed or made, as Her Majesty considers appropriate.

(2)   An Order in Council under subsection (1) above shall not be made unless a draft of the Order has been laid before Parliament and approved by a resolution of each House.

(3)   In subsection (1) above—
'modifications' includes additions, omissions and alterations;
'revision' means an omission from, addition to or alteration of any of the Conventions and includes replacement of any of the Conventions to any extent by another convention, protocol or other description of international agreement; and
'statutory provision' means any provision contained in an Act, or in any Northern Ireland legislation, or in—
  (a)   subordinate legislation (as defined in section 21(1) of the Interpretation Act 1978); or
  (b)   any instrument of a legislative character made under any Northern Ireland legislation.

### 5.   Consequential amendments

The enactments specified in Schedule 4 to this Act shall have effect subject to the amendments specified in that Schedule.

### 6. Application to Crown
This Act binds the Crown.

### 7. Commencement
This Act shall come into force on such day as the Lord Chancellor and the Lord Advocate may by order made by statutory instrument appoint; and different days may be appointed for different provisions or different purposes.

### 8. Extent
(1) This Act extends to Northern Ireland.

(2) Her Majesty may by Order in Council direct that all or any of the provisions of this Act shall extend to any of the following territories, namely—
    (a) the Isle of Man;
    (b) any of the Channel Islands;
    (c) Gibraltar;
    (d) the Sovereign Base Areas of Akrotiri and Dhekelia (that is to say, the areas mentioned in section 2(1) of the Cyprus Act 1960).

(3) An Order in Council under subsection (2) above may modify this Act in its application to any of the territories mentioned in that subsection and may contain such supplementary provisions as Her Majesty considers appropriate; and in this subsection 'modify' shall be construed in accordance with section 4 above.

### 9. Short title
This Act may be cited as the Contracts (Applicable Law) Act 1990.

## SCHEDULES

## SCHEDULE 1. THE ROME CONVENTION

The High Contracting Parties to the Treaty establishing the European Economic Community,

Anxious to continue in the field of private international law the work of unification of law which has already been done within the Community, in particular in the field of jurisdiction and enforcement of judgments,

Wishing to establish uniform rules concerning the law applicable to contractual obligations,

Have agreed as follows:

## TITLE I. SCOPE OF THE CONVENTION

### Article 1. Scope of the Convention
1. The rules of this Convention shall apply to contractual obligations in any situation involving a choice between the laws of different countries.

2. They shall not apply to:
    (a) questions involving the status or legal capacity of natural persons, without prejudice to Article 11;
    (b) contractual obligations relating to:
    —wills and succession,
    —rights in property arising out of a matrimonial relationship,
    —rights and duties arising out of a family relationship, parentage, marriage or affinity, including maintenance obligations in respect of children who are not legitimate;
    (c) obligations arising under bills of exchange, cheques and promissory notes and other negotiable instruments to the extent that the obligations under such other negotiable instruments arise out of their negotiable character;
    (d) arbitration agreements and agreements on the choice of court;

(e)   questions governed by the law of companies and other bodies corporate or unincorporate such as the creation, by registration or otherwise, legal capacity, internal organisation or winding up of companies and other bodies corporate or unincorporate and the personal liability of officers and members as such for the obligations of the company or body;

(f)   the question whether an agent is able to bind a principal or an organ to bind a company or body corporate or unincorporate, to a third party;

(g)   the constitution of trusts and the relationship between settlors, trustees and beneficiaries;

(h)   evidence and procedure, without prejudice to Article 14.

3.   The rules of this Convention do not apply to contracts of insurance which cover risks situated in the territories of the Member States of the European Economic Community. In order to determine whether a risk is situated in these territories the court shall apply its internal law.

4.   The preceding paragraph does not apply to contracts of re-insurance.

### Article 2. Application of law of non-contracting States
Any law specified by this Convention shall be applied whether or not it is the law of a Contracting State.

## TITLE II. UNIFORM RULES

### Article 3. Freedom of choice
1.   A contract shall be governed by the law chosen by the parties. The choice must be express or demonstrated with reasonable certainty by the terms of the contract or the circumstances of the case. By their choice the parties can select the law applicable to the whole or a part only of the contract.

2.   The parties may at any time agree to subject the contract to a law other than that which previously governed it, whether as a result of an earlier choice under this Article or of other provisions of this Convention. Any variation by the parties of the law to be applied made after the conclusion of the contract shall not prejudice its formal validity under Article 9 or adversely affect the rights of third parties.

3.   The fact that the parties have chosen a foreign law, whether or not accompanied by the choice of a foreign tribunal, shall not, where all the other elements relevant to the situation at the time of the choice are connected with one country only, prejudice the application of rules of the law of that country which cannot be derogated from by contract, hereinafter called 'mandatory rules'.

4.   The existence and validity of the consent of the parties as to the choice of the applicable law shall be determined in accordance with the provisions of Articles 8, 9 and 11.

### Article 4. Applicable law in the absence of choice
1.   To the extent that the law applicable to the contract has not been chosen in accordance with Article 3, the contract shall be governed by the law of the country with which it is most closely connected. Nevertheless, a severable part of the contract which has a closer connection with another country may by way of exception be governed by the law of that other country.

2.   Subject to the provisions of paragraph 5 of this Article, it shall be presumed that the contract is most closely connected with the country where the party who is to effect the performance which is characteristic of the contract has, at the time of conclusion of the contract, his habitual residence, or, in the case of a body corporate or unincorporate, its central administration. However, if the contract is entered into in the course of that party's trade or profession, that country shall be the country in which the principal place of business is situated or, where under the terms of the contract the performance is to be

effected through a place of business other than the principal place of business, the country in which that other place of business is situated.

3. Notwithstanding the provisions of paragraph 2 of this Article, to the extent that the subject matter of the contract is a right in immovable property or a right to use immovable property it shall be presumed that the contract is most closely connected with the country where the immovable property is situated.

4. A contract for the carriage of goods shall not be subject to the presumption in paragraph 2. In such a contract if the country in which, at the time the contract is concluded, the carrier has his principal place of business is also the country in which the place of loading or the place of discharge or the principal place of business of the consignor is situated, it shall be presumed that the contract is most closely connected with that country. In applying this paragraph single voyage charter-parties and other contracts the main purpose of which is the carriage of goods shall be treated as contracts for the carriage of goods.

5. Paragraph 2 shall not apply if the characteristic performance cannot be determined, and the presumptions in paragraphs 2, 3 and 4 shall be disregarded if it appears from the circumstances as a whole that the contract is more closely connected with another country.

### Article 5. Certain consumer contracts

1. This Article applies to a contract the object of which is the supply of goods or services to a person ('the consumer') for a purpose which can be regarded as being outside his trade or profession, or a contract for the provision of credit for that object.

2. Notwithstanding the provisions of Article 3, a choice of law made by the parties shall not have the result of depriving the consumer of the protection afforded to him by the mandatory rules of the law of the country in which he has his habitual residence:

—if in that country the conclusion of the contract was preceded by a specific invitation addressed to him or by advertising, and he had taken in that country all the steps necessary on his part for the conclusion of the contract, or

—if the other party or his agent received the consumer's order in that country, or

—if the contract is for the sale of goods and the consumer travelled from that country to another country and there gave his order, provided that the consumer's journey was arranged by the seller for the purpose of inducing the consumer to buy.

3. Notwithstanding the provisions of Article 4, a contract to which this Article applies shall, in the absence of choice in accordance with Article 3, be governed by the law of the country in which the consumer has his habitual residence if it is entered into in the circumstances described in paragraph 2 of this Article.

4. This Article shall not apply to:

(a) a contract of carriage;

(b) a contract for the supply of services where the services are to be supplied to the consumer exclusively in a country other than that in which he has his habitual residence.

5. Notwithstanding the provisions of paragraph 4, this Article shall apply to a contract which, for an inclusive price, provides for a combination of travel and accommodation.

### Article 6. Individual employment contracts

1. Notwithstanding the provisions of Article 3, in a contract of employment a choice of law made by the parties shall not have the result of depriving the

employee of the protection afforded to him by the mandatory rules of the law which would be applicable under paragraph 2 in the absence of choice.

2. Notwithstanding the provisions of Article 4, a contract of employment shall, in the absence of choice in accordance with Article 3, be governed:

(a) by the law of the country in which the employee habitually carries out his work in performance of the contract, even if he is temporarily employed in another country; or

(b) if the employee does not habitually carry out his work in any one country, by the law of the country in which the place of business through which he was engaged is situated;

unless it appears from the circumstances as a whole that the contract is more closely connected with another country, in which case the contract shall be governed by the law of that country.

### Article 7. Mandatory rules

1. When applying under this Convention the law of a country, effect may be given to the mandatory rules of the law of another country with which the situation has a close connection, if and in so far as, under the law of the latter country, those rules must be applied whatever the law applicable to the contract. In considering whether to give effect to these mandatory rules, regard shall be had to their nature and purpose and to the consequences of their application or non-application.

2. Nothing in this Convention shall restrict the application of the rules of the law of the forum in a situation where they are mandatory irrespective of the law otherwise applicable to the contract.

### Article 8. Material validity

1. The existence and validity of a contract, or of any term of a contract, shall be determined by the law which would govern it under this Convention if the contract or term were valid.

2. Nevertheless a party may rely upon the law of the country in which he has his habitual residence to establish that he did not consent if it appears from the circumstances that it would not be reasonable to determine the effect of his conduct in accordance with the law specified in the preceding paragraph.

### Article 9. Formal validity

1. A contract concluded between persons who are in the same country is formally valid if it satisfies the formal requirements of the law which governs it under this Convention or of the law of the country where it is concluded.

2 A contract concluded between persons who are in different countries is formally valid if it satisfies the formal requirements of the law which governs it under this Convention or of the law of one of those countries.

3. Where a contract is concluded by an agent, the country in which the agent acts is the relevant country for the purposes of paragraphs 1 and 2.

4. An act intended to have legal effect relating to an existing or contemplated contract is formally valid if it satisfies the formal requirements of the law which under this Convention governs or would govern the contract or of the law of the country where the act was done.

5. The provisions of the preceding paragraphs shall not apply to a contract to which Article 5 applies, concluded in the circumstances described in paragraph 2 of Article 5. The formal validity of such a contract is governed by the law of the country in which the consumer has his habitual residence.

6. Notwithstanding paragraphs 1 to 4 of this Article, a contract the subject matter of which is a right in immovable property or a right to use immovable property shall be subject to the mandatory requirements of form of the law of the country where the property is situated if by that law those requirements are

imposed irrespective of the country where the contract is concluded and irrespective of the law governing the contract.

### Article 10. Scope of the applicable law

1.   The law applicable to a contract by virtue of Articles 3 to 6 and 12 of this Convention shall govern in particular:

    (a)   interpretation;

    (b)   performance;

    (c)   within the limits of the powers conferred on the court by its procedural law, the consequences of breach, including the assessment of damages in so far as it is governed by rules of law;

    (d)   the various ways of extinguishing obligations, and prescription and limitation of actions;

    (e)   the consequences of nullity of the contract.

2.   In relation to the manner of performance and the steps to be taken in the event of defective performance regard shall be had to the law of the country in which performance takes place.

### Article 11. Incapacity

In a contract concluded between persons who are in the same country, a natural person who would have capacity under the law of that country may invoke his incapacity resulting from another law only if the other party to the contract was aware of this incapacity at the time of the conclusion of the contract or was not aware thereof as a result of negligence.

### Article 12. Voluntary assignment

1.   The mutual obligations of assignor and assignee under a voluntary assignment of a right against another person ('the debtor') shall be governed by the law which under this Convention applies to the contract between the assignor and assignee.

2.   The law governing the right to which the assignment relates shall determine its assignability, the relationship between the assignee and the debtor, the conditions under which the assignment can be invoked against the debtor and any question whether the debtor's obligations have been discharged.

### Article 13. Subrogation

1.   Where a person ('the creditor') has a contractual claim upon another ('the debtor'), and a third person has a duty to satisfy the creditor, or has in fact satisfied the creditor in discharge of that duty, the law which governs the third person's duty to satisfy the creditor shall determine whether the third person is entitled to exercise against the debtor the rights which the creditor had against the debtor under the law governing their relationship and, if so, whether he may do so in full or only to a limited extent.

2.   The same rule applies where several persons are subject to the same contractual claim and one of them has satisfied the creditor.

### Article 14. Burden of proof, etc

1.   The law governing the contract under this Convention applies to the extent that it contains, in the law of contract, rules which raise presumptions of law or determine the burden of proof.

2.   A contract or an act intended to have legal effect may be proved by any mode of proof recognised by the law of the forum or by any of the laws referred to in Article 9 under which that contract or act is formally valid, provided that such mode of proof can be administered by the forum.

### Article 15. Exclusion of renvoi

The application of the law of any country specified by this Convention means the application of the rules of law in force in that country other than its rules of private international law.

### Article 16. 'Ordre public'
The application of a rule of the law of any country specified by this Convention may be refused only if such application is manifestly incompatible with the public policy ('ordre public') of the forum.

### Article 17. No retrospective effect
This Convention shall apply in a Contracting State to contracts made after the date on which this Convention has entered into force with respect to that State.

### Article 18. Uniform interpretation
In the interpretation and application of the preceding uniform rules regard shall be had to their international character and to the desirability of achieving uniformity in their interpretation and application.

### Article 19. States with more than one legal system
1.   Where a State comprises several territorial units each of which has its own rules of law in respect of contractual obligations, each territorial unit shall be considered as a country for the purposes of identifying the law applicable under this Convention.

2.   A State within which different territorial units have their own rules of law in respect of contractual obligations shall not be bound to apply this Convention to conflicts solely between the laws of such units.

### Article 20. Precedence of Community law
This Convention shall not affect the application of provisions which, in relation to particular matters, lay down choice of law rules relating to contractual obligations and which are or will be contained in acts of the institutions of the European Communities or in national laws harmonised in implementation of such acts.

### Article 21. Relationship with other conventions
This Convention shall not prejudice the application of international conventions to which a Contracting State is, or becomes, a party.

### Article 22. Reservations
1.   Any Contracting State may, at the time of signature, ratification, acceptance or approval, reserve the right not to apply:
    (a)   the provisions of Article 7(1);
    (b)   the provisions of Article 10(1)(e).
    . . .
3.   Any Contracting State may at any time withdraw a reservation which it has made; the reservation shall cease to have effect on the first day of the third calendar month after notification of the withdrawal.

## TITLE III. FINAL PROVISIONS

### Article 23
1.   If, after the date on which this Convention has entered into force for a Contracting State, that State wishes to adopt any new choice of law rule in regard to any particular category of contract within the scope of this Convention, it shall communicate its intention to the other signatory States through the Secretary-General of the Council of the European Communities.

2.   Any signatory State may, within six months from the date of the communication made to the Secretary-General, request him to arrange consultations between signatory States in order to reach agreement.

3.   If no signatory State has requested consultations within this period or if within two years following the communication made to the Secretary-General no agreement is reached in the course of consultations, the Contracting State concerned may amend its law in the manner indicated. The measures taken by

that State shall be brought to the knowledge of the other signatory States through the Secretary-General of the Council of the European Communities.

## Article 24

1. If, after the date on which this Convention has entered into force with respect to a Contracting State, that State wishes to become a party to a multilateral convention whose principal aim or one of whose principal aims is to lay down rules of private international law concerning any of the matters governed by this Convention, the procedure set out in Article 23 shall apply. However, the period of two years, referred to in paragraph 3 of that Article, shall be reduced to one year.

2 The procedure referred to in the preceding paragraph need not be followed if a Contracting State or one of the European Communities is already a party to the multilateral convention, or if its object is to revise a convention to which the State concerned is already a party, or if it is a convention concluded within the framework of the Treaties establishing the European Communities.

## Article 25

If a Contracting State considers that the unification achieved by this Convention is prejudiced by the conclusion of agreements not covered by Article 24(1), that State may request the Secretary-General of the Council of the European Communities to arrange consultations between the signatory States of this Convention.

## Article 26

Any Contracting State may request the revision of this Convention. In this event a revision conference shall be convened by the President of the Council of the European Communities.

## Article 28

1. This Convention shall be open from 19 June 1980 for signature by the States party to the Treaty establishing the European Economic Community.

2. This Convention shall be subject to ratification, acceptance or approval by the signatory States. The instruments of ratification, acceptance or approval shall be deposited with the Secretary-General of the Council of the European Communities.

## Article 29

1. This Convention shall enter into force on the first day of the third month following the deposit of the seventh instrument of ratification, acceptance or approval.

2. This Convention shall enter into force for each signatory State ratifying, accepting or approving at a later date on the first day of the third month following the deposit of its instrument of ratification, acceptance or approval.

## Article 30

1. This Convention shall remain in force for 10 years from the date of its entry into force in accordance with Article 29(1), even for States for which it enters into force at a later date.

2. If there has been no denunciation it shall be renewed tacitly every five years.

3. A Contracting State which wishes to denounce shall, not less than six months before the expiration of the period of 10 or five years, as the case may be, give notice to the Secretary-General of the Council of the European Communities. . . .

4. The denunciation shall have effect only in relation to the State which has notified it. The Convention will remain in force as between all other Contracting States.

**Article 31**
The Secretary-General of the Council of the European Communities shall notify the States party to the Treaty establishing the European Economic Community of:
(a)  the signatures;
(b)  the deposit of each instrument of ratification, acceptance or approval;
(c)  the date of entry into force of this Convention;
(d)  communications made in pursuance of Articles 23, 24, 25, 26 and 30;
(e)  the reservations and withdrawals of reservations referred to in Article 22.

**Article 32**
The Protocol annexed to this Convention shall form an integral part thereof.

**Article 33**
This Convention, drawn up in a single original in the Danish, Dutch, English, French, German, Irish and Italian languages, these texts being equally authentic, shall be deposited in the archives of the Secretariat of the Council of the European Communities. The Secretary-General shall transmit a certified copy thereof to the Government of each signatory State.

[PROTOCOL

The High Contracting Parties have agreed upon the following provision which shall be annexed to the Convention:
Notwithstanding the provisions of the Convention, Denmark, Sweden and Finland may retain national provisions concerning the law applicable to questions relating to the carriage of goods by sea and may amend such provisions without following the procedure provided for in Article 23 of the Convention of Rome. The national provisions applicable in this respect are the following:
– in Denmark, paragraphs 252 and 321(3) and (4) of the 'Sølov' (maritime law);
– in Sweden, Chapter 13, Article 2(1) and (2), and Chapter 14, Article 1(3), of 'sjölagen' (maritime law);
– in Finland, Chapter 13, Article 2(1) and (2), and Chapter 14, Article 1(3) of 'merilaki'/'sjölagen' (maritime law).]

SCHEDULE 2. THE LUXEMBOURG CONVENTION

The High Contracting Parties to the Treaty establishing the European Economic Community,
Considering that the Hellenic Republic, in becoming a Member of the Community, undertook to accede to the Convention on the law applicable to contractual obligations, opened for signature in Rome on 19 June 1980,
Have decided to conclude this Convention, and to this end have designated as their plenipotentiaries:
(Designation of plenipotentiaries)
Who, meeting within the Council, having exchanged their full powers, found in good and due form,
Have agreed as follows:

**Article 1**
The Hellenic Republic hereby accedes to the Convention on the law applicable to contractual obligations, opened for signature in Rome on 19 June 1980.

**Article 2**
The Secretary-General of the Council of the European Communities shall transmit a certified copy of the Convention on the law applicable to contractual

obligations in the Danish, Dutch, English, French, German, Irish and Italian languages to the Government of the Hellenic Republic.

The text of the Convention on the law applicable to contractual obligations in the Greek language is annexed hereto. The text in the Greek language shall be authentic under the same conditions as the other texts of the Convention on the law applicable to contractual obligations.

### Article 3
This Convention shall be ratified by the Signatory States. The instruments of ratification shall be deposited with the Secretary-General of the Council of the European Communities.

### Article 4
This Convention shall enter into force, as between the States which have ratified it, on the first day of the third month following the deposit of the last instrument of ratification by the Hellenic Republic and seven States which have ratified the Convention on the law applicable to contractual obligations.

This Convention shall enter into force for each Contracting State which subsequently ratifies it on the first day of the third month following the deposit of its instrument of ratification.

### Article 5
The Secretary-General of the Council of the European Communities shall notify the Signatory States of:
  (a)   the deposit of each instrument of ratification;
  (b)   the dates of entry into force of this Convention for the Contracting States.

### Article 6
This Convention, drawn up in a single original in the Danish, Dutch, English, French, German, Greek, Irish and Italian languages, all eight texts being equally authentic, shall be deposited in the archives of the General Secretariat of the Council of the European Communities. The Secretary-General shall transmit a certified copy to the Government of each Signatory State.

## SCHEDULE 3. THE BRUSSELS PROTOCOL

The High Contracting Parties to the Treaty establishing the European Economic Community,

Having regard to the Joint Declaration annexed to the Convention on the law applicable to contractual obligations, opened for signature in Rome on 19 June 1980,

Have decided to conclude a Protocol conferring jurisdiction on the Court of Justice of the European Communities to interpret that Convention and to this end have designated as their Plenipotentiaries:

(Designation of plenipotentiaries)

Who, meeting within the Council of the European Communities, having exchanged their full powers, found in good and due form,

Have agreed as follows:

### Article 1
The Court of Justice of the European Communities shall have jurisdiction to give rulings on the interpretation of—
  (a)   the Convention on the law applicable to contractual obligations, opened for signature in Rome on 19 June 1980, hereinafter referred to as 'the Rome Convention';
  (b)   the Convention on accession to the Rome Convention by the States which have become Members of the European Communities since the date on which it was opened for signature;
  (c)   this Protocol.

**Article 2**
Any of the courts referred to below may request the Court of Justice to give a preliminary ruling on a question raised in a case pending before it and concerning interpretation of the provisions contained in the instruments referred to in Article 1 if that court considers that a decision on the question is necessary to enable it to give judgment:

(a)   —in Belgium:
        la Cour de cassation (het Hof van Cassatie) and le Conseil d'Etat (de Raad van State),
      —in Denmark:
        Højesteret,
      —in the Federal Republic of Germany:
        die obersten Gerichtschöfe des Bundes,
      —in Greece:
        τα ανώτατα Αικαστήρια,
      —in Spain:
        el Tribunal Supremo,
      —in France:
        la Cour de cassation and le Conseil d'Etat,
      —in Ireland:
        the Supreme Court,
      —in Italy:
        la Corte suprema di cassazione and il Consiglio di Stato,
      —in Luxembourg:
        la Cour Supérieure de Justice, when sitting as Cour de cassation,
      [—in Austria:
        the Oberste Gerichtshof, the Verwaltungsgerichtshof and the Verfassungsgerichtshof,]
      —in the Netherlands:
        de Hoge Raad,
      —in Portugal:
        o Supremo Tribunal de Justiça and o Supremo Tribunal Administrativo,
      [—in Finland:
        korkein oikeus/högsta domstolen, korkein hallinto-oikeus/högsta förvaltningsdomstolen, markkinatuomioistuin/marknadsdomstolen and työtuomioistuin/arbetsdomstolen,
      —in Sweden:
        Högsta domstolen, Regeringsrätten, Arbetsdomstolen and Marknadsdomstolen]
      —in the United Kingdom:
        the House of Lords and other courts from which no further appeal is possible;
(b)   the courts of the Contracting States when acting as appeal courts.

**Article 3**
1.  The competent authority of a Contracting State may request the Court of Justice to give a ruling on a question of interpretation of the provisions contained in the instruments referred to in Article 1 if judgments given by courts of that State conflict with the interpretation given either by the Court of Justice or in a judgment of one of the courts of another Contracting State referred to in Article 2. The provisions of this paragraph shall apply only to judgments which have become *res judicata*.
2.  The interpretation given by the Court of Justice in response to such a request shall not affect the judgments which gave rise to the request for interpretation.

3. The Procurators-General of the Supreme Courts of Appeal of the Contracting States, or any other authority designated by a Contracting State, shall be entitled to request the Court of Justice for a ruling on interpretation in accordance with paragraph 1.

4. The Registrar of the Court of Justice shall give notice of the request to the Contracting States, to the Commission and to the Council of the European Communities; they shall then be entitled within two months of the notification to submit statements of case or written observations to the Court.

5. No fees shall be levied or any costs or expenses awarded in respect of the proceedings provided for in this Article.

### Article 4

1. Except where this Protocol otherwise provides, the provisions of the Treaty establishing the European Economic Community and those of the Protocol on the Statute of the Court of Justice annexed thereto, which are applicable when the Court is requested to give a preliminary ruling, shall also apply to any proceedings for the interpretation of the instruments referred to in Article 1.

2. The Rules of Procedure of the Court of Justice shall, if necessary, be adjusted and supplemented in accordance with Article 188 of the Treaty establishing the European Economic Community.

### Article 5

This Protocol shall be subject to ratification by the Signatory States. The instruments of ratification shall be deposited with the Secretary-General of the Council of the European Communities.

### Article 6

1. To enter into force, this Protocol must be ratified by seven States in respect of which the Rome Convention is in force. This Protocol shall enter into force on the first day of the third month following the deposit of the instrument of ratification by the last such State to take this step. If, however, the Second Protocol conferring on the Court of Justice of the European Communities certain powers to interpret the Convention on the law applicable to contractual obligations, opened for signature in Rome on 19 June 1980, concluded in Brussels on 19 December 1988, enters into force on a later date, this Protocol shall enter into force on the date of entry into force of the Second Protocol.

2. Any ratification subsequent to the entry into force of this Protocol shall take effect on the first day of the third month following the deposit of the instrument of ratification provided that the ratification, acceptance or approval of the Rome Convention by the State in question has become effective.

### Article 7

The Secretary-General of the Council of the European Communities shall notify the Signatory States of:
(a)   the deposit of each instrument of ratification;
(b)   the date of entry into force of this Protocol;
(c)   any designation communicated pursuant to Article 3(3);
(d)   any communication made pursuant to Article 8.

### Article 8

The Contracting States shall communicate to the Secretary-General of the Council of the European Communities the texts of any provisions of their laws which necessitate an amendment to the list of courts in Article 2(a).

### Article 9

This Protocol shall have effect for as long as the Rome Convention remains in force under the conditions laid down in Article 30 of that Convention.

**Article 10**

Any Contracting State may request the revision of this Protocol. In this event, a revision conference shall be convened by the President of the Council of the European Communities.

**Article 11**

This Protocol, drawn up in a single original in the Danish, Dutch, English, French, German, Greek, Irish, Italian, Portuguese and Spanish languages, all 10 texts being equally authentic, shall be deposited in the archives of the General Secretariat of the Council of the European Communities. The Secretary-General shall transmit a certified copy to the Government of each Signatory State.

[SCHEDULE 3A. THE FUNCHAL CONVENTION

The High Contracting Parties to the Treaty establishing the European Economic Community.

Considering that the Kingdom of Spain and the Portuguese Republic, in becoming Members of the Community, undertook to accede to the Convention on the law applicable to contractual obligations, opened for signature in Rome on 19th June 1980.

Have decided to conclude this Convention, and to this end have designated as their plenipotentiaries:

(Designation of plenipotentiaries)

Who, meeting within the Council, having exchanged their full powers, found in good and due form.

Have agreed as follows:

**Article 1**

The Kingdom of Spain and the Portuguese Republic hereby accede to the Convention on the law applicable to contractual obligations, opened for signature in Rome on 19th June 1980.

**Article 2**

The Convention on the law applicable to contractual obligations is hereby amended as follows:

(1) Article 22(2), Article 27 and the second sentence of Article 30(3) shall be deleted.

(2) The reference to Article 27 in Article 31(d) shall be deleted.

**Article 3**

The Secretary-General of the Council of the European Communities shall transmit a certified copy of the Convention on the law applicable to contractual obligations in the Danish, Dutch, English, French, German, Greek, Irish and Italian languages to the Governments of the Kingdom of Spain and the Portuguese Republic.

**Article 4**

This Convention shall be ratified by the Signatory States. The instruments of ratification shall be deposited with the Secretary-General of the Council of the European Communities.

**Article 5**

This Convention shall enter into force, as between the States which have ratified it, on the first day of the third month following deposit of the last instrument of ratification by the Kingdom of Spain or the Portuguese Republic and by one State which has ratified the Convention on the law applicable to contractual obligations.

This Convention shall enter into force for each Contracting State which subsequently ratifies it on the first day of the third month following that of deposit of its instrument of ratification.

**Article 6**
The Secretary-General of the Council of the European Communities shall notify the Signatory States of:
(a)  the deposit of each instrument of ratification;
(b)  the dates of entry into force of this Convention for the Contracting States.

**Article 7**
This Convention, drawn up in a single original in the Danish, Dutch, English, French, German, Greek, Irish, Italian, Portuguese and Spanish languages, all ten texts being equally authentic, shall be deposited in the archives of the General Secretariat of the Council of the European Communities. The Secretary-General shall transmit a certified copy to the Government of each Signatory State.]

[SCHEDULE 3B. THE 1996 ACCESSION CONVENTION

*Section 2*

The High Contracting Parties to the Treaty establishing the European Community.

Considering that the Republic of Austria, the Republic of Finland and the Kingdom of Sweden, in becoming Members of the European Union, undertook to accede to the Convention on the Law applicable to Contractual Obligations, opened for signature in Rome on 19th June 1980, and to the First and Second Protocols on its interpretation by the Court of Justice,

Have agreed as follows:

### TITLE I. GENERAL PROVISIONS

**Article 1**
The Republic of Austria, the Republic of Finland and the Kingdom of Sweden hereby accede to:
(a)  the Convention on the Law applicable to Contractual Obligations, opened for signature in Rome on 19th June 1980, hereinafter referred to as 'the Convention of 1980', as it stands following incorporation of all the adjustments and amendments made thereto by:
—the Convention signed in Luxembourg on 10th April 1984, hereinafter referred to as 'the Convention of 1984', on the accession of the Hellenic Republic to the Convention on the Law applicable to Contractual Obligations;
—the Convention signed in Funchal on 18th May 1992, hereinafter referred to as 'the Convention of 1992', on the accession of the Kingdom of Spain and the Portuguese Republic to the Convention on the Law applicable to Contractual Obligations;
(b)  the First Protocol, signed on 19th December 1988, hereinafter referred to as 'the First Protocol of 1988', on the interpretation by the Court of Justice of the European Communities of the Convention on the Law applicable to Contractual Obligations;
(c)  the Second Protocol, signed on 19th December 1988, hereinafter referred to as 'the Second Protocol of 1988', conferring on the Court of Justice of the European Communities certain powers to interpret the Convention on the Law applicable to Contractual Obligations.

### TITLE II. ADJUSTMENTS TO THE PROTOCOL ANNEXED TO THE CONVENTION OF 1980

**Article 2**
The Protocol annexed to the Convention of 1980 is hereby replaced by the following:

'Notwithstanding the provisions of the Convention, Denmark, Sweden and Finland may retain national provisions concerning the law applicable to questions relating to the carriage of goods by sea and may amend such provisions without following the procedure provided for in Article 23 of the Convention of Rome. The national provisions applicable in this respect are the following:

— in Denmark, paragraphs 252 and 321(3) and (4) of the "Sølov" (maritime law);
— in Sweden, Chapter 13, Article 2(1) and (2), and Chapter 14, Article 1(3), of "sjölagen" (maritime law);
— in Finland, Chapter 13, Article 2(1) and (2), and Chapter 14, Article 1(3), of "merilaki"/"sjölagen" (maritime law).'

### TITLE III. ADJUSTMENTS TO THE FIRST PROTOCOL OF 1988

**Article 3**
The following indents shall be inserted in Article 2(a) of the First Protocol of 1988:
(a) between the tenth and eleventh indents:
'— in Austria:
the Oberste Gerìchtshof, the Verwaltungsgerichtshof and the Verfassungs-gerichtshof,'
(b) between the eleventh and twelfth indents:
'— in Finland:
Korkein oikeus/högsta domstolen, korkein hallinto-oikeus/högsta förvalt-ningsdomstolen, markkinatuomioistuin/marknadsdomstolen and työtuo-mioistuin/arbetsdomstolen,
— in Sweden:
Högsta domstolen, Regeringsrätten, Arbetsdomstolen and Marknadsdom-stolen,'.

### TITLE IV. FINAL PROVISIONS

**Article 4**
1. The Secretary-General of the Council of the European Union shall transmit a certified copy of the Convention of 1980, the Convention of 1984, the First Protocol of 1988, the Second Protocol of 1988 and the Convention of 1992 in the Danish, Dutch, English, French, German, Greek, Irish, Italian, Spanish and Portuguese languages to the Governments of the Republic of Austria, the Republic of Finland and the Kingdom of Sweden.
2. The text of the Convention of 1980, the Convention of 1984, the First Protocol of 1988, the Second Protocol of 1988 and the Convention of 1992 in the Finnish and Swedish languages shall be authentic under the same conditions as the other texts of the Convention of 1980, the Convention of 1984, the First Protocol of 1988, the Second Protocol of 1988 and the Convention of 1992.

**Article 5**
This Convention shall be ratified by the Signatory States. The instruments of ratification shall be deposited with the Secretary-General of the Council of the European Union.

**Article 6**
1. This Convention shall enter into force, as between the States which have ratified it, on the first day of the third month following the deposit of the last instrument of ratification by the Republic of Austria, the Republic of Finland or the Kingdom of Sweden and by one Contracting State which has ratified the Convention on the Law applicable to Contractual Obligations.
2. This Convention shall enter into force for each Contracting State which subsequently ratifies it on the first day of the third month following the deposit of its instrument of ratification.

**Article 7**

The Secretary-General of the Council of the European Union shall notify the Signatory States of:

(a) the deposit of each instrument of ratification;

(b) the dates of entry into force of this Convention for the Contracting States.

**Article 8**

This Convention, drawn up in a single original in the Danish, Dutch, English, Finnish, French, German, Greek, Irish, Italian, Portuguese, Spanish and Swedish languages, all twelve texts being equally authentic, shall be deposited in the archives of the General Secretariat of the Council of the European Union. The Secretary-General shall transmit a certified copy to the Government of each Signatory State.]

## AGE OF LEGAL CAPACITY (SCOTLAND) ACT 1991
### (1991, c 50)

**1.   Age of legal capacity**

(1)   As from the commencement of this Act—

(a)   a person under the age of 16 years shall, subject to section 2 below, have no legal capacity to enter into any transaction;

(b)   a person of or over the age of 16 years shall have legal capacity to enter into any transaction.

(2)   Subject to section 8 below, any reference in any enactment to a pupil (other than in the context of education or training) or to a person under legal disability or incapacity by reason of nonage shall, insofar as it relates to any time after the commencement of this Act, be construed as a reference to a person under the age of 16 years.

(3)   Nothing in this Act shall—

(a)   apply to any transaction entered into before the commencement of this Act;

(b)   confer any legal capacity on any person who is under legal disability or incapacity other than by reason of nonage;

(c)   affect the delictual or criminal responsibility of any person;

(d)   affect any enactment which lays down an age limit expressed in years for any particular purpose;

(e)   prevent any person under the age of 16 years from receiving or holding any right, title or interest;

(f)   affect any existing rule of law or practice whereby—

(i)   any civil proceedings may be brought or defended, or any step in civil proceedings may be taken, in the name of a person under the age of 16 years [in relation to whom there is no person entitled to act as his legal representative (within the meaning of Part I of the Children (Scotland) Act 1995), or where there is such a person,] is unable (whether by reason of conflict of interest or otherwise) or refuses to bring or defend such proceedings or take such step;

(ii)   the court may, in any civil proceedings, appoint a curator ad litem to a person under the age of 16 years;

(iii)   the court may, in relation to the approval of an arrangement under section 1 of the Trusts (Scotland) Act 1961, appoint a curator ad litem to a person of or over the age of 16 years but under the age of 18 years;

(iv)   the court may appoint a curator bonis to any person;

(g)   prevent any person under the age of 16 years from [exercising parental responsibilities and parental rights (within the meaning of sections 1(3) and 2(4) respectively of the Children (Scotland) Act 1995) in relation to any child of his.]

(4)   Any existing rule of law relating to the legal capacity of minors and pupils which is inconsistent with the provisions of this Act shall cease to have effect.

(5)   Any existing rule of law relating to reduction of a transaction on the ground of minority and lesion shall cease to have effect.

## 2.  Exceptions to general rule

(1)   A person under the age of 16 years shall have legal capacity to enter into a transaction—

(a)   of a kind commonly entered into by persons of his age and circumstances, and

(b)   on terms which are not unreasonable.

(2)   A person of or over the age of 12 years shall have testamentary capacity, including legal capacity to exercise by testamentary writing any power of appointment.

(3)   A person of or over the age of 12 years shall have legal capacity to consent to the making of an adoption order in relation to him; and accordingly—

(a)   for section 12(8) (adoption orders) of the Adoption (Scotland) Act 1978 there shall be substituted the following subsection—

'(8)   An adoption order shall not be made in relation to a child of or over the age of 12 years unless with the child's consent; except that, where the court is satisfied that the child is incapable of giving his consent to the making of the order, it may dispense with that consent.'; and

(b)   for section 18(8) (freeing child for adoption) of that Act there shall be substituted the following subsection—

'(8)   An order under this section shall not be made in relation to a child of or over the age of 12 years unless with the child's consent; except that where the court is satisfied that the child is incapable of giving his consent to the making of the order, it may dispense with that consent.'

(4)   A person under the age of 16 years shall have legal capacity to consent on his own behalf to any surgical, medical or dental procedure or treatment where, in the opinion of a qualified medical practitioner attending him, he is capable of understanding the nature and possible consequences of the procedure or treatment.

[(4A)   A person under the age of sixteen years shall have legal capacity to instruct a solicitor, in connection with any civil matter, where that person has a general understanding of what it means to do so; and without prejudice to the generality of this subsection a person twelve years of age or more shall be presumed to be of sufficient age and maturity to have such understanding.

(4B)   A person who by virtue of subsection (4A) above has legal capacity to instruct a solicitor shall also have legal capacity to sue, or to defend, in any civil proceedings.

(4C)   Subsections (4A) and (4B) above are without prejudice to any question of legal capacity arising in connection with any criminal matter.]

(5)   Any transaction—

(a)   which a person under the age of 16 years purports to enter into after the commencement of this Act, and

(b)   in relation to which that person does not have legal capacity by virtue of this section,

shall be void.

## 3.  Setting aside of transactions

(1)   A person under the age of 21 years ('the applicant') may make application to the court to set aside a transaction which he entered into while he was of or over the age of 16 years but under the age of 18 years and which is a prejudicial transaction.

(2)   In this section 'prejudicial transaction' means a transaction which—

(a)   an adult, exercising reasonable prudence, would not have entered into in the circumstances of the applicant at the time of entering into the transaction, and

(b)   has caused or is likely to cause substantial prejudice to the applicant.

(3)   Subsection (1) above shall not apply to—

(a)   the exercise of testamentary capacity;

(b)   the exercise by testamentary writing of any power of appointment;

(c)   the giving of consent to the making of an adoption order;

(d)   the bringing or defending of, or the taking of any step in, civil proceedings;

(e)   the giving of consent to any surgical, medical or dental procedure or treatment;

(f)   a transaction in the course of the applicant's trade, business or profession;

(g)   a transaction into which any other party was induced to enter by virtue of any fraudulent misrepresentation by the applicant as to age or other material fact;

(h)   a transaction ratified by the applicant after he attained the age of 18 years and in the knowledge that it could be the subject of an application to the court under this section to set it aside; or

(j)   a transaction ratified by the court under section 4 below.

(4)   Where an application to set aside a transaction can be made or could have been made under this section by the person referred to in subsection (1) above, such application may instead be made by that person's executor, trustee in bankruptcy, trustee acting under a trust deed for creditors or curator bonis at any time prior to the date on which that person attains or would have attained the age of 21 years.

(5)   An application under this section to set aside a transaction may be made—

(a)   by an action in the Court of Session or the sheriff court, or

(b)   by an incidental application in other proceedings in such court,

and the court may make an order setting aside the transaction and such further order, if any, as seems appropriate to the court in order to give effect to the rights of the parties.

## 4.   Ratification by court of proposed transaction

(1)   Where a person of or over the age of 16 years but under the age of 18 years proposes to enter into a transaction which, if completed, could be the subject of an application to the court under section 3 above to set aside, all parties to the proposed transaction may make a joint application to have it ratified by the court.

(2)   The court shall not grant an application under this section if it appears to the court that an adult, exercising reasonable prudence and in the circumstances of the person referred to in subsection (1) above, would not enter into the transaction.

(3)   An application under this section shall be made by means of a summary application—

(a)   to the sheriff of the sheriffdom in which any of the parties to the proposed transaction resides, or

(b)   where none of the said parties resides in Scotland, to the sheriff at Edinburgh,

and the decision of the sheriff on such application shall be final.

## 5.   Guardians of persons under 16

(1)   Except insofar as otherwise provided in Schedule 1 to this Act, as from the commencement of this Act any reference in any rule of law, enactment or document to the tutor . . . of a pupil child shall be construed as a reference to

[a person entitled to act as a child's legal representative (within the meaning of Part I of the Children (Scotland) Act 1995) and any reference to the tutory of such a child shall be construed as a reference to the entitlement to act as a child's legal representative enjoyed by a person, by, under or by virtue of the said Part I.]

(2) Subject to section 1(3)(f) above, as from the commencement of this Act no guardian of a person under the age of 16 years shall be appointed as such except under section [7 of the Children (Scotland) Act 1995.]

(3) As from the commencement of this Act, no person shall, by reason of age alone, be subject to the curatory of another person.

(4) As from the commencement of this Act, no person shall be appointed as factor loco tutoris.

## 6.  Attainment of age

(1) The time at which a person attains a particular age expressed in years shall be taken to be the beginning of the relevant anniversary of the date of his birth.

(2) Where a person has been born on 29th February in a leap year, the relevant anniversary in any year other than a leap year shall be taken to be 1st March.

(3) The provisions of this section shall apply only to a relevant anniversary which occurs after the commencement of this Act.

## 7.  Acquisition of domicile

The time at which a person first becomes capable of having an independent domicile shall be the date at which he attains the age of 16 years.

## 8.  Transitional provision

Where any person referred to in section 6(4)(b), 17(3), 18(3) or 18A(2) of the Prescription and Limitation (Scotland) Act 1973 as having been under legal disability by reason of nonage was of or over the age of 16 years but under the age of 18 years immediately before the commencement of this Act, any period prior to such commencement shall not be reckoned as, or as part of, the period of 5 years, or (as the case may be) 3 years, specified respectively in section 6, 17, 18 or 18A of that Act.

## 9.  Interpretation

In this Act, unless the context otherwise requires—

'existing' means existing immediately before the commencement of this Act;

. . .

'transaction' means a transaction having legal effect, and includes—

(a)   any unilateral transaction;

(b)   the exercise of testamentary capacity;

(c)   the exercise of any power of appointment;

(d)   the giving by a person of any consent having legal effect;

(e)   the bringing or defending of, or the taking of any step in, civil proceedings;

(f)   acting as arbiter or trustee;

(g)   acting as an instrumentary witness.

## 10.  Amendments and repeals

(1) The enactments mentioned in Schedule 1 to this Act shall have effect subject to the amendments therein specified.

(2) The enactments specified in Schedule 2 to this Act are repealed to the extent specified in the third column of that Schedule.

## 11.  Short title, commencement and extent

(1) This Act may be cited as the Age of Legal Capacity (Scotland) Act 1991.

(2) This Act shall come into force at the end of the period of two months beginning with the date on which it is passed.

(3) This Act shall extend to Scotland only.

# SCHEDULES

## SCHEDULE 1. AMENDMENT OF ENACTMENTS

*Defence Act 1842 (c. 94)*

1. In section 15, for the words 'persons within the age of twenty-one years' substitute the words 'or, being persons under legal disability by reason of nonage'; and for the words 'come and be at the age of twenty-one years' substitute the words 'cease to be under legal disability by reason of nonage or come and be'.

2. In section 27, for the words 'infancy or' substitute the words 'persons under legal disability by reason of nonage or of'.

*Lands Clauses Consolidation (Scotland) Act 1845 (c. 19)*

. . .

6. In section 70, for the word 'infancy' substitute the words 'legal disability by reason of nonage'.

. . .

*Improvement of Land Act 1864 (c. 114)*

16. In section 18, for the words 'an infant or infants, or a minor or minors' substitute the words 'a person under legal disability by reason of nonage'.

17. In section 24, for the words 'infants, minors' substitute the words 'persons under legal disability by reason of nonage'.

18. In section 68, for the word 'infant' substitute the words 'person under legal disability by reason of nonage'.

*Titles to Land Consolidation (Scotland) Act 1868 (c. 101)*

19. In section 24, for the words 'pupil, minor' wherever they occur substitute the words 'person under legal disability by reason of nonage'.

20. In section 62, for the words 'in nonage' substitute the words 'under legal disability by reason of nonage'.

21. In section 119, for the words 'of full age, or in pupillarity or minority, or although he should be subject to any legal incapacity' substitute the words 'subject to any legal incapacity or not'.

*Colonial Stock Act 1877 (c. 59)*

22. In section 26 (definitions) after the definition of 'colony' there shall be inserted—
    'The expression "infant", in relation to Scotland, means a person under legal disability by reason of nonage, and the expression "infancy" shall be construed accordingly:'

*Heritable Securities (Scotland) Act 1894 (c. 44)*

23. In section 13, for the words 'in pupillarity or minority, or subject to any legal incapacity' substitute the words 'subject to any legal disability by reason of nonage or otherwise'; and after the word 'curators,' insert the word 'guardians'.

*Merchant Shipping Act 1894 (c. 60)*

24.   In section 55(1), for the word 'infancy' substitute the words 'legal disability by reason of nonage'.

*Trusts (Scotland) Act 1921 (c. 58)*

25.   In section 2, in the definitions of 'trust' and 'trust deed', after the word 'curator' insert the word 'guardian', and, in the definition of 'trustee', for the words from 'tutor' to 'curator' substitute the words 'tutor, curator, guardian (including a father or mother acting as guardian of a child under the age of 16 years)'.

*Conveyancing (Scotland) Act 1924 (c. 27)*

26.   In section 41(1), for the words from 'in pupillarity' to 'incapacity' substitute the words 'subject to any legal disability by reason of nonage or otherwise'.

*Trusts (Scotland) Act 1961 (c. 57)*

27.   In section 1, in subsection (1)(a) after the word 'who' insert the words 'because of any legal disability', and, in subsection (2), for the words 'over the age of pupillarity' substitute the words 'of or over the age of 16 years'.

*Registration of Births, Deaths and Marriages (Scotland) Act 1965 (c. 49)*

28.   In section 20(3)(c), for '18' substitute '16'.
29.   In section 43(10), for the words 'tutor or curator' substitute the word 'guardian'.

*National Loans Act 1968 (c. 13)*

30.   In section 14(5)(a), for the words from 'of unsound' to 'disability' substitute the words 'under legal disability by reason of nonage or otherwise'.

*Social Work (Scotland) Act 1968 (c. 49)*

31.   In section 16(11)(c), for the words 'tutor or curator' substitute the word 'guardian'.
32.   In section 18(4), for the words 'tutor or curator of an infant' substitute the words 'guardian of a child'.

*Taxes Management Act 1970 (c. 9)*

33.   In section 73, for the words 'parent, guardian or tutor' substitute the words 'parent or guardian'.
34.   In section 118(1), in the appropriate alphabetical position, insert the following definition—
    '"infant", in relation to Scotland, except in section 73 of this Act, means a person under legal disability by reason of nonage, and, in the said section 73, means a person under the age of 18 years.'

*Sheriff Courts (Scotland) Act 1971 (c. 58)*

35.   In section 37(2A), for the words 'tutory, curatory' substitute the word 'guardianship'.

*Adoption (Scotland) Act 1978 (c. 28)*

36.   In section 65(1), in paragraph (b) of the definition of 'guardian' for the words 'tutory, curatory' substitute the word 'guardianship'.

*Matrimonial Homes (Family Protection) (Scotland) Act 1981 (c. 59)*

37.   In section 7(1)(d), for the words 'a minor' substitute the words 'under legal disability by reason of nonage'.

*Civil Jurisdiction and Judgments Act 1982 (c. 27)*

38.   In Schedule 9, in paragraph 3 for the words 'tutory and curatory' substitute the words 'guardianship of children'.

*Companies Act 1985 (c. 6)*

39.   In sections 203(1), 327(2)(b) and 328(8), for the words 'pupil or minor' substitute the words 'person under the age of 18 years'.

*Family Law (Scotland) Act 1985 (c. 37)*

40.   In section 2(4)(c)(i), for the words 'father or mother' substitute the words 'parent or guardian'.

*Law Reform (Parent and Child) (Scotland) Act 1986 (c. 9)*

41.   For section 4 substitute the following section—

**'4.   Power of parent to appoint guardian**
The parent of a child may appoint any person to be guardian of the child after his death, but any such appointment shall be of no effect unless—
(a)   the appointment is in writing and signed by the parent; and
(b)   the parent at the time of his death was guardian of the child or would have been such guardian if he had survived until after the birth of the child.'

42.   In section 6(2), for the words 'pupil child' substitute the words 'child under the age of 16 years'; and for the word 'tutor' substitute the word 'guardian'.

43.   In section 8, in paragraph (a) of the definition of 'child' after the words 'in relation to' insert the word 'guardianship,' and in paragraph (d) for the words from 'custody' to 'curatory' substitute the words 'guardianship, custody or access'; and in the definition of 'parental rights' for the words 'tutory, curatory' substitute the word 'guardianship'.

*Family Law Act 1986 (c. 55)*

44.   In section l(1)(b)(ix), for the words 'tutory or curatory' substitute the word 'guardianship'.

45.   In section 16, in subsections (1) and (4) for the words 'tutory or curatory' substitute the word 'guardianship' and for the words 'pupil or minor' substitute the word 'child'; and in subsection (2) for the words 'factor loco tutoris' substitute the words 'judicial factor'.

46.   In section 18(2), for the words 'tutory or curatory of a pupil or minor' substitute the words 'guardianship of a child'.

47.   In section 35(4)(b), for the words 'tutor or curator' substitute the word 'guardian'.

SCHEDULE 2. REPEALS

| Chapter | Short title | Extent of repeal |
| --- | --- | --- |
| 1474, c 6 | The Tutors Act 1474 | The whole Act |
| 1672, c 2 | The Tutors and Curators Act 1672 | The whole Act |
| 1681, c 85 | The Oaths of Minors Act 1681 | The whole Act |
| 1696, c 8 | The Tutors and Curators Act 1696 | The whole Act |
| 12 & 13 Vict. c 51 | The Judicial Factors Act 1849 | In section 1, the words 'factor loco tutoris', 'to any pupil' where first occurring and 'pupil or' where second occurring. In section 25(1), the words 'to any pupil' where first occurring and 'pupil or' where second occurring. In section 26, the words 'to a pupil' and 'pupils or'. Section 30. In section 31, the words 'loco tutoris'. |
| 31 & 32 Vict. c. 101 | The Titles to Land Consolidation (Scotland) Act 1868 | In section 3, the words 'factors loco tutoris'. In section 119, the words 'whether of full age or in pupillarity or minority, or'. In section 121, the words 'in pupillarity or minority or'. Section 139. |
| 43 & 44 Vict. c. 4 | The Judicial Factors (Scotland) Act 1880 | In section 3, the words 'a factor loco tutoris'. |
| 52 & 53 Vict. c. 39 | The Judicial Factors (Scotland) Act 1889 | Section 11 |
| 55 & 56 Vict. c. 4 | The Betting and Loans (Infants) Act 1892 | The whole Act |
| 23 & 24 Geo 5 c 41 | The Administration of Justice (Scotland) Act 1933 | Section 12 |
| 12, 13, & 14 Geo. 6 c 75 | The Agricultural Holdings (Scotland) Act 1949 | In section 84, the words 'a pupil or a minor or is'. |
| 9 & 10 Eliz. 2 c. 57 | The Trusts (Scotland) Act 1961 | In section 1, in subsection (2) the words '(whether acting with the concurrence of a curator, administrator-at-law, or other guardian or not)' and subsection (3). |
| 1964, c 41 | The Succession (Scotland) Act 1964 | Section 28. |

| Chapter | Short title | Extent of repeal |
|---|---|---|
| 1965, c 49 | The Registration of Births, Deaths and Marriages Act 1965 | In section 20(3), paragraph (b). In section 43, in subsections (5), (6) and (7) the words from 'and under' to 'over eighteen years of age'. In section 56(1), the definitions of 'guardian' and 'tutor or curator'. |
| 1968, c 49 | The Social Work (Scotland) Act 1968 | In section 94(1), in the definition of 'guardian' the words 'tutor, curator or'. |
| 1973, c 29 | The Guardianship Act 1973 | In section 13(1), the definition of 'guardian'. |
| 1974, c 39 | The Consumer Credit Act 1974 | In section 189(1), the definition of 'minor'. |
| 1974, c 53 | The Rehabilitation of Offenders Act 1974 | In section 7(2), the words 'including a pupil child'. |
| 1975, c 45 | The Finance (No. 2) Act 1975 | In section 73(5), the words 'pupil or'. |
| 1975, c 72 | The Children Act 1975 | In section 47(2), the words 'tutor, curator' in each place where they occur. |
| 1978, c 28 | The Adoption (Scotland) Act 1978 | In section 12(3)(a)(ii), the words 'tutor, curator or other'. |
| 1979, c 54 | The Sale of Goods Act 1979 | In section 3, in subsection (2) the words 'to a minor or' and in subsection (3) the words 'minor or other'. |
| 1982, c 50 | The Insurance Companies Act 1982 | In section 7(8) the definition of 'minor' in relation to Scotland. In section 31(7), the definition of 'minor' in relation to Scotland. |
| 1984, c 37 | The Child Abduction Act 1984 | In section 6(7), the words from 'a tutor' to '1986 or'. |
| 1985, c 37 | The Family Law (Scotland) Act 1985 | In section 2(4), in paragraph (b) the words 'or the curator of a minor who is an incapax' and in paragraph (c) head (ii). |
| 1986, c 9 | The Law Reform (Parent and Child) (Scotland) Act 1986 | Section 3(3). In section 8, in the definition of 'child' paragraphs (b) and (c), and the definitions of 'curator' and 'tutor'. In Schedule 1, in paragraph 9 in sub-paragraph (2) the words from 'and for' to the end, and in sub-paragraph (6) the words from 'for the words' where first occurring to 'and'; and paragraphs 11, 12, 14(1)(b) and 20(b). |
| 1986, c 33 | The Disabled Persons (Services, Consultation and Representation) Act 1986 | In section 16, in paragraph (b) of the definition of 'guardian' the words 'tutor, curator or'. |

## CARRIAGE OF GOODS BY SEA ACT 1992
### (1992, c 50)

**1.  Shipping documents etc. to which Act applies**

(1)   This Act applies to the following documents, that is to say—

(a)   any bill of lading;

(b)   any sea waybill; and

(c)   any ship's delivery order.

(2)   References in this Act to a bill of lading—

(a)   do not include references to a document which is incapable of transfer either by indorsement or, as a bearer bill, by delivery without indorsement; but

(b)   subject to that, do include references to a received for shipment bill of lading.

(3)   References in this Act to a sea waybill are references to any document which is not a bill of lading but—

(a)   is such a receipt for goods as contains or evidences a contract for the carriage of goods by sea; and

(b)   identifies the person to whom delivery of the goods is to be made by the carrier in accordance with that contract.

(4)   References in this Act to a ship's delivery order are references to any document which is neither a bill of lading nor a sea waybill but contains an undertaking which—

(a)   is given under or for the purposes of a contract for the carriage by sea of the goods to which the document relates, or of goods which include those goods; and

(b)   is an undertaking by the carrier to a person identified in the document to deliver the goods to which the document relates to that person.

(5)   The Secretary of State may by regulations make provision for the application of this Act to cases where a telecommunication system or any other information technology is used for effecting transactions corresponding to—

(a)   the issue of a document to which this Act applies;

(b)   the indorsement, delivery or other transfer of such a document; or

(c)   the doing of anything else in relation to such a document.

(6)   Regulations under subsection (5) above may—

(a)   make such modifications of the following provisions of this Act as the Secretary of State considers appropriate in connection with the application of this Act to any case mentioned in that subsection; and

(b)   contain supplemental, incidental, consequential and transitional provision;

and the power to make regulations under that subsection shall be exercisable by statutory instrument subject to annulment in pursuance of a resolution of either House of Parliament.

**2.  Rights under shipping documents**

(1)   Subject to the following provisions of this section, a person who becomes—

(a)   the lawful holder of a bill of lading;

(b)   the person who (without being an original party to the contract of carriage) is the person to whom delivery of the goods to which a sea waybill relates is to be made by the carrier in accordance with that contract; or

(c)   the person to whom delivery of the goods to which a ship's delivery order relates is to be made in accordance with the undertaking contained in the order,

shall (by virtue of becoming the holder of the bill or, as the case may be, the person to whom delivery is to be made) have transferred to and vested in him all rights of suit under the contract of carriage as if he had been a party to that contract.

(2) Where, when a person becomes the lawful holder of a bill of lading, possession of the bill no longer gives a right (as against the carrier) to possession of the goods to which the bill relates, that person shall not have any rights transferred to him by virtue of subsection (1) above unless he becomes the holder of the bill—

(a) by virtue of a transaction effected in pursuance of any contractual or other arrangements made before the time when such a right to possession ceased to attach to possession of the bill; or

(b) as a result of the rejection to that person by another person of goods or documents delivered to the other person in pursuance of any such arrangements.

(3) The rights vested in any person by virtue of the operation of subsection (1) above in relation to a ship's delivery order—

(a) shall be so vested subject to the terms of the order; and

(b) where the goods to which the order relates form a part only of the goods to which the contract of carriage relates, shall be confined to rights in respect of the goods to which the order relates.

(4) Where, in the case of any document to which this Act applies—

(a) a person with any interest or right in or in relation to goods to which the document relates sustains loss or damage in consequence of a breach of the contract of carriage; but

(b) subsection (1) above operates in relation to that document so that rights of suit in respect of that breach are vested in another person,

the other person shall be entitled to exercise those rights for the benefit of the person who sustained the loss or damage to the same extent as they could have been exercised if they had been vested in the person for whose benefit they are exercised.

(5) Where rights are transferred by virtue of the operation of subsection (1) above in relation to any document, the transfer for which that subsection provides shall extinguish any entitlement to those rights which derives—

(a) where that document is a bill of lading, from a person's having been an original party to the contract of carriage; or

(b) in the case of any document to which this Act applies, from the previous operation of that subsection in relation to that document;

but the operation of that subsection shall be without prejudice to any rights which derive from a person's having been an original party to the contract contained in, or evidenced by, a sea waybill and, in relation to a ship's delivery order, shall be without prejudice to any rights deriving otherwise than from the previous operation of that subsection in relation to that order.

## 3. Liabilities under shipping documents

(1) Where subsection (1) of section 2 of this Act operates in relation to any document to which this Act applies and the person in whom rights are vested by virtue of that subsection—

(a) takes or demands delivery from the carrier of any of the goods to which the document relates;

(b) makes a claim under the contract of carriage against the carrier in respect of any of those goods; or

(c) is a person who, at a time before those rights were vested in him, took or demanded delivery from the carrier of any of those goods,

that person shall (by virtue of taking or demanding delivery or making the claim or, in a case falling within paragraph (c) above, of having the rights vested in him) become subject to the same liabilities under that contract as if he had been a party to that contract.

(2) Where the goods to which a ship's delivery order relates form a part only of the goods to which the contract of carriage relates, the liabilities to which any person is subject by virtue of the operation of this section in relation to that order shall exclude liabilities in respect of any goods to which the order does not relate.

(3) This section, so far as it imposes liabilities under any contract on any person, shall be without prejudice to the liabilities under the contract of any person as an original party to the contract.

## 4. Representations in bills of lading

A bill of lading which—

(a) represents goods to have been shipped on board a vessel or to have been received for shipment on board a vessel; and

(b) has been signed by the master of the vessel or by a person who was not the master but had the express, implied or apparent authority of the carrier to sign bills of lading,

shall, in favour of a person who has become the lawful holder of the bill, be conclusive evidence against the carrier of the shipment of the goods or, as the case may be, of their receipt for shipment.

## 5. Interpretation etc.

(1) In this Act—

'bill of lading', 'sea waybill' and 'ship's delivery order' shall be construed in accordance with section 1 above;

'the contract of carriage'—

(a) in relation to a bill of lading or sea waybill, means the contract contained in or evidenced by that bill or waybill; and

(b) in relation to a ship's delivery order, means the contract under or for the purposes of which the undertaking contained in the order is given;

'holder', in relation to a bill of lading, shall be construed in accordance with subsection (2) below;

'information technology' includes any computer or other technology by means of which information or other matter may be recorded or communicated without being reduced to documentary form; and

'telecommunication system' has the same meaning as in the Telecommunications Act 1984.

(2) References in this Act to the holder of a bill of lading are references to any of the following persons, that is to say—

(a) a person with possession of the bill who, by virtue of being the person identified in the bill, is the consignee of the goods to which the bill relates;

(b) a person with possession of the bill as a result of the completion, by delivery of the bill, of any indorsement of the bill or, in the case of a bearer bill, of any other transfer of the bill;

(c) a person with possession of the bill as a result of any transaction by virtue of which he would have become a holder falling within paragraph (a) or (b) above had not the transaction been effected at a time when possession of the bill no longer gave a right (as against the carrier) to possession of the goods to which the bill relates;

and a person shall be regarded for the purposes of this Act as having become the lawful holder of a bill of lading wherever he has become the holder of the bill in good faith.

(3) References in this Act to a person's being identified in a document include references to his being identified by a description which allows for the identity of the person in question to be varied, in accordance with the terms of the document, after its issue; and the reference in section 1(3)(b) of this Act to a document's identifying a person shall be construed accordingly.

(4) Without prejudice to sections 2(2) and 4 above, nothing in this Act shall

preclude its operation in relation to a case where the goods to which a document relates—

(a) cease to exist after the issue of the document; or

(b) cannot be identified (whether because they are mixed with other goods or for any other reason);

and references in this Act to the goods to which a document relates shall be construed accordingly.

(5) The preceding provisions of this Act shall have effect without prejudice to the application, in relation to any case, of the rules (the Hague-Visby Rules) which for the time being have the force of law by virtue of section 1 of the Carriage of Goods by Sea Act 1971.

### 6. Short title, repeal, commencement and extent

(1) This Act may be cited as the Carriage of Goods by Sea Act 1992.

(2) The Bills of Lading Act 1855 is hereby repealed.

(3) This Act shall come into force at the end of the period of two months beginning with the day on which it is passed; but nothing in this Act shall have effect in relation to any document issued before the coming into force of this Act.

(4) This Act extends to Northern Ireland.

## CHILDREN (SCOTLAND) ACT 1995
### (1995, c 36)

## PART I. PARENTS, CHILDREN AND GUARDIANS

*Parental responsibilities and parental rights*

### 1. Parental responsibilities

(1) Subject to section 3(1)(b) and (3) of this Act, a parent has in relation to his child the responsibility—

(a) to safeguard and promote the child's health, development and welfare;

(b) to provide, in a manner appropriate to the stage of development of the child—

    (i) direction;

    (ii) guidance,

to the child;

(c) if the child is not living with the parent, to maintain personal relations and direct contact with the child on a regular basis; and

(d) to act as the child's legal representative,

but only in so far as compliance with this section is practicable and in the interests of the child.

(2) 'Child' means for the purposes of—

(a) paragraphs (a), (b)(i), (c) and (d) of subsection (1) above, a person under the age of sixteen years;

(b) paragraph (b)(ii) of that subsection, a person under the age of eighteen years.

(3) The responsibilities mentioned in paragraphs (a) to (d) of subsection (1) above are in this Act referred to as 'parental responsibilities'; and the child, or any person acting on his behalf, shall have title to sue, or to defend, in any proceedings as respects those responsibilities.

(4) The parental responsibilities supersede any analogous duties imposed on a parent at common law; but this section is without prejudice to any other duty so imposed on him or to any duty imposed on him by, under or by virtue of any other provision of this Act or of any other enactment.

### 6. Views of children

(1)  A person shall, in reaching any major decision which involves—

(a)  his fulfilling a parental responsibility or the responsibility mentioned in section 5(1) of this Act; or

(b)  his exercising a parental right or giving consent by virtue of that section,

have regard so far as practicable to the views (if he wishes to express them) of the child concerned, taking account of the child's age and maturity, and to those of any other person who has parental responsibilities or parental rights in relation to the child (and wishes to express those views); and without prejudice to the generality of this subsection a child twelve years of age or more shall be presumed to be of sufficient age and maturity to form a view.

(2)  A transaction entered into in good faith by a third party and a person acting as legal representative of a child shall not be challengeable on the ground only that the child, or a person with parental responsibilities or parental rights in relation to the child, was not consulted or that due regard was not given to his views before the transaction was entered into.

*Guardianship*

. . .

### 10.  Obligations and rights of person administering child's property

(1)  A person acting as a child's legal representative in relation to the administration of the child's property—

(a)  shall be required to act as a reasonable and prudent person would act on his own behalf; and

(b)  subject to any order made under section 11 of this Act, shall be entitled to do anything which the child, if of full age and capacity, could do in relation to that property;

and subject to subsection (2) below, on ceasing to act as legal representative, shall be liable to account to the child for his intromissions with the child's property.

(2)  No liability shall be incurred by virtue of subsection (1) above in respect of funds which have been used in the proper discharge of the person's responsibility to safeguard and promote the child's health, development and welfare.

### PRIVATE INTERNATIONAL LAW (MISCELLANEOUS PROVISIONS) ACT 1995 (1995, c 42)

### 7.  Validity and effect in Scots law of potentially polygamous marriages

(1)  A person domiciled in Scotland does not lack capacity to enter into a marriage by reason only that the marriage is entered into under a law which permits polygamy.

(2)  For the avoidance of doubt, a marriage valid by the law of Scotland and entered into—

(a)  under a law which permits polygamy; and

(b)  at a time when neither party to the marriage is already married,

has, so long as neither party marries a second spouse during the subsistence of the marriage, the same effects for all purposes of the law of Scotland as a marriage entered into under a law which does not permit polygamy.

### 8.  Part II: supplemental

(1)  Nothing in this Part affects any law or custom relating to the marriage of members of the Royal Family.

(2)   The enactments specified in the Schedule to this Act (which contains consequential amendments and amendments removing unnecessary references to potentially polygamous marriages) are amended in accordance with that Schedule.

(3)   Nothing in that Schedule affects either the generality of any enactment empowering the making of subordinate legislation or any such legislation made before the commencement of this Part.

## PART III. CHOICE OF LAW IN TORT AND DELICT

### 9.   Purpose of Part III

(1)   The rules in this Part apply for choosing the law (in this Part referred to as 'the applicable law') to be used for determining issues relating to tort or (for the purposes of the law of Scotland) delict.

(2)   The characterisation for the purposes of private international law of issues arising in a claim as issues relating to tort or delict is a matter for the courts of the forum.

(3)   The rules in this Part do not apply in relation to issues arising in any claim excluded from the operation of this Part by section 13 below.

(4)   The applicable law shall be used for determining the issues arising in a claim, including in particular the question whether an actionable tort or delict has occurred.

(5)   The applicable law to be used for determining the issues arising in a claim shall exclude any choice of law rules forming part of the law of the country or countries concerned.

(6)   For the avoidance of doubt (and without prejudice to the operation of section 14 below) this Part applies in relation to events occurring in the forum as it applies in relation to events occurring in any other country.

(7)   In this Part as it extends to any country within the United Kingdom, 'the forum' means England and Wales, Scotland or Northern Ireland, as the case may be.

(8)   In this Part 'delict' includes quasi-delict.

### 10.   Abolition of certain common law rules

The rules of the common law, in so far as they—

(a)   require actionability under both the law of the forum and the law of another country for the purpose of determining whether a tort or delict is actionable; or

(b)   allow (as an exception from the rules falling within paragraph (a) above) for the law of a single country to be applied for the purpose of determining the issues, or any of the issues, arising in the case in question,

are hereby abolished so far as they apply to any claim in tort or delict which is not excluded from the operation of this Part by section 13 below.

### 11.   Choice of applicable law: the general rule

(1)   The general rule is that the applicable law is the law of the country in which the events constituting the tort or delict in question occur.

(2)   Where elements of those events occur in different countries, the applicable law under the general rule is to be taken as being—

(a)   for a cause of action in respect of personal injury caused to an individual or death resulting from personal injury, the law of the country where the individual was when he sustained the injury;

(b)   for a cause of action in respect of damage to property, the law of the country where the property was when it was damaged; and

(c)   in any other case, the law of the country in which the most significant element or elements of those events occurred.

(3) In this section 'personal injury' includes disease or any impairment of physical or mental condition.

### 12. Choice of applicable law: displacement of general rule

(1) If it appears, in all the circumstances, from a comparison of—

(a) the significance of the factors which connect a tort or delict with the country whose law would be the applicable law under the general rule; and

(b) the significance of any factors connecting the tort or delict with another country,

that it is substantially more appropriate for the applicable law for determining the issues arising in the case, or any of those issues, to be the law of the other country, the general rule is displaced and the applicable law for determining those issues or that issue (as the case may be) is the law of that other country.

(2) The factors that may be taken into account as connecting a tort or delict with a country for the purposes of this section include, in particular, factors relating to the parties, to any of the events which constitute the tort or delict in question or to any of the circumstances or consequences of those events.

### 13. Exclusion of defamation claims from Part III

(1) Nothing in this Part applies to affect the determination of issues arising in any defamation claim.

(2) For the purposes of this section 'defamation claim' means—

(a) any claim under the law of any part of the United Kingdom for libel or slander or for slander of title, slander of goods or other malicious falsehood and any claim under the law of Scotland for verbal injury; and

(b) any claim under the law of any other country corresponding to or otherwise in the nature of a claim mentioned in paragraph (a) above.

### 14. Transitional provision and savings

(1) Nothing in this Part applies to acts or omissions giving rise to a claim which occur before the commencement of this Part.

(2) Nothing in this Part affects any rules of law (including rules of private international law) except those abolished by section 10 above.

(3) Without prejudice to the generality of subsection (2) above, nothing in this Part—

(a) authorises the application of the law of a country outside the forum as the applicable law for determining issues arising in any claim in so far as to do so—

(i) would conflict with principles of public policy; or

(ii) would give effect to such a penal, revenue or other public law as would not otherwise be enforceable under the law of the forum; or

(b) affects any rules of evidence, pleading or practice or authorises questions of procedure in any proceedings to be determined otherwise than in accordance with the law of the forum.

(4) This Part has effect without prejudice to the operation of any rule of law which either has effect notwithstanding the rules of private international law applicable in the particular circumstances or modifies the rules of private international law that would otherwise be so applicable.

### 15. Crown application

(1) This Part applies in relation to claims by or against the Crown as it applies in relation to claims to which the Crown is not a party.

(2) In subsection (1) above a reference to the Crown does not include a reference to Her Majesty in Her private capacity or to Her Majesty in right of Her Duchy of Lancaster or to the Duke of Cornwall.

(3) Without prejudice to the generality of section 14(2) above, nothing in this section affects any rule of law as to whether proceedings of any description may be brought against the Crown.

## REQUIREMENTS OF WRITING (SCOTLAND) ACT 1995
### (1995, c 7)

**1. Writing required for certain contracts, obligations, trusts, conveyances and wills**

(1)   Subject to subsection (2) below and any other enactment, writing shall not be required for the constitution of a contract, unilateral obligation or trust.

(2)   Subject to subsection (3) below, a written document complying with section 2 of this Act shall be required for—

    (a)   the constitution of—

      (i)   a contract or unilateral obligation for the creation, transfer, variation or extinction of [a real right] in land;

      (ii)   a gratuitous unilateral obligation except an obligation undertaken in the course of business; and

      (iii)   a trust whereby a person declares himself to be sole trustee of his own property or any property which he may acquire;

    (b)   the creation, transfer, variation or extinction of [a real right] in land otherwise than by the operation of a court decree, enactment or rule of law; and

    (c)   the making of any will, testamentary trust disposition and settlement or codicil.

(3)   Where a contract, obligation or trust mentioned in subsection (2)(a) above is not constituted in a written document complying with section 2 of this Act, but one of the parties to the contract, a creditor in the obligation or a beneficiary under the trust ('the first person') has acted or refrained from acting in reliance on the contract, obligation or trust with the knowledge and acquiescence of the other party to the contract, the debtor in the obligation or the truster ('the second person')—

    (a)   the second person shall not be entitled to withdraw from the contract, obligation or trust; and

    (b)   the contract, obligation or trust shall not be regarded as invalid, on the ground that it is not so constituted, if the condition set out in subsection (4) below is satisfied.

(4)   The condition referred to in subsection (3) above is that the position of the first person—

    (a)   as a result of acting or refraining from acting as mentioned in that subsection has been affected to a material extent; and

    (b)   as a result of such a withdrawal as is mentioned in that subsection would be adversely affected to a material extent.

(5)   In relation to the constitution of any contract, obligation or trust mentioned in subsection (2)(a) above, subsections (3) and (4) above replace the rules of law known as *rei interventus* and homologation.

(6)   This section shall apply to the variation of a contract, obligation or trust as it applies to the constitution thereof but as if in subsections (3) and (4) for the references to acting or refraining from acting in reliance on the contract, obligation or trust and withdrawing therefrom there were substituted respectively references to acting or refraining from acting in reliance on the variation of the contract, obligation or trust and withdrawing from the variation.

(7)   In this section ['real right in land' means any real] right in or over land, including any right to occupy or to use land or to restrict the occupation or use of land, but does not include—

    (a)   a tenancy;

    (b)   a right to occupy or use land; or

    (c)   a right to restrict the occupation or use of land,

if the tenancy or right is not granted for more than one year, unless the tenancy or right is for a recurring period or recurring periods and there is a gap of more than one year between the beginning of the first, and the end of the last, such period.

(8) For the purposes of subsection (7) above 'land' does not include—

(a) growing crops; or

(b) a moveable building or other moveable structure.

## 2. Type of writing required for formal validity of certain documents

(1) No document required by section 1(2) of this Act shall be valid in respect of the formalities of execution unless it is subscribed by the granter of it or, if there is more than one granter, by each granter, but nothing apart from such subscription shall be required for the document to be valid as aforesaid.

(2) A contract mentioned in section 1(2)(a)(i) of this Act may be regarded as constituted or varied (as the case may be) if the offer is contained in one or more documents and the acceptance is contained in another document or other documents, and each document is subscribed by the granter or granters thereof.

(3) Nothing in this section shall prevent a document which has not been subscribed by the granter or granters of it from being used as evidence in relation to any right or obligation to which the document relates.

(4) This section is without prejudice to any other enactment which makes different provision in respect of the formalities of execution of a document to which this section applies.

## 3. Presumption as to granter's subscription or date or place of subscription

(1) Subject to subsections (2) to (7) below, where—

(a) a document bears to have been subscribed by a granter of it;

(b) the document bears to have been signed by a person as a witness of that granter's subscription and the document, or the testing clause or its equivalent, bears to state the name and address of the witness; and

(c) nothing in the document, or in the testing clause or its equivalent, indicates—

(i) that it was not subscribed by that granter as it bears to have been so subscribed; or

(ii) that it was not validly witnessed for any reason specified in paragraphs (a) to (e) of subsection (4) below,

the document shall be presumed to have been subscribed by that granter.

(2) Where a testamentary document consists of more than one sheet, it shall not be presumed to have been subscribed by a granter as mentioned in subsection (1) above unless, in addition to it bearing to have been subscribed by him and otherwise complying with that subsection, it bears to have been signed by him on every sheet.

(3) For the purposes of subsection (1)(b) above—

(a) the name and address of a witness may be added at any time before the document is—

(i) founded on in legal proceedings; or

(ii) registered for preservation in the Books of Council and Session or in sheriff court books; and

(b) the name and address of a witness need not be written by the witness himself.

(4) Where, in any proceedings relating to a document in which a question arises as to a granter's subscription, it is established—

(a) that a signature bearing to be the signature of the witness of that granter's subscription is not such a signature, whether by reason of forgery or otherwise;

(b) that the person who signed the document as the witness of that granter's subscription is a person who is named in the document as a granter of it;

(c) that the person who signed the document as the witness of that granter's subscription, at the time of signing—

(i)   did not know the granter;

(ii)   was under the age of 16 years; or

(iii)   was mentally incapable of acting as a witness;

(d)   that the person who signed the document, purporting to be the witness of that granter's subscription, did not witness such subscription;

(e)   that the person who signed the document as the witness of that granter's subscription did not sign the document after him or that the granter's subscription or, as the case may be, acknowledgement of his subscription and the person's signature as witness of that subscription were not one continuous process;

(f)   that the name or address of the witness of that granter's subscription was added after the document was founded on or registered as mentioned in subsection (3)(a) above or is erroneous in any material respect; or

(g)   in the case of a testamentary document consisting of more than one sheet, that a signature on any sheet bearing to be the signature of the granter is not such a signature, whether by reason of forgery or otherwise,

then, for the purposes of those proceedings, there shall be no presumption that the document has been subscribed by that granter.

(5)   For the purposes of subsection (4)(c)(i) above, the witness shall be regarded as having known the person whose subscription he has witnessed at the time of witnessing if he had credible information at that time of his identity.

(6)   For the purposes of subsection (4)(e) above, where—

(a)   a document is granted by more than one granter; and

(b)   a person is the witness to the subscription of more than one granter,

the subscription or acknowledgement of any such granter and the signature of the person witnessing that granter's subscription shall not be regarded as not being one continuous process by reason only that, between the time of that subscription or acknowledgement and that signature, another granter has subscribed the document or acknowledged his subscription.

(7)   For the purposes of the foregoing provisions of this section a person witnesses a granter's subscription of a document—

(a)   if he sees the granter subscribe it; or

(b)   if the granter acknowledges his subscription to that person.

(8)   Where—

(a)   by virtue of subsection (1) above a document to which this subsection applies is presumed to have been subscribed by a granter of it;

(b)   the document, or the testing clause or its equivalent, bears to state the date or place of subscription of the document by that granter; and

(c)   nothing in the document, or in the testing clause or its equivalent, indicates that that statement as to date or place is incorrect,

there shall be a presumption that the document was subscribed by that granter on the date or at the place as stated.

(9)   Subsection (8) above applies to any document other than a testamentary document.

(10)   Where—

(a)   a testamentary document bears to have been subscribed and the document, or the testing clause or its equivalent, bears to state the date or place of subscription (whether or not it is presumed under subsections (1) to (7) above to have been subscribed by a granter of it); and

(b)   nothing in the document, or in the testing clause or its equivalent, indicates that that statement as to date or place is incorrect,

there shall be a presumption that the statement as to date or place is correct.

## 4.   Presumption as to granter's subscription or date or place of subscription when established in court proceedings

(1)   Where a document bears to have been subscribed by a granter of it, but

there is no presumption under section 3 of this Act that the document has been subscribed by that granter, then, if the court, on an application being made to it by any person who has an interest in the document, is satisfied that the document was subscribed by that granter, it shall—

(a)　cause the document to be endorsed with a certificate to that effect; or

(b)　where the document has already been registered in the Books of Council and Session or in sheriff court books, grant decree to that effect.

(2)　Where a document bears to have been subscribed by a granter of it, but there is no presumption under section 3 of this Act as to the date or place of subscription, then, if the court, on an application being made to it by any person who has an interest in the document, is satisfied as to the date or place of subscription, it shall—

(a)　cause the document to be endorsed with a certificate to that effect; or

(b)　where the document has already been registered in the Books of Council and Session or in sheriff court books, grant decree to that effect.

(3)　On an application under subsection (1) or (2) above evidence shall, unless the court otherwise directs, be given by affidavit.

(4)　An application under subsection (1) or (2) above may be made either as a summary application or as incidental to and in the course of other proceedings.

(5)　The effect of a certificate or decree—

(a)　under subsection (1) above shall be to establish a presumption that the document has been subscribed by the granter concerned;

(b)　under subsection (2) above shall be to establish a presumption that the statement in the certificate or decree as to date or place is correct.

(6)　In this section 'the court' means—

(a)　in the case of a summary application—

(i)　the sheriff in whose sheriffdom the applicant resides; or

(ii)　if the applicant does not reside in Scotland, the sheriff at Edinburgh; and

(b)　in the case of an application made in the course of other proceedings, the court before which those proceedings are pending.

## 5.　Alterations to documents: formal validity and presumptions

(1)　An alteration made to a document required by section 1(2) of this Act—

(a)　before the document is subscribed by the granter or, if there is more than one granter, by the granter first subscribing it, shall form part of the document as so subscribed;

(b)　after the document is so subscribed shall, if the alteration has been signed by the granter or (as the case may be) by all the granters, have effect as a formally valid alteration of the document as so subscribed,

but an alteration made to such a document otherwise than as mentioned in paragraphs (a) and (b) above shall not be formally valid.

(2)　Subsection (1) above is without prejudice to—

(a)　any rule of law enabling any provision in a testamentary document to be revoked by deletion or erasure without authentication of the deletion or erasure by the testator;

(b)　the Erasures in Deeds (Scotland) Act 1836 and section 54 of the Conveyancing (Scotland) Act 1874.

(3)　The fact that an alteration to a document was made before the document was subscribed by the granter of it, or by the granter first subscribing it, may be established by all relevant evidence, whether written or oral.

(4)　Where a document bears to have been subscribed by the granter or, if there is more than one granter, by all the granters of it, then, if subsection (5) or (6) below applies, an alteration made to the document shall be presumed to have been made before the document was subscribed by the granter or, if there is more than one granter, by the granter first subscribing it, and to form part of the document as so subscribed.

(5)  This subsection applies where—

(a)  the document is presumed under section 3 of this Act to have been subscribed by the granter or granters (as the case may be);

(b)  it is stated in the document, or in the testing clause or its equivalent, that the alteration was made before the document was subscribed; and

(c)  nothing in the document, or in the testing clause or its equivalent, indicates that the alteration was made after the document was subscribed.

(6)  This subsection applies where subsection (5) above does not apply, but the court is satisfied, on an application being made to it, that the alteration was made before the document was subscribed by the granter or, if there is more than one granter, by the granter first subscribing it, and causes the document to be endorsed with a certificate to that effect or, where the document has already been registered in the Books of Council and Session or in sheriff court books, grants decree to that effect.

(7)  Subsections (3), (4) and (6) of section 4 of this Act shall apply in relation to an application under subsection (6) above as they apply in relation to an application under subsection (1) of that section.

(8)  Where an alteration is made to a document after the document has been subscribed by a granter, Schedule 1 to this Act (presumptions as to granter's signature and date and place of signing in relation to such alterations) shall have effect.

## 6.  Registration of documents

(1)  Subject to subsection (3) below, it shall not be competent—

(a)  to record a document in the Register of Sasines; or

(b)  to register a document for execution or preservation in the Books of Council and Session or in sheriff court books,

unless subsection (2) below applies in relation to the document.

(2)  This subsection applies where—

(a)  the document is presumed under section 3 or 4 of this Act to have been subscribed by the granter; or

(b)  if there is more than one granter, the document is presumed under section 3 or 4 or partly under the one section and partly under the other to have been subscribed by at least one of the granters.

(3)  Subsection (1) above shall not apply in relation to—

(a)  the recording of a document in the Register of Sasines or the registration of a document in the Books of Council and Session or in sheriff court books, if such recording or registration is required or expressly permitted under any enactment;

(b)  the recording of a court decree in the Register of Sasines;

(c)  the registration in the Books of Council and Session or in sheriff court books of—

(i)  a testamentary document;

(ii)  a document which is directed by the Court of Session or (as the case may be) the sheriff to be so registered;

(iii)  a document whose formal validity is governed by a law other than Scots law, if the Keeper of the Registers of Scotland or (as the case may be) the sheriff clerk is satisfied that the document is formally valid according to the law governing such validity;

(iv)  a court decree granted under section 4 or 5 of this Act in relation to a document already registered in the Books of Council and Session or in sheriff court books (as the case may be); or

(d)  the registration of a court decree in a separate register maintained for that purpose.

(4) A document may be registered for preservation in the Books of Council and Session or in sheriff court books without a clause of consent to registration.

### 7. Subscription and signing

(1) Except where an enactment expressly provides otherwise, a document is subscribed by a granter of it if it is signed by him at the end of the last page (excluding any annexation, whether or not incorporated in the document as provided for in section 8 of this Act).

(2) Subject to paragraph 2(2) of Schedule 2 to this Act, a document, or an alteration to a document, is signed by an individual natural person as a granter or on behalf of a granter of it if it is signed by him—

(a) with the full name by which he is identified in the document or in any testing clause or its equivalent; or

(b) with his surname, preceded by at least one forename (or an initial or abbreviation or familiar form of a forename); or

(c) except for the purposes of section 3(1) to (7) of this Act, with a name (not in accordance with paragraph (a) or (b) above) or description or an initial or mark if it is established that the name, description, initial or mark—

(i) was his usual method of signing, or his usual method of signing documents or alterations of the type in question; or

(ii) was intended by him as his signature of the document or alteration.

(3) Where there is more than one granter, the requirement under subsection (1) above of signing at the end of the last page of a document shall be regarded as complied with if at least one granter signs at the end of the last page and any other granter signs on an additional page.

(4) Where a person grants a document in more than one capacity, one subscription of the document by him shall be sufficient to bind him in all such capacities.

(5) A document, or an alteration to a document, is signed by a witness if it is signed by him—

(a) with the full name by which he is identified in the document or in any testing clause or its equivalent; or

(b) with his surname, preceded by at least one forename (or an initial or abbreviation or familiar form of a forename),

and if the witness is witnessing the signature of more than one granter, it shall be unnecessary for him to sign the document or alteration more than once.

(6) This section is without prejudice to any rule of law relating to the subscription or signing of documents by members of the Royal Family, by peers or by the wives or the eldest sons of peers.

(7) Schedule 2 to this Act (special rules relating to subscription and signing of documents etc by partnerships, companies, [limited liability partnerships,] local authorities, other bodies corporate and Ministers) shall have effect.

### 8. Annexations to documents

(1) Subject to subsection (2) below and except where an enactment expressly otherwise provides, any annexation to a document shall be regarded as incorporated in the document if it is—

(a) referred to in the document; and

(b) identified on its face as being the annexation referred to in the document,

without the annexation having to be signed or subscribed.

(2) Where a document relates to land and an annexation to it describes or shows all or any part of the land to which the document relates, the annexation shall be regarded as incorporated in the document if and only if—

(a) it is referred to in the document; and

(b) it is identified on its face as being the annexation referred to in the document; and

(c) it is signed on—

(i)  each page, where it is a plan, drawing, photograph or other representation; or

(ii)  the last page, where it is an inventory, appendix, schedule or other writing.

(3)  Any annexation referred to in subsection (2) above which bears to have been signed by a granter of the document shall be presumed to have been signed by the person who subscribed the document as that granter.

(4)  Section 7(2) of this Act shall apply in relation to any annexation referred to in subsection (2) above as it applies in relation to a document as if for any reference to a document (except the reference in paragraph (a)) there were substituted a reference to an annexation.

(5)  It shall be competent to sign any annexation to a document at any time before the document is—

(a)  founded on in legal proceedings;

(b)  registered for preservation in the Books of Council and Session or in sheriff court books;

(c)  recorded in the Register of Sasines;

(d)  registered in the Land Register of Scotland.

(6)  Where there is more than one granter, the requirement under subsection (2)(c)(ii) above of signing on the last page shall be regarded as complied with (provided that at least one granter signs at the end of the last page) if any other granter signs on an additional page.

## 9.  Subscription on behalf of blind granter or granter unable to write

(1)  Where a granter of a document makes a declaration to a relevant person that he is blind or unable to write, the relevant person—

(a)  having read the document to that granter; or

(b)  if the granter makes a declaration that he does not wish him to do so, without having read it to the granter,

shall, if authorised by the granter, be entitled to subscribe it and, if it is a testamentary document, sign it as mentioned in section 3(2) of this Act, on the granter's behalf.

(2)  Subscription or signing by a relevant person under subsection (1) above shall take place in the presence of the granter.

(3)  This Act shall have effect in relation to subscription or signing by a relevant person under subsection (1) above subject to the modifications set out in Schedule 3 to this Act.

(4)  A document subscribed by a relevant person under subsection (1) above which confers on the relevant person or his spouse, son or daughter a benefit in money or money's worth (whether directly or indirectly) shall be invalid to the extent, but only to the extent, that it confers such benefit.

(5)  This section and Schedule 3 to this Act apply in relation to the signing of—

(a)  an annexation to a document as mentioned in section 8(2) of this Act;

(b)  an alteration made to a document or to any such annexation to a document,

as they apply in relation to the subscription of a document; and for that purpose, any reference to reading a document includes a reference to describing a plan, drawing, photograph or other representation in such an annexation or in an alteration to such an annexation.

(6)  In this Act 'relevant person' means a solicitor who has in force a practising certificate as defined in section 4(c) of the Solicitors (Scotland) Act 1980, an advocate, a justice of the peace or a sheriff clerk and, in relation to the execution of documents outwith Scotland, includes a notary public or any other person with official authority under the law of the place of execution to execute documents on behalf of persons who are blind or unable to write.

(7) Nothing in this section shall prevent the granter of a document who is blind from subscribing or signing the document as mentioned in section 7 of this Act.

## 10. Forms of testing clause

(1) Without prejudice to the effectiveness of any other means of providing information relating to the execution of a document, this information may be provided in such form of testing clause as may be prescribed in regulations made by the Secretary of State.

(2) Regulations under subsection (1) above shall be made by statutory instrument which shall be subject to annulment in pursuance of a resolution of either House of Parliament and may prescribe different forms for different cases or classes of case.

## 11. Abolition of proof by writ or oath, reference to oath and other common law rules

(1) Any rule of law and any enactment whereby the proof of any matter is restricted to proof by writ or by reference to oath shall cease to have effect.

(2) The procedure of proving any matter in any civil proceedings by reference to oath is hereby abolished.

(3) The following rules of law shall cease to have effect—

  (a) any rule whereby certain contracts and obligations and any variations of those contracts and obligations, and assignations of incorporeal moveables, are required to be in writing; and

  (b) any rule which confers any privilege—

    (i) on a document which is holograph or adopted as holograph; or

    (ii) on a writ *in re mercatoria*.

(4) Subsections (1) and (2) above shall not apply in relation to proceedings commenced before the commencement of this Act.

## 12. Interpretation

(1) In this Act, except where the context otherwise requires—

'alteration' includes interlineation, marginal addition, deletion, substitution, erasure or anything written on erasure;

'annexation' includes any inventory, appendix, schedule, other writing, plan, drawing, photograph or other representation annexed to a document;

'authorised' means expressly or impliedly authorised and any reference to a person authorised to sign includes a reference to a person authorised to sign generally or in relation to a particular document;

'company' has the same meaning as in section 735(1) of the Companies Act 1985;

'decree' includes a judgment or order, or an official certified copy, abbreviate or extract of a decree;

'director' includes any person occupying the position of director, by whatever name he is called;

'document' includes any annexation which is incorporated in it under section 8 of this Act and any reference, however expressed, to the signing of a document includes a reference to the signing of an annexation;

'enactment' includes an enactment contained in a statutory instrument [and an enactment comprised in, or in an instrument made under, an Act of the Scottish Parliament];

'governing board', in relation to a body corporate to which paragraph 5 of Schedule 2 to this Act applies, means any governing body, however described;

'local authority' means a local authority within the meaning of section 235(1) of the Local Government (Scotland) Act 1973 and a council constituted under section 2 of the Local Government etc. (Scotland) Act 1994;

'Minister' has the same meaning as 'Minister of the Crown' has in section 8 of the Ministers of the Crown Act 1975 [and also includes a Member of the Scottish Executive];

'office-holder' does not include a Minister but, subject to that, means—

(a)    the holder of an office created or continued in existence by a public general Act of Parliament;

(b)    the holder of an office the remuneration in respect of which is paid out of money provided by Parliament [or out of the Scottish Consolidated Fund];

(c)    the registrar of companies within the meaning of the Companies Act 1985;

'officer'—

(a)    in relation to a Minister, means any person in the civil service of the Crown who is serving in his Department [or as the case may be, as a member of the staff of the Scottish Ministers or the Lord Advocate];

(b)    in relation to an office-holder, means any member of his staff, or any person in the civil service of the Crown who has been assigned or appointed to assist him in the exercise of his functions;

'proper officer', in relation to a local authority, has the same meaning as in section 235(3) of the Local Government (Scotland) Act 1973; and

'secretary' means, if there are two or more joint secretaries, any one of them.

(2)    Any reference in this Act to subscription or signing by a granter of a document or an alteration made to a document, in a case where a person is subscribing or signing under a power of attorney on behalf of the granter, shall be construed as a reference to subscription or signing by that person of the document or alteration.

## 13.    Application of Act to Crown

(1)    Nothing in this Act shall—

(a)    prevent Her Majesty from authenticating—

(i)    a document by superscription; or

(ii)    a document relating to her private estates situated or arising in Scotland in accordance with section 6 of the Crown Private Estates Act 1862;

(b)    prevent authentication under the Writs Act 1672 of a document passing the seal appointed by the Treaty of Union to be kept and used in Scotland in place of the Great Seal of Scotland formerly in use; or

(c)    prevent any document mentioned in paragraph (a) or (b) above authenticated as aforesaid from being recorded in the Register of Sasines or registered for execution or preservation in the Books of Council and Session or in sheriff court books.

(2)    Nothing in this Act shall prevent a Crown writ from being authenticated or recorded in Chancery under section 78 of the Titles to Land Consolidation (Scotland) Act 1868.

(3)    Subject to subsections (1) and (2) above, this Act binds the Crown.

## 14.    Minor and consequential amendments, repeals, transitional provisions and savings

(1)    The enactments mentioned in Schedule 4 to this Act shall have effect subject to the minor and consequential amendments specified in that Schedule.

(2)    The enactments mentioned in Schedule 5 to this Act are hereby repealed to the extent specified in the third column of that Schedule.

(3)    Subject to subsection (4) below and without prejudice to subsection (5) below and section 11(4) of this Act, nothing in this Act shall—

(a)    apply to any document executed or anything done before the commencement of this Act; or

(b)    affect the operation, in relation to any document executed before such commencement, of any procedure for establishing the authenticity of such a document.

(4) In the repeal of the Blank Bonds and Trusts Act 1696 (provided for in Schedule 5 to this Act), the repeal of the words from 'And farder' to the end—

(a) shall have effect in relation to a deed of trust, whether executed before or after the commencement of this Act; but

(b) notwithstanding paragraph (a) above, shall not have effect in relation to proceedings commenced before the commencement of this Act in which a question arises as to the deed of trust.

(5) The repeal of certain provisions of the Lyon King of Arms Act 1672 (provided for in Schedule 5 to this Act) shall not affect any right of a person to add a territorial designation to his signature or the jurisdiction of the Lord Lyon King of Arms in relation to any such designation.

(6) For the purposes of this Act, if it cannot be ascertained whether a document was executed before or after the commencement of this Act, there shall be a presumption that it was executed after such commencement.

### 15. Short title, commencement and extent

(1) This Act may be cited as the Requirements of Writing (Scotland) Act 1995.

(2) This Act shall come into force at the end of the period of three months beginning with the date on which it is passed.

(3) This Act extends to Scotland only.

## SCHEDULES

## SCHEDULE 1. ALTERATIONS MADE TO A DOCUMENT AFTER IT HAS BEEN SUBSCRIBED

*Presumption as to granter's signature or date or place of signing*

1.—(1) Subject to sub-paragraphs (2) to (7) below, where—

(a) an alteration to a document bears to have been signed by a granter of the document;

(b) the alteration bears to have been signed by a person as a witness of that granter's signature and the alteration, or the testing clause or its equivalent, bears to state the name and address of the witness; and

(c) nothing in the document or alteration, or in the testing clause or its equivalent, indicates—

(i) that the alteration was not signed by that granter as it bears to have been so signed; or

(ii) that it was not validly witnessed for any reason specified in paragraphs (a) to (e) of sub-paragraph (4) below,

the alteration shall be presumed to have been signed by that granter.

(2) Where an alteration to a testamentary document consists of more than one sheet, the alteration shall not be presumed to have been signed by a granter as mentioned in sub-paragraph (1) above unless, in addition to it bearing to have been signed by him on the last sheet and otherwise complying with that sub-paragraph, it bears to have been signed by him on every other sheet.

(3) For the purposes of sub-paragraph (1)(b) above—

(a) the name and address of a witness may be added at any time before the alteration is—

(i) founded on in legal proceedings; or

(ii) registered for preservation in the Books of Council and Session or in sheriff court books; and

(b)   the name and address of a witness need not be written by the witness himself.

(4)   Where, in any proceedings relating to an alteration to a document in which a question arises as to a granter's signature, it is established—

(a)   that a signature bearing to be the signature of the witness of that granter's signature is not such a signature, whether by reason of forgery or otherwise;

(b)   that the person who signed the alteration as the witness of that granter's signature is a person who is named in the document as a granter of the document;

(c)   that the person who signed the alteration as the witness of that granter's signature, at the time of signing—

(i)   did not know the granter;

(ii)   was under the age of 16 years; or

(iii)   was mentally incapable of acting as a witness;

(d)   that the person who signed the alteration, purporting to be the witness of that granter's signature, did not witness such signature;

(e)   that the person who signed the alteration as the witness of that granter's signature did not sign the alteration after him or that the signing of the alteration by the granter or, as the case may be, the granter's acknowledgement of his signature and the signing by the person as witness were not one continuous process;

(f)   that the name or address of the witness of that granter's signature was added after the alteration was founded on or registered as mentioned in sub-paragraph (3)(a) above or is erroneous in any material respect; or

(g)   in the case of an alteration to a testamentary document consisting of more than one sheet, that a signature on any sheet of the alteration bearing to be the signature of the granter is not such a signature, whether by reason of forgery or otherwise,

then, for the purposes of those proceedings, there shall be no presumption that the alteration has been signed by that granter.

(5)   For the purposes of sub-paragraph (4)(c)(i) above, the witness shall be regarded as having known the person whose signature he has witnessed at the time of witnessing if he had credible information at that time of his identity.

(6)   For the purposes of sub-paragraph (4)(e) above, where—

(a)   an alteration to a document is made by more than one granter; and

(b)   a person is the witness to the signature of more than one granter,

the signing of the alteration by any such granter or the acknowledgement of his signature and the signing by the person witnessing that granter's signature shall not be regarded as not being one continuous process by reason only that, between the time of signing or acknowledgement by that granter and of signing by that witness, another granter has signed the alteration or acknowledged his signature.

(7)   For the purposes of the foregoing provisions of this paragraph a person witnesses a granter's signature of an alteration—

(a)   if he sees the granter sign it; or

(b)   if the granter acknowledges his signature to that person.

(8)   Where—

(a)   by virtue of sub-paragraph (1) above an alteration to a document to which this sub-paragraph applies is presumed to have been signed by a granter of the document;

(b)   the alteration, or the testing clause or its equivalent, bears to state the date or place of signing of the alteration by that granter; and

(c)   nothing in the document or alteration, or in the testing clause or its equivalent, indicates that that statement as to date or place is incorrect, there shall be a presumption that the alteration was signed by that granter on the date or at the place as stated.

(9) Sub-paragraph (8) above applies to any document other than a testamentary document.

(10) Where—

(a) an alteration to a testamentary document bears to have been signed and the alteration, or the testing clause or its equivalent, bears to state the date or place of signing (whether or not it is presumed under sub-paragraphs (1) to (7) above to have been signed by a granter of the document); and

(b) nothing in the document or alteration, or in the testing clause or its equivalent, indicates that that statement as to date or place is incorrect,

there shall be a presumption that the statement as to date or place is correct.

*Presumption as to granter's signature or date or place of signing when established in court proceedings*

2.—(1) Where an alteration to a document bears to have been signed by a granter of the document, but there is no presumption under paragraph 1 above that the alteration has been signed by that granter, then, if the court, on an application being made to it by any person having an interest in the document, is satisfied that the alteration was signed by that granter, it shall—

(a) cause the document to be endorsed with a certificate to that effect; or

(b) where the document has already been registered in the Books of Council and Session or in sheriff court books, grant decree to that effect.

(2) Where an alteration to a document bears to have been signed by a granter of the document, but there is no presumption under paragraph 1 above as to the date or place of signing, then, if the court, on an application being made to it by any person having an interest in the document, is satisfied as to the date or place of signing, it shall—

(a) cause the document to be endorsed with a certificate to that effect; or

(b) where the document has already been registered in the Books of Council and Session or in sheriff court books, grant decree to that effect.

(3) In relation to an application under sub-paragraph (1) or (2) above evidence shall, unless the court otherwise directs, be given by affidavit.

(4) An application under sub-paragraph (1) or (2) above may be made either as a summary application or as incidental to and in the course of other proceedings.

(5) The effect of a certificate or decree—

(a) under sub-paragraph (1) above shall be to establish a presumption that the alteration has been signed by the granter concerned;

(b) under sub-paragraph (2) above shall be to establish a presumption that the statement in the certificate or decree as to date or place is correct.

(6) In this paragraph 'the court' means—

(a) in the case of a summary application—

(i) the sheriff in whose sheriffdom the applicant resides; or

(ii) if the applicant does not reside in Scotland, the sheriff at Edinburgh; and

(b) in the case of an application made in the course of other proceedings, the court before which those proceedings are pending.

SCHEDULE 2. SUBSCRIPTION AND SIGNING: SPECIAL CASES

*General*

1. Any reference in this Act to subscription or signing by a granter of a document or an alteration to a document, in a case where the granter is a person to whom any of paragraphs 2 to 6 of this Schedule applies shall, unless

the context otherwise requires, be construed as a reference to subscription or, as the case may be, signing of the document or alteration by a person in accordance with that paragraph.

### Partnerships

2.—(1) Except where an enactment expressly provides otherwise, where a granter of a document is a partnership, the document is signed by the partnership if it is signed on its behalf by a partner or by a person authorised to sign the document on its behalf.

(2) A person signing on behalf of a partnership under this paragraph may use his own name or the firm name.

(3) Sub-paragraphs (1) and (2) of this paragraph apply in relation to the signing of an alteration made to a document as they apply in relation to the signing of a document.

(4) In this paragraph 'partnership' has the same meaning as in section 1 of the Partnership Act 1890.

### Companies

3.—(1) Except where an enactment expressly provides otherwise, where a granter of a document is a company, the document is signed by the company if it is signed on its behalf by a director, or by the secretary, of the company or by a person authorised to sign the document on its behalf.

(2) This Act is without prejudice to—

(a) section 283(3) of the Companies Act 1985; and

(b) paragraph 9 of Schedule 1, paragraph 9 of Schedule 2, and paragraph 7 of Schedule 4, to the Insolvency Act 1986.

(3) Sub-paragraphs (1) and (2) of this paragraph apply in relation to the signing of an alteration made to a document as they apply in relation to the signing of a document.

(4) Where a granter of a document is a company, section 3 of and Schedule 1 to this Act shall have effect subject to the modifications set out in sub-paragraphs (5) and (6) below.

(5) In section 3—

(a) for subsection (1) there shall be substituted the following subsections—

'(1) Subject to subsections (1A) to (7) below, where—

(a) a document bears to have been subscribed on behalf of a company by a director, or by the secretary, of the company or by a person bearing to have been authorised to subscribe the document on its behalf;

(b) the document bears to have been signed by a person as a witness of the subscription of the director, secretary or other person subscribing on behalf of the company and to state the name and address of the witness; and

(c) nothing in the document, or in the testing clause or its equivalent, indicates—

(i) that it was not subscribed on behalf of the company as it bears to have been so subscribed; or

(ii) that it was not validly witnessed for any reason specified in paragraphs (a) to (e) of subsection (4) below,

the document shall be presumed to have been subscribed by the company.

(1A) Where a document does not bear to have been signed by a person as a witness of the subscription of the director, secretary or other

person subscribing on behalf of the company it shall be presumed to have
been subscribed by the company if it bears to have been subscribed on
behalf of the company by—

    (a)   two directors of the company; or

    (b)   a director and secretary of the company; or

    (c)   two persons bearing to have been authorised to subscribe the
document on its behalf.

    (1B)  For the purposes of subsection (1)(b) above, the name and address
of the witness may bear to be stated in the document itself or in the
testing clause or its equivalent.

    (1C)  A presumption under subsection (1) or (1A) above as to
subscription of a document does not include a presumption—

    (a)   that a person bearing to subscribe the document as a director or
the secretary of the company was such director or secretary; or

    (b)   that a person subscribing the document on behalf of the
company bearing to have been authorised to do so was authorised to do
so.';

  (b)  in subsection (4) after paragraph (g) there shall be inserted the
following paragraph—

    '(h)  if the document does not bear to have been witnessed, but bears
to have been subscribed on behalf of the company by two of the directors
of the company, or by a director and secretary of the company, or by two
authorised persons, that a signature bearing to be the signature of a
director, secretary or authorised person is not such a signature, whether
by reason of forgery or otherwise;'.

  (6)  In paragraph 1 of Schedule 1—

  (a)  for sub-paragraph (1) there shall be substituted the following sub-
paragraphs—

    '(1)  Subject to sub-paragraphs (1A) to (7) below, where—

    (a)   an alteration to a document bears to have been signed on behalf
of a company by a director, or by the secretary, of the company or by a
person bearing to have been authorised to sign the alteration on its
behalf;

    (b)   the alteration bears to have been signed by a person as a witness
of the signature of the director, secretary or other person signing on
behalf of the company and to state the name and address of the
witness; and

    (c)   nothing in the document or alteration, or in the testing clause or
its equivalent, indicates—

       (i)   that the alteration was not signed on behalf of the company
as it bears to have been so signed; or

       (ii)  that the alteration was not validly witnessed for any reason
specified in paragraphs (a) to (e) of sub-paragraph (4) below,

the alteration shall be presumed to have been signed by the company.

    (1A)  Where an alteration does not bear to have been signed by a
person as a witness of the signature of the director, secretary or other
person signing on behalf of the company it shall be presumed to have
been signed by the company if it bears to have been signed on behalf of
the company by—

    (a)   two directors of the company; or

    (b)   a director and secretary of the company; or

    (c)   two persons bearing to have been authorised to sign the
alteration on its behalf.

    (1B)  For the purposes of sub-paragraph (1)(b) above, the name and
address of the witness may bear to be stated in the alteration itself or in
the testing clause or its equivalent.

(1C)  A presumption under sub-paragraph (1) or (1A) above as to signing of an alteration to a document does not include a presumption—

(a)  that a person bearing to sign the alteration as a director or the secretary of the company was such director or secretary; or

(b)  that a person signing the alteration on behalf of the company bearing to have been authorised to do so was authorised to do so.';

(b)  in sub-paragraph (4) after paragraph (g) there shall be inserted the following paragraph—

'(h)  if the alteration does not bear to have been witnessed, but bears to have been signed on behalf of the company by two of the directors of the company, or by a director and secretary of the company, or by two authorised persons, that a signature bearing to be the signature of a director, secretary or authorised person is not such a signature, whether by reason of forgery or otherwise;'.

*[Limited liability partnerships*

3A.  (1)  Except where an enactment expressly provides otherwise, where a granter of a document is a limited liability partnership, the document is signed by the limited liability partnership if it is signed on its behalf by a member of the limited liability partnership.

(2)  This Act is without prejudice to paragraph 9 of Schedule 1, paragraph 9 of Schedule 2, and paragraph 7 of Schedule 4, to the Insolvency Act 1986.

(3)  Sub-paragraphs (1) and (2) of this paragraph apply in relation to the signing of an alteration made to a document as they apply in relation to the signing of a document.

(4)  Where a granter of a document is a limited liability partnership, section 3 of and Schedule 1 to this Act shall have effect subject to the modifications set out in sub-paragraphs (5) and (6) below.

(5)  In section 3—

(a)  for subsection (1) there shall be substituted the following subsections—

'(1)  Subject to subsections (1A) to (7) below, where—

(a)  a document bears to have been subscribed on behalf of a limited liability partnership by a member of the limited liability partnership;

(b)  the document bears to have been signed by a person as a witness of the subscription of the member of the limited liability partnership and to state the name and address of the witness; and

(c)  nothing in the document, or in the testing clause or its equivalent, indicates—

(i)  that it was not subscribed on behalf of the limited liability partnership as it bears to have been so subscribed; or

(ii)  that it was not validly witnessed for any reason specified in paragraphs (a) to (e) of subsection (4) below,

the document shall be presumed to have been subscribed by the limited liability partnership.

(1A)  Where a document does not bear to have been signed by a person as a witness of the subscription of the member of the limited liability partnership it shall be presumed to have been subscribed by the limited liability partnership if it bears to have been subscribed on behalf of the limited liability partnership by two members of the limited liability partnership.

(1B)  A presumption under subsection (1) or (1A) above as to subscription of a document does not include a presumption that a person bearing to subscribe the document as a member of the limited liability partnership was such member.'

(b)  in subsection (4) after paragraph (g) there shall be inserted the following paragraph—

'(h)  if the document does not bear to have been witnessed, but bears to have been subscribed on behalf of the limited liability partnership by two of the members of the limited liability partnership, that a signature bearing to be the signature of a member is not such a signature, whether by reason of forgery or otherwise;'

(6)  In paragraph 1 of Schedule 1—

(a)  for sub-paragraph (1) there shall be substituted the following sub-paragraphs—

'(1)  Subject to sub-paragraphs (1A) to (7) below, where—

(a)  an alteration to a document bears to have been signed on behalf of a limited liability partnership by a member of the limited liability partnership;

(b)  the alteration bears to have been signed by a person as a witness of the signature of the member of the limited liability partnership and to state the name and address of the witness; and

(c)  nothing in the document or alteration, or in the testing clause or its equivalent, indicates—

(i)  that the alteration was not signed on behalf of the limited liability partnership as it bears to have been so signed; or

(ii)  that the alteration was not validly witnessed for any reason specified in paragraphs (a) to (e) of sub-paragraph (4) below,

the alteration shall be presumed to have been signed by the limited liability partnership.

(1A)  Where an alteration does not bear to have been signed by a person as a witness of the signature of the member of the limited liability partnership it shall be presumed to have been signed by the limited liability partnership if it bears to have been signed on behalf of the limited liability partnership by two members of the limited liability partnership.

(1B)  For the purposes of sub-paragraph (1)(b) above, the name and address of the witness may bear to be stated in the alteration itself or in the testing clause or its equivalent.

(1C)  A presumption under sub-paragraph (1) or (1A) above as to signing of an alteration to a document does not include a presumption that a person bearing to sign the alteration as a member of the limited liability partnership was such member';

(b)  in sub-paragraph (4) after paragraph (g) there shall be inserted the following—

'; or

(h)  if the alteration does not bear to have been witnessed, but bears to have been signed on behalf of the limited liability partnership by two of the members of the limited liability partnership, that a signature bearing to be the signature of a member is not such a signature, whether by reason of forgery or otherwise;']

*Local authorities*

4.—(1)  Except where an enactment expressly provides otherwise, where a granter of a document is a local authority, the document is signed by the authority if it is signed on their behalf by the proper officer of the authority.

(2)  For the purposes of the signing of a document under this paragraph, a

person purporting to sign on behalf of a local authority as an officer of the authority shall be presumed to be the proper officer of the authority.

(3) Sub-paragraphs (1) and (2) of this paragraph apply in relation to the signing of an alteration made to a document as they apply in relation to the signing of a document.

(4) Where a granter of a document is a local authority, section 3 of and Schedule 1 to this Act shall have effect subject to the modifications set out in sub-paragraphs (5) to (8) below.

(5) For section 3(1) there shall be substituted the following subsections—

'(1) Subject to subsections (1A) to (7) below, where—

(a) a document bears to have been subscribed on behalf of a local authority by the proper officer of the authority;

(b) the document bears—

(i) to have been signed by a person as a witness of the proper officer's subscription and to state the name and address of the witness; or

(ii) (if the subscription is not so witnessed), to have been sealed with the common seal of the authority; and

(c) nothing in the document, or in the testing clause or its equivalent, indicates—

(i) that it was not subscribed on behalf of the authority as it bears to have been so subscribed; or

(ii) that it was not validly witnessed for any reason specified in paragraphs (a) to (e) of subsection (4) below or that it was not sealed as it bears to have been sealed or that it was not validly sealed for the reason specified in subsection (4)(h) below,

the document shall be presumed to have been subscribed by the proper officer and by the authority.

(1A) For the purposes of subsection (1)(b)(i) above, the name and address of the witness may bear to be stated in the document itself or in the testing clause or its equivalent.'.

(6) In section 3(4) after paragraph (g) there shall be inserted the following paragraph—

'(h) if the document does not bear to have been witnessed, but bears to have been sealed with the common seal of the authority, that it was sealed by a person without authority to do so or was not sealed on the date on which it was subscribed on behalf of the authority;'.

(7) For paragraph 1(1) of Schedule 1 there shall be substituted the following sub-paragraphs—

'(1) Subject to sub-paragraphs (1A) to (7) below, where—

(a) an alteration to a document bears to have been signed on behalf of a local authority by the proper officer of the authority;

(b) the alteration bears—

(i) to have been signed by a person as a witness of the proper officer's signature and to state the name and address of the witness; or

(ii) (if the signature is not so witnessed), to have been sealed with the common seal of the authority; and

(c) nothing in the document or alteration, or in the testing clause or its equivalent, indicates—

(i) that the alteration was not signed on behalf of the authority as it bears to have been so signed; or

(ii) that the alteration was not validly witnessed for any reason specified in paragraphs (a) to (e) of sub-paragraph (4) below or that it was not sealed as it bears to have been sealed or that it was not validly sealed for the reason specified in sub-paragraph (4)(h) below, the alteration shall be presumed to have been signed by the proper officer and by the authority.

(1A) For the purposes of sub-paragraph (1)(b)(i) above, the name and address of the witness may bear to be stated in the alteration itself or in the testing clause or its equivalent.'.

(8) In paragraph 1(4) of Schedule 1 after paragraph (g) there shall be inserted the following paragraph—

'(h) if the alteration does not bear to have been witnessed, but bears to have been sealed with the common seal of the authority, that it was sealed by a person without authority to do so or was not sealed on the date on which it was signed on behalf of the authority;'.

*Other bodies corporate*

5.—(1) This paragraph applies to any body corporate other than a company or a local authority.

(2) Except where an enactment expressly provides otherwise, where a granter of a document is a body corporate to which this paragraph applies, the document is signed by the body if it is signed on its behalf by—

(a) a member of the body's governing board or, if there is no governing board, a member of the body;

(b) the secretary of the body by whatever name he is called; or

(c) a person authorised to sign the document on behalf of the body.

(3) Sub-paragraphs (1) and (2) of this paragraph apply in relation to the signing of an alteration made to a document as they apply in relation to the signing of a document.

(4) Where a granter of a document is a body corporate to which this paragraph applies, section 3 of and Schedule 1 to this Act shall have effect subject to the modifications set out in sub-paragraphs (5) to (8) below.

(5) For section 3(1) there shall be substituted the following subsections—

'(1) Subject to subsections (1A) to (7) below, where—

(a) a document bears to have been subscribed on behalf of a body corporate to which paragraph 5 of Schedule 2 to this Act applies by—

(i) a member of the body's governing board or, if there is no governing board, a member of the body;

(ii) the secretary of the body; or

(iii) a person bearing to have been authorised to subscribe the document on its behalf;

(b) the document bears—

(i) to have been signed by a person as a witness of the subscription of the member, secretary or other person signing on behalf of the body and to state the name and address of the witness; or

(ii) (if the subscription is not so witnessed), to have been sealed with the common seal of the body; and

(c) nothing in the document, or in the testing clause or its equivalent, indicates—

(i) that it was not subscribed on behalf of the body as it bears to have been so subscribed; or

(ii) that it was not validly witnessed for any reason specified in paragraphs (a) to (e) of subsection (4) below or that it was not sealed as it bears to have been sealed or that it was not validly sealed for the reason specified in subsection (4)(h) below,

the document shall be presumed to have been subscribed by the member, secretary or authorised person (as the case may be) and by the body.

(1A)  For the purposes of subsection (1)(b)(i) above, the name and address of the witness may bear to be stated in the document itself or in the testing clause or its equivalent.

(1B)  A presumption under subsection (1) above as to subscription of a document does not include a presumption—

(a)  that a person bearing to subscribe the document as a member of the body's governing board, a member of the body or the secretary of the body was such member or secretary; or

(b)  that a person subscribing the document on behalf of the body bearing to have been authorised to do so was authorised to do so.'.

(6)  In section 3(4) after paragraph (g) there shall be inserted the following paragraph—

'(h)  if the document does not bear to have been witnessed, but bears to have been sealed with the common seal of the body, that it was sealed by a person without authority to do so or was not sealed on the date on which it was subscribed on behalf of the body;'.

(7)  For paragraph 1(1) of Schedule 1 there shall be substituted the following sub-paragraphs—

'(1)  Subject to sub-paragraphs (1A) to (7) below, where—

(a)  an alteration to a document bears to have been signed on behalf of a body corporate to which paragraph 5 of Schedule 2 to this Act applies by—

(i)  a member of the body's governing board or, if there is no governing board, a member of the body;

(ii)  the secretary of the body; or

(iii)  a person bearing to have been authorised to sign the alteration on its behalf,

(b)  the alteration bears—

(i)  to have been signed by a person as a witness of the signature of the member, secretary or other person signing on behalf of the body and to state the name and address of the witness; or

(ii)  (if the signature is not so witnessed), to have been sealed with the common seal of the body; and

(c)  nothing in the document or alteration, or in the testing clause or its equivalent, indicates—

(i)  that the alteration was not signed on behalf of the body as it bears to have been so signed; or

(ii)  that the alteration was not validly witnessed for any reason specified in paragraphs (a) to (e) of sub-paragraph (4) below or that it was not sealed as it bears to have been sealed or that it was not validly sealed for the reason specified in sub-paragraph (4)(h) below,

the alteration shall be presumed to have been signed by the member, secretary or authorised person (as the case may be) and by the body.

(1A)  For the purposes of sub-paragraph (1)(b)(i) above, the name and address of the witness may bear to be stated in the alteration itself or in the testing clause or its equivalent.

(1B)  A presumption under sub-paragraph (1) above as to signing of an alteration to a document does not include a presumption—

(a)  that a person bearing to sign the alteration as a member of the body's governing board, a member of the body or the secretary of the body was such member or secretary; or

(b)  that a person signing the alteration on behalf of the body bearing to have been authorised to do so was authorised to do so.'.

(8)  In paragraph 1(4) of Schedule 1 after paragraph (g) there shall be inserted the following paragraph—

'(h)   if the alteration does not bear to have been witnessed, but bears to have been sealed with the common seal of the body, that it was sealed by a person without authority to do so or was not sealed on the date on which it was signed on behalf of the body;'.

*Ministers of the Crown and office-holders*

6.—(1)   Except where an enactment expressly provides otherwise, where a granter of a document is a Minister or an office-holder, the document is signed by the Minister or office-holder if it is signed—
   (a)   by him personally; or
   (b)   in a case where by virtue of any enactment or rule of law a document by a Minister may be signed by an officer of his or by any other Minister, by that officer or by that other Minister as the case may be; or
   (c)   in a case where by virtue of any enactment or rule of law a document by an office-holder may be signed by an officer of his, by that officer; or
   (d)   by any other person authorised to sign the document on his behalf.
   (2)   For the purposes of the signing of a document under this paragraph, a person purporting to sign—
   (a)   as an officer as mentioned in sub-paragraph (1)(b) or (1)(c) above;
   (b)   as another Minister as mentioned in sub-paragraph (1)(b) above;
   (c)   as a person authorised as mentioned in sub-paragraph (1)(d) above,
shall be presumed to be the officer, other Minister or authorised person, as the case may be.
   (3)   Sub-paragraphs (1) and (2) of this paragraph are without prejudice to section 3 of and Schedule 1 to the Ministers of the Crown Act 1975.
   (4)   Sub-paragraphs (1) to (3) of this paragraph apply in relation to the signing of an alteration made to a document as they apply in relation to the signing of a document.
   (5)   Where a granter of a document is a Minister or office-holder, section 3 of and Schedule 1 to this Act shall have effect subject to the modifications set out in sub-paragraphs (6) and (7) below.
   (6)   For section 3(1) there shall be substituted the following subsections—
   '(1)   Subject to subsections (1A) to (7) below, where—
      (a)   a document bears to have been subscribed—
         (i)   by a Minister or, in a case where by virtue of any enactment or rule of law a document by a Minister may be signed by an officer of his or by any other Minister, by that officer or by that other Minister; or
         (ii)   by an office-holder or, in a case where by virtue of any enactment or rule of law a document by an office-holder may be signed by an officer of his, by that officer; or
         (iii)   by any other person bearing to have been authorised to subscribe the document on behalf of the Minister or office-holder;
      (b)   the document bears to have been signed by a person as a witness of the subscription mentioned in paragraph (a) above and to state the name and address of the witness; and
      (c)   nothing in the document, or in the testing clause or its equivalent, indicates—
         (i)   that it was not subscribed as it bears to have been subscribed; or
         (ii)   that it was not validly witnessed for any reason specified in paragraphs (a) to (e) of subsection (4) below,
   the document shall be presumed to have been subscribed by the officer, other Minister or authorised person and by the Minister or office-holder, as the case may be.

(1A)  For the purposes of subsection (1)(b) above, the name and address of the witness may bear to be stated in the document itself or in the testing clause or its equivalent.'.

(7)  For paragraph 1(1) of Schedule 1 there shall be substituted the following sub-paragraphs—

'(1)  Subject to sub-paragraphs (1A) to (7) below, where—

(a)  an alteration to a document bears to have been signed by—

(i)  a Minister or, in a case where by virtue of any enactment or rule of law a document by a Minister may be signed by an officer of his or by any other Minister, by that officer or by that other Minister; or

(ii)  an office-holder or, in a case where by virtue of any enactment or rule of law a document by an office-holder may be signed by an officer of his, by that officer; or

(iii)  any other person bearing to have been authorised to sign the alteration on behalf of the Minister or office-holder;

(b)  the alteration bears to have been signed by a person as a witness of the signature mentioned in paragraph (a) above and to state the name and address of the witness; and

(c)  nothing in the document or alteration, or in the testing clause or its equivalent, indicates—

(i)  that the alteration was not signed as it bears to have been signed; or

(ii)  that the alteration was not validly witnessed for any reason specified in paragraphs (a) to (e) of sub-paragraph (4) below,

the alteration shall be presumed to have been signed by the officer, other Minister or authorised person and by the Minister or office-holder, as the case may be.

(1A)  For the purposes of sub-paragraph (1)(b) above, the name and address of the witness may bear to be stated in the alteration itself or in the testing clause or its equivalent.'.

## SCHEDULE 3. MODIFICATIONS OF THIS ACT IN RELATION TO SUBSCRIPTION OR SIGNING BY RELEVANT PERSON UNDER SECTION 9

1.  For any reference to the subscription or signing of a document by a granter there shall be substituted a reference to such subscription or signing by a relevant person under section 9(1).

2.  For section 3(1) there shall be substituted the following subsection—

'(1)  Subject to subsections (2) to (6) below, where—

(a)  a document bears to have been subscribed by a relevant person with the authority of a granter of it;

(b)  the document, or the testing clause or its equivalent, states that the document was read to that granter by the relevant person before such subscription or states that it was not so read because the granter made a declaration that he did not wish him to do so;

(c)  the document bears to have been signed by a person as a witness of the relevant person's subscription and the document, or the testing clause or its equivalent, bears to state the name and address of the witness; and

(d)  nothing in the document, or in the testing clause or its equivalent, indicates—

(i)  that it was not subscribed by the relevant person as it bears to have been so subscribed;

(ii)  that the statement mentioned in paragraph (b) above is incorrect; or

(iii)   that it was not validly witnessed for any reason specified in paragraphs (a) to (e) of subsection (4) below (as modified by paragraph 4 of Schedule 3 to this Act),

the document shall be presumed to have been subscribed by the relevant person and the statement so mentioned shall be presumed to be correct.'.

**3.**   In section 3(3) for the words 'subsection (1)(b)' there shall be substituted the words 'subsection (1)(c)'.

**4.**   For section 3(4) there shall be substituted the following subsection—

'(4)   Where, in any proceedings relating to a document in which a question arises as to a relevant person's subscription on behalf of a granter under section 9(1) of this Act, it is established—

(a)   that a signature bearing to be the signature of the witness of the relevant person's subscription is not such a signature, whether by reason of forgery or otherwise;

(b)   that the person who signed the document as the witness of the relevant person's subscription is a person who is named in the document as a granter of it;

(c)   that the person who signed the document as the witness of the relevant person's subscription, at the time of signing—

(i)   did not know the granter on whose behalf the relevant person had so subscribed;

(ii)   was under the age of 16 years; or

(iii)   was mentally incapable of acting as a witness;

(d)   that the person who signed the document, purporting to be the witness of the relevant person's subscription, did not see him subscribe it;

(dd)   that the person who signed the document as the witness of the relevant person's subscription did not witness the granting of authority by the granter concerned to the relevant person to subscribe the document on his behalf or did not witness the reading of the document to the granter by the relevant person or the declaration that the granter did not wish him to do so;

(e)   that the person who signed the document as the witness of the relevant person's subscription did not sign the document after him or that such subscription and signature were not one continuous process;

(f)   that the name or address of such a witness was added after the document was founded on or registered as mentioned in subsection (3)(a) above or is erroneous in any material respect; or

(g)   in the case of a testamentary document consisting of more than one sheet, that a signature on any sheet bearing to be the signature of the relevant person is not such a signature, whether by reason of forgery or otherwise,

then, for the purposes of those proceedings, there shall be no presumption that the document has been subscribed by the relevant person on behalf of the granter concerned.'.

**5.**   In section 3(6) the words 'or acknowledgement' in both places where they occur shall be omitted.

**6.**   Section 3(7) shall be omitted.

**7.**   For section 4(1) there shall be substituted the following subsection—

'(1)   Where—

(a)   a document bears to have been subscribed by a relevant person under section 9(1) of this Act on behalf of a granter of it; but

(b)   there is no presumption under section 3 of this Act (as modified by paragraph 2 of Schedule 3 to this Act) that the document has been subscribed by that person or that the procedure referred to section 3(1)(b) of this Act as so modified was followed,

then, if the court, on an application being made to it by any person who has an interest in the document, is satisfied that the document was so subscribed by the relevant person with the authority of the granter and that the relevant person read the document to the granter before subscription or did not so read it because the granter declared that he did not wish him to do so, it shall—

(i)  cause the document to be endorsed with a certificate to that effect; or

(ii)  where the document has already been registered in the Books of Council and Session or in sheriff court books, grant decree to that effect.'.

8.  At the end of section 4(5)(a) there shall be added the following words—
'and that the procedure referred to in section 3(1)(b) of this Act as modified by paragraph 2 of Schedule 3 to this Act was followed.'.

9.  For paragraph 1(1) of Schedule 1 there shall be substituted the following sub-paragraph—
'(1)  Subject to sub-paragraphs (2) to (6) below, where—

(a)  an alteration to a document bears to have been signed by a relevant person with the authority of a granter of the document;

(b)  the document or alteration, or the testing clause or its equivalent, states that the alteration was read to that granter by the relevant person before such signature or states that the alteration was not so read because the granter made a declaration that he did not wish him to do so;

(c)  the alteration bears to have been signed by a person as a witness of the relevant person's signature and the alteration, or the testing clause or its equivalent, bears to state the name and address of the witness; and

(d)  nothing in the document or alteration, or in the testing clause or its equivalent, indicates—

(i)  that the alteration was not signed by the relevant person as it bears to have been so signed;

(ii)  that the statement mentioned in paragraph (b) above is incorrect; or

(iii)  that the alteration was not validly witnessed for any reason specified in paragraphs (a) to (e) of sub-paragraph (4) below (as modified by paragraph 11 of Schedule 3 to this Act),

the alteration shall be presumed to have been signed by the relevant person and the statement so mentioned shall be presumed to be correct.'.

10.  In paragraph 1(3) of Schedule 1 for the words 'sub-paragraph (1)(b)' there shall be substituted the words 'sub-paragraph (1)(c)'.

11.  For paragraph 1(4) of Schedule 1 there shall be substituted the following sub-paragraph—
'(4)  Where, in any proceedings relating to an alteration to a document in which a question arises as to a relevant person's signature on behalf of a granter under section 9(1) of this Act, it is established—

(a)  that a signature bearing to be the signature of the witness of the relevant person's signature is not such a signature, whether by reason of forgery or otherwise;

(b)  that the person who signed the alteration as the witness of the relevant person's signature is a person who is named in the document as a granter of it;

(c)    that the person who signed the alteration as the witness of the relevant person's signature, at the time of signing—
(i)    did not know the granter on whose behalf the relevant person had so signed;
(ii)    was under the age of 16 years; or
(iii)    was mentally incapable of acting as a witness;
(d)    that the person who signed the alteration, purporting to be the witness of the relevant person's signature, did not see him sign it;
(dd)    that the person who signed the alteration as the witness of the relevant person's signature did not witness the granting of authority by the granter concerned to the relevant person to sign the alteration on his behalf or did not witness the reading of the alteration to the granter by the relevant person or the declaration that the granter did not wish him to do so;
(e)    that the person who signed the alteration as the witness of the relevant person's signature did not sign the alteration after him or that the signing of the alteration by the granter and the witness was not one continuous process;
(f)    that the name or address of such a witness was added after the alteration was founded on or registered as mentioned in sub-paragraph (3)(a) above or is erroneous in any material respect; or
(g)    in the case of an alteration to a testamentary document consisting of more than one sheet, that a signature on any sheet of the alteration bearing to be the signature of the relevant person is not such a signature, whether by reason of forgery or otherwise,
then, for the purposes of those proceedings, there shall be no presumption that the alteration has been signed by the relevant person on behalf of the granter concerned.'.

**12.**    In paragraph 1(6) of Schedule 1 the words 'or the acknowledgement of his signature' and the words 'or acknowledgement' shall be omitted.

**13.**    Paragraph 1(7) of Schedule 1 shall be omitted.

**14.**    For paragraph 2(1) of Schedule 1 there shall be substituted the following sub-paragraph—
'(1)    Where—
(a)    an alteration to a document bears to have been signed by a relevant person under section 9(1) of this Act on behalf of a granter of the document; but
(b)    there is no presumption under paragraph 1 of Schedule 1 to this Act (as modified by paragraph 9 of Schedule 3 to this Act) that the alteration has been signed by that person or that the procedure referred to in paragraph 1(1)(b) of Schedule 1 to this Act as so modified was followed,
then, if the court, on an application being made to it by any person who has an interest in the document, is satisfied that the alteration was so signed by the relevant person with the authority of the granter and that the relevant person read the alteration to the granter before signing or did not so read it because the granter declared that he did not wish him to do so, it shall—
(i)    cause the document to be endorsed with a certificate to that effect; or
(ii)    where the document has already been registered in the Books of Council and Session or in sheriff court books, grant decree to that effect.'.

**15.** At the end of paragraph 2(5)(a) of Schedule 1 there shall be added the following words—

'and that the procedure referred to in paragraph 1(1)(b) of Schedule 1 to this Act as modified by paragraph 9 of Schedule 3 to this Act was followed.'.

## SCHEDULE 4. MINOR AND CONSEQUENTIAL AMENDMENTS

### *General adaptation*

1.—(1)  Any reference in any other enactment to a probative document shall, in relation to a document executed after the commencement of this Act, be construed as a reference to a document in relation to which section 6(2) of this Act applies.

(2)  For the purposes of any enactment—

(a)  providing for a document to be executed by a body corporate by affixing its common seal; or

(b)  referring (in whatever terms) to a document so executed,

a document signed or subscribed by or on behalf of the body corporate in accordance with the provisions of the Requirements of Writing (Scotland) Act 1995 shall have effect as if so executed.

### Specific enactments

### *Lands Clauses Consolidation (Scotland) Act 1845*

**2.**  In Schedules (A) and (B) to the Lands Clauses Consolidation (Scotland) Act 1845 at the end of each of the forms there shall be added—

'Note—Subscription of the document by the granter of it will be sufficient for the document to be formally valid, but witnessing of it may be necessary or desirable for other purposes (see the Requirements of Writing (Scotland) Act 1995).'.

### *Infeftment Act 1845*

**3.**  In Schedules (A) and (B) to the Infeftment Act 1845 for the words from 'In witness' to the end there shall be substituted the words 'Testing clause +

+Note—Subscription of the document by the granter of it will be sufficient for the document to be formally valid, but witnessing of it may be necessary or desirable for other purposes (see the Requirements of Writing (Scotland) Act 1995).'.

### *Commissioners Clauses Act 1847*

**4.**  At the end of section 59 of the Commissioners Clauses Act 1847 there shall be added the following subsection—

'(2)  This section shall apply to Scotland as if—

(a)  for the words from "by deed under" to "recorded" there were substituted the words—

'by a document—

(a)  if they are a corporation, subscribed in accordance with section 7 of, and paragraph 5 of Schedule 2 to, the Requirements of Writing (Scotland) Act 1995;

(b)  if they are not a corporation, subscribed in accordance with the said section 7 by the commissioners or any two of them acting by the authority of and on behalf of the commissioners;

and a document so subscribed, followed by infeftment duly recorded,';

(b) for the words from "under such" to "acting" there were substituted the word "subscribed'.'.

5. At the end of section 75 of that Act there shall be added the following subsection—

'(2) This section shall apply to Scotland as if for the words "by deed" to "five of them" there were substituted the words—

"in a document—

(a) which is duly stamped;

(b) in which the consideration is truly stated; and

(c) which is subscribed, if the commissioners—

(i) are a corporation, in accordance with section 7 of, and paragraph 5 of Schedule 2 to, the Requirements of Writing (Scotland) Act 1995;

(ii) are not a corporation, in accordance with the said section 7 by the commissioners or any five of them,".'.

6. At the end of section 77 of that Act there shall be added the following subsection—

'(2) This section shall apply to Scotland as if for the words "by deed duly stamped" there were substituted the words "in a document which is duly stamped and which is subscribed in accordance with the Requirements of Writing (Scotland) Act 1995.".'.

7. In Schedule (B) to that Act—

(a) the words from 'or, if the deed' to 'case may be,' are hereby repealed;

(b) at the end there shall be added the words '[or, if the document is granted under Scots law, insert testing clause+]

+Note—As regards a document granted under Scots law, subscription of it by the granter will be sufficient for the document to be formally valid, but witnessing of it may be necessary or desirable for other purposes (see the Requirements of Writing (Scotland) Act 1995).'.

8. In Schedule (C) to that Act—

(a) the words from '[or, if the deed' to 'Scotland,]' are hereby repealed;

(b) at the end there shall be added the words '[or, if the document is granted under Scots law, insert testing clause+]

+Note—As regards a document granted under Scots law, subscription of it by the granter will be sufficient for the document to be formally valid, but witnessing of it may be necessary or desirable for other purposes (see the Requirements of Writing (Scotland) Act 1995).'.

*Entail Amendment Act 1848*

9. In section 50 of the Entail Amendment Act 1848 for the word 'tested' there shall be substituted the word 'subscribed'.

10. In the Schedule to that Act—

(a) the words 'and of the witnesses subscribing,' are hereby repealed;

(b) for the words from 'In witness whereof' to the end there shall be substituted the words 'Testing clause+

+Note—Subscription of the document by the heir of entail in possession and the notary public will be sufficient for the document to be formally valid, but witnessing of it may be necessary or desirable for other purposes (see the Requirements of Writing (Scotland) Act 1995).'.

*Ordnance Board Transfer Act 1855*

**11**. At the end of section 5 of the Ordnance Board Transfer Act 1855 there shall be added the following subsection—
'(2) This section shall apply to Scotland as if for the words from "signing" to "his deed" there were substituted the words "subscribing it in accordance with the Requirements of Writing (Scotland) Act 1995".

*Registration of Leases (Scotland) Act 1857*

**12.** In Schedule (A) to the Registration of Leases (Scotland) Act 1857 for the words 'in common form' there shall be substituted—
'+
+Note—Subscription of the document by the granter of it will be sufficient for the document to be formally valid, but witnessing of it may be necessary or desirable for other purposes (see the Requirements of Writing (Scotland) Act 1995).'.

**13.** In each of Schedules (B), (C), (D), (F), (G) and (H) to that Act after the words 'Testing clause' there shall be inserted ' +
+Note—Subscription of the document by the granter of it will be sufficient for the document to be formally valid, but witnessing of it may be necessary or desirable for other purposes (see the Requirements of Writing (Scotland) Act 1995).'.

*Transmission of Moveable Property (Scotland) Act 1862*

**14.** In each of Schedules A and B to the Transmission of Moveable Property (Scotland) Act 1862 for the words from 'In witness whereof' to the end there shall be substituted the words 'Testing clause +
+Note—Subscription of the document by the granter of it will be sufficient for the document to be formally valid, but witnessing of it may be necessary or desirable for other purposes (see the Requirements of Writing (Scotland) Act 1995).'.

**15.** In Schedule C to that Act for the words from 'and D' to the end there shall be substituted the words 'Testing clause'.

*Titles to Land Consolidation (Scotland) Act 1868*

**16.** In Schedule (B) nos. 1 and 2 and (AA) no. 3 to the Titles to Land Consolidation (Scotland) Act 1868 for the words from 'In witness whereof' to 'usual form]' there shall be substituted the words 'Testing clause +
+Note—Subscription of the document by the granter of it will be sufficient for the document to be formally valid, but witnessing of it may be necessary or desirable for other purposes (see the Requirements of Writing (Scotland) Act 1995).'.

**17.** In Schedules (J), (BB) no. 1, (CC) nos. 1 and 2 and (OO) to that Act for the words from 'In witness whereof' to the end there shall be substituted the words 'Testing clause +
+Note—Subscription of the document by the granter of it will be sufficient for the document to be formally valid, but witnessing of it may be necessary or desirable for other purposes (see the Requirements of Writing (Scotland) Act 1995).'.

**18.** In Schedule (FF) no. 1 to that Act—
(a) for the words from 'In witness whereof' to 'usual form]' there shall be substituted the words 'Testing clause+';
(b) at the end there shall be added '+ Subscription of the document by the granter of it will be sufficient for the document to be formally valid, but witnessing of it may be necessary or desirable for other purposes (see the Requirements of Writing (Scotland) Act 1995).'.

**19.** In Schedule (GG) to that Act—
(a) for the words from 'In witness whereof' to 'I K Witness' there shall be substituted the words 'Testing clause+';
(b) after Note (b) there shall be inserted—
  '+ (c) Subscription of the document by the granter of it will be sufficient for the document to be formally valid, but witnessing of it may be necessary or desirable for other purposes (see the Requirements of Writing (Scotland) Act 1995).'.

**20.** In Schedule (NN) to that Act—
(a) for the words from 'In witness whereof' to 'G H Witness' there shall be substituted the words 'Testing clause+';
(b) at the end there shall be added—
  '+ Subscription of the document by the granter if it will be sufficient for the document to be formally valid, but witnessing of it may be necessary or desirable for other purposes (see the Requirements of Writing (Scotland) Act 1995).'.

*Conveyancing (Scotland) Act 1874*

**21.** In Schedules C, F, L nos. 1 and 2 and N to the Conveyancing (Scotland) Act 1874 for the words 'In witness whereof [testing clause]' there shall be substituted the words 'Testing clause+
  +Note—Subscription of the document by the granter of it will be sufficient for the document to be formally valid, but witnessing of it may be necessary or desirable for other purposes (see the Requirements of Writing (Scotland) Act 1995).'.

**22.** In Schedule G to that Act—
(a) for the words 'In witness whereof [testing clause]' there shall be substituted the words 'Testing clause+';
(b) at the end of the Note there shall be added—
  '+ Subscription of the document by the granter of it will be sufficient for the document to be formally valid, but witnessing of it may be necessary or desirable for other purposes (see the Requirements of Writing (Scotland) Act 1995).'.

**23.** In Schedule M to that Act for the words 'and add testing clause]' there shall be substituted the words 'Testing clause+]
  +Note—Subscription of the document by the granter of it will be sufficient for the document to be formally valid, but witnessing of it may be necessary or desirable for other purposes (see the Requirements of Writing (Scotland) Act 1995).'.

*Colonial Stock Act 1877*

**24.** At the end of subsection (1) of section 4 of the Colonial Stock Act 1877 there shall be added the words 'or, in relation to Scotland, subscribed in accordance with section 7 of the Requirements of Writing (Scotland) Act 1995.'.

**25.**   At the end of section 6 of that Act there shall be added the following subsection—

'(2)   This section shall have effect in relation to Scotland as if for the words from "given" to "attested" there were substituted the words "subscribed by the person not under disability in accordance with section 7 of the Requirements of Writing (Scotland) Act 1995.'.'.

### Colonial Stock Act 1892

**26.**   After subsection (2) of section 2 of the Colonial Stock Act 1892 there shall be added the following subsection—

'(2A)   This section shall have effect in relation to Scotland as if—

(a)   in subsection (1) for the words from "deed according" to "parties" there were substituted the words "a document in the form set out in the Schedule to this Act or to the like effect and the document as executed";

(b)   in subsection (2) for the words "by deed" there were substituted the words "under this section".'

**27.**   At the end of the Schedule to that Act there shall be added the words '[If the document is granted under the law of Scotland, for the words from "Witness our hands" to the end substitute "[Testing clause +

+Note—Subscription of the document by the granter of it will be sufficient for the document to be formally valid, but witnessing of it may be necessary or desirable for other purposes (see the Requirements of Writing (Scotland) Act 1995).]"]'.

### Feudal Casualties (Scotland) Act 1914

**28.**   In each of Schedules B and C to the Feudal Casualties (Scotland) Act 1914—

(a)   for the words 'In witness whereof' there shall be substituted the words 'Testing clause'; and

(b)   at the end of the Note there shall be added the words 'Subscription of the document by the granter of it will be sufficient for the document to be formally valid, but witnessing of it may be necessary or desirable for other purposes (see the Requirements of Writing (Scotland) Act 1995).'.

### Trusts (Scotland) Act 1921

**29.**   In Schedule A to the Trusts (Scotland) Act 1921—

(a)   for the words '(To be attested)' there shall be substituted the words 'Testing clause +';

(b)   at the end there shall be added—

'+Note—Subscription of the document by the granter of it will be sufficient for the document to be formally valid, but witnessing of it may be necessary or desirable for other purposes (see the Requirements of Writing (Scotland) Act 1995).'.

**30.**   In Schedule B to that Act for the words '(To be attested)' there shall be substituted the words 'Testing clause +

+Note—Subscription of the document by the granter or granters of it will be sufficient for the document to be formally valid, but witnessing of it may be necessary or desirable for other purposes (see the Requirements of Writing (Scotland) Act 1995).'.

*Conveyancing (Scotland) Act 1924*

**31.**   In Schedule B to the Conveyancing (Scotland) Act 1924—
(a)   in forms nos. 1 to 6 for the words '[To be attested]' there shall be substituted the words 'Testing clause+';
(b)   at the end of the Notes there shall be added—
'+Note 8—Subscription of the document by the notary public (or law agent) on behalf of the granter of it will be sufficient for the document to be formally valid, but witnessing of it may be necessary or desirable for other purposes (see the Requirements of Writing (Scotland) Act 1995).'.

**32.**   In Schedule E to that Act for the words '[To be attested]' there shall be substituted the words 'Testing clause+
+Note—Subscription of the document by the granter of it will be sufficient for the document to be formally valid, but witnessing of it may be necessary or desirable for other purposes (see the Requirements of Writing (Scotland) Act 1995).'.

**33.**   In Schedules G and H to that Act for the words '[to be attested]' there shall be substituted the words 'Testing clause+
+Note—Subscription of the document by the granter of it will be sufficient for the document to be formally valid, but witnessing of it may be necessary or desirable for other purposes (see the Requirements of Writing (Scotland) Act 1995)'.

**34.**   In Schedule K to that Act—
(a)   in forms nos 1 to 7 for the words '[To be attested]' there shall be substituted the words 'Testing clause+';
(b)   at the end of the notes there shall be added—
'+Note 5—Subscription of the document by the granter of it will be sufficient for the document to be formally valid, but witnessing of it may be necessary or desirable for other purposes (see the Requirements of Writing (Scotland) Act 1995).'.

**35.**   In Schedule L to that Act, in form 4, for the words '[To be attested]' there shall be substituted the words 'Testing clause+
+Note—Subscription of the document by the notary public or law agent on behalf of the granter of it will be sufficient for the document to be formally valid, but witnessing of it may be necessary or desirable for other purposes (see the Requirements of Writing (Scotland) Act 1995).'.

**36.**   In Schedule N to that Act for the words '[To be attested]' there shall be substituted the words 'Testing clause+
+Note—Subscription of the document by the granter of it will be sufficient for the document to be formally valid, but witnessing of it may be necessary or desirable for other purposes (see the Requirements of Writing (Scotland) Act 1995).'.

*Long Leases (Scotland) Act 1954*

**37.**   In the Fourth Schedule to the Long Leases (Scotland) Act 1954—
(a)   for the words '[To be attested]' there shall be substituted the words 'Testing clause+';
(b)   at the end of the Notes there shall be added—
'+4 Subscription of the feu contract by the parties to it will be sufficient for the contract to be formally valid, but witnessing of it may be necessary or desirable for other purposes (see the Requirements of Writing (Scotland) Act 1995).'.

*Succession (Scotland) Act 1964*

**38.** At the end of section 21 of the Succession (Scotland) Act 1964 there shall be added the following subsection—

'(2) This section shall not apply to a testamentary document executed after the commencement of the Requirements of Writing (Scotland) Act 1995.'.

**39.** After section 21 of that Act there shall be inserted the following section—

**'21A. Evidence as to testamentary documents in commissary proceedings**

Confirmation of an executor to property disposed of in a testamentary document executed after the commencement of the Requirements of Writing (Scotland) Act 1995 shall not be granted unless the formal validity of the document is governed—

(a) by Scots law and the document is presumed under section 3 or 4 of that Act to have been subscribed by the granter so disposing of that property; or

(b) by a law other than Scots law and the court is satisfied that the document is formally valid according to the law governing such validity.'.

**40.** For section 32 of that Act there shall be substituted the following section—

**'32. Certain testamentary dispositions to be formally valid**

(1) For the purpose of any question arising as to entitlement, by virtue of a testamentary disposition, to any relevant property or to any interest therein, the disposition shall be treated as valid in respect of the formalities of execution.

(2) Subsection (1) above is without prejudice to any right to challenge the validity of the testamentary disposition on the ground of forgery or on any other ground of essential invalidity.

(3) In this section "relevant property" means property disposed of in the testamentary disposition in respect of which—

(a) confirmation has been granted; or

(b) probate, letters of administration or other grant of representation—

(i) has been issued, and has noted the domicile of the deceased to be, in England and Wales or Northern Ireland; or

(ii) has been issued outwith the United Kingdom and had been sealed in Scotland under section 2 of the Colonial Probates Act 1892.'.

**41.** In Schedule 1 to that Act for the words '[To be attested by two witnesses] [Signature of A B]' there shall be substituted the words 'Testing clause+

+Note—Subscription of the document by the granter of it will be sufficient for the document to be formally valid, but witnessing of it may be necessary or desirable for other purposes (see the Requirements of Writing (Scotland) Act 1995).'.

*Industrial and Provident Societies Act 1965*

**42.** In Schedule 3 to the Industrial and Provident Societies Act 1965 in each of Forms C, D and E for the words from 'Signed' to the end there shall be substituted the words 'Testing clause+

+Note—Subscription of the document by the granter of it will be sufficient for the document to be formally valid, but witnessing of it may be necessary or desirable for other purposes (see the Requirements of Writing (Scotland) Act 1995).'.

**43.** In Schedule 4 to that Act, in Form C for the words from 'Signed' to the end there shall be substituted the words 'Testing clause+
+Note—Subscription of the document by the cautioner will be sufficient for the document to be formally valid, but witnessing of it may be necessary or desirable for other purposes (see the Requirements of Writing (Scotland) Act 1995).'.

*Conveyancing and Feudal Reform (Scotland) Act 1970*

**44.** In Schedule 2 to the Conveyancing and Feudal Reform (Scotland) Act 1970—
(a) in forms A and B for the words '[To be attested]' there shall be substituted the words 'Testing clause+';
(b) at the end of the Notes there shall be added—
'+Note 8—Subscription of the document by the granter of it will be sufficient for the document to be formally valid, but witnessing of it may be necessary or desirable for other purposes (see the Requirements of Writing (Scotland) Act 1995).'.

**45.** In Schedule 4 to that Act—
(a) in form A and forms C to F for the words '[To be attested]' there shall be substituted the words 'Testing clause+';
(b) at the end of the Notes there shall be added—
'+Note 7—Subscription of the document by the granter of it, or in the case of form E the granter and the consenter to the variation, will be sufficient for the document to be formally valid, but witnessing of it may be necessary or desirable for other purposes (see the Requirements of Writing (Scotland) Act 1995).'.

**46.** In Schedule 5 to that Act, in form D—
(a) in nos 1 and 2 for the words '[To be attested]' there shall be substituted the words 'Testing clause+';
(b) at the end there shall be added—
'+Note—Subscription of the document by the granter of it will be sufficient for the document to be formally valid, but witnessing of it may be necessary or desirable for other purposes (see the Requirements of Writing (Scotland) Act 1995).'.

**47.** In Schedule 9 to that Act—
(a) for the words '[To be attested]' there shall be substituted the words 'Testing clause+';
(b) at the end of the Notes there shall be added—
'+Note 4—Subscription of the document by the granter of it will be sufficient for the document to be formally valid, but witnessing of it may be necessary or desirable for other purposes (see the Requirements of Writing (Scotland) Act 1995).'.
. . .

*Patents Act 1977*

**49.** In section 31(6) of the Patents Act 1977 for the words from 'probative' to the end there shall be substituted the words 'subscribed in accordance with the Requirements of Writing (Scotland) Act 1995.'.
. . .

*Companies Act 1985*

**51.** For section 36B of the Companies Act 1985 there shall be substituted the following section—

> **36B. 'Execution of documents by companies**
> (1) Notwithstanding the provisions of any enactment, a company need not have a company seal.
> (2) For the purposes of any enactment—
> (a) providing for a document to be executed by a company by affixing its common seal; or
> (b) referring (in whatever terms) to a document so executed,
> a document signed or subscribed by or on behalf of the company in accordance with the provisions of the Requirements of Writing (Scotland) Act 1995 shall have effect as if so executed.
> (3) In this section "enactment" includes an enactment contained in a statutory instrument.'.

**52.** At the end of section 38 of that Act there shall be added the following subsection—

> '(3) This section does not extend to Scotland.'.

**53.** In section 39 of that Act—
> (a) after subsection (2) there shall be inserted the following subsection—
> '(2A) Subsection (2) does not extend to Scotland.';
> (b) in subsection (3) after the words 'common seal' there shall be inserted the words 'or as respects Scotland by writing subscribed in accordance with the Requirements of Writing (Scotland) Act 1995'.

**54.** Section 40 of that Act shall become subsection (1) of that section and at the end there shall be added the following subsection—

> '(2) Nothing in this section shall affect the right of a company registered in Scotland to subscribe such securities and documents in accordance with the Requirements of Writing (Scotland) Act 1995.'.

**55.** Section 186 of that Act shall become subsection (1) of that section and at the end there shall be added the following subsection—

> '(2) Without prejudice to subsection (1), as respects Scotland a certificate specifying any shares held by a member and subscribed by the company in accordance with the Requirements of Writing (Scotland) Act 1995 is, unless the contrary is shown, sufficient evidence of his title to the shares.'.

**56.** In section 188 of that Act in subsection (2) after the words 'common seal' there shall be inserted the words '(or, in the case of a company registered in Scotland, subscribed in accordance with the Requirements of Writing (Scotland) Act 1995)'.

*Companies Consolidation (Consequential Provisions) Act 1985*

**57.** At the end of section 11 of the Companies Consolidation (Consequential Provisions) Act 1985 there shall be added the following subsection—

> '(3) The foregoing provisions of this section are without prejudice to the right of a company to subscribe such securities and documents in accordance with the Requirements of Writing (Scotland) Act 1995.'.

*Insolvency Act 1986*

**58.** In section 53 of the Insolvency Act 1986—
   (a) in subsection (1) for the words 'a validly executed instrument in writing' there shall be substituted the words 'an instrument subscribed in accordance with the Requirements of Writing (Scotland) Act 1995';
   (b) for subsection (4) there shall be substituted the following subsection—
      '(4) If the receiver is to be appointed by the holders of a series of secured debentures, the instrument of appointment may be executed on behalf of the holders of the floating charge by any person authorised by resolution of the debenture-holders to execute the instrument.'.

### SCHEDULE 5. REPEALS

| Chapter | Short title | Extent of repeal |
|---|---|---|
| 1540, c 37 (S.) | The Subscription of Deeds Act 1540 | The whole Act. |
| 1579, c 18 (S.) | The Subscription of Deeds Act 1579 | The whole Act. |
| 1672, c 47 (S.) | The Lyon King of Arms Act 1672 | The words from 'And his Maiestie with consent' to 'contraveiners heirof'. |
| 1681, c 5 (S.) | The Subscription of Deeds Act 1681 | The whole Act. |
| 1696, c 15 (S.) | The Deeds Act 1696 | The whole Act. |
| 1696, c 25 (S.) | The Blank Bonds and Trusts Act 1696 | The whole Act. |
| 1698, c 4 (S.) | The Registration Act 1698 | The whole Act. |
| 10 & 11 Vict. c. 16 | The Commissioners Clauses Act 1847 | In section 56, the words from '(that is to say,)' to 'discharge the same' where they first occur. In Schedule (B), the words from 'or, if the deed' to 'case may be,'. In Schedule (C), the words from '[or, if the deed' to 'Scotland,]'. |
| 11 & 12 Vict. c. 36 | The Entail Amendment Act 1848 | In the Schedule the words 'and of the witnesses subscribing,'. |
| 19 & 20 Vict. c. 60 | The Mercantile Law Amendment Act, Scotland 1856 | Section 6. |
| 31 & 32 Vict. c. 101 | The Titles to Land Consolidation (Scotland) Act 1868 | Sections 139 and 149. |
| 37 & 38 Vict. c. 94 | The Conveyancing (Scotland) Act 1874 | Sections 38 to 41. Schedule I. |

| Chapter | Short title | Extent of repeal |
|---|---|---|
| 7 Edw. 7 c 51 | The Sheriff Courts (Scotland) Act 1907 | In section 35 the words 'either holograph or attested by one witness'. In Schedule 1, paragraph 67 and in the Appendix in Form M the words from 'If not holograph' to the end of the form. |
| 4 & 5 Geo. 5 c. 48 | The Feudal Casualties (Scotland) Act 1914 | In section 8 the words 'which need not be tested or holograph'. |
| 14 & 15 Geo. 5 c 27 | The Conveyancing (Scotland) Act 1924 | Section 18. Schedule I. |
| 23 & 24 Geo. 5 c 44 | The Church of Scotland (Property and Endowments) (Amendment) Act 1933 | Section 13. |
| 2 & 3 Geo. 6 c. 20 | The Reorganisation of Offices (Scotland) Act 1939 | In section 1(8) the words from 'and any such' to the end. |
| 1959, c 40 | The Deer (Scotland) Act 1959 | In Schedule 1, paragraphs 12 and 13. |
| 1963, c 18 | The Stock Transfer Act 1963 | Section 2(4). |
| 1965, c 12 | The Industrial and Provident Societies Act 1965 | In section 34(5)(a), in the definition of 'receipt' the words from 'signed by two members' to 'as such'. Section 36. |
| 1967, c 10 | The Forestry Act 1967 | Section 39(5). |
| 1968, c 16 | The New Towns (Scotland) Act 1968 | In Schedule 2, paragraphs 10 and 11. |
| 1970, c 35 | The Conveyancing and Feudal Reform (Scotland) Act 1970 | Section 44. |
| 1973, c 52 | The Prescription and Limitation (Scotland) Act 1973 | Section 5(2). In Schedule 1, paragraphs 2(c), 3 and 4(b). |
| 1973, c 65 | The Local Government (Scotland) Act 1973 | Section 194, other than subsection (2). In Schedule 8, paragraph 5. |
| 1978, c 29 | The National Health Service (Scotland) Act 1978 | In section 79(1A) the words from 'and where' to the end of the subsection. In Schedule 1, paragraphs 9 and 10. In Schedule 5, paragraphs 10 and 11. |
| 1980, c 46 | The Solicitors (Scotland) Act 1980 | In Schedule 1, paragraph 12. |
| 1985, c 6 | The Companies Act 1985 | In section 2(6) the words from 'and that' to the end. |

| Chapter | Short title | Extent of repeal |
|---|---|---|
| | | In section 7(3)(c) the words from '(which attestation' to the end. Section 462(3). |
| 1985, c 16 | The National Heritage (Scotland) Act 1985 | In Schedule 1, paragraphs 8 and 19. |
| 1986, c 47 | The Legal Aid (Scotland) Act 1986 | In Schedule 1, paragraph 14. |
| 1988, c 43 | The Housing (Scotland) Act 1988 | In Schedule 1, paragraphs 18 and 19. |
| 1990, c 40 | The Law Reform (Miscellaneous Provisions) (Scotland) Act 1990 | Section 72. Section 75(6). In Schedule 8, paragraph 33. |
| 1990, c 35 | The Enterprise and New Towns (Scotland) Act 1990 | In Schedule 1, paragraph 23. |
| 1991, c 28 | The Natural Heritage (Scotland) Act 1991 | In Schedule 1, paragraph 18. |
| 1993, c 44 | The Crofters (Scotland) Act 1993 | In Schedule 1, paragraphs 14 and 15. |
| 1994, c 39 | The Local Government etc. (Scotland) Act 1994 | In section 172(4), paragraph (h). In Schedule 3, paragraph 11. In Schedule 5, in Part II, paragraph 8. In Schedule 7, paragraph 17. In Schedule 12, paragraph 13. In Schedule 13, paragraph 92(60). |

**EMPLOYMENT RIGHTS ACT 1996**
**(1996, c 18)**

## PART I. EMPLOYMENT PARTICULARS

*Right to statements of employment particulars*

**1. Statement of initial employment particulars**

(1) Where an employee begins employment with an employer, the employer shall give to the employee a written statement of particulars of employment.

(2) The statement may (subject to section 2(4)) be given in instalments and (whether or not given in instalments) shall be given not later than two months after the beginning of the employment.

(3) The statement shall contain particulars of—

(a) the names of the employer and employee,

(b) the date when the employment began, and

(c) the date on which the employee's period of continuous employment began (taking into account any employment with a previous employer which counts towards that period).

(4) The statement shall also contain particulars, as at a specified date not more than seven days before the statement (or the instalment containing them) is given, of—

(a)   the scale or rate of remuneration or the method of calculating remuneration,

(b)   the intervals at which remuneration is paid (that is, weekly, monthly or other specified intervals),

(c)   any terms and conditions relating to hours of work (including any terms and conditions relating to normal working hours),

(d)   any terms and conditions relating to any of the following—

(i)   entitlement to holidays, including public holidays, and holiday pay (the particulars given being sufficient to enable the employee's entitlement, including any entitlement to accrued holiday pay on the termination of employment, to be precisely calculated),

(ii)   incapacity for work due to sickness or injury, including any provision for sick pay, and

(iii)   pensions and pension schemes,

(e)   the length of notice which the employee is obliged to give and entitled to receive to terminate his contract of employment,

(f)   the title of the job which the employee is employed to do or a brief description of the work for which he is employed,

(g)   where the employment is not intended to be permanent, the period for which it is expected to continue or, if it is for a fixed term, the date when it is to end,

(h)   either the place of work or, where the employee is required or permitted to work at various places, an indication of that and of the address of the employer,

(j)   any collective agreements which directly affect the terms and conditions of the employment including, where the employer is not a party, the persons by whom they were made, and

(k)   where the employee is required to work outside the United Kingdom for a period of more than one month—

(i)   the period for which he is to work outside the United Kingdom,

(ii)   the currency in which remuneration is to be paid while he is working outside the United Kingdom,

(iii)   any additional remuneration payable to him, and any benefits to be provided to or in respect of him, by reason of his being required to work outside the United Kingdom, and

(iv)   any terms and conditions relating to his return to the United Kingdom.

(5)   Subsection (4)(d)(iii) does not apply to an employee of a body or authority if—

(a)   the employee's pension rights depend on the terms of a pension scheme established under any provision contained in or having effect under any Act, and

(b)   any such provision requires the body or authority to give to a new employee information concerning the employee's pension rights or the determination of questions affecting those rights.

## PART II. PROTECTION OF WAGES

### Deductions by employer

### 13.   Right not to suffer unauthorised deductions

(1)   An employer shall not make a deduction from wages of a worker employed by him unless—

(a)   the deduction is required or authorised to be made by virtue of a statutory provision or a relevant provision of the worker's contract, or

(b) the worker has previously signified in writing his agreement or consent to the making of the deduction.

(2) In this section 'relevant provision', in relation to a worker's contract, means a provision of the contract comprised—

(a) in one or more written terms of the contract of which the employer has given the worker a copy on an occasion prior to the employer making the deduction in question, or

(b) in one or more terms of the contract (whether express or implied and, if express, whether oral or in writing) the existence and effect, or combined effect, of which in relation to the worker the employer has notified to the worker in writing on such an occasion.

(3) Where the total amount of wages paid on any occasion by an employer to a worker employed by him is less than the total amount of the wages properly payable by him to the worker on that occasion (after deductions), the amount of the deficiency shall be treated for the purposes of this Part as a deduction made by the employer from the worker's wages on that occasion.

(4) Subsection (3) does not apply in so far as the deficiency is attributable to an error of any description on the part of the employer affecting the computation by him of the gross amount of the wages properly payable by him to the worker on that occasion.

(5) For the purposes of this section a relevant provision of a worker's contract having effect by virtue of a variation of the contract does not operate to authorise the making of a deduction on account of any conduct of the worker, or any other event occurring, before the variation took effect.

(6) For the purposes of this section an agreement or consent signified by a worker does not operate to authorise the making of a deduction on account of any conduct of the worker, or any other event occurring, before the agreement or consent was signified.

(7) This section does not affect any other statutory provision by virtue of which a sum payable to a worker by his employer but not constituting 'wages' within the meaning of this Part is not to be subject to a deduction at the instance of the employer.

## DEFAMATION ACT 1996
### (1996, c 31)

**1. Responsibility for publication**

(1) In defamation proceedings a person has a defence if he shows that—

(a) he was not the author, editor or publisher of the statement complained of,

(b) he took reasonable care in relation to its publication, and

(c) he did not know, and had no reason to believe, that what he did caused or contributed to the publication of a defamatory statement.

(2) For this purpose 'author', 'editor' and 'publisher' have the following meanings, which are further explained in subsection (3)—

'author' means the originator of the statement, but does not include a person who did not intend that his statement be published at all;

'editor' means a person having editorial or equivalent responsibility for the content of the statement or the decision to publish it; and

'publisher' means a commercial publisher, that is, a person whose business is issuing material to the public, or a section of the public, who issues material containing the statement in the course of that business.

(3) A person shall not be considered the author, editor or publisher of a statement if he is only involved—

(a) in printing, producing, distributing or selling printed material containing the statement;

(b)   in processing, making copies of, distributing, exhibiting or selling a film or sound recording (as defined in Part I of the Copyright, Designs and Patents Act 1988) containing the statement;

(c)   in processing, making copies of, distributing or selling any electronic medium in or on which the statement is recorded, or in operating or providing any equipment, system or service by means of which the statement is retrieved, copied, distributed or made available in electronic form;

(d)   as the broadcaster of a live programme containing the statement in circumstances in which he has no effective control over the maker of the statement;

(e)   as the operator of or provider of access to a communications system by means of which the statement is transmitted, or made available, by a person over whom he has no effective control.

In a case not within paragraphs (a) to (e) the court may have regard to those provisions by way of analogy in deciding whether a person is to be considered the author, editor or publisher of a statement.

(4)   Employees or agents of an author, editor or publisher are in the same position as their employer or principal to the extent that they are responsible for the content of the statement or the decision to publish it.

(5)   In determining for the purposes of this section whether a person took reasonable care, or had reason to believe that what he did caused or contributed to the publication of a defamatory statement, regard shall be had to—

(a)   the extent of his responsibility for the content of the statement or the decision to publish it,

(b)   the nature or circumstances of the publication, and

(c)   the previous conduct or character of the author, editor or publisher.

(6)   This section does not apply to any cause of action which arose before the section came into force.

## 2.   Offer to make amends

(1)   A person who has published a statement alleged to be defamatory of another may offer to make amends under this section.

(2)   The offer may be in relation to the statement generally or in relation to a specific defamatory meaning which the person making the offer accepts that the statement conveys ('a qualified offer').

(3)   An offer to make amends—

(a)   must be in writing

(b)   must be expressed to be an offer to make amends under section 2 of the Defamation Act 1996, and

(c)   must state whether it is a qualified offer and, if so, set out the defamatory meaning in relation to which it is made.

(4)   An offer to make amends under this section is an offer—

(a)   to make a suitable correction of the statement complained of and a sufficient apology to the aggrieved party;

(b)   to publish the correction and apology in a manner that is reasonable and practicable in the circumstances, and

(c)   to pay to the aggrieved party such compensation (if any), and such costs, as may be agreed or determined to be payable.

The fact that the offer is accompanied by an offer to take specific steps does not affect the fact that an offer to make amends under this section is an offer to do all the things mentioned in paragraphs (a) to (c).

(5)   An offer to make amends under this section may not be made by a person after serving a defence in defamation proceedings brought against him by the aggrieved party in respect of the publication in question.

(6)   An offer to make amends under this section may be withdrawn before it

is accepted; and a renewal of an offer which has been withdrawn shall be treated as a new offer.

### 3.  Accepting an offer to make amends

(1)  If an offer to make amends under section 2 is accepted by the aggrieved party, the following provisions apply.

(2)  The party accepting the offer may not bring or continue defamation proceedings in respect of the publication concerned against the person making the offer, but he is entitled to enforce the offer to make amends, as follows.

(3)  If the parties agree on the steps to be taken in fulfilment of the offer, the aggrieved party may apply to the court for an order that the other party fulfil his offer by taking the steps agreed.

(4)  If the parties do not agree on the steps to be taken by way of correction, apology and publication, the party who made the offer may take such steps as he thinks appropriate, and may in particular—

(a)  make the correction and apology by a statement in open court in terms approved by the court, and

(b)  give an undertaking to the court as to the manner of their publication.

(5)  If the parties do not agree on the amount to be paid by way of compensation, it shall be determined by the court on the same principles as damages in defamation proceedings.

The court shall take account of any steps taken in fulfilment of the offer and (so far as not agreed between the parties) of the suitability of the correction, the sufficiency of the apology and whether the manner of their publication was reasonable in the circumstances, and may reduce or increase the amount of compensation accordingly.

(6)  If the parties do not agree on the amount to be paid by way of costs, it shall be determined by the court on the same principles as costs awarded in court proceedings.

(7)  The acceptance of an offer by one person to make amends does not affect any cause of action against another person in respect of the same publication, subject as follows.

(8)  [*applies to England and Wales only*]

(9)  In Scotland—

(a)  subsection (2) of section 3 of the Law Reform (Miscellaneous Provisions) (Scotland) Act 1940 (right of one joint wrongdoer as respects another to recover contribution towards damages) applies in relation to compensation paid under an offer to make amends as it applies in relation to damages in an action to which that section applies; and

(b)  where another person is liable in respect of the same damage (whether jointly or otherwise), the person whose offer to make amends was accepted is not required to pay by virtue of any contribution under section 3(2) of that Act a greater amount than the amount of compensation payable in pursuance of the offer.

(10)  Proceedings under this section shall be heard and determined without a jury.

### 4.  Failure to accept offer to make amends

(1)  If an offer to make amends under section 2, duly made and not withdrawn, is not accepted by the aggrieved party, the following provisions apply.

(2)  The fact that the offer was made is a defence (subject to subsection (3)) to defamation proceedings in respect of the publication in question by that party against the person making the offer.

A qualified offer is only a defence in respect of the meaning to which the offer related.

(3)   There is no such defence if the person by whom the offer was made knew or had reason to believe that the statement complained of—

(a)   referred to the aggrieved party or was likely to be understood as referring to him, and

(b)   was both false and defamatory of that party;

but it shall be presumed until the contrary is shown that he did not know and had no reason to believe that was the case.

(4)   The person who made the offer need not rely on it by way of defence, but if he does he may not rely on any other defence.

If the offer was a qualified offer, this applies only in respect of the meaning to which the offer related.

(5)   The offer may be relied on in mitigation of damages whether or not it was relied on as a defence.

. . .

## The meaning of a statement

### 7.   Ruling on the meaning of a statement

In defamation proceedings the court shall not be asked to rule whether a statement is arguably capable, as opposed to capable, of bearing a particular meaning or meanings attributed to it.

. . .

## Evidence of convictions

### 12.   Evidence of convictions

(1)   [*applies to England and Wales only*]

(2)   In section 12 of the Law Reform (Miscellaneous Provisions) (Scotland) Act 1968 (conclusiveness of convictions for purposes of defamation actions), in subsections (1) and (2) for 'a person' substitute 'the pursuer' and for 'that person' substitute 'he'; and after subsection (2) insert—

'(2A) In the case of an action for defamation in which there is more than one pursuer—

(a)   the references in subsections (1) and (2) above to the pursuer shall be construed as references to any of the pursuers, and

(b)   proof that any of the pursuers stands convicted of an offence shall be conclusive evidence that he committed that offence so far as that fact is relevant to any issue arising in relation to his cause of action or that of any other pursuer.'.

The amendments made by this subsection apply only for the purposes of an action begun after this section comes into force, whenever the cause of action arose.

(3)   [*applies to Northern Ireland only*]

## Evidence concerning proceedings in Parliament

### 13.   Evidence concerning proceedings in Parliament

(1)   Where the conduct of a person in or in relation to proceedings in Parliament is in issue in defamation proceedings, he may waive for the purposes of those proceedings, so far as concerns him, the protection of any enactment or rule of law which prevents proceedings in Parliament being impeached or questioned in any court or place out of Parliament.

(2)   Where a person waives that protection—

(a)   any such enactment or rule of law shall not apply to prevent evidence being given, questions being asked or statements, submissions, comments or findings being made about his conduct, and

(b)   none of those things shall be regarded as infringing the privilege of either House of Parliament.

(3)   The waiver by one person of that protection does not affect its operation in relation to another person who has not waived it.

(4)   Nothing in this section affects any enactment or rule of law so far as it protects a person (including a person who has waived the protection referred to above) from legal liability for words spoken or things done in the course of, or for the purposes of or incidental to, any proceedings in Parliament.

(5)   Without prejudice to the generality of subsection (4), that subsection applies to—

(a)   the giving of evidence before either House or a committee;

(b)   the presentation or submission of a document to either House or a committee;

(c)   the preparation of a document for the purposes of or incidental to the transacting of any such business;

(d)   the formulation, making or publication of a document, including a report, by or pursuant to an order of either House or a committee; and

(e)   any communication with the Parliamentary Commissioner for Standards or any person having functions in connection with the registration of members' interests.

In this subsection 'a committee' means a committee of either House or a joint committee of both Houses of Parliament.

*Statutory privilege*

**14.   Reports of court proceedings absolutely privileged**

(1)   A fair and accurate report of proceedings in public before a court to which this section applies, if published contemporaneously with the proceedings, is absolutely privileged.

(2)   A report of proceedings which by an order of the court, or as a consequence of any statutory provision, is required to be postponed shall be treated as published contemporaneously if it is published as soon as practicable after publication is permitted.

(3)   This section applies to—

(a)   any court in the United Kingdom,

(b)   the European Court of Justice or any court attached to that court,

(c)   the European Court of Human Rights, and

(d)   any international criminal tribunal established by the Security Council of the United Nations or by an international agreement to which the United Kingdom is a party.

In paragraph (a) 'court' includes any tribunal or body exercising the judicial power of the State.

(4)   In section 8(6) of the Rehabilitation of Offenders Act 1974 and in Article 9(6) of the Rehabilitation of Offenders (Northern Ireland) Order 1978 (defamation actions: reports of court proceedings), for 'section 3 of the Law of Libel Amendment Act 1888' substitute 'section 14 of the Defamation Act 1996'.

**15.   Reports, etc protected by qualified privilege**

(1)   The publication of any report or other statement mentioned in Schedule 1 to this Act is privileged unless the publication is shown to be made with malice, subject as follows.

(2)   In defamation proceedings in respect of the publication of a report or other statement mentioned in Part II of that Schedule, there is no defence under this section if the plaintiff shows that the defendant—

(a)   was requested by him to publish in a suitable manner a reasonable letter or statement by way of explanation or contradiction, and

(b)   refused or neglected to do so.

For this purpose 'in a suitable manner' means in the same manner as the publication complained of or in a manner that is adequate and reasonable in the circumstances.

(3)   This section does not apply to the publication to the public, or a section of the public, of matter which is not of public concern and the publication of which is not for the public benefit.

(4)   Nothing in this section shall be construed—

(a)   as protecting the publication of matter the publication of which is prohibited by law, or

(b)   as limiting or abridging any privilege subsisting apart from this section.

*Supplementary provisions*

. . .

### 17.   Interpretation

(1)   In this Act—

'publication' and 'publish', in relation to a statement, have the meaning they have for the purposes of the law of defamation generally, but 'publisher' is specially defined for the purposes of section 1;

'statement' means words, pictures, visual images, gestures or any other method of signifying meaning; and

'statutory provision' means—

(a)   a provision contained in an Act or in subordinate legislation within the meaning of the Interpretation Act 1978, or

(b)   a statutory provision within the meaning given by section 1(f) of the Interpretation Act (Northern Ireland) 1954.

(2)   In this Act as it applies to proceedings in Scotland—

'costs' means expenses; and

'plaintiff' and 'defendant' mean pursuer and defender.

*General provisions*

### 18.   Extent

. . .

(2)   The following provisions of this Act extend to Scotland—

section 1 (responsibility for publication),

sections 2 to 4 (offer to make amends), except section 3(8),

section 12(2) (evidence of convictions),

section 13 (evidence concerning proceedings in Parliament),

sections 14 and 15 and Schedule 1 (statutory privilege),

section 16 and Schedule 2 (repeals) so far as relating to enactments extending to Scotland,

section 17 (interpretation),

this subsection,

section 19 (commencement) so far as relating to provisions which extend to Scotland, and

section 20 (short title and saving).

. . .

### 20.   Short title and saving

(1)   This Act may be cited as the Defamation Act 1996.

(2)   Nothing in this Act affects the law relating to criminal libel.

# SCHEDULES

## SCHEDULE 1. QUALIFIED PRIVILEGE

### PART I. STATEMENTS HAVING QUALIFIED PRIVILEGE WITHOUT EXPLANATION OR CONTRADICTION

1.   A fair and accurate report of proceedings in public of a legislature anywhere in the world.

2.   A fair and accurate report of proceedings in public before a court anywhere in the world.

3.   A fair and accurate report of proceedings in public of a person appointed to hold a public inquiry by a government or legislature anywhere in the world.

4.   A fair and accurate report of proceedings in public anywhere in the world of an international organisation or an international conference.

5.   A fair and accurate copy of or extract from any register or other document required by law to be open to public inspection.

6.   A notice or advertisement published by or on the authority of a court, or of a judge or officer of a court, anywhere in the world.

7.   A fair and accurate copy of or extract from matter published by or on the authority of a government or legislature anywhere in the world.

8.   A fair and accurate copy of or extract from matter published anywhere in the world by an international organisation or an international conference.

### PART II. STATEMENTS PRIVILEGED SUBJECT TO EXPLANATION OR CONTRADICTION

9.   (1)   A fair and accurate copy of or extract from a notice or other matter issued for the information of the public by or on behalf of—
   (a)   a legislature in any member State or the European Parliament;
   (b)   the government of any member State, or any authority performing governmental functions in any member State or part of a member State, or the European Commission;
   (c)   an international organisation or international conference.
   (2)   In this paragraph 'governmental functions' includes police functions.

10.   A fair and accurate copy of or extract from a document made available by a court in any member State or the European Court of Justice (or any court attached to that court), or by a judge or officer of any such court.

11.   (1)   A fair and accurate report of proceedings at any public meeting or sitting in the United Kingdom of—
   (a)   a local authority or local authority committee;
   (b)   a justice or justices of the peace acting otherwise than as a court exercising judicial authority;
   (c)   a commission, tribunal, committee or person appointed for the purposes of any inquiry by any statutory provision, by Her Majesty or by a Minister of the Crown or a Northern Ireland Department;
   (d)   a person appointed by a local authority to hold a local inquiry in pursuance of any statutory provision;
   (e)   any other tribunal, board, committee or body constituted by or under, and exercising functions under, any statutory provision.
   (2)   In sub-paragraph (1)(a)—
   'local authority' means—
      (a)   in relation to England and Wales, a principal council within the meaning of the Local Government Act 1972, any body falling within any paragraph of section 100J(1) of that Act or an authority or body to which the Public Bodies (Admission to Meetings) Act 1960 applies,

(b)   in relation to Scotland, a council constituted under section 2 of the Local Government etc (Scotland) Act 1994 or an authority or body to which the Public Bodies (Admission to Meetings) Act 1960 applies,

(c)   in relation to Northern Ireland, any authority or body to which sections 23 to 27 of the Local Government Act (Northern Ireland) 1972 apply; and

'local authority committee' means any committee of a local authority or of local authorities, and includes—

(a)   any committee or sub-committee in relation to which sections 100A to 100D of the Local Government Act 1972 apply by virtue of section 100E of that Act (whether or not also by virtue of section 100J of that Act), and

(b)   any committee or sub-committee in relation to which sections 50A to 50D of the Local Government (Scotland) Act 1973 apply by virtue of section 50E of that Act.

(3)   A fair and accurate report of any corresponding proceedings in any of the Channel Islands or the Isle of Man or in another member State.

12.   (1)   A fair and accurate report of proceedings at any public meeting held in a member State.

(2)   In this paragraph a 'public meeting' means a meeting bona fide and lawfully held for a lawful purpose and for the furtherance or discussion of a matter of public concern, whether admission to the meeting is general or restricted.

13.   (1)   A fair and accurate report of proceedings at a general meeting of a UK public company.

(2)   A fair and accurate copy of or extract from any document circulated to members of a UK public company—

(a)   by or with the authority of the board of directors of the company,

(b)   by the auditors of the company, or

(c)   by any member of the company in pursuance of a right conferred by any statutory provision.

(3)   A fair and accurate copy of or extract from any document circulated to members of a UK public company which relates to the appointment, resignation, retirement or dismissal of directors of the company.

(4)   In this paragraph 'UK public company' means—

(a)   a public company within the meaning of section 1(3) of the Companies Act 1985 or Article 12(3) of the Companies (Northern Ireland) Order 1986, or

(b)   a body corporate incorporated by or registered under any other statutory provision, or by Royal Charter, or formed in pursuance of letters patent.

(5)   A fair and accurate report of proceedings at any corresponding meeting of, or copy of or extract from any corresponding document circulated to members of, a public company formed under the law of any of the Channel Islands or the Isle of Man or of another member State.

14.   A fair and accurate report of any finding or decision of any of the following descriptions of association, formed in the United Kingdom or another member State, or of any committee or governing body of such an association—

(a)   an association formed for the purpose of promoting or encouraging the exercise of or interest in any art, science, religion or learning, and empowered by its constitution to exercise control over or adjudicate on matters of interest or concern to the association, or the actions or conduct of any person subject to such control or adjudication;

(b)   an association formed for the purpose of promoting or safeguarding the interests of any trade, business, industry or profession, or of the persons carrying on or engaged in any trade, business, industry or profession, and empowered by its constitution to exercise control over or adjudicate upon matters connected with that trade, business, industry or profession, or the actions or conduct of those persons;

(c)   an association formed for the purpose of promoting or safeguarding the interests of a game, sport or pastime to the playing or exercise of which members of the public are invited or admitted, and empowered by its constitution to exercise control over or adjudicate upon persons connected with or taking part in the game, sport or pastime;

(d)   an association formed for the purpose of promoting charitable objects or other objects beneficial to the community and empowered by its constitution to exercise control over or to adjudicate on matters of interest or concern to the association, or the actions or conduct of any person subject to such control or adjudication.

15.   (1)   A fair and accurate report of, or copy of or extract from, any adjudication, report, statement or notice issued by a body, officer or other person designated for the purposes of this paragraph—

(a)   for England and Wales or Northern Ireland, by order of the Lord Chancellor, and

(b)   for Scotland, by order of the Secretary of State.

(2)   An order under this paragraph shall be made by statutory instrument which shall be subject to annulment in pursuance of a resolution of either House of Parliament.

## PART III. SUPPLEMENTARY PROVISIONS

16.   (1)   In this Schedule—

'court' includes any tribunal or body exercising the judicial power of the State;

'international conference' means a conference attended by representatives of two or more governments;

'international organisation' means an organisation of which two or more governments are members, and includes any committee or other subordinate body of such an organisation; and

'legislature' includes a local legislature.

(2)   References in this Schedule to a member State include any European dependent territory of a member State.

(3)   In paragraphs 2 and 6 'court' includes—

(a)   the European Court of Justice (or any court attached to that court) and the Court of Auditors of the European Communities,

(b)   the European Court of Human Rights,

(c)   any international criminal tribunal established by the Security Council of the United Nations or by an international agreement to which the United Kingdom is a party, and

(d)   the International Court of Justice and any other judicial or arbitral tribunal deciding matters in dispute between States.

(4)   In paragraphs 1, 3 and 7 'legislature' includes the European Parliament.

17.   (1)   Provision may be made by order identifying—

(a)   for the purposes of paragraph 11, the corresponding proceedings referred to in sub-paragraph (3);

(b)   for the purposes of paragraph 13, the corresponding meetings and documents referred to in sub-paragraph (5).

(2)   An order under this paragraph may be made—

(a)   for England and Wales or Northern Ireland, by the Lord Chancellor, and

(b)   for Scotland, by the Secretary of State.

(3)   An order under this paragraph shall be made by statutory instrument which shall be subject to annulment in pursuance of a resolution of either House of Parliament.

## DAMAGES ACT 1996
### (1996, c 48)

**1. Assumed rate of return on investment of damages**

(1) In determining the return to be expected from the investment of a sum awarded as damages for future pecuniary loss in an action for personal injury the court shall, subject to and in accordance with rules of court made for the purposes of this section, take into account such rate of return (if any) as may from time to time be prescribed by an order made by the Lord Chancellor.

(2) Subsection (1) above shall not however prevent the court taking a different rate of return into account if any party to the proceedings shows that it is more appropriate in the case in question.

(3) An order under subsection (1) above may prescribe different rates of return for different classes of case.

(4) Before making an order under subsection (1) above the Lord Chancellor shall consult the Government Actuary and the Treasury; and any order under that subsection shall be made by statutory instrument subject to annulment in pursuance of a resolution of either House of Parliament.

(5) In the application of this section to Scotland—

(a) for the reference to the Lord Chancellor in subsections (1) and (4) there is substituted a reference to the Scottish Ministers; and

(b) in subsection (4)—

(i) 'and the Treasury' is omitted; and

(ii) for 'either House of Parliament' there is substituted 'the Scottish Parliament'.

## HOUSING GRANTS, CONSTRUCTION AND REGENERATION ACT 1996
### (1996, c 53)

**113. Prohibition of conditional payment provisions**

(1) A provision making payment under a construction contract conditional on the payer receiving payment from a third person is ineffective, unless that third person, or any other person payment by whom is under the contract (directly or indirectly) a condition of payment by that third person, is insolvent.

(2) For the purposes of this section a company becomes insolvent—

(a) on the making of an administration order against it under Part II of the Insolvency Act 1986,

(b) on the appointment of an administrative receiver or a receiver or manager of its property under Chapter I of Part III of that Act, or the appointment of a receiver under Chapter II of that Part,

(c) on the passing of a resolution for voluntary winding-up without a declaration of solvency under section 89 of that Act, or

(d) on the making of a winding-up order under Part IV or V of that Act.

(3) For the purposes of this section a partnership becomes insolvent—

(a) on the making of a winding-up order against it under any provision of the Insolvency Act 1986 as applied by an order under section 420 of that Act, or

(b) when sequestration is awarded on the estate of the partnership under section 12 of the Bankruptcy (Scotland) Act 1985 or the partnership grants a trust deed for its creditors.

(4) For the purposes of this section an individual becomes insolvent—

(a) on the making of a bankruptcy order against him under Part IX of the Insolvency Act 1986, or

(b) on the sequestration of his estate under the Bankruptcy (Scotland) Act 1985 or when he grants a trust deed for his creditors.

(5) A company, partnership or individual shall also be treated as insolvent

on the occurrence of any event corresponding to those specified in subsection (2), (3) or (4) under the law of Northern Ireland or of a country outside the United Kingdom.

(6) Where a provision is rendered ineffective by subsection (1), the parties are free to agree other terms for payment.

In the absence of such agreement, the relevant provisions of the Scheme for Construction Contracts apply.

## CONTRACT (SCOTLAND) ACT 1997
### (1997, c 34)

**1. Extrinsic evidence of additional contract term etc.**

(1) Where a document appears (or two or more documents appear) to comprise all the express terms of a contract or unilateral voluntary obligation, it shall be presumed, unless the contrary is proved, that the document does (or the documents do) comprise all the express terms of the contract or unilateral voluntary obligation.

(2) Extrinsic oral or documentary evidence shall be admissible to prove, for the purposes of subsection (1) above, that the contract or unilateral voluntary obligation includes additional express terms (whether or not written terms).

(3) Notwithstanding the foregoing provisions of this section, where one of the terms in the document (or in the documents) is to the effect that the document does (or the documents do) comprise all the express terms of the contract or unilateral voluntary obligation, that term shall be conclusive in the matter.

(4) This section is without prejudice to any enactment which makes provision as respects the constitution, or formalities of execution, of a contract or unilateral voluntary obligation.

**2. Supersession**

(1) Where a deed is executed in implement, or purportedly in implement, of a contract, an unimplemented, or otherwise unfulfilled, term of the contract shall not be taken to be superseded by virtue only of that execution or of the delivery and acceptance of the deed.

(2) Subsection (1) above is without prejudice to any agreement which the parties to a contract may reach (whether or not an agreement incorporated into the contract) as to supersession of the contract.

**3. Damages for breach of contract of sale**

Any rule of law which precludes the buyer in a contract of sale of property from obtaining damages for breach of that contract by the seller unless the buyer rejects the property and rescinds the contract shall cease to have effect.

**4. Short title, extent etc.**

(1) This Act may be cited as the Contract (Scotland) Act 1997.

(2) This Act shall come into force at the end of that period of three months which begins with the day on which the Act is passed.

(3) Section 1 of this Act applies only for the purposes of proceedings commenced on or after, and sections 2 and 3 only as respects contracts entered into on or after, the date on which this Act comes into force.

(4) This Act extends to Scotland only.

## PROTECTION FROM HARASSMENT ACT 1997
### (1997, c 40)

*Scotland*

### 8.  Harassment

(1)   Every individual has a right to be free from harassment and, accordingly, a person must not pursue a course of conduct which amounts to harassment of another and—

(a)   is intended to amount to harassment of that person; or

(b)   occurs in circumstances where it would appear to a reasonable person that it would amount to harassment of that person.

(2)   An actual or apprehended breach of subsection (1) may be the subject of a claim in civil proceedings by the person who is or may be the victim of the course of conduct in question; and any such claim shall be known as an action of harassment.

(3)   For the purposes of this section—

'conduct' includes speech;

'harassment' of a person includes causing the person alarm or distress; and a course of conduct must involve conduct on at least two occasions.

(4)   It shall be a defence to any action of harassment to show that the course of conduct complained of—

(a)   was authorised by, under or by virtue of any enactment or rule of law;

(b)   was pursued for the purpose of preventing or detecting crime; or

(c)   was, in the particular circumstances, reasonable.

(5)   In an action of harassment the court may, without prejudice to any other remedies which it may grant—

(a)   award damages;

(b)   grant—

(i)   interdict or interim interdict;

(ii)   if it is satisfied that it is appropriate for it to do so in order to protect the person from further harassment, an order, to be known as a 'non-harassment order', requiring the defender to refrain from such conduct in relation to the pursuer as may be specified in the order for such period (which includes an indeterminate period) as may be so specified,

but a person may not be subjected to the same prohibitions in an interdict or interim interdict and a non-harassment order at the same time.

(6)   The damages which may be awarded in an action of harassment include damages for any anxiety caused by the harassment and any financial loss resulting from it.

(7)   Without prejudice to any right to seek review of any interlocutor, a person against whom a non-harassment order has been made, or the person for whose protection the order was made, may apply to the court by which the order was made for revocation of or a variation of the order and, on any such application, the court may revoke the order or vary it in such manner as it considers appropriate.

(8)   In section 10(1) of the Damages (Scotland) Act 1976 (interpretation), in the definition of 'personal injuries', after 'to reputation' there is inserted ', or injury resulting from harassment actionable under section 8 of the Protection from Harassment Act 1997'.

### 9.  Breach of non-harassment order

(1)   Any person who is found to be in breach of a non-harassment order made under section 8 is guilty of an offence and liable—

(a)   on conviction on indictment, to imprisonment for a term not exceeding five years or to a fine, or to both such imprisonment and such fine; and

(b)   on summary conviction, to imprisonment for a period not exceeding six months or to a fine not exceeding the statutory maximum, or to both such imprisonment and such fine.

(2)   A breach of a non-harassment order shall not be punishable other than in accordance with subsection (1).

## SOCIAL SECURITY (RECOVERY OF BENEFITS) ACT 1997
### (1997, c 27)

**3.  'The relevant period'**

(1)   In relation to a person ('the claimant') who has suffered any accident, injury or disease, 'the relevant period' has the meaning given by the following subsections.

(2)   Subject to subsection (4), if it is a case of accident or injury, the relevant period is the period of five years immediately following the day on which the accident or injury in question occurred.

(3)   Subject to subsection (4), if it is a case of disease, the relevant period is the period of five years beginning with the date on which the claimant first claims a listed benefit in consequence of the disease.

(4)   If at any time before the end of the period referred to in subsection (2) or (3)—

(a)   a person makes a compensation payment in final discharge of any claim made by or in respect of the claimant and arising out of the accident, injury or disease, or

(b)   an agreement is made under which an earlier compensation payment is treated as having been made in final discharge of any such claim,

the relevant period ends at that time.

**6.  Liability to pay Secretary of State amount of benefits**

(1)   A person who makes a compensation payment in any case is liable to pay to the Secretary of State an amount equal to the total amount of the recoverable benefits.

(2)   The liability referred to in subsection (1) arises immediately before the compensation payment or, if there is more than one, the first of them is made.

(3)   No amount becomes payable under this section before the end of the period of 14 days following the day on which the liability arises.

**7.  Recovery of payments due under section 6**

(1)   This section applies where a person has made a compensation payment but—

(a)   has not applied for a certificate of recoverable benefits, or

(b)   has not made a payment to the Secretary of State under section 6 before the end of the period allowed under that section.

(2)   The Secretary of State may—

(a)   issue the person who made the compensation payment with a certificate of recoverable benefits, if none has been issued, or

(b)   issue him with a copy of the certificate of recoverable benefits or (if more than one has been issued) the most recent one,

and (in either case) issue him with a demand that payment of any amount due under section 6 be made immediately.

(3)   The Secretary of State may, in accordance with subsections (4) and (5), recover the amount for which a demand for payment is made under subsection (2) from the person who made the compensation payment.

(4)   If the person who made the compensation payment resides or carries on business in England and Wales and a county court so orders, any amount recoverable under subsection (3) is recoverable by execution issued from the county court or otherwise as if it were payable under an order of that court.

(5) If the person who made the payment resides or carries on business in Scotland, any amount recoverable under subsection (3) may be enforced in like manner as an extract registered decree arbitral bearing a warrant for execution issued by the sheriff court of any sheriffdom in Scotland.

(6) A document bearing a certificate which—

(a) is signed by a person authorised to do so by the Secretary of State, and

(b) states that the document, apart from the certificate, is a record of the amount recoverable under subsection (3),

is conclusive evidence that that amount is so recoverable.

(7) A certificate under subsection (6) purporting to be signed by a person authorised to do so by the Secretary of State is to be treated as so signed unless the contrary is proved.

# SCHEDULES

## SCHEDULE 1. COMPENSATION PAYMENTS

### PART I. EXEMPTED PAYMENTS

1. Any small payment (defined in Part II of this Schedule).

2. Any payment made to or for the injured person under section [130 of the Powers of Criminal Courts (Sentencing) Act 2000] or section 249 of the Criminal Procedure (Scotland) Act 1995 (compensation orders against convicted persons).

3. Any payment made in the exercise of a discretion out of property held subject to a trust in a case where no more than 50 per cent. by value of the capital contributed to the trust was directly or indirectly provided by persons who are, or are alleged to be, liable in respect of—

(a) the accident, injury or disease suffered by the injured person, or

(b) the same or any connected accident, injury or disease suffered by another.

4. Any payment made out of property held for the purposes of any prescribed trust (whether the payment also falls within paragraph 3 or not).

5. (1) Any payment made to the injured person by an [insurer] under the terms of any contract of insurance entered into between the injured person and the [insurer] before—

(a) the date on which the injured person first claims a listed benefit in consequence of the disease in question, or

(b) the occurrence of the accident or injury in question.

[(2) 'Insurer' means—

(a) a person who has permission under Part 4 of the Financial Services and Markets Act 2000 to effect or carry out contracts of insurance; or

(b) an EEA firm of the kind mentioned in paragraph 5(d) of Schedule 3 to that Act which has permission under paragraph 15 of that Schedule (as a result of qualifying for authorisation under paragraph 12 of that Schedule) to effect or carry out contracts of insurance.

(3) Sub-paragraph (2) must be read with—

(a) section 22 of the Financial Services and Markets Act 2000;

(b) any relevant order under that section; and

(c) Schedule 2 to that Act.]

6. Any redundancy payment falling to be taken into account in the assessment of damages in respect of an accident, injury or disease.

7. So much of any payment as is referable to costs.

8. Any prescribed payment.

PART II. POWER TO DISREGARD SMALL PAYMENTS

9.—(1) Regulations may make provision for compensation payments to be disregarded for the purposes of sections 6 and 8 in prescribed cases where the amount of the compensation payment, or the aggregate amount of two or more connected compensation payments, does not exceed the prescribed sum.

(2) A compensation payment disregarded by virtue of this paragraph is referred to in paragraph 1 as a 'small payment'.

(3) For the purposes of this paragraph—

(a) two or more compensation payments are 'connected' if each is made to or in respect of the same injured person and in respect of the same accident, injury or disease, and

(b) any reference to a compensation payment is a reference to a payment which would be such a payment apart from paragraph 1.

SCHEDULE 2. CALCULATION OF COMPENSATION PAYMENT

| (1) Head of compensation | (2) Benefit |
|---|---|
| 1. Compensation for earnings lost during the relevant period | . . . Disablement pension payable under section 103 of the 1992 Act Incapacity benefit Income support Invalidity pension and allowance Jobseeker's allowance Reduced earnings allowance Severe disablement allowance Sickness benefit Statutory sick pay Unemployability supplement Unemployment benefit |
| 2. Compensation for cost of care incurred during the relevant period | Attendance allowance Care component of disability living allowance Disablement pension increase payable under section 104 or 105 of the 1992 Act |
| 3. Compensation for loss of mobility during the relevant period | Mobility allowance Mobility component of disability living allowance |

**HUMAN RIGHTS ACT 1998**
**(1998, c 42)**

*Introduction*

**1.  The Convention Rights**

(1) In this Act 'the Convention rights' means the rights and fundamental freedoms set out in—

(a) Articles 2 to 12 and 14 of the Convention,

(b) Articles 1 to 3 of the First Protocol, and

(c) Articles 1 and 2 of the Sixth Protocol,

as read with Articles 16 to 18 of the Convention.

(2) Those Articles are to have effect for the purposes of this Act subject to any designated derogation or reservation (as to which see sections 14 and 15).

(3) The Articles are set out in Schedule 1.

(4) The [Lord Chancellor] may by order make such amendments to this Act as he considers appropriate to reflect the effect, in relation to the United Kingdom, of a protocol.

(5) In subsection (4) 'protocol' means a protocol to the Convention—

(a) which the United Kingdom has ratified; or

(b) which the United Kingdom has signed with a view to ratification.

(6) No amendment may be made by an order under subsection (4) so as to come into force before the protocol concerned is in force in relation to the United Kingdom.

## 2. Interpretation of Convention rights

(1) A court or tribunal determining a question which has arisen in connection with a Convention right must take into account any—

(a) judgment, decision, declaration or advisory opinion of the European Court of Human Rights,

(b) opinion of the Commission given in a report adopted under Article 31 of the Convention,

(c) decision of the Commission in connection with Article 26 or 27(2) of the Convention, or

(d) decision of the Committee of Ministers taken under Article 46 of the Convention,

whenever made or given, so far as, in the opinion of the court or tribunal, it is relevant to the proceedings in which that question has arisen.

(2) Evidence of any judgment, decision, declaration or opinion of which account may have to be taken under this section is to be given in proceedings before any court or tribunal in such manner as may be provided by rules.

(3) In this section 'rules' means rules of court or, in the case of proceedings before a tribunal, rules made for the purposes of this section—

(a) by the Lord Chancellor or the Secretary of State, in relation to any proceedings outside Scotland;

(b) by the Secretary of State, in relation to proceedings in Scotland; or

(c) by a Northern Ireland department, in relation to proceedings before a tribunal in Northern Ireland—

(i) which deals with transferred matters; and

(ii) for which no rules made under paragraph (a) are in force.

*Legislation*

## 3. Interpretation of legislation

(1) So far as it is possible to do so, primary legislation and subordinate legislation must be read and given effect in a way which is compatible with the Convention rights.

(2) This section—

(a) applies to primary legislation and subordinate legislation whenever enacted;

(b) does not affect the validity, continuing operation or enforcement of any incompatible primary legislation; and

(c) does not affect the validity, continuing operation or enforcement of any incompatible subordinate legislation if (disregarding any possibility of revocation) primary legislation prevents removal of the incompatibility.

## 4. Declaration of incompatibility

(1) Subsection (2) applies in any proceedings in which a court determines

whether a provision of primary legislation is compatible with a Convention right.

(2) If the court is satisfied that the provision is incompatible with a Convention right, it may make a declaration of that incompatibility.

(3) Subsection (4) applies in any proceedings in which a court determines whether a provision of subordinate legislation, made in the exercise of a power conferred by primary legislation, is compatible with a Convention right.

(4) If the court is satisfied—

    (a) that the provision is incompatible with a Convention right, and

    (b) that (disregarding any possibility of revocation) the primary legislation concerned prevents removal of the incompatibility,

it may make a declaration of that incompatibility.

(5) In this section 'court' means—

    (a) the House of Lords;

    (b) the Judicial Committee of the Privy Council;

    (c) the Courts-Martial Appeal Court;

    (d) in Scotland, the High Court of Justiciary sitting otherwise than as a trial court or the Court of Session;

    (e) in England and Wales or Northern Ireland, the High Court or the Court of Appeal.

(6) A declaration under this section ('a declaration of incompatibility')—

    (a) does not affect the validity, continuing operation or enforcement of the provision in respect of which it is given; and

    (b) is not binding on the parties to the proceedings in which it is made.

## 5. Right of Crown to intervene

(1) Where a court is considering whether to make a declaration of incompatibility, the Crown is entitled to notice in accordance with rules of court.

(2) In any case to which subsection (1) applies—

    (a) a Minister of the Crown (or a person nominated by him),

    (b) a member of the Scottish Executive,

    (c) a Northern Ireland Minister,

    (d) a Northern Ireland department,

is entitled, on giving notice in accordance with rules of court, to be joined as a party to the proceedings.

(3) Notice under subsection (2) may be given at any time during the proceedings.

(4) A person who has been made a party to criminal proceedings (other than in Scotland) as the result of a notice under subsection (2) may, with leave, appeal to the House of Lords against any declaration of incompatibility made in the proceedings.

(5) In subsection (4)—

'criminal proceedings' includes all proceedings before the Courts-Martial Appeal Court; and

'leave' means leave granted by the court making the declaration of incompatibility or by the House of Lords.

*Remedial action*

## 10. Power to take remedial action

(1) This section applies if—

    (a) a provision of legislation has been declared under section 4 to be incompatible with a Convention right and, if an appeal lies—

        (i) all persons who may appeal have stated in writing that they do not intend to do so;

(ii)   the time for bringing an appeal has expired and no appeal has been brought within that time; or

(iii)   an appeal brought within that time has been determined or abandoned; or

(b)   it appears to a Minister of the Crown or Her Majesty in Council that, having regard to a finding of the European Court of Human Rights made after the coming into force of this section in proceedings against the United Kingdom, a provision of legislation is incompatible with an obligation of the United Kingdom arising from the Convention.

(2)   If a Minister of the Crown considers that there are compelling reasons for proceeding under this section, he may by order make such amendments to the legislation as he considers necessary to remove the incompatibility.

(3)   If, in the case of subordinate legislation, a Minister of the Crown considers—

(a)   that it is necessary to amend the primary legislation under which the subordinate legislation in question was made, in order to enable the incompatibility to be removed, and

(b)   that there are compelling reasons for proceeding under this section, he may by order make such amendments to the primary legislation as he considers necessary.

(4)   This section also applies where the provision in question is in subordinate legislation and has been quashed, or declared invalid, by reason of incompatibility with a Convention right and the Minister proposes to proceed under paragraph 2(b) of Schedule 2.

(5)   If the legislation is an Order in Council, the power conferred by subsection (2) or (3) is exercisable by Her Majesty in Council.

(6)   In this section 'legislation' does not include a Measure of the Church Assembly or of the General Synod of the Church of England.

(7)   Schedule 2 makes further provision about remedial orders.

## 21.   Interpretation, etc.

(1)   In this Act—

'amend' includes repeal and apply (with or without modifications);

'the appropriate Minister' means the Minister of the Crown having charge of the appropriate authorised government department (within the meaning of the Crown Proceedings Act 1947);

'the Commission' means the European Commission of Human Rights;

'the Convention' means the Convention for the Protection of Human Rights and Fundamental Freedoms, agreed by the Council of Europe at Rome on 4th November 1950 as it has effect for the time being in relation to the United Kingdom;

'declaration of incompatibility' means a declaration under section 4;

'Minister of the Crown' has the same meaning as in the Ministers of the Crown Act 1975;

'Northern Ireland Minister' includes the First Minister and the deputy First Minister in Northern Ireland;

'primary legislation' means any—

(a)   public general Act;

(b)   local and personal Act;

(c)   private Act;

(d)   Measure of the Church Assembly;

(e)   Measure of the General Synod of the Church of England;

(f)   Order in Council—

(i)   made in exercise of Her Majesty's Royal Prerogative;

(ii)   made under section 38(1)(a) of the Northern Ireland Constitution

Act 1973 or the corresponding provision of the Northern Ireland Act 1998; or

(iii)   amending an Act of a kind mentioned in paragraph (a), (b) or (c); and includes an order or other instrument made under primary legislation (otherwise than by the National Assembly for Wales, a member of the Scottish Executive, a Northern Ireland Minister or a Northern Ireland department) to the extent to which it operates to bring one or more provisions of that legislation into force or amends any primary legislation;

'the First Protocol' means the protocol to the Convention agreed at Paris on 20th March 1952;

'the Sixth Protocol' means the protocol to the Convention agreed at Strasbourg on 28th April 1983;

'the Eleventh Protocol' means the protocol to the Convention (restructuring the control machinery established by the Convention) agreed at Strasbourg on 11th May 1994;

'remedial order' means an order under section 10;

'subordinate legislation' means any—

(a)   Order in Council other than one—

(i)   made in exercise of Her Majesty's Royal Prerogative;

(ii)   made under section 38(1)(a) of the Northern Ireland Constitution Act 1973 or the corresponding provision of the Northern Ireland Act 1998; or

(iii)   amending an Act of a kind mentioned in the definition of primary legislation;

(b)   Act of the Scottish Parliament;

(c)   Act of the Parliament of Northern Ireland;

(d)   Measure of the Assembly established under section 1 of the Northern Ireland Assembly Act 1973;

(e)   Act of the Northern Ireland Assembly;

(f)   order, rules, regulations, scheme, warrant, byelaw or other instrument made under primary legislation (except to the extent to which it operates to bring one or more provisions of that legislation into force or amends any primary legislation);

(g)   order, rules, regulations, scheme, warrant, byelaw or other instrument made under legislation mentioned in paragraph (b), (c), (d) or (e) or made under an Order in Council applying only to Northern Ireland;

(h)   order, rules, regulations, scheme, warrant, byelaw or other instrument made by a member of the Scottish Executive, a Northern Ireland Minister or a Northern Ireland department in exercise of prerogative or other executive functions of Her Majesty which are exercisable by such a person on behalf of Her Majesty;

'transferred matters' has the same meaning as in the Northern Ireland Act 1998; and

'tribunal' means any tribunal in which legal proceedings may be brought.

(2)   The references in paragraphs (b) and (c) of section 2(1) to Articles are to Articles of the Convention as they had effect immediately before the coming into force of the Eleventh Protocol.

(3)   The reference in paragraph (d) of section 2(1) to Article 46 includes a reference to Articles 32 and 54 of the Convention as they had effect immediately before the coming into force of the Eleventh Protocol.

(4)   The references in section 2(1) to a report or decision of the Commission or a decision of the Committee of Ministers include references to a report or decision made as provided by paragraphs 3, 4 and 6 of Article 5 of the Eleventh Protocol (transitional provisions).

(5)   Any liability under the Army Act 1955, the Air Force Act 1955 or the Naval Discipline Act 1957 to suffer death for an offence is replaced by a liability

to imprisonment for life or any less punishment authorised by those Acts; and those Acts shall accordingly have effect with the necessary modifications.

**22. Short title, commencement, application and extent**
(1)   This Act may be cited as the Human Rights Act 1998.
. . .

# SCHEDULES

## SCHEDULE 1. THE ARTICLES

### PART I. THE CONVENTION

*Rights and Freedoms*

**Article 2. Right to Life**
l.   Everyone's right to life shall be protected by law. No one shall be deprived of his life intentionally save in the execution of a sentence of a court following his conviction of a crime for which this penalty is provided by law.
2.   Deprivation of life shall not be regarded as inflicted in contravention of this Article when it results from the use of force which is no more than absolutely necessary:
(a)   in defence of any person from unlawful violence;
(b)   in order to effect a lawful arrest or to prevent the escape of a person lawfully detained;
(c)   in action lawfully taken for the purpose of quelling a riot or insurrection.

**Article 3. Prohibition of Torture**
No one shall be subjected to torture or to inhuman or degrading treatment or punishment.

**Article 4. Prohibition of Slavery and Forced Labour**
l.   No one shall be held in slavery or servitude.
2.   No one shall be required to perform forced or compulsory labour.
3.   For the purpose of this Article the term 'forced or compulsory labour' shall not include:
(a)   any work required to be done in the ordinary course of detention imposed according to the provisions of Article 5 of this Convention or during conditional release from such detention;
(b)   any service of a military character or, in case of conscientious objectors in countries where they are recognised, service exacted instead of compulsory military service;
(c)   any service exacted in case of an emergency or calamity threatening the life or well-being of the community;
(d)   any work or service which forms part of normal civic obligations.

**Article 5. Right to Liberty and Security**
1.   Everyone has the right to liberty and security of person. No one shall be deprived of his liberty save in the following cases and in accordance with a procedure prescribed by law:
(a)   the lawful detention of a person after conviction by a competent court;
(b)   the lawful arrest or detention of a person for non-compliance with the lawful order of a court or in order to secure the fulfilment of any obligation prescribed by law;
(c)   the lawful arrest or detention of a person effected for the purpose of bringing him before the competent legal authority on reasonable suspicion of

having committed an offence or when it is reasonably considered necessary to prevent his committing an offence or fleeing after having done so;

(d) the detention of a minor by lawful order for the purpose of educational supervision or his lawful detention for the purpose of bringing him before the competent legal authority;

(e) the lawful detention of persons for the prevention of the spreading of infectious diseases, of persons of unsound mind, alcoholics or drug addicts or vagrants;

(f) the lawful arrest or detention of a person to prevent his effecting an unauthorised entry into the country or of a person against whom action is being taken with a view to deportation or extradition.

2. Everyone who is arrested shall be informed promptly, in a language which he understands, of the reasons for his arrest and of any charge against him.

3. Everyone arrested or detained in accordance with the provisions of paragraph 1(c) of this Article shall be brought promptly before a judge or other officer authorised by law to exercise judicial power and shall be entitled to trial within a reasonable time or to release pending trial. Release may be conditioned by guarantees to appear for trial.

4. Everyone who is deprived of his liberty by arrest or detention shall be entitled to take proceedings by which the lawfulness of his detention shall be decided speedily by a court and his release ordered if the detention is not lawful.

5. Everyone who has been the victim of arrest or detention in contravention of the provisions of this Article shall have an enforceable right to compensation.

### Article 6. Right to a Fair Trial

1. In the determination of his civil rights and obligations or of any criminal charge against him, everyone is entitled to a fair and public hearing within a reasonable time by an independent and impartial tribunal established by law. Judgment shall be pronounced publicly but the press and public may be excluded from all or part of the trial in the interest of morals, public order or national security in a democratic society, where the interests of juveniles or the protection of the private life of the parties so require, or to the extent strictly necessary in the opinion of the court in special circumstances where publicity would prejudice the interests of justice.

2. Everyone charged with a criminal offence shall be presumed innocent until proved guilty according to law.

3. Everyone charged with a criminal offence has the following minimum rights:

(a) to be informed promptly, in a language which he understands and in detail, of the nature and cause of the accusation against him;

(b) to have adequate time and facilities for the preparation of his defence;

(c) to defend himself in person or through legal assistance of his own choosing or, if he has not sufficient means to pay for legal assistance, to be given it free when the interests of justice so require;

(d) to examine or have examined witnesses against him and to obtain the attendance and examination of witnesses on his behalf under the same conditions as witnesses against him;

(e) to have the free assistance of an interpreter if he cannot understand or speak the language used in court.

### Article 7. No Punishment Without Law

1. No one shall be held guilty of any criminal offence on account of any act or omission which did not constitute a criminal offence under national or international law at the time when it was committed. Nor shall a heavier penalty be imposed than the one that was applicable at the time the criminal offence was committed.

2. This Article shall not prejudice the trial and punishment of any person for

any act or omission which, at the time when it was committed, was criminal according to the general principles of law recognised by civilised nations.

## Article 8. Right to Respect for Private and Family Life

1. Everyone has the right to respect for his private and family life, his home and his correspondence.

2. There shall be no interference by a public authority with the exercise of this right except such as is in accordance with the law and is necessary in a democratic society in the interests of national security, public safety or the economic well-being of the country, for the prevention of disorder or crime, for the protection of health or morals, or for the protection of the rights and freedoms of others.

## Article 9. Freedom of Thought, Conscience and Religion

1. Everyone has the right to freedom of thought, conscience and religion; this right includes freedom to change his religion or belief and freedom, either alone or in community with others and in public or private, to manifest his religion or belief, in worship, teaching, practice and observance.

2. Freedom to manifest one's religion or beliefs shall be subject only to such limitations as are prescribed by law and are necessary in a democratic society in the interests of public safety, for the protection of public order, health or morals, or for the protection of the rights and freedoms of others.

## Article 10. Freedom of Expression

1. Everyone has the right to freedom of expression. This right shall include freedom to hold opinions and to receive and impart information and ideas without interference by public authority and regardless of frontiers. This Article shall not prevent States from requiring the licensing of broadcasting, television or cinema enterprises.

2. The exercise of these freedoms, since it carries with it duties and responsibilities, may be subject to such formalities, conditions, restrictions or penalties as are prescribed by law and are necessary in a democratic society, in the interests of national security, territorial integrity or public safety, for the prevention of disorder or crime, for the protection of health or morals, for the protection of the reputation or rights of others, for preventing the disclosure of information received in confidence, or for maintaining the authority and impartiality of the judiciary.

## Article 11. Freedom of Assembly and Association

1. Everyone has the right to freedom of peaceful assembly and to freedom of association with others, including the right to form and to join trade unions for the protection of his interests.

2. No restrictions shall be placed on the exercise of these rights other than such as are prescribed by law and are necessary in a democratic society in the interests of national security or public safety, for the prevention of disorder or crime, for the protection of health or morals or for the protection of the rights and freedoms of others. This Article shall not prevent the imposition of lawful restrictions on the exercise of these rights by members of the armed forces, of the police or of the administration of the State.

## Article 12. Right to Marry

Men and women of marriageable age have the right to marry and to found a family, according to the national laws governing the exercise of this right.

## Article 14. Prohibition of Discrimination

The enjoyment of the rights and freedoms set forth in this Convention shall be secured without discrimination on any ground such as sex, race, colour, language, religion, political or other opinion, national or social origin, association with a national minority, property, birth or other status.

### Article 16. Restrictions on Political Activity of Aliens
Nothing in Articles 10, 11 and 14 shall be regarded as preventing the High Contracting Parties from imposing restrictions on the political activity of aliens.

### Article 17. Prohibition of Abuse of Rights
Nothing in this Convention may be interpreted as implying for any State, group or person any right to engage in any activity or perform any act aimed at the destruction of any of the rights and freedoms set forth herein or at their limitation to a greater extent than is provided for in the Convention.

### Article 18. Limitation on Use of Restrictions on Rights
The restrictions permitted under this Convention to the said rights and freedoms shall not be applied for any purpose other than those for which they have been prescribed.

## PART II. THE FIRST PROTOCOL

### Article 1. Protection of Property
Every natural or legal person is entitled to the peaceful enjoyment of his possessions. No one shall be deprived of his possessions except in the public interest and subject to the conditions provided for by law and by the general principles of international law.

The preceding provisions shall not, however, in any way impair the right of a State to enforce such laws as it deems necessary to control the use of property in accordance with the general interest or to secure the payment of taxes or other contributions or penalties.

### Article 2. Right to Education
No person shall be denied the right to education. In the exercise of any functions which it assumes in relation to education and to teaching, the State shall respect the right of parents to ensure such education and teaching in conformity with their own religious and philosophical convictions.

### Article 3. Right to Free Elections
The High Contracting Parties undertake to hold free elections at reasonable intervals by secret ballot, under conditions which will ensure the free expression of the opinion of the people in the choice of the legislature.

## PART III. THE SIXTH PROTOCOL

### Article 1. Abolition of the Death Penalty
The death penalty shall be abolished. No one shall be condemned to such penalty or executed.

### Article 2. Death Penalty in Time of War
A State may make provision in its law for the death penalty in respect of acts committed in time of war or of imminent threat of war; such penalty shall be applied only in the instances laid down in the law and in accordance with its provisions. The State shall communicate to the Secretary General of the Council of Europe the relevant provisions of that law.

## SCHEDULE 2. REMEDIAL ORDERS

### 1. Orders
(1) A remedial order may—

(a) contain such incidental, supplemental, consequential or transitional provision as the person making it considers appropriate;

(b) be made so as to have effect from a date earlier than that on which it is made;

(c) make provision for the delegation of specific functions;

(d) make different provision for different cases.

(2) The power conferred by sub-paragraph (1)(a) includes—

(a) power to amend primary legislation (including primary legislation other than that which contains the incompatible provision); and

(b) power to amend or revoke subordinate legislation (including subordinate legislation other than that which contains the incompatible provision).

(3) A remedial order may be made so as to have the same extent as the legislation which it affects.

(4) No person is to be guilty of an offence solely as a result of the retrospective effect of a remedial order.

## 2. Procedure

No remedial order may be made unless—

(a) a draft of the order has been approved by a resolution of each House of Parliament made after the end of the period of 60 days beginning with the day on which the draft was laid; or

(b) it is declared in the order that it appears to the person making it that, because of the urgency of the matter, it is necessary to make the order without a draft being so approved.

## 3. Orders laid in draft

(1) No draft may be laid under paragraph 2(a) unless—

(a) the person proposing to make the order has laid before Parliament a document which contains a draft of the proposed order and the required information; and

(b) the period of 60 days, beginning with the day on which the document required by this sub-paragraph was laid, has ended.

(2) If representations have been made during that period, the draft laid under paragraph 2(a) must be accompanied by a statement containing—

(a) a summary of the representations; and

(b) if, as a result of the representations, the proposed order has been changed, details of the changes.

## 4. Urgent cases

(1) If a remedial order ('the original order') is made without being approved in draft, the person making it must lay it before Parliament, accompanied by the required information, after it is made.

(2) If representations have been made during the period of 60 days beginning with the day on which the original order was made, the person making it must (after the end of that period) lay before Parliament a statement containing—

(a) a summary of the representations; and

(b) if, as a result of the representations, he considers it appropriate to make changes to the original order, details of the changes.

(3) If sub-paragraph (2)(b) applies, the person making the statement must—

(a) make a further remedial order replacing the original order; and

(b) lay the replacement order before Parliament.

(4) If, at the end of the period of 120 days beginning with the day on which the original order was made, a resolution has not been passed by each House approving the original or replacement order, the order ceases to have effect (but without that affecting anything previously done under either order or the power to make a fresh remedial order).

## 5. Definitions

In this Schedule—

'representations' means representations about a remedial order (or proposed remedial order) made to the person making (or proposing to make) it and includes any relevant Parliamentary report or resolution; and 'required information' means—

(a) an explanation of the incompatibility which the order (or proposed order) seeks to remove, including particulars of the relevant declaration, finding or order; and

(b) a statement of the reasons for proceeding under section 10 and for making an order in those terms.

## 6. Calculating periods

In calculating any period for the purposes of this Schedule, no account is to be taken of any time during which—

(a) Parliament is dissolved or prorogued; or

(b) both Houses are adjourned for more than four days.

[7. (1) This paragraph applies in relation to—

(a) any remedial order made, and any draft of such an order proposed to be made,—

    (i) by the Scottish Ministers; or

    (ii) within devolved competence (within the meaning of the Scotland Act 1998) by Her Majesty in Council; and

(b) any document or statement to be laid in connection with such an order (or proposed order).

(2) This Schedule has effect in relation to any such order (or proposed order), document or statement subject to the following modifications.

(3) Any reference to Parliament, each House of Parliament or both Houses of Parliament shall be construed as a reference to the Scottish Parliament.

(4) Paragraph 6 does not apply and instead, in calculating any period for the purposes of this Schedule, no account is to be taken of any time during which the Scottish Parliament is dissolved or is in recess for more than four days.]

## LATE PAYMENT OF COMMERCIAL DEBTS (INTEREST) ACT 1998
### (1998, c 20)

### PART I. STATUTORY INTEREST ON QUALIFYING DEBTS

## 1. Statutory interest

(1) It is an implied term in a contract to which this Act applies that any qualifying debt created by the contract carries simple interest subject to and in accordance with this Part.

(2) Interest carried under that implied term (in this Act referred to as 'statutory interest') shall be treated, for the purposes of any rule of law or enactment (other than this Act) relating to interest on debts, in the same way as interest carried under an express contract term.

(3) This Part has effect subject to Part II (which in certain circumstances permits contract terms to oust or vary the right to statutory interest that would otherwise be conferred by virtue of the term implied by subsection (1)).

## 2. Contracts to which Act applies

(1) This Act applies to a contract for the supply of goods or services where the purchaser and the supplier are each acting in the course of a business, other than an excepted contract.

(2) In this Act 'contract for the supply of goods or services' means—

(a) a contract of sale of goods; or

(b) a contract (other than a contract of sale of goods) by which a person does any, or any combination, of the things mentioned in subsection (3) for a consideration that is (or includes) a money consideration.

(3) Those things are—

(a) transferring or agreeing to transfer to another the property in goods;

(b)   bailing or agreeing to bail goods to another by way of hire or, in Scotland, hiring or agreeing to hire goods to another; and

(c)   agreeing to carry out a service.

(4)   For the avoidance of doubt a contract of service or apprenticeship is not a contract for the supply of goods or services.

(5)   The following are excepted contracts—

(a)   a consumer credit agreement;

(b)   a contract intended to operate by way of mortgage, pledge, charge or other security.

(c)   (*repealed*)

(6)   (*repealed*)

(7)   In this section—

'business' includes a profession and the activities of any government department or local or public authority;

'consumer credit agreement' has the same meaning as in the Consumer Credit Act 1974;

'contract of sale of goods' and 'goods' have the same meaning as in the Sale of Goods Act 1979;

['government department' includes any part of the Scottish Administration].

'property in goods' means the general property in them and not merely a special property.

## [2A.   Application of the Act to advocates

The provisions of this Act apply to a transaction in respect of which fees are paid for professional services to a member of the Faculty of Advocates as they apply to a contract for the supply of services for the purpose of this Act.]

## 3.   Qualifying debts

(1)   A debt created by virtue of an obligation under a contract to which this Act applies to pay the whole or any part of the contract price is a 'qualifying debt' for the purposes of this Act, unless (when created) the whole of the debt is prevented from carrying statutory interest by this section.

(2)   A debt does not carry statutory interest if or to the extent that it consists of a sum to which a right to interest or to charge interest applies by virtue of any enactment (other than section 1 of this Act).

This subsection does not prevent a sum from carrying statutory interest by reason of the fact that a court, arbitrator or arbiter would, apart from this Act, have power to award interest on it.

(3)   A debt does not carry (and shall be treated as never having carried) statutory interest if or to the extent that a right to demand interest on it, which exists by virtue of any rule of law, is exercised.

(4), (5)   (*repealed*)

## 4.   Period for which statutory interest runs

(1)   Statutory interest runs in relation to a qualifying debt in accordance with this section (unless section 5 applies).

(2)   Statutory interest starts to run on the day after the relevant day for the debt, at the rate prevailing under section 6 at the end of the relevant day.

(3)   Where the supplier and the purchaser agree a date for payment of the debt (that is, the day on which the debt is to be created by the contract), that is the relevant day unless the debt relates to an obligation to make an advance payment.

A date so agreed may be a fixed one or may depend on the happening of an event or the failure of an event to happen.

(4)   Where the debt relates to an obligation to make an advance payment, the relevant day is the day on which the debt is treated by section 11 as having been created.

(5) In any other case, the relevant day is the last day of the period of 30 days beginning with—

(a) the day on which the obligation of the supplier to which the debt relates is performed; or

(b) the day on which the purchaser has notice of the amount of the debt or (where that amount is unascertained) the sum which the supplier claims is the amount of the debt,

whichever is the later.

(6) Where the debt is created by virtue of an obligation to pay a sum due in respect of a period of hire of goods, subsection (5)(a) has effect as if it referred to the last day of that period.

(7) Statutory interest ceases to run when the interest would cease to run if it were carried under an express contract term.

(8) In this section 'advance payment' has the same meaning as in section 11.

## 5. Remission of statutory interest

(1) This section applies where, by reason of any conduct of the supplier, the interests of justice require that statutory interest should be remitted in whole or part in respect of a period for which it would otherwise run in relation to a qualifying debt.

(2) If the interests of justice require that the supplier should receive no statutory interest for a period, statutory interest shall not run for that period.

(3) If the interests of justice require that the supplier should receive statutory interest at a reduced rate for a period, statutory interest shall run at such rate as meets the justice of the case for that period.

(4) Remission of statutory interest under this section may be required—

(a) by reason of conduct at any time (whether before or after the time at which the debt is created); and

(b) for the whole period for which statutory interest would otherwise run or for one or more parts of that period.

(5) In this section 'conduct' includes any act or omission.

## [5A. Compensation arising out of late payment

(1) Once statutory interest begins to run in relation to a qualifying debt, the supplier shall be entitled to a fixed sum (in addition to the statutory interest on the debt).

(2) That sum shall be—

(a) for a debt less than £1,000, the sum of £40;

(b) for a debt of £1,000 or more, but less than £10,000, the sum of £70;

(c) for a debt of £10,000 or more, the sum of £100.

(3) The obligation to pay an additional fixed sum under this section in respect of a qualifying debt shall be treated as part of the term implied by section 1(1) in the contract creating the debt.]

## 6. Rate of statutory interest

(1) The Secretary of State shall by order made with the consent of the Treasury set the rate of statutory interest by prescribing—

(a) a formula for calculating the rate of statutory interest; or

(b) the rate of statutory interest.

(2) Before making such an order the Secretary of State shall, among other things, consider the extent to which it may be desirable to set the rate so as to—

(a) protect suppliers whose financial position makes them particularly vulnerable if their qualifying debts are paid late; and

(b) deter generally the late payment of qualifying debts.

## PART II. CONTRACT TERMS RELATING TO LATE PAYMENT OF QUALIFYING DEBTS

### 7.  Purpose of Part II

(1)   This Part deals with the extent to which the parties to a contract to which this Act applies may by reference to contract terms oust or vary the right to statutory interest that would otherwise apply when a qualifying debt created by the contract (in this Part referred to as 'the debt') is not paid.

(2)   This Part applies to contract terms agreed before the debt is created; after that time the parties are free to agree terms dealing with the debt.

(3)   This Part has effect without prejudice to any other ground which may affect the validity of a contract term.

### 8.  Circumstances where statutory interest may be ousted or varied

(1)   Any contract terms are void to the extent that they purport to exclude the right to statutory interest in relation to the debt, unless there is a substantial contractual remedy for late payment of the debt.

(2)   Where the parties agree a contractual remedy for late payment of the debt that is a substantial remedy, statutory interest is not carried by the debt (unless they agree otherwise).

(3)   The parties may not agree to vary the right to statutory interest in relation to the debt unless either the right to statutory interest as varied or the overall remedy for late payment of the debt is a substantial remedy.

(4)   Any contract terms are void to the extent that they purport to—

(a)   confer a contractual right to interest that is not a substantial remedy for late payment of the debt, or

(b)   vary the right to statutory interest so as to provide for a right to statutory interest that is not a substantial remedy for late payment of the debt,

unless the overall remedy for late payment of the debt is a substantial remedy.

(5)   Subject to this section, the parties are free to agree contract terms which deal with the consequences of late payment of the debt.

### 9.  Meaning of 'substantial remedy'

(1)   A remedy for the late payment of the debt shall be regarded as a substantial remedy unless—

(a)   the remedy is insufficient either for the purpose of compensating the supplier for late payment or for deterring late payment; and

(b)   it would not be fair or reasonable to allow the remedy to be relied on to oust or (as the case may be) to vary the right to statutory interest that would otherwise apply in relation to the debt.

(2)   In determining whether a remedy is not a substantial remedy, regard shall be had to all the relevant circumstances at the time the terms in question are agreed.

(3)   In determining whether subsection (1)(b) applies, regard shall be had (without prejudice to the generality of subsection (2)) to the following matters—

(a)   the benefits of commercial certainty;

(b)   the strength of the bargaining positions of the parties relative to each other;

(c)   whether the term was imposed by one party to the detriment of the other (whether by the use of standard terms or otherwise); and

(d)   whether the supplier received an inducement to agree to the term.

### 10.  Interpretation of Part II

In this Part—

'contract term' means a term of the contract creating the debt or any other contract term binding the parties (or either of them);

'contractual remedy' means a contractual right to interest or any contractual remedy other than interest;

'contractual right to interest' includes a reference to a contractual right to charge interest;

'overall remedy', in relation to the late payment of the debt, means any combination of a contractual right to interest, a varied right to statutory interest or a contractual remedy other than interest;

'substantial remedy' shall be construed in accordance with section 9.

(2)   In this Part a reference (however worded) to contract terms which vary the right to statutory interest is a reference to terms altering in any way the effect of Part I in relation to the debt (for example by postponing the time at which interest starts to run or by imposing conditions on the right to interest).

(3)   In this Part a reference to late payment of the debt is a reference to late payment of the sum due when the debt is created (excluding any part of that sum which is prevented from carrying statutory interest by section 3).

## PART III. GENERAL AND SUPPLEMENTARY

### 11.   Treatment of advance payments of the contract price

(1)   A qualifying debt created by virtue of an obligation to make an advance payment shall be treated for the purposes of this Act as if it was created on the day mentioned in subsection (3), (4) or (5) (as the case may be).

(2)   In this section 'advance payment' means a payment falling due before the obligation of the supplier to which the whole contract price relates ('the supplier's obligation') is performed, other than a payment of a part of the contract price that is due in respect of any part performance of that obligation and payable on or after the day on which that part performance is completed.

(3)   Where the advance payment is the whole contract price, the debt shall be treated as created on the day on which the supplier's obligation is performed.

(4)   Where the advance payment is a part of the contract price, but the sum is not due in respect of any part performance of the supplier's obligation, the debt shall be treated as created on the day on which the supplier's obligation is performed.

(5)   Where the advance payment is a part of the contract price due in respect of any part performance of the supplier's obligation, but is payable before that part performance is completed, the debt shall be treated as created on the day on which the relevant part performance is completed.

(6)   Where the debt is created by virtue of an obligation to pay a sum due in respect of a period of hire of goods, this section has effect as if—

(a)   references to the day on which the supplier's obligation is performed were references to the last day of that period; and

(b)   references to part performance of that obligation were references to part of that period.

(7)   For the purposes of this section an obligation to pay the whole outstanding balance of the contract price shall be regarded as an obligation to pay the whole contract price and not as an obligation to pay a part of the contract price.

### 12.   Conflict of laws

(1)   This Act does not have effect in relation to a contract governed by the law of a part of the United Kingdom by choice of the parties if—

(a)   there is no significant connection between the contract and that part of the United Kingdom; and

(b)   but for that choice, the applicable law would be a foreign law.

(2)   This Act has effect in relation to a contract governed by a foreign law by choice of the parties if—

(a)   but for that choice, the applicable law would be the law of a part of the United Kingdom; and

(b)   there is no significant connection between the contract and any country other than that part of the United Kingdom.

(3)   In this section—

'contract' means a contract falling within section 2(1); and

'foreign law' means the law of a country outside the United Kingdom.

### 13.   Assignments, etc.

(1)   The operation of this Act in relation to a qualifying debt is not affected by—

(a)   any change in the identity of the parties to the contract creating the debt; or

(b)   the passing of the right to be paid the debt, or the duty to pay it (in whole or in part) to a person other than the person who is the original creditor or the original debtor when the debt is created.

(2)   Any reference in this Act to the supplier or the purchaser is a reference to the person who is for the time being the supplier or the purchaser or, in relation to a time after the debt in question has been created, the person who is for the time being the creditor or the debtor, as the case may be.

(3)   Where the right to be paid part of a debt passes to a person other than the person who is the original creditor when the debt is created, any reference in this Act to a debt shall be construed as (or, if the context so requires, as including) a reference to part of a debt.

(4)   A reference in this section to the identity of the parties to a contract changing, or to a right or duty passing, is a reference to it changing or passing by assignment or assignation, by operation of law or otherwise.

### 14.   Contract terms relating to the date for payment of the contract price

(1)   This section applies to any contract term which purports to have the effect of postponing the time at which a qualifying debt would otherwise be created by a contract to which this Act applies.

(2)   Sections 3(2)(b) and 17(1)(b) of the Unfair Contract Terms Act 1977 (no reliance to be placed on certain contract terms) shall apply in cases where such a contract term is not contained in written standard terms of the purchaser as well as in cases where the term is contained in such standard terms.

(3)   In this section 'contract term' has the same meaning as in section 10(1).

### 15.   Orders and regulations

(1)   Any power to make an order or regulations under this Act is exercisable by statutory instrument.

(2)   Any statutory instrument containing an order or regulations under this Act, other than an order under section 17(2), shall be subject to annulment in pursuance of a resolution of either House of Parliament.

### 16.   Interpretation

(1)   In this Act—

'contract for the supply of goods or services' has the meaning given in section 2(2);

'contract price' means the price in a contract of sale of goods or the money consideration referred to in section 2(2)(b) in any other contract for the supply of goods or services;

'purchaser' means (subject to section 13(2)) the buyer in a contract of sale or the person who contracts with the supplier in any other contract for the supply of goods or services;

'qualifying debt' means a debt falling within section 3(1);

'statutory interest' means interest carried by virtue of the term implied by section 1(1); and

'supplier' means (subject to section 13(2)) the seller in a contract of sale of goods or the person who does one or more of the things mentioned in section 2(3) in any other contract for the supply of goods or services.

(2) In this Act any reference (however worded) to an agreement or to contract terms includes a reference to both express and implied terms (including terms established by a course of dealing or by such usage as binds the parties).

### 17. Short title, commencement and extent

(1) This Act may be cited as the Late Payment of Commercial Debts (Interest) Act 1998.

(2) This Act (apart from this section) shall come into force on such day as the Secretary of State may by order appoint; and different days may be appointed for different descriptions of contract or for other different purposes.

An order under this subsection may specify a description of contract by reference to any feature of the contract (including the parties).

(3) The Secretary of State may by regulations make such transitional, supplemental or incidental provision (including provision modifying any provision of this Act) as the Secretary of State may consider necessary or expedient in connection with the operation of this Act while it is not fully in force.

(4) This Act does not affect contracts of any description made before this Act comes into force for contracts of that description.

(5) This Act extends to Northern Ireland.

## SCOTLAND ACT 1998
### (1998, c 46)

*Legislation*

### 28. Acts of the Scottish Parliament

(1) Subject to section 29, the Parliament may make laws, to be known as Acts of the Scottish Parliament.

(2) Proposed Acts of the Scottish Parliament shall be known as Bills; and a Bill shall become an Act of the Scottish Parliament when it has been passed by the Parliament and has received Royal Assent.

(3) A Bill receives Royal Assent at the beginning of the day on which Letters Patent under the Scottish Seal signed with Her Majesty's own hand signifying Her Assent are recorded in the Register of the Great Seal.

(4) The date of Royal Assent shall be written on the Act of the Scottish Parliament by the Clerk, and shall form part of the Act.

(5) The validity of an Act of the Scottish Parliament is not affected by any invalidity in the proceedings of the Parliament leading to its enactment.

(6) Every Act of the Scottish Parliament shall be judicially noticed.

(7) This section does not affect the power of the Parliament of the United Kingdom to make laws for Scotland.

### 29. Legislative competence

(1) An Act of the Scottish Parliament is not law so far as any provision of the Act is outside the legislative competence of the Parliament.

(2) A provision is outside that competence so far as any of the following paragraphs apply—

(a) it would form part of the law of a country or territory other than Scotland, or confer or remove functions exercisable otherwise than in or as regards Scotland,

(b) it relates to reserved matters,

(c) it is in breach of the restrictions in Schedule 4,

(d) it is incompatible with any of the Convention rights or with Community law,

(e)   it would remove the Lord Advocate from his position as head of the systems of criminal prosecution and investigation of deaths in Scotland.

(3)   For the purposes of this section, the question whether a provision of an Act of the Scottish Parliament relates to a reserved matter is to be determined, subject to subsection (4), by reference to the purpose of the provision, having regard (among other things) to its effect in all the circumstances.

(4)   A provision which—
   (a)   would otherwise not relate to reserved matters, but
   (b)   makes modifications of Scots private law, or Scots criminal law, as it applies to reserved matters,
is to be treated as relating to reserved matters unless the purpose of the provision is to make the law in question apply consistently to reserved matters and otherwise.

## 30.   Legislative competence: supplementary

(1)   Schedule 5 (which defines reserved matters) shall have effect.

(2)   Her Majesty may by Order in Council make any modifications of Schedule 4 or 5 which She considers necessary or expedient.

(3)   Her Majesty may by Order in Council specify functions which are to be treated, for such purposes of this Act as may be specified, as being, or as not being, functions which are exercisable in or as regards Scotland.

(4)   An Order in Council under this section may also make such modifications of—
   (a)   any enactment or prerogative instrument (including any enactment comprised in or made under this Act), or
   (b)   any other instrument or document,
as Her Majesty considers necessary or expedient in connection with other provision made by the Order.

## 31.   Scrutiny of Bills before introduction

(1)   A member of the Scottish Executive in charge of a Bill shall, on or before introduction of the Bill in the Parliament, state that in his view the provisions of the Bill would be within the legislative competence of the Parliament.

(2)   The Presiding Officer shall, on or before the introduction of a Bill in the Parliament, decide whether or not in his view the provisions of the Bill would be within the legislative competence of the Parliament and state his decision.

(3)   The form of any statement, and the manner in which it is to be made, shall be determined under standing orders, and standing orders may provide for any statement to be published.

## 41.   Defamatory statements

(1)   For the purposes of the law of defamation—
   (a)   any statement made in proceedings of the Parliament, and
   (b)   the publication under the authority of the Parliament of any statement,
shall be absolutely privileged.

(2)   In subsection (1), 'statement' has the same meaning as in the Defamation Act 1996.

## 57.   Community law and Convention rights

(1)   Despite the transfer to the Scottish Ministers by virtue of section 53 of functions in relation to observing and implementing obligations under Community law, any function of a Minister of the Crown in relation to any matter shall continue to be exercisable by him as regards Scotland for the purposes specified in section 2(2) of the European Communities Act 1972.

(2)   A member of the Scottish Executive has no power to make any subordinate legislation, or to do any other act, so far as the legislation or act is incompatible with any of the Convention rights or with Community law.

(3)   Subsection (2) does not apply to an act of the Lord Advocate—

(a)   in prosecuting any offence, or
(b)   in his capacity as head of the systems of criminal prosecution and
investigation of deaths in Scotland,
which, because of subsection (2) of section 6 of the Human Rights Act 1998, is
not unlawful under subsection (1) of that section.

**126.  Interpretation**
(1)   In this Act—
'body' includes unincorporated association,
'constituencies' and 'regions', in relation to the Parliament, mean the
constituencies and regions provided for by Schedule l,
'constituency member' means a member of the Parliament for a constituency,
'the Convention rights' has the same meaning as in the Human Rights Act 1998,
'document' means anything in which information is recorded in any form
(and references to producing a document are to be read accordingly),
'enactment' includes an Act of the Scottish Parliament, Northern Ireland
legislation (within the meaning of the Northern Ireland Act 1998) and an
enactment comprised in subordinate legislation, and includes an enactment
comprised in, or in subordinate legislation under, an Act of Parliament,
whenever passed or made,
'financial year' means a year ending with 31st March,
'functions' includes powers and duties, and 'confer', in relation to functions,
includes impose,
'government department' means any department of the Government of the
United Kingdom,
'the Human Rights Convention' means—
(a)   the Convention for the Protection of Human Rights and Fundamental
Freedoms, agreed by the Council of Europe at Rome on 4th November 1950,
and
(b)   the Protocols to the Convention,
as they have effect for the time being in relation to the United Kingdom,
'Minister of the Crown' includes the Treasury,
'modify' includes amend or repeal,
'occupational pension scheme', 'personal pension scheme' and 'public service
pension scheme' have the meanings given by section 1 of the Pension Schemes
Act 1993, . . .
'the Parliament' means the Scottish Parliament,
'parliamentary', in relation to constituencies, elections and electors, is to be
taken to refer to the Parliament of the United Kingdom,
'prerogative instrument' means an Order in Council, warrant, charter or other
instrument made under the prerogative,
'the principal appointed day' means the day appointed by an order under
section 130 which is designated by the order as the principal appointed day,
'proceedings', in relation to the Parliament, includes proceedings of any
committee or sub-committee,
'property' includes rights and interests of any description,
'regional member' means a member of the Parliament for a region,
'Scotland' includes so much of the internal waters and territorial sea of the
United Kingdom as are adjacent to Scotland,
'Scottish public authority' means any public body (except the Parliamentary
corporation), public office or holder of such an office whose functions (in each
case) are exercisable only in or as regards Scotland,
'the Scottish zone' means the sea within British fishery limits (that is, the
limits set by or under section 1 of the Fishery Limits Act 1976) which is
adjacent to Scotland,
'standing orders' means standing orders of the Parliament,

'subordinate legislation' has the same meaning as in the Interpretation Act 1978 and also includes an instrument made under an Act of the Scottish Parliament,

'tribunal' means any tribunal in which legal proceedings may be brought.

(2)   Her Majesty may by Order in Council determine, or make provision for determining, for the purposes of this Act any boundary between waters which are to be treated as internal waters or territorial sea of the United Kingdom, or sea within British fishery limits, adjacent to Scotland and those which are not.

(3)   For the purposes of this Act—

(a)   the question whether any function of a body, government department, office or office-holder relates to reserved matters is to be determined by reference to the purpose for which the function is exercisable, having regard (among other things) to the likely effects in all the circumstances of any exercise of the function, but

(b)   bodies to which paragraph 3 of Part III of Schedule 5 applies are to be treated as if all their functions were functions which relate to reserved matters.

(4)   References in this Act to Scots private law are to the following areas of the civil law of Scotland—

(a)   the general principles of private law (including private international law),

(b)   the law of persons (including natural persons, legal persons and unincorporated bodies),

(c)   the law of obligations (including obligations arising from contract, unilateral promise, delict, unjustified enrichment and negotiorum gestio),

(d)   the law of property (including heritable and moveable property, trusts and succession), and

(e)   the law of actions (including jurisdiction, remedies, evidence, procedure, diligence, recognition and enforcement of court orders, limitation of actions and arbitration),

and include references to judicial review of administrative action.

(5)   References in this Act to Scots criminal law include criminal offences, jurisdiction, evidence, procedure and penalties and the treatment of offenders.

(6)   References in this Act and in any other enactment to the Scottish Administration are to the office-holders in the Scottish Administration and the members of the staff of the Scottish Administration.

(7)   For the purposes of this Act—

(a)   references to office-holders in the Scottish Administration are to—

(i)   members of the Scottish Executive and junior Scottish Ministers, and

(ii)   the holders of offices in the Scottish Administration which are not ministerial offices, and

(b)   references to members of the staff of the Scottish Administration are to the staff of the persons referred to in paragraph (a).

(8)   For the purposes of this Act, the offices in the Scottish Administration which are not ministerial offices are—

(a)   the Registrar General of Births, Deaths and Marriages for Scotland, the Keeper of the Registers of Scotland and the Keeper of the Records of Scotland, and

(b)   any other office of a description specified in an Order in Council made by Her Majesty under this subsection.

(9)   In this Act—

(a)   all those rights, powers, liabilities, obligations and restrictions from time to time created or arising by or under the Community Treaties, and

(b)   all those remedies and procedures from time to time provided for by or under the Community Treaties,

are referred to as 'Community law'.

(10) In this Act, 'international obligations' means any international obligations of the United Kingdom other than obligations to observe and implement Community law or the Convention rights.

(11) In this Act, 'by virtue of' includes 'by' and 'under'.

## SCHEDULE 5. RESERVED MATTERS

## PART I. GENERAL RESERVATIONS

### *The constitution*

1. The following aspects of the constitution are reserved matters, that is—
    (a) the Crown, including succession to the Crown and a regency,
    (b) the Union of the Kingdoms of Scotland and England,
    (c) the Parliament of the United Kingdom,
    (d) the continued existence of the High Court of Justiciary as a criminal court of first instance and of appeal,
    (e) the continued existence of the Court of Session as a civil court of first instance and of appeal.

2. (1) Paragraph 1 does not reserve—
    (a) Her Majesty's prerogative and other executive functions,
    (b) functions exercisable by any person acting on behalf of the Crown, or
    (c) any office in the Scottish Administration.
    (2) Sub-paragraph (1) does not affect the reservation by paragraph 1 of honours and dignities or the functions of the Lord Lyon King of Arms so far as relating to the granting of arms; but this sub-paragraph does not apply to the Lord Lyon King of Arms in his judicial capacity.
    (3) Sub-paragraph (1) does not affect the reservation by paragraph 1 of the management (in accordance with any enactment regulating the use of land) of the Crown Estate.
    (4) Sub-paragraph (1) does not affect the reservation by paragraph 1 of the functions of the Security Service, the Secret Intelligence Service and the Government Communications Headquarters.

3. (1) Paragraph 1 does not reserve property belonging to Her Majesty in right of the Crown or belonging to any person acting on behalf of the Crown or held in trust for Her Majesty for the purposes of any person acting on behalf of the Crown.
    (2) Paragraph 1 does not reserve the ultimate superiority of the Crown or the superiority of the Prince and Steward of Scotland.
    (3) Sub-paragraph (1) does not affect the reservation by paragraph 1 of—
    (a) the hereditary revenues of the Crown, other than revenues from bona vacantia, ultimus haeres and treasure trove,
    (b) the royal arms and standard,
    (c) the compulsory acquisition of property held or used by a Minister of the Crown or government department.

4. (1) Paragraph 1 does not reserve property held by Her Majesty in Her private capacity.
    (2) Sub-paragraph (1) does not affect the reservation by paragraph 1 of the subject-matter of the Crown Private Estates Acts 1800 to 1873.

5. Paragraph 1 does not reserve the use of the Scottish Seal.

### *Political parties*

6. The registration and funding of political parties is a reserved matter.

*Foreign affairs etc*

**7.** (1) International relations, including relations with territories outside the United Kingdom, the European Communities (and their institutions) and other international organisations, regulation of international trade, and international development assistance and co-operation are reserved matters.

(2) Sub-paragraph (1) does not reserve—

(a) observing and implementing international obligations, obligations under the Human Rights Convention and obligations under Community law,

(b) assisting Ministers of the Crown in relation to any matter to which that sub-paragraph applies.

*Public service*

**8.** (1) The Civil Service of the State is a reserved matter.

(2) Sub-paragraph (1) does not reserve the subject-matter of—

(a) Part I of the Sheriff Courts and Legal Officers (Scotland) Act 1927 (appointment of sheriff clerks and procurators fiscal etc),

(b) Part III of the Administration of Justice (Scotland) Act 1933 (officers of the High Court of Justiciary and of the Court of Session).

*Defence*

**9.** (1) The following are reserved matters—

(a) the defence of the realm,

(b) the naval, military or air forces of the Crown, including reserve forces,

(c) visiting forces,

(d) international headquarters and defence organisations,

(e) trading with the enemy and enemy property.

(2) Sub-paragraph (1) does not reserve—

(a) the exercise of civil defence functions by any person otherwise than as a member of any force or organisation referred to in sub-paragraph (1)(b) to (d) or any other force or organisation reserved by virtue of sub-paragraph (1)(a),

(b) the conferral of enforcement powers in relation to sea fishing.

*Treason*

**10.** Treason (including constructive treason), treason felony and misprision of treason are reserved matters.

## PART II. SPECIFIC RESERVATIONS

*Preliminary*

1. The matters to which any of the Sections in this Part apply are reserved matters for the purposes of this Act.

2. A Section applies to any matter described or referred to in it when read with any illustrations, exceptions or interpretation provisions in that Section.

3. Any illustrations, exceptions or interpretation provisions in a Section relate only to that Section (so that an entry under the heading 'exceptions' does not affect any other Section).

*Reservations*

## Head A—Financial and Economic Matters

**A1. Fiscal, economic and monetary policy.** Fiscal, economic and monetary policy, including the issue and circulation of money, taxes and excise duties, government borrowing and lending, control over United Kingdom public expenditure, the exchange rate and the Bank of England.

*Exception.* Local taxes to fund local authority expenditure (for example, council tax and non-domestic rates).

**A2. The currency.** Coinage, legal tender and bank notes.

**A3. Financial services.** Financial services, including investment business, banking and deposit-taking, collective investment schemes and insurance.

*Exception.* The subject-matter of section 1 of the Banking and Financial Dealings Act 1971 (bank holidays).

**A4. Financial markets.** Financial markets, including listing and public offers of securities and investments, transfer of securities and insider dealing.

**A5. Money laundering.** The subject-matter of the Money Laundering Regulations 1993, but in relation to any type of business.

## Head B—Home Affairs

**B1. Misuse of drugs.** The subject-matter of—
    (a)   the Misuse of Drugs Act 1971,
    (b)   sections 12 to 14 of the Criminal Justice (International Co-operation) Act 1990 (substances useful for manufacture of controlled drugs), and
    (c)   Part V of the Criminal Law (Consolidation) (Scotland) Act 1995 (drug trafficking) and, so far as relating to drug trafficking, the Proceeds of Crime (Scotland) Act 1995.

**B2. Data protection.** The subject-matter of—
    (a)   the Data Protection Act 1998, and
    (b)   Council Directive 95/46/EC (protection of individuals with regard to the processing of personal data and on the free movement of such data).

*Interpretation.* If any provision of the Data Protection Act 1998 is not in force on the principal appointed day, it is to be treated for the purposes of this reservation as if it were.

**B3. Elections.** Elections for membership of the House of Commons, the European Parliament and the Parliament, including the subject-matter of—
    (a)   the European Parliamentary Elections Act 1978,
    (b)   the Representation of the People Act 1983 and the Representation of the People Act 1985, and
    (c)   the Parliamentary Constituencies Act 1986
so far as those enactments apply, or may be applied, in respect of such membership.
    The franchise at local government elections

**B4. Firearms.** The subject-matter of the Firearms Acts 1968 to 1997.

**B5. Entertainment.** The subject-matter of—
    (a)   the Video Recordings Act 1984, and
    (b)   sections 1 to 3 and 5 to 16 of the Cinemas Act 1985 (control of exhibitions).

The classification of films for public exhibition by reference to their suitability for viewing by persons generally or above a particular age, with or without any advice as to the desirability of parental guidance.

**B6.  Immigration and nationality.**  Nationality; immigration, including asylum and the status and capacity of persons in the United Kingdom who are not British citizens; free movement of persons within the European Economic Area; issue of travel documents.

**B7.  Scientific procedures on live animals.**  The subject-matter of the Animals (Scientific Procedures) Act 1986.

**B8.  National security, interception of communications, official secrets and terrorism.**  National security.

The interception of communications; but not the subject-matter of Part III of the Police Act 1997 (authorisation to interfere with property etc) or surveillance not involving interference with property.

The subject-matter of—
  (a)  the Official Secrets Acts 1911 and 1920, and
  (b)  the Official Secrets Act 1989, except so far as relating to any information, document or other article protected against disclosure by section 4(2) (crime) and not by any other provision of sections 1 to 4.

Special powers, and other special provisions, for dealing with terrorism.

**B9.  Betting, gaming and lotteries.**  Betting, gaming and lotteries.

**B10.  Emergency powers.**  Emergency powers.

**B11.  Extradition.**  Extradition.

**B12.  Lieutenancies.**  The subject-matter of the Lieutenancies Act 1997.

### Head C—Trade and Industry

**C1.  Business associations.**  The creation, operation, regulation and dissolution of types of business association.

*Exceptions.*  The creation, operation, regulation and dissolution of—
  (a)  particular public bodies, or public bodies of a particular type, established by or under any enactment, and
  (b)  charities.

*Interpretation.*  'Business association' means any person (other than an individual) established for the purpose of carrying on any kind of business, whether or not for profit; and 'business' includes the provision of benefits to the members of an association.

**C2.  Insolvency.**  In relation to business associations—
  (a)  the modes of, the grounds for and the general legal effect of winding up, and the persons who may initiate winding up,
  (b)  liability to contribute to assets on winding up,
  (c)  powers of courts in relation to proceedings for winding up, other than the power to sist proceedings,
  (d)  arrangements with creditors, and
  (e)  procedures giving protection from creditors.

Preferred or preferential debts for the purposes of the Bankruptcy (Scotland) Act 1985, the Insolvency Act 1986, and any other enactment relating to the sequestration of the estate of any person or to the winding up of business associations, the preference of such debts against other such debts and the extent of their preference over other types of debt.

Regulation of insolvency practitioners.

Co-operation of insolvency courts.

*Exceptions.* In relation to business associations—

(a)   the process of winding up, including the person having responsibility for the conduct of a winding up or any part of it, and his conduct of it or of that part,

(b)   the effect of winding up on diligence, and

(c)   avoidance and adjustment of prior transactions on winding up.

Floating charges and receivers, except in relation to preferential debts, regulation of insolvency practitioners and co-operation of insolvency courts.

*Interpretation.*

'Business association' has the meaning given in Section C1 of this Part of this Schedule, but does not include any person whose estate may be sequestrated under the Bankruptcy (Scotland) Act 1985 or any public body established by or under an enactment.

'Winding up', in relation to business associations, includes winding up of solvent, as well as insolvent, business associations.

**C3. Competition.** Regulation of anti-competitive practices and agreements; abuse of dominant position; monopolies and mergers.

*Exception.* Regulation of particular practices in the legal profession for the purpose of regulating that profession or the provision of legal services.

*Interpretation.* 'The legal profession' means advocates, solicitors and qualified conveyancers and executry practitioners within the meaning of Part II of the Law Reform (Miscellaneous Provisions) (Scotland) Act 1990.

**C4. Intellectual property.** Intellectual property.

*Exception.* The subject-matter of Parts I and II of the Plant Varieties Act 1997 (plant varieties and the Plant Varieties and Seeds Tribunal).

**C5.   Import and export control.** The subject-matter of the Import, Export and Customs Powers (Defence) Act 1939.

Prohibition and regulation of the import and export of endangered species of animals and plants.

*Exceptions.* Prohibition and regulation of movement into and out of Scotland of—

(a)   food, animals, animal products, plants and plant products for the purposes of protecting human, animal or plant health, animal welfare or the environment or observing or implementing obligations under the Common Agricultural Policy, and

(b)   animal feeding stuffs, fertilisers and pesticides for the purposes of protecting human, animal or plant health or the environment.

**C6.   Sea fishing.** Regulation of sea fishing outside the Scottish zone (except in relation to Scottish fishing boats).

*Interpretation.* 'Scottish fishing boat' means a fishing vessel which is registered in the register maintained under section 8 of the Merchant Shipping Act 1995 and whose entry in the register specifies a port in Scotland as the port to which the vessel is to be treated as belonging.

**C7.   Consumer protection.** Regulation of—

(a)   the sale and supply of goods and services to consumers,

(b)   guarantees in relation to such goods and services,

(c)   hire-purchase, including the subject-matter of Part III of the Hire-Purchase Act 1964,

(d)   trade descriptions, except in relation to food,

(e)   misleading and comparative advertising, except regulation specifically in relation to food, tobacco and tobacco products,

(f)   price indications,

(g)   trading stamps,

(h)   auctions and mock auctions of goods and services, and

(i)   hallmarking and gun barrel proofing.

Safety of, and liability for, services supplied to consumers.

The subject-matter of—

(a)   the Hearing Aid Council Act 1968,

(b)   the Unsolicited Goods and Services Acts 1971 and 1975,

(c)   Parts I to III and XI of the Fair Trading Act 1973,

(d)   the Consumer Credit Act 1974,

(e)   the Estate Agents Act 1979,

(f)   the Timeshare Act 1992,

(g)   the Package Travel, Package Holidays and Package Tours Regulations 1992, and

(h)   the Commercial Agents (Council Directive) Regulations 1993.

*Exception.*   The subject-matter of section 16 of the Food Safety Act 1990 (food safety and consumer protection).

**C8. Product standards, safety and liability.** Technical standards and requirements in relation to products in pursuance of an obligation under Community law.

Product safety and liability.

Product labelling.

*Exceptions.*   Food, agricultural and horticultural produce, fish and fish products, seeds, animal feeding stuffs, fertilisers and pesticides.

In relation to food safety, materials which come into contact with food.

**C9. Weights and measures.**   Units and standards of weight and measurement.

Regulation of trade so far as involving weighing, measuring and quantities.

**C10. Telecommunications and wireless telegraphy.**   Telecommunications and wireless telegraphy.

Internet services.

Electronic encryption.

The subject-matter of Part II of the Wireless Telegraphy Act 1949 (electro-magnetic disturbance).

*Exception.*   The subject-matter of Part III of the Police Act 1997 (authorisation to interfere with property etc).

**C11. Post Office, posts and postal services.**   The Post Office, posts (including postage stamps, postal orders and postal packets) and regulation of postal services.

**C12. Research Councils.**   Research Councils within the meaning of the Science and Technology Act 1965.

The subject-matter of section 5 of that Act (funding of scientific research) so far as relating to Research Councils.

**C13. Designation of assisted areas.**   The subject-matter of section 1 of the Industrial Development Act 1982.

**C14. Industrial Development Advisory Board.**   The Industrial Development Advisory Board.

**C15.  Protection of trading and economic interests.**  The subject-matter of—
(a)  section 2 of the Emergency Laws (Re-enactments and Repeals) Act 1964 (Treasury power in relation to action damaging to economic position of United Kingdom),
(b)  Part II of the Industry Act 1975 (powers in relation to transfer of control of important manufacturing undertakings), and
(c)  the Protection of Trading Interests Act 1980.

*Head D—Energy*

**D1.  Electricity.**  Generation, transmission, distribution and supply of electricity. The subject-matter of Part II of the Electricity Act 1989.

*Exception.*  The subject-matter of Part I of the Environmental Protection Act 1990.

**D2.  Oil and gas.**  Oil and gas, including—
(a)  the ownership of, exploration for and exploitation of deposits of oil and natural gas,
(b)  the subject-matter of section 1 of the Mineral Exploration and Investment Grants Act 1972 (contributions in connection with mineral exploration) so far as relating to exploration for oil and gas,
(c)  offshore installations and pipelines,
(d)  the subject-matter of the Pipe-lines Act 1962 (including section 5 (deemed planning permission)) so far as relating to pipelines within the meaning of section 65 of that Act,
(e)  the application of Scots law and the jurisdiction of the Scottish courts in relation to offshore activities,
(f)  pollution relating to oil and gas exploration and exploitation, but only outside controlled waters (within the meaning of section 30A(1) of the Control of Pollution Act 1974),
(g)  the subject-matter of Part II of the Food and Environment Protection Act 1985 so far as relating to oil and gas exploration and exploitation, but only in relation to activities outside such controlled waters,
(h)  restrictions on navigation, fishing and other activities in connection with offshore activities,
(i)  liquefaction of natural gas, and
(j)  the conveyance, shipping and supply of gas through pipes.

*Exceptions.*  The subject-matter of—
(a)  sections 10 to 12 of the Industry Act 1972 (credits and grants for construction of ships and offshore installations),
(b)  the Offshore Petroleum Development (Scotland) Act 1975, other than sections 3 to 7, and
(c)  Part I of the Environmental Protection Act 1990.
The manufacture of gas.
The conveyance, shipping and supply of gas other than through pipes.

**D3.  Coal.**  Coal, including its ownership and exploitation, deep and opencast coal mining and coal mining subsidence.

*Exceptions.*  The subject-matter of—
(a)  Part I of the Environmental Protection Act 1990, and
(b)  sections 53 (environmental duties in connection with planning) and 54 (obligation to restore land affected by coal-mining operations) of the Coal Industry Act 1994.

**D4.  Nuclear energy.**  Nuclear energy and nuclear installations, including—
(a)  nuclear safety, security and safeguards, and
(b)  liability for nuclear occurrences.

*Exceptions.* The subject-matter of—
  (a)   Part I of the Environmental Protection Act 1990, and
  (b)   the Radioactive Substances Act 1993.

**D5.  Energy conservation.**  The subject-matter of the Energy Act 1976, other than section 9.

*Exception.*  The encouragement of energy efficiency other than by prohibition or regulation.

### Head E—Transport

**E1.  Road transport.**  The subject-matter of—
  (a)   the Motor Vehicles (International Circulation) Act 1952,
  (b)   the Public Passenger Vehicles Act 1981 and the Transport Act 1985, so far as relating to public service vehicle operator licensing,
  (c)   section 17 (traffic regulation on special roads), section 25 (pedestrian crossings), Part V (traffic signs) and Part VI (speed limits) of the Road Traffic Regulation Act 1984,
  (d)   the Road Traffic Act 1988 and the Road Traffic Offenders Act 1988,
  (e)   the Vehicle Excise and Registration Act 1994,
  (f)   the Road Traffic (New Drivers) Act 1995, and
  (g)   the Goods Vehicles (Licensing of Operators) Act 1995.
Regulation of proper hours or periods of work by persons engaged in the carriage of passengers or goods by road.
The conditions under which international road transport services for passengers or goods may be undertaken.
Regulation of the instruction of drivers of motor vehicles.

*Exceptions.*  The subject-matter of sections 39 and 40 (road safety information and training) and 157 to 159 (payments for treatment of traffic casualties) of the Road Traffic Act 1988.

**E2.  Rail transport.**  Provision and regulation of railway services.
Rail transport security.
The subject-matter of the Channel Tunnel Act 1987.
The subject-matter of the Railway Heritage Act 1996.

*Exceptions.*  Grants so far as relating to railway services; but this exception does not apply in relation to—
  (a)   the subject-matter of section 63 of the Railways Act 1993 (government financial assistance where railway administration orders made),
  (b)   'railway services' as defined in section 82(1)(b) of the Railways Act 1993 (carriage of goods by railway), or
  (c)   the subject-matter of section 136 of the Railways Act 1993 (grants and subsidies).

*Interpretation.*  'Railway services' has the meaning given by section 82 of the Railways Act 1993 (excluding the wider meaning of 'railway' given by section 81(2) of that Act).

**E3.  Marine transport.**  The subject-matter of—
  (a)   the Coastguard Act 1925,
  (b)   the Hovercraft Act 1968, except so far as relating to the regulation of noise and vibration caused by hovercraft,
  (c)   the Carriage of Goods by Sea Act 1971,
  (d)   section 2 of the Protection of Wrecks Act 1973 (prohibition on approaching dangerous wrecks),
  (e)   the Merchant Shipping (Liner Conferences) Act 1982,
  (f)   the Dangerous Vessels Act 1985,

(g)   the Aviation and Maritime Security Act 1990, other than Part I (aviation security),

(h)   the Carriage of Goods by Sea Act 1992,

(i)   the Merchant Shipping Act 1995,

(j)   the Shipping and Trading Interests (Protection) Act 1995, and

(k)   sections 24 (implementation of international agreements relating to protection of wrecks), 26 (piracy) and 27 and 28 (international bodies concerned with maritime matters) of the Merchant Shipping and Maritime Security Act 1997.

Navigational rights and freedoms.

Financial assistance for shipping services which start or finish or both outside Scotland.

*Exceptions.*   Ports, harbours, piers and boatslips, except in relation to the matters reserved by virtue of paragraph (d), (f), (g) or (i).

Regulation of works which may obstruct or endanger navigation.

The subject-matter of the Highlands and Islands Shipping Services Act 1960 in relation to financial assistance for bulk freight services.

**E4.  Air transport.**   Regulation of aviation and air transport, including the subject-matter of—

(a)   the Carriage by Air Act 1961,

(b)   the Carriage by Air (Supplementary Provisions) Act 1962,

(c)   the Carriage by Air and Road Act 1979 so far as relating to carriage by air,

(d)   the Civil Aviation Act 1982,

(e)   the Aviation Security Act 1982,

(f)   the Airports Act 1986, and

(g)   sections 1 (endangering safety at aerodromes) and 48 (powers in relation to certain aircraft) of the Aviation and Maritime Security Act 1990,

and arrangements to compensate or repatriate passengers in the event of an air transport operator's insolvency.

*Exceptions.*   The subject-matter of the following sections of the Civil Aviation Act 1982—

(a)   section 25 (Secretary of State's power to provide aerodromes),

(b)   section 30 (provision of aerodromes and facilities at aerodromes by local authorities),

(c)   section 31 (power to carry on ancillary business in connection with local authority aerodromes),

(d)   section 34 (financial assistance for certain aerodromes),

(e)   section 35 (facilities for consultation at certain aerodromes),

(f)   section 36 (health control at Secretary of State's aerodromes and aerodromes of Civil Aviation Authority), and

(g)   sections 41 to 43 and 50 (powers in relation to land exercisable in connection with civil aviation) where land is to be or was acquired for the purpose of airport development or expansion.

The subject-matter of Part II (transfer of airport undertakings of local authorities), sections 63 and 64 (airport byelaws) and 66 (functions of operators of designated airports as respects abandoned vehicles) of the Airports Act 1986.

The subject-matter of sections 59 (acquisition of land and rights over land) and 60 (disposal of compulsorily acquired land) of the Airports Act 1986 where land is to be or was acquired for the purpose of airport development or expansion.

**E5.  Other matters.**   Transport of radioactive material.

Technical specifications for public passenger transport for disabled persons, including the subject-matter of—

(a)    section 125(7) and (8) of the Transport Act 1985 (Secretary of State's guidance and consultation with the Disabled Persons Transport Advisory Committee), and

(b)    Part V of the Disability Discrimination Act 1995 (public transport).

Regulation of the carriage of dangerous goods.

*Interpretation.*   'Radioactive material' has the same meaning as in section 1(1) of the Radioactive Material (Road Transport) Act 1991.

## Head F—Social Security

**F1.  Social security schemes.**   Schemes supported from central or local funds which provide assistance for social security purposes to or in respect of individuals by way of benefits.

Requiring persons to—

(a)    establish and administer schemes providing assistance for social security purposes to or in respect of individuals, or

(b)    make payments to or in respect of such schemes, and to keep records and supply information in connection with such schemes.

The circumstances in which a person is liable to maintain himself or another for the purposes of the enactments relating to social security and the Child Support Acts 1991 and 1995.

The subject-matter of the Vaccine Damage Payment Scheme.

*Illustrations.*   National Insurance; Social Fund; administration and funding of housing benefit and council tax benefit; recovery of benefits for accident, injury or disease from persons paying damages; deductions from benefits for the purpose of meeting an individual's debts; sharing information between government departments for the purposes of the enactments relating to social security; making decisions for the purposes of schemes mentioned in the reservation and appeals against such decisions.

*Exceptions.*   The subject-matter of Part II of the Social Work (Scotland) Act 1968 (social welfare services), section 2 of the Chronically Sick and Disabled Persons Act 1970 (provision of welfare services), section 50 of the Children Act 1975 (payments towards maintenance of children), section 15 of the Enterprise and New Towns (Scotland) Act 1990 (industrial injuries benefit), and sections 22 (promotion of welfare of children in need), 29 and 30 (advice and assistance for young persons formerly looked after by local authorities) of the Children (Scotland) Act 1995.

*Interpretation.*   'Benefits' includes pensions, allowances, grants, loans and any other form of financial assistance.

Providing assistance for social security purposes to or in respect of individuals includes (among other things) providing assistance to or in respect of individuals—

(a)    who qualify by reason of old age, survivorship, disability, sickness, incapacity, injury, unemployment, maternity or the care of children or others needing care,

(b)    who qualify by reason of low income, or

(c)    in relation to their housing costs or liabilities for local taxes.

**F2.  Child support.**   The subject-matter of the Child Support Acts 1991 and 1995.

*Exception.*   The subject-matter of sections 1 to 7 of the Family Law (Scotland) Act 1985 (aliment).

*Interpretation.*   If section 30(2) of the Child Support Act 1991 (collection of payments other than child support maintenance) is not in force on the principal appointed day, it is to be treated for the purposes of this reservation as if it were.

**F3. Occupational and personal pensions.** The regulation of occupational pension schemes and personal pension schemes, including the obligations of the trustees or managers of such schemes.

Provision about pensions payable to, or in respect of, any persons, except—
    (a)   the persons referred to in section 81(3),
    (b)   in relation to a Scottish public authority with mixed functions or no reserved functions, persons who are or have been a member of the public body, the holder of the public office, or a member of the staff of the body, holder or office.

The subject-matter of the Pensions (Increase) Act 1971.

Schemes for the payment of pensions which are listed in Schedule 2 to that Act, except those mentioned in paragraphs 38A and 38AB.

Where pension payable to or in respect of any class of persons under a public service pension scheme is covered by this reservation, so is making provision in their case—
    (a)   for compensation for loss of office or employment, for their office or employment being affected by constitutional changes, or circumstances arising from such changes, in any territory or territories or for loss or diminution of emoluments, or
    (b)   for benefits in respect of death or incapacity resulting from injury or disease.

*Interpretation.* 'Pension' includes gratuities and allowances.

**F4. War pensions.** Schemes for the payment of pensions for or in respect of persons who have a disablement or have died in consequence of service as members of the armed forces of the Crown.

The subject-matter of any scheme under the Personal Injuries (Emergency Provisions) Act 1939, sections 3 to 5 and 7 of the Pensions (Navy, Army, Air Force and Mercantile Marine) Act 1939 or section 1 of the Polish Resettlement Act 1947.

*Illustration.* The provision of pensions under the Naval, Military and Air Forces Etc (Disablement and Death) Service Pensions Order 1983.

*Interpretation.* 'Pension' includes grants, allowances, supplements and gratuities.

### Head G—Regulation of the Professions

**G1. Architects.** Regulation of the profession of architect.

**G2. Health professions.** Regulation of the health professions.

*Exceptions.* The subject-matter of—
    (a)   section 21 of the National Health Service (Scotland) Act 1978 (requirement of suitable experience for medical practitioners), and
    (b)   section 25 of that Act (arrangements for the provision of general dental services), so far as it relates to vocational training and disciplinary proceedings.

*Interpretation.* 'The health professions' means the professions regulated by—
    (a)   the Pharmacy Act 1954,
    (b)   the Professions Supplementary to Medicine Act 1960,
    (c)   the Veterinary Surgeons Act 1966,
    (d)   the Medical Act 1983,
    (e)   the Dentists Act 1984,
    (f)   the Opticians Act 1989,

(g) the Osteopaths Act 1993,
(h) the Chiropractors Act 1994, and
(i) the Nurses, Midwives and Health Visitors Act 1997.

**G3. Auditors.** Regulation of the profession of auditor.

### Head H—Employment

**H1. Employment and industrial relations.** Employment rights and duties and industrial relations, including the subject-matter of—
(a) the Employers' Liability (Compulsory Insurance) Act 1969,
(b) the Employment Agencies Act 1973,
(c) the Pneumoconiosis etc. (Workers' Compensation) Act 1979,
(d) the Transfer of Undertakings (Protection of Employment) Regulations 1981,
(e) the Trade Union and Labour Relations (Consolidation) Act 1992,
(f) the Industrial Tribunals Act 1996,
(g) the Employment Rights Act 1996, and
(h) the National Minimum Wage Act 1998.

*Exception.* The subject-matter of the Agricultural Wages (Scotland) Act 1949.

**H2. Health and safety.** The subject-matter of the following Parts of the Health and Safety at Work etc Act 1974—
(a) Part I (health, safety and welfare in connection with work, and control of dangerous substances) as extended or applied by section 36 of the Consumer Protection Act 1987, sections 1 and 2 of the Offshore Safety Act 1992 and section 117 of the Railways Act 1993, and
(b) Part II (the Employment Medical Advisory Service).

*Exception.* Public safety in relation to matters which are not reserved.

**H3. Job search and support.** The subject-matter of—
(a) the Disabled Persons (Employment) Act 1944, and
(b) the Employment and Training Act 1973, except so far as relating to training for employment.

*Exception.* The subject-matter of—
(a) sections 8 to 10A of the Employment and Training Act 1973 (careers services), and
(b) the following sections of Part I of the Enterprise and New Towns (Scotland) Act 1990 (Scottish Enterprise and Highlands and Islands Enterprise)—
(i) section 2(3)(c) (arrangements for the purpose of assisting persons to establish themselves as self-employed persons), and
(ii) section 12 (disclosure of information).

### Head J—Health and Medicines

**J1. Abortion.** Abortion.

**J2. Xenotransplantation.** Xenotransplantation.

**J3. Embryology, surrogacy and genetics.** Surrogacy arrangements, within the meaning of the Surrogacy Arrangements Act 1985, including the subject-matter of that Act.
The subject-matter of the Human Fertilisation and Embryology Act 1990.
Human genetics.

**J4. Medicines, medical supplies and poisons.** The subject-matter of—

(a)   the Medicines Act 1968, the Marketing Authorisations for Veterinary Medicinal Products Regulations 1994 and the Medicines for Human Use (Marketing Authorisations Etc) Regulations 1994,
   (b)   the Poisons Act 1972, and
   (c)   the Biological Standards Act 1975.
Regulation of prices charged for medical supplies or medicinal products which (in either case) are supplied for the purposes of the health service established under section 1 of the National Health Service (Scotland) Act 1978.

*Interpretation.* 'Medical supplies' has the same meaning as in section 49(3) of the National Health Service (Scotland) Act 1978.
   'Medicinal products' has the same meaning as in section 130(1) of the Medicines Act 1968.

**J5.  Welfare foods.**   Schemes made by regulations under section 13 of the Social Security Act 1988 (schemes for distribution of welfare foods).

## Head K—Media and Culture

**K1.  Broadcasting.**   The subject-matter of the Broadcasting Act 1990 and the Broadcasting Act 1996.
   The British Broadcasting Corporation.

**K2.  Public lending right.**   The subject-matter of the Public Lending Right Act 1979.

**K3.  Government Indemnity Scheme.**   The subject-matter of sections 16 and 16A of the National Heritage Act 1980 (public indemnities for objects on loan to museums, art galleries, etc).

**K4.  Property accepted in satisfaction of tax.**   The subject-matter of sections 8 and 9 of the National Heritage Act 1980 (payments to Inland Revenue in respect of property accepted in satisfaction of tax, and disposal of such property).

## Head L—Miscellaneous

**L1.  Judicial remuneration.**   Determination of the remuneration of—
   (a)   judges of the Court of Session,
   (b)   sheriffs principal and sheriffs,
   (c)   members of the Lands Tribunal for Scotland, and
   (d)   the Chairman of the Scottish Land Court.

**L2.  Equal opportunities.**   Equal opportunities, including the subject-matter of—
   (a)   the Equal Pay Act 1970,
   (b)   the Sex Discrimination Act 1975,
   (c)   the Race Relations Act 1976, and
   (d)   the Disability Discrimination Act 1995.

*Exceptions.* The encouragement (other than by prohibition or regulation) of equal opportunities, and in particular of the observance of the equal opportunity requirements.
   Imposing duties on—
   (a)   any office-holder in the Scottish Administration, or any Scottish public authority with mixed functions or no reserved functions, to make arrangements with a view to securing that the functions of the office-holder or authority are carried out with due regard to the need to meet the equal opportunity requirements, or

(b)   any cross-border public authority to make arrangements with a view to securing that its Scottish functions are carried out with due regard to the need to meet the equal opportunity requirements.

*Interpretation.*   'Equal opportunities' means the prevention, elimination or regulation of discrimination between persons on grounds of sex or marital status, on racial grounds, or on grounds of disability, age, sexual orientation, language or social origin, or of other personal attributes, including beliefs or opinions, such as religious beliefs or political opinions.
   'Equal opportunity requirements' means the requirements of the law for the time being relating to equal opportunities.
   'Scottish functions' means functions which are exercisable in or as regards Scotland and which do not relate to reserved matters.

**L3.  Control of weapons.**   Control of nuclear, biological and chemical weapons and other weapons of mass destruction.

**L4.  Ordnance survey.**   The subject-matter of the Ordnance Survey Act 1841.

**L5.  Time Timescales, time zones and the subject-matter of the Summer Time Act 1972.**   The calendar; units of time; the date of Easter.

*Exceptions.*   The computation of periods of time.
   The subject-matter of—
      (a)   section 1 of the Banking and Financial Dealings Act 1971 (bank holidays), and
      (b)   the Term and Quarter Days (Scotland) Act 1990.

**L6.  Outer space.**   Regulation of activities in outer space.


PART III. GENERAL PROVISIONS

*Scottish public authorities*
   1.   (1)   This Schedule does not reserve any Scottish public authority if some of its functions relate to reserved matters and some do not, unless it is a cross-border public authority.
   (2)   Sub-paragraph (1) has effect as regards—
      (a)   the constitution of the authority, including its establishment and dissolution, its assets and liabilities and its funding and receipts,
      (b)   conferring or removing any functions specifically exercisable in relation to the authority.
   (3)   Sub-paragraph (2)(b) does not apply to any function which is specifically exercisable in relation to a particular function of the authority if the particular function relates to reserved matters.
   (4)   An authority to which this paragraph applies is referred to in this Act as a Scottish public authority with mixed functions.
   2.   Paragraph 1 of Part I of this Schedule does not reserve any Scottish public authority with functions none of which relate to reserved matters (referred to in this Act as a Scottish public authority with no reserved functions).

*Reserved bodies*
   3.   (1)   The reservation of any body to which this paragraph applies has effect to reserve—
      (a)   its constitution, including its establishment and dissolution, its assets and liabilities and its funding and receipts,
      (b)   conferring functions on it or removing functions from it,
      (c)   conferring or removing any functions specifically exercisable in relation to it.

(2)   This paragraph applies to—
   (a)   a body reserved by name by Part II of this Schedule,
   (b)   each of the councils reserved by Section C12 of that Part,
   (c)   the Commission for Racial Equality, the Equal Opportunities Commission and the National Disability Council.

*Financial assistance to industry*
4.   (1)   This Schedule does not reserve giving financial assistance to commercial activities for the purpose of promoting or sustaining economic development or employment.
   (2)   Sub-paragraph (1)—
   (a)   does not apply to giving financial assistance to any activities in pursuance of a power exercisable only in relation to activities which are reserved,
   (b)   does not apply to Part I of this Schedule, except paragraph 9, or to a body to which paragraph 3 of this Part of this Schedule applies,
   (c)   is without prejudice to the exceptions from the reservations in Sections E2 and E3 of Part II of this Schedule.
   (3)   Sub-paragraph (1) does not affect the question whether any matter other than financial assistance to which that sub-paragraph applies is reserved.

*Interpretation*
5.   (1)   References in this Schedule to the subject-matter of any enactment are to be read as references to the subject-matter of that enactment as it has effect on the principal appointed day or, if it ceased to have effect at any time within the period ending with that day and beginning with the day on which this Act is passed, as it had effect immediately before that time.
   (2)   Subordinate legislation under section 129(1) may, in relation to the operation of this Schedule at any time before the principal appointed day, modify the references to that day in sub-paragraph (1).

# PART II
# DRAFT LEGISLATION

## CONTRACT (SCOTLAND) BILL
### (SLC Report no 174)

*An Act of the Scottish Parliament to reform certain rules of law relating to rights arising on, and remedies for, breach of contract and unilateral voluntary obligation.*

**1. Restriction of right to payment for unwanted performance**

(1) Where—

(a) a party to a contract or the beneficiary under a conditional unilateral voluntary obligation (the 'performing party') is, before completion of performance, informed by another party to the contract or the person undertaking the obligation that performance is no longer required;

(b) the performing party is able to proceed or continue with performance without the co-operation of that other party or that person; and

(c) either—

(i) the performing party can, without unreasonable effort or expense, secure a reasonable substitute transaction; or

(ii) it is unreasonable for the performing party to proceed or continue with performance,

then the performing party is not entitled, on so proceeding or continuing, to recover the consideration due under the contract or benefit due under the obligation in respect of performance occurring after the performing party has been so informed.

(2) Subsection (1) above does not affect any right of the performing party to recover damages for breach of contract or conditional unilateral voluntary obligation.

**2. Non-patrimonial loss recoverable on breach**

(1) Non-patrimonial loss or harm is included within the heads of damages which may be awarded for breach of contract or for breach of a unilateral voluntary obligation.

(2) The following are examples of the kinds of loss or harm referred to in subsection (1) above: injury to feelings, loss of reputation, loss of amenity, loss of satisfaction in obtaining performance of the contract or obligation, grief and distress.

**3. Damages where losses etc. caused also by party not in breach**

(1) Where loss or harm is caused to a party to a contract or a beneficiary of a unilateral voluntary obligation—

(a) partly by breach of the contract by another party to it or breach of the obligation by the person undertaking it; and

(b) partly by an act or omission of the first mentioned party or the beneficiary,

the damages recoverable in respect of the breach may be reduced proportionately to the extent that the loss or harm was caused by that act or omission.

(2)   In considering whether to reduce damages under subsection (1) above and the extent to which loss or harm was caused by a person's act or omission, a court shall have regard to the whole circumstances of the case, including the conduct of both or all persons concerned.

### 4.   Interim specific implement
It is competent for the Court of Session or the sheriff to order interim specific implement of a contractual or unilateral voluntary obligation.

### 5.   Application, commencement and citation
(1)   Section 1 of this Act applies as respects contracts and conditional unilateral voluntary obligations in respect of which the performing party is, after this Act comes into force, informed by another party to the contract or, as the case may be, the person undertaking the obligation that performance is not required.

(2)   Sections 2 to 4 above apply for the purposes of proceedings begun after this Act comes into force.

(3)   This Act (except this subsection and subsection (4) below) comes into force on the expiry of two months after it has received Royal Assent.

(4)   This Act may be cited as the Contract (Scotland) Act 1999.

## PRIVATE LAW (INTERPRETATION) (SCOTLAND) BILL
### (SLC Report no 160)

*Draft of a Bill to provide rules for interpreting juridical acts and to make provision relating to the admissibility of extrinsic evidence for the purpose of interpreting juridical acts; and for connected purposes.*

### 1.   Interpretation of juridical acts
(1)   The Schedule to this Act (rules for interpretation of juridical acts) shall have effect.

(2)   The Schedule is without prejudice to any other enactment or rule of law which makes provision as respects the interpretation of an expression or a type of expression.

(3)   Subject to subsection (2), any rule of law as to the interpretation of a juridical act which is in force before the commencement of this Act and is inconsistent with the rules in the Schedule shall cease to have effect.

### 2.   Admissibility of relevant extrinsic evidence
Evidence of any description relevant to the interpretation of a juridical act shall be admissible notwithstanding that it is extrinsic evidence.

### 3.   Interpretation
In this Act—

   'judicial act' means any act of a court or tribunal established by law, but does not include the act of an arbiter whether appointed in pursuance of any enactment or otherwise;

   'juridical act' means any act of will or intention which has, or which is intended by the maker of the act to have, legal effect, but does not include any legislative or judicial act;

   'legislative act' includes subordinate legislation (within the meaning of the Interpretation Act 1978).

### 4.   Short title, extent etc.
(1)   This Act may be cited as the Private Law (Interpretation) (Scotland) Act 1997.

(2)   This Act applies to every juridical act whenever made (including juridical acts made before the date on which this Act comes into force).

(3) Section 2 of this Act does not apply to proceedings instituted before the date on which the Act comes into force.

(4) This Act shall come into force at the end of the period of two months beginning with the day on which the Act is passed.

(5) This Act extends to Scotland only.

## SCHEDULE. RULES FOR INTERPRETATION OF JURIDICAL ACTS

### General rule

1.—(1) Any expression which forms part of a juridical act shall have the meaning which would reasonably be given to it in its context; and in determining that meaning, regard may be had to—

(a) the surrounding circumstances; and

(b) in so far as they can be objectively ascertained, the nature and purpose of the juridical act.

(2) For the purposes of this rule the surrounding circumstances do not include—

(a) statements of intention;

(b) instructions, communings or negotiations forming part of the process of preparation of the juridical act;

(c) conduct subsequent to the juridical act.

(3) The rule set out in sub-paragraph (1) above is referred to in this Schedule as 'the general rule'.

### Contracts

2.—(1) Any expression which forms part of a contract shall be interpreted in accordance with the general rule unless the rule in sub-paragraph (2) below has effect.

(2) Subject to sub-paragraph (3) below, any expression forming part of a contract which is used by one party in a particular sense (whether or not it is also used in that sense by any other party) shall be interpreted in that sense if every other party at the time of contracting knew, or could reasonably have been assumed to know, that it was being used in that sense.

(3) Sub-paragraph (2) above does not apply—

(a) to a contract which is recorded, or intended by the parties to be recorded, in the Register of Sasines or which is presented, or intended by the parties to be presented, in support of an application for registration in the Land Register; or

(b) in any question with a person, not being a party to the contract, who has reasonably relied on the meaning which would be given to the expression by the application of the general rule.

### Testamentary writings

3.—(1) Any expression in a testamentary writing shall be interpreted in accordance with the general rule unless the rule in sub-paragraph (2) below has effect.

(2) Any expression in a testamentary writing which describes a beneficiary or a bequest in terms which are applicable to two or more persons or, as the case may be, things shall be interpreted as applying to such one of those persons or things as corresponds to the intention of the testator.

Schedule
The Schedule contains the basic rules on the interpretation of juridical acts. The

general aim is not to change the underlying policy of the existing law but to
restate the main rules of interpretation as rules of substantive law rather than as
rules of evidence and to clear the way for the radical simplification of the law
of evidence effected by clause 2 of the Bill.

*General rule*
Paragraph 1(1) states the general rule that an expression in a juridical act is to
have the meaning which would reasonably be given to it in its context, having
regard, where appropriate, to the surrounding circumstances and, in so far as
they can be objectively ascertained, to the nature and purpose of the juridical
act.

   Paragraph 1(2) provides that surrounding circumstances do not include
statements of intention; or instructions, communings or negotiations forming
part of the process of preparation of the juridical act; or conduct subsequent to
the juridical act. Surrounding circumstances would, however, include any well-
known trade practices or customs in the field of activity concerned and any
usages adopted between the parties in previous similar transactions. See
paragraphs 2.19–2.34 of the report. These rules reflect the same policy as the
existing law. The benefits of the objective approach, in interpreting, say, a
disposition, would be lost if reference could be made to prior communings.

*Contracts*
Paragraph 2 of the Schedule deals with the special rule for certain contracts
which is discussed in Part 3 of the report.

   Paragraph 2(1) provides that contracts are to be interpreted according to the
general rule unless the special rule in sub-paragraph (2) has effect. The words
'has effect' are used to indicate that even if sub-paragraph (2) could be said to
apply to the situation in an abstract way, the general objective rule is not
displaced unless sub-paragraph (2) actually produces a result. See paragraph
3.10 of the report.

   Paragraph 2(2) states the special rule for contracts which applies where an
expression is used by one party in a particular sense and at the time of
contracting the other parties know, or could reasonably be assumed to know,
that it is being used in that sense. This is probably the existing law in Scotland
(see *Houldsworth v Gordon Cumming* 1910 SC (HL) 49) and is also the policy
adopted (using a slightly different drafting formula) in recent international
instruments like the United Nations Convention on Contracts for the
International Sale of Goods.

   Paragraph 2(3)(a) provides that an objective approach is to be taken to
contracts destined for the Register of Sasines or for presentation in support of
an application for registration in the Land Register. The need for the public to
be able to rely on the ordinary meaning of terms appearing in these registers
justifies this approach. An objective approach is also to be adopted (by virtue of
sub-paragraph (3)(b)) in any question with third parties who have reasonably
relied on the ordinary meaning of any expression in a contract.

*Testamentary writings*
Paragraph 3 of the Schedule deals with the special rule for testamentary
writings which is discussed in Part 4 of the report.

   Paragraph 3(1) provides that the general rule applies to testamentary writings
unless the special rule in sub-paragraph (2) has effect. See above for the
significance of 'has effect'.

   Paragraph 3(2) provides that an expression in a testamentary writing which
describes a beneficiary or bequest in terms which are equally applicable to two
or more persons or things is to be interpreted in accordance with the actual
intention of the testator. There is a very similar rule in the existing law. See
paragraphs 4.2–4.6 of the report.

## Rules of preference for cases of doubt in the construction of a juridical act

(1)   A construction of the juridical act which gives effect to all its terms is preferred to one which does not.

(2)   Where, in an onerous juridical act, terms supplied by one party are unclear, there is a preference for their interpretation against that party.

(3)   Where a list of items, all of which are members of the same class, is followed by a general term, there is a preference for interpreting the general term as applying only to items of the same class as those in the specific list.

(4)   A construction which gives effect to precise terms is preferred to one which gives effect to general language.

(5)   A construction which gives effect to operative or essential terms is preferred to one which is in accordance with narrative or incidental terms.

(6)   A construction which gives effect to separately negotiated terms is preferred to one which gives effect to standard terms not separately negotiated.

(7)   There is a preference for a construction which favours a result other than donation and which, in the case of a gratuitous unilateral act, favours the result least burdensome to the granter.

(8)   There is a preference for a construction in favour of freedom from burdens or restrictions.

(9)   There is a preference for a construction which leads to results which are lawful, fair and reasonable.

(10)   Where a juridical act is executed in two or more linguistic versions, and where it does not itself provide a rule for resolving discrepancies between them, there is, in case of discrepancy, a preference for construction according to the version in which the act was originally drawn up.

## PENALTY CLAUSES (SCOTLAND) BILL
### (SLC Report no 171)

*Draft of a Bill to make new provision for Scotland as respects the enforceability of penalty clauses in contracts and in unilateral voluntary obligations; and for connected purposes.*

### 1.   Enforceability of penalty clauses

(1)   A penalty clause in a contract is unenforceable in a particular case if the penalty which the clause provides for is manifestly excessive (whether or not having regard to any loss suffered) in that case.

(2)   Any rule of law whereby such a clause is unenforceable if it is not founded in a pre-estimate of damages shall cease to have effect.

(3)   In subsection (1) above—
'penalty' means a penalty of any kind whatsoever (including, without prejudice to that generality, a forfeiture or an obligation to transfer); and
'penalty clause'—
    (a)   does not include a clause of irritancy of a lease of land; but
    (b)   means any other clause, in whatever form, the substance of which is that a penalty is incurred in the event of breach of, or early termination of, the contract or failure to do, or to do in a particular way, something provided for in the contract.

(4)   In determining, for the purposes of subsection (1) above, whether a penalty is manifestly excessive all circumstances which appear relevant shall be taken into account; and without prejudice to the generality of this subsection such circumstances may include circumstances arising after the contract is entered into.

### 2. Onus of proof

The onus of proving that a penalty is manifestly excessive shall lie on the party so contending.

### 3. Purported evasion

Where a term of a contract would (but for this section) have the effect of excluding or restricting the application of a provision of this Act in respect of that or any other contract, the term shall be void.

### 4. Power to modify a penalty

(1) Where a court determines that a penalty provided for in a contract is manifestly excessive in a particular case then on application it may, if it thinks fit, modify the penalty in that case so as to make the penalty clause enforceable in the case.

(2) In subsection (1) above, the reference to modifying a penalty shall be construed as including a reference to imposing a condition as respects the penalty.

(3) Subsection (1) above applies to a tribunal or arbiter as it applies to a court (provided that the tribunal or arbiter has power to adjudicate on the enforceability of the penalty).

### 5. Application of Act to unilateral voluntary obligations

This Act applies to unilateral voluntary obligations as it applies to contracts.

### 6. Short title, commencement and extent

(1) This Act may be cited as the Penalty Clauses (Scotland) Act 1999.

(2) This Act shall come into force at the end of that period of three months which begins with the day on which the Act is passed.

(3) This Act applies only as respects a penalty clause agreed to on or after the date on which the Act comes into force.

(4) This Act extends to Scotland only.

# PART III
# STATUTORY INSTRUMENTS

## COMMERCIAL AGENTS (COUNCIL DIRECTIVE) REGULATIONS 1993
### (SI 1993/3053)

*(as amended by the Commercial Agents (Council Directive) (Amendment) Regulations 1993 (SI 1993/3173) and 1998 (SI 1998/2868).)*

### PART I. GENERAL

**1.  Citation, commencement and applicable law**

(1)  These Regulations may be cited as the Commercial Agents (Council Directive) Regulations 1993 and shall come into force on 1st January 1994.

(2)  These Regulations govern the relations between commercial agents and their principals and, subject to paragraph (3), apply in relation to the activities of commercial agents in Great Britain.

[(3)  A court or tribunal shall:

(a)  apply the law of the other member State concerned in place of regulations 3 to 22 where the parties have agreed that the agency contract is to be governed by the law of that member State;

(b)  (whether or not it would otherwise be required to do so) apply these Regulations where the law of another member State corresponding to these Regulations enables the parties to agree that the agency contract is to be governed by the law of a different member State and the parties have agreed that it is to be governed by the law of England and Wales or Scotland.]

**2.  Interpretation, application and extent**

(1)  In these Regulations—

'commercial agent' means a self-employed intermediary who has continuing authority to negotiate the sale or purchase of goods on behalf of another person (the 'principal'), or to negotiate and conclude the sale or purchase of goods on behalf of and in the name of that principal; but shall be understood as not including in particular:

(i)  a person who, in his capacity as an officer of a company or association, is empowered to enter into commitments binding on that company or association;

(ii)  a partner who is lawfully authorised to enter into commitments binding on his partners;

(iii)  a person who acts as an insolvency practitioner (as that expression is defined in section 388 of the Insolvency Act 1986) or the equivalent in any other jurisdiction;

'commission' means any part of the remuneration of a commercial agent which varies with the number or value of business transactions;

['EEA Agreement' means the Agreement on the European Economic Area signed at Oporto on 2nd May 1992 as adjusted by the Protocol signed at Brussels on 17th March 1993;

'member State' includes a State which is a contracting party to the EEA Agreement;]

'restraint of trade clause' means an agreement restricting the business activities of a commercial agent following termination of the agency contract.

(2)   These Regulations do not apply to—

(a)   commercial agents whose activities are unpaid;

(b)   commercial agents when they operate on commodity exchanges or in the commodity market;

(c)   the Crown Agents for Overseas Governments and Administrations, as set up under the Crown Agents Act 1979, or its subsidiaries.

(3)   The provisions of the Schedule to these Regulations have effect for the purpose of determining the persons whose activities as commercial agents are to be considered secondary.

(4)   These Regulations shall not apply to the persons referred to in paragraph (3) above.

(5)   These Regulations do not extend to Northern Ireland.

## PART II. RIGHTS AND OBLIGATIONS

### 3.   Duties of a commercial agent to his principal

(1)   In performing his activities a commercial agent must look after the interests of his principal and act dutifully and in good faith.

(2)   In particular, a commercial agent must—

(a)   make proper efforts to negotiate and, where appropriate, conclude the transactions he is instructed to take care of;

(b)   communicate to his principal all the necessary information available to him;

(c)   comply with reasonable instructions given by his principal.

### 4.   Duties of a principal to his commercial agent

(1)   In his relations with his commercial agent a principal must act dutifully and in good faith.

(2)   In particular, a principal must—

(a)   provide his commercial agent with the necessary documentation relating to the goods concerned;

(b)   obtain for his commercial agent the information necessary for the performance of the agency contract, and in particular notify his commercial agent within a reasonable period once he anticipates that the volume of commercial transactions will be significantly lower than that which the commercial agent could normally have expected.

(3)   A principal shall, in addition, inform his commercial agent within a reasonable period of his acceptance or refusal of, and of any non-execution by him of, a commercial transaction which the commercial agent has procured for him.

### 5.   Prohibition on derogation from regulations 3 and 4 and consequence of breach

(1)   The parties may not derogate from regulations 3 and 4 above.

(2)   The law applicable to the contract shall govern the consequence of breach of the rights and obligations under regulations 3 and 4 above.

## PART III. REMUNERATION

### 6.   Form and amount of remuneration in absence of agreement

(1)   In the absence of any agreement as to remuneration between the parties, a commercial agent shall be entitled to the remuneration that commercial agents appointed for the goods forming the subject of his agency contract are customarily allowed in the place where he carries on his activities and, if there is no such customary practice, a commercial agent shall be entitled to reasonable remuneration taking into account all the aspects of the transaction.

(2) This regulation is without prejudice to the application of any enactment or rule of law concerning the level of remuneration.

(3) Where a commercial agent is not remunerated (wholly or in part) by commission, regulations 7 to 12 below shall not apply.

### 7. Entitlement to commission on transactions concluded during agency contract

(1) A commercial agent shall be entitled to commission on commercial transactions concluded during the period covered by the agency contract—

(a) where the transaction has been concluded as a result of his action; or

(b) where the transaction is concluded with a third party whom he has previously acquired as a customer for transactions of the same kind.

(2) A commercial agent shall also be entitled to commission on transactions concluded during the period covered by the agency contract where he has an exclusive right to a specific geographical area or to a specific group of customers and where the transaction has been entered into with a customer belonging to that area or group.

### 8. Entitlement to commission on transactions concluded after agency contract has terminated

Subject to regulation 9 below, a commercial agent shall be entitled to commission on commercial transactions concluded after the agency contract has terminated if—

(a) the transaction is mainly attributable to his efforts during the period covered by the agency contract and if the transaction was entered into within a reasonable period after that contract terminated; or

(b) in accordance with the conditions mentioned in regulation 7 above, the order of the third party reached the principal or the commercial agent before the agency contract terminated.

### 9. Apportionment of commission between new and previous commercial agents

(1) A commercial agent shall not be entitled to the commission referred to in regulation 7 above if that commission is payable, by virtue of regulation 8 above, to the previous commercial agent, unless it is equitable because of the circumstances for the commission to be shared between the commercial agents.

(2) The principal shall be liable for any sum due under paragraph (1) above to the person entitled to it in accordance with that paragraph, and any sum which the other commercial agent receives to which he is not entitled shall be refunded to the principal.

### 10. When commission due and date for payment

(1) Commission shall become due as soon as, and to the extent that, one of the following circumstances occurs:

(a) the principal has executed the transaction; or

(b) the principal should, according to his agreement with the third party, have executed the transaction; or

(c) the third party has executed the transaction.

(2) Commission shall become due at the latest when the third party has executed his part of the transaction or should have done so if the principal had executed his part of the transaction, as he should have.

(3) The commission shall be paid not later than on the last day of the month following the quarter in which it became due, and, for the purposes of these Regulations, unless otherwise agreed between the parties, the first quarter period shall run from the date the agency contract takes effect, and subsequent periods shall run from that date in the third month thereafter or the beginning of the fourth month, whichever is the sooner.

(4) Any agreement to derogate from paragraphs (2) and (3) above to the detriment of the commercial agent shall be void.

**11. Extinction of right to commission**

(1) The right to commission can be extinguished only if and to the extent that—

(a) it is established that the contract between the third party and the principal will not be executed; and

(b) that fact is due to a reason for which the principal is not to blame.

(2) Any commission which the commercial agent has already received shall be refunded if the right to it is extinguished.

(3) any agreement to derogate from paragraph (1) above to the detriment of the commercial agent shall be void.

**12. Periodic supply of information as to commission due and right of inspection of principal's books**

(1) The principal shall supply his commercial agent with a statement of the commission due, not later than the last day of the month following the quarter in which the commission has become due, and such statement shall set out the main components used in calculating the amount of the commission.

(2) A commercial agent shall be entitled to demand that he be provided with all the information (and in particular an extract from the books) which is available to his principal and which he needs in order to check the amount of the commission due to him.

(3) Any agreement to derogate from paragraphs (1) and (2) above shall be void.

(4) Nothing in this regulation shall remove or restrict the effect of, or prevent reliance upon, any enactment or rule of law which recognises the right of an agent to inspect the books of a principal.

PART IV. CONCLUSION AND TERMINATION OF THE AGENCY CONTRACT

**13. Right to signed written statement of terms of agency contract**

(1) The commercial agent and principal shall each be entitled to receive from the other, on request, a signed written document setting out the terms of the agency contract including any terms subsequently agreed.

(2) Any purported waiver of the right referred to in paragraph (1) above shall be void.

**14. Conversion of agency contract after expiry of fixed period**

An agency contract for a fixed period which continues to be performed by both parties after that period has expired shall be deemed to be converted into an agency contract for an indefinite period.

**15. Minimum periods of notice for termination of agency contract**

(1) Where an agency contract is concluded for an indefinite period either party may terminate it by notice.

(2) The period of notice shall be—

(a) 1 month for the first year of the contract;

(b) 2 months for the second year commenced;

(c) 3 months for the third year commenced and for the subsequent years;

and the parties may not agree on any shorter periods of notice.

(3) If the parties agree on longer periods than those laid down in paragraph (2) above, the period of notice to be observed by the principal must not be shorter than that to be observed by the commercial agent.

(4) Unless otherwise agreed by the parties, the end of the period of notice must coincide with the end of a calendar month.

(5) The provisions of this regulation shall also apply to an agency contract

for a fixed period where it is converted under regulation 14 above into an agency contract for an indefinite period subject to the proviso that the earlier fixed period must be taken into account in the calculation of the period of notice.

**16.  Savings with regard to immediate termination**
These Regulations shall not affect the application of any enactment or rule of law which provides for the immediate termination of the agency contract—
  (a)  because of the failure of one party to carry out all or part of his obligations under that contract; or
  (b)   where exceptional circumstances arise.

**17.   Entitlement of commercial agent to indemnity or compensation on termination of agency contract**
  (1)   This regulation has effect for the purpose of ensuring that the commercial agent is, after termination of the agency contract, indemnified in accordance with paragraphs (3) to (5) below or compensated for damage in accordance with paragraphs (6) and (7) below.
  (2)   Except where the agency [contract] otherwise provides, the commercial agent shall be entitled to be compensated rather than indemnified.
  (3)   Subject to paragraph (9) and to regulation 18 below, the commercial agent shall be entitled to an indemnity if and to the extent that—
    (a)   he has brought the principal new customers or has significantly increased the volume of business with existing customers and the principal continues to derive substantial benefits from the business with such customers; and
    (b)   the payment of this indemnity is equitable having regard to all the circumstances and, in particular, the commission lost by the commercial agent on the business transacted with such customers.
  (4)   The amount of the indemnity shall not exceed a figure equivalent to an indemnity for one year calculated from the commercial agent's average annual remuneration over the preceding five years and if the contract goes back less than five years the indemnity shall be calculated on the average for the period in question.
  (5)   The grant of an indemnity as mentioned above shall not prevent the commercial agent from seeking damages.
  (6)   Subject to paragraph (9) and to regulation 18 below, the commercial agent shall be entitled to compensation for the damage he suffers as a result of the termination of his relations with his principal.
  (7)   For the purpose of these Regulations such damage shall be deemed to occur particularly when the termination takes place in either or both of the following circumstances, namely circumstances which—
    (a)   deprive the commercial agent of the commission which proper performance of the agency contract would have procured for him whilst providing his principal with substantial benefits linked to the activities of the commercial agent; or
    (b)   have not enabled the commercial agent to amortize the costs and expenses that he had incurred in the performance of the agency contract on the advice of his principal.
  (8)   Entitlement to the indemnity or compensation for damage as provided for under paragraphs (2) to (7) above shall also arise where the agency contract is terminated as a result of the death of the commercial agent.
  (9)   The commercial agent shall lose his entitlement to the indemnity or compensation for damage in the instances provided for in paragraphs (2) to (8) above if within one year following termination of his agency contract he has not notified his principal that he intends pursuing his entitlement.

### 18. Grounds for excluding payment of indemnity or compensation under regulation 17

The [indemnity or] compensation referred to in regulation 17 above shall not be payable to the commercial agent where—

(a)  the principal has terminated the agency contract because of default attributable to the commercial agent which would justify immediate termination of the agency contract pursuant to regulation 16 above; or

(b)  the commercial agent has himself terminated the agency contract, unless such termination is justified—

    (i)  by circumstances attributable to the principal, or

    (ii)  on grounds of the age, infirmity or illness of the commercial agent in consequence of which he cannot reasonably be required to continue his activities; or

(c)  the commercial agent, with the agreement of his principal, assigns his rights and duties under the agency contract to another person.

### 19. Prohibition on derogation from regulations 17 and 18

The parties may not derogate from regulations 17 and 18 to the detriment of the commercial agent before the agency contract expires.

### 20. Restraint of trade clauses

(1)  A restraint of trade clause shall be valid only if and to the extent that—

(a)  it is concluded in writing; and

(b)  it relates to the geographical area or the group of customers and the geographical area entrusted to the commercial agent and to the kind of goods covered by his agency under the contract.

(2)  A restraint of trade clause shall be valid for not more than two years after termination of the agency contract.

(3)  Nothing in this regulation shall affect any enactment or rule of law which imposes other restrictions on the validity or enforceability of restraint of trade clauses or which enables a court to reduce the obligations on the parties resulting from such clauses.

## PART V. MISCELLANEOUS AND SUPPLEMENTAL

### 21. Disclosure of information

Nothing in these Regulations shall require information to be given where such disclosure would be contrary to public policy.

### 22. Service of notice etc

(1)  Any notice, statement or other document to be given or supplied to a commercial agent or to be given or supplied to the principal under these Regulations may be so given or supplied:

(a)  by delivering it to him;

(b)  by leaving it at his proper address addressed to him by name;

(c)  by sending it by post to him addressed either to his registered address or to the address of his registered or principal office;

or by any other means provided for in the agency contract.

(2)  Any such notice, statement or document may—

(a)  in the case of a body corporate, be given or served on the secretary or clerk of that body;

(b)  in the case of a partnership, be given to or served on any partner or on any person having the control or management of the partnership business.

### 23. Transitional provisions

(1)  Notwithstanding any provision in an agency contract made before 1st January 1994, these Regulations shall apply to that contract after that date and,

accordingly any provision which is inconsistent with these Regulations shall have effect subject to them.

(2) Nothing in these Regulations shall affect the rights and liabilities of a commercial agent or a principal which have accrued before 1st January 1994.

**Regulation 2(3)**                    THE SCHEDULE

1. The activities of a person as a commercial agent are to be considered secondary where it may reasonably be taken that the primary purpose of the arrangement with his principal is other than as set out in paragraph 2 below.

2. An arrangement falls within this paragraph if—
(a) the business of the principal is the sale, or as the case may be purchase, of goods of a particular kind; and
(b) the goods concerned are such that—
(i) transactions are normally individually negotiated and concluded on a commercial basis, and
(ii) procuring a transaction on one occasion is likely to lead to further transactions in those goods with that customer on future occasions, or to transactions in those goods with other customers in the same geographical area or among the same group of customers, and
that accordingly it is in the commercial interests of the principal in developing the market in those goods to appoint a representative to such customers with a view to the representative devoting effort, skill and expenditure from his own resources to that end.

3. The following are indications that an arrangement falls within paragraph 2 above, and the absence of any of them is an indication to the contrary—
(a) the principal is the manufacturer, importer or distributor of the goods;
(b) the goods are specifically identified with the principal in the market in question rather than, or to a greater extent than, with any other person;
(c) the agent devotes substantially the whole of his time to representative activities (whether for one principal or for a number of principals whose interests are not conflicting);
(d) the goods are not normally available in the market in question other than by means of the agent;
(e) the arrangement is described as one of commercial agency.

4. The following are indications that an arrangement does not fall within paragraph 2 above—
(a) promotional material is supplied direct to potential customers;
(b) persons are granted agencies without reference to existing agents in a particular area or in relation to a particular group;
(c) customers normally select the goods for themselves and merely place their orders through the agent.

5. The activities of the following categories of persons are presumed, unless the contrary is established, not to fall within paragraph 2 above—
Mail order catalogue agents for consumer goods.
Consumer credit agents.

## GENERAL PRODUCT SAFETY REGULATIONS 1994
### (SI 1994/2328)

**1. Citation and commencement**
[(1)] These Regulations may be cited as the General Product Safety Regulations 1994 and shall come into force on 3rd October 1994.
[(2) Nothing in these Regulations applies to a medicinal product for human use to which the Medicines for Human Use (Marketing Authorisations Etc.) Regulations 1994 apply.]

## 2. Interpretation

(1)  In these Regulations—

'the 1968 Act' means the Medicines Act 1968;

'the 1987 Act' means the Consumer Protection Act 1987;

'the 1990 Act' means the Food Safety Act 1990;

'commercial activity' includes a business and a trade;

'consumer' means a consumer acting otherwise than in the course of a commercial activity;

'dangerous product' means any product other than a safe product;

'distributor' means any professional in the supply chain whose activity does not affect the safety properties of a product;

'enforcement authority' means the Secretary of State, any other Minister of the Crown in charge of a Government Department, any such department and any authority, council and other person on whom functions under these Regulations are imposed by or under regulation 11;

'general safety requirement' means the requirement in regulation 7;

'the GPS Directive' means Council Directive 92/59/EEC on general product safety;

'the 1991 Order' means the Food Safety (Northern Ireland) Order 1991;

'producer' means

(a)  the manufacturer of the product, when he is established in the Community, and includes any person presenting himself as the manufacturer by affixing to the product his name, trade mark or other distinctive mark, or the person who reconditions the product;

(b)  when the manufacturer is not established in the Community—

(i)  if the manufacturer does not have a representative established in the Community, the importer of the product;

(ii)  in all other cases, the manufacturer's representative; and

(c)  other professionals in the supply chain, insofar as their activities may affect the safety properties of a product placed on the market;

'product' means any product intended for consumers or likely to be used by consumers, supplied whether for consideration or not in the course of a commercial activity and whether new, used or reconditioned; provided, however, a product which is used exclusively in the context of a commercial activity even if it is used for or by a consumer shall not be regarded as a product for the purposes of these Regulations provided always and for the avoidance of doubt this exception shall not extend to the supply of such a product to a consumer;

'safe product' means any product which, under normal or reasonably foreseeable conditions of use, including duration, does not present any risk or only the minimum risks compatible with the product's use, considered as acceptable and consistent with a high level of protection for the safety and health of persons, taking into account in particular—

(a)  the characteristics of the product, including its composition, packaging, instructions for assembly and maintenance;

(b)  the effect on other products, where it is reasonably foreseeable that it will be used with other products;

(c)  the presentation of the product, the labelling, any instructions for its use and disposal and any other indication or information provided by the producer; and

(d)  the categories of consumers at serious risk when using the product, in particular children,

and the fact that higher levels of safety may be obtained or other products presenting a lesser degree of risk may be available shall not of itself cause the product to be considered other than a safe product.

(2)  References in these Regulations to the 'Community' are references to the

European Economic Area established under the Agreement signed at Oporto on 2nd May 1992 as adjusted by the Protocol signed at Brussels on 17th March 1993.

**Application and revocation**
3.  These Regulations do not apply to—
(a)   second-hand products which are antiques;
(b)   products supplied for repair or reconditioning before use, provided the supplier clearly informs the person to whom he supplies the product to that effect; or
(c)   any product where there are specific provisions in rules of Community law governing all aspects of the safety of the product.

4.  The requirements of these Regulations apply to a product where the product is the subject of provisions of Community law other than the GPS Directive insofar as those provisions do not make specific provision governing an aspect of the safety of the product.

5.  For the purposes of these Regulations the provisions of section 10 of the 1987 Act to the extent that they impose general safety requirements which must be complied with if products are to be—
(i)   placed on the market, offered or agreed to be placed on the market or exposed or possessed to be placed on the market by producers; or
(ii)   supplied, offered or agreed to be supplied or exposed or possessed to be supplied by distributors,
are hereby disapplied.

6.—(1)   Sub-paragraph (ii) of paragraph (b) of sub-section (3) of section 10 of the 1987 Act is hereby repealed.
(2)   The Approval of Safety Standards Regulations 1987 are hereby revoked.

**7.   General safety requirement**
No producer shall place a product on the market unless the product is a safe product.

**8.   Requirement as to information**
(1)   Within the limits of his activity, a producer shall—
(a)   provide consumers with the relevant information to enable them to assess the risks inherent in a product throughout the normal or reasonably foreseeable period of its use, where such risks are not immediately obvious without adequate warnings, and to take precautions against those risks; and
(b)   adopt measures commensurate with the characteristics of the products which he supplies, to enable him to be informed of the risks which these products might present and to take appropriate action, including, if necessary, withdrawing the product in question from the market to avoid those risks.
(2)   The measures referred to in sub-paragraph (b) of paragraph (1) above may include, whenever appropriate—
(i)   marking of the products or product batches in such a way that they can be identified;
(ii)   sample testing of marketed products;
(iii)   investigating complaints; and
(iv)   keeping distributors informed of such monitoring.

**9.   Requirements of distributors**
A distributor shall act with due care in order to help ensure compliance with the requirements of regulation 7 above and, in particular, without limiting the generality of the foregoing—
(a)   a distributor shall not supply products to any person which he knows, or should have presumed, on the basis of the information in his possession and as a professional, are dangerous products; and

(b) within the limits of his activities, a distributor shall participate in monitoring the safety of products placed on the market, in particular by passing on information on the product risks and cooperating in the action taken to avoid those risks.

**10. Presumption of conformity and product assessment**
(1) Where in relation to any product such product conforms to the specific rules of the law of the United Kingdom laying down the health and safety requirements which the product must satisfy in order to be marketed there shall be a presumption that, until the contrary is proved, the product is a safe product.
(2) Where no specific rules as are mentioned or referred to in paragraph (1) exist, the conformity of a product to the general safety requirement shall be assessed taking into account—
   (i) voluntary national standards of the United Kingdom giving effect to a European standard; or
   (ii) Community technical specifications; or
   (iii) if there are no such voluntary national standards of the United Kingdom or Community technical specifications—
      (aa) standards drawn up in the United Kingdom; or
      (bb) the codes of good practice in respect of health and safety in the product sector concerned; or
      (cc) the state of the art and technology and the safety which consumers may reasonably expect.

**11. Enforcement**
For the purposes of providing for the enforcement of these Regulations—
   (a) section 13 of the 1987 Act (prohibition notices and notices to warn) shall (to the extent that it does not already do so) apply to products as it applies to relevant goods under that section;
   (b) the requirements of these Regulations shall constitute safety provisions for the purposes of sections 14 (suspension notices), 15 (appeals against suspension notices), 16 (forfeiture: England, Wales and Northern Ireland), 17 (forfeiture: Scotland) and 18 (power to obtain information) of the 1987 Act;
   (c) (i) subject to paragraph (ii) below a weights and measures authority in Great Britain and a district council in Northern Ireland shall have the same duty to enforce these Regulations as they have in relation to Part II of the 1987 Act, and Part IV, sections 37 and 38 and subsections (3) and (4) of section 42 of that Act shall apply accordingly;
   (ii) without prejudice to the provisions of paragraphs (a) and (b) above and sub-paragraph (i) above, insofar as these Regulations apply—
      (aa) to products licensed in accordance with the provisions of the 1968 Act [or which are the subject of a marketing authorisation within the meaning of the Medicines for Human Use (Marketing Authorisations Etc.) Regulations 1994], it shall be the duty of the enforcement authority as defined in section 132(1) of the 1968 Act to enforce or to secure the enforcement of these Regulations and sections 108 to 115 and section 119 of and Schedule 3 to that Act shall apply accordingly as if these Regulations were regulations made under the said Act;
      (bb) in relation to food within the meaning of section 1 of the 1990 Act, it shall be the duty of each food authority as defined in section 5 of the 1990 Act to enforce or to secure the enforcement of these Regulations, within its area, in Great Britain and sections 9, 29, 30 and 32 of that Act shall apply accordingly as if these Regulations were food safety requirements made under the said Act and section 10 of that Act shall apply as if these Regulations were regulations made under Part II of that Act; and

(cc) in relation to food within the meaning of article 2 of the 1991 Order, it shall be the duty of the relevant enforcement authority as provided for in article 26 of that Order to enforce or to secure enforcement of these Regulations in Northern Ireland and articles 8, 29, 30, 31 and 33 of that Order shall apply accordingly as if these Regulations were food safety requirements made under that Order and article 9 of that Order shall apply as if these Regulations were regulations made under Part II of that Order;

(d) in sections 13(4) and 14(6) of the 1987 Act for the words 'six months' there shall be substituted 'three months'; and

(e) nothing in this regulation shall authorise any enforcement authority to bring proceedings in Scotland for an offence.

### Offences and preparatory acts

**12**. Any person who contravenes regulation 7 or 9(a) shall be guilty of an offence.

**13**. No producer or distributor shall—

(a) offer or agree to place on the market any dangerous product or expose or possess any such product for placing on the market; or

(b) offer or agree to supply any dangerous product or expose or possess any such product for supply,

and any person who contravenes the requirements of this regulation shall be guilty of an offence.

### 14. Defence of due diligence

(1) Subject to the following paragraphs of this regulation, in proceedings against any person for an offence under these Regulations it shall be a defence for that person to show that he took all reasonable steps and exercised all due diligence to avoid committing the offence.

(2) Where in any proceedings against any person for such an offence the defence provided by paragraph (1) above involves an allegation that the commission of the offence was due—

(a) to the act or default of another, or

(b) to reliance on information given by another,

that person shall not, without leave of the court, be entitled to rely on the defence unless, not less than seven days before, in England, Wales and Northern Ireland, the hearing of the proceedings or, in Scotland, the trial diet, he has served a notice under paragraph (3) below on the person bringing the proceedings.

(3) A notice under this paragraph shall give such information identifying or assisting in the identification of the person who committed the act or default or gave the information as is in the possession of the person serving the notice at the time he serves it.

(4) It is hereby declared that a person shall not be entitled to rely on the defence provided in paragraph (1) above by reason of his reliance on information supplied by another, unless he shows that it was reasonable in all the circumstances for him to have relied on the information, having regard in particular—

(a) to the steps which he took, and those which might reasonably have been taken, for the purpose of verifying the information; and

(b) to whether he had any reason to disbelieve the information.

(5) It is hereby declared that a person shall not be entitled to rely on the defence provided by paragraph (1) above or by section 39(1) of the 1987 Act (defence of due diligence) if he has contravened regulation 9(b).

### 15. Liability of persons other than principal offender

(1) Where the commission by any person of an offence to which regulation 14 above applies is due to the act or default committed by some other

person in the course of a commercial activity of his, the other person shall be guilty of an offence and may be proceeded against and punished by virtue of this paragraph whether or not proceedings are taken against the first-mentioned person.

(2) Where a body corporate is guilty of an offence under these Regulations (including where it is so guilty by virtue of paragraph (1) above) in respect of any act or default which is shown to have been committed with the consent or connivance of, or to be attributable to any neglect on the part of any director, manager, secretary or other similar officer of the body corporate or any person who was purporting to act in any such capacity he, as well as the body corporate, shall be guilty of that offence and shall be liable to be proceeded against and punished accordingly.

(3) Where the affairs of a body corporate are managed by its members, paragraph (2) above shall apply in relation to the acts and defaults of a member in connection with his functions of management as if he were a director of the body corporate.

(4) Where a Scottish partnership is guilty of an offence under regulation 14 above (including where it is so guilty by virtue of paragraph (1) above) in respect of any act or default which is shown to have been committed with the consent or connivance of, or to be attributable to any neglect on the part of, a partner in the partnership, he, as well as the partnership, shall be guilty of that offence and shall be liable to be proceeded against and punished accordingly.

## 16. Extension of the time for bringing summary proceedings

(1) Notwithstanding section 127 of the Magistrates' Courts Act 1980 and article 19 of the Magistrates' Courts (Northern Ireland) Order 1981 in England, Wales and Northern Ireland a magistrates' court may try an information (in the case of England and Wales) or a complaint (in the case of Northern Ireland) in respect of proceedings for an offence under regulation 12 or 13 above if (in the case of England and Wales) the information is laid or (in the case of Northern Ireland) the complaint is made within twelve months from the date of the offence.

(2) Notwithstanding section 331 of the Criminal Procedure (Scotland) Act 1975, in Scotland summary proceedings for an offence under regulation 12 or 13 above may be commenced at any time within twelve months from the date of the offence.

(3) For the purposes of paragraph (2) above, section 331(3) of the Criminal Procedure (Scotland) Act 1975 shall apply as it applies for the purposes of that section.

## 17. Penalties

A person guilty of an offence under regulation 12 or 13 above shall be liable on summary conviction to—

(a) imprisonment for a term not exceeding three months; or

(b) a fine not exceeding level 5 on the standard scale;

or to both.

## 18. Duties of enforcement authorities

(1) Every enforcement authority shall give immediate notice to the Secretary of State of any action taken by it to prohibit or restrict the supply of any product or forfeit or do any other thing in respect of any product for the purposes of these Regulations.

(2) The requirements of paragraph (1) above shall not apply in the case of any action taken in respect of any second-hand product.

## AIR CARRIER LIABILITY ORDER 1998
### (SI 1998/1751)

**Interpretation**

**2.** In this Order—

'Council Regulation' means Council Regulation (EC) No 2027/97 of 9th October 1997 on air carrier liability in the event of accidents;

'non-Community air carrier' means an air carrier established outside the Community operating to, from or within the Community; and

other expressions have, in so far as the context admits, the same meaning as in the Council Regulation.

. . .

**Offences**

**6.**—(1) A Community air carrier which fails to include the provisions contained in Articles 3 and 5 of the Council Regulation in its conditions of carriage in accordance with Article 6.1 of that Regulation shall be guilty of an offence.

(2) A Community air carrier which fails to ensure that:

(a) the information required to be made available on request to passengers by paragraph 2 of Article 6 of the Council Regulations is so made available; or

(b) its ticket document or an equivalent contains the summary of the requirements contained in Articles 3 and 5 of the Council Regulation as required by paragraph 2 of Article 6 of that Regulation,

shall be guilty of an offence unless it proves that the failure to do so occurred without its consent or connivance and that it exercised all due diligence to prevent the failure.

(3) A non-Community carrier which does not apply the provisions in Articles 3 and 5 of the Council Regulation and which fails to ensure that the information or the form required to be provided to passengers by paragraph 3 of Article 6 of the Council Regulation is so provided shall be guilty of an offence unless it proves that the failure to do so occurred without its consent or connivance and that it exercised all due diligence to prevent the failure.

**7.**—(1) A person guilty of an offence under this Order shall be liable—

(a) on summary conviction, to a fine not exceeding level 5 on the standard scale, and

(b) on conviction on indictment, to a fine.

(2) Where an offence under these Regulations has been committed by a body corporate and is proved to have been committed with the consent or connivance of or to be attributable to any neglect on the part of any director, manager, secretary or other similar officer of the body corporate or any such person who was purporting to act in such capacity, he, as well as the body corporate, shall be guilty of that offence and be liable to be proceeded against and punished accordingly.

(3) Where the affairs of a body corporate are managed by its members, paragraph (2) above shall apply in relation to the acts and defaults of a member in connection with his functions of management as if he were a director of the body corporate.

(4) Where a Scottish partnership is guilty of an offence under these Regulations in Scotland and that offence is proved to have been committed with the consent or connivance of or to be attributable to any neglect on the part of a partner, he, as well as the partnership, shall be guilty of that offence and shall be liable to be proceeded against and punished accordingly.

## PROVISION AND USE OF WORK EQUIPMENT REGULATIONS 1998
### (SI 1998/2306)

**2. Interpretation**

(1) In these Regulations, unless the context otherwise requires—

'the 1974 Act' means the Health and Safety at Work etc. Act 1974;

'employer' except in regulation 3(2) and (3) includes a person to whom the requirements imposed by the Regulations apply by virtue of regulation 3(3)(a) and (b);

'essential requirements' means requirements described in regulation 10(1);

'the Executive' means the Health and Safety Executive;

'inspection' in relation to an inspection under paragraph (1) or (2) of regulation 6—

(a)   means such visual or more rigorous inspection by a competent person as is appropriate for the purpose described in the paragraph;

(b)   where it is appropriate to carry out testing for the purpose, includes testing the nature and extent of which are appropriate for the purpose;

'power press' means a press or press brake for the working of metal by means of tools, or for die proving, which is power driven and which embodies a flywheel and clutch;

'thorough examination' in relation to a thorough examination under paragraph (1), (2), (3) or (4) of regulation 32—

(a)   means a thorough examination by a competent person;

(b)   includes testing the nature and extent of which are appropriate for the purpose described in the paragraph;

'use' in relation to work equipment means any activity involving work equipment and includes starting, stopping, programming, setting, transporting, repairing, modifying, maintaining, servicing and cleaning;

'work equipment' means any machinery, appliance, apparatus, tool or installation for use at work (whether exclusively or not);

and related expressions shall be construed accordingly.

**4. Suitability of work equipment**

(1) Every employer shall ensure that work equipment is so constructed or adapted as to be suitable for the purpose for which it is used or provided.

(2) In selecting work equipment, every employer shall have regard to the working conditions and to the risks to the health and safety of persons which exist in the premises or undertaking in which that work equipment is to be used and any additional risk posed by the use of that work equipment.

(3) Every employer shall ensure that work equipment is used only for operations for which, and under conditions for which, it is suitable.

(4) In this regulation 'suitable' [—

(a)   subject to paragraph (b), means suitable in any respect which it is reasonably foreseeable will affect the health and safety of any person; . . .]

**5. Maintenance**

(1) Every employer shall ensure that work equipment is maintained in an efficient state, in efficient working order and in good repair.

(2) Every employer shall ensure that where any machinery has a maintenance log, the log is kept up to date.

**6. Inspection**

(1) Every employer shall ensure that, where the safety of work equipment depends on the installation conditions, it is inspected—

(a)   after installation and before being put into service for the first time; or

(b)   after assembly at a new site or in a new location,

to ensure that it has been installed correctly and is safe to operate.

(2) Every employer shall ensure that work equipment exposed to conditions

causing deterioration which is liable to result in dangerous situations is inspected—

(a)   at suitable intervals; and

(b)   each time that exceptional circumstances which are liable to jeopardise the safety of the work equipment have occurred,

to ensure that health and safety conditions are maintained and that any deterioration can be detected and remedied in good time.

(3)   Every employer shall ensure that the result of an inspection made under this regulation is recorded and kept until the next inspection under this regulation is recorded.

(4)   Every employer shall ensure that no work equipment—

(a)   leaves his undertaking; or

(b)   if obtained from the undertaking of another person, is used in his undertaking, unless it is accompanied by physical evidence that the last inspection required to be carried out under this regulation has been carried out.

### 7.   Specific risks

(1)   Where the use of work equipment is likely to involve a specific risk to health or safety, every employer shall ensure that—

(a)   the use of that work equipment is restricted to those persons given the task of using it; and

(b)   repairs, modifications, maintenance or servicing of that work equipment is restricted to those persons who have been specifically designated to perform operations of that description (whether or not also authorised to perform other operations).

(2)   The employer shall ensure that the persons designated for the purposes of sub-paragraph (b) of paragraph (1) have received adequate training related to any operations in respect of which they have been so designated.

### 8.   Information and instructions

(1)   Every employer shall ensure that all persons who use work equipment have available to them adequate health and safety information and, where appropriate, written instructions pertaining to the use of the work equipment.

(2)   Every employer shall ensure that any of his employees who supervises or manages the use of work equipment has available to him adequate health and safety information and, where appropriate, written instructions pertaining to the use of the work equipment.

(3)   Without prejudice to the generality of paragraph (1) or (2), the information and instructions required by either of those paragraphs shall include information and, where appropriate, written instructions on—

(a)   the conditions in which and the methods by which the work equipment may be used;

(b)   foreseeable abnormal situations and the action to be taken if such a situation were to occur; and

(c)   any conclusions to be drawn from experience in using the work equipment.

(4)   Information and instructions required by this regulation shall be readily comprehensive to those concerned.

### 9.   Training

(1)   Every employer shall ensure that all persons who use work equipment have received adequate training for purposes of health and safety, including training in the methods which may be adopted when using the work equipment, any risks which such use may entail and precautions to be taken.

(2)   Every employer shall ensure that any of his employees who supervises or manages the use of work equipment has received adequate training for purposes

of health and safety, including training in the methods which may be adopted when using the work equipment, any risks which such use may entail and precautions to be taken.

**10. Conformity with Community requirements**

(1) Every employer shall ensure that an item of work equipment has been designed and constructed in compliance with any essential requirements, that is to say requirements relating to its design or construction in any of the instruments listed in Schedule 1 (being instruments which give effect to Community directives concerning the safety of products).

(2) Where an essential requirement applied to the design or construction of an item of work equipment, the requirements of regulations 11 to 19 and 22 to 29 shall apply in respect of that item only to the extent that the essential requirement did not apply to it.

(3) This regulation applies to items of work equipment provided for use in the premises or undertaking of the employer for the first time after 31 December 1992.

**11. Dangerous parts of machinery**

(1) Every employer shall ensure that measures are taken in accordance with paragraph (2) which are effective—

(a) to prevent access to any dangerous part of machinery or to any rotating stock-bar; or

(b) to stop the movement of any dangerous part of machinery or rotating stock-bar before any part of a person enters a danger zone.

(2) The measures required by paragraph (1) shall consist of—

(a) the provision of fixed guards enclosing every dangerous part or rotating stock-bar where and to the extent that it is practicable to do so, but where or to the extent that it is not, then

(b) the provision of other guards or protection devices where and to the extent that it is practicable to do so, but where or to the extent that it is not, then

(c) the provision of jigs, holders, push-sticks or similar protection appliances used in conjunction with the machinery where and to the extent that it is practicable to do so, but where or to the extent that it is not, then

(d) the provision of information, instruction, training and supervision.

(3) All guards and protection devices provided under sub-paragraphs (a) or (b) of paragraph (2) shall—

(a) be suitable for the purpose for which they are provided;

(b) be of good construction, sound material and adequate strength;

(c) be maintained in an efficient state, in efficient working order and in good repair;

(d) not give rise to any increased risk to health or safety;

(e) not be easily bypassed or disabled;

(f) be situated at sufficient distance from the danger zone;

(g) not unduly restrict the view of the operating cycle of the machinery, where such a view is necessary;

(h) be so constructed or adapted that they allow operations necessary to fit or replace parts and for maintenance work, restricting access so that it is allowed only to the area where the work is to be carried out and, if possible, without having to dismantle the guard or protection device.

(4) All protection appliances provided under sub-paragraph (c) of paragraph (2) shall comply with sub-paragraphs (a) to (d) and (g) of paragraph (3).

(5) In this regulation—

'danger zone' means any zone in or around machinery in which a person is exposed to a risk to health or safety from contact with a dangerous part of machinery or a rotating stock-bar;

'stock-bar' means any part of a stock-bar which projects beyond the head-stock of a lathe.

## 12. Protection against specified hazards

(1) Every employer shall take measures to ensure that the exposure of a person using work equipment to any risk to his health or safety from any hazard specified in paragraph (3) is either prevented, or, where that is not reasonably practicable, adequately controlled.

(2) The measures required by paragraph (1) shall—

(a) be measures other than the provision of personal protective equipment or of information, instruction, training and supervision, so far as is reasonably practicable; and

(b) include, where appropriate, measures to minimise the effects of the hazard as well as to reduce the likelihood of the hazard occurring.

(3) The hazards referred to in paragraph (1) are—

(a) any article or substance falling or being ejected from work equipment;

(b) rupture or disintegration of parts of work equipment;

(c) work equipment catching fire or overheating;

(d) the unintended or premature discharge of any article or of any gas, dust, liquid, vapour or other substance which, in each case, is produced, used or stored in the work equipment;

(e) the unintended or premature explosion of the work equipment or any article or substance produced, used or stored in it.

(4) For the purposes of this regulation 'adequately' means adequately having regard only to the nature of the hazard and the nature and degree of exposure to the risk.

(5) This regulation shall not apply where any of the following Regulations apply in respect of any risk to a person's health or safety for which such Regulations require measures to be taken to prevent or control such risk, namely—

(a) the Ionising Radiations Regulations 1985;

(b) the Control of Asbestos at Work Regulations 1987;

(c) the Control of Substances Hazardous to Health Regulations 1994;

(d) the Noise at Work Regulations 1989;

(e) the Construction (Head Protection) Regulations 1989;

(f) the Control of Lead at Work Regulations 1998.

## 13. High or very low temperature

Every employer shall ensure that work equipment, parts of work equipment and any article or substance produced, used or stored in work equipment which, in each case, is at a high or very low temperature shall have protection where appropriate so as to prevent injury to any person by burn, scald or sear.

## 14. Controls for starting or making a significant change in operating conditions

(1) Every employer shall ensure that, where appropriate, work equipment is provided with one or more controls for the purposes of—

(a) starting the work equipment (including re-starting after a stoppage for any reason); or

(b) controlling any change in the speed, pressure or other operating conditions of the work equipment where such conditions after the change result in risk to health and safety which is greater than or of a different nature from such risks before the change.

(2) Subject to paragraph (3), every employer shall ensure that, where a control is required by paragraph (1), it shall not be possible to perform any operation mentioned in sub-paragraph (a) or (b) of that paragraph except by a deliberate action on such control.

(3) Paragraph (1) shall not apply to re-starting or changing operating conditions as a result of the normal operating cycle of an automatic device.

### 15. Stop controls

(1) Every employer shall ensure that, where appropriate, work equipment is provided with one or more readily accessible controls the operation of which will bring the work equipment to a safe condition in a safe manner.

(2) Any control required by paragraph (1) shall bring the work equipment to a complete stop where necessary for reasons of health and safety.

(3) Any control required by paragraph (1) shall, if necessary for reasons of health and safety, switch off all sources of energy after stopping the functioning of the work equipment.

(4) Any control required by paragraph (1) shall operate in priority to any control which starts or changes the operating conditions of the work equipment.

### 16. Emergency stop controls

(1) Every employer shall ensure that, where appropriate, work equipment is provided with one or more readily accessible emergency stop controls unless it is not necessary by reason of the nature of the hazards and the time taken for the work equipment to come to a complete stop as a result of the action of any control provided by virtue of regulation 15(1).

(2) Any control required by paragraph (1) shall operate in priority to any control required by regulation 15(1).

### 17. Controls

(1) Every employer shall ensure that all controls for work equipment are clearly visible and identifiable, including by appropriate marking where necessary.

(2) Except where necessary, the employer shall ensure that no control for work equipment is in a position where any person operating the control is exposed to a risk to his health or safety.

(3) Every employer shall ensure where appropriate—

(a) that, so far as is reasonably practicable, the operator of any control is able to ensure from the position of that control that no person is in a place where he would be exposed to any risk to his health or safety as a result of the operation of that control, but where or to the extent that it is not reasonably practicable;

(b) that, so far as is reasonably practicable, systems of work are effective to ensure that, when work equipment is about to start, no person is in a place where he would be exposed to a risk to his health or safety as a result of the work equipment starting, but where neither of these is reasonably practicable;

(c) that an audible, visible or other suitable warning is given by virtue of regulation 24 whenever work equipment is about to start,

(4) Every employer shall take appropriate measures to ensure that any person who is in a place where he would be exposed to a risk to his health or safety as a result of the starting or stopping of work equipment has sufficient time and suitable means to avoid that risk.

### 18. Control systems

(1) Every employer shall—

(a) ensure, so far as is reasonably practicable, that all control systems of work equipment are safe; and

(b) are chosen making due allowance for the failures, faults and constraints to be expected in the planned circumstances of use.

(2) Without prejudice to the generality of paragraph (1), a control system shall not be safe unless—

(a) its operation does not create any increased risk to health or safety;

(b) it ensures, so far as is reasonably practicable, that any fault in or damage to any part of the control system or the loss of supply of any source of energy used by the work equipment cannot result in additional or increased risk to health or safety;

(c)   it does not impede the operation of any control required by regulation 15 or 16.

### 19.   Isolation from sources of energy

(1)   Every employer shall ensure that where appropriate work equipment is provided with suitable means to isolate it from all its sources of energy.

(2)   Without prejudice to the generality of paragraph (1), the means mentioned in that paragraph shall not be suitable unless they are clearly identifiable and readily accessible.

(3)   Every employer shall take appropriate measures to ensure that re-connection of any energy source to work equipment does not expose any person using the work equipment to any risk to his health or safety.

### 20.   Stability

Every employer shall ensure that work equipment or any part of work equipment is stabilised by clamping or otherwise where necessary for purposes of health or safety.

### 21.   Lighting

Every employer shall ensure that suitable and sufficient lighting, which takes account of the operations to be carried out, is provided at any place where a person uses work equipment.

### 22.   Maintenance operations

Every employer shall take appropriate measures to ensure that work equipment is so constructed or adapted that, so far as is reasonably practicable, main-tenance operations which involve a risk to health or safety can be carried out while the work equipment is shut down, or in other cases—

(a)   maintenance operations can be carried out without exposing the person carrying them out to a risk to his health or safety; or

(b)   appropriate measures can be taken for the protection of any person carrying out maintenance operations which involve a risk to his health or safety.

### 23.   Markings

Every employer shall ensure that work equipment is marked in a clearly visible manner with any marking appropriate for reasons of health and safety.

### 24.   Warnings

(1)   Every employer shall ensure that work equipment incorporates any warnings or warning devices which are appropriate for reasons of health and safety.

(2)   Without prejudice to the generality of paragraph (1), warnings given by warning devices on work equipment shall not be appropriate unless they are unambiguous, easily perceived and easily understood.

### EMPLOYERS' LIABILITY (COMPULSORY INSURANCE)
### REGULATIONS 1998
### (SI 1998/2573)

### 1.   Citation, commencement and interpretation

. . .

(2)   In these Regulations—

'the 1969 Act' means the Employers' Liability (Compulsory Insurance) Act 1969;

. . .

**2. Prohibition of certain conditions in policies of insurance**

(1)   For the purposes of the 1969 Act, there is prohibited in any contract of insurance any condition which provides (in whatever terms) that no liability (either generally or in respect of a particular claim) shall arise under the policy, or that any such liability so arising shall cease, if—

(a)   some specified thing is done or omitted to be done after the happening of the event giving rise to a claim under the policy,

(b)   the policy holder does not take reasonable care to protect his employees against the risk of bodily injury or disease in the course of their employment;

(c)   the policy holder fails to comply with the requirements of any enactment for the protection of employees against the risk of bodily injury or disease in the course of their employment; or

(d)   the policy holder does not keep specified records or fails to provide the insurer with or make available to him information from such records.

(2)   For the purposes of the 1969 Act there is also prohibited in a policy of insurance any condition which requires—

(a)   a relevant employee to pay; or

(b)   an insured employer to pay the relevant employee,

the first amount of any claim or any aggregation of claims.

(3)   Paragraphs (1) and (2) above do not prohibit for the purposes of the 1969 Act a condition in a policy of insurance which requires the employer to pay or contribute any sum to the insurer in respect of the satisfaction of any claim made under the contract of insurance by a relevant employee or any costs and expenses incurred in relation to any such claim.

**3. Limit of amount of compulsory insurance**

(1)   Subject to paragraph (2) below, the amount for which an employer is required by the 1969 Act to insure and maintain insurance in respect of relevant employees under one or more policies of insurance shall be, or shall in aggregate be not less than £5 million in respect of—

(a)   a claim relating to any one or more of those employees arising out of any one occurrence; and

(b)   any costs and expenses incurred in relation to any such claim.

### UNFAIR TERMS IN CONSUMER CONTRACTS REGULATIONS 1999
### (SI 1999/2083)

*(as amended by the Unfair Terms in Consumer Contracts (Amendment) Regulations 2001 (SI 2001/1186))*

**3. Interpretation**

(1)   In these Regulations—

'the Community' means the European Community;

'consumer' means any natural person who, in contracts covered by these Regulations, is acting for purposes which are outside his trade, business or profession;

'court' in relation to England and Wales and Northern Ireland means a county court or the High Court, and in relation to Scotland, the Sheriff or the Court of Session;

'Director' means the Director General of Fair Trading;

'EEA Agreement' means the Agreement on the European Economic Area signed at Oporto on 2nd May 1992 as adjusted by the protocol signed at Brussels on 17th March 1993;

'Member State' means a State which is a contracting party to the EEA Agreement;

'notified' means notified in writing;

'qualifying body' means a person specified in Schedule 1;

'seller or supplier' means any natural or legal person who, in contracts covered by these Regulations, is acting for purposes relating to his trade, business or profession, whether publicly owned or privately owned;

'unfair terms' means the contractual terms referred to in regulation 5.

(2)   In the application of these Regulations to Scotland for references to an 'injunction' or an 'interim injunction' there shall be substituted references to an 'interdict' or 'interim interdict' respectively.

### 4.   Terms to which these Regulations apply

(1)   These Regulations apply in relation to unfair terms in contracts concluded between a seller or a supplier and a consumer.

(2)   These Regulations do not apply to contractual terms which reflect—

(a)   mandatory statutory or regulatory provisions (including such provisions under the law of any Member State or in Community legislation having effect in the United Kingdom without further enactment);

(b)   the provisions or principles of international conventions to which the Member States or the Community are party.

### 5.   Unfair terms

(1)   A contractual term which has not been individually negotiated shall be regarded as unfair if, contrary to the requirement of good faith, it causes a significant imbalance in the parties' rights and obligations arising under the contract, to the detriment of the consumer.

(2)   A term shall always be regarded as not having been individually negotiated where it has been drafted in advance and the consumer has therefore not been able to influence the substance of the term.

(3)   Notwithstanding that a specific term or certain aspects of it in a contract has been individually negotiated, these Regulations shall apply to the rest of a contract if an overall assessment of it indicates that it is a pre-formulated standard contract.

(4)   It shall be for any seller or supplier who claims that a term was individually negotiated to show that it was.

(5)   Schedule 2 to these Regulations contains an indicative and non-exhaustive list of the terms which may be regarded as unfair.

### 6.   Assessment of unfair terms

(1)   Without prejudice to regulation 12, the unfairness of a contractual term shall be assessed, taking into account the nature of the goods or services for which the contract was concluded and by referring, at the time of conclusion of the contract, to all the circumstances attending the conclusion of the contract and to all the other terms of the contract or of another contract on which it is dependent.

(2)   In so far as it is in plain intelligible language, the assessment of fairness of a term shall not relate—

(a)   to the definition of the main subject matter of the contract, or

(b)   to the adequacy of the price or remuneration, as against the goods or services supplied in exchange.

### 7.   Written contracts

(1)   A seller or supplier shall ensure that any written term of a contract is expressed in plain, intelligible language.

(2)   If there is doubt about the meaning of a written term, the interpretation which is most favourable to the consumer shall prevail but this rule shall not apply in proceedings brought under regulation 12.

### 8.  Effect of unfair term

(1)   An unfair term in a contract concluded with a consumer by a seller or supplier shall not be binding on the consumer.

(2)   The contract shall continue to bind the parties if it is capable of continuing in existence without the unfair term.

### 9.  Choice of law clauses

These Regulations shall apply notwithstanding any contract term which applies or purports to apply the law of a non-Member State, if the contract has a close connection with the territory of the Member States.

### 10.  Complaints—consideration by Director

(1)   It shall be the duty of the Director to consider any complaint made to him that any contract term drawn up for general use is unfair, unless—

(a)   the complaint appears to the Director to be frivolous or vexatious; or

(b)   a qualifying body has notified the Director that it agrees to consider the complaint.

(2)   The Director shall give reasons for his decision to apply or not to apply, as the case may be, for an injunction under regulation 12 in relation to any complaint which these Regulations require him to consider.

(3)   In deciding whether or not to apply for an injunction in respect of a term which the Director considers to be unfair, he may, if he considers it appropriate to do so, have regard to any undertakings given to him by or on behalf of any person as to the continued use of such a term in contracts concluded with consumers.

### 11.  Complaints—consideration by qualifying bodies

(1)   If a qualifying body specified in Part One of Schedule I notifies the Director that it agrees to consider a complaint that any contract term drawn up for general use is unfair, it shall be under a duty to consider that complaint.

(2)   Regulation 10(2) and (3) shall apply to a qualifying body which is under a duty to consider a complaint as they apply to the Director.

### 12.  Injunctions to prevent continued use of unfair terms

(1)   The Director or, subject to paragraph (2), any qualifying body may apply for an injunction (including an interim injunction) against any person appearing to the Director or that body to be using, or recommending use of, an unfair term drawn up for general use in contracts concluded with consumers.

(2)   A qualifying body may apply for an injunction only where—

(a)   it has notified the Director of its intention to apply at least fourteen days before the date on which the application is made, beginning with the date on which the notification was given; or

(b)   the Director consents to the application being made within a shorter period.

(3)   The court on an application under this regulation may grant an injunction on such terms as it thinks fit.

(4)   An injunction may relate not only to use of a particular contract term drawn up for general use but to any similar term, or a term having like effect, used or recommended for use by any person.

### 13.  Powers of the Director and qualifying bodies to obtain documents and information

(1)   The Director may exercise the power conferred by this regulation for the purpose of—

(a)   facilitating his consideration of a complaint that a contract term drawn up for general use is unfair; or

(b)   ascertaining whether a person has complied with an undertaking or court order as to the continued use, or recommendation for use, of a term in contracts concluded with consumers.

(2) A qualifying body specified in Part One of Schedule 1 may exercise the power conferred by this regulation for the purpose of—

(a) facilitating its consideration of a complaint that a contract term drawn up for general use is unfair; or

(b) ascertaining whether a person has complied with—

(i) an undertaking given to it or to the court following an application by that body, or

(ii) a court order made on an application by that body,

as to the continued use, or recommendation for use, of a term in contracts concluded with consumers.

(3) The Director may require any person to supply to him, and a qualifying body specified in Part One of Schedule 1 may require any person to supply to it—

(a) a copy of any document which that person has used or recommended for use, at the time the notice referred to in paragraph (4) below is given, as a pre-formulated standard contract in dealings with consumers;

(b) information about the use, or recommendation for use, by that person of that document or any other such document in dealings with consumers.

(4) The power conferred by this regulation is to be exercised by a notice in writing which may—

(a) specify the way in which and the time within which it is to be complied with; and

(b) be varied or revoked by a subsequent notice.

(5) Nothing in this regulation compels a person to supply any document or information which he would be entitled to refuse to produce or give in civil proceedings before the court.

(6) If a person makes default in complying with a notice under this regulation, the court may, on the application of the Director or of the qualifying body, make such order as the court thinks fit for requiring the default to be made good, and any such order may provide that all the costs or expenses of and incidental to the application shall be borne by the person in default or by any officers of a company or other association who are responsible for its default.

### 14. Notification of undertakings and orders to Director

A qualifying body shall notify the Director—

(a) of any undertaking given to it by or on behalf of any person as to the continued use of a term which that body considers to be unfair in contracts concluded with consumers,

(b) of the outcome of any application made by it under regulation 12, and of the terms of any undertaking given to, or order made by, the court;

(c) of the outcome of any application made by it to enforce a previous order of the court.

### 15. Publication, information and advice

(1) The Director shall arrange for the publication in such form and manner as he considers appropriate, of—

(a) details of any undertaking or order notified to him under regulation 14;

(b) details of any undertaking given to him by or on behalf of any persons to the continued use of a term which the Director considers to be unfair in contracts concluded with consumers;

(c) details of any application made by him under regulation 12, and of the terms of any undertaking given to, or order made by, the court;

(d)   details of any application made by the Director to enforce a previous order of the court.

(2)   The Director shall inform any person on request whether a particular term to which these Regulations apply has been—

(a)   the subject of an undertaking given to the Director or notified to him by a qualifying body; or

(b)   the subject of an order of the court made upon application by him or notified to him by a qualifying body;

and shall give that person details of the undertaking or a copy of the order, as the case may be, together with a copy of any amendments which the person giving the undertaking has agreed to make to the term in question.

(3)   The Director may arrange for the dissemination in such form and manner as he considers appropriate of such information and advice concerning the operation of these Regulations as may appear to him to be expedient to give to the public and to all persons likely to be affected by these Regulations.

**[16.   The functions of the Financial Services Authority**
The functions of the Financial Services Authority under these Regulations shall be treated as functions of the Financial Services Authority under the Financial Services Act 1986.]

**Regulation 3**          SCHEDULE 1. QUALIFYING BODIES

PART ONE

[1.   The Information Commissioner.
2.   The Gas and Electricity Markets Authority.
3.   The Director General of Electricity Supply for Northern Ireland.
4.   The Director General of Gas for Northern Ireland.
5.   The Director General of Telecommunications.
6.   The Director General of Water Services.
7.   The Rail Regulator.
8.   Every weights and measures authority in Great Britain.
9.   The Department of Enterprise, Trade and Investment in Northern Ireland.
10.   The Financial Services Authority.

PART TWO

11.   Consumers' Association.]

**Regulation 5(5)**          SCHEDULE 2

INDICATIVE AND NON-EXHAUSTIVE LIST OF TERMS WHICH MAY BE REGARDED AS UNFAIR

1.   Terms which have the object or effect of—

(a)   excluding or limiting the legal liability of a seller or supplier in the event of the death of a consumer or personal injury to the latter resulting from an act or omission of that seller or supplier;

(b)   inappropriately excluding or limiting the legal rights of the consumer vis-à-vis the seller or supplier or another party in the event of total or partial non-performance or inadequate performance by the seller or supplier of any of the contractual obligations, including the option of offsetting a debt owed to the seller or supplier against any claim which the consumer may have against him;

(c)   making an agreement binding on the consumer whereas provision of services by the seller or supplier is subject to a condition whose realisation depends on his own will alone;

(d)   permitting the seller or supplier to retain sums paid by the consumer where the latter decides not to conclude or perform the contract, without providing for the consumer to receive compensation of an equivalent amount from the seller or supplier where the latter is the party cancelling the contract;

(e)   requiring any consumer who fails to fulfil his obligation to pay a disproportionately high sum in compensation;

(f)   authorising the seller or supplier to dissolve the contract on a discretionary basis where the same facility is not granted to the consumer, or permitting the seller or supplier to retain the sums paid for services not yet supplied by him where it is the seller or supplier himself who dissolves the contract;

(g)   enabling the seller or supplier to terminate a contract of indeterminate duration without reasonable notice except where there are serious grounds for doing so;

(h)   automatically extending a contract of fixed duration where the consumer does not indicate otherwise, when the deadline fixed for the consumer to express his desire not to extend the contract is unreasonably early;

(i)   irrevocably binding the consumer to terms with which he had no real opportunity of becoming acquainted before the conclusion of the contract;

(j)   enabling the seller or supplier to alter the terms of the contract unilaterally without a valid reason which is specified in the contract;

(k)   enabling the seller or supplier to alter unilaterally without a valid reason any characteristics of the product or service to be provided;

(l)   providing for the price of goods to be determined at the time of delivery or allowing a seller of goods or supplier of services to increase their price without in both cases giving the consumer the corresponding right to cancel the contract if the final price is too high in relation to the price agreed when the contract was concluded;

(m)   giving the seller or supplier the right to determine whether the goods or services supplied are in conformity with the contract, or giving him the exclusive right to interpret any term of the contract;

(n)   limiting the seller's or supplier's obligation to respect commitments undertaken by his agents or making his commitments subject to compliance with a particular formality;

(o)   obliging the consumer to fulfil all his obligations where the seller or supplier does not perform his;

(p)   giving the seller or supplier the possibility of transferring his rights and obligations under the contract, where this may serve to reduce the guarantees for the consumer, without the latter's agreement,

(q)   excluding or hindering the consumer's right to take legal action or exercise any other legal remedy, particularly by requiring the consumer to take disputes exclusively to arbitration not covered by legal provisions, unduly restricting the evidence available to him or imposing on him a burden of proof which, according to the applicable law, should lie with another party to the contract.

2.   Scope of paragraphs 1(g), (j) and (1)—

(a)   Paragraph 1(g) is without hindrance to terms by which a supplier of financial services reserves the right to terminate unilaterally a contract of indeterminate duration without notice where there is a valid reason provided that the supplier is required to inform the other contracting party or parties thereof immediately.

(b)   Paragraph 1(j) is without hindrance to terms under which a supplier of financial services reserves the right to alter the rate of interest payable by the consumer or due to the latter, or the amount of other charges for financial services without notice where there is a valid reason, provided that the supplier is required to inform the other contracting party or parties thereof at the earliest opportunity and that the latter are free to dissolve the contract immediately.

Paragraph 1(j) is also without hindrance to terms under which a seller or supplier reserves the right to alter unilaterally the conditions of a contract of indeterminate duration, provided that he is required to inform the consumer with reasonable notice and that the consumer is free to dissolve the contract.

(c) Paragraphs 1(g), (j) and (l) do not apply to:

—transactions in transferable securities, financial instruments and other products or services where the price is linked to fluctuations in a stock exchange quotation or index or a financial market rate that the seller or supplier does not control;

—contracts for the purchase or sale of foreign currency, traveller's cheques or international money orders denominated in foreign currency;

(d) Paragraph 1(1) is without hindrance to price indexation clauses, where lawful, provided that the method by which prices vary is explicitly described.

## CONSUMER PROTECTION (DISTANCE SELLING) REGULATIONS 2000
### (SI 2000/2334)

**1. Title, commencement and extent**

(1) These Regulations may be cited as the Consumer Protection (Distance Selling) Regulations 2000 and shall come into force on 31 October 2000.

(2) These Regulations extend to Northern Ireland.

**2. Revocation**

The Mail Order Transactions (Information) Order 1976 is hereby revoked.

**3. Interpretation**

(1) In these Regulations—

'breach' means contravention by a supplier of a prohibition in, or failure to comply with a requirement of, these Regulations;

'business' includes a trade or profession;

'consumer' means any natural person who, in contracts to which these Regulations apply, is acting for purposes which are outside his business;

'court' in relation to England and Wales and Northern Ireland means a county court or the High Court, and in relation to Scotland means the Sheriff Court or the Court of Session;

'credit' includes a cash loan and any other form of financial accommodation, and for this purpose 'cash' includes money in any form;

'Director' means the Director General of Fair Trading;

'distance contract' means any contract concerning goods or services concluded between a supplier and a consumer under an organised distance sales or service provision scheme run by the supplier who, for the purpose of the contract, makes exclusive use of one or more means of distance communication up to and including the moment at which the contract is concluded;

'EEA Agreement' means the Agreement on the European Economic Area signed at Oporto on 2 May 1992 as adjusted by the Protocol signed at Brussels on 17 March 1993;

'enactment' includes an enactment comprised in, or in an instrument made under, an Act of the Scottish Parliament;

'enforcement authority' means the Director, every weights and measures authority in Great Britain, and the Department of Enterprise, Trade and Investment in Northern Ireland;

'excepted contract' means a contract such as is mentioned in regulation 5(1);

'means of distance communication' means any means which, without the simultaneous physical presence of the supplier and the consumer, may be used for the conclusion of a contract between those parties; and an indicative list of such means is contained in Schedule 1;

'Member State' means a State which is a contracting party to the EEA Agreement;

'operator of a means of communication' means any public or private person whose business involves making one or more means of distance communication available to suppliers;

'period for performance' has the meaning given by regulation 19(2);

'personal credit agreement' has the meaning given by regulation 14(8);

'related credit agreement' has the meaning given by regulation 15(5);

'supplier' means any person who, in contracts to which these Regulations apply, is acting in his commercial or professional capacity; and

'working days' means all days other than Saturdays, Sundays and public holidays.

(2)   In the application of these Regulations to Scotland, for references to an 'injunction' or an 'interim injunction' there shall be substituted references to an 'interdict' or an 'interim interdict' respectively.

### 4.   Contracts to which these Regulations apply
These Regulations apply, subject to regulation 6, to distance contracts other than excepted contracts.

### 5.   Excepted contracts
(1)   The following are excepted contracts, namely any contract—

(a)   for the sale or other disposition of an interest in land except for a rental agreement;

(b)   for the construction of a building where the contract also provides for a sale or other disposition of an interest in land on which the building is constructed, except for a rental agreement;

(c)   relating to financial services, a non-exhaustive list of which is contained in Schedule 2;

(d)   concluded by means of an automated vending machine or automated commercial premises;

(e)   concluded with a telecommunications operator through the use of a public pay-phone;

(f) concluded at an auction.

(2)   References in paragraph (1) to a rental agreement—

(a)   if the land is situated in England and Wales, are references to any agreement which does not have to be made in writing (whether or not in fact made in writing) because of section 2(5)(a) of the Law of Property (Miscellaneous Provisions) Act 1989;

(b)   if the land is situated in Scotland, are references to any agreement for the creation, transfer, variation or extinction of an interest in land, which does not have to be made in writing (whether or not in fact made in writing) as provided for in section 1(2) and (7) of the Requirements of Writing (Scotland) Act 1995; and

(c)   if the land is situated in Northern Ireland, are references to any agreement which is not one to which section II of the Statute of Frauds, (Ireland) 1695 applies.

(3)   Paragraph (2) shall not be taken to mean that a rental agreement in respect of land situated outside the United Kingdom is not capable of being a distance contract to which these Regulations apply.

### 6.   Contracts to which only part of these Regulations apply
(1)   Regulations 7 to 20 shall not apply to a contract which is a 'timeshare

agreement' within the meaning of the Timeshare Act 1992 and to which that Act applies.

(2) Regulations 7 to 19(1) shall not apply to—

(a) contracts for the supply of food, beverages or other goods intended for everyday consumption supplied to the consumer's residence or to his workplace by regular roundsmen; or

(b) contracts for the provision of accommodation, transport, catering or leisure services, where the supplier undertakes, when the contract is concluded, to provide these services on a specific date or within a specific period.

(3) Regulations 19(2) to (8) and 20 do not apply to a contract for a 'package' within the meaning of the Package Travel, Package Holidays and Package Tours Regulations 1992 which is sold or offered for sale in the territory of the Member States.

## 7. Information required prior to the conclusion of the contract

(1) Subject to paragraph (4), in good time prior to the conclusion of the contract the supplier shall—

(a) provide to the consumer the following information—

(i) the identity of the supplier and, where the contract requires payment in advance, the supplier's address;

(ii) a description of the main characteristics of the goods or services;

(iii) the price of the goods or services including all taxes;

(iv) delivery costs where appropriate;

(v) the arrangements for payment, delivery or performance;

(vi) the existence of a right of cancellation except in the cases referred to in regulation 13;

(vii) the cost of using the means of distance communication where it is calculated other than at the basic rate;

(viii) the period for which the offer or the price remains valid; and

(ix) where appropriate, the minimum duration of the contract, in the case of contracts for the supply of goods or services to be performed permanently or recurrently;

(b) inform the consumer if he proposes, in the event of the goods or services ordered by the consumer being unavailable, to provide substitute goods or services (as the case may be) of equivalent quality and price; and

(c) inform the consumer that the cost of returning any such substitute goods to the supplier in the event of cancellation by the consumer would be met by the supplier.

(2) The supplier shall ensure that the information required by paragraph (1) is provided in a clear and comprehensible manner appropriate to the means of distance communication used, with due regard in particular to the principles of good faith in commercial transactions and the principles governing the protection of those who are unable to give their consent such as minors.

(3) Subject to paragraph (4), the supplier shall ensure that his commercial purpose is made clear when providing the information required by paragraph (1).

(4) In the case of a telephone communication, the identity of the supplier and the commercial purpose of the call shall be made clear at the beginning of the conversation with the consumer.

## 8. Written and additional information

(1) Subject to regulation 9, the supplier shall provide to the consumer in writing, or in another durable medium which is available and accessible to the consumer, the information referred to in paragraph (2), either—

(a) prior to the conclusion of the contract, or

(b) thereafter, in good time and in any event—

(i) during the performance of the contract, in the case of services; and

(ii) at the latest at the time of delivery where goods not for delivery to third parties are concerned.

(2) The information required to be provided by paragraph (1) is—

(a) the information set out in paragraphs (i) to (vi) of regulation 7(1)(a);

(b) information about the conditions and procedures for exercising the right to cancel under regulation 10, including—

(i) where a term of the contract requires (or the supplier intends that it will require) that the consumer shall return the goods to the supplier in the event of cancellation, notification of that requirement; and

(ii) information as to whether the consumer or the supplier would be responsible under these Regulations for the cost of returning any goods to the supplier, or the cost of his recovering them, if the consumer cancels the contract under regulation 10;

(c) the geographical address of the place of business of the supplier to which the consumer may address any complaints;

(d) information about any after-sales services and guarantees; and

(e) the conditions for exercising any contractual right to cancel the contract, where the contract is of an unspecified duration or a duration exceeding one year.

(3) Subject to regulation 9, prior to the conclusion of a contract for the supply of services, the supplier shall inform the consumer in writing or in another durable medium which is available and accessible to the consumer that, unless the parties agree otherwise, he will not be able to cancel the contract under regulation 10 once the performance of the services has begun with his agreement.

**9. Services performed through the use of a means of distance communication**

(1) Regulation 8 shall not apply to a contract for the supply of services which are performed through the use of a means of distance communication, where those services are supplied on only one occasion and are invoiced by the operator of the means of distance communication.

(2) But the supplier shall take all necessary steps to ensure that a consumer who is a party to a contract to which paragraph (1) applies is able to obtain the supplier's geographical address and the place of business to which the consumer may address any complaints.

**10. Right to cancel**

(1) Subject to regulation 13, if within the cancellation period set out in regulations 11 and 12, the consumer gives a notice of cancellation to the supplier, or any other person previously notified by the supplier to the consumer as a person to whom notice of cancellation may be given, the notice of cancellation shall operate to cancel the contract.

(2) Except as otherwise provided by these Regulations, the effect of a notice of cancellation is that the contract shall be treated as if it had not been made.

(3) For the purposes of these Regulations, a notice of cancellation is a notice in writing or in another durable medium available and accessible to the supplier (or to the other person to whom it is given) which, however expressed, indicates the intention of the consumer to cancel the contract.

(4) A notice of cancellation given under this regulation by a consumer to a supplier or other person is to be treated as having been properly given if the consumer—

(a) leaves it at the address last known to the consumer and addressed to the supplier or other person by name (in which case it is to be taken to have been given on the day on which it was left);

(b) sends it by post to the address last known to the consumer and addressed to the supplier or other person by name (in which case, it is to be taken to have been given on the day on which it was posted);

(c)   sends it by facsimile to the business facsimile number last known to the consumer (in which case it is to be taken to have been given on the day on which it is sent); or

(d)   sends it by electronic mail, to the business electronic mail address last known to the consumer (in which case it is to be taken to have been given on the day on which it is sent).

(5)   Where a consumer gives a notice in accordance with paragraph (4)(a) or (b) to a supplier who is a body corporate or a partnership, the notice is to be treated as having been properly given if—

(a)   in the case of a body corporate, it is left at the address of, or sent to, the secretary or clerk of that body; or

(b)   in the case of a partnership, it is left with or sent to a partner or a person having control or management of the partnership business.

## 11.   Cancellation period in the case of contracts for the supply of goods

(1)   For the purposes of regulation 10, the cancellation period in the case of contracts for the supply of goods begins with the day on which the contract is concluded and ends as provided in paragraphs (2) to (5).

(2)   Where the supplier complies with regulation 8, the cancellation period ends on the expiry of the period of seven working days beginning with the day after the day on which the consumer receives the goods.

(3)   Where a supplier who has not complied with regulation 8 provides to the consumer the information referred to in regulation 8(2), and does so in writing or in another durable medium available and accessible to the consumer, within the period of three months beginning with the day after the day on which the consumer receives the goods, the cancellation period ends on the expiry of the period of seven working days beginning with the day after the day on which the consumer receives the information.

(4)   Where neither paragraph (2) nor (3) applies, the cancellation period ends on the expiry of the period of three months and seven working days beginning with the day after the day on which the consumer receives the goods.

(5)   In the case of contracts for goods for delivery to third parties, paragraphs (2) to (4) shall apply as if the consumer had received the goods on the day on which they were received by the third party.

## 12.   Cancellation period in the case of contracts for the supply of services

(1)   For the purposes of regulation 10, the cancellation period in the case of contracts for the supply of services begins with the day on which the contract is concluded and ends as provided in paragraphs (2) to (4).

(2)   Where the supplier complies with regulation 8 on or before the day on which the contract is concluded, the cancellation period ends on the expiry of the period of seven working days beginning with the day after the day on which the contract is concluded.

(3)   Where a supplier who has not complied with regulation 8 on or before the day on which the contract is concluded provides to the consumer the information referred to in regulation 8(2) and (3), and does so in writing or in another durable medium available and accessible to the consumer, within the period of three months beginning with the day after the day on which the contract is concluded, the cancellation period ends on the expiry of the period of seven working days beginning with the day after the day on which the consumer receives the information.

(4)   Where neither paragraph (2) nor (3) applies, the cancellation period ends on the expiry of the period of three months and seven working days beginning with the day after the day on which the contract is concluded.

## 13.   Exceptions to the right to cancel

(1)   Unless the parties have agreed otherwise, the consumer will not have the

right to cancel the contract by giving notice of cancellation pursuant to regulation 10 in respect of contracts—

(a)   for the supply of services if the supplier has complied with regulation 8(3) and performance of the contract has begun with the consumer's agreement before the end of the cancellation period applicable under regulation 12;

(b)   for the supply of goods or services the price of which is dependent on fluctuations in the financial market which cannot be controlled by the supplier;

(c)   for the supply of goods made to the consumer's specifications or clearly personalised or which by reason of their nature cannot be returned or are liable to deteriorate or expire rapidly;

(d)   for the supply of audio or video recordings or computer software if they are unsealed by the consumer;

(e)   for the supply of newspapers, periodicals or magazines; or

(f)   for gaming, betting or lottery services.

**14.   Recovery of sums paid by or on behalf of the consumer on cancellation, and return of security**

(1)   On the cancellation of a contract under regulation 10, the supplier shall reimburse any sum paid by or on behalf of the consumer under or in relation to the contract to the person by whom it was made free of any charge, less any charge made in accordance with paragraph (5).

(2)   The reference in paragraph (1) to any sum paid on behalf of the consumer includes any sum paid by a creditor who is not the same person as the supplier under a personal credit agreement with the consumer.

(3)   The supplier shall make the reimbursement referred to in paragraph (1) as soon as possible and in any case within a period not exceeding 30 days beginning with the day on which the notice of cancellation was given.

(4)   Where any security has been provided in relation to the contract, the security (so far as it is so provided) shall, on cancellation under regulation 10, be treated as never having had effect and any property lodged with the supplier solely for the purposes of the security as so provided shall be returned by him forthwith.

(5)   Subject to paragraphs (6) and (7), the supplier may make a charge, not exceeding the direct costs of recovering any goods supplied under the contract, where a term of the contract provides that the consumer must return any goods supplied if he cancels the contract under regulation 10 but the consumer does not comply with this provision or returns the goods at the expense of the supplier.

(6)   Paragraph (5) shall not apply where—

(a)   the consumer cancels in circumstances where he has the right to reject the goods under a term of the contract, including a term implied by virtue of any enactment, or

(b)   the term requiring the consumer to return any goods supplied if he cancels the contract is an 'unfair term' within the meaning of the Unfair Terms in Consumer Contracts Regulations 1999.

(7)   Paragraph (5) shall not apply to the cost of recovering any goods which were supplied as substitutes for the goods ordered by the consumer.

(8)   For the purposes of these Regulations, a personal credit agreement is an agreement between the consumer and any other person ('the creditor') by which the creditor provides the consumer with credit of any amount.

**15.   Automatic cancellation of a related credit agreement**

(1)   Where a notice of cancellation is given under regulation 10 which has the effect of cancelling the contract, the giving of the notice shall also have the effect of cancelling any related credit agreement.

(2)   Where a related credit agreement is cancelled by virtue of paragraph (1),

the supplier shall, if he is not the same person as the creditor under that agreement, forthwith on receipt of the notice of cancellation inform the creditor that the notice has been given.

(3)  Where a related credit agreement is cancelled by virtue of paragraph (1)—

(a)  any sum paid by or on behalf of the consumer under, or in relation to, the credit agreement which the supplier is not obliged to reimburse under regulation 14(1) shall be reimbursed, except for any sum which, if it had not already been paid, would have to be paid under sub-paragraph (b);

(b)  the agreement shall continue in force so far as it relates to repayment of the credit and payment of interest, subject to regulation 16; and

(c)  subject to sub-paragraph (b), the agreement shall cease to be enforceable.

(4)  Where any security has been provided under a related credit agreement, the security, so far as it is so provided, shall be treated as never having had effect and any property lodged with the creditor solely for the purposes of the security as so provided shall be returned by him forthwith.

(5)  For the purposes of this regulation and regulation 16, a 'related credit agreement' means an agreement under which fixed sum credit which fully or partly covers the price under a contract cancelled under regulation 10 is granted—

(a)  by the supplier, or

(b)  by another person, under an arrangement between that person and the supplier.

(6)  For the purposes of this regulation and regulation 16—

(a)  'creditor' is a person who grants credit under a related credit agreement;

(b)  'fixed sum credit' has the same meaning as in section 10 of the Consumer Credit Act 1974;

(c)  'repayment' in relation to credit means repayment of money received by the consumer, and cognate expressions shall be construed accordingly; and

(d)  'interest' means interest on money so received.

## 16.  Repayment of credit and interest after cancellation of a related credit agreement

(1)  This regulation applies following the cancellation of a related credit agreement by virtue of regulation 15(1).

(2)  If the consumer repays the whole or a portion of the credit—

(a)  before the expiry of one month following the cancellation of the credit agreement, or

(b)  in the case of a credit repayable by instalments, before the date on which the first instalment is due,

no interest shall be payable on the amount repaid.

(3)  If the whole of a credit repayable by instalments is not repaid on or before the date referred to in paragraph (2)(b), the consumer shall not be liable to repay any of the credit except on receipt of a request in writing, signed by the creditor, stating the amounts of the remaining instalments (recalculated by the creditor as nearly as may be in accordance with the agreement and without extending the repayment period), but excluding any sum other than principal and interest.

(4)  Where any security has been provided under a related credit agreement the duty imposed on the consumer to repay credit and to pay interest shall not be enforceable before the creditor has discharged any duty imposed on him by regulation 15(4) to return any property lodged with him as security on cancellation.

## 17.  Restoration of goods by consumer after cancellation

(1)  This regulation applies where a contract is cancelled under regulation 10 after the consumer has acquired possession of any goods under the contract other than any goods mentioned in regulation 13(1)(b) to (e).

(2)   The consumer shall be treated as having been under a duty throughout the period prior to cancellation—
(a)   to retain possession of the goods, and
(b)   to take reasonable care of them.

(3)   On cancellation, the consumer shall be under a duty to restore the goods to the supplier in accordance with this regulation, and in the meanwhile to retain possession of the goods and take reasonable care of them.

(4)   The consumer shall not be under any duty to deliver the goods except at his own premises and in pursuance of a request in writing, or in another durable medium available and accessible to the consumer, from the supplier and given to the consumer either before, or at the time when, the goods are collected from those premises.

(5)   If the consumer—
(a)   delivers the goods (whether at his own premises or elsewhere) to any person to whom, under regulation 10(1), a notice of cancellation could have been given; or
(b)   sends the goods at his own expense to such a person,
he shall be discharged from any duty to retain possession of the goods or restore them to the supplier.

(6)   Where the consumer delivers the goods in accordance with paragraph (5)(a), his obligation to take care of the goods shall cease; and if he sends the goods in accordance with paragraph (5)(b), he shall be under a duty to take reasonable care to see that they are received by the supplier and not damaged in transit, but in other respects his duty to take care of the goods shall cease when he sends them.

(7)   Where, at any time during the period of 21 days beginning with the day notice of cancellation was given, the consumer receives such a request as is mentioned in paragraph (4), and unreasonably refuses or unreasonably fails to comply with it, his duty to retain possession and take reasonable care of the goods shall continue until he delivers or sends the goods as mentioned in paragraph (5), but if within that period he does not receive such a request his duty to take reasonable care of the goods shall cease at the end of that period.

(8)   Where—
(a)   a term of the contract provides that if the consumer cancels the contract, he must return the goods to the supplier, and
(b)   the consumer is not otherwise entitled to reject the goods under the terms of the contract or by virtue of any enactment,
paragraph (7) shall apply as if for the period of 21 days there were substituted the period of 6 months.

(9)   Where any security has been provided in relation to the cancelled contract, the duty to restore goods imposed on the consumer by this regulation shall not be enforceable before the supplier has discharged any duty imposed on him by regulation 14(4) to return any property lodged with him as security on cancellation.

(10)   Breach of a duty imposed by this regulation on a consumer is actionable as a breach of statutory duty.

**18.   Goods given in part-exchange**
(1)   This regulation applies on the cancellation of a contract under regulation 10 where the supplier agreed to take goods in part-exchange (the 'part-exchange goods') and those goods have been delivered to him.

(2)   Unless, before the end of the period of 10 days beginning with the date of cancellation, the part-exchange goods are returned to the consumer in a condition substantially as good as when they were delivered to the supplier, the consumer shall be entitled to recover from the supplier a sum equal to the part-exchange allowance.

(3)　In this regulation the part-exchange allowance means the sum agreed as such in the cancelled contract, or if no such sum was agreed, such sum as it would have been reasonable to allow in respect of the part-exchange goods if no notice of cancellation had been served.

(4)　Where the consumer recovers from the supplier a sum equal to the part-exchange allowance, the title of the consumer to the part-exchange goods shall vest in the supplier (if it has not already done so) on recovery of that sum.

### 19.　Performance

(1)　Unless the parties agree otherwise, the supplier shall perform the contract within a maximum of 30 days beginning with the day after the day the consumer sent his order to the supplier.

(2)　Subject to paragraphs (7) and (8), where the supplier is unable to perform the contract because the goods or services ordered are not available, within the period for performance referred to in paragraph (1) or such other period as the parties agree ('the period for performance'), he shall—

　　(a)　inform the consumer; and

　　(b)　reimburse any sum paid by or on behalf of the consumer under or in relation to the contract to the person by whom it was made.

(3)　The reference in paragraph (2)(b) to any sum paid on behalf of the consumer includes any sum paid by a creditor who is not the same person as the supplier under a personal credit agreement with the consumer.

(4)　The supplier shall make the reimbursement referred to in paragraph (2)(b) as soon as possible and in any event within a period of 30 days beginning with the day after the day on which the period for performance expired.

(5)　A contract which has not been performed within the period for performance shall be treated as if it had not been made, save for any rights or remedies which the consumer has under it as a result of the non-performance.

(6)　Where any security has been provided in relation to the contract, the security (so far as it is so provided) shall, where the supplier is unable to perform the contract within the period for performance, be treated as never having had any effect and any property lodged with the supplier solely for the purposes of the security as so provided shall be returned by him forthwith.

(7)　Where the supplier is unable to supply the goods or services ordered by the consumer, the supplier may perform the contract for the purposes of these Regulations by providing substitute goods or services (as the case may be) of equivalent quality and price provided that—

　　(a)　this possibility was provided for in the contract;

　　(b)　prior to the conclusion of the contract the supplier gave the consumer the information required by regulation 7(1)(b) and (c) in the manner required by regulation 7(2).

(8)　In the case of outdoor leisure events which by their nature cannot be rescheduled, paragraph 2(b) shall not apply where the consumer and the supplier so agree.

### 20.　Effect of non-performance on related credit agreement

Where a supplier is unable to perform the contract within the period for performance—

　　(a)　regulations 15 and 16 shall apply to any related credit agreement as if the consumer had given a valid notice of cancellation under regulation 10 on the expiry of the period for performance; and

　　(b)　the reference in regulation 15(3)(a) to regulation 14(1) shall be read, for the purposes of this regulation, as a reference to regulation 19(2).

### 21.　Payment by card

(1)　Subject to paragraph (4), the consumer shall be entitled to cancel a payment where fraudulent use has been made of his payment card in connection with a contract to which this regulation applies by another person not acting, or to be treated as acting, as his agent.

(2)   Subject to paragraph (4), the consumer shall be entitled to be recredited, or to have all sums returned by the card issuer, in the event of fraudulent use of his payment card in connection with a contract to which this regulation applies by another person not acting, or to be treated as acting, as the consumer's agent.

(3)   Where paragraphs (1) and (2) apply, in any proceedings if the consumer alleges that any use made of the payment card was not authorised by him it is for the card issuer to prove that the use was so authorised.

(4)   Paragraphs (1) and (2) shall not apply to an agreement to which section 83(1) of the Consumer Credit Act 1974 applies.

(5)   Section 84 of the Consumer Credit Act 1974 (misuse of credit-tokens) is amended by the insertion after subsection (3) of—

'(3A)   Subsections (1) and (2) shall not apply to any use, in connection with a distance contract (other than an excepted contract), of a card which is a credit-token.

(3B)   In subsection (3A), "distance contract" and "excepted contract" have the meanings given in the Consumer Protection (Distance Selling) Regulations 2000.'

(6)   For the purposes of this regulation—
   'card issuer' means the owner of the card; and
   'payment card' includes credit cards, charge cards, debit cards and store cards.

## 22.   Amendments to the Unsolicited Goods and Services Act 1971
(1)   The Unsolicited Goods and Services Act 1971 is amended as follows.
(2)   Omit section 1 (rights of recipient of unsolicited goods).
(3)   In subsection (1) of section 2 (demands and threats regarding payment), after 'them' insert 'for the purposes of his trade or business'.
(4)   The amendments made by this regulation apply only in relation to goods sent after the date on which it comes into force.

## 23.   Amendments to the Unsolicited Goods and Services (Northern Ireland) Order 1976
(1)   The Unsolicited Goods and Services (Northern Ireland) Order 1976 is amended as follows.
(2)   Omit Article 3 (rights of recipient of unsolicited goods).
(3)   In paragraph (1) of Article 4 (demands and threats regarding payment), after 'them' insert 'for the purposes of his trade or business'.
(4)   The amendments made by this regulation apply only in relation to goods sent after the date on which it comes into force.

## 24.   Inertia Selling
(1)   Paragraphs (2) and (3) apply if—
   (a)   unsolicited goods are sent to a person ('the recipient') with a view to his acquiring them;
   (b)   the recipient has no reasonable cause to believe that they were sent with a view to their being acquired for the purposes of a business; and
   (c)   the recipient has neither agreed to acquire nor agreed to return them.
(2)   The recipient may, as between himself and the sender, use, deal with or dispose of the goods as if they were an unconditional gift to him.
(3)   The rights of the sender to the goods are extinguished.
(4)   A person who, not having reasonable cause to believe there is a right to payment, in the course of any business makes a demand for payment, or asserts a present or prospective right to payment, for what he knows are—

(a)   unsolicited goods sent to another person with a view to his acquiring them for purposes other than those of his business, or

(b)   unsolicited services supplied to another person for purposes other than those of his business,

is guilty of an offence and liable, on summary conviction, to a fine not exceeding level 4 on the standard scale.

(5)   A person who, not having reasonable cause to believe there is a right to payment, in the course of any business and with a view to obtaining payment for what he knows are unsolicited goods sent or services supplied as mentioned in paragraph (4)—

(a)   threatens to bring any legal proceedings, or

(b)   places or causes to be placed the name of any person on a list of defaulters or debtors or threatens to do so, or

(c)   invokes or causes to be invoked any other collection procedure or threatens to do so,

is guilty of an offence and liable, on summary conviction, to a fine not exceeding level 5 on the standard scale.

(6)   In this regulation—

'acquire' includes hire;

'send' includes deliver;

'sender', in relation to any goods, includes—

(a)   any person on whose behalf or with whose consent the goods are sent;

(b)   any other person claiming through or under the sender or any person mentioned in paragraph (a); and

(c)   any person who delivers the goods; and

'unsolicited' means, in relation to goods sent or services supplied to any person, that they are sent or supplied without any prior request made by or on behalf of the recipient.

(7)   For the purposes of this regulation, an invoice or similar document which—

(a)   states the amount of a payment, and

(b)   fails to comply with the requirements of regulations made under section 3A of the Unsolicited Goods and Services Act 1971 or, as the case may be, Article 6 of the Unsolicited Goods and Services (Northern Ireland) Order 1976 applicable to it,

is to be regarded as asserting a right to the payment.

(8)   Section 3A of the Unsolicited Goods and Services Act 1971 applies for the purposes of this regulation in its application to England, Wales and Scotland as it applies for the purposes of that Act.

(9)   Article 6 of the Unsolicited Goods and Services (Northern Ireland) Order 1976 applies for the purposes of this regulation in its application to Northern Ireland as it applies for the purposes of that Order.

(10)   This regulation applies only to goods sent and services supplied after the date on which it comes into force.

## 25.  No contracting-out

(1)   A term contained in any contract to which these Regulations apply is void if, and to the extent that, it is inconsistent with a provision for the protection of the consumer contained in these Regulations.

(2)   Where a provision of these Regulations specifies a duty or liability of the consumer in certain circumstances, a term contained in a contract to which these Regulations apply, other than a term to which paragraph (3) applies, is inconsistent with that provision if it purports to impose, directly or indirectly, an additional duty or liability on him in those circumstances.

(3)   This paragraph applies to a term which requires the consumer to return any goods supplied to him under the contract if he cancels it under regulation 10.

(4) A term to which paragraph (3) applies shall, in the event of cancellation by the consumer under regulation 10, have effect only for the purposes of regulations 14(5) and 17(8).

(5) These Regulations shall apply notwithstanding any contract term which applies or purports to apply the law of a non-Member State if the contract has a close connection with the territory of a Member State.

## 26. Consideration of complaints

(1) It shall be the duty of an enforcement authority to consider any complaint made to it about a breach unless—

(a) the complaint appears to the authority to be frivolous or vexatious; or

(b) another enforcement authority has notified the Director that it agrees to consider the complaint.

(2) If an enforcement authority notifies the Director that it agrees to consider a complaint made to another enforcement authority, the first mentioned authority shall be under a duty to consider the complaint.

(3) An enforcement authority which is under a duty to consider a complaint shall give reasons for its decision to apply or not to apply, as the case may be, for an injunction under regulation 27.

(4) In deciding whether or not to apply for an injunction in respect of a breach an enforcement authority may, if it considers it appropriate to do so, have regard to any undertaking given to it or another enforcement authority by or on behalf of any person as to compliance with these Regulations.

## 27. Injunctions to secure compliance with these Regulations

(1) The Director or, subject to paragraph (2), any other enforcement authority may apply for an injunction (including an interim injunction) against any person who appears to the Director or that authority to be responsible for a breach.

(2) An enforcement authority other than the Director may apply for an injunction only where—

(a) it has notified the Director of its intention to apply at least fourteen days before the date on which the application is to be made, beginning with the date on which the notification was given; or

(b) the Director consents to the application being made within a shorter period.

(3) The court on an application under this regulation may grant an injunction on such terms as it thinks fit to secure compliance with these Regulations.

## 28. Notification of undertakings and orders to the Director

An enforcement authority other than the Director shall notify the Director—

(a) of any undertaking given to it by or on behalf of any person who appears to it to be responsible for a breach;

(b) of the outcome of any application made by it under regulation 27 and of the terms of any undertaking given to or order made by the court;

(c) of the outcome of any application made by it to enforce a previous order of the court.

## 29. Publication, information and advice

(1) The Director shall arrange for the publication in such form and manner as he considers appropriate of—

(a) details of any undertaking or order notified to him under regulation 28;

(b) details of any undertaking given to him by or on behalf of any person as to compliance with these Regulations;

(c) details of any application made by him under regulation 27, and of the terms of any undertaking given to, or order made by, the court;

(d) details of any application made by the Director to enforce a previous order of the court.

(2) The Director may arrange for the dissemination in such form and manner as he considers appropriate of such information and advice concerning the operation of these Regulations as it may appear to him to be expedient to give to the public and to all persons likely to be affected by these Regulations.

**Regulation 3** SCHEDULE 1.
INDICATIVE LIST OF MEANS OF DISTANCE COMMUNICATION

1. Unaddressed printed matter.
2. Addressed printed matter.
3. Letter.
4. Press advertising with order form.
5. Catalogue.
6. Telephone with human intervention.
7. Telephone without human intervention (automatic calling machine, audio-text).
8. Radio.
9. Videophone (telephone with screen).
10. Videotext (microcomputer and television screen) with keyboard or touch screen.
11. Electronic mail.
12. Facsimile machine (fax).
13. Television (teleshopping).

**Regulation 5(1)(c)** SCHEDULE 2.
NON-EXHAUSTIVE LIST OF FINANCIAL SERVICES

1. Investment services.
2. Insurance and reinsurance operations.
3. Banking services.
4. Services relating to dealings in futures or options.
Such services include in particular:
 – investment services referred to in the Annex to Directive 93/22/EEC; services of collective investment undertakings;
 – services covered by the activities subject to mutual recognition referred to in the Annex to Directive 89/846/EEC;
 – operations covered by the insurance and reinsurance activities referred to in:
  – Article 1 of Directive 73/239/EEC;
  – the Annex to Directive 79/267/EEC;
  – Directive 64/225/EEC;
  – Directives 92/49/EEC and 92/96/EEC.

## LATE PAYMENT OF COMMERCIAL DEBTS (SCOTLAND) REGULATIONS 2002
### (SSI 2002/335)

**1. Citation, commencement and extent**
(1) These Regulations may be cited as the Late Payment of Commercial Debts (Scotland) Regulations 2002 and shall come into force on 7th August 2002.
(2) These Regulations extend to Scotland only.

**2.** *(amends Late Payment of Commercial Debts (Interest) Act 1998)*

**3. Proceedings restraining use of grossly unfair terms**
(1) In this regulation—

(a)   'small and medium-sized enterprises' means those enterprises defined in Annex 1 to Commission Regulation (EC) No 70/2001 of 12th January 2001 on the application of Articles 87 and 88 of the EC Treaty to State aid to small and medium-sized enterprises;

(b)   'representative body' means an organisation established to represent the collective interests of small and medium-sized enterprises in general or in a particular sector or area.

(2)   This regulation applies where a person acting in the course of a business has written standard terms on which he or she enters (or intends to enter) as purchaser into contracts to which the Late Payment of Commercial Debts (Interest) Act 1998 applies which include a term purporting to oust or vary the right to statutory interest in relation to qualifying debts created by those contracts.

(3)   If it appears to the Court of Session that in all or any circumstances the purported use of such a term in a relevant contract would be void under the Late Payment of Commercial Debts (Interest) Act 1998, the court on the application of a representative body may grant an interdict against that person prohibiting that person in those circumstances from using the offending term, on such terms as the court may think fit.

(4)   Only a representative body may apply to the Court of Session under this regulation.

**4.   Saving for existing contracts**
These Regulations do not affect contracts made before 7th August 2002.

### LATE PAYMENT OF COMMERCIAL DEBTS (RATE OF INTEREST) (SCOTLAND) ORDER 2002
### (SSI 2002/336)

**1.   Citation, commencement and extent**
(1)   This Order may be cited as the Late Payment of Commercial Debts (Rate of Interest) (Scotland) Order 2002 and shall come into force on 7th August 2002.

(2)   This Order extends to Scotland only.

**2.   Revocation**
The Late Payment of Commercial Debts (Rate of Interest) (No 2) Order 1998 is revoked.

**3.   Interpretation**
In this Order, 'the official dealing rate' means the rate announced from time to time by the Monetary Policy Committee of the Bank of England ('the Bank') and for the time being in force as the official dealing rate, being the rate at which the Bank is willing to enter into transactions for providing short term liquidity in the money markets.

**4.   Rate of statutory interest**
The rate of interest for the purposes of the Late Payment of Commercial Debts (Interest) Act 1998 shall be 8 per cent per annum over the official dealing rate in force on the 30th June (in respect of interest which starts to run between 1st July and 31st December) or the 31st December (in respect of interest which starts to run between 1st January and 30th June) immediately before the day on which statutory interest starts to run.

## SALE AND SUPPLY OF GOODS TO CONSUMERS REGULATIONS 2002
### (SI 2002/3045)

*[These regulations, which implement Directive 1999/44/EC, became available too late to allow their provisions to be incorporated into the principal statutes. It is hoped, however, that the inclusion of the regulations here in their entirety will be useful for readers.]*

### 1. Title, commencement and extent
(1) These Regulations may be cited as the Sale and Supply of Goods to Consumers Regulations 2002 and shall come into force on 31st March 2003.

(2) These Regulations extend to Northern Ireland.

### 2. Interpretation
In these Regulations—

'consumer' means any natural person who, in the contracts covered by these Regulations, is acting for purposes which are outside his trade, business or profession;

'consumer guarantee' means any undertaking to a consumer by a person acting in the course of his business, given without extra charge, to reimburse the price paid or to replace, repair or handle consumer goods in any way if they do not meet the specifications set out in the guarantee statement or in the relevant advertising;

'court' in relation to England and Wales and Northern Ireland means a county court or the High Court, and in relation to Scotland, the sheriff or the Court of Session;

'enforcement authority' means the Director General of Fair Trading, every local weights and measures authority in Great Britain and the Department of Enterprise, Trade and Investment for Northern Ireland;

'goods' has the same meaning as in section 61 of the Sale of Goods Act 1979;

'guarantor' means a person who offers a consumer guarantee to a consumer; and

'supply' includes supply by way of sale, lease, hire or hire-purchase.

## AMENDMENTS TO THE SALE OF GOODS ACT 1979

### 3. Additional implied terms in consumer cases
(1) Section 14 of the Sale of Goods Act 1979 is amended as follows.

(2) After subsection (2C) insert—

'(2D) If the buyer deals as consumer or, in Scotland, if a contract of sale is a consumer contract, the relevant circumstances mentioned in subsection (2A) above include any public statements on the specific characteristics of the goods made about them by the seller, the producer or his representative, particularly in advertising or on labelling.

(2E) A public statement is not by virtue of subsection (2D) above a relevant circumstance for the purposes of subsection (2A) above in the case of a contract of sale, if the seller shows that—

(a) at the time the contract was made, he was not, and could not reasonably have been, aware of the statement,

(b) before the contract was made, the statement had been withdrawn in public or, to the extent that it contained anything which was incorrect or misleading, it had been corrected in public, or

(c) the decision to buy the goods could not have been influenced by the statement.

(2F) Subsections (2D) and (2E) above do not prevent any public statement from being a relevant circumstance for the purposes of subsection (2A) above (whether or not the buyer deals as consumer or, in Scotland, whether or not the contract of sale is a consumer contract) if the statement would have been such a circumstance apart from those subsections.'.

### 4. Amendments to rules on passing of risk and acceptance of goods in consumer cases

(1)   Section 20 of the Sale of Goods Act 1979 is amended as follows. For the marginal note there is substituted 'Passing of risk'.

(2)   After subsection (3) there is inserted—

'(4)   In a case where the buyer deals as consumer or, in Scotland, where there is a consumer contract in which the buyer is a consumer, subsections (1) to (3) above must be ignored and the goods remain at the seller's risk until they are delivered to the consumer.'.

(3)   In section 32 of the Sale of Goods Act 1979, after subsection (3) there is inserted—

'(4)   In a case where the buyer deals as consumer or, in Scotland, where there is a consumer contract in which the buyer is a consumer, subsections (1) to (3) above must be ignored, but if in pursuance of a contract of sale the seller is authorised or required to send the goods to the buyer, delivery of the goods to the carrier is not delivery of the goods to the buyer.'.

### 5. Buyer's additional remedies in consumer cases

After Part 5 of the Sale of Goods Act 1979 insert—

'PART 5A

ADDITIONAL RIGHTS OF BUYER IN CONSUMER CASES

#### 48A.   Introductory

(1)   This section applies if—

(a)   the buyer deals as consumer or, in Scotland, there is a consumer contract in which the buyer is a consumer, and

(b)   the goods do not conform to the contract of sale at the time of delivery.

(2)   If this section applies, the buyer has the right—

(a)   under and in accordance with section 48B below, to require the seller to repair or replace the goods, or

(b)   under and in accordance with section 48C below—

(i)   to require the seller to reduce the purchase price of the goods to the buyer by an appropriate amount, or

(ii)   to rescind the contract with regard to the goods in question.

(3)   For the purposes of subsection (1)(b) above goods which do not conform to the contract of sale at any time within the period of six months starting with the date on which the goods were delivered to the buyer must be taken not to have so conformed at that date.

(4)   Subsection (3) above does not apply if—

(a)   it is established that the goods did so conform at that date;

(b)   its application is incompatible with the nature of the goods or the nature of the lack of conformity.

#### 48B.   Repair or replacement of the goods

(1)   If section 48A above applies, the buyer may require the seller—

(a)   to repair the goods, or

(b)   to replace the goods.

(2)   If the buyer requires the seller to repair or replace the goods, the seller must—

(a) repair or, as the case may be, replace the goods within a reasonable time but without causing significant inconvenience to the buyer;

(b) bear any necessary costs incurred in doing so (including in particular the cost of any labour, materials or postage).

(3) The buyer must not require the seller to repair or, as the case may be, replace the goods if that remedy is—

(a) impossible, or

(b) disproportionate in comparison to the other of those remedies, or

(c) disproportionate in comparison to an appropriate reduction in the purchase price under paragraph (a), or rescission under paragraph (b), of section 48C(1) below.

(4) One remedy is disproportionate in comparison to the other if the one imposes costs on the seller which, in comparison to those imposed on him by the other, are unreasonable, taking into account—

(a) the value which the goods would have if they conformed to the contract of sale,

(b) the significance of the lack of conformity, and

(c) whether the other remedy could be effected without significant inconvenience to the buyer.

(5) Any question as to what is a reasonable time or significant inconvenience is to be determined by reference to—

(a) the nature of the goods, and

(b) the purpose for which the goods were acquired.

### 48C. Reduction of purchase price or rescission of contract

(1) If section 48A above applies, the buyer may—

(a) require the seller to reduce the purchase price of the goods in question to the buyer by an appropriate amount, or

(b) rescind the contract with regard to those goods,

if the condition in subsection (2) below is satisfied.

(2) The condition is that—

(a) by virtue of section 48B(3) above the buyer may require neither repair nor replacement of the goods; or

(b) the buyer has required the seller to repair or replace the goods, but the seller is in breach of the requirement of section 48B(2)(a) above to do so within a reasonable time and without significant inconvenience to the buyer.

(3) For the purposes of this Part, if the buyer rescinds the contract, any reimbursement to the buyer may be reduced to take account of the use he has had of the goods since they were delivered to him.

### 48D. Relation to other remedies etc

(1) If the buyer requires the seller to repair or replace the goods the buyer must not act under subsection (2) until he has given the seller a reasonable time in which to repair or replace (as the case may be) the goods.

(2) The buyer acts under this subsection if—

(a) in England and Wales or Northern Ireland he rejects the goods and terminates the contract for breach of condition;

(b) in Scotland he rejects any goods delivered under the contract and treats it as repudiated;

(c) he requires the goods to be replaced or repaired (as the case may be).

### 48E. Powers of the court

(1) In any proceedings in which a remedy is sought by virtue of this

Part the court, in addition to any other power it has, may act under this section.

(2) On the application of the buyer the court may make an order requiring specific performance or, in Scotland, specific implement by the seller of any obligation imposed on him by virtue of section 48B above.

(3) Subsection (4) applies if—

(a) the buyer requires the seller to give effect to a remedy under section 48B or 48C above or has claims to rescind under section 48C, but

(b) the court decides that another remedy under section 48B or 48C is appropriate.

(4) The court may proceed—

(a) as if the buyer had required the seller to give effect to the other remedy, or if the other remedy is rescission under section 48C

(b) as if the buyer had claimed to rescind the contract under that section.

(5) If the buyer has claimed to rescind the contract the court may order that any reimbursement to the buyer is reduced to take account of the use he has had of the goods since they were delivered to him.

(6) The court may make an order under this section unconditionally or on such terms and conditions as to damages, payment of the price and otherwise as it thinks just.

**48F. Conformity with the contract**
For the purposes of this Part, goods do not conform to a contract of sale if there is, in relation to the goods, a breach of an express term of the contract or a term implied by section 13, 14 or 15 above.'.

## 6. Other amendments to the 1979 Act

(1) In section 61(1) after the definition of 'plaintiff' there is inserted—

'"producer" means the manufacturer of goods, the importer of goods into the European Economic Area or any person purporting to be a producer by placing his name, trade mark or other distinctive sign on the goods;';

(2) in section 61(1) after the definition of 'property' there is inserted—

'"repair" means, in cases where there is a lack of conformity in goods for the purposes of section 48F of this Act, to bring the goods into conformity with the contract;'.

AMENDMENTS TO THE SUPPLY OF GOODS AND SERVICES ACT 1982

## 7. Additional implied terms in cases where goods are transferred to consumers—England, Wales and Northern Ireland

(1) Section 4 of the Supply of Goods and Services Act 1982 is amended as follows.

(2) After subsection (2A) insert—

'(2B) If the transferee deals as consumer, the relevant circumstances mentioned in subsection (2A) above include any public statements on the specific characteristics of the goods made about them by the transferor, the producer or his representative, particularly in advertising or on labelling.

(2C) A public statement is not by virtue of subsection (2B) above a relevant circumstance for the purposes of subsection (2A) above in the case of a contract for the transfer of goods, if the transferor shows that—

(a) at the time the contract was made, he was not, and could not reasonably have been, aware of the statement,

(b) before the contract was made, the statement had been withdrawn in public or, to the extent that it contained anything which was incorrect or misleading, it had been corrected in public, or

(c)   the decision to acquire the goods could not have been influenced by the statement.

(2D)   Subsections (2B) and (2C) above do not prevent any public statement from being a relevant circumstance for the purposes of subsection (2A) above (whether or not the transferee deals as consumer) if the statement would have been such a circumstance apart from those subsections.'.

**8.   Additional implied terms in cases where goods are transferred to consumers—Scotland**

(1)   Section 11D of the Supply of Goods and Services Act 1982 is amended as follows.

(2)   After subsection (3) insert—

'(3A)   If the contract for the transfer of goods is a consumer contract, the relevant circumstances mentioned in subsection (3) above include any public statements on the specific characteristics of the goods made about them by the transferor, the producer or his representative, particularly in advertising or on labelling.

(3B)   A public statement is not by virtue of subsection (3A) above a relevant circumstance for the purposes of subsection (3) above in the case of a contract for the transfer of goods, if the transferor shows that—

(a)   at the time the contract was made, he was not, and could not reasonably have been, aware of the statement,

(b)   before the contract was made, the statement had been withdrawn in public or, to the extent that it contained anything which was incorrect or misleading, it had been corrected in public, or

(c)   the decision to acquire the goods could not have been influenced by the statement.

(3C)   Subsections (3A) and (3B) above do not prevent any public statement from being a relevant circumstance for the purposes of subsection (3) above (whether or not the contract for the transfer of goods is a consumer contract) if the statement would have been such a circumstance apart from those subsections.'.

(3)   After subsection (9) insert—

'(10)   For the purposes of this section, 'consumer contract' has the same meaning as in section 11F(3) below.'.

**9.   Transferee's additional remedies in consumer cases**

(1)   After Part 1A of the Supply off Goods and Services Act 1982 insert—

'PART 1B

ADDITIONAL RIGHTS OF TRANSFEREE IN CONSUMER CASES

**11M.   Introductory**

(1)   This section applies if—

(a)   the transferee deals as consumer or, in Scotland, there is a consumer contract in which the transferee is a consumer, and

(b)   the goods do not conform to the contract for the transfer of goods at the time of delivery.

(2)   If this section applies, the transferee has the right—

(a)   under and in accordance with section 11N below, to require the transferor to repair or replace the goods, or

(b)   under and in accordance with section 11P below—

(i)   to require the transferor to reduce the amount to be paid for the transfer by the transferee by an appropriate amount, or

(ii)   to rescind the contract with regard to the goods in question.

(3)   For the purposes of subsection (1)(b) above, goods which do not conform to the contract for the transfer of goods at any time within the period of six months starting with the date on which the goods were delivered to the transferee must be taken not to have so conformed at that date.

(4)   Subsection (3) above does not apply if—

(a)   it is established that the goods did so conform at that date;

(b)   its application is incompatible with the nature of the goods or the nature of the lack of conformity.

(5)   For the purposes of this section, 'consumer contract' has the same meaning as in section 11F(3) above.

**11N.   Repair or replacement of the goods**

(1)   If section 11M above applies, the transferee may require the transferor—

(a)   to repair the goods, or

(b)   to replace the goods.

(2)   If the transferee requires the transferor to repair or replace the goods, the transferor must—

(a)   repair or, as the case may be, replace the goods within a reasonable time but without causing significant inconvenience to the transferee;

(b)   bear any necessary costs incurred in doing so (including in particular the cost of any labour, materials or postage).

(3)   The transferee must not require the transferor to repair or, as the case may be, replace the goods if that remedy is—

(a)   impossible,

(b)   disproportionate in comparison to the other of those remedies, or

(c)   disproportionate in comparison to an appropriate reduction in the purchase price under paragraph (a), or rescission under paragraph (b), of section 11P(1) below.

(4)   One remedy is disproportionate in comparison to the other if the one imposes costs on the transferor which, in comparison to those imposed on him by the other, are unreasonable, taking into account—

(a)   the value which the goods would have if they conformed to the contract for the transfer of goods,

(b)   the significance of the lack of conformity to the contract for the transfer of goods, and

(c)   whether the other remedy could be effected without significant inconvenience to the transferee.

(5)   Any question as to what is a reasonable time or significant inconvenience is to be determined by reference to—

(a)   the nature of the goods, and

(b)   the purpose for which the goods were acquired.

**11P.   Reduction of purchase price or rescission of contract**

(1)   If section 11M above applies, the transferee may—

(a)   require the transferor to reduce the purchase price of the goods in question to the transferee by an appropriate amount, or

(b)   rescind the contract with regard to those goods,

if the condition in subsection (2) below is satisfied.

(2)   The condition is that—

(a)   by virtue of section 11N(3) above the transferee may require neither repair nor replacement of the goods, or

(b)   the transferee has required the transferor to repair or replace the goods, but the transferor is in breach of the requirement of section 11N(2)(a) above to do so within a reasonable time and without significant inconvenience to the transferee.

(3)   If the transferee rescinds the contract, any reimbursement to the transferee may be reduced to take account of the use he has had of the goods since they were delivered to him.

**11Q.   Relation to other remedies etc**

(1)   If the transferee requires the transferor to repair or replace the goods the transferee must not act under subsection (2) until he has given the transferor a reasonable time in which to repair or replace (as the case may be) the goods.

(2)   The transferee acts under this subsection if—

(a)   in England and Wales or Northern Ireland he rejects the goods and terminates the contract for breach of condition;

(b)   in Scotland he rejects any goods delivered under the contract and treats it as repudiated; or

(c)   he requires the goods to be replaced or repaired (as the case may be).

**11R.   Powers of the court**

(1)   In any proceedings in which a remedy is sought by virtue of this Part the court, in addition to any other power it has, may act under this section.

(2)   On the application of the transferee the court may make an order requiring specific performance or, in Scotland, specific implement by the transferor of any obligation imposed on him by virtue of section 11N above.

(3)   Subsection (4) applies if—

(a)   the transferee requires the transferor to give effect to a remedy under section 11N or 11P above or has claims to rescind under section 11P, but

(b)   the court decides that another remedy under section 11N or 11P is appropriate.

(4)   The court may proceed—

(a)   as if the transferee had required the transferor to give effect to the other remedy, or if the other remedy is rescission under section 11P,

(b)   as if the transferee had claimed to rescind the contract under that section.

(5)   If the transferee has claimed to rescind the contract the court may order that any reimbursement to the transferee is reduced to take account of the use he has had of the goods since they were delivered to him.

(6)   The court may make an order under this section unconditionally or on such terms and conditions as to damages, payment of the price and otherwise as it thinks just.

**11S.   Conformity with the contract**

(1)   Goods do not conform to a contract for the supply or transfer of goods if—

(a)   there is, in relation to the goods, a breach of an express term of the contract or a term implied by section 3, 4 or 5 above or, in Scotland, by section 11C, 11D or 11E above, or

(b)   installation of the goods forms part of the contract for the transfer of goods, and the goods were installed by the transferor, or under his responsibility, in breach of the term implied by section 13 below or (in Scotland) in breach of any term implied by any rule of law as to the manner in which the installation is carried out.'.

**10.  Additional implied terms where goods are hired to consumers—England, Wales and Northern Ireland**

(1)  Section 9 of the Supply of Goods and Services Act 1982 is amended as follows.

(2)  After subsection (2A) insert—

'(2B)  If the bailee deals as consumer, the relevant circumstances mentioned in subsection (2A) above include any public statements on the specific characteristics of the goods made about them by the bailor, the producer or his representative, particularly in advertising or on labelling.

(2C)  A public statement is not by virtue of subsection (2B) above a relevant circumstance for the purposes of subsection (2A) above in the case of a contract for the hire of goods, if the bailor shows that—

(a)  at the time the contract was made, he was not, and could not reasonably have been, aware of the statement,

(b)  before the contract was made, the statement had been withdrawn in public or, to the extent that it contained anything which was incorrect or misleading, it had been corrected in public, or

(c)  the decision to acquire the goods could not have been influenced by the statement.

(2D)  Subsections (2B) and (2C) above do not prevent any public statement from being a relevant circumstance for the purposes of subsection (2A) above (whether or not the bailee deals as consumer) if the statement would have been such a circumstance apart from those subsections.'.

**11.  Additional implied terms where goods are hired to consumers—Scotland**

(1)  Section 11J of the Supply of Goods and Services Act 1982 is amended as follows.

(2)  After subsection (3) insert—

'(3A)  If the contract for the hire of goods is a consumer contract, the relevant circumstances mentioned in subsection (3) above include any public statements on the specific characteristics of the goods made about them by the hirer, the producer or his representative, particularly in advertising or on labelling.

(3B)  A public statement is not by virtue of subsection (3A) above a relevant circumstance for the purposes of subsection (3) above in the case of a contract for the hire of goods, if the hirer shows that—

(a)  at the time the contract was made, he was not, and could not reasonably have been, aware of the statement,

(b)  by the time the contract was made, the statement had been withdrawn in public or, to the extent that it contained anything which was incorrect or misleading, it had been corrected in public, or

(c)  the decision to acquire the goods could not have been influenced by the statement.

(3C)  Subsections (3A) and (3B) above do not prevent any public statement from being a relevant circumstance for the purposes of subsection (3) above (whether or not the contract for the hire of goods is a consumer contract) if the statement would have been such a circumstance apart from those subsections.'.

(3)  At the end of the section add—

'(10)  For the purposes of this section, 'consumer contract' has the same meaning as in section 11F(3) above.'.

**12.  Other amendments to 1982 Act**

(1)  In section 18(1) after the definition of 'hire purchase agreement' there is inserted—

'"producer" means the manufacturer of goods, the importer of goods into the European Economic Area or any person purporting to be a producer by placing his name, trade mark or other distinctive sign on the goods;'.

(2)   In section 18(1) after the definition of 'redemption' there is inserted—

'"repair" means, in cases where there is a lack of conformity in goods for the purposes of this Act, to bring the goods into conformity with the contract.'.

## AMENDMENTS TO THE SUPPLY OF GOODS (IMPLIED TERMS) ACT 1973

**13.   Additional implied terms in consumer cases**
(1)   Section 10 of the Supply of Goods (Implied Terms) Act 1973 is amended as follows.
(2)   After subsection (2C) insert—

'(2D)   If the person to whom the goods are bailed or hired deals as consumer or, in Scotland, if the goods are hired to a person under a consumer contract, the relevant circumstances mentioned in subsection (2A) above include any public statements on the specific characteristics of the goods made about them by the creditor, the producer or his representative, particularly in advertising or on labelling.
(2E)   A public statement is not by virtue of subsection (2D) above relevant circumstance for the purposes of subsection (2A) above in the case of a contract of hire-purchase, if the creditor shows that—
(a)   at the time the contract was made, he was not, and could not reasonably have been, aware of the statement,
(b)   before the contract was made, the statement had been withdrawn in public or, to the extent that it contained anything which was incorrect or misleading, it had been corrected in public, or
(c)   the decision to acquire the goods could not have been influenced by the statement.
(2F)   Subsections (2D) and (2E) above do not prevent any public statement from being a relevant circumstance for the purposes of subsection (2A) above (whether or not the person to whom the goods are bailed or hired deals as consumer or, in Scotland, whether or not the goods are hired to a person under a consumer contract) if the statement would have been such a circumstance apart from those subsections.'.

(3)   At the end of the section add—

'(8)   In Scotland, "consumer contract" in this section has the same meaning as in section 12A(3) below.'.

(4)   In section 15(1) after the definition of 'hire purchase agreement' there is inserted—

'"producer" means the manufacturer of goods, the importer of goods into the European Economic Area or any person purporting to be a producer by placing his name, trade mark or other distinctive sign on the goods;'.

**14.   Amendments to the Unfair Contract Terms Act 1977**
(1)   The Unfair Contract Terms Act 1977 is amended as follows.
(2)   In section 12, after subsection (1) there is inserted the following subsection—

'(1A)   But if the first party mentioned in subsection (1) is an individual paragraph (c) of that subsection must be ignored.'.

(3) For subsection (2) of section 12 there is substituted the following subsection—

'(2) But the buyer is not in any circumstances to be regarded as dealing as consumer—
(a) if he is an individual and the goods are second hand goods sold at public auction at which individuals have the opportunity of attending the sale in person;
(b) if he is not an individual and the goods are sold by auction or by competitive tender.'.

(4) In section 25—
(a) in subsection (1), the definition of 'consumer contract'—
(i) after the word 'means' there is inserted 'subject to subsections (1A) and (1B) below';
(ii) the words '(not being a contract of sale by auction or competitive tender)' are repealed.
(b) after subsection (1) there is inserted—

'(1A) Where the consumer is an individual, paragraph (b) in the definition of "consumer contract" in subsection (1) must be disregarded.
(1B) The expression of 'consumer contract' does not include a contract in which—
(a) the buyer is an individual and the goods are second hand goods sold by public auction at which individuals have the opportunity of attending in person; or
(b) the buyer is not an individual and the goods are sold by auction or competitive tender.'.

## 15. Consumer guarantees

(1) Where goods are sold or otherwise supplied to a consumer which are offered with a consumer guarantee, the consumer guarantee takes effect at the time the goods are delivered as a contractual obligation owed by the guarantor under the conditions set out in the guarantee statement and the associated advertising.

(2) The guarantor shall ensure that the guarantee sets out in plain intelligible language the contents of the guarantee and the essential particulars necessary for making claims under the guarantee, notably the duration and territorial scope of the guarantee as well as the name and address of the guarantor.

(3) On request by the consumer to a person to whom paragraph (4) applies, the guarantee shall within a reasonable time be made available in writing or in another durable medium available and accessible to him.

(4) This paragraph applies to the guarantor and any other person who offers to consumers the goods which are the subject of the guarantee for sale or supply.

(5) Where consumer goods are offered with a consumer guarantee, and where those goods are offered within the territory of the United Kingdom, then the guarantor shall ensure that the consumer guarantee is written in English.

(6) If the guarantor fails to comply with the provisions of paragraphs (2) or (5) above, or a person to whom paragraph (4) applies fails to comply with paragraph (3) then the enforcement authority may apply for an injunction or (in Scotland) an order of specific implement against that person requiring him to comply.

(7) The court on application under this Regulation may grant an injunction or (in Scotland) an order of specific implement on such terms as it thinks fit.

# PART IV
# EC MATERIALS

**COUNCIL DIRECTIVE OF 25 JULY 1985**
**on the approximation of the laws, regulations and administrative provisions**
**of the Member States concerning liability for defective products**
**(85/374/EEC)**

*(amended by Directive 99/34 EC)*

THE COUNCIL OF THE EUROPEAN COMMUNITIES,

Having regard to the Treaty establishing the European Economic Community, and in particular Article 100 thereof,

Having regard to the proposal from the Commission,

Having regard to the opinion of the European Parliament,

Having regard to the opinion of the Economic and Social Committee,

Whereas approximation of the laws of the Member States concerning the liability of the producer for damage caused by the defectiveness of his products is necessary because the existing divergences may distort competition and affect the movement of goods within the common market and entail a differing degree of protection of the consumer against damage caused by a defective product to his health or property;

Whereas liability without fault on the part of the producer is the sole means of adequately solving the problem, peculiar to our age of increasing technicality, of a fair apportionment of the risks inherent in modern technological production;

Whereas liability without fault should apply only to movables which have been industrially produced;

Whereas, as a result, it is appropriate to exclude liability for agricultural products and game, except where they have undergone a processing of an industrial nature which could cause a defect in these products; whereas the liability provided for in this Directive should also apply to movables which are used in the construction of immovables or are installed in immovables;

Whereas protection of the consumer requires that all producers involved in the production process should be made liable, in so far as their finished product, component part or any raw material supplied by them was defective; whereas, for the same reason, liability should extend to importers of products into the Community and to persons who present themselves as producers by affixing their name, trade mark or other distinguishing feature or who supply a product the producer of which cannot be identified;

Whereas, in situations where several persons are liable for the same damage, the protection of the consumer requires that the injured person should be able to claim full compensation for the damage from any one of them;

Whereas, to protect the physical well-being and property of the consumer, the defectiveness of the product should be determined by reference not to its fitness for use but to the lack of the safety which the public at large is entitled to expect; whereas the safety is assessed by excluding any misuse of the product not reasonable under the circumstances;

Whereas a fair apportionment of risk between the injured person and the producer implies that the producer should be able to free himself from liability if he furnishes proof as to the existence of certain exonerating circumstances;

Whereas the protection of the consumer requires that the liability of the producer remains unaffected by acts or omissions of other persons having contributed to cause the damage; whereas, however, the contributory negligence of the injured person may be taken into account to reduce or disallow such liability;

Whereas the protection of the consumer requires compensation for death and personal injury as well as compensation for damage to property; whereas the latter should nevertheless be limited to goods for private use or consumption and be subject to a deduction of a lower threshold of a fixed amount in order to avoid litigation in an excessive number of cases; whereas this Directive should not prejudice compensation for pain and suffering and other non-material damages payable, where appropriate, under the law applicable to the case;

Whereas a uniform period of limitation for the bringing of action for compensation is in the interests both of the injured person and of the producer;

Whereas products age in the course of time, higher safety standards are developed and the state of science and technology progresses; whereas, therefore, it would not be reasonable to make the producer liable for an unlimited period for the defectiveness of his product; whereas, therefore, liability should expire after a reasonable length of time, without prejudice to claims pending at law;

Whereas, to achieve effective protection of consumers, no contractual derogation should be permitted as regards the liability of the producer in relation to the injured person;

Whereas under the legal systems of the Member States an injured party may have a claim for damages based on grounds of contractual liability or on grounds of non-contractual liability other than that provided for in this Directive; in so far as these provisions also serve to attain the objective of effective protection of consumers, they should remain unaffected by this Directive; whereas, in so far as effective protection of consumers in the sector of pharmaceutical products is already also attained in a Member State under a special liability system, claims based on this system should similarly remain possible;

Whereas, to the extent that liability for nuclear injury or damage is already covered in all Member States by adequate special rules, it has been possible to exclude damage of this type from the scope of this Directive;

Whereas, since the exclusion of primary agricultural products and game from the scope of this Directive may be felt, in certain Member States, in view of what is expected for the protection of consumers, to restrict unduly such protection, it should be possible for a Member State to extend liability to such products;

Whereas, for similar reasons, the possibility offered to a producer to free himself from liability if he proves that the state of scientific and technical knowledge at the time when he put the product into circulation was not such as to enable the existence of a defect to be discovered may be felt in certain Member States to restrict unduly the protection of the consumer; whereas it should therefore be possible for a Member State to maintain in its legislation or to provide by new legislation that this exonerating circumstance is not admitted; whereas, in the case of new legislation, making use of this derogation should, however, be subject to a Community stand-still procedure, in order to raise, if possible, the level of protection in a uniform manner throughout the Community;

Whereas, taking into account the legal traditions in most of the Member States, it is inappropriate to set any financial ceiling on the producer's liability without fault; whereas, in so far as there are, however, differing traditions, it seems possible to admit that a Member State may derogate from the principle of unlimited liability by providing a limit for the total liability of the producer for damage resulting from a death or personal injury and caused by identical items with the same defect, provided that this limit is established at a level sufficiently high to guarantee adequate protection of the consumer and the correct functioning of the common market;

Whereas the harmonization resulting from this cannot be total at the present stage, but opens the way towards greater harmonization; whereas it is therefore necessary that the Council receive at regular intervals, reports from the Commission on the application of this Directive, accompanied, as the case may be, by appropriate proposals;

Whereas it is particularly important in this respect that a re-examination be carried out of those parts of the Directive relating to the derogations open to the Member States, at the expiry of a period of sufficient length to gather practical experience on the effects of these derogations on the protection of consumers and on the functioning of the common market,

HAS ADOPTED THIS DIRECTIVE:

### Article 1
The producer shall be liable for damage caused by a defect in his product.

### [Article 2
For the purpose of this Directive 'product' means all movables even if incorporated into another movable or into an immovable. 'Product' includes electricity.]

### Article 3
1. 'Producer' means the manufacturer of a finished product, the producer of any raw material or the manufacturer of a component part and any person who, by putting his name, trade mark or other distinguishing feature on the product presents himself as its producer.

2. Without prejudice to the liability of the producer, any person who imports into the Community a product for sale, hire, leasing or any form of distribution in the course of his business shall be deemed to be a producer within the meaning of this Directive and shall be responsible as a producer.

3. Where the producer of the product cannot be identified, each supplier of the product shall be treated as its producer unless he informs the injured person, within a reasonable time, of the identity of the producer or of the person who supplied him with the product. The same shall apply, in the case of an imported product, if this product does not indicate the identity of the importer referred to in paragraph 2, even if the name of the producer is indicated.

### Article 4
The injured person shall be required to prove the damage, the defect and the causal relationship between defect and damage.

### Article 5
Where, as a result of the provisions of this Directive, two or more persons are liable for the same damage, they shall be liable jointly and severally, without prejudice to the provisions of national law concerning the rights of contribution or recourse.

### Article 6
1. A product is defective when it does not provide the safety which a person is entitled to expect, taking all circumstances into account, including:
    (a)   the presentation of the product;

(b) the use to which it could reasonably be expected that the product would be put;

(c) the time when the product was put into circulation.

2. A product shall not be considered defective for the sole reason that a better product is subsequently put into circulation.

## Article 7

The producer shall not be liable as a result of this Directive if he proves:

(a) that he did not put the product into circulation; or

(b) that, having regard to the circumstances, it is probable that the defect which caused the damage did not exist at the time when the product was put into circulation by him or that this defect came into being afterwards; or

(c) that the product was neither manufactured by him for sale or any form of distribution for economic purpose nor manufactured or distributed by him in the course of his business; or

(d) that the defect is due to compliance of the product with mandatory regulations issued by the public authorities; or

(e) that the state of scientific and technical knowledge at the time when he put the product into circulation was not such as to enable the existence of the defect to be discovered; or

(f) in the case of a manufacturer of a component, that the defect is attributable to the design of the product in which the component has been fitted or to the instructions given by the manufacturer of the product.

## Article 8

1. Without prejudice to the provisions of national law concerning the right of contribution or recourse, the liability of the producer shall not be reduced when the damage is caused both by a defect in product and by the act or omission of a third party.

2. The liability of the producer may be reduced or disallowed when, having regard to all the circumstances, the damage is caused both by a defect in the product and by the fault of the injured person or any person for whom the injured person is responsible.

## Article 9

For the purpose of Article 1, 'damage' means:

(a) damage caused by death or by personal injuries;

(b) damage to, or destruction of, any item of property other than the defective product itself, with a lower threshold of 500 ECU, provided that the item of property:

(i) is of a type ordinarily intended for private use or consumption, and

(ii) was used by the injured person mainly for his own private use or consumption.

This Article shall be without prejudice to national provisions relating to non-material damage.

## Article 10

1. Member States shall provide in their legislation that a limitation period of three years shall apply to proceedings for the recovery of damages as provided for in this Directive. The limitation period shall begin to run from the day on which the plaintiff became aware, or should reasonably have become aware, of the damage, the defect and the identity of the producer.

2. The laws of Member States regulating suspension or interruption of the limitation period shall not be affected by this Directive.

## Article 11

Member States shall provide in their legislation that the rights conferred upon the injured person pursuant to this Directive shall be extinguished upon the expiry of a period of 10 years from the date on which the producer put into circulation the actual product which caused the damage, unless the injured person has in the meantime instituted proceedings against the producer.

### Article 12
The liability of the producer arising from this Directive may not, in relation to the injured person, be limited or excluded by a provision limiting his liability or exempting him from liability.

### Article 13
This Directive shall not affect any rights which an injured person may have according to the rules of the law of contractual or non-contractual liability or a special liability system existing at the moment when this Directive is notified.

### Article 14
This Directive shall not apply to injury or damage arising from nuclear accidents and covered by international conventions ratified by the Member States.

### Article 15
1.  Each Member State may:
    (a)  [*repealed*]
    (b)  by way of derogation from Article 7(e), maintain or, subject to the procedure set out in paragraph 2 of this Article, provide in this legislation that the producer shall be liable even if he proves that the state of scientific and technical knowledge at the time when he put the product into circulation was not such as to enable the existence of a defect to be discovered.
2.  A Member State wishing to introduce the measure specified in paragraph 1(b) shall communicate the text of the proposed measure to the Commission. The Commission shall inform the other Member States thereof.

The Member State concerned shall hold the proposed measure in abeyance for nine months after the Commission is informed and provided that in the meantime the Commission has not submitted to the Council a proposal amending this Directive on the relevant matter. However, if within three months of receiving the said information, the Commission does not advise the Member State concerned that it intends submitting such a proposal to the Council, the Member State may take the proposed measure immediately.

If the Commission does submit to the Council such a proposal amending this Directive within the aforementioned nine months, the Member State concerned shall hold the proposed measure in abeyance for a further period of 18 months from the date on which the proposal is submitted.
3.  Ten years after the date of notification of this Directive, the Commission shall submit to the Council a report on the effect that rulings by the courts as to the application of Article 7(e) and of paragraph 1(b) of this Article have on consumer protection and the functioning of the common market. In the light of this report the Council, acting on a proposal from the Commission and pursuant to the terms of Article 100 of the Treaty, shall decide whether to repeal Article 7(e).

### Article 16
1.  Any Member State may provide that a producer's total liability for damage resulting from a death or personal injury and caused by identical items with the same defect shall be limited to an amount which may not be less than 70 million ECU.
2.  Ten years after the date of notification of this Directive, the Commission shall submit to the Council a report on the effect on consumer protection and the functioning of the common market of the implementation of the financial limit on liability by those Member States which have used the option provided for in paragraph 1. In the light of this report the Council, acting on a proposal

from the Commission and pursuant to the terms of Article 100 of the Treaty, shall decide whether to repeal paragraph 1.

**Article 17**
This Directive shall not apply to products put into circulation before the date on which the provisions referred to in Article 19 enter into force.

**Article 18**
1. For the purposes of this Directive, the ECU shall be that defined by Regulation (EEC) No 3180/78, as amended by Regulation (EEC) No 2626/84. The equivalent in national currency shall initially be calculated at the rate obtaining on the date of adoption of this Directive.
2. Every five years the Council, acting on a proposal from the Commission, shall examine and, if need be, revise the amounts in this Directive, in the light of economic and monetary trends in the Community.

**Article 19**
1. Member States shall bring into force, not later than three years from the date of notification of this Directive, the laws, regulations and administrative provisions necessary to comply with this Directive. They shall forthwith inform the Commission thereof.
2. The procedure set out in Article 15(2) shall apply from the date of notification of this Directive.

**Article 20**
Member States shall communicate to the Commission the texts of the main provisions of national law which they subsequently adopt in the field governed by this Directive.

**Article 21**
Every five years the Commission shall present a report to the Council on the application of this Directive and, if necessary, shall submit appropriate proposals to it.

**Article 22**
This Directive is addressed to the Member States.

Done at Brussels, 25 July 1985.


### COUNCIL DIRECTIVE OF 5 APRIL 1993
### on unfair terms in consumer contracts
### (93/13 EEC)

THE COUNCIL OF THE EUROPEAN COMMUNITIES,

Having regard to the Treaty establishing the European Economic Community, and in particular Article 100A thereof,
   Having regard to the proposal from the Commission,
   In cooperation with the European Parliament,
   Having regard to the opinion of the Economic and Social Committee,
   Whereas it is necessary to adopt measures with the aim of progressively establishing the internal market before 31 December 1992; whereas the internal market comprises an area without internal frontiers in which goods, persons, services and capital move freely;
   Whereas the laws of Member States relating to the terms of contract between the seller of goods or supplier of services, on the one hand, and the consumer of them, on the other hand, show many disparities, with the result that the national markets for the sale of goods and services to consumers differ from

each other and that distortions of competition may arise amongst the sellers and suppliers, notably when they sell and supply in other Member States;

Whereas, in particular, the laws of Member States relating to unfair terms in consumer contracts show marked divergences;

Whereas it is the responsibility of the Member States to ensure that contracts concluded with consumers do not contain unfair terms;

Whereas, generally speaking, consumers do not know the rules of law which, in Member States other than their own, govern contracts for the sale of goods or services; whereas this lack of awareness may deter them from direct transactions for the purchase of goods or services in another Member State;

Whereas, in order to facilitate the establishment of the internal market and to safeguard the citizen in his role as consumer when acquiring goods and services under contracts which are governed by the laws of Member States other than his own, it is essential to remove unfair terms from those contracts;

Whereas sellers of goods and suppliers of services will thereby be helped in their task of selling goods and supplying services, both at home and throughout the internal market; whereas competition will thus be stimulated, so contributing to increased choice for Community citizens as consumers;

Whereas the two Community programmes for a consumer protection and information policy underlined the importance of safeguarding consumers in the matter of unfair terms of contract; whereas this protection ought to be provided by laws and regulations which are either harmonized at Community level or adopted directly at that level;

Whereas in accordance with the principle laid down under the heading 'Protection of the economic interests of the consumers', as stated in those programmes: 'acquirers of goods and services should be protected against the abuse of power by the seller or supplier, in particular against one-sided standard contracts and the unfair exclusion of essential rights in contracts';

Whereas more effective protection of the consumer can be achieved by adopting uniform rules of law in the matter of unfair terms;

Whereas those rules should apply to all contracts concluded between sellers or suppliers and consumers; whereas as a result inter alia contracts relating to employment, contracts relating to succession rights, contracts relating to rights under family law and contracts relating to the incorporation and organization of companies or partnership agreements must be excluded from this Directive;

Whereas the consumer must receive equal protection under contracts concluded by word of mouth and written contracts regardless, in the latter case, of whether the terms of the contract are contained in one or more documents;

Whereas, however, as they now stand, national laws allow only partial harmonization to be envisaged;

Whereas, in particular, only contractual terms which have not been individually negotiated are covered by this Directive;

Whereas Member States should have the option, with due regard for the Treaty, to afford consumers a higher level of protection through national provisions that are more stringent than those of this Directive;

Whereas the statutory or regulatory provisions of the Member States which directly or indirectly determine the terms of consumer contracts are presumed not to contain unfair terms; whereas, therefore, it does not appear to be necessary to subject the terms which reflect mandatory statutory or regulatory provisions and the principles or provisions of international conventions to which the Member States or the Community are party; whereas in that respect the wording 'mandatory statutory or regulatory provisions' in Article 1(2) also covers rules which, according to the law, shall apply between the contracting parties provided that no other arrangements have been established;

Whereas Member States must however ensure that unfair terms are not included, particularly because this Directive also applies to trades, business or professions of a public nature;

Whereas it is necessary to fix in a general way the criteria for assessing the unfair character of contract terms;

Whereas the assessment, according to the general criteria chosen, of the unfair character of terms, in particular in sale or supply activities of a public nature providing collective services which take account of solidarity among users, must be supplemented by a means of making an overall evaluation of the different interests involved; whereas this constitutes the requirement of good faith; whereas, in making an assessment of good faith, particular regard shall be had to the strength of the bargaining positions of the parties, whether the consumer had an inducement to agree to the term and whether the goods or services were sold or supplied to the special order of the consumer; whereas the requirement of good faith may be satisfied by the seller or supplier where he deals fairly and equitably with the other party whose legitimate interests he has to take into account;

Whereas, for the purposes of this Directive, the annexed list of terms can be of indicative value only and, because of the cause of the minimal character of the Directive, the scope of these terms may be the subject of amplification or more restrictive editing by the Member States in their national laws;

Whereas the nature of goods or services should have an influence on assessing the unfairness of contractual terms;

Whereas, for the purposes of this Directive, assessment of unfair character shall not be made of terms which describe the main subject matter of the contract nor the quality/price ratio of the goods or services supplied; whereas the main subject matter of the contract and the price/quality ratio may nevertheless be taken into account in assessing the fairness of other terms; whereas it follows, inter alia, that in insurance contracts, the terms which clearly define or circumscribe the insured risk and the insurer's liability shall not be subject to such assessment since these restrictions are taken into account in calculating the premium paid by the consumer;

Whereas contracts should be drafted in plain, intelligible language, the consumer should actually be given an opportunity to examine all the terms and, if in doubt, the interpretation most favourable to the consumer should prevail;

Whereas Member States should ensure that unfair terms are not used in contracts concluded with consumers by a seller or supplier and that if, nevertheless, such terms are so used, they will not bind the consumer, and the contract will continue to bind the parties upon those terms if it is capable of continuing in existence without the unfair provisions;

Whereas there is a risk that, in certain cases, the consumer may be deprived of protection under this Directive by designating the law of a non-Member country as the law applicable to the contract; whereas provisions should therefore be included in this Directive designed to avert this risk;

Whereas persons or organizations, if regarded under the law of a Member State as having a legitimate interest in the matter, must have facilities for initiating proceedings concerning terms of contract drawn up for general use in contracts concluded with consumers, and in particular unfair terms, either before a court or before an administrative authority competent to decide upon complaints or to initiate appropriate legal proceedings; whereas this possibility does not, however, entail prior verification of the general conditions obtaining in individual economic sectors;

Whereas the courts or administrative authorities of the Member States must have at their disposal adequate and effective means of preventing the continued application of unfair terms in consumer contracts,

HAS ADOPTED THIS DIRECTIVE:

### Article 1

1.  The purpose of this Directive is to approximate the laws, regulations and administrative provisions of the Member States relating to unfair terms in contracts concluded between a seller or supplier and a consumer.

2.  The contractual terms which reflect mandatory statutory or regulatory provisions and the provisions or principles of international conventions to which the Member States or the Community are party, particularly in the transport area, shall not be subject to the provisions of this Directive.

### Article 2

For the purposes of this Directive:

(a)  'unfair terms' means the contractual terms defined in Article 3;

(b)  'consumer' means any natural person who, in contracts covered by this Directive, is acting for purposes which are outside his trade, business or profession;

(c)  'seller or supplier' means any natural or legal person who, in contracts covered by this Directive, is acting for purposes relating to his trade, business or profession, whether publicly owned or privately owned.

### Article 3

1.  A contractual term which has not been individually negotiated shall be regarded as unfair if, contrary to the requirement of good faith, it causes a significant imbalance in the parties' rights and obligations arising under the contract, to the detriment of the consumer.

2.  A term shall always be regarded as not individually negotiated where it has been drafted in advance and the consumer has therefore not been able to influence the substance of the term, particularly in the context of a pre-formulated standard contract.

The fact that certain aspects of a term or one specific term have been individually negotiated shall not exclude the application of this Article to the rest of a contract if an overall assessment of the contract indicates that it is nevertheless a pre-formulated standard contract.

Where any seller or supplier claims that a standard term has been individually negotiated, the burden of proof in this respect shall be incumbent on him.

3.  The Annex shall contain an indicative and non-exhaustive list of the terms which may be regarded as unfair.

### Article 4

1.  Without prejudice to Article 7, the unfairness of a contractual term shall be assessed, taking into account the nature of the goods or services for which the contract was concluded and by referring, at the time of conclusion of the contract, to all the circumstances attending the conclusion of the contract and to all the other terms of the contract or of another contract on which it is dependent.

2.  Assessment of the unfair nature of the terms shall relate neither to the definition of the main subject matter of the contract nor to the adequacy of the price and remuneration, on the one hand, as against the services or goods supplied in exchange, on the other, in so far as these terms are in plain intelligible language.

### Article 5

In the case of contracts where all or certain terms offered to the consumer are in writing, these terms must always be drafted in plain, intelligible language. Where there is doubt about the meaning of a term, the interpretation most favourable to the consumer shall prevail. This rule on interpretation shall not apply in the context of the procedures laid down in Article 7(2).

## Article 6

1. Member States shall lay down that unfair terms used in a contract concluded with a consumer by a seller or supplier shall, as provided for under their national law, not be binding on the consumer and that the contract shall continue to bind the parties upon those terms if it is capable of continuing in existence without the unfair terms.

2. Member States shall take the necessary measures to ensure that the consumer does not lose the protection granted by this Directive by virtue of the choice of the law of a non-Member country as the law applicable to the contract if the latter has a close connection with the territory of the Member States.

## Article 7

1. Member States shall ensure that, in the interests of consumers and of competitors, adequate and effective means exist to prevent the continued use of unfair terms in contracts concluded with consumers by sellers or suppliers.

2. The means referred to in paragraph 1 shall include provisions whereby persons or organizations, having a legitimate interest under national law in protecting consumers, may take action according to the national law concerned before the courts or before competent administrative bodies for a decision as to whether contractual terms drawn up for general use are unfair, so that they can apply appropriate and effective means to prevent the continued use of such terms.

3. With due regard for national laws, the legal remedies referred to in paragraph 2 may be directed separately or jointly against a number of sellers or suppliers from the same economic sector or their associations which use or recommend the use of the same general contractual terms or similar terms.

## Article 8

Member States may adopt or retain the most stringent provisions compatible with the Treaty in the area covered by this Directive, to ensure a maximum degree of protection for the consumer.

## Article 9

The Commission shall present a report to the European Parliament and to the Council concerning the application of this Directive five years at the latest after the date in Article 10(1).

## Article 10

1. Member States shall bring into force the laws, regulations and administrative provisions necessary to comply with this Directive no later than 31 December 1994. They shall forthwith inform the Commission thereof.

These provisions shall be applicable to all contracts concluded after 31 December 1994.

2. When Member States adopt these measures, they shall contain a reference to this Directive or shall be accompanied by such reference on the occasion of their official publication. The methods of making such a reference shall be laid down by the Member States.

3. Member States shall communicate the main provisions of national law which they adopt in the field covered by this Directive to the Commission.

## Article 11

This Directive is addressed to the Member States.

Done at Luxembourg, 5 April 1993.

ANNEX. TERMS REFERRED TO IN ARTICLE 3(3)

1. Terms which have the object or effect of:

(a) excluding or limiting the legal liability of a seller or supplier in the event of the death of a consumer or personal injury to the latter resulting from an act or omission of that seller or supplier;

(b) inappropriately excluding or limiting the legal rights of the consumer vis-à-vis the seller or supplier or another party in the event of total or partial non-performance or inadequate performance by the seller or supplier of any of the contractual obligations, including the option of offsetting a debt owed to the seller or supplier against any claim which the consumer may have against him;

(c) making an agreement binding on the consumer whereas provision of services by the seller or supplier is subject to a condition whose realization depends on his own will alone;

(d) permitting the seller or supplier to retain sums paid by the consumer where the latter decides not to conclude or perform the contract, without providing for the consumer to receive compensation of an equivalent amount from the seller or supplier where the latter is the party cancelling the contract;

(e) requiring any consumer who fails to fulfil his obligation to pay a disproportionately high sum in compensation;

(f) authorizing the seller or supplier to dissolve the contract on a discretionary basis where the same facility is not granted to the consumer, or permitting the seller or supplier to retain the sums paid for services not yet supplied by him where it is the seller or supplier himself who dissolves the contract;

(g) enabling the seller or supplier to terminate a contract of indeterminate duration without reasonable notice except where there are serious grounds for doing so;

(h) automatically extending a contract of fixed duration where the consumer does not indicate otherwise, when the deadline fixed for the consumer to express this desire not to extend the contract is unreasonably early;

(i) irrevocably binding the consumer to terms with which he had no real opportunity of becoming acquainted before the conclusion of the contract;

(j) enabling the seller or supplier to alter the terms of the contract unilaterally without a valid reason which is specified in the contract;

(k) enabling the seller or supplier to alter unilaterally without a valid reason any characteristics of the product or service to be provided;

(l) providing for the price of goods to be determined at the time of delivery or allowing a seller of goods or supplier of services to increase their price without in both cases giving the consumer the corresponding right to cancel the contract if the final price is too high in relation to the price agreed when the contract was concluded;

(m) giving the seller or supplier the right to determine whether the goods or services supplied are in conformity with the contract, or giving him the exclusive right to interpret any term of the contract;

(n) limiting the seller's or supplier's obligation to respect commitments undertaken by his agents or making his commitments subject to compliance with a particular formality;

(o) obliging the consumer to fulfil all his obligations where the seller or supplier does not perform his;

(p) giving the seller or supplier the possibility of transferring his rights and obligations under the contract, where this may serve to reduce the guarantees for the consumer, without the latter's agreement;

(q) excluding or hindering the consumer's right to take legal action or exercise any other legal remedy, particularly by requiring the consumer to take disputes exclusively to arbitration not covered by legal provisions, unduly restricting the evidence available to him or imposing on him a burden of proof which, according to the applicable law, should lie with another party to the contract.

2. Scope of subparagraphs (g), (j) and (l)

(a) Subparagraph (g) is without hindrance to terms by which a supplier of financial services reserves the right to terminate unilaterally a contract of indeterminate duration without notice where there is a valid reason, provided that the supplier is required to inform the other contracting party or parties thereof immediately.

(b) Subparagraph (j) is without hindrance to terms under which a supplier of financial services reserves the right to alter the rate of interest payable by the consumer or due to the latter, or the amount of other charges for financial services without notice where there is a valid reason, provided that the supplier is required to inform the other contracting party or parties thereof at the earliest opportunity and that the latter are free to dissolve the contract immediately.

Subparagraph (j) is also without hindrance to terms under which a seller or supplier reserves the right to alter unilaterally the conditions of a contract of indeterminate duration, provided that he is required to inform the consumer with reasonable notice and that the consumer is free to dissolve the contract.

(c) Subparagraphs (g), (j) and (l) do not apply to:
– transactions in transferable securities, financial instruments and other products or services where the price is linked to fluctuations in a stock exchange quotation or index or a financial market rate that the seller or supplier does not control;
– contracts for the purchase or sale of foreign currency, traveller's cheques or international money orders denominated in foreign currency;

(d) Subparagraph (l) is without hindrance to price-indexation clauses, where lawful, provided that the method by which prices vary is explicitly described.

## DIRECTIVE OF THE EUROPEAN PARLIAMENT AND OF THE COUNCIL
### OF 25 MAY 1999
### on certain aspects of the sale of consumer goods and associated guarantees (1999/44/EC)

THE EUROPEAN PARLIAMENT AND THE COUNCIL OF THE EUROPEAN UNION,

Having regard to the Treaty establishing the European Community, and in particular Article 95 thereof,

Having regard to the proposal from the Commission,

Having regard to the opinion of the Economic and Social Committee,

Acting in accordance with the procedure laid down in Article 251 of the Treaty in the light of the joint text approved by the Conciliation Committee on 18 May 1999,

(1) Whereas Article 153(1) and (3) of the Treaty provides that the Community should contribute to the achievement of a high level of consumer protection by the measures it adopts pursuant to Article 95 thereof;

(2) Whereas the internal market comprises an area without internal frontiers in which the free movement of goods, persons, services and capital is guaranteed; whereas free movement of goods concerns not only transactions by persons acting in the course of a business but also transactions by private

individuals; whereas it implies that consumers resident in one Member State should be free to purchase goods in the territory of another Member State on the basis of a uniform minimum set of fair rules governing the sale of consumer goods;

(3)   Whereas the laws of the Member States concerning the sale of consumer goods are somewhat disparate, with the result that national consumer goods markets differ from one another and that competition between sellers may be distorted;

(4)   Whereas consumers who are keen to benefit from the large market by purchasing goods in Member States other than their State of residence play a fundamental role in the completion of the internal market; whereas the artificial reconstruction of frontiers and the compartmentalisation of markets should be prevented; whereas the opportunities available to consumers have been greatly broadened by new communication technologies which allow ready access to distribution systems in other Member States or in third countries; whereas, in the absence of minimum harmonisation of the rules governing the sale of consumer goods, the development of the sale of goods through the medium of new distance communication technologies risks being impeded;

(5)   Whereas the creation of a common set of minimum rules of consumer law, valid no matter where goods are purchased within the Community, will strengthen consumer confidence and enable consumers to make the most of the internal market;

(6)   Whereas the main difficulties encountered by consumers and the main source of disputes with sellers concern the non-conformity of goods with the contract; whereas it is therefore appropriate to approximate national legislation governing the sale of consumer goods in this respect, without however impinging on provisions and principles of national law relating to contractual and non-contractual liability;

(7)   Whereas the goods must, above all, conform with the contractual specifications; whereas the principle of conformity with the contract may be considered as common to the different national legal traditions; whereas in certain national legal traditions it may not be possible to rely solely on this principle to ensure a minimum level of protection for the consumer; whereas under such legal traditions, in particular, additional national provisions may be useful to ensure that the consumer is protected in cases where the parties have agreed no specific contractual terms or where the parties have concluded contractual terms or agreements which directly or indirectly waive or restrict the rights of the consumer and which, to the extent that these rights result from this Directive, are not binding on the consumer;

(8)   Whereas, in order to facilitate the application of the principle of conformity with the contract, it is useful to introduce a rebuttable presumption of conformity with the contract covering the most common situations; whereas that presumption does not restrict the principle of freedom of contract; whereas, furthermore, in the absence of specific contractual terms, as well as where the minimum protection clause is applied, the elements mentioned in this presumption may be used to determine the lack of conformity of the goods with the contract; whereas the quality and performance which consumers can reasonably expect will depend inter alia on whether the goods are new or second-hand; whereas the elements mentioned in the presumption are cumulative; whereas, if the circumstances of the case render any particular element manifestly inappropriate, the remaining elements of the presumption nevertheless still apply;

(9)   Whereas the seller should be directly liable to the consumer for the conformity of the goods with the contract; whereas this is the traditional solution enshrined in the legal orders of the Member States; whereas nevertheless the seller should be free, as provided for by national law, to pursue

remedies against the producer, a previous seller in the same chain of contracts or any other intermediary, unless he has renounced that entitlement; whereas this Directive does not affect the principle of freedom of contract between the seller, the producer, a previous seller or any other intermediary; whereas the rules governing against whom and how the seller may pursue such remedies are to be determined by national law;

(10)   Whereas, in the case of non-conformity of the goods with the contract, consumers should be entitled to have the goods restored to conformity with the contract free of charge, choosing either repair or replacement, or, failing this, to have the price reduced or the contract rescinded;

(11)   Whereas the consumer in the first place may require the seller to repair the goods or to replace them unless those remedies are impossible or disproportionate; whereas whether a remedy is disproportionate should be determined objectively; whereas a remedy would be disproportionate if it imposed, in comparison with the other remedy, unreasonable costs; whereas, in order to determine whether the costs are unreasonable, the costs of one remedy should be significantly higher than the costs of the other remedy;

(12)   Whereas in cases of a lack of conformity, the seller may always offer the consumer, by way of settlement, any available remedy; whereas it is for the consumer to decide whether to accept or reject this proposal;

(13)   Whereas, in order to enable consumers to take advantage of the internal market and to buy consumer goods in another Member State, it should be recommended that, in the interests of consumers, the producers of consumer goods that are marketed in several Member States attach to the product a list with at least one contact address in every Member State where the product is marketed;

(14)   Whereas the references to the time of delivery do not imply that Member States have to change their rules on the passing of the risk;

(15)   Whereas Member States may provide that any reimbursement to the consumer may be reduced to take account of the use the consumer has had of the goods since they were delivered to him; whereas the detailed arrangements whereby rescission of the contract is effected may be laid down in national law;

(16)   Whereas the specific nature of second-hand goods makes it generally impossible to replace them; whereas therefore the consumer's right of replacement is generally not available for these goods; whereas for such goods, Member States may enable the parties to agree a shortened period of liability;

(17)   Whereas it is appropriate to limit in time the period during which the seller is liable for any lack of conformity which exists at the time of delivery of the goods; whereas Member States may also provide for a limitation on the period during which consumers can exercise their rights, provided such a period does not expire within two years from the time of delivery; whereas where, under national legislation, the time when a limitation period starts is not the time of delivery of the goods, the total duration of the limitation period provided for by national law may not be shorter than two years from the time of delivery;

(18)   Whereas Member States may provide for suspension or interruption of the period during which any lack of conformity must become apparent and of the limitation period, where applicable and in accordance with their national law, in the event of repair, replacement or negotiations between seller and consumer with a view to an amicable settlement;

(19)   Whereas Member States should be allowed to set a period within which the consumer must inform the seller of any lack of conformity; whereas Member States may ensure a higher level of protection for the consumer by not introducing such an obligation; whereas in any case consumers throughout the Community should have at least two months in which to inform the seller that a lack of conformity exists;

(20)   Whereas Member States should guard against such a period placing at a disadvantage consumers shopping across borders; whereas all Member States should inform the Commission of their use of this provision; whereas the Commission should monitor the effect of the varied application of this provision on consumers and on the internal market; whereas information on the use made of this provision by a Member State should be available to the other Member States and to consumers and consumer organisations throughout the Community; whereas a summary of the situation in all Member States should therefore be published in the Official Journal of the European Communities;

(21)   Whereas, for certain categories of goods, it is current practice for sellers and producers to offer guarantees on goods against any defect which becomes apparent within a certain period; whereas this practice can stimulate competition; whereas, while such guarantees are legitimate marketing tools, they should not mislead the consumer; whereas, to ensure that consumers are not misled, guarantees should contain certain information, including a statement that the guarantee does not affect the consumer's legal rights;

(22)   Whereas the parties may not, by common consent, restrict or waive the rights granted to consumers, since otherwise the legal protection afforded would be thwarted; whereas this principle should apply also to clauses which imply that the consumer was aware of any lack of conformity of the consumer goods existing at the time the contract was concluded; whereas the protection granted to consumers under this Directive should not be reduced on the grounds that the law of a non-member State has been chosen as being applicable to the contract;

(23)   Whereas legislation and case-law in this area in the various Member States show that there is growing concern to ensure a high level of consumer protection; whereas, in the light of this trend and the experience acquired in implementing this Directive, it may be necessary to envisage more far-reaching harmonisation, notably by providing for the producer's direct liability for defects for which he is responsible;

(24)   Whereas Member States should be allowed to adopt or maintain in force more stringent provisions in the field covered by this Directive to ensure an even higher level of consumer protection;

(25)   Whereas, according to the Commission recommendation of 30 March 1998 on the principles applicable to the bodies responsible for out-of-court settlement of consumer disputes, Member States can create bodies that ensure impartial and efficient handling of complaints in a national and cross-border context and which consumers can use as mediators;

(26)   Whereas it is appropriate, in order to protect the collective interests of consumers, to add this Directive to the list of Directives contained in the Annex to Directive 98/27/EC of the European Parliament and of the Council of 19 May 1998 on injunctions for the protection of consumers' interests,

HAVE ADOPTED THIS DIRECTIVE:

### Article 1. Scope and definitions

1.   The purpose of this Directive is the approximation of the laws, regulations and administrative provisions of the Member States on certain aspects of the sale of consumer goods and associated guarantees in order to ensure a uniform minimum level of consumer protection in the context of the internal market.

2.   For the purposes of this Directive:

(a)   consumer: shall mean any natural person who, in the contracts covered by this Directive, is acting for purposes which are not related to his trade, business or profession;

(b)   consumer goods: shall mean any tangible movable item, with the exception of:

– goods sold by way of execution or otherwise by authority of law,

– water and gas where they are not put up for sale in a limited volume or set quantity,

– electricity;

(c)    seller: shall mean any natural or legal person who, under a contract, sells consumer goods in the course of his trade, business or profession;

(d)    producer: shall mean the manufacturer of consumer goods, the importer of consumer goods into the territory of the Community or any person purporting to be a producer by placing his name, trade mark or other distinctive sign on the consumer goods;

(e)    guarantee: shall mean any undertaking by a seller or producer to the consumer, given without extra charge, to reimburse the price paid or to replace, repair or handle consumer goods in any way if they do not meet the specifications set out in the guarantee statement or in the relevant advertising;

(f)    repair: shall mean, in the event of lack of conformity, bringing consumer goods into conformity with the contract of sale.

3.    Member States may provide that the expression 'consumer goods' does not cover second-hand goods sold at public auction where consumers have the opportunity of attending the sale in person.

4.    Contracts for the supply of consumer goods to be manufactured or produced shall also be deemed contracts of sale for the purpose of this Directive.

### Article 2. Conformity with the contract

1.    The seller must deliver goods to the consumer which are in conformity with the contract of sale.

2.    Consumer goods are presumed to be in conformity with the contract if they:

(a)    comply with the description given by the seller and possess the qualities of the goods which the seller has held out to the consumer as a sample or model;

(b)    are fit for any particular purpose for which the consumer requires them and which he made known to the seller at the time of conclusion of the contract and which the seller has accepted;

(c)    are fit for the purposes for which goods of the same type are normally used;

(d)    show the quality and performance which are normal in goods of the same type and which the consumer can reasonably expect, given the nature of the goods and taking into account any public statements on the specific characteristics of the goods made about them by the seller, the producer or his representative, particularly in advertising or on labelling.

3.    There shall be deemed not to be a lack of conformity for the purposes of this Article if, at the time the contract was concluded, the consumer was aware, or could not reasonably be unaware of, the lack of conformity, or if the lack of conformity has its origin in materials supplied by the consumer.

4.    The seller shall not be bound by public statements, as referred to in paragraph 2(d) if he:

– shows that he was not, and could not reasonably have been, aware of the statement in question,

– shows that by the time of conclusion of the contract the statement had been corrected, or

– shows that the decision to buy the consumer goods could not have been influenced by the statement.

5.    Any lack of conformity resulting from incorrect installation of the consumer goods shall be deemed to be equivalent to lack of conformity of the goods if installation forms part of the contract of sale of the goods and the goods were installed by the seller or under his responsibility. This shall apply

equally if the product, intended to be installed by the consumer, is installed by the consumer and the incorrect installation is due to a shortcoming in the installation instructions.

### Article 3. Rights of the consumer

1. The seller shall be liable to the consumer for any lack of conformity which exists at the time the goods were delivered.

2. In the case of a lack of conformity, the consumer shall be entitled to have the goods brought into conformity free of charge by repair or replacement, in accordance with paragraph 3, or to have an appropriate reduction made in the price or the contract rescinded with regard to those goods, in accordance with paragraphs 5 and 6.

3. In the first place, the consumer may require the seller to repair the goods or he may require the seller to replace them, in either case free of charge, unless this is impossible or disproportionate.

A remedy shall be deemed to be disproportionate if it imposes costs on the seller which, in comparison with the alternative remedy, are unreasonable, taking into account:

    – the value the goods would have if there were no lack of conformity,

    – the significance of the lack of conformity, and

    – whether the alternative remedy could be completed without significant inconvenience to the consumer.

Any repair or replacement shall be completed within a reasonable time and without any significant inconvenience to the consumer, taking account of the nature of the goods and the purpose for which the consumer required the goods.

4. The terms 'free of charge' in paragraphs 2 and 3 refer to the necessary costs incurred to bring the goods into conformity, particularly the cost of postage, labour and materials.

5. The consumer may require an appropriate reduction of the price or have the contract rescinded:

    – if the consumer is entitled to neither repair nor replacement, or

    – if the seller has not completed the remedy within a reasonable time, or

    – if the seller has not completed the remedy without significant inconvenience to the consumer.

6. The consumer is not entitled to have the contract rescinded if the lack of conformity is minor.

### Article 4. Right of redress

Where the final seller is liable to the consumer because of a lack of conformity resulting from an act or omission by the producer, a previous seller in the same chain of contracts or any other intermediary, the final seller shall be entitled to pursue remedies against the person or persons liable in the contractual chain. The person or persons liable against whom the final seller may pursue remedies, together with the relevant actions and conditions of exercise, shall be determined by national law.

### Article 5. Time limits

1. The seller shall be held liable under Article 3 where the lack of conformity becomes apparent within two years as from delivery of the goods. If, under national legislation, the rights laid down in Article 3(2) are subject to a limitation period, that period shall not expire within a period of two years from the time of delivery.

2. Member States may provide that, in order to benefit from his rights, the consumer must inform the seller of the lack of conformity within a period of two months from the date on which he detected such lack of conformity.

Member States shall inform the Commission of their use of this paragraph.

The Commission shall monitor the effect of the existence of this option for the Member States on consumers and on the internal market.

Not later than 7 January 2003, the Commission shall prepare a report on the use made by Member States of this paragraph. This report shall be published in the Official Journal of the European Communities.

3. Unless proved otherwise, any lack of conformity which becomes apparent within six months of delivery of the goods shall be presumed to have existed at the time of delivery unless this presumption is incompatible with the nature of the goods or the nature of the lack of conformity.

### Article 6. Guarantees

1. A guarantee shall be legally binding on the offerer under the conditions laid down in the guarantee statement and the associated advertising.

2. The guarantee shall:
– state that the consumer has legal rights under applicable national legislation governing the sale of consumer goods and make clear that those rights are not affected by the guarantee,
– set out in plain intelligible language the contents of the guarantee and the essential particulars necessary for making claims under the guarantee, notably the duration and territorial scope of the guarantee as well as the name and address of the guarantor.

3. On request by the consumer, the guarantee shall be made available in writing or feature in another durable medium available and accessible to him.

4. Within its own territory, the Member State in which the consumer goods are marketed may, in accordance with the rules of the Treaty, provide that the guarantee be drafted in one or more languages which it shall determine from among the official languages of the Community.

5. Should a guarantee infringe the requirements of paragraphs 2, 3 or 4, the validity of this guarantee shall in no way be affected, and the consumer can still rely on the guarantee and require that it be honoured.

### Article 7. Binding nature

1. Any contractual terms or agreements concluded with the seller before the lack of conformity is brought to the seller's attention which directly or indirectly waive or restrict the rights resulting from this Directive shall, as provided for by national law, not be binding on the consumer.

Member States may provide that, in the case of second-hand goods, the seller and consumer may agree contractual terms or agreements which have a shorter time period for the liability of the seller than that set down in Article 5(1). Such period may not be less than one year.

2. Member States shall take the necessary measures to ensure that consumers are not deprived of the protection afforded by this Directive as a result of opting for the law of a non-member State as the law applicable to the contract where the contract has a close connection with the territory of the Member States.

### Article 8. National law and minimum protection

1. The rights resulting from this Directive shall be exercised without prejudice to other rights which the consumer may invoke under the national rules governing contractual or non-contractual liability.

2. Member States may adopt or maintain in force more stringent provisions, compatible with the Treaty in the field covered by this Directive, to ensure a higher level of consumer protection.

### Article 9

Member States shall take appropriate measures to inform the consumer of the national law transposing this Directive and shall encourage, where appropriate, professional organisations to inform consumers of their rights.

**Article 10**

The Annex to Directive 98/27/EC shall be completed as follows: '10. Directive 1999/44/EC of the European Parliament and of the Council of 25 May 1999 on certain aspects of the sale of consumer goods and associated guarantees (OJ L 171, 7.7.1999, p. 12).'.

**Article 11. Transposition**

1. Member States shall bring into force the laws, regulations and administrative provisions necessary to comply with this Directive not later than 1 January 2002. They shall forthwith inform the Commission thereof.

When Member States adopt these measures, they shall contain a reference to this Directive, or shall be accompanied by such reference at the time of their official publication. The procedure for such reference shall be adopted by Member States.

2. Member States shall communicate to the Commission the provisions of national law which they adopt in the field covered by this Directive.

**Article 12. Review**

The Commission shall, not later than 7 July 2006, review the application of this Directive and submit to the European Parliament and the Council a report. The report shall examine, inter alia, the case for introducing the producer's direct liability and, if appropriate, shall be accompanied by proposals.

**Article 13. Entry into force**

This Directive shall enter into force on the day of its publication in the Official Journal of the European Communities.

**Article 14**

This Directive is addressed to the Member States.

Done at Brussels, 25 May 1999.

## DIRECTIVE OF THE EUROPEAN PARLIAMENT AND OF THE COUNCIL OF 29 JUNE 2000
### on combating late payment in commercial transactions
### (2000/35/EC)

THE EUROPEAN PARLIAMENT AND THE COUNCIL OF THE EUROPEAN UNION,

Having regard to the Treaty establishing the European Community, and in particular Article 95 thereof,

Having regard to the proposal from the Commission,

Having regard to the opinion of the Economic and Social Committee,

Acting in accordance with the procedure laid down in Article 251 of the Treaty, in the light of the joint text approved by the Conciliation Committee on 4 May 2000,

Whereas:

(1) In its resolution on the integrated programme in favour of SMEs and the craft sector, the European Parliament urged the Commission to submit proposals to deal with the problem of late payment.

(2) On 12 May 1995 the Commission adopted a recommendation on payment periods in commercial transactions.

(3) In its resolution on the Commission recommendation on payment periods in commercial transactions, the European Parliament called on the Commission to consider transforming its recommendation into a proposal for a Council directive to be submitted as soon as possible.

(4) On 29 May 1997 the Economic and Social Committee adopted an

opinion on the Commission's Green Paper on Public Procurement in the European Union: Exploring the way forward.

(5) On 4 June 1997 the Commission published an action plan for the single market, which underlined that late payment represents an increasingly serious obstacle for the success of the single market.

(6) On 17 July 1997 the Commission published a report on late payments in commercial transactions, summarising the results of an evaluation of the effects of the Commission's recommendation of 12 May 1995.

(7) Heavy administrative and financial burdens are placed on businesses, particularly small and medium-sized ones, as a result of excessive payment periods and late payment. Moreover, these problems are a major cause of insolvencies threatening the survival of businesses and result in numerous job losses.

(8) In some Member States contractual payment periods differ significantly from the Community average.

(9) The differences between payment rules and practices in the Member States constitute an obstacle to the proper functioning of the internal market.

(10) This has the effect of considerably limiting commercial transactions between Member States. This is in contradiction with Article 14 of the Treaty as entrepreneurs should be able to trade throughout the internal market under conditions which ensure that transborder operations do not entail greater risks than domestic sales. Distortions of competition would ensue if substantially different rules applied to domestic and transborder operations.

(11) The most recent statistics indicate that there has been, at best, no improvement in late payments in many Member States since the adoption of the recommendation of 12 May 1995.

(12) The objective of combating late payments in the internal market cannot be sufficiently achieved by the Member States acting individually and can, therefore, be better achieved by the Community. This Directive does not go beyond what is necessary to achieve that objective. This Directive complies therefore, in its entirety, with the requirements of the principles of subsidiarity and proportionality as laid down in Article 5 of the Treaty.

(13) This Directive should be limited to payments made as remuneration for commercial transactions and does not regulate transactions with consumers, interest in connection with other payments, eg payments under the laws on cheques and bills of exchange, payments made as compensation for damages including payments from insurance companies.

(14) The fact that the liberal professions are covered by this Directive does not mean that Member States have to treat them as undertakings or merchants for purposes not covered by this Directive.

(15) This Directive only defines the term 'enforceable title' but does not regulate the various procedures of forced execution of such a title and the conditions under which forced execution of such a title can be stopped or suspended.

(16) Late payment constitutes a breach of contract which has been made financially attractive to debtors in most Member States by low interest rates on late payments and/or slow procedures for redress. A decisive shift, including compensation of creditors for the costs incurred, is necessary to reverse this trend and to ensure that the consequences of late payments are such as to discourage late payment.

(17) The reasonable compensation for the recovery costs has to be considered without prejudice to national provisions according to which a national judge can award to the creditor any additional damage caused by the debtor's late payment, taking also into account that such incurred costs may be already compensated for by the interest for late payment.

(18) This Directive takes into account the issue of long contractual payment

periods and, in particular, the existence of certain categories of contracts where a longer payment period in combination with a restriction of freedom of contract or a higher interest rate can be justified.

(19) This Directive should prohibit abuse of freedom of contract to the disadvantage of the creditor. Where an agreement mainly serves the purpose of procuring the debtor additional liquidity at the expense of the creditor, or where the main contractor imposes on his suppliers and subcontractors terms of payment which are not justified on the grounds of the terms granted to himself, these may be considered to be factors constituting such an abuse. This Directive does not affect national provisions relating to the way contracts are concluded or regulating the validity of contractual terms which are unfair to the debtor.

(20) The consequences of late payment can be dissuasive only if they are accompanied by procedures for redress which are rapid and effective for the creditor. In conformity with the principle of non-discrimination contained in Article 12 of the Treaty, those procedures should be available to all creditors who are established in the Community.

(21) It is desirable to ensure that creditors are in a position to exercise a retention of title on a non-discriminatory basis throughout the Community, if the retention of title clause is valid under the applicable national provisions designated by private international law.

(22) This Directive should regulate all commercial transactions irrespective of whether they are carried out between private or public undertakings or between undertakings and public authorities, having regard to the fact that the latter handle a considerable volume of payments to business. It should therefore also regulate all commercial transactions between main contractors and their suppliers and subcontractors.

(23) Article 5 of this Directive requires that the recovery procedure for unchallenged claims be completed within a short period of time in conformity with national legislation, but does not require Member States to adopt a specific procedure or to amend their existing legal procedures in a specific way.

HAVE ADOPTED THIS DIRECTIVE:

### Article 1. Scope
This Directive shall apply to all payments made as remuneration for commercial transactions.

### Article 2. Definitions
For the purposes of this Directive:

1. 'commercial transactions' means transactions between undertakings or between undertakings and public authorities which lead to the delivery of goods or the provision of services for remuneration,

'public authority' means any contracting authority or entity, as defined by the Public Procurement Directives (92/50/EEC, 93/36/EEC, 93/37/EEC and 93/38/EEC),

'undertaking' means any organisation acting in the course of its independent economic or professional activity, even where it is carried on by a single person;

2. 'late payment' means exceeding the contractual or statutory period of payment;

3. 'retention of title' means the contractual agreement according to which the seller retains title to the goods in question until the price has been paid in full;

4. 'interest rate applied by the European Central Bank to its main refinancing operations' means the interest rate applied to such operations in the case of fixed-rate tenders. In the event that a main refinancing operation was conducted according to a variable-rate tender procedure, this interest rate refers to the

marginal interest rate which resulted from that tender. This applies both in the case of single-rate and variable-rate auctions;

5. 'enforceable title' means any decision, judgment or order for payment issued by a court or other competent authority, whether for immediate payment or payment by instalments, which permits the creditor to have his claim against the debtor collected by means of forced execution; it shall include a decision, judgment or order for payment that is provisionally enforceable and remains so even if the debtor appeals against it.

### Article 3. Interest in case of late payment

1. Member States shall ensure that:

(a)  interest in accordance with point (d) shall become payable from the day following the date or the end of the period for payment fixed in the contract;

(b)  if the date or period for payment is not fixed in the contract, interest shall become payable automatically without the necessity of a reminder:

(i)  30 days following the date of receipt by the debtor of the invoice or an equivalent request for payment; or

(ii)  if the date of the receipt of the invoice or the equivalent request for payment is uncertain, 30 days after the date of receipt of the goods or services; or

(iii)  if the debtor receives the invoice or the equivalent request for payment earlier than the goods or the services, 30 days after the receipt of the goods or services; or

(iv)  if a procedure of acceptance or verification, by which the conformity of the goods or services with the contract is to be ascertained, is provided for by statute or in the contract and if the debtor receives the invoice or the equivalent request for payment earlier or on the date on which such acceptance or verification takes place, 30 days after this latter date;

(c)  the creditor shall be entitled to interest for late payment to the extent that:

(i)  he has fulfilled his contractual and legal obligations; and

(ii)  he has not received the amount due on time, unless the debtor is not responsible for the delay;

(d)  the level of interest for late payment ('the statutory rate'), which the debtor is obliged to pay, shall be the sum of the interest rate applied by the European Central Bank to its most recent main refinancing operation carried out before the first calendar day of the half-year in question ('the reference rate'), plus at least seven percentage points ('the margin'), unless otherwise specified in the contract. For a Member State which is not participating in the third stage of economic and monetary union, the reference rate referred to above shall be the equivalent rate set by its national central bank. In both cases, the reference rate in force on the first calendar day of the half-year in question shall apply for the following six months;

(e)  unless the debtor is not responsible for the delay, the creditor shall be entitled to claim reasonable compensation from the debtor for all relevant recovery costs incurred through the latter's late payment. Such recovery costs shall respect the principles of transparency and proportionality as regards the debt in question. Member States may, while respecting the principles referred to above, fix maximum amounts as regards the recovery costs for different levels of debt.

2. For certain categories of contracts to be defined by national law, Member States may fix the period after which interest becomes payable to a maximum of 60 days provided that they either restrain the parties to the contract from exceeding this period or fix a mandatory interest rate that substantially exceeds the statutory rate.

3.  Member States shall provide that an agreement on the date for payment or on the consequences of late payment which is not in line with the provisions of paragraphs 1(b) to (d) and 2 either shall not be enforceable or shall give rise to a claim for damages if, when all circumstances of the case, including good commercial practice and the nature of the product, are considered, it is grossly unfair to the creditor. In determining whether an agreement is grossly unfair to the creditor, it will be taken, inter alia, into account whether the debtor has any objective reason to deviate from the provisions of paragraphs 1(b) to (d) and 2. If such an agreement is determined to be grossly unfair, the statutory terms will apply, unless the national courts determine different conditions which are fair.

4.  Member States shall ensure that, in the interests of creditors and of competitors, adequate and effective means exist to prevent the continued use of terms which are grossly unfair within the meaning of paragraph 3.

5.  The means referred to in paragraph 4 shall include provisions whereby organisations officially recognised as, or having a legitimate interest in, representing small and medium-sized enterprises may take action according to the national law concerned before the courts or before competent administrative bodies on the grounds that contractual terms drawn up for general use are grossly unfair within the meaning of paragraph 3, so that they can apply appropriate and effective means to prevent the continued use of such terms.

### Article 4. Retention of title

1.  Member States shall provide in conformity with the applicable national provisions designated by private international law that the seller retains title to goods until they are fully paid for if a retention of title clause has been expressly agreed between the buyer and the seller before the delivery of the goods.

2.  Member States may adopt or retain provisions dealing with down payments already made by the debtor.

### Article 5. Recovery procedures for unchallenged claims

1.  Member States shall ensure that an enforceable title can be obtained, irrespective of the amount of the debt, normally within 90 calendar days of the lodging of the creditor's action or application at the court or other competent authority, provided that the debt or aspects of the procedure are not disputed. This duty shall be carried out by Member States in conformity with their respective national legislation, regulations and administrative provisions.

2.  The respective national legislation, regulations and administrative provisions shall apply the same conditions for all creditors who are established in the European Community.

3.  The 90 calendar day period referred to in paragraph 1 shall not include the following:

(a)  periods for service of documents;

(b)  any delays caused by the creditor, such as periods devoted to correcting applications.

4.  This Article shall be without prejudice to the provisions of the Brussels Convention on jurisdiction and enforcement of judgments in civil and commercial matters.

### Article 6. Transposition

1.  Member States shall bring into force the laws, regulations and administrative provisions necessary to comply with this Directive before 8 August 2002. They shall forthwith inform the Commission thereof.

When Member States adopt these measures, they shall contain a reference to this Directive or shall be accompanied by such reference on the occasion of their official publication. The methods of making such reference shall be laid down by Member States.

2. Member States may maintain or bring into force provisions which are more favourable to the creditor than the provisions necessary to comply with this Directive.

3. In transposing this Directive, Member States may exclude:

   (a) debts that are subject to insolvency proceedings instituted against the debtor;

   (b) contracts that have been concluded prior to 8 August 2002; and

   (c) claims for interest of less than EUR 5.

4. Member States shall communicate to the Commission the text of the main provisions of national law which they adopt in the field covered by this Directive.

5. The Commission shall undertake two years after 8 August 2002 a review of, inter alia, the statutory rate, contractual payment periods and late payments, to assess the impact on commercial transactions and the operation of the legislation in practice. The results of this review and of other reviews will be made known to the European Parliament and the Council, accompanied where appropriate by proposals for improvement of this Directive.

### Article 7. Entry into force
This Directive shall enter into force on the day of its publication in the Official Journal of the European Communities.

### Article 8. Addressees
This Directive is addressed to the Member States.

Done at Luxembourg, 29 June 2000.

## DIRECTIVE OF THE EUROPEAN PARLIAMENT AND OF THE COUNCIL
### OF 3 DECEMBER 2001
### on general product safety
### (2001/95/EC: Text with EEA relevance)

THE EUROPEAN PARLIAMENT AND THE COUNCIL OF THE EUROPEAN UNION,

Having regard to the Treaty establishing the European Community, and in particular Article 95 thereof,

   Having regard to the proposal from the Commission,

   Having regard to the opinion of the Economic and Social Committee,

   Acting in accordance with the procedure referred to in Article 251 of the Treaty, in the light of the joint text approved by the Conciliation Committee on 2 August 2001,

   Whereas:

   (1) Under Article 16 of Council Directive 92/59/EEC of 29 June 1992 on general product safety, the Council was to decide, four years after the date set for the implementation of the said Directive, on the basis of a report of the Commission on the experience acquired, together with appropriate proposals, whether to adjust Directive 92/59/EEC. It is necessary to amend Directive 92/59/EEC in several respects, in order to complete, reinforce or clarify some of its provisions in the light of experience as well as new and relevant developments on consumer product safety, together with the changes made to the Treaty, especially in Articles 152 concerning public health and 153 concerning consumer protection, and in the light of the precautionary principle. Directive 92/59/EEC should therefore be recast in the interest of clarity. This recasting leaves the safety of services outside the scope of this Directive, since the Commission intends to identify the needs, possibilities and

priorities for Community action on the safety of services and liability of service providers, with a view to presenting appropriate proposals.

(2) It is important to adopt measures with the aim of improving the functioning of the internal market, comprising an area without internal frontiers in which the free movement of goods, persons, services and capital is assured.

(3) In the absence of Community provisions, horizontal legislation of the Member States on product safety, imposing in particular a general obligation on economic operators to market only safe products, might differ in the level of protection afforded to consumers. Such disparities, and the absence of horizontal legislation in some Member States, would be liable to create barriers to trade and distortion of competition within the internal market.

(4) In order to ensure a high level of consumer protection, the Community must contribute to protecting the health and safety of consumers. Horizontal Community legislation introducing a general product safety requirement, and containing provisions on the general obligations of producers and distributors, on the enforcement of Community product safety requirements and on rapid exchange of information and action at Community level in certain cases, should contribute to that aim.

(5) It is very difficult to adopt Community legislation for every product which exists or which may be developed; there is a need for a broad-based, legislative framework of a horizontal nature to deal with such products, and also to cover lacunae, in particular pending revision of the existing specific legislation, and to complement provisions in existing or forthcoming specific legislation, in particular with a view to ensuring a high level of protection of safety and health of consumers, as required by Article 95 of the Treaty.

(6) It is therefore necessary to establish at Community level a general safety requirement for any product placed on the market, or otherwise supplied or made available to consumers, intended for consumers, or likely to be used by consumers under reasonably foreseeable conditions even if not intended for them. In all these cases the products under consideration can pose risks for the health and safety of consumers which must be prevented. Certain second-hand goods should nevertheless be excluded by their very nature.

(7) This Directive should apply to products irrespective of the selling techniques, including distance and electronic selling.

(8) The safety of products should be assessed taking into account all the relevant aspects, in particular the categories of consumers which can be particularly vulnerable to the risks posed by the products under consideration, in particular children and the elderly.

(9) This Directive does not cover services, but in order to secure the attainment of the protection objectives in question, its provisions should also apply to products that are supplied or made available to consumers in the context of service provision for use by them. The safety of the equipment used by service providers themselves to supply a service to consumers does not come within the scope of this Directive since it has to be dealt with in conjunction with the safety of the service provided. In particular, equipment on which consumers ride or travel which is operated by a service provider is excluded from the scope of this Directive.

(10) Products which are designed exclusively for professional use but have subsequently migrated to the consumer market should be subject to the requirements of this Directive because they can pose risks to consumer health and safety when used under reasonably foreseeable conditions.

(11) In the absence of more specific provisions, within the framework of Community legislation covering safety of the products concerned, all the

provisions of this Directive should apply in order to ensure consumer health and safety.

(12) If specific Community legislation sets out safety requirements covering only certain risks or categories of risks, with regard to the products concerned the obligations of economic operators in respect of these risks are those determined by the provisions of the specific legislation, while the general safety requirement of this Directive should apply to the other risks.

(13) The provisions of this Directive relating to the other obligations of producers and distributors, the obligations and powers of the Member States, the exchanges of information and rapid intervention situations and dissemination of information and confidentiality apply in the case of products covered by specific rules of Community law, if those rules do not already contain such obligations.

(14) In order to facilitate the effective and consistent application of the general safety requirement of this Directive, it is important to establish European voluntary standards covering certain products and risks in such a way that a product which conforms to a national standard transposing a European standard is to be presumed to be in compliance with the said requirement.

(15) With regard to the aims of this Directive, European standards should be established by European standardisation bodies, under mandates set by the Commission assisted by appropriate Committees. In order to ensure that products in compliance with the standards fulfil the general safety requirement, the Commission assisted by a committee composed of representatives of the Member States, should fix the requirements that the standards must meet. These requirements should be included in the mandates to the standardisation bodies.

(16) In the absence of specific regulations and when the European standards established under mandates set by the Commission are not available or recourse is not made to such standards, the safety of products should be assessed taking into account in particular national standards transposing any other relevant European or international standards, Commission recommendations or national standards, international standards, codes of good practice, the state of the art and the safety which consumers may reasonably expect. In this context, the Commission's recommendations may facilitate the consistent and effective application of this Directive pending the introduction of European standards or as regards the risks and/or products for which such standards are deemed not to be possible or appropriate.

(17) Appropriate independent certification recognised by the competent authorities may facilitate proof of compliance with the applicable product safety criteria.

(18) It is appropriate to supplement the duty to observe the general safety requirement by other obligations on economic operators because action by such operators is necessary to prevent risks to consumers under certain circumstances.

(19) The additional obligations on producers should include the duty to adopt measures commensurate with the characteristics of the products, enabling them to be informed of the risks that these products may present, to supply consumers with information enabling them to assess and prevent risks, to warn consumers of the risks posed by dangerous products already supplied to them, to withdraw those products from the market and, as a last resort, to recall them when necessary, which may involve, depending on the provisions applicable in the Member States, an appropriate form of compensation, for example exchange or reimbursement.

(20) Distributors should help in ensuring compliance with the applicable safety requirements. The obligations placed on distributors apply in pro-

portion to their respective responsibilities. In particular, it may prove impossible, in the context of charitable activities, to provide the competent authorities with information and documentation on possible risks and origin of the product in the case of isolated used objects provided by private individuals.

(21) Both producers and distributors should cooperate with the competent authorities in action aimed at preventing risks and inform them when they conclude that certain products supplied are dangerous. The conditions regarding the provision of such information should be set in this Directive to facilitate its effective application, while avoiding an excessive burden for economic operators and the authorities.

(22) In order to ensure the effective enforcement of the obligations incumbent on producers and distributors, the Member States should establish or designate authorities which are responsible for monitoring product safety and have powers to take appropriate measures, including the power to impose effective, proportionate and dissuasive penalties, and ensure appropriate coordination between the various designated authorities.

(23) It is necessary in particular for the appropriate measures to include the power for Member States to order or organise, immediately and efficiently, the withdrawal of dangerous products already placed on the market and as a last resort to order, coordinate or organise the recall from consumers of dangerous products already supplied to them. Those powers should be applied when producers and distributors fail to prevent risks to consumers in accordance with their obligations. Where necessary, the appropriate powers and procedures should be available to the authorities to decide and apply any necessary measures rapidly.

(24) The safety of consumers depends to a great extent on the active enforcement of Community product safety requirements. The Member States should, therefore, establish systematic approaches to ensure the effectiveness of market surveillance and other enforcement activities and should ensure their openness to the public and interested parties.

(25) Collaboration between the enforcement authorities of the Member States is necessary in ensuring the attainment of the protection objectives of this Directive. It is, therefore, appropriate to promote the operation of a European network of the enforcement authorities of the Member States to facilitate, in a coordinated manner with other Community procedures, in particular the Community Rapid Information System (RAPEX), improved collaboration at operational level on market surveillance and other enforcement activities, in particular risk assessment, testing of products, exchange of expertise and scientific knowledge, execution of joint surveillance projects and tracing, withdrawing or recalling dangerous products.

(26) It is necessary, for the purpose of ensuring a consistent, high level of consumer health and safety protection and preserving the unity of the internal market, that the Commission be informed of any measure restricting the placing on the market of a product or requiring its withdrawal or recall from the market. Such measures should be taken in compliance with the provisions of the Treaty, and in particular Articles 28, 29 and 30 thereof.

(27) Effective supervision of product safety requires the setting-up at national and Community levels of a system of rapid exchange of information in situations of serious risk requiring rapid intervention in respect of the safety of a product. It is also appropriate in this Directive to set out detailed procedures for the operation of the system and to give the Commission, assisted by an advisory committee, power to adapt them.

(28) This Directive provides for the establishment of non-binding guidelines aimed at indicating simple and clear criteria and practical rules which may change, in particular for the purpose of allowing efficient notification of

measures restricting the placing on the market of products in the cases referred to in this Directive, whilst taking into account the range of situations dealt with by Member States and economic operators. The guidelines should in particular include criteria for the application of the definition of serious risks in order to facilitate consistent implementation of the relevant provisions in case of such risks.

(29) It is primarily for Member States, in compliance with the Treaty and in particular with Articles 28, 29 and 30 thereof, to take appropriate measures with regard to dangerous products located within their territory.

(30) However, if the Member States differ as regards the approach to dealing with the risk posed by certain products, such differences could entail unacceptable disparities in consumer protection and constitute a barrier to intra-Community trade.

(31) It may be necessary to deal with serious product-safety problems requiring rapid intervention which affect or could affect, in the immediate future, all or a significant part of the Community and which, in view of the nature of the safety problem posed by the product, cannot be dealt with effectively in a manner commensurate with the degree of urgency, under the procedures laid down in the specific rules of Community law applicable to the products or category of products in question.

(32) It is therefore necessary to provide for an adequate mechanism allowing, as a last resort, for the adoption of measures applicable throughout the Community, in the form of a decision addressed to the Member States, to cope with situations created by products presenting a serious risk. Such a decision should entail a ban on the export of the product in question, unless in the case in point exceptional circumstances allow a partial ban or even no ban to be decided upon, particularly when a system of prior consent is established. In addition, the banning of exports should be examined with a view to preventing risks to the health and safety of consumers. Since such a decision is not directly applicable to economic operators, Member States should take all necessary measures for its implementation. Measures adopted under such a procedure are interim measures, save when they apply to individually identified products or batches of products. In order to ensure the appropriate assessment of the need for, and the best preparation of such measures, they should be taken by the Commission, assisted by a committee, in the light of consultations with the Member States, and, if scientific questions are involved falling within the competence of a Community scientific committee, with the scientific committee competent for the risk concerned.

(33) The measures necessary for the implementation of this Directive should be adopted in accordance with Council Decision 1999/468/EC of 28 June 1999 laying down the procedures for the exercise of implementing powers conferred on the Commission.

(34) In order to facilitate effective and consistent application of this Directive, the various aspects of its application may need to be discussed within a committee.

(35) Public access to the information available to the authorities on product safety should be ensured. However, professional secrecy, as referred to in Article 287 of the Treaty, must be protected in a way which is compatible with the need to ensure the effectiveness of market surveillance activities and of protection measures.

(36) This Directive should not affect victims' rights within the meaning of Council Directive 85/374/EEC of 25 July 1985 on the approximation of the laws, regulations and administrative provisions of the Member States concerning liability for defective products.

(37) It is necessary for Member States to provide for appropriate means of redress before the competent courts in respect of measures taken by the

competent authorities which restrict the placing on the market of a product or require its withdrawal or recall.

(38) In addition, the adoption of measures concerning imported products, like those concerning the banning of exports, with a view to preventing risks to the safety and health of consumers must comply with the Community's international obligations.

(39) The Commission should periodically examine the manner in which this Directive is applied and the results obtained, in particular in relation to the functioning of market surveillance systems, the rapid exchange of information and measures adopted at Community level, together with other issues relevant for consumer product safety in the Community, and submit regular reports to the European Parliament and the Council on the subject.

(40) This Directive should not affect the obligations of Member States concerning the deadline for transposition and application of Directive 92/59/EEC.

HAVE ADOPTED THIS DIRECTIVE:

## CHAPTER I. OBJECTIVE—SCOPE—DEFINITIONS

### Article 1

1. The purpose of this Directive is to ensure that products placed on the market are safe.

2. This Directive shall apply to all the products defined in Article 2(a). Each of its provisions shall apply in so far as there are no specific provisions with the same objective in rules of Community law governing the safety of the products concerned.

Where products are subject to specific safety requirements imposed by Community legislation, this Directive shall apply only to the aspects and risks or categories of risks not covered by those requirements. This means that:

   (a)   Articles 2(b) and (c), 3 and 4 shall not apply to those products in so far as concerns the risks or categories of risks covered by the specific legislation;

   (b)   Articles 5 to 18 shall apply except where there are specific provisions governing the aspects covered by the said Articles with the same objective.

### Article 2

For the purposes of this Directive:

   (a)   'product' shall mean any product—including in the context of providing a service—which is intended for consumers or likely, under reasonably foreseeable conditions, to be used by consumers even if not intended for them, and is supplied or made available, whether for consideration or not, in the course of a commercial activity, and whether new, used or reconditioned.

This definition shall not apply to second-hand products supplied as antiques or as products to be repaired or reconditioned prior to being used, provided that the supplier clearly informs the person to whom he supplies the product to that effect;

   (b)   'safe product' shall mean any product which, under normal or reasonably foreseeable conditions of use including duration and, where applicable, putting into service, installation and maintenance requirements, does not present any risk or only the minimum risks compatible with the product's use, considered to be acceptable and consistent with a high level of protection for the safety and health of persons, taking into account the following points in particular:

      (i)   the characteristics of the product, including its composition, packaging, instructions for assembly and, where applicable, for installation and maintenance;

      (ii)   the effect on other products, where it is reasonably foreseeable that it will be used with other products;

(iii) the presentation of the product, the labelling, any warnings and instructions for its use and disposal and any other indication or information regarding the product;

(iv) the categories of consumers at risk when using the product, in particular children and the elderly.

The feasibility of obtaining higher levels of safety or the availability of other products presenting a lesser degree of risk shall not constitute grounds for considering a product to be 'dangerous';

(c) 'dangerous product' shall mean any product which does not meet the definition of 'safe product' in (b);

(d) 'serious risk' shall mean any serious risk, including those the effects of which are not immediate, requiring rapid intervention by the public authorities;

(e) 'producer' shall mean:

(i) the manufacturer of the product, when he is established in the Community, and any other person presenting himself as the manufacturer by affixing to the product his name, trade mark or other distinctive mark, or the person who reconditions the product;

(ii) the manufacturer's representative, when the manufacturer is not established in the Community or, if there is no representative established in the Community, the importer of the product;

(iii) other professionals in the supply chain, in so far as their activities may affect the safety properties of a product;

(f) 'distributor' shall mean any professional in the supply chain whose activity does not affect the safety properties of a product;

(g) 'recall' shall mean any measure aimed at achieving the return of a dangerous product that has already been supplied or made available to consumers by the producer or distributor;

(h) 'withdrawal' shall mean any measure aimed at preventing the distribution, display and offer of a product dangerous to the consumer.

## CHAPTER II. GENERAL SAFETY REQUIREMENT, CONFORMITY ASSESSMENT CRITERIA AND EUROPEAN STANDARDS

**Article 3**

1. Producers shall be obliged to place only safe products on the market.

2. A product shall be deemed safe, as far as the aspects covered by the relevant national legislation are concerned, when, in the absence of specific Community provisions governing the safety of the product in question, it conforms to the specific rules of national law of the Member State in whose territory the product is marketed, such rules being drawn up in conformity with the Treaty, and in particular Articles 28 and 30 thereof, and laying down the health and safety requirements which the product must satisfy in order to be marketed.

A product shall be presumed safe as far as the risks and risk categories covered by relevant national standards are concerned when it conforms to voluntary national standards transposing European standards, the references of which have been published by the Commission in the Official Journal of the European Communities in accordance with Article 4. The Member States shall publish the references of such national standards.

3. In circumstances other than those referred to in paragraph 2, the conformity of a product to the general safety requirement shall be assessed by taking into account the following elements in particular, where they exist:

(a) voluntary national standards transposing relevant European standards other than those referred to in paragraph 2;

(b) the standards drawn up in the Member State in which the product is marketed;

(c)   Commission recommendations setting guidelines on product safety assessment;

(d)   product safety codes of good practice in force in the sector concerned;

(e)   the state of the art and technology;

(f)   reasonable consumer expectations concerning safety.

4.   Conformity of a product with the criteria designed to ensure the general safety requirement, in particular the provisions mentioned in paragraphs 2 or 3, shall not bar the competent authorities of the Member States from taking appropriate measures to impose restrictions on its being placed on the market or to require its withdrawal from the market or recall where there is evidence that, despite such conformity, it is dangerous.

**Article 4**

1.   For the purposes of this Directive, the European standards referred to in the second subparagraph of Article 3(2) shall be drawn up as follows:

(a)   the requirements intended to ensure that products which conform to these standards satisfy the general safety requirement shall be determined in accordance with the procedure laid down in Article 15(2);

(b)   on the basis of those requirements, the Commission shall, in accordance with Directive 98/34/EC of the European Parliament and of the Council of 22 June 1998 laying down a procedure for the provision of information in the field of technical standards and regulations and of rules on information society services call on the European standardisation bodies to draw up standards which satisfy these requirements;

(c)   on the basis of those mandates, the European standardisation bodies shall adopt the standards in accordance with the principles contained in the general guidelines for cooperation between the Commission and those bodies;

(d)   the Commission shall report every three years to the European Parliament and the Council, within the framework of the report referred to in Article 19(2), on its programmes for setting the requirements and the mandates for standardisation provided for in subparagraphs (a) and (b) above. This report will, in particular, include an analysis of the decisions taken regarding requirements and mandates for standardisation referred to in subparagraphs (a) and (b) and regarding the standards referred to in subparagraph (c). It will also include information on the products for which the Commission intends to set the requirements and the mandates in question, the product risks to be considered and the results of any preparatory work launched in this area.

2.   The Commission shall publish in the Official Journal of the European Communities the references of the European standards adopted in this way and drawn up in accordance with the requirements referred to in paragraph 1.

If a standard adopted by the European standardisation bodies before the entry into force of this Directive ensures compliance with the general safety requirement, the Commission shall decide to publish its references in the Official Journal of the European Communities.

If a standard does not ensure compliance with the general safety requirement, the Commission shall withdraw reference to the standard from publication in whole or in part.

In the cases referred to in the second and third subparagraphs, the Commission shall, on its own initiative or at the request of a Member State, decide in accordance with the procedure laid down in Article 15(2) whether the standard in question meets the general safety requirement. The Commission shall decide to publish or withdraw after consulting the Committee established by Article 5 of Directive 98/34/EC. The Commission shall notify the Member States of its decision.

## CHAPTER III. OTHER OBLIGATIONS OF PRODUCERS AND OBLIGATIONS OF DISTRIBUTORS

**Article 5**

1. Within the limits of their respective activities, producers shall provide consumers with the relevant information to enable them to assess the risks inherent in a product throughout the normal or reasonably foreseeable period of its use, where such risks are not immediately obvious without adequate warnings, and to take precautions against those risks.

The presence of warnings does not exempt any person from compliance with the other requirements laid down in this Directive.

Within the limits of their respective activities, producers shall adopt measures commensurate with the characteristics of the products which they supply, enabling them to:

(a)   be informed of risks which these products might pose;

(b)   choose to take appropriate action including, if necessary to avoid these risks, withdrawal from the market, adequately and effectively warning consumers or recall from consumers.

The measures referred to in the third subparagraph shall include, for example:

(a)   an indication, by means of the product or its packaging, of the identity and details of the producer and the product reference or, where applicable, the batch of products to which it belongs, except where not to give such indication is justified and

(b)   in all cases where appropriate, the carrying out of sample testing of marketed products, investigating and, if necessary, keeping a register of complaints and keeping distributors informed of such monitoring.

Action such as that referred to in (b) of the third subparagraph shall be undertaken on a voluntary basis or at the request of the competent authorities in accordance with Article 8(1)(f). Recall shall take place as a last resort, where other measures would not suffice to prevent the risks involved, in instances where the producers consider it necessary or where they are obliged to do so further to a measure taken by the competent authority. It may be effected within the framework of codes of good practice on the matter in the Member State concerned, where such codes exist.

2. Distributors shall be required to act with due care to help to ensure compliance with the applicable safety requirements, in particular by not supplying products which they know or should have presumed, on the basis of the information in their possession and as professionals, do not comply with those requirements. Moreover, within the limits of their respective activities, they shall participate in monitoring the safety of products placed on the market, especially by passing on information on product risks, keeping and providing the documentation necessary for tracing the origin of products, and cooperating in the action taken by producers and competent authorities to avoid the risks. Within the limits of their respective activities they shall take measures enabling them to cooperate efficiently.

3. Where producers and distributors know or ought to know, on the basis of the information in their possession and as professionals, that a product that they have placed on the market poses risks to the consumer that are incompatible with the general safety requirement, they shall immediately inform the competent authorities of the Member States thereof under the conditions laid down in Annex I, giving details, in particular, of action taken to prevent risk to the consumer.

The Commission shall, in accordance with the procedure referred to in Article 15(3), adapt the specific requirements relating to the obligation to provide information laid down in Annex I.

4. Producers and distributors shall, within the limits of their respective

activities, cooperate with the competent authorities, at the request of the latter, on action taken to avoid the risks posed by products which they supply or have supplied. The procedures for such cooperation, including procedures for dialogue with the producers and distributors concerned on issues related to product safety, shall be established by the competent authorities.

## CHAPTER IV. SPECIFIC OBLIGATIONS AND POWERS OF THE MEMBER STATES

**Article 6**
1.   Member States shall ensure that producers and distributors comply with their obligations under this Directive in such a way that products placed on the market are safe.
2.   Member States shall establish or nominate authorities competent to monitor the compliance of products with the general safety requirements and arrange for such authorities to have and use the necessary powers to take the appropriate measures incumbent upon them under this Directive.
3.   Member States shall define the tasks, powers, organisation and cooperation arrangements of the competent authorities. They shall keep the Commission informed, and the Commission shall pass on such information to the other Member States.

**Article 7**
Member States shall lay down the rules on penalties applicable to infringements of the national provisions adopted pursuant to this Directive and shall take all measures necessary to ensure that they are implemented. The penalties provided for shall be effective, proportionate and dissuasive. Member States shall notify those provisions to the Commission by 15 January 2004 and shall also notify it, without delay, of any amendment affecting them.

**Article 8**
1.   For the purposes of this Directive, and in particular of Article 6 thereof, the competent authorities of the Member States shall be entitled to take, inter alia, the measures in (a) and in (b) to (f) below, where appropriate:
   (a)   for any product:
      (i)   to organise, even after its being placed on the market as being safe, appropriate checks on its safety properties, on an adequate scale, up to the final stage of use or consumption;
      (ii)   to require all necessary information from the parties concerned;
      (iii)   to take samples of products and subject them to safety checks;
   (b)   for any product that could pose risks in certain conditions:
      (i)   to require that it be marked with suitable, clearly worded and easily comprehensible warnings, in the official languages of the Member State in which the product is marketed, on the risks it may present;
      (ii)   to make its marketing subject to prior conditions so as to make it safe;
   (c)   for any product that could pose risks for certain persons: to order that they be given warning of the risk in good time and in an appropriate form, including the publication of special warnings;
   (d)   for any product that could be dangerous: for the period needed for the various safety evaluations, checks and controls, temporarily to ban its supply, the offer to supply it or its display;
   (e)   for any dangerous product: to ban its marketing and introduce the accompanying measures required to ensure the ban is complied with;
   (f)   for any dangerous product already on the market:
      (i)   to order or organise its actual and immediate withdrawal, and alert consumers to the risks it presents;

    (ii)  to order or coordinate or, if appropriate, to organise together with producers and distributors its recall from consumers and its destruction in suitable conditions.

2.   When the competent authorities of the Member States take measures such as those provided for in paragraph 1, in particular those referred to in (d) to (f), they shall act in accordance with the Treaty, and in particular Articles 28 and 30 thereof, in such a way as to implement the measures in a manner proportional to the seriousness of the risk, and taking due account of the precautionary principle.

In this context, they shall encourage and promote voluntary action by producers and distributors, in accordance with the obligations incumbent on them under this Directive, and in particular Chapter III thereof, including where applicable by the development of codes of good practice.

If necessary, they shall organise or order the measures provided for in paragraph 1(f) if the action undertaken by the producers and distributors in fulfilment of their obligations is unsatisfactory or insufficient. Recall shall take place as a last resort. It may be effected within the framework of codes of good practice on the matter in the Member State concerned, where such codes exist.

3.   In particular, the competent authorities shall have the power to take the necessary action to apply with due dispatch appropriate measures such as those mentioned in paragraph 1, (b) to (f), in the case of products posing a serious risk. These circumstances shall be determined by the Member States, assessing each individual case on its merits, taking into account the guidelines referred to in point 8 of Annex II.

4.   The measures to be taken by the competent authorities under this Article shall be addressed, as appropriate, to:

    (a)  the producer;

    (b)  within the limits of their respective activities, distributors and in particular the party responsible for the first stage of distribution on the national market;

    (c)  any other person, where necessary, with a view to cooperation in action taken to avoid risks arising from a product.

## Article 9

1.   In order to ensure effective market surveillance, aimed at guaranteeing a high level of consumer health and safety protection, which entails cooperation between their competent authorities, Member States shall ensure that approaches employing appropriate means and procedures are put in place, which may include in particular:

    (a)  establishment, periodical updating and implementation of sectoral surveillance programmes by categories of products or risks and the monitoring of surveillance activities, findings and results;

    (b)  follow-up and updating of scientific and technical knowledge concerning the safety of products;

    (c)  periodical review and assessment of the functioning of the control activities and their effectiveness and, if necessary, revision of the surveillance approach and organisation put in place.

2.   Member States shall ensure that consumers and other interested parties are given an opportunity to submit complaints to the competent authorities on product safety and on surveillance and control activities and that these complaints are followed up as appropriate. Member States shall actively inform consumers and other interested parties of the procedures established to that end.

## Article 10

1.   The Commission shall promote and take part in the operation in a

European network of the authorities of the Member States competent for product safety, in particular in the form of administrative cooperation.

2. This network operation shall develop in a coordinated manner with the other existing Community procedures, particularly RAPEX. Its objective shall be, in particular, to facilitate:

(a) the exchange of information on risk assessment, dangerous products, test methods and results, recent scientific developments as well as other aspects relevant for control activities;

(b) the establishment and execution of joint surveillance and testing projects;

(c) the exchange of expertise and best practices and cooperation in training activities;

(d) improved cooperation at Community level with regard to the tracing, withdrawal and recall of dangerous products.

## CHAPTER V. EXCHANGES OF INFORMATION AND RAPID INTERVENTION SITUATIONS

### Article 11

1. Where a Member State takes measures which restrict the placing on the market of products—or require their withdrawal or recall—such as those provided for in Article 8(1)(b) to (f), the Member State shall, to the extent that such notification is not required under Article 12 or any specific Community legislation, inform the Commission of the measures, specifying its reasons for adopting them. It shall also inform the Commission of any modification or lifting of such measures.

If the notifying Member State considers that the effects of the risk do not or cannot go beyond its territory, it shall notify the measures concerned in so far as they involve information likely to be of interest to Member States from the product safety standpoint, and in particular if they are in response to a new risk which has not yet been reported in other notifications.

In accordance with the procedure laid down in Article 15(3) of this Directive, the Commission shall, while ensuring the effectiveness and proper functioning of the system, adopt the guidelines referred to in point 8 of Annex II. These shall propose the content and standard form for the notifications provided for in this Article, and, in particular, shall provide precise criteria for determining the conditions for which notification is relevant for the purposes of the second subparagraph.

2. The Commission shall forward the notification to the other Member States, unless it concludes, after examination on the basis of the information contained in the notification, that the measure does not comply with Community law. In such a case, it shall immediately inform the Member State which initiated the action.

### Article 12

1. Where a Member State adopts or decides to adopt, recommend or agree with producers and distributors, whether on a compulsory or voluntary basis, measures or actions to prevent, restrict or impose specific conditions on the possible marketing or use, within its own territory, of products by reason of a serious risk, it shall immediately notify the Commission thereof through RAPEX. It shall also inform the Commission without delay of modification or withdrawal of any such measure or action.

If the notifying Member State considers that the effects of the risk do not or cannot go beyond its territory, it shall follow the procedure laid down in Article 11, taking into account the relevant criteria proposed in the guidelines referred to in point 8 of Annex II.

Without prejudice to the first subparagraph, before deciding to adopt such measures or to take such action, Member States may pass on to the Commission any information in their possession regarding the existence of a serious risk.

In the case of a serious risk, they shall notify the Commission of the voluntary measures laid down in Article 5 of this Directive taken by producers and distributors.

2.   On receiving such notifications, the Commission shall check whether they comply with this Article and with the requirements applicable to the functioning of RAPEX, and shall forward them to the other Member States, which, in turn, shall immediately inform the Commission of any measures adopted.

3.   Detailed procedures for RAPEX are set out in Annex II. They shall be adapted by the Commission in accordance with the procedure referred to in Article 15(3).

4.   Access to RAPEX shall be open to applicant countries, third countries or international organisations, within the framework of agreements between the Community and those countries or international organisations, according to arrangements defined in these agreements. Any such agreements shall be based on reciprocity and include provisions on confidentiality corresponding to those applicable in the Community.

### Article 13

1.   If the Commission becomes aware of a serious risk from certain products to the health and safety of consumers in various Member States, it may, after consulting the Member States, and, if scientific questions arise which fall within the competence of a Community Scientific Committee, the Scientific Committee competent to deal with the risk concerned, adopt a decision in the light of the result of those consultations, in accordance with the procedure laid down in Article 15(2), requiring Member States to take measures from among those listed in Article 8(1)(b) to (f) if, at one and the same time:

(a)   it emerges from prior consultations with the Member States that they differ significantly on the approach adopted or to be adopted to deal with the risk; and

(b)   the risk cannot be dealt with, in view of the nature of the safety issue posed by the product, in a manner compatible with the degree of urgency of the case, under other procedures laid down by the specific Community legislation applicable to the products concerned; and

(c)   the risk can be eliminated effectively only by adopting appropriate measures applicable at Community level, in order to ensure a consistent and high level of protection of the health and safety of consumers and the proper functioning of the internal market.

2.   The decisions referred to in paragraph 1 shall be valid for a period not exceeding one year and may be confirmed, under the same procedure, for additional periods none of which shall exceed one year.

However, decisions concerning specific, individually identified products or batches of products shall be valid without a time limit.

3.   Export from the Community of dangerous products which have been the subject of a decision referred to in paragraph 1 shall be prohibited unless the decision provides otherwise.

4.   Member States shall take all necessary measures to implement the decisions referred to in paragraph 1 within less than 20 days, unless a different period is specified in those decisions.

5.   The competent authorities responsible for carrying out the measures referred to in paragraph 1 shall, within one month, give the parties concerned an opportunity to submit their views and shall inform the Commission accordingly.

## CHAPTER VI. COMMITTEE PROCEDURES

**Article 14**

1.   The measures necessary for the implementation of this Directive relating to the matters referred to below shall be adopted in accordance with the regulatory procedure provided for in Article 15(2):

   (a)   the measures referred to in Article 4 concerning standards adopted by the European standardisation bodies;

   (b)   the decisions referred to in Article 13 requiring Member States to take measures as listed in Article 8(1)(b) to (f).

2.   The measures necessary for the implementation of this Directive in respect of all other matters shall be adopted in accordance with the advisory procedure provided for in Article 15(3).

**Article 15**

1.   The Commission shall be assisted by a Committee.

2.   Where reference is made to this paragraph, Articles 5 and 7 of Decision 1999/468/EC shall apply, having regard to the provisions of Article 8 thereof.

The period laid down in Article 5(6) of Decision 1999/468/EC shall be set at 15 days.

3.   Where reference is made to this paragraph, Articles 3 and 7 of Decision 1999/468/EC shall apply, having regard to the provisions of Article 8 thereof.

4.   The Committee shall adopt its rules of procedure.

## CHAPTER VII. FINAL PROVISIONS

**Article 16**

1.   Information available to the authorities of the Member States or the Commission relating to risks to consumer health and safety posed by products shall in general be available to the public, in accordance with the requirements of transparency and without prejudice to the restrictions required for monitoring and investigation activities. In particular the public shall have access to information on product identification, the nature of the risk and the measures taken.

However, Member States and the Commission shall take the steps necessary to ensure that their officials and agents are required not to disclose information obtained for the purposes of this Directive which, by its nature, is covered by professional secrecy in duly justified cases, except for information relating to the safety properties of products which must be made public if circumstances so require, in order to protect the health and safety of consumers.

2.   Protection of professional secrecy shall not prevent the dissemination to the competent authorities of information relevant for ensuring the effectiveness of market monitoring and surveillance activities. The authorities receiving information covered by professional secrecy shall ensure its protection.

**Article 17**

This Directive shall be without prejudice to the application of Directive 85/374/EEC.

**Article 18**

1.   Any measure adopted under this Directive and involving restrictions on the placing of a product on the market or requiring its withdrawal or recall must state the appropriate reasons on which it is based. It shall be notified as soon as possible to the party concerned and shall indicate the remedies available under the provisions in force in the Member State in question and the time limits applying to such remedies.

The parties concerned shall, whenever feasible, be given an opportunity to submit their views before the adoption of the measure. If this has not been done in advance because of the urgency of the measures to be taken, they shall be given such opportunity in due course after the measure has been implemented.

Measures requiring the withdrawal of a product or its recall shall take into consideration the need to encourage distributors, users and consumers to contribute to the implementation of such measures.

2. Member States shall ensure that any measure taken by the competent authorities involving restrictions on the placing of a product on the market or requiring its withdrawal or recall can be challenged before the competent courts.

3. Any decision taken by virtue of this Directive and involving restrictions on the placing of a product on the market or requiring its withdrawal or its recall shall be without prejudice to assessment of the liability of the party concerned, in the light of the national criminal law applying in the case in question.

### Article 19

1. The Commission may bring before the Committee referred to in Article 15 any matter concerning the application of this Directive and particularly those relating to market monitoring and surveillance activities.

2. Every three years, following 15 January 2004, the Commission shall submit a report on the implementation of this Directive to the European Parliament and the Council.

The report shall in particular include information on the safety of consumer products, in particular on improved traceability of products, the functioning of market surveillance, standardisation work, the functioning of RAPEX and Community measures taken on the basis of Article 13. To this end the Commission shall conduct assessments of the relevant issues, in particular the approaches, systems and practices put in place in the Member States, in the light of the requirements of this Directive and the other Community legislation relating to product safety. The Member States shall provide the Commission with all the necessary assistance and information for carrying out the assessments and preparing the reports.

### Article 20

The Commission shall identify the needs, possibilities and priorities for Community action on the safety of services and submit to the European Parliament and the Council, before 1 January 2003, a report, accompanied by proposals on the subject as appropriate.

### Article 21

1. Member States shall bring into force the laws, regulations and administrative provisions necessary in order to comply with this Directive with effect from 15 January 2004. They shall forthwith inform the Commission thereof.

When Member States adopt those measures, they shall contain a reference to this Directive or be accompanied by such reference on the occasion of their official publication. The methods of making such reference shall be laid down by Member States.

2. Member States shall communicate to the Commission the provisions of national law which they adopt in the field covered by this Directive.

### Article 22

Directive 92/59/EEC is hereby repealed from 15 January 2004, without prejudice to the obligations of Member States concerning the deadlines for transposition and application of the said Directive as indicated in Annex III.

References to Directive 92/59/EEC shall be construed as references to this Directive and shall be read in accordance with the correlation table in Annex IV.

**Article 23**
This Directive shall enter into force on the day of its publication in the Official Journal of the European Communities.

**Article 24**
This Directive is addressed to the Member States.

Done at Brussels, 3 December 2001.

## ANNEX I

### REQUIREMENTS CONCERNING INFORMATION ON PRODUCTS THAT DO NOT COMPLY WITH THE GENERAL SAFETY REQUIREMENT TO BE PROVIDED TO THE COMPETENT AUTHORITIES BY PRODUCERS AND DISTRIBUTORS

1. The information specified in Article 5(3), or where applicable by specific requirements of Community rules on the product concerned, shall be passed to the competent authorities appointed for the purpose in the Member States where the products in question are or have been marketed or otherwise supplied to consumers.

2. The Commission, assisted by the Committee referred to in Article 15, shall define the content and draw up the standard form of the notifications provided for in this Annex, while ensuring the effectiveness and proper functioning of the system. In particular, it shall put forward, possibly in the form of a guide, simple and clear criteria for determining the special conditions, particularly those concerning isolated circumstances or products, for which notification is not relevant in relation to this Annex.

3. In the event of serious risks, this information shall include at least the following:

(a) information enabling a precise identification of the product or batch of products in question;

(b) a full description of the risk that the products in question present;

(c) all available information relevant for tracing the product;

(d) a description of the action undertaken to prevent risks to consumers.

## ANNEX II

### PROCEDURES FOR THE APPLICATION OF RAPEX AND GUIDELINES FOR NOTIFICATIONS

1. RAPEX covers products as defined in Article 2(a) that pose a serious risk to the health and safety of consumers.

Pharmaceuticals, which come under Directives 75/319/EEC and 81/851/EEC, are excluded from the scope of RAPEX.

2. RAPEX is essentially aimed at a rapid exchange of information in the event of a serious risk. The guidelines referred to in point 8 define specific criteria for identifying serious risks.

3. Member States notifying under Article 12 shall provide all available details. In particular, the notification shall contain the information stipulated in the guidelines referred to in point 8 and at least:

(a) information enabling the product to be identified;

(b) a description of the risk involved, including a summary of the results of any tests/analyses and of their conclusions which are relevant to assessing the level of risk;

(c)   the nature and the duration of the measures or action taken or decided on, if applicable;

(d)   information on supply chains and distribution of the product, in particular on destination countries.

Such information must be transmitted using the special standard notification form and by the means stipulated in the guidelines referred to in point 8.

When the measure notified pursuant to Article 11 or Article 12 seeks to limit the marketing or use of a chemical substance or preparation, the Member States shall provide as soon as possible either a summary or the references of the relevant data relating to the substance or preparation considered and to known and available substitutes, where such information is available. They will also communicate the anticipated effects of the measure on consumer health and safety together with the assessment of the risk carried out in accordance with the general principles for the risk evaluation of chemical substances as referred to in Article 10(4) of Regulation (EEC) No 793/93 in the case of an existing substance or in Article 3(2) of Directive 67/548/EEC in the case of a new substance. The guidelines referred to in point 8 shall define the details and procedures for the information requested in that respect.

4.   When a Member State has informed the Commission, in accordance with Article 12(1), third subparagraph, of a serious risk before deciding to adopt measures, it must inform the Commission within 45 days whether it confirms or modifies this information.

5.   The Commission shall, in the shortest time possible, verify the conformity with the provisions of the Directive of the information received under RAPEX and, may, when it considers it to be necessary and in order to assess product safety, carry out an investigation on its own initiative. In the case of such an investigation, Member States shall supply the Commission with the requested information to the best of their ability.

6.   Upon receipt of a notification referred to in Article 12, the Member States are requested to inform the Commission, at the latest within the set period of time stipulated in the guidelines referred to in point 8, of the following:

(a)   whether the product has been marketed in their territory;

(b)   what measures concerning the product in question they may be adopting in the light of their own circumstances, stating the reasons, including any differing assessment of risk or any other special circumstance justifying their decision, in particular lack of action or of follow-up;

(c)   any relevant supplementary information they have obtained on the risk involved, including the results of any tests or analyses carried out.

The guidelines referred to in point 8 shall provide precise criteria for notifying measures limited to national territory and shall specify how to deal with notifications concerning risks which are considered by the Member State not to go beyond its territory.

7.   Member States shall immediately inform the Commission of any modification or lifting of the measure(s) or action(s) in question.

8.   The Commission shall prepare and regularly update, in accordance with the procedure laid down in Article 15(3), guidelines concerning the management of RAPEX by the Commission and the Member States.

9.   The Commission may inform the national contact points regarding products posing serious risks, imported into or exported from the Community and the European Economic Area.

10.   Responsibility for the information provided lies with the notifying Member State.

11.   The Commission shall ensure the proper functioning of the system, in particular classifying and indexing notifications according to the degree of urgency. Detailed procedures shall be laid down by the guidelines referred to in point 8.

# PART V
# CODES

CONTRACT CODE

**Drawn up on behalf of the English Law Commission**

*Introductory*

**1. Definition of contract**

A contract is an agreement between two or more persons which the law recognises as creating, altering or extinguishing legal rights and duties.

**2. Agreements which are contracts**

Every agreement is a contract except where—
  (a)   the terms of the agreement are too uncertain,
  (b)   the persons making the agreement do not intend to be legally bound by it, or
  (c)   the agreement lacks the necessary formal characteristics.

PART I. VALID CONTRACTS

FORMATION

*Agreement*

*General rules*

**11. Method of making agreement**

An agreement may be inferred from the written statements, the oral statements or the conduct of the parties, or from any combination of these.

**12. Agreement by offer and acceptance**

An agreement will be inferred whenever an offer is met by an acceptance which relates to the offer and assents to its terms.

**13. Agreement without offer and acceptance**

(1)   The existence of an agreement may be inferred even though there is no clearly identifiable offer and acceptance and even though the precise time at which the agreement is concluded cannot be identified.

(2)   The rules which follow as to the making of agreements by way of offer and acceptance apply, so far as circumstances permit, to agreements made without offer and acceptance.

**14. Communication in relation to offer and acceptance**

For the purpose of sections 15 to 27
  (a)   a communication shall be taken to have reached the person to whom it is addressed when it comes to his attention or to that of a person having his authority to receive it and, in the case of a written communication, when it comes into the possession of either of such persons or is delivered to any place authorised for the delivery of such a communication; and

(b) a communication may be cancelled or varied by a communication subsequently despatched which comes to the attention of the person to whom it is addressed or to that of any person having his authority to receive it before or at the same time as the former communication does.

*The offer*

### 15. Meaning of offer

(1) An offer is a statement of terms which the offeror proposes to the offeree as the basis of an agreement; coupled with a promise, express or implied, to adhere to those terms if the offer is accepted.

(2) An invitation to make an offer is a statement of terms for an agreement where no promise is made and where the person to whom it is made is himself invited to make an offer.

(3) An advertisement inviting performance of an act shall be presumed to be an offer but an advertisement not inviting performance of an act shall be presumed to be an invitation to make an offer.

### 16. Number of potential offerees

An offer may be made to a specific person, to a class of persons or to the general public.

### 17. Number of potential agreements

An offer may be made so as to invite a single acceptance thereby forming a single agreement or so as to invite a series of acceptances thereby forming as many agreements as there are acceptances.

### 18. Time when offer takes effect

An offer takes effect only when it reaches the offeree; and remains effective until it is revoked, is rejected or lapses.

### 19. Revocation

(1) An offer may be revoked except where
  (a) by the express terms of the offer, or
  (b) by implication from the circumstances, the preliminary negotiations, the practices which the parties have established between themselves or the customs and usages applicable to their relationship
the offer is irrevocable for a period which has not expired.

(2) A revocation takes effect when it reaches the offeree through a communication of the offeror at any time prior to either the acceptance of the offer or the despatch by the offeree of an acceptance of the offer.

### 20. Rejection

(1) An offer ceases to have effect on its rejection by the offeree, whether or not the rejection is coupled with a counter-offer, unless it is stipulated by the offeror that the offer will continue despite any rejection.

(2) A rejection of an offer may be made in any form but an ambiguous reply or a request for information or for a variation of the offer is not to be construed as a rejection.

(3) A rejection takes effect only when it reaches the offeror and is of no effect if an acceptance of the offer or a withdrawal of the rejection reaches the offeror before or at the same time as the original rejection.

### 21. Lapse

(1) An offer, whether revocable or irrevocable, lapses upon
  (a) the expiry of the specified period for acceptance or, where no time is specified, of a reasonable time;
  (b) the failure of an express or implied condition of acceptance.

(2) What is a reasonable time for acceptance is to be calculated from the

moment the offeror despatches his offer to the moment he receives a communication of acceptance, except that where the offer is delayed, and delay is the fault of the offeror and could not reasonably have been known to the offeree, the offer shall not lapse until the expiry of a reasonable time from the receipt of the offer.

(3)   In determining what is a reasonable time, regard shall be had to all the circumstances, including the nature of the transaction, custom and usage, and the rapidity of the means of communication employed by the offeror.

(4)   An offer does not lapse merely because the offeror or offeree dies or becomes incapable of contracting but only where the situation is so changed as to frustrate the purpose of the offer according to its terms.

*The acceptance*

## 22.   Meaning of acceptance

(1)   Acceptance of an offer is an assent by the offeree to its terms coupled, where relevant, with a promise, express or implied, by the offeree to fulfil any obligations which may fall upon him under the proposed contract.

(2)   Even though the assent is not express, it shall be inferred

(a)   where the terms of the offer require or permit the indication of assent by performance and the offeree starts or continues performance with the intention of accepting, or

(b)   where the offeree takes the benefit of an offered performance which he has had a reasonable opportunity to reject.

(3)   Assent is not to be inferred from a failure to reply to an offer merely because the offeror has indicated to the offeree that no communication of assent is required or that silence will be treated as assent, except where

(a)   the offeree intends by his silence to indicate assent, or

(b)   the parties have already agreed either expressly or by a course of dealing between them that there need be no communication of acceptance.

(4)   Where it is not clear whether an offer calls for an express assent or assent to be inferred from performance of an act, the offeree in accepting may choose between the two.

## 23.   Time when acceptance takes effect

An acceptance by express assent takes effect only when the communication of assent reaches the offeror and is of no effect if a withdrawal of the acceptance reaches the offeror before or at the same time as the original acceptance.

## 24.   Form and method of acceptance

Communication of acceptance may be in any form or by any method unless the offeror unambiguously states that he requires a special form or method, in which event acceptance by a different form or method shall not bind the offeror.

## 25.   Late and imperfect acceptance

(1)   An acceptance which is late or, being an acceptance which requires communication, is late in reaching the offeror or does not comply with a special form or method required may nevertheless be treated by the offeror as a valid acceptance.

(2)   Where the offeror is aware that an acceptance, if the system of transmission had been normal, would have reached him in due time, he shall be bound by the acceptance unless he promptly advises the acceptor by an appropriate communication that he regards the offer as having lapsed.

## 26.   Acceptances containing qualifications

A reply by the offeree which, while relating to the same subject matter as the offer, contains proposals which differ from those in the offer constitutes a rejection of the offer coupled with a counter-offer, except that

(a)   there is neither a rejection nor an acceptance if the offeree indicates that his proposal of different terms is an alternative offer not to be taken as a rejection of the original offer;

(b)   there is an acceptance if the different terms do not materially alter the terms of the offer unless the offeror promptly communicates his objection to the discrepancy and, if no such objection is communicated, the terms of the contract consist of the terms of the offer with the modifications contained in the acceptance.

### 27.   Potential acceptors

An offer can be accepted only by a person to whom it is made.

## *Certainty*

### 41.   Indefinite or incomplete agreements

An agreement is not a contract if its terms are indefinite or incomplete except where there is a reasonably certain basis, by reference to methods agreed by the parties or prescribed by law or custom, upon which the court can resolve the uncertainties and supply the omissions.

## *Intention to be legally bound*

### 51.   Agreements not intended to be legally binding

(1)   An agreement is not a contract where the parties do not intend to be legally bound by it; an intention to be legally bound is, however, presumed.

(2)   This presumption may be displaced

(a)   if the agreement is of a type the legal enforcement of which is not usually contemplated, or

(b)   by the words or conduct of the parties or the circumstances in which the agreement is made.

## *Form*

### 61.   Agreements not made in prescribed form

An agreement is not a contract where it is not in the form which a statute or custom makes mandatory for a contract to come into existence but otherwise an agreement is a contract in whatever form it is made.

### 62.   When contract created despite lack of form

(1)   An agreement which fails as a contract of one type through non-compliance with a requirement that such a contract be in writing or in a sealed writing may yet be a contract of another type.

(2)   An agreement which fails to comply with a requirement

(a)   that it be evidenced in writing or that it be in writing signed by the party against whom it is otherwise unenforceable, or

(b)   that it be in writing, without indication that failure to comply with the requirement of writing prevents a contract coming into existence

is a contract, but a defective one.

CONTENT

*Nature of a contract's provisions*

### 101.  Types of provision

(1)  A contract contains one or more of the following obligations:

(a)   promises as to future conduct of the contracting parties,

(b)   undertakings as to future events beyond the control of the contracting parties,

(c)   representations as to existing or past events, fact or law, and

(d)   obligations imposed by law or custom,

and may contain provisions suspending, ending or otherwise affecting the operation of the contract.

(2)  Each of the parties to a contract is bound to fulfil the obligations assumed by or imposed on him by the contract.

### 102.  Express provisions unknown to one contracting party

The express provisions of a contract include not only those to which each party has knowingly agreed but also any provisions which one party may reasonably assume the other to have accepted because:

(a)   they were included in a document signed as a memorandum of the contract by the other party, or

(b)   reasonable steps were taken to draw them to the other party's attention on or before the making of the contract.

### 103.  Representations

(1)  A representation, however expressed, as to an existing or past state of fact or law made by one contracting party to the other shall be presumed to be a provision of the contract, and hence constitute an undertaking as to the truth of the representation, where the contracting party to whom it was made reasonably relied on it in entering into the contract.

(2)  Factors relevant in determining whether it is reasonable for one contracting party to rely on a representation made by another are:

(a)   whether the representation is incorporated in any writing evidencing the contract, although the mere absence of such incorporation shall not preclude the representation from being a provision of the contract;

(b)   whether in the circumstances the advice of a person possessing expert knowledge or special skill is normally sought;

(c)   whether one contracting party has expert knowledge or special skill not possessed by the other; and

(d)   whether the representation was on a matter of importance to the contracting party to whom it was made.

(3)  A representation which is not a provision of the contract gives rise to no contractual remedy.

### 104.  Provisions not expressly stated in the contract

The express provisions of a contract are not exhaustive and provisions shall be implied:

(a)   when, in the light of the surrounding circumstances including the general law and any course of dealing between the parties, such provision must be taken to have been intended by the parties,

(b)   when required to enable the contract to operate reasonably,

(c)   when required by any applicable statute, trade custom or local usage.

### 105.  Incidence of promises and obligations

(1)  The parties to a contract may provide that the whole or any part of its provisions shall not come into operation until the occurrence of an event; the contract is already in existence and neither party can withdraw, but it is a

question of construction whether either party undertakes any obligation in respect of the occurrence of the event, although it shall be presumed that both undertake not unreasonably to hinder or prevent its occurrence.

(2)   The parties to a contract may provide that the whole or any part of its provisions shall cease to operate for the future upon the occurrence of an event; it is then a question of construction whether either party undertakes any obligation in respect of the occurrence of the event, but it shall be presumed that both undertake not unreasonably to cause or promote its occurrence.

(3)   The parties to a contract may provide that an obligation to perform one or more of the promises contained in the contract shall not arise before the occurrence of an event.

### 106.   Gradations of promises and obligations

Obligations of the contracting parties are of varying importance but the importance of an obligation is of no practical significance until breach or alleged breach and therefore falls to be ascertained only at that point in time.

*Contracting out of provisions*

### 107.   Freedom to contract out

Contracting parties are free to exclude from their contract, or limit the extent of, any obligation imposed by law except as provided in section 108.

### 108.   Limits upon contracting out

The exclusion or limitation by agreement between the parties of an obligation imposed by law is of no effect if such exclusion or limitation or reliance on it
  (a)   has been expressly prohibited by statute, or
  (b)   is held to be unreasonable by the court.

*Proving the contract's provisions*

### 109.   Oral modification of written contracts

Where contracting parties have reduced their agreement to writing there is a presumption that the whole contract is contained in the writing; but extraneous evidence, both oral and written, may be introduced to defeat this presumption.

### 110.   Oral evidence that contract inaccurately reduced to writing

Where the provisions of a contract are recorded inaccurately in writing and its true provisions can be established the contract shall be enforced in accordance with the true provisions.

*Interpreting the contract's provisions*

### 111.   Rules of interpretation

The words used by contracting parties are to be taken to be used in their natural meaning in the context in which they appear unless a special meaning is attributed to any of them by the parties themselves, or by trade custom or local usage not inconsistent with the words of the contract taken as a whole.

## PERFORMANCE

### 201.   Method of performance

(1)   Performance must be in accordance with the standards of fair dealing reasonably to be expected in the circumstances and, so far as is consistent with such standards, in accordance with the method agreed by the contracting parties.

(2)   Unless the contract expressly or by implication provides otherwise, then subject to the provisions of subsection (1)
  (a)   performance in several parts at different times is not permissible,

(b)   performance consisting in the payment of money must be in legal tender.

(3)   If in accordance with sub-section (1) payment by cheque or other negotiable instrument is permissible or required or if such instrument is accepted by the payee, then, unless otherwise agreed, performance takes place when the instrument is delivered to the payee or his agent authorised to receive it but is ineffective if the instrument is dishonoured.

## 202.   Alternative performances

(1)   Where a contract provides for money, property or services to be available for one of two or more periods of time without specifying which party has the choice between them, the choice is that of the party entitled to have the money, property or services made available to him.

(2)   Otherwise, where a contract provides for performance to be made in one of two or more different ways, it is a matter of construction which party has the choice between them.

## 203.   Appropriation of particular performance to particular contract

(1)   Where money is due from one party to another by virtue of two or more contractual obligations, the payer may, at the time he makes any payment, specifically appropriate it to any of such obligations, even if unenforceable or invalid, and the payee is then not entitled to treat the payment as performance of another such obligation.

(2)   Where the payer fails to make such an appropriation at the time of payment, the payee may at any time treat the payment as performance of whichever of the obligations he chooses, provided that the obligation is valid and enforceable, but once he has made such an appropriation he is not entitled afterwards to make a different appropriation.

(3)   Where neither payer nor payee makes any appropriation the payment is to be treated as performance of whichever of two valid and enforceable obligations is due for performance earlier in time or, if such obligations are due for performance at the same time, as proportionate part performance of each of them.

(4)   Such appropriation may be by words or conduct communicated to the other party.

## 204.   Demand for performance

Performance is due without being demanded unless the contract provides otherwise.

## 205.   Time for performance

(1)   Where a contract provides, expressly or by implication, for performance at or within a specified time, then subject to the provisions of section 201(1) performance must be at or within that time, but a provision for performance at a specified time may permit performance before that time has arrived.

(2)   Where no time for performance is specified, the contract must be performed within a reasonable time and, in deciding what is reasonable, custom, usage and the previous dealings of the parties may be taken into consideration.

(3)   Unless otherwise provided expressly or by implication, performance must be made at a reasonable hour.

## 206.   Place of performance

(1)   Where a contract provides, expressly or by implication, for performance at a particular place, then subject to the provisions of section 201(1) performance must be at that place.

(2)   Where no place for performance is specified, performance must be at whatever place is reasonable and in particular

(a)   performance of a promise to supply goods is satisfied by making them available to the recipient at the supplier's place of business at the time of contracting,

    (b)   performance of a promise to pay money is satisfied by making the payment at the payee's place of business at the time of contracting.

## 207. Tender of performance

(1)   Where one party's performance requires the concurrence of the other party for its completion, he must tender to the other unless the other has made it clear that he will not accept the tender.

(2)   Tender is an unqualified offer of exact performance, accompanied by production of the money or property necessary for such performance or, in the case of services, by readiness and ability to render them.

(3)   Tender of an inexact performance does not necessarily preclude the contracting party from subsequently tendering, or rendering, exact performance within the time permitted by the contract.

## 208. Performance other than by a contracting party

Except where the contract provides that a party shall perform his obligations personally or the nature of his performance is such as to require the application of skill, judgment or other qualifications personal to him

    (a)   a contracting party may delegate the performance required of him to another, and

    (b)   a contracting party's performance may be effected without his knowledge or consent by another.

## 209. Performance other than to the contracting party

A contracting party may render performance to the other party or to anyone whom the latter has authorised to receive performance, whether such person be indicated in the contract or not.

## 210. Requirement of performance terminated by agreement

(1)   The parties to a contract may, before it has been fully performed on both sides, agree to a release from the as yet unperformed obligations; further performance is not then required and the contract is at an end.

(2)   The parties to a contract may, before it has been fully performed on both sides, agree to alter its provisions in respect of the as yet unperformed obligations, whether by substituting a new contract bringing the original one to an end or by varying the original contract; whatever the degree of alteration, performance is then required only of the obligations as altered.

(3)   The new contract or the variation of the original contract may be in any form even if the original contract was by deed or made in writing but when such formality was required by law

    (a)   a new contract or a variation of the original contract must comply with the formality;

    (b)   the original contract may be terminated without formality where no new contract is substituted;

    (c)   the original contract remains in effect where the parties purport to substitute a new contract which is ineffective for lack of formality;

    (d)   a purported variation of the original contract which is ineffective only for lack of formality shall, where possible, take effect as a waiver in accordance with the provisions of section 211.

(4)   Where one party who has fully performed agrees to an alteration in the other party's as yet unperformed promises or other obligations, it is a question of construction whether he is agreeing to the substitution of new obligations in his favour in place of the original ones or only to abandon his entitlement in respect of the original obligations upon the performance of the new ones.

(5)   The provisions of this section apply whether the new agreement is

entered into after breach by one or both of the contracting parties or before breach by either contracting party.

### 211.  Requirement of performance terminated by waiver

A party to a contract cannot require due performance of the other party's obligations to the extent that, by words or conduct, he

(a)   has agreed with the other, or led the other reasonably to believe, that he will not insist upon due performance, or

(b)   has otherwise rendered it contrary to good faith for him to insist upon due performance;

such behaviour constitutes a waiver of the provisions in the original contract subject to their future reinstatement by the giving of reasonable notice, and until such reinstatement performance is required only of the obligations as altered.

### 212.  Requirement of performance terminated by notice

(1)   Where a contract expressly or impliedly provides that a party can cancel it, whether as to the future only or as from the start, he may bring the contract to an end by giving appropriate notice of cancellation to the other.

(2)   Where parties enter into a contract of such a nature that it will continue indefinitely until put an end to, it shall be presumed that either party may bring it to an end by giving appropriate notice of termination to the other.

(3)   Appropriate notice may require a period of notice and whether such a period is required and how long it must be depends

(a)   upon the express or implied provisions of the contract or any relevant statute, or

(b)   in the absence of any such provisions, upon custom and usage and what is reasonable in the light of all the circumstances existing at the time the notice is given.

## BREACH

### *Forms of breach*

### 301.  Failure to perform

A party to a contract who totally fails to perform any of the obligations which he is liable to perform or who performs late, or only in part, or in any other way which does not comply with his obligations commits a breach of contract.

### 302.  Unfulfilled undertakings

A party to a contract any of whose undertakings as to an event or to a state of fact or law is not duly fulfilled commits a breach of contract.

### 303.  Anticipation of non-performance

(1)   A party to a contract who, before the due time for performance of all or any of his contractual promises or other obligations, indicates a definite intention not to perform all or any separate and distinct part of them, or becomes unable to do so in circumstances not terminating the contract by frustration in accordance with sections 591 to 597, commits a breach of contract if the other party elects to treat such intention or inability as an immediate breach; this type of breach is called an anticipatory breach.

(2)   Such election by the other party

(a)   is precluded once the one who has declined or become unable to perform has, to the knowledge of the other party, reasserted his intention or regained his ability to perform;

(b)   is presumed where it would be unreasonable for him to continue with his own performance and so aggravate his loss;

(c)   otherwise requires words or conduct showing an unequivocal intention to treat the other party as in breach.

#### 304.  Failure to give assurance of performance
(1)  Where, before the due time for performance of all or any of the contractual promises or other contractual obligations of a party to a contract, the other party has reasonable grounds for believing that there may be a failure of performance in all or any separate part of them, he is entitled to request an assurance that future performance will be forthcoming in the proper manner and may then suspend his performance until a reasonable assurance is given to him.

(2)  The party to whom the request is made commits a breach of contract if the other elects to treat as an immediate breach any failure to provide a reasonable assurance within such time as is reasonable in all the circumstances.

#### 305.  Obstruction of other party's performance
A party to a contract who unreasonably prevents or obstructs the other party's performance commits a breach of contract.

*Effect of breach*

#### 306.  Substantial breach: relevance and definition
(1)  The effect of breach of contract depends upon whether it is substantial or not.

(2)  A breach of contract is substantial either where there is total non-performance by a contracting party or where there is such other failure to perform as to make it unreasonable to require the other party to continue with his own performance.

#### 307.  Effect of substantial breach
(1)  Where a breach of contract is substantial within the meaning given to that term by section 306, either the contract is automatically at an end if the consequences are such that, had the contract not been broken, it would have been frustrated or the victim of the breach is entitled to elect to treat it as at an end; in either case he may then both decline to accept any performance or further performance from the other party and refuse to perform or to continue performance of his own side of the contract.

(2)  The fact that the contract has been brought to an end does not affect the right to claim damages for the breach or prevent either party from claiming restitution of benefits conferred by him.

#### 308.  Duration of election given by substantial breach
It is too late for a contracting party to treat the contract as at an end once he has behaved in such a way as to indicate that he does not intend to do so despite a substantial breach.

#### 309.  Effect of breach which is not substantial
(1)  Where a breach of contract is not substantial within the meaning given to that term by section 306, the victim of the breach cannot treat the contract as at an end and remains under an obligation both to perform himself and to accept performance from the other party.

(2)  He is entitled only to seek specific enforcement of the contract or to claim damages for its breach.

#### 310.  Effect of breach on provisions excluding or limiting liability
It is a question of construction whether provisions of the contract designed to exclude or limit the liability of the party in breach apply to the particular breach which has occurred but, where the breach is substantial and either the contract is automatically at an end or the victim of the breach elects to treat it as an end, the party in breach cannot rely upon or enforce any such provision.

# REMEDIES

## *Specific Enforcement*

### *General rules as to availability of specific enforcement*

**401.  Entitlement as of right**
(1)  A party to a contract upon the other party's breach is entitled to an order requiring the other party specifically to perform his affirmative promises under the contract, subject to the limitations set out in sections 403 to 412.
(2)  No limitation upon the availability of the remedy arises from the sole fact that damages may appear to provide an adequate alternative remedy.
(3)  The granting of the remedy is not precluded by the existence of a provision in the contract for payment of a stipulated sum in the event of breach.

**402.  Terms, conditions and enforcement of order**
The court may make its order for specific enforcement of a contract unconditionally or grant it upon such terms and conditions as to mode of performance and otherwise as it considers reasonable, except that the court cannot impose criminal penalties for a failure to carry out its order.

### *Grounds of practicality and policy for refusing specific enforcement*

**403.  Impossibility of performance**
(1)  Specific enforcement of a contract will not be granted where it is impossible for the person against whom the claim is made to perform.
(2)  Specific enforcement of a contract will not be granted where the rights of third parties acquired in good faith make performance impossible without infringing those rights.

**404.  Right to withhold performance**
(1)  Specific enforcement is not available where the person against whom the claim is made is at the time entitled, although already in breach, to terminate the contract as to the future.
(2)  Where the person against whom the claim is made is entitled under the terms of the contract to choose between two or more different performances he retains that choice notwithstanding that he is in breach by failure to carry out any of them and specific enforcement will be granted only of the performance which he chooses.

**405.  Uncertainty of performance promised**
Specific enforcement is not available where the terms of the contract are not sufficiently precise to permit the formulation of a suitable order.

**406.  Difficulty of supervising performance**
Specific enforcement is not available where undue supervision would be necessary to ensure that the contractual performance is properly carried out.

**407.  Performance an infringement of personal freedom**
Specific enforcement is not available where it would force upon the parties to the contract an unduly close personal relationship and in particular where such relationship will involve one party in rendering personal services to the other against his will.

**408.  Hardship out of proportion to benefit of performance**
Specific enforcement is not available where it would occasion hardship to the person against whom the claim is made out of all proportion to the benefit likely to be gained by the claimant.

*Grounds relating to the claimant's performance for refusing specific enforcement*

### 409.  Claimant's own performance not assured

Specific enforcement of a contract is not available unless the court is satisfied that the person against whom the claim is made will not be left in the position of having performed his side of the contract without the claimant having performed his.

### 410.  Breach of claimant's own performance

Specific enforcement of a contract is not available where the claimant has committed a substantial breach of his own obligations under the contract but where his breach is minor specific enforcement is available to him subject to his paying compensation for the breach.

*Availability of partial specific enforcement*

### 411.  Partial specific enforcement with compensation for the remainder

Where specific enforcement of part of the promised performance cannot be granted because one or more of the grounds of practicality or policy for non-enforcement set out in sections 403 to 408 applies to it, specific enforcement of the remainder of the promised performance will still be granted together with the award of compensation for that part which cannot be enforced except in the limited circumstances set out in section 412.

### 412.  Limitations on partial specific enforcement

(1)  Specific enforcement of part of a contract will not be granted if the partial performance would be of no material benefit without performance of the remainder.

(2)  Specific enforcement of part of a contract will not be granted if this would produce hardship which would not have resulted from specific enforcement of the whole.

### Restraint of Breach

### 421.  General rule as to availability of restraint of breach

(1)  A party to a contract upon the other party's breach is entitled to an order requiring the other party to restrain from breach of his negative promises under the contract, whether such promises are express or implied, subject to the limitations set out in sections 403 to 412 and in section 422.

(2)  The provisions of section 401(2) and (3) and section 402 shall apply to claims for restraint of breach.

### 422.  Restraint an infringement of personal freedom

Where specific enforcement of an affirmative promise is prevented because it would impose restrictions on personal freedom within the meaning of section 407, restraint of breach of the promise which forms the negative side of such affirmative promise is not available unless the restrictions imposed by the negative promise only cover, or are only valid within, a sufficiently limited ambit as to afford the person in breach of the affirmative promise adequate scope and opportunity for rendering personal services elsewhere without being in breach of the negative promise.

### 423.  Ancillary orders

Where restraint of breach of a negative promise is available but the promise has been broken before the appropriate order has been obtained, the court may order the person in breach, in a suitable case, to remove the positive effects of his breach.

*Damages*

*General rules as to availability of damages*

### 431.  Entitlement to damages to compensate for loss

(1)  A party to a contract upon the other party's breach is entitled to damages to compensate him for loss resulting from the breach assessed in accordance with the rules set out in sections 434 to 448.

(2)  Damages are generally awarded by way of a lump sum of money expressed in sterling.

### 432.  No action for damages where no loss

No action for damages lies where the claimant fails to prove any loss resulting to him from the breach of contract.

### 433.  No award of damages beyond loss

Damages are not awarded for a breach of contract, however wilful, either as a punishment of the party in breach or as an example to others.

*General rules as to assessment of damages*

### 434.  Basic measure: loss of bargain

The governing object of damages is to place the claimant in the position, so far as money can do it, that he would have been in if the contract had been performed by both parties, but this basic entitlement of the claimant is subject to the limits set out in sections 436 to 440.

### 435.  Alternative measure: restoration of pre-contract position

(1)  As an alternative to damages calculated under section 434 the claimant is entitled to damages which will place him in the position, so far as money can do it, that he would have been in if the contract had never been made.

(2)  This alternative entitlement of the claimant is subject both to the limits set out in sections 436 to 440 and to the limit that damages so calculated must not place him in a better position than he would have been in if the contract had been fully performed by both parties, the burden of proving that the claimant would thus be placed in a better position being on the party against whom the claim is made.

*Limits placed on the availability and assessment of damages*

### 436.  Loss not caused by the breach

Damages are available only for loss caused by the breach of contract and the mere fact that loss would not have occurred but for the breach does not give an entitlement to damages.

### 437.  Unforeseeable loss

Damages are available only for loss which the party against whom the claim is made

(a)  foresaw or had reason to foresee at the time of contracting as liable to result from the breach of contract because its occurrence was a serious possibility, and

(b)  could reasonably be regarded as having contracted to be liable.

### 438.  Uncertain loss

(1)  Damages are available only for loss which is proved by the claimant and, where the amount of such loss is uncertain, are limited to a sum which is a fair assessment of the loss likely to arise.

(2)  Damages are available for the loss of the chance of realising a particular gain and are measured by the value of the chance at the time of breach.

### 439. Avoidable and avoided loss

(1) Damages are not available for loss which the claimant could have avoided by reasonable steps.

(2) Damages are not available for loss which the claimant has avoided by steps, taken before or after the breach, which are outside the requirements of sub-section (1).

(3) Damages are available for loss, and in particular for expenses, incurred in taking reasonable steps to avoid loss resulting from the breach both where the steps succeed in reducing the overall loss and also where they are unsuccessful and so either increase the overall loss or leave it unreduced.

(4) In deciding whether there has been a failure to take reasonable steps to avoid loss, the standard of reasonableness is not a rigorous one, requiring the claimant to incur neither undue financial risk nor undue personal humiliation, and the burden of proof lies upon the party in breach.

(5) Where the breach of contract consists of a repudiation before the due time for performance, the claimant is required to act reasonably from the time of repudiation.

### 440. Prospective loss

(1) Damages for loss resulting from a single breach of contract must be claimed in a single action but the court may postpone the assessment of damages for part or all of the loss which has not occurred at the time of judgment in the action.

(2) The claimant is not limited to a single action in the event of
    (a)   separate breaches of the contract, or
    (b)   a continuing breach of the contract,
but in an action brought for a separate breach damages are awarded for loss from that breach only and in an action brought for a continuing breach damages are awarded for loss down to the time of judgment in the action.

*Various general factors in the assessment of damages*

### 441. Taxation

(1) Where damages themselves not subject to tax are awarded in respect of the loss of an amount which would have been subject to tax, the court is entitled to take this into account in calculating the damages.

(2) Where damages are themselves subject to tax, the court is not entitled to increase the damages on that account.

### 442. Interest

Where the loss which the claimant has suffered as a result of the breach of contract includes deprivation of a specific sum of money, the court may award him damages by way of interest for any period from the time of breach but damages in these circumstances are not necessarily limited to an award of interest.

### 443. Legal expenses

(1) Damages are available for legal expenses reasonably incurred by the claimant in disputes between him and third parties which result from the breach of contract and which the party in breach at the time of contracting had reason to foresee as liable to result from the breach, except where to allow such compensation would be against public policy.

(2) Legal expenses to which this section applies are damages awarded, amounts agreed in settlement of damages claims, and costs both judicial and extra-judicial.

*Damages agreed by the parties in advance*

### 444. Damages agreed in advance generally recoverable
Where the parties to a contract agree in advance that a stipulated sum shall be payable on a breach of contract, then, subject to the provisions of sections 445 and 446, the stipulated sum is recoverable on breach, without proof of loss and irrespective of the amount of the provable loss.

### 445. Agreed damages greater than loss
If the party in breach proves that the stipulated sum is not only greater than but also manifestly disproportionate to the amount which could be recovered by the other party in the absence of a stipulated sum, then
    (a)  if the court is satisfied that in all the circumstances (which in this section are taken to include the circumstances at the time of contracting, breach and trial, and in particular to include any relevant commercial or trade practices and customs) it is reasonable for the stipulated sum to be recovered, the court shall award the stipulated sum;
    (b)  if the court is satisfied that in the circumstances at the time of contracting it was reasonable for the parties to agree that the stipulated sum should be payable on breach but that in all the circumstances it would be unreasonable for the whole stipulated sum to be recovered, the court shall substitute and award any lesser sum that it considers reasonable, even if the sum awarded would not have been recoverable under the general law relating to damages;
    (c)  otherwise the court shall award damages in the ordinary way as if there had been no agreement for the payment of a stipulated sum.

### 446. Agreed damages less than loss
If the stipulated sum proves to be less than the amount which could be recovered in the absence of a stipulated sum, the court shall nevertheless award the stipulated sum unless
    (a)  the limitation of recovery to the stipulated sum has been expressly prohibited by statute or is held to be unreasonable
    (b)  the claimant proves that the stipulated sum was intended to represent only the minimum amount recoverable.

### 447. Money payable on an event other than breach
Where a contract contains provisions either
    (a)  for the payment of a stipulated sum upon the determination of the contract other than by full performance, or
    (b)  for alternative modes of performance at least one of which is the payment of a stipulated sum, and the more onerous mode of performance involves a payment of money and is intended as a sanction to induce the less onerous mode of performance in any action claiming the stipulated sum the court shall have the same powers as it would have where the victim of a breach is claiming an agreed sum payable on breach.

### 448. Deposits and forfeiture clauses
Where a contract contains an express or implied provision that sums already paid or payable before breach, or before determination of the contract, or a part of them, are to be forfeited by the payer upon his breach or upon the contract's determination, in any action reclaiming sums so paid or claiming sums so payable the court shall have the same powers as it would have in an action claiming an agreed sum payable upon breach or upon determination.

*Restitution*

*Meaning and scope of restitution*

### 461. Restitution of benefits upon breach of contract

Where a contract has been broken, restitution is available to the parties in accordance with the rules set out in sections 462 to 471 in order to effect a return of benefits to the party conferring them, by an order for a sum of money representing their value or, where appropriate, for their specific restitution.

*General rules as to availability of restitution of benefits*

### 462. Restitution where the party against whom the claim is made is in substantial breach

(1) A party to a contract who is released from the duty of further performance by a substantial breach by the other party, or who at the time of such breach has already fully performed his side of the contract, is entitled to restitution of benefits already conferred by him on the other party in performing the contract to the extent that these benefits exceed any benefits conferred upon him by the other party in part performance.

(2) The provisions of this section do not apply, and no right to restitution exists, in relation to benefits conferred by the claimant in full performance of a separable part of a contract where the other party is not in substantial breach of that separate part but only of other parts of the contract.

### 463. Restitution where the claimant is himself in substantial breach

A party to a contract whose substantial breach of his obligations under it has led the other party properly to refuse performance, or to continue performance, is nevertheless entitled to restitution of benefits already conferred by him on the other party in performing the contract to the extent that these benefits exceed any loss suffered by the other party.

### 464. No restitution where neither party is in substantial breach

Restitution upon breach of contract is not available where neither party is in substantial breach of his obligations under the contract.

*Meaning and measurement of benefit*

### 465. Meaning of benefit

Anything received by a party to a contract in its performance constitutes a benefit conferred on him but expenditure incurred by a party to a contract in its performance does not in itself constitute a benefit conferred on the other party.

### 466. Contract consideration as a ceiling on benefit

(1) Where the benefit is conferred by the party in substantial breach, the measure of it cannot exceed such proportion of the consideration for full performance as the benefit conferred bears to the benefit that would have been conferred by full performance.

(2) No such limitation applies in measuring the benefit conferred by the party not in substantial breach.

### 467. Measurement of money benefit

Subject to the limitations of section 466, a benefit which consists of money is measured by an equivalent sum of money together with, where appropriate, interest at the commercial rate from the time of payment to the time of judgment.

### 468. Measurement of property benefit

Subject to the limitations of section 466, a benefit which consists of property is measured

(a)    where the property is retained, by the reasonable value of the interest transferred at the time of its transfer together with, where appropriate, a reasonable sum for the use of the property from the time of its transfer to the time of judgment, and

(b)    where the property is not retained, by a reasonable sum for the use of the property from the time of its transfer to the time when it is relinquished.

### 469.   Measurement of services benefit

Subject to the limitations of section 466, a benefit which consists of services is measured by the reasonable value of the services at the time they were rendered and received together with, where appropriate, interest at the commercial rate on that value from the time of receipt to the time of judgment.

*Specific restitution of property*

### 470.   Right of the victim of a substantial breach to require property to be returned to him

(1)    Where a party to a contract who is not in substantial breach is claiming restitution in respect of property transferred to the other party by him, he is entitled, subject to sub-section (3), to claim specific restitution of such property in lieu of claiming its value.

(2)    Where a claim for restitution is made against a party to a contract who is not in substantial breach and property has been transferred to the other party by him, he is entitled, subject to sub-section (3), to require the other party to make specific restitution to him of such property in lieu of a money deduction representing its value from the amount awarded against him by way of restitution.

(3)    If the court is satisfied that specific restitution of property to the victim of the substantial breach would cause disproportionate harm to the other party or would infringe upon the rights of third parties acquired in good faith, it may refuse to grant specific restitution or impose conditions upon its award.

### 471.   Right of the victim of a substantial breach to return property transferred to him

(1)    Where a party to a contract who is not in substantial breach is claiming restitution and has had property transferred by the other party to him, he is entitled, in lieu of retaining the property and suffering a money deduction in the amount awarded to him by way of restitution, to return the property provided that he has tendered it within a reasonable time of the other party's breach and provided that it is in substantially no worse condition than when received or that its deteriorated condition results from the other party's breach.

(2)    Where a claim for restitution is made against a party to a contract who is not in substantial breach in respect of property which has been transferred by the other party to him, he is entitled, in lieu of retaining the property and paying its value, to require the other party to accept its return provided that he tenders it within a reasonable time and provided that it is in substantially no worse condition than when received or that its deteriorated condition results from the other party's breach.

*Declarations*

### 481.   Declarations of breach of contract

A party to a contract upon the other party's breach is entitled to a judicial declaration that the other party has committed a breach of contract whether or not the claimant can prove that he has suffered any loss from the breach.

### 482.   Declarations as to matters other than breach

Where any question arises as to the existence or subsistence of a contract or as to the rights or obligations of the parties under the contract, either party is entitled to a judicial declaration resolving the question unless the court considers a declaration to be unnecessary.

### *Interrelation of Remedies*

#### 491.  Complementary nature of remedies
A claimant may be awarded any one remedy in conjunction with any one or more of the others except that the court cannot give two or more remedies which would result in benefits to the claimant exceeding his loss.

#### 492.  Election between remedies
The institution of a claim for one remedy does not in itself bar the claimant from pursuing another remedy, either by making a fresh claim or by amendment of the old, except
  (a)   where an election between substantive rights is thereby involved, or
  (b)   where the court is of the opinion that the party in breach is prejudiced by the claimant's vacillation.

## PART II. DEFECTIVE CONTRACTS

### *Introductory*

#### 501.  Defective contracts in general
Where a contract
  (a)   is illegal or is otherwise affected by public policy
  (b)   fails to comply with prescribed formalities
  (c)   is entered into by a person lacking full contractual capacity
  (d)   lacks the free consent of a contracting party because his field of choice is curtailed by pressure or influence
  (e)   lacks the full consent of a contracting party because he has misunderstood the contract
  (f)   is entered into under a common mistake as to existing circumstances
  (g)   is frustrated by changed circumstances after it has been entered into
it is not a nullity but is unenforceable, and gives rise to rights of restitution, to the extent provided in the following sections.

## CONTRACTS AFFECTED BY PUBLIC POLICY

### *Illegal Contracts*

#### 511.  General rule
Subject to the qualifications contained in sections 515 to 519, a contract which is illegal is unenforceable against either party to the contract and gives rise to no rights of restitution in respect of benefits conferred under it.

### *Types of illegality*

#### 512.  Definition of illegal contracts
  (1)   A contract
  (a)   declared to be illegal or unlawful, or otherwise specifically prohibited by statute, or
  (b)   to do something, or intended to enable something to be done, which is illegal.
  (2)   Something is illegal if it is forbidden by statute, is a common law wrong or is contrary to public policy.
  (3)   A contract is not rendered illegal solely by reason of the occurrence of a

breach of the law in the course of its performance; it will be illegal only if the law which is broken prohibits, expressly or by implication, that type of contract.

### 513.  Contracts illegal in formation or performance
A contract
    (a)   the making of which constitutes a criminal or civil wrong
    (b)   to commit a criminal or civil wrong
    (c)   to sell public offices
    (d)   to trade with the enemy or do other acts harmful to the state in its external affairs
    (e)   to abuse the legal process, interfere with the course of justice or oust the jurisdiction of the courts
    (f)   to make payments in consequence of the deliberate commission of a crime or of a civil wrong
    (g)   unreasonably to restrain a marriage
    (h)   to commit sexual immorality
    (i)   in unreasonable restraint of trade
    (j)   the making or performance of which would be manifestly contrary to public policy in any other way
is illegal.

### 514.  Contracts illegal in purpose
A contract which is intended by one or both of the contracting parties
    (a)   to assist in the commission of a crime
    (b)   to defraud the revenue or any other fiscal authority
    (c)   to enable sexual immorality to be practised
    (d)   unreasonably to restrict personal liberty, or to promote any of the acts listed in section 513, is illegal.

*Exceptional cases*

### 515.  Enforcement and restitution where one party innocent of the illegality
Where, whether through ignorance of the facts or of the law, a contracting party neither knows nor ought reasonably to have known that the contract is illegal, he may, if the other contracting party does know or ought reasonably to have known of the illegality,
    (a)   obtain specific enforcement of any severable part of the contract which can be performed without doing something that is illegal
    (b)   claim such compensation as will put both in the same position as if the contract had been performed
    (c)   claim restitution, including specific restitution, of benefits conferred by him in performing the contract subject to his restoring, specifically or otherwise and to the extent that the court thinks fit, benefits conferred on him under it.

### 516.  Restitution where both parties innocent of the illegality
Where, whether through ignorance of the facts or of the law, neither contracting party knows or ought reasonably to know that the contract is illegal, the contract, while remaining unenforceable against either contracting party, entitles both to restitution, including specific restitution, of benefits conferred under it.

### 517.  Restitution where one party less at fault than the other
A party to an illegal contract is entitled to restitution, including specific restitution, of benefits conferred by him in performing the contract subject to his restoring, specifically or otherwise and to the extent that the court thinks fit, benefits conferred on him in part performance where
    (a)   he repudiates the contract of his own volition before the com-

mencement of the performance of the illegal act or purpose and the illegality is not such as to make it contrary to public policy to allow restitution, or

(b)   his entry into the contract has been induced by fraud or by improper pressure or influence, or

(c)   he is one of the class of persons for whose protection statute has made the contract illegal.

### 518.   Restitution where no reliance on illegal contract

A party to an illegal contract is entitled to specific restitution of property where by the contract he has transferred only a limited interest in it and the limited interest

(a)   has expired, or

(b)   was given by way of security for the better enforcement of the contract and the illegality is not such as to make it contrary to public policy to allow specific restitution.

### 519.   Enforcement of part of illegal contract

(1)   Where a contract is illegal only because some provision in the contract falls within section 512(1)(b) the court may sever and enforce as if it were a separate contract the part of the contract which is not illegal, unless the illegality is such as to make it contrary to public policy to allow severance and enforcement.

(2)   The court is entitled to sever a contracting party's illegal promises from his legal promises and enforce the latter, whether the illegal promises are contained in a separate provision or from part of a single provision which it is necessary for the court to recast in order to excise the offending part.

*Other contracts affected by public policy*

### 521.   Contractual rights arising by virtue of an illegal act

Where a contract provides for rights to arise in favour of a contracting party upon the occurrence of an event, those rights are unenforceable by him if he has brought about the event by a consciously committed act which is illegal within the meaning of section 512(2) and it would be contrary to public policy to enforce them.

### 522.   Contracts unworthy of recognition by the law

Instead of declaring a contract to be illegal, a statute may on grounds of public policy provide that it will not be accorded recognition by the law: such a contract is unenforceable against either party to it and neither is entitled to restitution in respect of benefits conferred under it.

## CONTRACTS LACKING FORMALITIES

### 531.   General rule

(1)   A contract which

(a)   fails to comply with all or any of the formalities prescribed by a statute, whether as to the form of the contract or as to the evidence by which it shall be proved, and

(b)   is of a type for which the statute provides

(i)   in whatever form of words, that no action may be brought upon it against either contracting party or against a particular contracting party unless the prescribed formalities are complied with, or

(ii)   without specifying the effect of non-compliance or without indicating that non-compliance prevents a contract coming into existence, that it must comply with the prescribed formalities

is unenforceable against either contracting party or against the particular contracting party as the case may be, gives rise to no rights of restitution after full performance in respect of benefits conferred under it, but one or other contracting party may be entitled to restitution where the contract has only been performed in part.

(2)   Performance in part of a contract for the disposition of an interest in land, if consistent with the contract alleged and explicable only on the basis that some contract exists, acts as a substitute for the prescribed formality of writing and renders the contract fully enforceable.

### 532.   Rights of restitution
(1)   Except to the extent that the contrary is provided in existing or future statutes, where a contracting party who is entitled not to proceed with the contract fails to perform, the other contracting party, subject to his restoring, specifically or otherwise, benefits conferred on him under it, may claim restitution including specific restitution of benefit conferred by him under it.

(2)   Benefit is to be interpreted in accordance with section 465 and measured in accordance with sections 467 to 469.

### 533.   Limits to restitution
It is in the discretion of the court whether to order specific restitution or restitution in money and, in either case, whether to require the claimant to make specific restoration of benefits received or restoration of their value in money, and, in particular, if the court is satisfied that specific restitution or specific restoration would cause disproportionate harm to either party, it shall not order or require specific restitution or specific restoration.

## CONTRACTS LACKING CAPACITY

### *Minors*

### 541.   General rule
(1)   A contract made by a minor is unenforceable against him if it can be shown that enforcement would be unfair or unreasonable.

(2)   A minor is entitled to restitution of benefits conferred by him under a contract in accordance with sections 543 and 544 if it can be shown that it would be unfair or unreasonable to hold him to the contract.

(3)   The court may refuse to allow a particular provision of a contract to be enforced against a minor if satisfied that it would be unfair or unreasonable to enforce that provision against him, but in that event neither party is entitled to restitution of any benefits conferred by him under the contract except to the extent, if any, that the court may order and on such terms as it may direct.

(4)   Otherwise, a contract made by a minor is as effective as one made by an adult of full capacity and is enforceable by and against him.

### 542.   Criteria of unfairness or unreasonableness
In determining whether it would be unfair or unreasonable to enforce against the minor the contract or a particular provision of it or to hold the minor to the contract where he has wholly or partly performed it, all the circumstances shall be taken into account and in particular:

(a)   the nature and value of the benefits to which the minor is entitled under the contract;

(b)   the burden which the obligations of the contract impose upon the minor;

(c)   the actual and apparent ability of the minor to discharge those obligations;

(d)   the actual and apparent age and intelligence of the minor;

(e)   whether the minor's parent or guardian has consented to or approved the making of the contract;

(f) any misrepresentations made by the minor relating to any of the matters referred to in (c), (d) and (e).

### 543. Rights of restitution

(1) Where the minor is entitled to restitution of benefits under section 541(2), he may claim restitution, including specific restitution, of benefits conferred by him in performing the contract subject to his restoring, specifically or otherwise, benefits conferred on him under it.

(2) Where the minor fails to perform a contract which is unenforceable against him under section 541(1), the other contracting party, subject to his restoring, specifically or otherwise, benefits conferred on him under the contract, may claim restitution, including specific restitution, of benefits conferred by him under it, but the court may relieve the minor from liability in restitution to the extent, if any, that it thinks fit.

(3) Benefit is to be interpreted in accordance with section 465 and measured in accordance with sections 467 to 469.

### 544. Limits to restitution

(1) The minor is not entitled to restitution unless he claims it during minority or within a reasonable time after attaining majority.

(2) It is in the discretion of the court whether to order specific restitution or restitution in money and, in either case, whether to require the claimant to make specific restoration of benefits received or restoration of their value in money, and, in particular, if the court is satisfied that specific restitution or specific restoration would cause disproportionate harm to either party, it shall order or require specific restitution or specific restoration.

### 545. Enforceability after affirmation

(1) If the minor affirms the contract after attaining majority, it becomes fully binding upon him as to both performance already made or due and performance due in the future to the same extent as if made by a person of full capacity.

(2) Affirmation may be by express words or may be inferred from conduct.

### 546. Enforceability of guarantees

(1) Where the performance of a minor under a contract is guaranteed by a person of full capacity, the guarantee is enforceable against the guarantor whether or not the contract is enforceable against the minor.

(2) Where the contract is unenforceable against the minor, the guarantor, upon rendering due performance under the guarantee, is entitled to pursue such rights of restitution against the minor as were available to the other party to the contract.

(3) The fact that the other party to the contract has not himself pursued his rights of restitution against the minor in no way operates to release the guarantor from his obligations under the guarantee to the other party to the contract.

### 547. Liability in tort or delict

A minor shall not be liable in tort or delict for a misrepresentation of a type referred to in section 542(f) but otherwise a minor's liability in tort or delict is unaffected by the fact that the tort or delict was committed in connection with the formation or performance of a contract.

*Persons Mentally Affected*

### 551. General rule where no court control

(1) A contract made by a person mentally affected is unenforceable against him and he is entitled to restitution of benefits conferred by him under it if it

can be shown that at the time of contracting the other party was aware that he was mentally affected.

(2)   A person mentally affected is one who, by reason of mental disorder or the influence of drink or drugs, is incapable of understanding the nature and consequences of the contract or is prevented from acting reasonably in entering into the contract.

### 552.   General rule where court control
A contract made by a person who by reason of mental disorder has had his property and affairs placed under the control and management of the court, and which is not one which has been made on his behalf in accordance with the powers under Part VIII of the Mental Health Act 1959, is unenforceable against him and entitles him to claim restitution of benefits conferred by him under it.

### 553.   Rights of restitution
(1)   Where the person mentally affected is entitled to restitution of benefits under sections 551(1) or 552, he may claim restitution, including specific restitution, of benefits conferred by him in performing the contract subject to his restoring, specifically or otherwise, benefits conferred on him under it.

(2)   Where the person mentally affected fails to perform a contract which is unenforceable against him under sections 551(1) or 552, the other contracting party, subject to his restoring, specifically or otherwise, benefits conferred on him under the contract, may claim restitution, including specific restitution, of benefits conferred by him under it, but the court may relieve the person mentally affected from liability in restitution to the extent, if any, that it thinks fit.

(3)   Benefit is to be interpreted in accordance with section 465 and measured in accordance with sections 467 to 469.

### 554.   Limits to restitution
It is in the discretion of the court whether to order specific restitution or restitution in money and, in either case, whether to require the claimant to make specific restoration of benefits received or restoration of their value in money and, in particular, if the court is satisfied that specific restitution or specific restoration would cause disproportionate harm to either party, it shall not order or require specific restitution or specific restoration.

### 555.   Enforceability after affirmation
(1)   If the person mentally affected affirms the contract at a time when he is capable of understanding its nature and consequences and of acting reasonably in affirming it, it becomes fully binding upon him as to both performance already made or due and performance due in the future to the same extent as if made by a person of full capacity.

(2)   Affirmation may be by express words or may be inferred from conduct.

### 556.   Enforceability of guarantees
(1)   Where the performance of a person mentally affected under a contract is guaranteed by a person of full capacity, the guarantee is enforceable against the guarantor whether or not the contract is enforceable against the person mentally affected.

(2)   Where the contract is unenforceable against the person mentally affected, the guarantor, upon rendering due performance under the guarantee, is entitled to pursue such rights of restitution against the person mentally affected as were available to the other party to the contract.

(3)   The fact that the other party to the contract has not himself pursued his rights of restitution against the person mentally affected in no way operates to release the guarantor from his obligations under the guarantee to the other party to the contract.

## CONTRACTS LACKING FREE CONSENT

### 561.  General rule
A contract made by a person under improper pressure or influence, or because the circumstances permit improper economic advantage to be taken of him, is unenforceable against him and he is entitled to restitution of benefits conferred by him under it if the other contracting party has exerted, or at the time of contracting was aware of, the improper pressure or influence or has taken the improper economic advantage.

*Forms which lack of free consent may take*

### 562.  Improper pressure
Improper pressure may be exerted upon a contracting party in a number of ways, and in particular
    (a)  by actual or threatened unlawful physical violence against, or unlawful detention of, his person
    (b)  by actual or threatened unlawful damage to, or unlawful detention of, his property or unlawful withholding of money due to him
    (c)  by threats to prosecute him, to make him bankrupt, to force into liquidation a company with which he is substantially identified or to take other legal proceedings, wherever the threatened proceedings are unrelated to the matter to which the contract relates
and also by similar acts or threats of action against any other person.

### 563.  Improper influence
(1)  Improper influence is exerted upon a contracting party wherever there is a relationship of confidence between him and another person and that person exerts influence arising from the confidence reposed in him in order to take advantage of the contracting party.

(2)  Where the relationship between the contracting parties is that of parent and minor child, guardian and ward, solicitor and client, doctor and patient or spiritual adviser and pupil, the exertion of improper influence by the former is presumed unless the contrary is proved.

(3)  This presumption is displaced if the party in the position of confidence shows that the other, by reason of the receipt of adequate advice from an outside source or otherwise, acted with a free and independent mind in concluding the contract.

### 564.  Improper economic advantage
Improper economic advantage is taken of a contracting party where a person knows that he is under pressure of circumstances to enter into the contract and takes advantage of that pressure to obtain manifestly unfair terms.

*Remedial rights*

### 565.  Rights of restitution of protected party
(1)  Where the victim of the pressure or influence exerted or the economic advantage taken is entitled to restitution of benefits, he may claim restitution, including specific restitution, of benefits conferred by him in performing the contract subject to his restoring, specifically or otherwise, benefits conferred on him under it.

(2)  Benefit is to be interpreted in accordance with section 465 and measured in accordance with sections 467 to 469.

### 566.  Rights of restitution of other contracting party
(1)  Where the victim of the pressure or influence exerted or the economic advantage taken fails to perform the contract, the other contracting party, subject to his restoring, specifically or otherwise, benefits conferred on him under it,

may claim restitution, including specific restitution, of benefits conferred by him under it.

(2)  Benefit is to be interpreted in accordance with section 465 and measured in accordance with sections 467 to 469, except that the measurement of any benefit conferred by the other contracting party cannot exceed such proportion of the consideration for full performance as the benefit conferred bears to the benefit that would have been conferred by full performance.

### 567.  Limits to restitution
It is in the discretion of the court whether to order specific restitution or restitution in money and, in either case, whether to require the claimant to make specific restoration of benefits received or restoration of their value in money and, in particular, if the court is satisfied that specific restitution or specific restoration would cause disproportionate harm to either party, it shall not order or require specific restitution or specific restoration.

### 568.  Enforceability after affirmation
(1)  If, once the pressure upon the contracting party has been removed, the relationship of confidence placing him in a position to be influenced has come to an end or the circumstances placing him at an economic disadvantage have ceased to exist, he affirms the contract, it becomes fully binding upon him as to both performance already made or due and performance falling due in the future to the same extent as if pressure or influence had never been exerted on him or economic advantage taken of him.

(2)  Affirmation may be by express words or may be inferred from conduct.

## CONTRACTS LACKING FULL CONSENT

### 571.  General rule for unilateral mistake
(1)  Where, objectively interpreted, an agreement is sufficiently certain to be regarded as a valid contract but one contracting party is under a mistake as to
   (a)   the identity or characteristics of the other or
   (b)   the character, provisions or meaning of the contract
and he would not have entered into the contract but for the mistake, and the mistake is known or ought to have been known to the other contracting party, the contract is unenforceable against the mistaken party and he is entitled to restitution of benefits conferred by him under it, unless the mistake is of type (b) and the other contracting party is prepared to have the contract interpreted in the way in which it was understood by the mistaken party.

(2)  Otherwise, the existence of a mistake of one contracting party cannot affect a contract's validity.

### 572.  General rule for non-disclosure
Where, in making a contract, one party is in a relationship of confidence to the other or the contract is one whereby the other insures him against a risk, and he fails to disclose all facts known to him which are material to the contract or the risk, the contract is unenforceable against the other party and he is entitled to restitution of benefits conferred by him under it.

### 573.  Rights of restitution
(1)  Where a contracting party is entitled to restitution of benefits under section 571 or section 572, he may claim restitution, including specific restitution, of benefits conferred by him in performing the contract subject to his restoring, specifically or otherwise, benefits conferred on him under it.

(2)  Where a contracting party fails to perform a contract which is unenforceable against him under section 571 or section 572, the other party to the contract, subject to his restoring, specifically or otherwise, benefits conferred

on him under it, may claim restitution, including specific restitution, of benefits conferred by him under it.

(3)  Benefit is to be interpreted in accordance with section 465 and measured in accordance with sections 467 to 469.

### 574.  Limits to restitution

It is in the discretion of the court whether to order specific restitution or restitution in money and, in either case, whether to require the claimant to make specific restoration of benefits received or restoration of their value in money and, in particular, if the court is satisfied that specific restitution or specific restoration would cause disproportionate harm to either party, it shall not order or require specific restitution or specific restoration.

## CONTRACTS INITIALLY AFFECTED BY COMMON MISTAKE

### 581.  General rule

(1)  Where before a contract has been entered into
   (a)  the performance of a contracting party is impossible and neither contracting party knows of such impossibility or
   (b)  circumstances exist which are radically different from what both contracting parties believe them to be
then, unless in the case of impossibility one contracting party has assumed the risk of that impossibility, the contract is unenforceable against either and both are entitled to restitution and reimbursement of expenses so far as sections 585 to 587 allow.

(2)  Otherwise, the existence of a mistake common to both contracting parties cannot affect a contract's validity.

*Range of application*

### 582.  Performance impossible

Performance is impossible where under the contract
   (a)  acts are to be performed personally by either party to the contract or some other person and he is unable substantially to perform them because of his death or because of incapacity or unavailability in such circumstances that it is unlikely that he will be able substantially to perform them within a reasonable time
   (b)  a particular piece of property or property of a particular description is to be provided or made available by a contracting party if the contract is to be substantially performed and that property has been destroyed or become unavailable to that party in such circumstances that it is unlikely that he will be able substantially to perform within a reasonable time.

### 583.  Assumption of risk

It is a question of construction of the contract whether the risk of impossibility has been assumed by one party to the contract and, if so, by which party, and the fact that one of the contracting parties should have foreseen the impossibility as likely to result may be relevant in establishing that he has assumed the risk of its occurring.

### 584.  Radical difference in circumstances

Circumstances are radically different where it would be unfair to require a contracting party to perform, but the court may refuse him relief if the other contracting party is prepared to offer to enter into a contract on such terms as the court considers reasonable in the light of the true facts.

*Remedial rights*

### 585. Rights of restitution

(1) Where a contracting party is entitled to restitution of benefits under section 581, he may claim restitution, including specific restitution, of benefits conferred by him in performing the contract subject to his restoring, specifically or otherwise, benefits conferred on him under it.

(2) Where a contracting party fails to perform a contract which is unenforceable against him under section 581, the other party to the contract, subject to his restoring, specifically or otherwise, benefits conferred on him under it, may claim restitution, including specific restitution, of benefits conferred by him under it.

(3) Benefit is to be interpreted in accordance with section 465 and measured in accordance with sections 467 to 469.

### 586. Limits to restitution

It is in the discretion of the court whether to order specific restitution or restitution in money and, in either case, whether to require the claimant to make specific restoration of benefits received or restoration of their value in money and, in particular, if the court is satisfied that specific restitution or specific restoration would cause disproportionate harm to either party, it shall not order or require specific restitution or specific restoration.

### 587. Rights of reimbursement of expenses

(1) Except where the contract indicates a contrary intention, a party to a contract to which section 581 applies who is entitled to claim restitution and who has incurred expenditure in, or in connection with, its performance may claim reimbursement of such part of the expenditure, if any, as the court taking all the circumstances into account considers reasonable.

(2) Expenditure includes overhead expenses and the value of time and effort expended in performance of the contract.

## CONTRACTS SUBSEQUENTLY FRUSTRATED

### 591. General rule

Where a contract is frustrated because after it has been entered into

(a)   the performance of a contracting party becomes impossible or illegal and neither party can show that the other has assumed the risk of impossibility or illegality, or

(b)   a radical change of circumstances has occurred,

the parties are excused from the moment of frustration from further performance and are entitled to restitution and reimbursement of expenses so far as sections 598 and 599 allow.

*Range of application*

### 592. Performance impossible

Performance is impossible where under the contract

(a)   acts are to be performed personally by either party to the contract or some other person and he is unable substantially to perform them because of his death or because of incapacity or unavailability in such circumstances that it is unlikely that he will be able substantially to perform them within a reasonable time

(b)   a particular piece of property or property of a particular description is to be provided or made available by a contracting party if the contract is to be substantially performed and that property has been destroyed or become unavailable to that party in such circumstances that it is unlikely that he will be able substantially to perform within a reasonable time.

### 593. Performance illegal
Performance is illegal where a contracting party cannot substantially perform without committing an act which is illegal within the meaning of section 512(1)(b) and which is unlikely to become legal within a reasonable time.

### 594. Assumption of risk
(1)  It is a question of construction of the contract whether the risk of impossibility or illegality has been assumed by one party to the contract and, if so, by which party, but the fact that the impossibility or illegality was foreseen by the contracting parties or that they must, as reasonable men, have expected it as likely to result does not establish that either has assumed the risk of its occurring.

(2)  A party assumes the risk of impossibility where he brings it about by an unreasonable act or omission which was intended or likely to cause it to occur.

(3)  A party may not assume the risk of illegality where to do so would be contrary to public policy.

### 595. Radical change in circumstances
Circumstances have radically changed where it would be unfair for one contracting party to require the other to perform; and in determining whether it would be unfair account shall be taken of whether one contracting party has made a reasonable offer to modify the terms of the contract in the light of the changed circumstances and of the other party's response to that offer.

*Special cases*

### 596. Part illegality
Where a contracting party can substantially but not fully perform without committing an act which is illegal within section 512(1)(b), then, although he must not perform the act so long as it remains illegal, he is liable in damages for breach unless in the circumstances to impose such liability would be contrary to public policy.

### 597. Part frustration
(1)  Where a person has entered into more than one contract, whether with the same person or different persons, and performance of one or more but not all of the contracts has become impossible or illegal because of circumstances that would have frustrated a single contract if all the contracts had been one, then, except to the extent that he can show that there are sound commercial or other reasons why he should give preference to any such contract or contracts by rendering full performance or offering more than *pro rata* performance, he must offer the other party to each contract *pro rata* performance of it.

(2)  If any such offer is accepted within a reasonable time, the contract to which it relates continues in existence as so varied; otherwise it is frustrated.

*Remedial rights*

### 598. Rights of restitution
(1)  Except where the contract indicates a contrary intention, a party to a frustrated contract may claim restitution, including specific restitution, of benefits conferred by him in performing the contract subject to his restoring, specifically or otherwise, benefits conferred on him under it.

(2)  Benefit is to be interpreted in accordance with section 465 and measured in accordance with sections 467 to 469.

(3)  It is in the discretion of the court whether to order specific restitution or restitution in money and, in either case, whether to require the claimant to make specific restoration of benefits received or restoration of their value in money and, in particular, if the court is satisfied that specific restitution or

specific restoration would cause disproportionate harm to either party, it shall not order or require specific restitution or specific restoration.

**599.  Rights of reimbursement of expenses**
(1)  Except where the contract indicates a contrary intention, a party to a frustrated contract who has incurred expenditure in, or in connection with, its performance may claim reimbursement of such part of the expenditure, if any, as the court taking all the circumstances into account considers reasonable.
(2)  Expenditure includes overhead expenses and the value of time and effort expended in performance of the contract.

## PART III. THREE PARTY SITUATIONS

### MULTIPLE PARTY CONTRACTS

**601.  Application of Code provisions to multiple party contracts**
The preceding provisions of the Code apply to contracts between three or more persons; the rules set out in sections 603 to 606 are however particular to, and have relevance only for, multiple party contracts.

**602.  Types of multiple party contracts**
In contracts made between three or more persons
(a)  the same promises may be made by each contracting party to each other contracting party;
(b)  the same promises may be made by one or more contracting parties to the other contracting party or parties;
(c)  some promises may be made between some contracting parties and other promises between other contracting parties.

*Obligations incurred by more than one person*

**603.  Promises of the same performance and promises of different performances**
Where two or more persons promise another to render a performance
(a)  it is a question of construction of the contract whether the promisee or other intended beneficiary is entitled to that performance only once or to as many performances as there are promisors, but of these alternative constructions the first is to be presumed until the contrary is shown;
(b)  where this presumption prevails, it is a further question of construction whether the promisee or other intended beneficiary is entitled to claim that same performance from any of the promisors or only a *pro rata* share of it from each of them, but of these alternative constructions the first is to be presumed until the contrary is shown.

**604.  Consequences of promises of the same performance**
Where two or more persons promise another to render the same performance
(a)  they may be sued separately or together, whether all together or some together;
(b)  judgment against one or some does not, while unsatisfied, bar proceedings against the others;
(c)  the death of one leaves his estate liable on the contract to the same extent as if he had been the only promisor;
(d)  a defence of one is available to the others unless it is personal to him;
(e)  a release of one deprives the others of their rights of contribution or indemnity against him but releases them from liability to the extent that their rights of contribution or indemnity against him are cut down.

*Rights conferred on more than one person*

### 605. Promises of the same performance and promises of different performances

Where a person promises to render a performance to or for the benefit of two or more other persons

(a) it is a question of construction of the contract whether the promisees or beneficiaries are entitled to that performance only once or to as many performances as there are promisees or beneficiaries but of these alternative constructions the first is to be presumed until the contrary is shown;

(b) where this presumption prevails, it is a further question of construction whether each promisee or beneficiary is entitled to claim that same performance from the promisor or only a *pro rata* share of it but of these alternative constructions the second is to be presumed until the contrary is shown.

### 606. Consequences of promises of the same performance

Where a person promises to render the same performance to or for the benefit of two or more other persons

(a) they may sue separately or together, whether all together or some together;

(b) the death of one brings his entitlement to an end and his rights pass to the surviving promisees or beneficiaries until the last promisee or beneficiary is reached;

(c) a defence against one is available against the others unless it is personal to him;

(d) a release by one cuts off the rights of contribution and survivorship and cuts down *pro rata* the rights of the others to claim the full performance;

(e) performance to one is performance to all unless the contract provides otherwise.

## CONTRACTS CONCLUDED THROUGH AGENTS

*Creation of rights and duties in principal*

### 621. Agent with authority to contract

(1) Where, in negotiating a contract, a person is authorised to act for and is acting on behalf of another and it is apparent to the other negotiating party that such person is acting as agent on behalf of a principal, a contract is made between the principal and the other party unless it can be shown that the agent and the other party intended to contract only with each other.

(2) Where the other party is unaware, and it is not apparent, that the agent is acting on behalf of a principal, no contract is made between the principal and the other party.

### 622. Agent with apparent or usual authority to contract

Where the agent does not have authority to contract on behalf of the principal but the principal has acted so as to lead the other party to contract in the reasonable belief that

(a) the agent has such authority or

(b) the agent has power to enter into the contract on behalf of whomever turns out to be his principal

a contract is made between the principal and the other party.

### 623. Principal's affirmation of unauthorised contract

(1) Where an agent purports to contract on behalf of a principal at a time when he does not have actual, apparent or usual authority to do so, but his acts are later affirmed by the principal for whom he purported to contract or, where there is no such person, by any person to whom he offers the position of

principal in the contract he has negotiated, a contract is made between the principal and the other party.

(2) Affirmation may be by express words or may be inferred from conduct and must be within a reasonable time.

*Creation of rights and duties in agent*

### 624. Agent contracting personally

When the agent does not indicate to the other party that he is, or purports to be, acting on behalf of a principal, a contract is made between the agent and the other party; but where the agent does indicate to the other party that he is, or purports to be, acting on behalf of a principal, it is a question of construction whether a contract is made between the agent and the other party in addition to the contract made between the principal and the other party.

### 625. Agent misrepresenting authority

Where, in circumstances giving rise to no contract between the agent and the other party, the agent has represented to him, whether by representation of fact or law, that he has authority to contract on behalf of the principal but, because he has neither actual nor apparent authority, no contract is made between the principal and the other party, the agent is liable, if the other party has relied on the representation of authority, to pay him damages to the extent necessary to place him, subject to the rules of remoteness and mitigation of damage, into the position in which he would have been if the agent had had authority or, alternatively, had not misrepresented his authority.

## CREATION OF RIGHTS AND DUTIES IN THIRD PARTIES BY CONTRACT

*General rules as to creation of rights and duties*

### 641. Creation of rights in third parties

(1) The parties to a contract may by the contract create rights in a third party against a contracting party who has promised to confer a benefit on him.

(2) Rights thus created against a contracting party are governed by the contract and are valid only to the extent that it is valid, and may be conditional upon the other contracting party performing his obligations under it.

### 642. Rights which may be created

Rights which may be created in a third party extend

(a) to the right to receive the promised performance from the promisor and also to the right to pursue any remedies for delayed or defective performance, and

(b) to the right to rely on any provisions in the contract restricting or excluding the third party's liability to a contracting party

as if the third party were a party to the contract.

### 643. No creation of duties in third parties

The parties to a contract cannot by the contract impose duties on a third party but may impose conditions upon the enjoyment of any benefit by him.

*Method of creating rights*

### 644. Basic requirement: manifestation of intention

Rights are created in a third party where the parties to the contract agree to confer a benefit on him with the intention of entitling him to claim the performance and otherwise to enforce the promise for his benefit, but the creation of a right in a third party is not to be inferred from the mere fact that he will derive benefit from performance of the contract.

### 645.  Communication and acceptance

Neither communication of the promise to the third party nor agreement by him to accept it is necessary to confer rights on him.

### 646.  Ascertainment of third party

Rights may be created in a third party even though he is not in existence or ascertained at the time the contract is made.

### 647.  Time of creation, variation and cancellation

(1)   It is a question of construction whether the parties to the contract intend to create rights in the third party immediately or only upon the happening of a subsequent event.

(2)   Rights once created in a third party cannot be varied or cancelled by subsequent agreement without the concurrence of the third party unless the contract so permits expressly or by implication.

(3)   A power reserved by the parties to the contract to vary or cancel the third party's right is personal to the contractual promisee and cannot be exercised by his personal representatives on his death unless the contract otherwise provides expressly or by implication.

*Overlap of remedies*

### 648.  Overlap of remedies of third party and contractual promisee

The promisor's duty to perform is owed both to the third party and the contractual promisee but, so far as he makes performance to or is released from performance by the third party, he discharges his duty under the contract, and all remedies against him for any breach of the contract are available to the third party and may be pursued by him in preference to the contractual promisee.

### 649.  Overlap of remedies against promisor and contractual promisee

Where the promisor's performance is designed to discharge an existing obligation of the contractual promisee to the third party, the third party may pursue claims against either the promisor or the contractual promisee, and the third party's acceptance of benefits under the contract discharges his rights against the contractual promisee only to the extent that such obligation is thereby fulfilled.

## TRANSFER OF CONTRACTUAL RIGHTS AND DUTIES

*General rules as to transfer of rights and duties*

### 661.  Transfer of rights to third parties

(1)   Subject to the limitations set out in sections 663 to 665 a party to a contract may transfer to a third party the rights created in him by the contract so that the transferee acquires, and the transferor ceases to possess, the right to receive the performance due under the contract and to any remedies for its breach.

(2)   Except where the transfer is of rights under a negotiable instrument the transferee can acquire only such rights as the transferor himself has against the other party to the contract.

### 662.  No transfer of duties to third parties

A party to a contract cannot transfer to a third party the duties created in him by the contract so as to make the transferee liable to render the performance under the contract or to any remedies for its breach, but can only impose conditions upon the enjoyment of any benefit by him.

*Rights which may not be transferred*

### 663. Transfer prohibited or restricted by the contract
(1) A right cannot be transferred if the contract prohibits, or to the extent that the contract restricts, transfer.

(2) A contractual prohibition of transfer or restriction on transfer only prevents the transferee from acquiring rights against the promisor and does not prevent either the transferee from acquiring rights against the transferor or the promisor from discharging his duty by rendering performance to the transferee.

### 664. Transfer prohibited by public policy or statute
(1) A contractual right cannot be transferred if transfer is against public policy or forbidden by statute.

(2) Transfer of a right of action for damages for breach of contract is not against public policy except where damages for non-pecuniary loss can be recovered.

### 665. Transfer altering promisor's duty
(1) A right cannot be transferred if the nature of the right is such that the substitution of the transferee for the transferor would substantially alter the duty of the promisor under the contract.

(2) If the promisor consents to the transfer of the promisee's rights under the contract, this overrides any objection on his part that the transfer falls within the prohibition of sub-section (1).

*Method of transferring rights*

### 666. Basic requirement: manifestation of intention
Rights created by contract are transferred to a third party once the party to the contract has manifested his intention to make a present transfer of them, without his complying with any further requirements except to the extent indicated by the rules as to transfer of property generally.

### 667. Effect of notice to promisor
(1) After the promisor is notified of the transfer he becomes liable to the transferee if he renders performance to the transferor or in any other way fails to render performance to the transferee.

(2) Notification may be given by the transferor or transferee or the agent of either, may be in writing or oral, and is effective when communicated to the promisor.

*Particular types of transfer*

### 668. Partial transfer
Part of a right created by contract is as capable of transfer as the whole, except that the promisor in any claim made against him can insist that both transferor and transferee be joined wherever possible.

### 669. Conditional transfer
A right created by contract may be transferred conditionally as well as absolutely but the promisor in any claim made against him can insist that both transferor and transferee be joined wherever possible.

### 670. Transfer of conditional rights
A right created by contract which is in any way conditional, and in particular which is conditional upon the transferor performing his own obligations under the contract, is as capable of transfer as an absolute right.

### 671. Transfer of future rights
A right created by contract which is expected to arise out of a contract to be made in the future cannot be presently transferred but an attempt at present

transfer will operate as a transfer from the moment that the right comes into existence.

## Transfer by operation of law

### 672. Transfer on death
Subject to contrary agreement between the contracting parties, the death of either operates to transfer all his rights and duties arising out of the contract to his personal representatives, except that

(a) where damages for breach of contract would include compensation for non-pecuniary loss, the right to such damages does not survive the death of the contracting party entitled to them;

(b) where the contract is of a personal nature so that one party cannot transfer his rights under it and the other cannot delegate his duties under it, the death of either contracting party operates to transfer to his personal representatives only such rights and liabilities as have accrued before his death.

### 673. Transfer on bankruptcy
The adjudication in bankruptcy of a party to a contract operates to transfer all his rights and duties arising out of the contract to his trustee in bankruptcy, except that

(a) where damages for breach of contract would include compensation for non-pecuniary loss, the right to such damages remains with the contracting party entitled to them and is not transferred by his bankruptcy;

(b) where the contract is of a personal nature so that one party cannot transfer his rights under it and the other cannot delegate his duties under it, the bankruptcy of either contracting party operates to transfer to his trustee in bankruptcy only such rights and liabilities as have accrued before his bankruptcy and leaves unaccrued rights and liabilities remaining in the bankrupt.

## THE PRINCIPLES OF EUROPEAN CONTRACT LAW*

### CHAPTER 1. GENERAL PROVISIONS

### Section 1. Scope of the Principles

### Article 1.101. Application of the principles
(1) These Principles are intended to be applied as general rules of contract law in the European Union.

(2) These Principles will apply when the parties have agreed to incorporate them into their contract or that their contract is to be governed by them.

(3) These Principles may be applied when the parties:

(a) have agreed that their contract is to be governed by 'general principles of law', the 'lex mercatoria' or the like; or

(b) have not chosen any system or rules of law to govern their contract.

(4) These Principles may provide a solution to the issue raised where the system or rules of law applicable do not do so.

### Article 1.102. Freedom of contract
(1) Parties are free to enter into a contract and to determine its contents,

---

subject to the requirements of good faith and fair dealing, and the mandatory rules established by these Principles.

(2)   The parties may exclude the application of any of the Principles or derogate from or vary their effects, except as otherwise provided by these Principles.

### Article 1.103.   Mandatory law

(1)   Where the law otherwise applicable so allows, the parties may choose to have their contract governed by the Principles, with the effect that national mandatory rules are not applicable.

(2)   Effect should nevertheless be given to those mandatory rules of national, supranational and international law which, according to the relevant rules of private international law, are applicable irrespective of the law governing the contract.

### Article 1.104.   Application to questions of consent

(1)   The existence and validity of the agreement of the parties to adopt or incorporate these Principles shall be determined by these Principles.

(2)   Nevertheless, a party may rely upon the law of the country in which it has its habitual residence to establish that it did not consent if it appears from the circumstances that it would not be reasonable to determine the effect of its conduct in accordance with these Principles.

### Article 1.105.   Usages and practices

(1)   The parties are bound by any usage to which they have agreed and by any practice they have established between themselves.

(2)   The parties are bound by a usage which would be considered generally applicable by persons in the same situation as the parties, except where the application of such usage would be unreasonable.

### Article 1.106.   Interpretation and supplementation

(1)   These Principles should be interpreted and developed in accordance with their purposes. In particular, regard should be had to the need to promote good faith and fair dealing, certainty in contractual relationships and uniformity of application.

(2)   Issues within the scope of these Principles but not expressly settled by them are so far as possible to be settled in accordance with the ideas underlying the Principles. Failing this, the legal system applicable by virtue of the rules of private international law is to be applied.

### Article 1.107.   Application of the principles by way of analogy

These Principles apply with appropriate modifications to agreements to modify or end a contract, to unilateral promises and other statements and conduct indicating intention.

## Section 2. General duties

### Article 1.201.   Good faith and fair dealing

(1)   Each party must act in accordance with good faith and fair dealing.

(2)   The parties may not exclude or limit this duty.

### Article 1.202.   Duty to co-operate

Each party owes to the other a duty to co-operate in order to give full effect to the contract.

## Section 3. Terminology and other provisions

### Article 1.301.   Meaning of terms

In these Principles, except where the context otherwise requires:

(1)   'act' includes omission;

(2)   'court' includes arbitral tribunal;

(3)   an 'intentional' act includes an act done recklessly;

(4)   'non-performance' denotes any failure to perform an obligation under the contract, whether or not excused, and includes delayed performance, defective performance and failure to co-operate in order to give full effect to the contract;

(5)   a matter is 'material' if it is one which a reasonable person in the same situation as one party ought to have known would influence the other party in its decision whether to contract on the proposed terms or to contract at all;

(6)   'written' statements include communications made by telegram, telex, telefax and electronic mail and other means of communication capable of providing a readable record of the statement on both sides.

### Article 1.302.   Reasonableness

Under these Principles reasonableness is to be judged by what persons acting in good faith and in the same situation as the parties would consider to be reasonable. In particular, in assessing what is reasonable the nature and purpose of the contract, the circumstances of the case, and the usages and practices of the trades or professions involved should be taken into account.

### Article 1.303.   Notice

(1)   Any notice may be given by any means, whether in writing or otherwise, appropriate to the circumstances.

(2)   Subject to paragraphs (4) and (5), any notice becomes effective when it reaches the addressee.

(3)   A notice reaches the addressee when it is delivered to it or to its place of business or mailing address, or, if it does not have a place of business or mailing address, to its habitual residence.

(4)   If one party gives notice to the other because of the other's non-performance or because such non-performance is reasonably anticipated by the first party, and the notice is properly dispatched or given, a delay or inaccuracy in the transmission of the notice or its failure to arrive does not prevent it from having effect. The notice shall have effect from the time at which it would have arrived in normal circumstances.

(5)   A notice has no effect if a withdrawal of it reaches the addressee before or at the same time as the notice.

(6)   In this Article, 'notice' includes the communication of a promise, statement, offer, acceptance, demand, request or other declaration.

### Article 1.304.   Computation of time

(1)   A period of time set by a party in a written document for the addressee to reply or take other action begins to run from the date stated as the date of the document. If no date is shown, the period begins to run from the moment the document reaches the addressee.

(2)   Official holidays and official non-working days occurring during the period are included in calculating the period. However, if the last day of the period is an official holiday or official non-working day at the address of the addressee, or at the place where a prescribed act is to be performed, the period is extended until the first following working day in that place.

(3)   Periods of time expressed in days, weeks, months or years shall begin at 00.00 on the next day and shall end at 24.00 on the last day of the period; but any reply that has to reach the party who set the period must arrive, or other act which is to be done must be completed, by the normal close of business in the relevant place on the last day of the period.

### Article 1.305.   Imputed knowledge and intention

If any person who with a party's assent was involved in making a contract, or who was entrusted with performance by a party or who performed with its assent:

(a)    knew or foresaw a fact, or ought to have known or foreseen it; or
(b)    acted intentionally or with gross negligence, or not in accordance with
good faith and fair dealing,
this knowledge, foresight or behaviour is imputed to the party itself.

## CHAPTER 2. FORMATION

### Section 1. General provisions

### Article 2.101.  Conditions for the conclusion of a contract
(1)    A contract is concluded if:
(a)    the parties intend to be legally bound, and
(b)    they reach a sufficient agreement
without any further requirement.
(2)    A contract need not be concluded or evidenced in writing nor is it
subject to any other requirement as to form. The contract may be proved by any
means, including witnesses.

### Article 2.102.  Intention
The intention of a party to be legally bound by contract is to be determined
from the party's statements or conduct as they were reasonably understood by
the other party.

### Article 2.103.  Sufficient agreement
(1)    There is sufficient agreement if the terms:
(a)    have been sufficiently defined by the parties so that the contract can
be enforced, or
(b)    can be determined under these Principles.
(2)    However, if one of the parties refuses to conclude a contract unless the
parties have agreed on some specific matter, there is no contract unless
agreement on that matter has been reached.

### Article 2.104.  Terms not individually negotiated
(1)    Contract terms which have not been individually negotiated may be
invoked against a party who did not know of them only if the party invoking
them took reasonable steps to bring them to the other party's attention before or
when the contract was concluded.
(2)    Terms are not brought appropriately to a party's attention by a mere
reference to them in a contract document, even if that party signs the document.

### Article 2.105.  Merger clause
(1)    If a written contract contains an individually negotiated clause stating
that the writing embodies all the terms of the contract (a merger clause), any
prior statements, undertakings or agreements which are not embodied in the
writing do not form part of the contract.
(2)    If the merger clause is not individually negotiated it will only establish a
presumption that the parties intended that their prior statements, undertakings
or agreements were not to form part of the contract. This rule may not be
excluded or restricted.
(3)    The parties' prior statements may be used to interpret the contract. This
rule may not be excluded or restricted except by an individually negotiated
clause.
(4)    A party may by its statements or conduct be precluded from asserting a
merger clause to the extent that the other party has reasonably relied on them.

### Article 2.106.  Written modification only
(1)    A clause in a written contract requiring any modification or ending by
agreement to be made in writing establishes only a presumption that an

agreement to modify or end the contract is not intended to be legally binding unless it is in writing.

(2)   A party may by its statements or conduct be precluded from asserting such a clause to the extent that the other party has reasonably relied on them.

### Article 2.107.   Promises binding without acceptance
A promise which is intended to be legally binding without acceptance is binding.

## Section 2. Offer and Acceptance

### Article 2.201.   Offer
(1)   A proposal amounts to an offer if:
   (a)   it is intended to result in a contract if the other party accepts it, and
   (b)   it contains sufficiently definite terms to form a contract.
(2)   An offer may be made to one or more specific persons or to the public.
(3)   A proposal to supply goods or services at stated prices made by a professional supplier in a public advertisement or a catalogue, or by a display of goods, is presumed to be an offer to sell or supply at that price until the stock of goods, or the supplier's capacity to supply the service, is exhausted.

### Article 2.202.   Revocation of an offer
(1)   An offer may be revoked if the revocation reaches the offeree before it has dispatched its acceptance or, in cases of acceptance by conduct, before the contract has been concluded under Article 2.205(2) or (3).
(2)   An offer made to the public can be revoked by the same means as were used to make the offer.
(3)   However, a revocation of an offer is ineffective if:
   (a)   the offer indicates that it is irrevocable; or
   (b)   it states a fixed time for its acceptance; or
   (c)   it was reasonable for the offeree to rely on the offer as being irrevocable and the offeree has acted in reliance on the offer.

### Article 2.203.   Rejection
When a rejection of an offer reaches the offeror, the offer lapses.

### Article 2.204.   Acceptance
(1)   Any form of statement or conduct by the offeree is an acceptance if it indicates assent to the offer.
(2)   Silence or inactivity does not in itself amount to acceptance.

### Article 2.205.   Time of conclusion of the contract
(1)   If an acceptance has been dispatched by the offeree the contract is concluded when the acceptance reaches the offeror.
(2)   In case of acceptance by conduct, the contract is concluded when notice of the conduct reaches the offeror.
(3)   If by virtue of the offer, of practices which the parties have established between themselves, or of a usage, the offeree may accept the offer by performing an act without notice to the offeror, the contract is concluded when the performance of the act begins.

### Article 2.206.   Time limit for acceptance
(1)   In order to be effective, acceptance of an offer must reach the offeror within the time fixed by it.
(2)   If no time has been fixed by the offeror acceptance must reach it within a reasonable time.
(3)   In the case of an acceptance by an act of performance under article 2.205(3), that act must be performed within the time for acceptance fixed by the offeror or, if no such time is fixed, within a reasonable time.

### Article 2.207.  Late acceptance

(1)  A late acceptance is nonetheless effective as an acceptance if without delay the offeror informs the offeree that he treats it as such.

(2)  If a letter or other writing containing a late acceptance shows that it has been sent in such circumstances that if its transmission had been normal it would have reached the offeror in due time, the late acceptance is effective as an acceptance unless, without delay, the offeror informs the offeree that it considers its offer as having lapsed.

### Article 2.208.  Modified acceptance

(1)  A reply by the offeree which states or implies additional or different terms which would materially alter the terms of the offer is a rejection and a new offer.

(2)  A reply which gives a definite assent to an offer operates as an acceptance even if it states or implies additional or different terms, provided these do not materially alter the terms of the offer. The additional or different terms then become part of the contract.

(3)  However, such a reply will be treated as a rejection of the offer if:

    (a)  the offer expressly limits acceptance to the terms of the offer; or

    (b)  the offeror objects to the additional or different terms without delay; or

    (c)  the offeree makes its acceptance conditional upon the offeror's assent to the additional or different terms, and the assent does not reach the offeree within a reasonable time.

### Article 2.209.  Conflicting general conditions

(1)  If the parties have reached agreement except that the offer and acceptance refer to conflicting general conditions of contract, a contract is nonetheless formed. The general conditions form part of the contract to the extent that they are common in substance.

(2)  However, no contract is formed if one party:

    (a)  has indicated in advance, explicitly, and not by way of general conditions, that it does not intend to be bound by a contract on the basis of paragraph (1); or

    (b)  without delay, informs the other party that it does not intend to be bound by such contract.

(3)  General conditions of contract are terms which have been formulated in advance for an indefinite number of contracts of a certain nature, and which have not been individually negotiated between the parties.

### Article 2.210.  Professional's written confirmation

If professionals have concluded a contract but have not embodied it in a final document, and one without delay sends the other a writing which purports to be a confirmation of the contract but which contains additional or different terms, such terms will become part of the contract unless:

    (a)  the terms materially alter the terms of the contract, or

    (b)  the addressee objects to them without delay.

### Article 2.211.  Contracts not concluded through offer and acceptance

The rules in this section apply with appropriate adaptations even though the process of conclusion of a contract cannot be analysed into offer and acceptance.

## Section 3. Liability for Negotiations

### Article 2.301.  Negotiations contrary to good faith

(1)  A party is free to negotiate and is not liable for failure to reach an agreement.

(2)   However, a party who has negotiated or broken off negotiations contrary to good faith and fair dealing is liable for the losses caused to the other party.

(3)   It is contrary to good faith and fair dealing, in particular, for a party to enter into or continue negotiations with no real intention of reaching an agreement with the other party.

### Article 2.302.   Breach of confidentiality

If confidential information is given by one party in the course of negotiations, the other party is under a duty not to disclose that information or use it for its own purposes whether or not a contract is subsequently concluded. The remedy for breach of this duty may include compensation for loss suffered and restitution of the benefit received by the other party.

## CHAPTER 3. AUTHORITY OF AGENTS

### Section 1. General provisions

### Article 3.101.   Scope of the chapter

(1)   This Chapter governs the authority of an agent or other intermediary to bind its principal in relation to a contract with a third party.

(2)   This Chapter does not govern an agent's authority bestowed by law or the authority of an agent appointed by a public or judicial authority.

(3)   This Chapter does not govern the internal relationship between the agent or intermediary and its principal.

### Article 3.102.   Categories of representation

(1)   Where an agent acts in the name of a principal, the rules on direct representation apply (Section 2). It is irrelevant whether the principal's identity is revealed at the time the agent acts or is to be revealed later.

(2)   Where an intermediary acts on instructions and on behalf of, but not in the name of, a principal, or where the third party neither knows nor has reason to know that the intermediary acts as an agent, the rules on indirect representation apply (Section 3).

### Section 2. Direct Representation

### Article 3.201.   Express, implied and apparent authority

(1)   The principal's grant of authority to an agent to act in its name may be express or may be implied from the circumstances.

(2)   The agent has authority to perform all acts necessary in the circumstances to achieve the purposes for which the authority was granted.

(3)   A person is to be treated as having granted authority to an apparent agent if the person's statements or conduct induce the third party reasonably and in good faith to believe that the apparent agent has been granted authority for the act performed by it.

### Article 3.202.   Agent acting in exercise of its authority

Where an agent is acting within its authority as defined by article 3.201, its acts bind the principal and the third party directly to each other. The agent itself is not bound to the third party.

### Article 3.203.   Unidentified principal

If an agent enters into a contract in the name of a principal whose identity is to be revealed later, but fails to reveal that identity within a reasonable time after a request by the third party, the agent itself is bound by the contract.

### Article 3.204.   Agent acting without or outside its authority

(1)   Where a person acting as an agent acts without authority or outside the

scope of its authority, its acts are not binding upon the principal and the third party.

(2)   Failing ratification by the principal according to article 3.207, the agent is liable to pay the third party such damages as will place the third party in the same position as if the agent had acted with authority. This does not apply if the third party knew or could not have been unaware of the agent's lack of authority.

### Article 3.205.   Conflict of interest

(1)   If a contract concluded by an agent involves the agent in a conflict of interests of which the third party knew or could not have been unaware, the principal may avoid the contract according to the provisions of articles 4.112 to 4.116.

(2)   There is presumed to be a conflict of interest where:
   (a)   the agent also acted as agent for the third party; or
   (b)   the contract was with itself in its personal capacity.

(3)   However, the principal may not avoid the contract:
   (a)   if it had consented to, or could not have been unaware of, the agent's so acting; or
   (b)   if the agent had disclosed the conflict of interest to it and it had not objected within a reasonable time.

### Article 3.206.   Subagency

An agent has implied authority to appoint a subagent to carry out tasks which are not of a personal character and which it is not reasonable to expect the agent to carry out itself. The rules of this Section apply to the subagency; acts of the subagent which are within its and the agent's authority bind the principal and the third party directly to each other.

### Article 3.207.   Ratification by principal

(1)   Where a person acting as an agent acts without authority or outside its authority, the principal may ratify the agent's acts.

(2)   Upon ratification, the agent's acts are considered as having been authorised, without prejudice to the rights of other persons.

### Article 3.208.   Third party's right with respect to confirmation of authority

Where the statements or conduct of the principal gave the third party reason to believe that an act performed by the agent was authorised, but the third party is in doubt about the authorisation, it may send a written confirmation to the principal or request ratification from it. If the principal does not object or answer the request without delay, the agent's act is treated as having been authorised.

### Article 3.209.   Duration of authority

(1)   An agent's authority continues until the third party knows or ought to know that:
   (a)   the agent's authority has been brought to an end by the principal, the agent, or both; or
   (b)   the acts for which the authority had been granted have been completed, or the time for which it had been granted has expired; or
   (c)   the agent has become insolvent or, where a natural person, has died or become incapacitated; or
   (d)   the principal has become insolvent.

(2)   The third party is considered to know that the agent's authority has been brought to an end under paragraph (1)(a) above if this has been communicated or publicised in the same manner in which the authority was originally communicated or publicised.

(3)   However, the agent remains authorised for a reasonable time to perform

those acts which are necessary to protect the interests of the principal or its successors.

## Section 3. Indirect Representation

### Article 3.301.  Intermediaries not acting in the name of a principal
(1)   Where an intermediary acts:
    (a)   on instructions and on behalf, but not in the name, of a principal, or
    (b)   on instructions from a principal but the third party does not know and has no reason to know this,
the intermediary and the third party are bound to each other.
(2)   The principal and the third party are bound to each other only under the conditions set out in Articles 3.302 to 3.304.

### Article 3.302.  Intermediary's insolvency or fundamental non-performance to principal
If the intermediary becomes insolvent, or if it commits a fundamental non-performance towards the principal, or if prior to the time for performance it is clear that there will be a fundamental non-performance:
    (a)   on the principal's demand, the intermediary shall communicate the name and address of the third party to the principal; and
    (b)   the principal may exercise against the third party the rights acquired on the principal's behalf by the intermediary, subject to any defences which the third party may set up against the intermediary.

### Article 3.303.  Intermediary's insolvency or fundamental non-performance to third party
If the intermediary becomes insolvent, or if it commits a fundamental non-performance towards the third party, or if prior to the time for performance it is clear that there will be a fundamental non-performance:
    (a)   on the third party's demand, the intermediary shall communicate the name and address of the principal to the third party; and
    (b)   the third party may exercise against the principal the rights which the third party has against the intermediary, subject to any defences which the intermediary may set up against the third party and those which the principal may set up against the intermediary.

### Article 3.304.  Requirement of notice
The rights under Articles 3.302 and 3.303 may be exercised only if notice of intention to exercise them is given to the intermediary and to the third party or principal, respectively. Upon receipt of the notice, the third party or the principal is no longer entitled to render performance to the intermediary.

## CHAPTER 4. VALIDITY

### Article 4.101.  Matters not covered
This Chapter does not deal with invalidity arising from illegality, immorality or lack of capacity.

### Article 4.102.  Initial impossibility
A contract is not invalid merely because at the time it was concluded performance of the obligation assumed was impossible, or because a party was not entitled to dispose of the assets to which the contract relates.

### Article 4.103.  Mistake as to facts or law
(1)   A party may avoid a contract for mistake of fact or law existing when the contract was concluded if:
    (a) (i)   the mistake was caused by information given by the other party; or
        (ii)   the other party knew or ought to have known of the mistake and it

was contrary to good faith and fair dealing to leave the mistaken party in error; or

    (iii)   the other party made the same mistake, and

   (b)   the other party knew or ought to have known that the mistaken party, had it known the truth, would not have entered the contract or would have done so only on fundamentally different terms.

(2)   However a party may not avoid the contract if:

    (a)   in the circumstances its mistake was inexcusable, or

    (b)   the risk of the mistake was assumed, or in the circumstances should be borne, by it.

### Article 4.104.   Inaccuracy in communication

An inaccuracy in the expression or transmission of a statement is to be treated as a mistake of the person who made or sent the statement and Article 4.103 applies.

### Article 4.105.   Adaptation of contract

(1)   If a party is entitled to avoid the contract for mistake but the other party indicates that it is willing to perform, or actually does perform, the contract as it was understood by the party entitled to avoid it, the contract is to be treated as if it had been concluded as the that [*sic*] party understood it. The other party must indicate its willingness to perform, or render such performance, promptly after being informed of the manner in which the party entitled to avoid it understood the contract and before that party acts in reliance on any notice of avoidance.

(2)   After such indication or performance the right to avoid is lost and any earlier notice of avoidance is ineffective.

(3)   Where both parties have made the same mistake, the court may at the request of either party bring the contract into accordance with what might reasonably have been agreed had the mistake not occurred.

### Article 4.106.   Incorrect information

A party who has concluded a contract relying on incorrect information given it by the other party may recover damages in accordance with Article 4.117(2) and (3) even if the information does not give rise to a right to avoid the contract on the ground of mistake under Article 4.103, unless the party who gave the information had reason to believe that the information was correct.

### Article 4.107.   Fraud

(1)   A party may avoid a contract when it has been led to conclude it by the other party's fraudulent representation, whether by words or conduct, or fraudulent non-disclosure of any information which in accordance with good faith and fair dealing it should have disclosed.

(2)   A party's representation or non-disclosure is fraudulent if it was intended to deceive.

(3)   In determining whether good faith and fair dealing required that a party disclose particular information, regard should be had to all the circumstances, including:

    (a)   whether the party had special expertise;

    (b)   the cost to it of acquiring the relevant information;

    (c)   whether the other party could reasonably acquire the information for itself; and

    (d)   the apparent importance of the information to the other party.

### Article 4.108.   Threats

A party may avoid a contract when it has been led to conclude it by the other party's imminent and serious threat of an act:

    (a)   which is wrongful in itself, or

(b)   which it is wrongful to use as a means to obtain the conclusion of the contract, unless in the circumstances the first party had a reasonable alternative.

### Article 4.109.   Excessive benefit or unfair advantage

(1)   A party may avoid a contract if, at the time of the conclusion of the contract:

(a)   it was dependent on or had a relationship of trust with the other party, was in economic distress or had urgent needs, was improvident, ignorant, inexperienced or lacking in bargaining skill, and

(b)   the other party knew or ought to have known of this and, given the circumstances and purpose of the contract, took advantage of the first party's situation in a way which was grossly unfair or took an excessive benefit.

(2)   Upon the request of the party entitled to avoidance, a court may if it is appropriate adapt the contract in order to bring it into accordance with what might have been agreed had the requirements of good faith and fair dealing been followed.

(3)   A court may similarly adapt the contract upon the request of a party receiving notice of avoidance for excessive benefit or unfair advantage, provided that this party informs the party who gave the notice promptly after receiving it and before that party has acted in reliance on it.

### Article 4.110.   Unfair terms not individually negotiated

(1)   A party may avoid a term which has not been individually negotiated if, contrary to the requirements of good faith and fair dealing, it causes a significant imbalance in the parties' rights and obligations arising under the contract to the detriment of that party, taking into account the nature of the performance to be rendered under the contract, all the other terms of the contract and the circumstances at the time the contract was concluded.

(2)   This Article does not apply to:

(a)   a term which defines the main subject matter of the contract, provided the term is in plain and intelligible language; or to

(b)   the adequacy in value of one party's obligations compared to the value of the obligations of the other party.

### Article 4.111.   Third persons

(1)   Where a third person for whose acts a party is responsible, or who with a party's assent is involved in the making of a contract:

(a)   causes a mistake by giving information, or knows of or ought to have known of a mistake,

(b)   gives incorrect information,

(c)   commits fraud,

(d)   makes a threat, or

(e)   takes excessive benefit or unfair advantage,

remedies under this Chapter will be available under the same conditions as if the behaviour or knowledge had been that of the party itself.

(2)   Where any other third person:

(a)   gives incorrect information,

(b)   commits fraud,

(c)   makes a threat, or

(d)   takes excessive benefit or unfair advantage,

remedies under this Chapter will be available if the party knew or ought to have known of the relevant facts, or at the time of avoidance it has not acted in reliance on the contract.

### Article 4.112.   Notice of avoidance

Avoidance must be by notice to the other party.

**Article 4.113.  Time limits**
(1)  Notice of avoidance must be given within a reasonable time, with due regard to the circumstances, after the avoiding party knew or ought to have known of the relevant facts or became capable of acting freely.
(2)  However, a party may avoid an individual term under Article 4.110 if it gives notice of avoidance within a reasonable time after the other party has invoked the term.

**Article 4.114.  Confirmation**
If the party who is entitled to avoid a contract confirms it, expressly or impliedly, after it knows of the ground for avoidance, or becomes capable of acting freely, avoidance of the contract is excluded.

**Article 4.115.  Effect of avoidance**
On avoidance either party may claim restitution of whatever it has supplied under the contract, provided it makes concurrent restitution of whatever it has received. If restitution cannot be made in kind for any reason, a reasonable sum must be paid for what has been received.

**Article 4.116.  Partial avoidance**
If a ground of avoidance affects only particular terms of a contract, the effect of an avoidance is limited to those terms unless, giving due consideration to all the circumstances of the case, it is unreasonable to uphold the remaining contract.

**Article 4.117.  Damages**
(1)  A party who avoids a contract under this Chapter may recover from the other party damages so as to put the avoiding party as nearly as possible into the same position as if it had not concluded the contract, provided that the other party knew or ought to have known of the mistake, fraud, threat or taking of excessive benefit or unfair advantage.
(2)  If a party has the right to avoid a contract under this Chapter, but does not exercise its right, or has lost its right under the provisions of Articles 4.113 or 4.114, it may recover, subject to paragraph (1), damages limited to the loss caused to it by the mistake, fraud, threat or taking of excessive benefit or unfair advantage. The same measure of damages shall apply when the party was misled by incorrect information in the sense of Article 4.106.
(3)  In other respects, the damages shall be in accordance with the relevant provisions of Chapter 9, Section 5, with appropriate adaptations.

**Article 4.118.  Exclusion or restriction of remedies**
(1)  Remedies for fraud, threats and excessive benefit or unfair advantage-taking, and the right to avoid an unfair term which has not been individually negotiated, cannot be excluded or restricted.
(2)  Remedies for mistake and incorrect information may be excluded or restricted unless the exclusion or restriction is contrary to good faith and fair dealing.

**Article 4.119.  Remedies for non-performance**
A party who is entitled to a remedy under this Chapter in circumstances which afford that party a remedy for non-performance may pursue either remedy.

## CHAPTER 5. INTERPRETATION

**Article 5.101.  General rules of interpretation**
(1)  A contract is to be interpreted according to the common intention of the parties even if this differs from the literal meaning of the words.
(2)  If it is established that one party intended the contract to have a particular meaning, and at the time of the conclusion of the contract the other

party could not have been unaware of the first party's intention, the contract is to be interpreted in the way intended by the first party.

(3)   If an intention cannot be established according to (1) or (2), the contract is to be interpreted according to the meaning that reasonable persons of the same kind as the parties would give to it in the same circumstances.

### Article 5.102.   Relevant circumstances
In interpreting the contract, regard shall be had, in particular, to:

(a)   the circumstances in which it was concluded, including the preliminary negotiations;

(b)   the conduct of the parties, even subsequent to the conclusion of the contract;

(c)   the nature and purpose of the contract;

(d)   the interpretation which has already been given to similar clauses by the parties and the practices they have established between themselves;

(e)   the meaning commonly given to terms and expressions in the branch of activity concerned and the interpretation similar clauses may already have received;

(f)   usages; and

(g)   good faith and fair dealing.

### Article 5.103.   Contra proferentem rule
Where there is doubt about the meaning of a contract term not individually negotiated, an interpretation of the term against the party who supplied it is to be preferred.

### Article 5.104.   Preference to negotiated terms
Terms which have been individually negotiated take preference over those which are not.

### Article 5.105.   Reference to contract as a whole
Terms are to be interpreted in the light of the whole contract in which they appear.

### Article 5.106.   Terms to be given effect
An interpretation which renders the terms of the contract lawful, or effective, is to be preferred to one which would not.

### Article 5.107.   Linguistic discrepancies
Where a contract is drawn up in two or more language versions none of which is stated to be authoritative, there is, in case of discrepancy between the versions, a preference for the interpretation according to the version in which the contract was originally drawn up.

## CHAPTER 6. CONTENTS AND EFFECTS

### Article 6.101.   Statements giving rise to contractual obligations

(1)   A statement made by one party before or when the contract is concluded is to be treated as giving rise to a contractual obligation if that is how the other party reasonably understood it in the circumstances, taking into account:

(a)   the apparent importance of the statement to the other party;

(b)   whether the party was making the statement in the course of business; and

(c)   the relative expertise of the parties.

(2)   If one of the parties is a professional supplier who gives information about the quality or use of services or goods or other property when marketing or advertising them or otherwise before the contract for them is concluded, the statement is to be treated as giving rise to a contractual obligation unless it is

shown that the other party knew or could not have been unaware that the statement was incorrect.

(3) Such information and other undertakings given by a person advertising or marketing services, goods or other property for the professional supplier, or by a person in earlier links of the business chain, are to be treated as giving rise to a contractual obligation on the part of the professional supplier unless it did not know and had no reason to know of the information or undertaking.

### Article 6.102. Implied terms
In addition to the express terms, a contract may contain implied terms which stem from
  (a)   the intention of the parties,
  (b)   the nature and purpose of the contract, and
  (c)   good faith and fair dealing.

### Article 6.103. Simulation
When the parties have concluded an apparent contract which was not intended to reflect their true agreement, as between the parties the true agreement prevails.

### Article 6.104. Determination of price
Where the contract does not fix the price or the method of determining it, the parties are to be treated as having agreed on a reasonable price.

### Article 6.105. Unilateral determination by a party
Where the price or any other contractual term is to be determined by one party whose determination is grossly unreasonable, then notwithstanding any provision to the contrary, a reasonable price or other term shall be substituted.

### Article 6.106. Determination by a third person
(1) Where the price or any other contractual term is to be determined by a third person, and it cannot or will not do so, the parties are presumed to have empowered the court to appoint another person to determine it.

(2) If a price or other term fixed by a third person is grossly unreasonable, a reasonable price or term shall be substituted.

### Article 6.107. Reference to a non-existent factor
Where the price or any other contractual term is to be determined by reference to a factor which does not exist or has ceased to exist or to be accessible, the nearest equivalent factor shall be substituted.

### Article 6.108. Quality of performance
If the contract does not specify the quality, a party must tender performance of at least average quality.

### Article 6.109. Contract for an indefinite period
A contract for an indefinite period may be ended by either party by giving notice of reasonable length.

### Article 6.110. Stipulation in favour of a third party
(1) A third party may require performance of a contractual obligation when its right to do so has been expressly agreed upon between the promisor and the promisee, or when such agreement is to be inferred from the purpose of the contract or the circumstances of the case. The third party need not be identified at the time the agreement is concluded.

(2) If the third party renounces the right to performance the right is treated as never having accrued to it.

(3) The promisee may by notice to the promisor deprive the third party of the right to performance unless:

(a)   the third party has received notice from the promisee that the right has been made irrevocable, or

(b)   the promisor or the promisee has received notice from the third party that the latter accepts the right.

**Article 6.111.   Change of circumstances**

(1)   A party is bound to fulfil its obligations even if performance has become more onerous, whether because the cost of performance has increased or because the value of the performance it receives has diminished.

(2)   If, however, performance of the contract becomes excessively onerous because of a change of circumstances, the parties are bound to enter into negotiations with a view to adapting the contract or terminating it, provided that:

(a)   the change of circumstances occurred after the time of conclusion of the contract,

(b)   the possibility of a change of circumstances was not one which could reasonably have been taken into account at the time of conclusion of the contract, and

(c)   the risk of the change of circumstances is not one which, according to the contract, the party affected should be required to bear.

(3)   If the parties fail to reach agreement within a reasonable period, the court may:

(a)   terminate the contract at a date and on terms to be determined by the court; or

(b)   adapt the contract in order to distribute between the parties in a just and equitable manner the losses and gains resulting from the change of circumstances.

In either case, the court may award damages for the loss suffered through a party refusing to negotiate or breaking off negotiations contrary to good faith and fair dealing.

## CHAPTER 7. PERFORMANCE

**Article 7.101.   Place of performance**

(1)   If the place of performance of a contractual obligation is not fixed by or determinable from the contract it shall be:

(a)   in the case of an obligation to pay money, the creditor's place of business at the time of the conclusion of the contract;

(b)   in the case of an obligation other than to pay money, the obligor's place of business at the time of the conclusion of the contract.

(2)   If a party has more than one place of business, the place of business for the purpose of the preceding paragraph is that which has the closest relationship to the contract, having regard to the circumstances known to or contemplated by the parties at the time of conclusion of the contract.

(3)   If a party does not have a place of business its habitual residence is to be treated as its place of business.

**Article 7.102.   Time of performance**

A party has to effect its performance:

(1)   if a time is fixed by or determinable from the contract, at that time;

(2)   if a period of time is fixed by or determinable from the contract, at any time within that period unless the circumstances of the case indicate that the other party is to choose the time;

(3)   in any other case, within a reasonable time after the conclusion of the contract.

**Article 7.103.   Early performance**

(1)   A party may decline a tender of performance made before it is due

except where acceptance of the tender would not unreasonably prejudice its interests.

(2) A party's acceptance of early performance does not affect the time fixed for the performance of its own obligation.

### Article 7.104. Order of performance

To the extent that the performances of the parties can be rendered simultaneously, the parties are bound to render them simultaneously unless the circumstances indicate otherwise.

### Article 7.105. Alternative performance

(1) Where an obligation may be discharged by one of alternative performances, the choice belongs to the party who is to perform, unless the circumstances indicate otherwise.

(2) If the party who is to make the choice fails to do so by the time required by the contract, then:

    (a) if the delay in choosing is fundamental, the right to choose passes to the other party;

    (b) if the delay is not fundamental, the other party may give a notice fixing an additional period of reasonable length in which the party to choose must do so. If the latter fails to do so, the right to choose passes to the other party.

### Article 7.106. Performance by a third person

(1) Except where the contract requires personal performance the obligee cannot refuse performance by a third person if:

    (a) the third person acts with the assent of the obligor; or

    (b) the third person has a legitimate interest in performance and the obligor has failed to perform or it is clear that it will not perform at the time performance is due.

(2) Performance by the third person in accordance with paragraph (1) discharges the obligor.

### Article 7.107. Form of payment

(1) Payment of money due may be made in any form used in the ordinary course of business.

(2) A creditor who, pursuant to the contract or voluntarily, accepts a cheque or other order to pay or a promise to pay is presumed to do so only on condition that it will be honoured. The creditor may not enforce the original obligation to pay unless the order or promise is not honoured.

### Article 7.108. Currency of payment

(1) The parties may agree that payment shall be made only in a specified currency.

(2) In the absence of such agreement, a sum of money expressed in a currency other than that of the place where payment is due may be paid in the currency of that place according to the rate of exchange prevailing there at the time when payment is due.

(3) If, in a case falling within the preceding paragraph, the debtor has not paid at the time when payment is due, the creditor may require payment in the currency of the place where payment is due according to the rate of exchange prevailing there either at the time when payment is due or at the time of actual payment.

### Article 7.109. Appropriation of performance

(1) Where a party has to perform several obligations of the same nature and the performance tendered does not suffice to discharge all of the obligations, then subject to paragraph 4 the party may at the time of its performance declare to which obligation the performance is to be appropriated.

(2)   If the performing party does not make such a declaration, the other party may within a reasonable time appropriate the performance to such obligation as it chooses. It shall inform the performing party of the choice. However, any such appropriation to an obligation which:
(a)   is not yet due, or
(b)   is illegal, or
(c)   is disputed,
is invalid.

(3)   In the absence of an appropriation by either party, and subject to paragraph 4, the performance is appropriated to that obligation which satisfies one of the following criteria in the sequence indicated:
(a)   the obligation which is due or is the first to fall due;
(b)   the obligation for which the obligee has the least security;
(c)   the obligation which is the most burdensome for the obligor,
(d)   the obligation which has arisen first.
If none of the preceding criteria applies, the performance is appropriated proportionately to all obligations.

(4)   In the case of a monetary obligation, a payment by the debtor is to be appropriated, first, to expenses, secondly, to interest, and thirdly, to principal, unless the creditor makes a different appropriation.

### Article 7.110.   Property not accepted
(1)   A party who is left in possession of tangible property other than money because of the other party's failure to accept or retake the property must take reasonable steps to protect and preserve the property.

(2)   The party left in possession may discharge its duty to deliver or return:
(a)   by depositing the property on reasonable terms with a third person to be held to the order of the other party, and notifying the other party of this; or
(b)   by selling the property on reasonable terms after notice to the other party, and paying the net proceeds to that party.

(3)   Where, however, the property is liable to rapid deterioration or its preservation is unreasonably expensive, the party must take reasonable steps to dispose of it. It may discharge its duty to deliver or return by paying the net proceeds to the other party.

(4)   The party left in possession is entitled to be reimbursed or to retain out of the proceeds of sale any expenses reasonably incurred.

### Article 7.111.   Money not accepted
Where a party fails to accept money properly tendered by the other party, that party may after notice to the first party discharge its obligation to pay by depositing the money to the order of the first party in accordance with the law of the place where payment is due.

### Article 7.112.   Costs of performance
Each party shall bear the costs of performance of its obligations.

## CHAPTER 8. NON-PERFORMANCE AND REMEDIES IN GENERAL

### Article 8.101.   Remedies available
(1)   Whenever a party does not perform an obligation under the contract and the non-performance is not excused under Article 8.108, the aggrieved party may resort to any of the remedies set out in Chapter 9.

(2)   Where a party's non-performance is excused under Article 8.108, the aggrieved party may resort to any of the remedies set out in Chapter 9 except claiming performance and damages.

(3)   A party may not resort to any of the remedies set out in Chapter 9 to the extent that its own act caused the other party's non-performance.

### Article 8.102.   Cumulation of remedies
Remedies which are not incompatible may be cumulated. In particular, a party is not deprived of its right to damages by exercising its right to any other remedy.

### Article 8.103.   Fundamental non-performance
A non-performance of an obligation is fundamental to the contract if:

(a)   strict compliance with the obligation is of the essence of the contract; or

(b)   the non-performance substantially deprives the aggrieved party of what it was entitled to expect under the contract, unless the other party did not foresee and could not reasonably have foreseen that result; or

(c)   the non-performance is intentional and gives the aggrieved party reason to believe that it cannot rely on the other party's future performance.

### Article 8.104.   Cure by non-performing party
A party whose tender of performance is not accepted by the other party because it does not conform to the contract may make a new and conforming tender where the time for performance has not yet arrived or the delay would not be such as to constitute a fundamental non-performance.

### Article 8.105.   Assurance of performance
(1)   A party who reasonably believes that there will be a fundamental non-performance by the other party may demand adequate assurance of due performance and meanwhile may withhold performance of its own obligations so long as such reasonable belief continues.

(2)   Where this assurance is not provided within a reasonable time, the party demanding it may terminate the contract if it still reasonably believes that there will be a fundamental non-performance by the other party and gives notice of termination without delay.

### Article 8.106.   Notice fixing additional period for performance
(1)   In any case of non-performance the aggrieved party may by notice to the other party allow an additional period of time for performance.

(2)   During the additional period the aggrieved party may withhold performance of its own reciprocal obligations and may claim damages, but it may not resort to any other remedy. If it receives notice from the other party that the latter will not perform within that period, or if upon expiry of that period due performance has not been made, the aggrieved party may resort to any of the remedies that may be available under Chapter 9.

(3)   If in a case of delay in performance which is not fundamental the aggrieved party has given a notice fixing an additional period of time of reasonable length, it may terminate the contract at the end of the period of notice. The aggrieved party may in its notice provide that if the other party does not perform within the period fixed by the notice the contract shall terminate automatically. If the period stated is too short, the aggrieved party may terminate, or, as the case may be, the contract shall terminate automatically, only after a reasonable period from the time of the notice.

### Article 8.107.   Performance entrusted to another
A party who entrusts performance of the contract to another person remains responsible for performance.

### Article 8.108.   Excuse due to an impediment
(1)   A party's non-performance is excused if it proves that it is due to an impediment beyond its control and that it could not reasonably have been expected to take the impediment into account at the time of the conclusion of the contract, or to have avoided or overcome the impediment or its consequences.

(2)   Where the impediment is only temporary the excuse provided by this article has effect for the period during which the impediment exists. However, if the delay amounts to a fundamental non-performance, the obligee may treat it as such.

(3)   The non-performing party must ensure that notice of the impediment and of its effect on its ability to perform is received by the other party within a reasonable time after the non-performing party knew or ought to have known of these circumstances. The other party is entitled to damages for any loss resulting from the non-receipt of such notice.

### Article 8.109.   Clause excluding or restricting remedies

Remedies for non-performance may be excluded or restricted unless it would be contrary to good faith and fair dealing to invoke the exclusion or restriction.

## CHAPTER 9. PARTICULAR REMEDIES FOR NON-PERFORMANCE

### Section 1. Right to Performance

### Article 9.101.   Monetary obligations

(1)   The creditor is entitled to recover money which is due.

(2)   Where the creditor has not yet performed its obligation and it is clear that the debtor will be unwilling to receive performance, the creditor may nonetheless proceed with its performance and may recover any sum due under the contract unless:

(a)   it could have made a reasonable substitute transaction without significant effort or expense; or

(b)   performance would be unreasonable in the circumstances.

### Article 9.102.   Non-monetary obligations

(1)   The aggrieved party is entitled to specific performance of an obligation other than one to pay money, including the remedying of a defective performance.

(2)   Specific performance cannot, however, be obtained where:

(a)   performance would be unlawful or impossible; or

(b)   performance would cause the obligor unreasonable effort or expense; or

(c)   the performance consists in the provision of services or work of a personal character or depends upon a personal relationship, or

(d)   the aggrieved party may reasonably obtain performance from another source.

(3)   The aggrieved party will lose the right to specific performance if it fails to seek it within a reasonable time after it has or ought to have become aware of the non-performance.

### Article 9.103.   Damages not precluded

The fact that a right to performance is excluded under this Section does not preclude a claim for damages.

### Section 2. Withholding Performance

### Article 9.201.   Right to withhold performance

(1)   A party who is to perform simultaneously with or after the other party may withhold performance until the other has tendered performance or has performed. The first party may withhold the whole of its performance or a part of it as may be reasonable in the circumstances.

(2)   A party may similarly withhold performance for as long as it is clear that there will be a non-performance by the other party when the other party's performance becomes due.

## Section 3. Termination of the Contract

**Article 9.301.  Right to terminate the contract**

(1)   A party may terminate the contract if the other party's non-performance is fundamental.

(2)   In the case of delay the aggrieved party may also terminate the contract under Article 8.106(3).

**Article 9.302.  Contract to be performed in parts**

If the contract is to be performed in separate parts and in relation to a part to which a counter-performance can be apportioned, there is a fundamental non-performance, the aggrieved party may exercise its right to terminate under this Section in relation to the part concerned. It may terminate the contract as a whole only if the non-performance is fundamental to the contract as a whole.

**Article 9.303.  Notice of termination**

(1)   A party's right to terminate the contract is to be exercised by notice to the other party.

(2)   The aggrieved party loses its right to terminate the contract unless it gives notice within a reasonable time after it has or ought to have become aware of the non-performance.

(3)(a)   When performance has not been tendered by the time it was due, the aggrieved party need not give notice of termination before a tender has been made. If a tender is later made it loses its right to terminate if it does not give such notice within a reasonable time after it has or ought to have become aware of the tender.

 (b)   If, however, the aggrieved party knows or has reason to know that the other party still intends to tender within a reasonable time, and the aggrieved party unreasonably fails to notify the other party that it will not accept performance, it loses its right to terminate if the other party in fact tenders within a reasonable time.

(4)   If a party is excused under Article 8.108 through an impediment which is total and permanent, the contract is terminated automatically and without notice at the time the impediment arises.

**Article 9.304.  Anticipatory non-performance**

Where prior to the time for performance by a party it is clear that there will be a fundamental non-performance by it the other party may terminate the contract.

**Article 9.305.  Effects of termination in general**

(1)   Termination of the contract releases both parties from their obligation to effect and to receive future performance, but, subject to Articles 9.306 to 9.308, does not affect the rights and liabilities that have accrued up to the time of termination.

(2)   Termination does not affect any provision of the contract for the settlement of disputes or any other provision which is to operate even after termination.

**Article 9.306.  Property reduced in value**

A party who terminates the contract may reject property previously received from the other party if its value to the first party has been fundamentally reduced as a result of the other party's non-performance.

**Article 9.307.  Recovery of money paid**

On termination of the contract a party may recover money paid for a performance which it did not receive or which it properly rejected.

**Article 9.308.  Recovery of property**

On termination of the contract a party who has supplied property which can be returned and for which it has not received payment or other counter-performance may recover the property.

### Article 9.309.  Recovery for performance that cannot be returned
On termination of the contract a party who has rendered a performance which cannot be returned and for which it has not received payment or other counter-performance may recover a reasonable amount for the value of the performance to the other party.

## Section 4. Price Reduction

### Article 9.401.  Right to reduce price
(1)  A party who accepts a tender of performance not conforming to the contract may reduce the price. This reduction shall be proportionate to the decrease in the value of the performance at the time this was tendered compared to the value which a conforming tender would have had at that time.

(2)  A party who is entitled to reduce the price under the preceding paragraph and who has already paid a sum exceeding the reduced price may recover the excess from the other party.

(3)  A party who reduces the price cannot also recover damages for reduction in the value of the performance but remains entitled to damages for any further loss it has suffered so far as these are recoverable under Section 5 of this Chapter.

## Section 5. Damages and Interest

### Article 9.501.  Right to damages
(1)  The aggrieved party is entitled to damages for loss caused by the other party's non-performance which is not excused under Article 8.108.

(2)  The loss for which damages are recoverable includes:
  (a)   non-pecuniary loss; and
  (b)   future loss which is reasonably likely to occur.

### Article 9.502.  General measure of damages
The general measure of damages is such sum as will put the aggrieved party as nearly as possible into the position in which it would have been if the contract had been duly performed. Such damages cover the loss which the aggrieved party has suffered and the gain of which it has been deprived.

### Article 9.503.  Foreseeability
The non-performing party is liable only for loss which it foresaw or could reasonably have foreseen at the time of conclusion of the contract as a likely result of its non-performance, unless the non-performance was intentional or grossly negligent.

### Article 9.504.  Loss attributable to aggrieved party
The non-performing party is not liable for loss suffered by the aggrieved party to the extent that the aggrieved party contributed to the non-performance or its effects.

### Article 9.505.  Reduction of loss
(1)  The non-performing party is not liable for loss suffered by the aggrieved party to the extent that the aggrieved party could have reduced the loss by taking reasonable steps.

(2)  The aggrieved party is entitled to recover any expenses reasonably incurred in attempting to reduce the loss.

### Article 9.506.  Substitute transaction
Where the aggrieved party has terminated the contract and has made a substitute transaction within a reasonable time and in a reasonable manner, it

may recover the difference between the contract price and the price of the substitute transaction as well as damages for any further loss so far as these are recoverable under this Section.

### Article 9.507. Current price

Where the aggrieved party has terminated the contract and has not made a substitute transaction but there is a current price for the performance contracted for, it may recover the difference between the contract price and the price current at the time the contract is terminated as well as damages for any further loss so far as these are recoverable under this Section.

### Article 9.508. Delay in payment of money

(1) If payment of a sum of money is delayed, the aggrieved party is entitled to interest on that sum from the time when payment is due to the time of payment at the average commercial bank short-term lending rate to prime borrowers prevailing for the contractual currency of payment at the place where payment is due.

(2) The aggrieved party may in addition recover damages for any further loss so far as these are recoverable under this Section.

### Article 9.509. Agreed Payment for non-performance

(1) Where the contract provides that a party who fails to perform is to pay a specified sum to the aggrieved party for such non-performance, the aggrieved party shall be awarded that sum irrespective of its actual loss.

(2) However, despite any agreement to the contrary the specified sum may be reduced to a reasonable amount where it is grossly excessive in relation to the loss resulting from the non-performance and the other circumstances.

### Article 9.510. Currency by which damages are to be measured

Damages are to be measured by the currency which most appropriately reflects the aggrieved party's loss.

## UNIDROIT PRINCIPLES FOR INTERNATIONAL COMMERCIAL CONTRACTS*

### PREAMBLE (ex Arts. 1.1 and 1.2)

*(Purpose of the Principles)*

These Principles set forth general rules for international commercial contracts.
They shall be applied when the parties have agreed that their contract be governed by them.
They may be applied when the parties have agreed that their contract be governed by 'general principles of law', the 'lex mercatoria' or the like.

---

They may provide a solution to an issue raised when it proves impossible to establish the relevant rule of the applicable law.

They may be used to interpret or supplement international uniform law instruments.

They may serve as a model for national and international legislators.

## CHAPTER 1. GENERAL PROVISIONS

### 1.1. Freedom of contract
The parties are free to enter into a contract and to determine its content.

### 1.2. No form required
Nothing in these Principles requires a contract to be concluded in or evidenced by writing. It may be proved by any means, including witnesses.

### 1.3. Binding character of contract
A contract validly entered into is binding upon the parties. It can only be modified or terminated in accordance with its terms or by agreement or as otherwise provided under these Principles.

### 1.4. Mandatory rules
Nothing in these Principles shall restrict the application of mandatory rules, whether of national, international, or supranational origin, which are applicable in accordance with the relevant rules of private international law.

### 1.5. Exclusion or modification by the parties
The parties may exclude the application of these Principles or derogate from or vary the effect of any of their provisions, except as otherwise provided in the Principles.

### 1.6. Interpretation and supplementation of the Principles
(1) In the interpretation of these Principles, regard is to be had to their international character and to their purposes including the need to promote uniformity in their application.

(2) Issues within the scope of these Principles but not expressly settled by them are as far as possible to be settled in accordance with their underlying general principles.

### 1.7. Good faith and fair dealing
(1) Each party must act in accordance with good faith and fair dealing in international trade.

(2) The parties may not exclude or limit this duty.

### 1.8. Usages and practices
(1) The parties are bound by any usage to which they have agreed and by any practices which they have established between themselves.

(2) The parties are bound by a usage that is widely known to and regularly observed in international trade by parties in the particular trade concerned except where the application of such a usage would be unreasonable.

### 1.9. Notice
(1) Where notice is required it may be given by any means appropriate to the circumstances.

(2) A notice is effective when it reaches the person to whom it is given.

(3) For the purpose of paragraph (2) a notice 'reaches' a person when given to the person orally or delivered at that person's place of business or mailing address.

(4) For the purpose of this article 'notice' includes a declaration, demand, request or any other communication of intention.

### 1.10. Definitions
In these Principles
  —'court' includes arbitration tribunal;
  —where a party has more than one place of business the relevant 'place of business' is that which has the closest relationship to the contract and its performance, having regard to the circumstances known to or contemplated by the parties at any time before or at the conclusion of the contract.
  —'obligor' refers to the party who is to perform an obligation and 'obligee' refers to the party who is entitled to performance of that obligation.
  —'writing' means any mode of communication that preserves a record of the information contained therein and is capable of being reproduced in tangible form.

## CHAPTER 2. FORMATION

### 2.1. Manner of formation
A contract may be concluded either by the acceptance of an offer or by conduct of the parties that is sufficient to show agreement.

### 2.2. Definition of offer
A proposal for concluding a contract constitutes an offer if it is sufficiently definite and indicates the intention of the offeror to be bound in case of acceptance.

### 2.3. Withdrawal of offer
  (1)  An offer becomes effective when it reaches the offeree.
  (2)  An offer, even if it is irrevocable, may be withdrawn if the withdrawal reaches the offeree before or at the same time as the offer.

### 2.4. Revocation of offer
  (1)  Until a contract is concluded an offer may be revoked if the revocation reaches the offeree before it has dispatched an acceptance.
  (2)  However, an offer cannot be revoked
    (a)  if it indicates, whether by stating a fixed time for acceptance or otherwise, that it is irrevocable; or
    (b)  if it was reasonable for the offeree to rely on the offer as being irrevocable and the offeree has acted in reliance on the offer.

### 2.5. Rejection of offer
An offer is terminated when a rejection reaches the offeror.

### 2.6. Mode of acceptance
  (1)  A statement made by or other conduct of the offeree indicating assent to an offer is an acceptance. Silence or inactivity does not in itself amount to acceptance.
  (2)  An acceptance of an offer becomes effective at the moment the indication of assent reaches the offeror.
  (3)  However, if, by virtue of the offer or as a result of practices which the parties have established between themselves or of usage, the offeree may indicate assent by performing an act without notice to the offeror, the acceptance is effective at the moment the act is performed.

### 2.7. Time of acceptance
An offer must be accepted within the time the offeror has fixed or, if no time is fixed, within a reasonable time having regard to the circumstances, including the rapidity of the means of communication employed by the offeror. An oral offer must be accepted immediately unless the circumstances indicate otherwise.

### 2.8. Acceptance within a fixed period of time
  (1)  A period of time for acceptance fixed by the offeror in a telegram or a

letter begins to run from the moment the telegram is handed in for dispatch or from the date shown on the letter or, if no such date is shown, from the date shown on the envelope. A period of time for acceptance fixed by the offeror by means of instantaneous communication begins to run from the moment that the offer reaches the offeree.

(2)  Official holidays or non-business days occurring during the period for acceptance are included in calculating the period. However, if a notice of acceptance cannot be delivered at the address of the offeror on the last day of the period because that day falls on an official holiday or a non-business day at the place of business of the offeror, the period is extended until the first business day which follows.

### 2.9.  Late acceptance. Delay in transmission

(1)  A late acceptance is nevertheless effective as an acceptance if without undue delay the offeror so informs the offeree or gives a notice to that effect.

(2)  If a letter or other writing containing a late acceptance shows that it has been sent in such circumstances that if its transmission had been normal it would have reached the offeror in due time, the late acceptance is effective as an acceptance unless, without undue delay, the offeror informs the offeree that it considers the offer as having lapsed.

### 2.10.  Withdrawal of acceptance

An acceptance may be withdrawn if the withdrawal reaches the offeror before or at the same time as the acceptance would have become effective.

### 2.11.  Modified acceptance

(1)  A reply to an offer which purports to be an acceptance but contains additions, limitations or other modifications is a rejection of the offer and constitutes a counter-offer.

(2)  However, a reply to an offer which purports to be an acceptance but contains additional or different terms which do not materially alter the terms of the offer constitutes an acceptance, unless the offeror, without undue delay, objects to the discrepancy. If the offeror does not object, the terms of the contract are the terms of the offer with the modifications contained in the acceptance.

### 2.12.  Writings in confirmation

If a writing which is sent within a reasonable time after the conclusion of the contract and which purports to be a confirmation of the contract contains additional or different terms, such terms become part of the contract, unless they materially alter the contract or the recipient, without undue delay, objects to the discrepancy.

### 2.13.  Conclusion of contract dependent on agreement on specific matters or in a specific form

Where in the course of negotiations one of the parties insists that the contract is not concluded until there is agreement on specific matters or in a specific form, no contract is concluded before there is agreement on those matters or in that form.

### 2.14.  Contract with terms deliberately left open

(1)  If the parties intend to conclude a contract, the fact that they intentionally leave a term to be agreed upon in further negotiations or to be determined by a third person does not prevent a contract from coming into existence.

(2)  The existence of the contract is not affected by the fact that subsequently
  (a)  the parties reach no agreement on the term, or
  (b)  the third person does not determine the term,
provided that there is an alternative means of rendering the term definite that is reasonable in the circumstances, having regard to the intention of the parties.

### 2.15.   Negotiations in bad faith

(1)   A party is free to negotiate and is not liable for failure to reach an agreement.

(2)   However, a party who has negotiated or breaks off negotiations in bad faith is liable for the losses caused to the other party.

(3)   It is bad faith, in particular, for a party to enter into or continue negotiations when intending not to make an agreement with the other party.

### 2.16.   Duty of confidentiality

Where information is given as confidential by one party in the course of negotiations, the other party is under a duty not to disclose that information or to use it improperly for his own purposes, whether or not a contract is subsequently concluded. Where appropriate, the remedy for breach of that duty may include compensation based on the benefit received by the other party.

### 2.17.   Merger clauses

A contract in writing which contains a clause indicating that the writing completely embodies the terms on which the parties have agreed cannot be contradicted or supplemented by evidence of prior statement or agreements. However, such statements or agreements may be used to interpret the writing.

### 2.18.   Written modification clauses

A contract in writing which contains a clause requiring any modification or termination by agreement to be in writing may not be otherwise modified or terminated. However, a party may be precluded by its conduct from asserting such a clause to the extent that the other party has acted in reliance on that conduct.

### 2.19.   Contracting under standard terms

(1)   Where one party or both parties use standard terms in concluding a contract, the general rules on formation apply, subject to Articles 2.20–2.22.

(2)   Standard terms are provisions which are prepared in advance for general and repeated use by one party and which are actually used without negotiation with the other party.

### 2.20.   Surprising terms

(1)   No term contained in standard terms which is of such a character that the other party could not reasonably have expected it, is effective unless it has been expressly accepted by that party.

(2)   In determining whether a term is of such a character regard is to be had to its content, language and presentation.

### 2.21.   Conflict between standard terms and non-standard terms

In the case of conflict between a standard term and a term which is not a standard term the latter prevails.

### 2.22.   Battle of forms

Where both parties use standard terms and reach agreement except on those terms, a contract is concluded on the basis of the agreed terms and of any standard terms which are common in substance unless one party clearly indicates in advance, or later and without undue delay informs the other party that it does not intend to be bound by such a contract.

## CHAPTER 3. VALIDITY

### 3.1.   Matters not covered

These Principles do not deal with invalidity arising from
- (a)   lack of capacity;
- (b)   lack of authority;
- (c)   immorality or illegality.

### 3.2. Validity of mere agreement

A contract is concluded, modified or terminated by the mere agreement of the parties, without any further requirement.

### 3.3. Initial impossibility

(1) The mere fact that at the time of the conclusion of the contract the performance of the obligation assumed was impossible shall not affect the validity of the contract.

(2) The mere fact that at the time of the conclusion of the contract a party was not entitled to dispose of the assets to which the contract relates, does not affect the validity of the contract.

### 3.4. Definition of mistake

Mistake is an erroneous assumption relating to facts or to law existing when the contract was concluded.

### 3.5. Relevant mistake

(1) A party may only avoid the contract for mistake if, when the contract was concluded, the mistake was of such importance that a reasonable person in the same situation as the party in error would only have contracted the contract on materially different terms or would not have contracted at all if the true state of affairs had been known, and

(a) the other party made the same mistake, or caused the mistake, or knew or ought to have known of the mistake and it was contrary to reasonable commercial standards of fair dealing to leave the mistaken party in error; or

(b) the other party had not at the time of avoidance acted in reliance on the contract.

(2) However, a party may not avoid the contract, if

(a) it was grossly negligent in committing the mistake; or

(b) the mistake relates to a matter in regard to which the risk of mistake was assumed or, having regard to the circumstances, should be borne by the mistaken party.

### 3.6. Error in expression or transmission

An error occurring in the expression or transmission of a declaration is considered to be a mistake of the person from whom the declaration emanated.

### 3.7. Remedies for non-performance

A party is not entitled to avoid the contract on the ground of mistake if the circumstances on which that party relies afford, or could have afforded, him a remedy for non-performance.

### 3.8. Fraud

A party may avoid the contract when it has been led to conclude the contract by the other party's fraudulent representation, including language or practices, or fraudulent non-disclosure of circumstances which, according to reasonable commercial standards of fair dealing, the latter party should have disclosed.

### 3.9. Threat

A party may avoid the contract when he has been led to conclude the contract by the other party's unjustified threat which, having regard to the circumstances, is so imminent and serious as to leave the first party no reasonable alternative. In particular, a threat is unjustified if the act or omission with which a party has been threatened is wrongful in itself, or it is wrongful to use it as a means to obtain the conclusion of the contract.

### 3.10. Gross disparity

(1) A party may avoid a contract or an individual term of it if, at the time

of the conclusion of the contract, the contract or term unjustifiably gave the other party an excessive advantage. Regard is to be had, among other factors, to
    (a)   the fact that the other party has taken unfair advantage of the first party's dependence, economic distress or urgent needs, or of its improvidence, ignorance, inexperience or lack of bargaining skill; and
    (b)   the nature and purpose of the contract.
    (2)   Upon the request of the party entitled to avoidance, a court may adapt the contract or term in order to make it accord with reasonable commercial standards of fair dealing.
    (3)   A court may also adapt the contract or term upon the request of the party receiving notice of avoidance, provided that that party informs the other party of its request promptly after receiving such notice and before the other party has acted in reliance on it. The provisions of Article 3.13(2) apply accordingly.

### 3.11.  Third persons

    (1)   Where fraud, threat, gross disparity or a party's mistake is imputable to, or is known or ought to be known by, a third person for whose acts the other party is responsible, the contract may be avoided under the same conditions as if the behaviour or knowledge had been that of the party itself.
    (2)   Where fraud, threat or gross disparity is imputable to a third person for whose acts the other party is not responsible, the contract may be avoided if that party knew or ought to have known of the fraud, threat or disparity, or has not at the time of avoidance acted in reliance on the contract.

### 3.12.  Confirmation

If the party entitled to avoid the contract expressly or impliedly confirms the contract after the period of time for giving notice of avoidance has begun to run, avoidance of the contract is excluded.

### 3.13.  Loss of right to avoid

    (1)   If a party is entitled to avoid the contract for mistake but the other party declares itself willing to perform or performs the contract as it was understood by the party entitled to avoidance, the contract is considered to have been concluded as the latter party understood it. The other party must make such a declaration or render such performance promptly after having been informed of the manner in which the party entitled to avoidance had understood the contract and before that party has acted in reliance on a notice of avoidance.
    (2)   After such a declaration or performance the right to avoidance is lost and any earlier notice of avoidance is ineffective.

### 3.14.  Notice of avoidance

The right of a party to avoid the contract is exercised by notice to the other party.

### 3.15.  Time limits

    (1)   Notice of avoidance shall be given within a reasonable time, having regard to the circumstances, after the avoiding party knew or could not have been unaware of the relevant facts or became capable of acting freely.
    (2)   Where an individual term of the contract may be avoided by a party under Article 3.10, the period of time for giving notice of avoidance begins to run when that term is asserted by the other party.

### 3.16.  Partial avoidance

If a ground of avoidance affects only individual terms of the contract, the effect of avoidance is limited to those terms unless, having regard to the circumstances, it is unreasonable to uphold the remaining contract.

### 3.17.  Retroactive effect of avoidance
(1)  Avoidance takes effect retroactively.
(2)  On avoidance either party may claim restitution of whatever it has supplied under the contract or the part of it avoided, provided that it concurrently makes restitution of whatever it has received under the contract or the part of it avoided or, if it cannot make restitution in kind, it must make an allowance for what it has received.

### 3.18.  Damages
Irrespective of whether or not the contract has been avoided, the party who knew or ought to have known of the ground for avoidance is liable for damages so as to put the other party into the same position in which it would have been if it had not concluded the contract.

### 3.19.  Mandatory character of the provisions
The provisions of this Chapter are mandatory, except insofar as they relate to the binding force of mere agreement, initial impossibility or mistake.

### 3.20.  Unilateral declarations
The provisions of this Chapter apply with appropriate adaptations to any communication of intention addressed by one party to the other.

## CHAPTER 4. INTERPRETATION

### 4.1.  Intention of parties
(1)  A contract shall be interpreted according to the common intention of the parties.
(2)  If such an intention cannot be established, the contract shall be interpreted according to the meaning that reasonable persons of the same kind as the parties would give to it in the same circumstances.

### 4.2.  Interpretation of statements and other conduct
(1)  The statements and other conduct of a party shall be interpreted according to that party's intention if the other party knew or could not have been unaware of that intention.
(2)  If the preceding paragraph is not applicable, such statements and other conduct shall be interpreted according to the meaning that a reasonable person of the same kind as the other party would give to it in the same circumstances.

### 4.3.  Relevant circumstances
(1)  In applying Articles 4.1 and 4.2, regard shall be had to all the circumstances, including
  (a)  any preliminary negotiations between the parties;
  (b)  any practices which the parties have established between themselves;
  (c)  any conduct of the parties subsequent to the conclusion of the contract;
  (d)  the nature and purpose of the contract;
  (e)  the meaning commonly given to terms and expressions in the trade concerned; and
  (f)  usages.

### 4.4.  Reference to contract or statement as a whole
Terms and expressions shall be interpreted in the light of the whole contract or statement in which they appear.

### 4.5.  All terms to be given effect
Contract terms shall be interpreted so as to give effect to all the terms rather than to deprive some of them of effect.

### 4.6. *Contra proferentem* rule

If contract terms supplied by one party are unclear, an interpretation against that party is preferred.

### 4.7. Linguistic discrepancies

Where a contract is drawn up in two or more language versions which are equally authoritative there is, in case of discrepancy between the versions, a preference for the interpretation according to the version in which the contract was originally drawn up.

### 4.8. Supplying an omitted term

(1) Where the parties to a contract have not agreed with respect to a term which is important for a determination of their rights and duties, a term which is appropriate in the circumstances shall be supplied.

(2) In determining what is an appropriate term regard shall be had, among other factors, to
    (a)   the intention of the parties;
    (b)   the nature and purpose of the contract;
    (c)   good faith and fair dealing;
    (d)   reasonableness.

## CHAPTER 5. CONTENT

### 5.1. Express and implied obligations

The contractual obligations of the parties may be express or implied.

### 5.2. Implied obligations

Implied obligations stem from
    (a)   the nature and purpose of the contract;
    (b)   practices established between the parties and usages;
    (c)   good faith and fair dealing;
    (d)   reasonableness.

### 5.3. Co-operation between the parties

Each party shall co-operate with the other party, when such co-operation may reasonably be expected for the performance of that party's obligations.

### 5.4. Duty to achieve a specific result, duty of best efforts

(1) To the extent that an obligation of a party involves a duty to achieve a specific result, that party is bound to achieve that result.

(2) To the extent that an obligation of a party involves a duty of best efforts in the performance of an activity, that party is bound to make such efforts as would be made by a reasonable person of the same kind in the same circumstances.

### 5.5. Determination of kind of duty involved

In determining the extent to which an obligation of a party involves a duty of best efforts in the performance of an activity or a duty to achieve a specific result, regard shall be had, among other factors, to
    (a)   the way in which the obligation is expressed in the contract;
    (b)   the contractual price and other terms of the contract;
    (c)   the degree of risk normally involved in achieving the expected result;
    (d)   the ability of the other party to influence the performance of the obligation.

### 5.6. Determination of quality of performance

Where the quality of performance is neither fixed by, nor determinable from, the contract, a party is bound to render a performance of a quality that is reasonable and not less than average in the circumstances.

### 5.7.  Price determination

(1)  Where a contract does not fix or make provision for determining the price, the parties are considered, in the absence of any indication to the contrary, to have made reference to the price generally charged at the time of the conclusion of the contract for such performance under comparable circumstances in the trade concerned or, if no such price is available, to a reasonable price.

(2)  Where the price is to be determined by one party and that determination is manifestly unreasonable, a reasonable price shall be substituted notwithstanding any contract term to the contrary.

(3)  Where the price is to be fixed by a third person, and that person cannot or will not do so, the price shall be a reasonable price.

(4)  Where the price is to be fixed by reference to factors which do not exist or have ceased to exist or to be accessible, the nearest equivalent factor shall be treated as a substitute.

### 5.8.  Contract for an indefinite period

A contract for an indefinite period may be ended by either party by giving notice a reasonable time in advance.

## CHAPTER 6. PERFORMANCE

### Section 1. Performance in General

### 6.1.1.  Time of performance

A party must perform its obligations:

(a)  if a time is fixed by or determinable from the contract, at that time;

(b)  if a period of time is fixed by or determinable from the contract, at any time within that period unless circumstances indicate that the other party is to choose a time; or

(c)  in any other case, within a reasonable time after the conclusion of the contract.

### 6.1.2.  Performance at one time or in instalments

In cases under Article 6.1.1(b) or (c), a party must perform its obligations at one time if that performance can be rendered at one time and the circumstances do not indicate otherwise.

### 6.1.3.  Partial performance

(1)  The obligee may reject an offer to perform in part at the time performance is due, whether or not such offer is coupled with an assurance as to the balance of the performance, unless the obligee has no legitimate interest in so doing.

(2)  Additional expenses caused to the obligee by partial performance are to be borne by the obligor without prejudice to any other remedy.

### 6.1.4.  Order of performance

(1)  To the extent that the performances of the parties can be rendered simultaneously, the parties are bound to render them simultaneously unless the circumstances indicate otherwise

(2)  To the extent that the performance of only one party requires a period of time, that party is bound to render its performance first, unless the circumstances indicate otherwise.

### 6.1.5.  Earlier performance

(1)  The obligee may reject an earlier performance unless it has no legitimate interest in so doing.

(2)  Acceptance by a party of an earlier performance does not affect the time

for the performance of its own obligation if that time has been fixed irrespective of the performance of the other party's obligations.

(3)   Additional expenses caused to the obligee by earlier performance are to be borne by the obligor, without prejudice to any other remedy.

### 6.1.6.   Place of performance

(1)   If the place of performance is neither fixed by, nor determinable from, the contract, a party is to perform:
    (a)   a monetary obligation, at the obligee's place of business;
    (b)   any other obligation, at its own place of business.

(2)   A party must bear any increase in the expenses incidental to performance which is caused by a change in its place of business subsequent to the conclusion of the contract.

### 6.1.7.   Payment by cheque or other instruments

(1)   Payment may be made in any form used in the ordinary course of business at the place for payment.

(2)   However, an obligee who accepts, either by virtue of paragraph (1) or voluntarily, a cheque, another order to pay or a promise to pay, is presumed to do so only on condition that it will be honoured.

### 6.1.8.   Payment by funds transfer

(1)   Unless the obligee has indicated a particular account, payment may be made by a transfer to any of the financial institutions in which the obligee has made it known that it has an account.

(2)   In case of payment by a transfer the obligation of the obligor is discharged when the transfer to the obligee's financial institution becomes effective.

### 6.1.9.   Currency of payment

(1)   If a monetary obligation is expressed in a currency other than that of the place for payment, it may be paid by the obligor in the currency of the place for payment unless
    (a)   that currency is not freely convertible; or
    (b)   the parties have agreed that payment should be made only in the currency in which the monetary obligation is expressed.

(2)   If it is impossible for the obligor to make payment in the currency in which the monetary obligation is expressed, the obligee may require payment in the currency of the place for payment, even in the case referred to in paragraph (1)(b).

(3)   Payment in the currency of the place for payment is to be made according to the applicable rate of exchange prevailing there when payment is due.

(4)   However, if the obligor has not paid at the time when payment is due, the obligee may require payment according to the applicable rate of exchange prevailing either when payment is due or at the time of actual payment.

### 6.1.10.   Currency not expressed

Where a monetary obligation is not expressed in a particular currency, payment must be made in the currency of the place where payment is to be made.

### 6.1.11.   Costs of performance

Each party shall bear the costs of performance of its obligations.

### 6.1.12.   Imputation of payments

(1)   An obligor owing several monetary obligations to the same obligee may specify at the time of payment the debt to which it intends the payment to be applied. However, the payment discharges first any expenses, then interests due and finally the principal.

(2) If the obligor makes no such specification, the obligee may, within a reasonable time after payment, declare to the obligor the obligation to which it imputes the payment, provided that the obligation is due and undisputed.

(3) In the absence of imputation under paragraphs (1) or (2), payment is imputed to that obligation which satisfies one of the following criteria in the order indicated:

    (a) an obligation which is due or which is the first to fall due;
    (b) an obligation for which the obligee has least security;
    (c) the obligation which is the most burdensome for the obligor;
    (d) the obligation which has arisen first.

If none of the preceding criteria applies, payment is imputed to all the obligations proportionally.

### 6.1.13. Imputation of non-monetary obligations

Article 6.1.11 applies with appropriate adaptations to the imputation of performances of non-monetary obligations.

### 6.1.14. Application for public permission

Where the law of a State requires a public permission affecting the validity of the contract or its performance and neither that law nor the circumstances indicate otherwise

    (a) if only one party has his place of business in that State, that party shall take the measures necessary to obtain the permission;

    (b) in any other case the party whose performance requires permission shall take the necessary measures.

### 6.1.15. Procedure in applying for permission

(1) The party required to take the measures necessary to obtain the permission shall do so without undue delay and shall bear any expenses incurred.

(2) That party shall whenever appropriate give the other party notice of the grant or refusal of such permission without undue delay.

### 6.1.16. Permission neither granted nor refused

(1) If, notwithstanding the fact that the party responsible has taken all measures required, permission is neither granted nor refused within an agreed period or, where no period has been agreed, within a reasonable time from the conclusion of the contract, either party is entitled to terminate the contract.

(2) Where the permission affects some terms only, paragraph (1) does not apply if, having regard to the circumstances, it is reasonable to uphold the remaining contract even if the permission is refused.

### 6.1.17. Permission refused

(1) The refusal of a permission affecting the validity of the contract renders the contract void. If the refusal affects the validity of some terms only, only such terms are void if, having regard to the circumstances of the case, it is reasonable to uphold the remaining contract.

(2) Where the refusal of a permission renders the performance of the contract impossible in whole or in part, the rules on non-performance apply.

## Section 2. Hardship

### 6.2.1. Contract to be observed

Where the performance of a contract becomes more onerous for one of the parties, that party is nevertheless bound to perform its obligations subject to the following provisions on hardship.

### 6.2.2. Definition of hardship

There is hardship where the occurrence of events fundamentally alters the equilibrium of the contract either because the cost of a party's performance has increased or because the value of the performance a party receives has diminished, and

(a) the events occur or become known to the disadvantaged party after the conclusion of the contract;

(b) the events could not reasonably have been taken into account by the disadvantaged party at the time of the conclusion of the contract;

(c) the events are beyond the control of the disadvantaged party; and

(d) the risk of the events was not assumed by the disadvantaged party.

### 6.2.3. Effects of hardship

(1) In a case of hardship the disadvantaged party is entitled to request renegotiations. The request shall be made without undue delay and shall indicate the grounds on which it is based.

(2) The request for renegotiation does not in itself entitle the disadvantaged party to withhold performance.

(3) Upon failure to reach agreement within a reasonable time either party may resort to the court.

(4) If a court finds hardship it may, if reasonable,

(a) terminate the contract at a date and on terms to be fixed; or

(b) adapt the contract with a view to restoring its equilibrium.

## CHAPTER 7. NON-PERFORMANCE

### Section 1. General provisions

### 7.1.1. Non-performance defined

Non-performance is failure by a party to perform any of its obligations under the contract, including defective performance or late performance.

### 7.1.2. Interference by the other party

A party may not rely on the non-performance of the other party to the extent that such non-performance was caused by the first party's act or omission or by another event as to which the first party bears the risk.

### 7.1.3. Withholding performance

(1) Where the parties are to perform simultaneously, either party may withhold performance until the other party tenders its performance.

(2) Where the parties are to perform consecutively, the party that is to perform later may withhold its performance until the first party has performed.

### 7.1.4. Cure by non-performing party

(1) The non-performing party may, at its own expense, cure any non-performance, provided that

(a) without undue delay, it gives notice indicating the proposed manner and timing of the cure;

(b) cure is appropriate in the circumstances;

(c) the aggrieved party has no legitimate interest in refusing cure; and

(d) cure is effected promptly.

(2) The right to cure is not precluded by notice of termination.

(3) Upon effective notice of cure, rights of the aggrieved party that are inconsistent with the non-performing party's performance are suspended until the time for cure has expired.

(4) The aggrieved party may withhold performance pending cure.

(5) Notwithstanding cure, the aggrieved party retains the right to claim damages for delay as well as for any harm caused or not prevented by the cure.

### 7.1.5. Additional period for performance

(1) In a case of non-performance the aggrieved party may by notice to the other party allow an additional period of time for performance.

(2) During the additional period the aggrieved party may withhold performance of its own reciprocal obligations and may claim damages but may not resort to any other remedy. If it receives notice from the other party that the latter will not perform within that period, or if upon expiry of that period due performance has not been made, the aggrieved party may resort to any of the remedies that may be available under this Chapter.

(3) Where in a case of delay in performance which is not fundamental the aggrieved party has given notice allowing an additional period of time of reasonable length, it may terminate the contract at the end of that period. If the additional period is not of reasonable length it shall be extended to a reasonable length. The aggrieved party may in its notice provide that if the other party fails to perform within the period allowed by the notice the contract shall automatically terminate.

(4) Paragraph (3) does not apply when the obligation which has not been performed is only a minor part of the non-performing party.

### 7.1.6. Exemption clauses

A term which limits or excludes one party's liability for non-performance or which permits one party to render performance substantially different from what the other party reasonably expected may not be invoked if it would be grossly unfair to do so, having regard to the purpose of the contract.

### 7.1.7. Force majeure

(1) Non-performance by a party is excused if that party proves that the non-performance was due to an impediment beyond its control and that it could not reasonably be expected to have taken the impediment into account at the time of the conclusion of the contract or to have avoided or overcome it or its consequences.

(2) When the impediment is only temporary, the excuse shall have effect for such period as is reasonable having regard to the effect of the impediment on performance of the contract.

(3) A party who fails to perform must give notice to the other party of the impediment and its effect on its ability to perform. If the notice is not received by the other party within a reasonable time after the party who fails to perform knew or ought to have known of the impediment, it is liable for damages resulting from such non-receipt.

(4) Nothing in this article prevents a party from exercising a right to terminate the contract or withhold performance or request interest on money due.

## Section 2. Right to Performance

### 7.2.1. Performance of monetary obligation

Where a party who is obliged to pay money does not do so, the other party may require payment.

### 7.2.2. Performance of non-monetary obligation

Where a party who owes an obligation other than one to pay money does not perform, the other party may require performance, unless

(a) performance is impossible in law or in fact;

(b) performance or, when relevant, enforcement is unreasonably burdensome or expensive;

(c) the party entitled to performance may reasonably obtain performance from another source;

(d) performance is of an exclusively personal character; or

(e) the party entitled to performance does not require performance within a reasonable time after it has, or ought to have, become aware of the non-performance.

### 7.2.3. Repair and replacement of defective performance
The right to performance includes in appropriate cases the right to require repair, replacement or other cure of a defective performance. The provisions of Articles 7.2.1 and 7.2.2 apply accordingly.

### 7.2.4. Judicial penalty
(1) Where the court orders a party to perform, it may also direct that this party pay a penalty if it does not comply with the order.

(2) The penalty shall be paid to the aggrieved party unless mandatory provisions of the law of the forum provide otherwise. Payment of the penalty to the aggrieved party does not exclude any claim for damages.

### 7.2.5. Change of remedy
(1) An aggrieved party who has required performance of a non-monetary obligation and who has not received performance within a period fixed or otherwise within a reasonable period of time may invoke any other remedy.

(2) Where the decision of a court for performance of a non-monetary obligation cannot be enforced, the aggrieved party may invoke any other remedy.

### Section 3. Termination

### 7.3.1. Right to terminate the contract
(1) A party may terminate the contract where the failure of the other party to perform an obligation under the contract amounts to a fundamental non-performance.

(2) In determining whether a failure to perform an obligation amounts to a fundamental non-performance regard shall be had, in particular, to whether

(a) the non-performance substantially deprives the aggrieved party of what it was entitled to expect under the contract unless the other party did not foresee and could not reasonably have foreseen such result;

(b) strict compliance with the obligation which has not been performed is of essence under the contract;

(c) the non-performance is intentional or reckless;

(d) the non-performance gives the aggrieved party reason to believe that it cannot rely on the other party's future performance;

(e) the non-performing party will suffer disproportionate loss as a result of the preparation or performance if the contract is terminated.

(3) In the case of delay the aggrieved party may also terminate the contract if the other party fails to perform before the time allowed it under Article 7.1.5 has expired.

### 7.3.2. Notice of termination
(1) The right of a party to terminate the contract is to be exercised by notice to the other party.

(2) If performance has been offered late or otherwise does not conform to the contract the aggrieved party will lose its right to terminate the contract unless it gives notice to the other party within a reasonable time after it has or ought to have become aware of the offer or of the non-conforming performance.

### 7.3.3. Anticipatory non-performance
Where prior to the date for performance by one of the parties it is clear that there will be a fundamental non-performance by that party, the other party may terminate the contract.

### 7.3.4. Adequate assurance of due performance
A party who reasonably believes that there will be a fundamental non-performance by the other party may demand adequate assurance of due performance and may meanwhile withhold its own performance. Where this

assurance is not provided within a reasonable time the party demanding it may terminate the contract.

### 7.3.5.  Effects of termination in general
(1)  Termination of the contract releases both parties from their obligation to effect and to receive future performance.

(2)  Termination does not preclude a claim for damages for non-performance.

(3)  Termination does not affect any provision in the contract for the settlement of disputes or any other term of the contract which is to operate even after termination.

### 7.3.6.  Restitution
(1)  On termination of the contract either party may claim restitution of whatever it has supplied, provided that such party concurrently makes restitution of whatever it has received. If restitution in kind is not possible or appropriate allowance should be made in money whenever reasonable.

(2)  However, if performance of the contract has extended over a period of time and the contract is divisible, such restitution can only be claimed for the period after termination has taken effect.

### Section 4. Damages

### 7.4.1.  Right to damages
Any non-performance gives the aggrieved party a right to damages either exclusively or in conjunction with any other remedies except where the non-performance is excused under these Principles.

### 7.4.2.  Full compensation
(1)  The aggrieved party is entitled to full compensation for harm as a result of the non-performance. Such harm includes both any loss which it suffered and any gain of which it was deprived, taking into account any gain to the aggrieved party resulting from its avoidance of cost or harm.

(2)  Such harm may be non-pecuniary and includes, for instance, physical suffering or emotional distress.

### 7.4.3.  Certainty of harm
(1)  Compensation is due only for harm, including future harm, that is established with a reasonable degree of certainty.

(2)  Compensation may be due for the loss of a chance in proportion to the probability of its occurrence.

(3)  Where the amount of damages cannot be established with a sufficient degree of certainty, the assessment is at the discretion of the court.

### 7.4.4.  Foreseeability of harm
The non-performing party is liable only for harm which it foresaw or could reasonably have foreseen at the time of the conclusion of the contract as being likely to result from its non-performance.

### 7.4.5.  Proof of harm in case of replacement transaction
Where the aggrieved party has terminated the contract and has made a replacement transaction within a reasonable time and in a reasonable manner it may recover the difference between the contract price and the price of the replacement transaction as well as damages for any further harm.

### 7.4.6.  Proof of harm by current price
(1)  Where the aggrieved party has terminated the contract and has not made a replacement transaction but there is a current price for the performance contracted for, it may recover the difference between the contract price and the price current at the time the contract is terminated as well as damages for any further harm.

(2) Current price is the price generally charged for goods delivered or services rendered in comparable circumstances at the place where the contract should have been performed or, if there is no current price at that place, the current price at such other place that appears reasonable to take as a reference.

### 7.4.7.  Harm due in part to aggrieved party
Where the harm is due in part to an act or omission of the aggrieved party or to another event as to which that party bears the risk, the amount of damages shall be reduced to the extent these factors have contributed to the harm, having regard to the conduct of each of the parties.

### 7.4.8.  Mitigation of harm
(1) The non-performing party is not liable for harm suffered by the aggrieved party to the extent that the harm could have been reduced by the latter party's taking reasonable steps.
(2) The aggrieved party is entitled to recover any expenses reasonably incurred in attempting to reduce the harm.

### 7.4.9.  Interest for failure to pay money
(1)  If a party does not pay a sum of money when it falls due the aggrieved party is entitled to interest upon that sum from the time when payment is due to the time of payment whether or not the non-payment is excused.
(2)  The rate of interest shall be the average bank short-term lending rate to prime borrowers prevailing for the currency of payment at the place for payment, or where no such rate exists at that place, then the same rate in the State of the currency of payment. In the absence of such a rate at either place the rate of interest shall be the appropriate rate fixed by the law of the State of the currency of payment.
(3)  The aggrieved party is entitled to additional damages if the non-payment caused it a greater harm.

### 7.4.10.  Interest on damages
Unless otherwise agreed, interest on damages for non-performance of non-monetary obligations accrues as from the time of non-performance.

### 7.4.11.  Manner of monetary redress
(1)  Damages are to be paid in a lump sum. However, they may be payable in instalments when the nature of the harm makes this appropriate.
(2)  Damages to be paid in instalments may be indexed.

### 7.4.12.  Currency in which to assess damages
Damages are to be assessed either in the currency in which the monetary obligation was expressed or in the currency in which the harm was suffered, whichever is more appropriate.

### 7.4.13.  Agreed payment for non-performance
(1)  Where the contract provides that a party who does not perform is to pay a specified sum to the aggrieved party for such non-performance, the aggrieved party is entitled to that sum irrespective of its actual harm.
(2)  However, notwithstanding any agreement to the contrary the specified sum may be reduced to a reasonable amount where it is grossly excessive in relation to the harm resulting from the non-performance and to the other circumstances.

## DRAFT RULES ON UNJUSTIFIED ENRICHMENT
### (SLC Discussion Paper No 99, Appendix)

**1. General principle**

A person who has been enriched at the expense of another person is bound, if the enrichment is unjustified, to redress the enrichment.

**2. Enrichment**

(1) A person is enriched if he acquires an economic benefit.

(2) A person acquires an economic benefit if his net worth is increased or is prevented from being decreased, and accordingly a person may be enriched, among other ways, by

   (a) acquiring money or other property

   (b) having value added to property

   (c) being freed, in whole or in part, from an obligation, or

   (d) being saved from a loss or expenditure

(3) A person is treated as acquiring an economic benefit under a void contract, or under a voidable contract which has been reduced, rescinded or otherwise set aside, or under a contract which has been terminated by frustration or rescission for breach or by some other means (apart from full performance) or under any other transaction or purported transaction which does not provide legal cause for the acquisition, if he would have acquired an economic benefit but for the fact that he gave consideration, and accordingly in such circumstances both parties to the transaction or purported transaction may be regarded as being enriched.

**3. At the expense of another person**

(1) The enrichment of one person is at the expense of another person if it is the direct result of

   (a) a payment, grant, transfer, incurring of liability, or rendering of services by the other person

     (i) to the enriched person

     (ii) in fulfilment of an obligation of the enriched person

     (iii) in adding value to the enriched person's property, or

     (iv) in acquiring some other economic benefit for the enriched person,

   or

   (b) in any case not covered by paragraph (a), an interference with the patrimonial rights of the other person otherwise than by the operation of natural forces.

(2) A person interferes with the patrimonial rights of another person if, among other things, he

   (a) extinguishes those rights or acts in such a way that they are extinguished

   (b) disposes or purports to dispose of property belonging to that other person

   (c) uses property which that other person has the right to use to the exclusion of the interferer, or

   (d) actively intercepts a benefit due to the other person

but a person does not interfere with the patrimonial rights of another person merely because he breaches a contract between himself and the other person.

(3) A person who claims redress or any unjustified enrichment resulting from an interference with his patrimonial rights is treated for the purpose of any claims by or against third parties as thereby ratifying the interference.

(4) A person who purchases property in good faith from someone who is not the owner of the property is not treated as being enriched at the expense of the owner or of any former owner by reason only of any economic benefit derived by him from the purchase of the property; and the same rule applies to any other acquirer, in good faith and for value, of the right, or of what purports

to be the right, to deal with the property or rights of another, and to anyone deriving title from such a purchaser or acquirer.

(5) Where a person (E) has been enriched indirectly as a result of performance by another person (C) under a contract between C and a third party (T), E's enrichment is not regarded as being at the expense of C, even if C is unable to recover under his contract with T.

(6)  This rule is subject to rule 8 (which deals with certain exceptional cases where redress is due for indirect enrichment).

## 4.  Unjustified
An enrichment is unjustified unless it is justified under rules 5 or 6.

## 5.  Enrichment justified by legal cause
(1)   An enrichment is justified if the enriched person is entitled to it by virtue of
    (a)   an enactment
    (b)   a rule of law
    (c)   a court decree
    (d)   a contract (whether or not the person claiming redress is a party) or unilateral voluntary obligation
    (e)   a will or trust
    (f)   a gift, or
    (g)   some other legal cause.

(2)  The reference to an enactment or rule of law in rule 5(1) is to an enactment or rule of law which confers rights directly and not to an enactment or rule of law in so far as it operates indirectly by regulating the effects of court decrees, contracts, wills, trusts, gifts or other legal causes.

(3)  A purported or apparent legal cause does not justify an enrichment if it is void or if, being voidable, it has been reduced, rescinded or otherwise set aside.

(4)  An acquisition of property is not a justified enrichment merely because legal title to the property has been acquired.

## 6.  Enrichment justified by public policy
(1)   An enrichment is justified if it is the result of
    (a)   work or expenditure which was undertaken or incurred by the other person for his own benefit, or for the benefit of a third party or the public at large, which has incidentally conferred a benefit on the enriched person, and which was undertaken or incurred when the person knew or could reasonably have been expected to know that there would be a benefit to the enriched person and accepted, or could reasonably be supposed to have accepted, the risk that the enriched person would not pay for the benefit
    (b)   the voluntary and deliberate conferring by the other person of a benefit on the enriched person, in the knowledge that it is not due and in acceptance of the risk that the enriched person may choose not to pay or do anything in return
    (c)   a voluntary performance by the other person of an obligation which has prescribed, even if he erroneously believed that the obligation was still due, provided that any due counter-performance has been given
    (d)   a voluntary performance by the other person of an obligation which is invalid for some formal reason only, even if he erroneously believed that the obligation was valid, provided that any due counter-performance has been given
or if there is some other consideration of public policy which requires it to be regarded as justified.

(2)  For the purpose of rule 6(1)(a) 'benefit', in relation to a person who has done work or provided services in tendering for a contract or in the anticipation

of obtaining a contract, includes the benefit to the person of having, or improving, the chance of obtaining the contract.

### 7. Exceptions to rules 5 and 6

(1)   Rule 5(1)(b) does not apply in so far as the enrichment is the result of any rule of law on the acquisition of property by accession or specification, or any analogous rule whereby one person may acquire another's property when it becomes attached to or mixed with his own.

(2)   Rule 5(1)(d) does not apply in so far as the contract or obligation,

(a)   is unenforceable because of an enactment or rule of law (whether or not it is also illegal), unless allowing redress for the enrichment would contravene the policy underlying the enactment or rule of law,

(b)   has been terminated by rescission or frustration or some other means (apart from full performance) and the contract or obligation does not, expressly or impliedly, exclude redress in respect of the benefit in question.

(3)   For the purpose of rule 7(2)(b) a contract which provides for performance in several parts or stages is presumed, unless the contract indicates the contrary, to exclude redress in so far as performance by one party under, and substantially in accordance with, the contract has been met by performance by the other party under, and substantially in accordance with, the contract.

(4)   Rule 5(1)(f) does not apply where the gift

(a)   was made in error, whether of fact or law, or

(b)   was subject to a condition, which has been met, that it would be returned.

(5)   Rule 6(1)(a) and (b) do not apply where the other person has, in circumstances where it was reasonable to do so,

(a)   paid a monetary debt due by the enriched person

(b)   fulfilled an alimentary obligation due by the enriched person

(c)   incurred expenditure or performed services necessary for preserving the life, health or welfare of the enriched person, or

(d)   incurred expenditure or performed services urgently necessary for preserving the property of the enriched person or preventing it from being dangerous.

### 8. Redress for indirect enrichment

(1)(a)   Where a person (E) has acquired money or money's worth from a third party (T) by disposing or purporting to dispose of property belonging to another person (C), or by otherwise interfering with C's patrimonial rights, or by disposing of property acquired by him from C under a transaction voidable at C's instance, E's enrichment is treated, notwithstanding anything in the preceding rules, as being at the expense of C and as not being justified by any contract between himself and T.

(b)   Paragraph (a) does not apply if E was a purchaser in good faith of the property in question, or had otherwise acquired, in good faith and for value, the right, or what purported to be the right, to deal with the property or rights in question, or had derived title from such a purchaser or acquirer.

(2)   Where a person (T) has been enriched at the expense of another person (C) and T has transferred to another person (E) any benefit arising out of the enrichment then, notwithstanding anything in the preceding rules, E is taken to be enriched at the expense of C and neither the transfer by T to E, nor any voluntary obligation underlying the transfer, justifies the enrichment if

(a)   T's enrichment at the expense of C was unjustified or was justified only by a transaction voidable at C's instance

(b)   C is unable to recover from T, or cannot reasonably be expected to attempt to recover from T, and

(c)   the acquisition by E from T was not in good faith and for value.

(3)   Where a person (E) has been enriched by receiving a benefit from a trust

estate or from the estate of a deceased person, the fact that E's enrichment is the result of a transfer from a trustee or executor does not prevent him from being liable to make redress to

(a)   a creditor of the estate to the extent that the creditor, because of the transfer to the beneficiary, has been unable to recover from the trustee or executor, or

(b)   a person (the true beneficiary) who is legally entitled to the benefit in question.

(4)   Where a debtor pays the wrong person, that person is enriched at the expense of the true creditor in so far as the payment extinguishes the liability of the debtor to the true creditor.

(5)   Nothing in these rules affects any procedural rule designed to avoid duplication of proceedings.

## 9.  Redress due

(1)   The redress due by an enriched person under these rules is such transfer of property or payment of money, or both, as is required to redress the enriched person's unjustified enrichment at the expense of the claimant.

(2)   The redress due is assessed in accordance with the rules in the schedule in any case where those rules are applicable.

(3)   Where the enriched person has been enriched at the expense of the claimant in more than one way, the rules in the schedule apply cumulatively unless there would be double redress in respect of the same enrichment.

(4)   This rule is subject to the provisions of rule 10.

## 10.  Court's powers to refuse or modify award

(1)   Where, in an action for unjustified enrichment, it appears to the court that each party is bound to make redress to the other, the court may

(a)   refuse to grant decree against the defender until satisfied that the pursuer has made, or will make, the redress due by him, or

(b)   where both obligations are to pay money, set off one entitlement against the other and grant decree for the difference.

(2)   Where, in an action for unjustified enrichment based on the passive receipt of a benefit by the enriched person, it appears to the court

(a)   that the enriched person had no reasonable opportunity to refuse the benefit

(b)   that the enriched person would have refused the benefit if he had had such an opportunity

(c)   that the enriched person cannot, or cannot reasonably be expected to, convert the value of the benefit into money or money's worth, and

(d)   that it would be inequitable to make a full award

the court may refuse or modify the award accordingly.

(3)   Where, in an action for unjustified enrichment based on the defender's acquisition of the pursuer's property by accession or specification or any analogous rule, it appears to the court that the pursuer has acted in good faith and that, having regard to the respective values of the properties involved, the conduct of the parties and all other relevant factors, the most appropriate and equitable solution would be for the defender to be ordered to sell to the pursuer such property at such a price as would enable the pursuer to regain his property without prejudice to the defender, the court may grant decree accordingly.

(4)   Notwithstanding anything in the preceding rules, a court deciding an action for unjustified enrichment may refuse to make an award, or may make a reduced award, or may grant decree subject to conditions, if it considers

(a)   that the person enriched, where he did not know, and could not reasonably be expected to know, that redress was due, changed his position (whether by spending money, disposing of property, consuming property or its fruits, abandoning rights, failing to exercise rights in time, or otherwise) in reliance on his enrichment, and it would for that reason be inequitable to make a full award or grant decree unconditionally

(b) that the claimant was so culpable or negligent in causing the unjustified enrichment that it would be inequitable or contrary to public policy to make a full award or grant decree unconditionally

(c) that the claimant would be unjustly enriched if a full award were made or if decree were granted unconditionally, or

(d) that, for any other reason, it would be inequitable or contrary to public policy to make a full award or grant decree unconditionally.

## 11. Bars to proceedings

(1)(a) An action for unjustified enrichment cannot be brought under these rules if there is, or was,

(i) a special statutory or contractual procedure for dealing with the situation giving rise to the enrichment or

(ii) another legal remedy for the enrichment

and if the claimant could reasonably have been expected to use that procedure or remedy.

(b) Paragraph (a) does not apply if the enactment or contract providing the other procedure or remedy indicates expressly or impliedly that it is intended to be in addition to any remedy available under the general law on unjustified enrichment.

(c) The availability of damages for loss does not preclude an action for redress of unjustified enrichment but, without prejudice to his right to claim damages for any consequential or other loss, the claimant cannot claim both redress of the other party's unjustified enrichment and damages for his corresponding loss.

(2)(a) A person who, before a court decision in proceedings to which he was not a party, has made a payment or transfer which was apparently due under the law as it was commonly supposed to be at that time cannot bring an action for unjustified enrichment in respect of that payment or transfer on the ground that the decision has shown that the law was not as it was commonly supposed to be and that the payment or transfer was accordingly not in fact due.

(b) In the preceding paragraph, 'decision' in any case where a decision is affirmed or restored on appeal means the decision so affirmed or restored and not the decision affirming or restoring it.

(3) The bars mentioned in this rule are in addition to any bar resulting from the operation of the general law on personal bar.

## 12. Areas of law not affected

(1) These rules replace the existing Scottish common law on unjustified enrichment, including

(a) the common law on restitution in so far as it is part of the law on unjustified enrichment

(b) the common law on repetition and recompense, and

(c) the *condictio indebiti*; the *condictio causa data causa non secuta*; the *condictio ob turpem vel iniustam causam*; the *condictio ob non causam*; the *condictio sine causa*; the *actio in quantum locupletior factus est*; and the *actio de in rem verso* in so far as they form part of the existing law.

(2) Nothing in these rules affects

(a) any enacted law

(b) the law on rights of relief of cautioners and co-obligants

(c) the law on subrogation of insurers or those who have paid an indemnity

(d) the law derived from the case of *Walker v Milne* (whereby loss suffered or expenditure incurred in the expectation of a contract may in certain circumstances be recovered)

(e)   the law on the rights of a defrauded person as against the creditors of the person who defrauded him

(f)   the law on the recovery by a person of the possession or control of his own property or of any other property to the possession or control of which he is entitled

(g)   the law on the special obligations of those in a fiduciary position

(h)   the law on general average or salvage

(i)   the law on *negotiorum gestio*.

## 13.   Interpretation

(1)   In these rules, and in the schedule where applicable,

(a)   'court decree' includes the decision of any tribunal, quasi-judicial body or arbiter having jurisdiction

(b)   'enactment' includes subordinate legislation

(c)   'gift' includes a gratuitous waiver, renunciation or discharge of a right

(d)   'he' means he, she or it; 'him' means him, her or it; and 'his' means his, hers or its

(e)   'patrimonial rights' include rights flowing from the ownership of property, rights to protect confidential information and other rights having an economic value but do not include purely personal rights, such as the rights to life, liberty, bodily integrity or reputation, and

(f)   'property' means property of any kind, corporeal or incorporeal, heritable or moveable.

(2)   Any reference in these rules to a contract which has been terminated by rescission or frustration includes a reference to a contract which has been substantially terminated by rescission or frustration and a reference to a severable part of a contract which has been terminated by rescission or frustration.

SCHEDULE. REDRESS DUE

PART I

*E acquires benefit directly from C*

1.   This part of the schedule applies where the enriched person (E) has been enriched by acquiring a benefit directly from the claimant (C).

2(1)   Where the unjustified enrichment resulted from the acquisition of money by E from C, the redress due by E to C is the amount acquired, with interest from the time of acquisition.

(2)   Where the unjustified enrichment resulted from the acquisition of other property by E from C, the redress due by E to C is

(a)   if the property is corporeal and can be returned in substantially the same condition as it was in at the time of the acquisition, the return of the property in that condition along with a sum of money to take account of any benefit derived by E from the ownership, use or possession of the property and interest on that sum where appropriate

(b)   if the property is corporeal and cannot be returned in substantially the same condition as it was in at the time of the acquisition, the amount which it would have been reasonable to expect E to pay C for the property at the time of its acquisition by E, with interest on that amount from the time of acquisition

(c)   if the property is incorporeal, the return of the property where possible and, whether or not return is possible, a sum of money to take account of any benefit derived by E from the ownership of the property and interest on that sum where appropriate.

3. Where the unjustified enrichment resulted from the addition of value by C to E's property, the redress due by E to C is the amount which it would have been reasonable to expect E to pay C for his work or expenditure in adding that value, or the amount of value added (at the time when the addition was made), if less, with interest where appropriate.

4. Where the unjustified enrichment resulted from the discharge or reduction of any liability of E by means of a payment by C, the redress due by E to C is the amount paid, with interest from the date of payment.

5. Where the unjustified enrichment resulted from E's being saved a loss or expenditure by receiving C's services, the redress due by E to C is the amount which it would have been reasonable to expect E to pay for those services, or the amount of loss or expenditure saved, if less, with interest where appropriate.

6(1) Where the unjustified enrichment resulted from E's being saved a loss or expenditure by using or possessing C's property, the redress due by E to C is the amount which it would have been reasonable to expect E to pay for that use or possession, or the amount of loss or expenditure saved, if less, with interest where appropriate.

(2) Where the unjustified enrichment resulted from E's being saved a loss or expenditure by consuming C's property, the redress due by E to C is the amount which it would have been reasonable to expect E to pay for the property at the time of consumption, or the amount of loss or expenditure saved, if less, with interest where appropriate.

(3) Where the unjustified enrichment resulted from E's being saved a loss or expenditure by interfering with C's patrimonial rights in any other way, the redress due by E to C is the amount which it would have been reasonable to expect E to pay C, at the time of the interference, for permission to interfere with those rights in that way in the circumstances, or the amount of loss or expenditure saved, if less, with interest where appropriate.

7. Where the unjustified enrichment resulted from the acquisition of any other benefit by E from C, the redress due by E to C is the amount which it would have been reasonable to expect E to pay C for the benefit at the time or acquisition, or the amount of E's actual enrichment, if less, with interest where appropriate.

## PART II

*E acquires benefit from T at indirect expense of C*

8. This part of the schedule applies where the enriched person (E) has been enriched indirectly at the expense of the claimant (C).

9. Where E has enriched himself by using or disposing of C's property, or otherwise interfering with C's patrimonial rights, in order to obtain money or money's worth from a third party (T) the redress due by E to C is the amount which it would have been reasonable for E to pay C at the time of the use, disposal or interference for permission to use or dispose of C's property or to interfere with his rights in that way, or the amount of E's actual enrichment attributable to the use, disposal or interference, if less, with interest where appropriate.

10. Where E has been indirectly enriched at the expense of C as a result of the transfer of a benefit from a third party (T) in the circumstances covered by rule 8(2) (transfer of benefit arising from unjustified enrichment to person taking otherwise than in good faith and for value) T is treated as if he had been acting as E's agent and accordingly the redress due by E to C is the same, and is due

on the same conditions, as it would have been if E had acquired the benefit directly from C.

11. Where E has been indirectly enriched at the expense of C in the circumstances covered by rule 8(3) (transfers from trusts or executries) the redress due by E to C is

(1) where C is a creditor claiming under rule 8(3)(a) the amount of the debt due to C out of the estate or the amount of E's enrichment out of the estate, whichever is the less, with interest where appropriate

(2) where C is a true beneficiary claiming under rule 8(3)(b), and the benefit due to him out of the estate and received by E was a special legacy, the transfer of the subject matter of the legacy along with a sum to take account of any benefit derived by E from its use or possession or, if the subject matter of the legacy cannot be transferred in substantially the same condition as it was in when acquired by E, an amount representing its value when acquired by E, with interest from that date

(3) where C is a true beneficiary claiming under rule 8(3)(b), and the benefit due to him out of the estate and received by E was not a special legacy, the amount of the benefit due to C out of the estate or the amount of E's unjustified enrichment out of the estate, whichever is the less, with interest where appropriate.

## PART III

### *General*

12. Any reference in this schedule to the return of property includes a reference to a return by reconveyance or by any other means by which ownership can be restored to the other person.

13. For the purposes of paragraph 2(2) corporeal property acquired by the enriched person by accession or specification, or any analogous rule whereby one person may acquire another's property when it becomes attached to or mixed with his own, is treated as property which cannot be returned in substantially the same condition as it was in at the time of acquisition.

14. Where property is to be returned or transferred to the claimant by the enriched person under these rules, the expenses of the return or transfer are to be borne

(1) by the claimant if the enrichment was in good faith, or

(2) by the enriched person if the enrichment was in bad faith unless a court dealing with the claim orders otherwise.

15. In assessing what it would have been reasonable for E to pay C for any interference with C's rights or for permission to interfere with those rights regard may be had to any factors which would have made C reluctant or unwilling to permit the interference.

# INDEX

# INDEX OF STATUTES